WEST GROUP
HIGH COURT
CASE SUMMARIES

YO-ART-011

Editor in Chief   **Dana L. Blatt, J.D., Esq.**

Managing Editor   **Marie H. Stedman**

Briefs Written By   **Sunil Gupta, J.D., Esq.**
Thomas G. Hardin, J.D., Esq.
Jennifer McDonough, J.D., Esq.
Anna-Elise Price, J.D., Esq.
J. Cai Ryan, J.D., Esq.
Xavier Tan-Sanchez, J.D., Esq.
Jennifer A. Weinzierl, J.D., Esq.

Memory Graphics   **Norman Vance**

Page Design   **Terri Asher**

Adaptable to Courses Utilizing Dressler's Casebook on Criminal Law, 2nd Edition

Published by **WEST GROUP**
610 Opperman Drive
Eagan, MN
55123

Copyright © 2001 West Group
610 Opperman Drive
P.O. Box 64526
St. Paul, MN 55164-0526

ISBN 0-314-25695-4

2nd reprint 2003

A Message from Dana L. Blatt, J.D., Editor In Chief
West Group High Court Case Summaries

As Editor in Chief of West Group's High Court Case Summaries, I am pleased to be associated with West Group and its tradition of providing the highest quality law student study aids such as Nutshells, Hornbooks, the Black Letter Series, and Sum and Substance products.   I am also pleased that West Group, as the new publisher of High Court Case Summaries, will continue its tradition of providing students with the best quality student briefs available today. When you use these High Court Case Summaries, you will know that you have the advantage of using the best-written and most comprehensive student briefs available, with the most thorough analyses.   Law students cannot afford to waste a minute of their time. That's why you need High Court Case Summaries. You'll find that with High Court you not only save time, but also have the competitive edge with our exclusive features such as memory graphics, "party lines," overview outlines, and case vocabulary. The following two pages will introduce you to the format of a High Court Brief.

Dana L. Blatt, J.D., Editor In Chief

FORMAT FOR A HIGH COURT BRIEF

THE HEADNOTE

Like a headline in a newspaper, the headnote provides you with a brief statement highlighting the importance of the case to the course.

"PARTY" LINE

A quick memory aid. For instantaneous recollection of the names of the parties and their relationship to each other.

MEMORY GRAPHIC

"A picture is worth a thousand words." Our professional cartoonists have created an entertaining "picture of the facts." To assist you in remembering what a particular case is about, simply glance at the picture.

INSTANT FACTS

Another great memory aid. A quick scan of a single sentence will instantly remind you of all of the facts of the case.

BLACK LETTER RULE

This section contains the single most important rule of the case (determined by reference to the chapter of the casebook where the case can be found). Read together with instant facts, you have a perfect mini brief.

CASE VOCABULARY

Every new or unusual legal, Latin or English word found in the original case is briefly defined in this section. This timesaver eliminates constant references to separate dictionaries.

PROCEDURAL BASIS

In a single sentence we summarize what happened, procedurally, to cause the case to be on appeal.

FACTS

"Just the facts ma'am..." Our facts are clearer and easier to understand than the original case. In fact, you can have a complete understanding of the original case without ever having to read it. Just read our brief.

ISSUE

Utilizing our I.R.A.C. format (Issue, Rule, Application, Conclusion), we put it all in focus by simply stating the single most important question of every case.

DECISION AND RATIONALE

We know you need to understand the rationale of every case to learn the law. In a clear, concise, and meticulous fashion we lay it all out for you. We do the work of separating what is important from what is not. Yet, we provide you with a thorough summary of every essential element of every case. Every concurrence and dissent is summarized as well.

ANALYSIS

We provide you with an extensive analysis of every single case. Here you will learn what you want to know about every case. What is the history or background of the litigation? What do authorities say about the opinion? How does it fit in with the course? How does each case compare with others in the casebook? Is it a majority or minority opinion? What is the importance of the case and why did the casebook author choose to include it as a major opinion in the casebook? What types of things will the professor be asking about the case? What will be said about the opinion in class? Will people criticize or applaud it? What would you want to say about the case if called upon in class to brief it? In other words, what are the "secret" essential things that one must know and understand about each case in order to do well in the course? We answer these and many other questions for you. Nobody else comes close to giving you the in-depth analysis that we give!

A Great All-Around Study Aid!

IMPLIED WARRANTIES OF MERCHANTABILITY SURVIVE EXPRESS CONTRACTUAL PROVISIONS TO THE CONTRARY

Henningsen v. Bloomfield Motors, Inc.

(Auto Purchaser) v. (Auto Dealer)
32 N.J. 358, 161 A.2d 69 (N.J. 1960)

M E M O R Y   G R A P H I C

Instant Facts
An automobile purchaser sued the dealer and manufacturer for breach of an implied warranty of merchantability, although the express contractual terms of the sale disclaimed all implied warranties.

Black Letter Rule
A contract of adhesion does not trump statutory implied warranties of merchantability.

Case Vocabulary
CAVEAT EMPTOR: Let the buyer beware.
CONTRACT OF ADHESION: A contract between parties of unequal bargaining position, where the buyer must "take it or leave it."
IMPLIED WARRANTY OF MERCHANTABILITY: A warranty that means that the thing sold must be reasonably fit for the general purpose for which it is manufactured and sold.

Procedural Basis: Certification to New Jersey Supreme Court of appeal of judgment awarding damages for breach of implied warranty.

Facts: Mr. Henningsen purchased a car from Bloomfield Motors Inc. (D), a retail dealer. The car had been manufactured by Chrysler Corporation (D). Mr. Henningsen gave the car to his wife for Christmas. Mrs. Henningsen (P) was badly injured a few days later when the steering gear failed and the car turned right into a wall. When he purchased the car, Mr. Henningsen signed a contract without reading the fine print. The fine print contained a "warranty" clause which disclaimed all implied warranties and which granted an express warranty for all defects within 90 days or 4000 miles, whichever came first. Mrs. Henningsen (P) sued Bloomfield (D) and Chrysler (D). The trial court dismissed her negligence counts but ruled for Mrs. Henningsen (P) based on the implied warranty of merchantability. Bloomfield (D) and Chrysler (D) appealed.

Issue: Does a contract of adhesion trump statutory implied warranties of merchantability?

Decision and Rationale: (Francis, J.) No. A contract of adhesion does not trump statutory implied warranties of merchantability. In order to ameliorate the harsh effects of the doctrine of caveat emptor, most states have imposed an implied warranty of merchantability on all sales transactions. This warranty simply means that the thing sold must be reasonably fit for the general purpose for which it is manufactured and sold. The warranty extends to all foreseeable users of the product, not merely those in privity of contract with the seller. In order to avoid the implied warranty obligations, many manufacturers, including Chrysler (D) and all other automobile manufacturers, include an express warranty provision which disclaims all statutory implied warranties. We must determine what effect to give this express warranty. Under traditional principles of freedom of contract, the law allows parties to contract away obligations. However, in the auto sales context, the fine-print disclaimer of implied warranties is a contract of adhesion. It is a standardized form contract, and the purchaser has no opportunity to bargain for different terms. He must "take it or leave it," and he cannot shop around to different dealers because all of them use the same standard contract. Because the purchaser and seller occupy grossly inequal bargaining positions, we feel that justice must trump the principle of freedom of contract. Chrysler's (D) attempted disclaimer of an implied warranty of merchantability is so inimical to the public good as to compel an adjudication of its invalidity. Affirmed.

Analysis:

This well-written opinion presents an excellent exegesis of several areas of law, ranging from products liability to various contract principles. The opinion notes several conflicting interests and principles which the court must weigh. First, the traditional principle of caveat emptor faces the modern doctrine of implied warranties of merchantability. The court has little difficulty in holding that modern commercial transactions require protection for purchasers. An implied warranty of merchantability is imposed in all auto sales transactions in order to protect the buyer. Second, the requirement of privity of contract is weighed against an implied warranty. The court notes that, in modern sales transactions, a warranty safeguards all consumers of a product, not merely those in direct contractual privity with the seller. Third, the principle of freedom of contract is weighed against this implied warranty. Freedom of contract is one of the fundamental tenets of the law. Parties should be free to contract for any provisions, and generally parties are bound by the terms of their contract. However, an important exception exists when a contract is one of adhesion. Contracts of adhesion typically involve terms in fine print, written by a powerful seller to limit liabilities or impose responsibilities upon an unsuspecting buyer. No bargaining occurs for these terms, and indeed the buyer is in no position to bargain. If the buyer attempts to change the terms of the contract, the seller simply will not complete the transaction. In order for a contract to be considered "adhesive" or "unconscionable," the buyer usually has nowhere else to go. As in the case at bar, all sellers of a particular type of goods may include similar terms in their adhesive contracts. Weighing all of these factors, a court may rule that the express contractual terms are invalid, notwithstanding the principle of freedom of contract. The arguments for and against this approach are easy to see. On one hand, a buyer should not be allowed to benefit from his failure to read the terms of a contract or to attempt to change some unwanted terms. On the other hand, social justice requires that the buyer be protected from an all-powerful seller, especially where the buyer has no other option but to accept the contract as written. All in all, public policy, and not traditional law, shapes this court's opinion.

Table of Contents

Alphabetical Table of Cases

Chapter 1

A "crime" can easily be defined as any social harm which the lawmakers choose to call a crime, and is punishable by law. However, this circular definition does little to distinguish criminal law from other areas of law. Although, the line between criminal and civil law has faded, as both take on characteristics of the other, the distinction between a crime and a civil wrong, such as a tort or breach of contract, is more complex.

Unlike civil wrongs, a crime is a social harm. Although the direct and immediate victim of a crime may be a private party, the injury suffered involves a violation of public rights and duties owed to the entire community. Therefore, criminal law involves public law, and is prosecuted by public attorneys who represent the community at large. Moreover, unlike a civil wrong, a person convicted of a crime is punished by a formal and solemn pronouncement of the moral condemnation of the community. It is this societal condemnation and stigma that accompanies the conviction that most of all distinguishes civil from the criminal process.

Since a crime is a social harm, and because of the societal stigma attached to a criminal conviction, in only fits that a person accused of a crime is tried by the community. For this reason, the Sixth Amendment of the United States Constitution provides that in all criminal prosecutions, the accused shall enjoy the right to speedy public trial, by an impartial jury. The right to a jury trial not only protects against governmental oppression, but also provides the accused with a common-sense judgment from the community. However, despite the sixth amendment, the Supreme Court of the United States has determined that the right to a trial by jury only applies to non-petty offenses. More specifically, when the penalty for a crime involves imprisonment for more than six months.

Furthermore, because the accused in a criminal prosecution has so much at stake, including the loss of his or her liberty, and the stigma attached to a conviction, the burden of proof at trial is necessarily high. The Supreme Court has ruled that the due process clause of the United States Constitution, requires the prosecutor to persuade the factfinder, "beyond a reasonable doubt," of every fact necessary to constitute the crime charged. It is a requirement that is founded upon the belief that it is better to let a guilty person go free, than to convict an innocent man.

Lastly, because the jury is seen as the "conscience of the community," they have the ultimate power to determine whether the accused is deserving of the societal condemnation and formal punishment, that results from a conviction. Juries have the power to nullify the law, and may set the accused free, despite having proof beyond a reasonable doubt of a crime. The jury may use this power of jury nullification, to protect against socially undesirable convictions, and to protect against governmental oppression. However, because this power may do more harm than good, the overwhelming rule is that arguments and jury instructions regarding the power of jury nullification are not permissible.

Chapter 1

NOTE: THE PURPOSE OF THIS OUTLINE IS TO ORGANIZE THE CASES SO THAT ONE CAN QUICKLY UNDERSTAND THE RELEVANCE OF EACH CASE TO THE COURSE. NO ATTEMPT IS MADE IN THIS OVERVIEW TO ADDRESS EVERY CONCEPT THAT MUST BE STUDIED. BE SURE TO READ THE ENTIRE CASEBOOK AND/OR OTHER MATERIALS TO GAIN A FULL UNDERSTANDING OF ALL CONCEPTS.

I. Nature, Sources, and Limits of the Criminal Law
  A. Criminal Law operates as a series of directions or commands that tell people what they must or must not do. *Henry M. Hart, Jr.*
    1. The commands are taken as valid and binding upon all those who fall within their terms, when the time comes for compliance.
    2. Although this is also true for noncriminal or civil law, crimes can be distinguished on the ground that they constitute injuries to society in general.
    3. It is not simply anything which a legislature chooses to call a "crime", or to which a legislature chooses to attach a "criminal" penalty.
    4. Nor is it simply antisocial conduct which public officers are given responsibility to suppress.
    5. It is conduct which will incur a formal and solemn pronouncement of the moral condemnation of the community.
  B. Of course, criminal law involves more than the threat of community condemnation of antisocial behavior. It also involves punishment, or in other words, the threat of unpleasant physical consequences. *Henry M. Hart, Jr.*

II. The Pre-Trial Procedure of Criminal Law
  A. Though it is easy to think that the commission of a crime inevitably results in a prosecution, culminating in a trial, this would be misleading. Trials are more the exception than the rule in the justice system.
  B. The criminal process begins when an alleged crime is reported to the police. However, there is no way of knowing exactly how many crimes go unreported.
  C. Although a crime occurs and is reported, this does not ensure that an arrest will be made. Police may doubt the authenticity of the claim and not investigate the report with vigor. Police may also give the investigation low priority because of the lack of resources to investigate every offense. Furthermore, even if police investigate a crime thoroughly, there may be insufficient evidence to make an arrest.
  D. If a suspect is arrested, the prosecutor must overcome various hurdles before a trial may be held.
    1. A person arrested may be entitled to a preliminary hearing to determine whether the arrest was justified.
    2. If justified, the prosecutor is permitted in some states to file an "information" in the trial court and proceed to trial.
    3. In most states and in the federal system, even if a preliminary hearing judge rules that the arrest was justified, the accused may not be brought to trial unless he or she is indicted by a grand jury.
    4. The jury determines whether there is sufficient evidence to prosecute the accused.
  E. Even if an indictment is issued or an information is filed, a trial might still not be held. The accused is entitled to make various pretrial motions which, if successful, sometimes require the dismissal of charges.
  F. Finally, a defendant may plead guilty rather than proceed to trial. Nearly always, a guilty plea is the result of a bargain between the prosecutor and defendant's lawyer.

III. The Criminal Law Procedure Of A Trial By Jury
  A. The Sixth Amendment to the United States Constitution provides that "in all criminal prosecutions, the accused shall enjoy the right to a speedy and public trial, by an impartial jury."
  B. This right is essential to preventing oppression by the government. It gives the accused the right to be tried by a jury of his peers, avoiding the corrupt or overzealous prosecutor, or a biased, eccentric, or less sympathetic judge. *Duncan v. Louisiana.*
  C. Despite this, the Supreme Court has determined that this right only applies to non-petty offenses, where the penalty to be imposed includes imprisonment for more than six months. *Sullivan v. Louisiana.*
  D. In the federal system and in most states, a jury in a criminal trial is composed of 12 people.
    1. However, juries as small as six have been held to be constitutionally permissible.
    2. Verdicts that acquit or convict must either be

unanimous, or when state law permits, must constitute a substantial majority of the jurors.

E. Juries must be impartial.

1. In order to discover possible bias prior to trial, the judge and the attorney must examine prospective jurors, or "venirepersons", regarding their attitudes and beliefs.

2. The examination is called a "voir dire." If a "venire person's" response demonstrates partiality, the juror is excused for cause.

IV. Proving Guilt at Trial

A. According to the Supreme Court of the United States, the Due Process Clause of the United States Constitution requires the prosecutor to persuade the factfinder "beyond a reasonable doubt of every fact necessary to constitute a crime."

1. This burden of proof is a prime instrument for reducing the risk of conviction resting on factual error.

2. The accused has interest of immense importance at stake, including the possibility of the loss of liberty, and stigmatization.

3. Accordingly, a society that values the good name and freedom of every individual should not condemn the accused if there is reasonable doubt about his guilt.

4. Moreover, the use if the reasonable-doubt standard is indispensable to command the respect and confidence of the community.

   a. It is critical that the moral force of the criminal not be diluted by a standard that leaves people in doubt whether innocent men are being condemned.

   b. Thus, it is far worse to convict an innocent man than to let a guilty man go free.

B. Although the burden of proof, "beyond a reasonable doubt", is necessarily high, it may be satisfied by circumstantial evidence alone. Thus a conviction may be sustained, even if based solely on circumstantial evidence, if the circumstances are inconsistent with any reasonable hypothesis of innocence. *Owens v. State.*

V. Jury Nullification

A. The jury, seen as the "conscience of the community," has the ultimate power to determine whether the accused is deserving of societal condemnation and formal punishment, that results from a conviction.

1. Juries have the power to nullify the law, and may set the accused free, despite having proof beyond a reasonable doubt of a crime.

2. The jury may use this power of jury nullification, to protect against socially undesirable convictions, and to protect against governmental oppression.

B. However, the power of jury nullification is not a precious attribute of a right to trial by Jury. *State v. Ragland.*

1. The juries power to disregard the law, casts aside our basic belief that only our elected representatives may determine what a crime is, and revise laws found to be unfair.

2. Finally, it is a confusing instruction to inform the jury that they must obey the law, yet are free to disregard it if they so wish.

3. For these reasons, the overwhelming rule is that arguments and jury instructions regarding the power of jury nullification are not permissible.

Owens v. State

(Drunk Driver) v. (Judge)
93 Md. App. 162, 611 A.2d 1043 (MD 1992)

M E M O R Y   G R A P H I C

 Instant Facts

An intoxicated person, found asleep behind the wheel of a car parked in a driveway, with its motor running and lights on, is convicted of drunk driving, even though there was only circumstantial evidence that the car was driven on the highway.

Black Letter Rule

A conviction based upon circumstantial evidence alone, may be sustained if the circumstances are inconsistent with any reasonable hypothesis of innocence.

Case Vocabulary

CIRCUMSTANTIAL EVIDENCE: Particular circumstances or indirect evidence, which would allow the inference that a particular event or action had taken place.

Procedural Basis: Appeal to the Maryland Court of Special Appeals, of a conviction by the trial court, sitting without a jury, for driving while intoxicated.

Facts: On March 17, 1991, Christopher Columbus Owens, Jr. (Owens) (D), was asleep in the driver's seat of a truck. The truck was parked in the driveway of a private residence, with its engine running and the lights turned on. At 11 P.M. Trooper Samuel Cottman (Cottman), responding to a complaint about a "suspicious vehicle", approached the truck and found Owens (D) with an open can of Budweiser clasped between his legs, and two more empty beers cans in the back seat. Cottman awakened Owens (D), who appeared lost and confused with a strong odor of alcohol on his breath. Then Owens (D) stumbled out of the truck, with his face flushed and eyes red. When asked to recite the alphabet, Owens (D) mumbled the letters, and failed to recite them in the correct order. His speech was generally slurred and unclear. A check with the Motor Vehicle Administration revealed that Owens (D) had an alcohol restriction on his license. Owens (D) then declined to submit to a blood test for alcohol. At trial, Owens (D) contended that the law he was charged with violating did not extend to driving on a "private driveway," and that there was insufficient evidence of driving while intoxicated. The trial court, sitting without a jury, convicted Owens (D) of driving while intoxicated. Owens (D) appealed.

Issue: May a conviction based upon circumstantial evidence alone, be sustained when the circumstances are inconsistent with any reasonable hypothesis of innocence?

Decision and Rationale: (Moylan, J.) Yes. A conviction based upon circumstantial evidence alone, may be sustained if the circumstances are inconsistent with any reasonable hypothesis of innocence. We are called upon, here, to examine the circumstantial evidence, and to ascertain whether there were any attendant and ancillary circumstances to render less likely, and therefore less reasonable the hypothesis of innocence. We agree with Owens (D) that he could not properly have been convicted, no matter how intoxicated, for driving back and forth on a driveway. However Owens (D) was convicted not for driving on a private driveway, but for driving on a public highway before coming to rest on a private driveway. It is a classic case of circumstantial evidence. From his presence behind the wheel of a vehicle with its engine running and lights turned on, it can reasonably be inferred that, 1) he just arrived by way of public highway, or 2) was just about to set forth upon the public highway. These two probabilities are strengthened by the lack of evidence of any third reasonable explanation. The first inference would render Owens (D) guilty, while the second would not. With either inference equally likely, a fact finder could not fairly draw the guilty inference and reject the innocent with the requisite certainty beyond a reasonable doubt. For the State to prevail, there has to be some other factor to enhance the likelihood of the first inference and diminish the second. If Owens (D) was parked in someone else's driveway with the motor still running, it would be more likely that he had just driven there a short time before. If Owens (D) was parked in his own driveway it is more likely that he was on his way out. Although it is routine procedure, Owens' (D) license, which showed the alcohol restriction and Owens' (D) address, was not offered into evidence. Therefore for the purposes of the present analysis, Owens' (D) address is not in this case, and we must look for a tiebreaker elsewhere. Three beer cans were in evidence. Since one does not typically drink in the house and then carry the empty cans out to the car, it may be inferred that some significant drinking had taken place while Owens (D) was in the car. One passes out on the steering wheel after one has been drinking for some time. It is not a reasonable hypothesis that one would leave the house, get in the car, turn on the lights and motor, then, before driving off, consume enough alcohol to pass out on the steering wheel. Furthermore, Trooper Cottman came to the scene because of a complaint about a suspicious looking vehicle. The inference is reasonable that the vehicle had been observed driving in some sort of erratic fashion. Had the appellant simply been sitting, with his motor idling, on the driveway of his own residence, it is not likely that someone from the immediate vicinity would have found suspicious the presence of a familiar neighbor in a familiar car sitting in his own driveway. This does not prove guilt in and of itself, but simply makes one of two alternative inferences less reasonable, and its alternative inference thereby more reasonable. The totality of circumstances are inconsistent with a reasonable hypothesis of innocence. It makes the drawing of the inference of guilt more than a mere flip of a coin between guilt and innocence. It makes it rational and therefore within the proper purview of the factfinder. Affirmed.

Analysis:

This case first raises a concern about the sufficiency of evidence needed for a conviction. Because of factors, such as negative social stigma, that necessarily follow a criminal conviction, the burden of proof is necessarily high. Thus prosecutors have the burden of proving every fact of a case necessary for the conviction, beyond a reasonable doubt. This case exemplifies that this burden of proof can be met, even if only circumstantial evidence is available. It is possible for the fact finding body to conclude that certain events did or did not take place, based on circumstantial evidence. Therefore, the fact finding body may infer guilt beyond a reasonable doubt, just as it may infer that a surgeon was negligent when a sponge is found inside the body of one of his patients. It is important to remember that Owens (D) did not present any evidence in his defense, but stood solely on the presumption of his innocence. A second concern this case raises, deals with the sufficiency of evidence needed to sustain a conviction. The appellate court must assume that the trier of fact, usually the jury, resolved any conflicts between factual claims in favor of the prosecution. Thus, the standard on appeal is whether a rational trier of fact could reasonably have reached the result that it did. Since the conviction in the instant case was based on circumstantial evidence alone, the appellate court was required to find that the circumstances were inconsistent with any reasonable hypothesis of innocence. The appellate court first deduced that Owens (D) was either leaving the driveway, which would make him innocent since he did not actually drive on the highway intoxicated, or had just arrived, which would make him guilty of driving on the highway intoxicated. Then the appellate court reasoned that the empty beer cans made it more likely that he had been inside the car while drinking, and that the driveway in which he was parked was not the driveway of his home. Therefore, it is more likely that he had just arrived, and his conviction may be properly sustained. A third issue this case raises is the Sixth Amendment right to a trial by jury. In the instant case, Owens (D) was convicted by the trial court judge, sitting without a jury. However, despite the sixth amendment, it has been established that the right to a trial by jury only applies to "non-petty" offenses, usually when imprisonment for more than six months is authorized, or the legislature determines that an offense is a "serious one". Therefore, Owens' (D) right to a trial by jury, turns upon the penalty that was imposed.

State v. Ragland

(Jury) v. (Felon)

105 N.J. 189, 519 A.2d 1361 (N.J. 1986)

M E M O R Y   G R A P H I C

Instant Facts

A convicted felon charged with possession of a weapon, contends that the judge erred in instructing the jury that they "must" convict, which conflicted with the jury's nullification power.

 ## Black Letter Rule

The power of jury nullification is not a precious attribute of a right to trial by jury.

Case Vocabulary

JURY NULLIFICATION: The power of a jury to deliberately disregard the law and acquit a defendant, even if the prosecutor proves beyond a reasonable doubt that the accused committed the offense charged.

Facts: Ragland (D), a previously convicted felon, was prosecuted for various offenses, including armed robbery and possession of a weapon by a convicted felon. At the conclusion of the trial for the latter offense, the judge instructed the jury that if it found that the defendant was in possession of a weapon during the commission of the robbery, it "must" find him guilty of the "possession" charge. The trial court found Ragland (D) guilty. Ragland (D) appealed arguing first, that the judges use of the word "must" in the instruction conflicted with the jury's nullification power, which Ragland (D) claimed was an essential attribute of his constitutional right to a jury trial. Second, Ragland (D) argued that the judge should have informed the jury regarding its power of nullification.

Issue: Is the jury's nullification power, an essential attribute of the constitutional right to a jury trial, which the jury must be informed of?

Decision and Rationale: (Wilentz, J.) No. The overwhelming weight of authority is contrary to Ragland's (D) argument. Even where the use of the word "must" is discouraged, it is not a result of a constitutional command. It is only relatively recently that some scholars have characterized this power as part of a defendant's right to trial by jury. Like Ragland (D), they take the position that the exercise of the power is essential to preserve the jury's role as the "conscience of the community." Some laws are said to be unfair, while other laws may do injustice in specific applications. Only the jury, it is thought, is capable of correcting that unfairness or injustice through its nullification power. Cast aside is our basic belief that only our elected representatives, may determine what is a crime, what is not, and what laws need revision. Furthermore, it is their belief that a person is entitled to *more* than a fair trial even when such a trial is pursuant to fair law. In other words, a person is entitled to the right to be found guilty beyond a reasonable doubt, but then acquitted and set free because of the beliefs of the jury. If jury nullification has proven to serve society well, that proof has been kept a deep secret. We know so little about this power that it is impossible to evaluate it in terms of result. Since, there is neither constitutional nor other legal authority mandating a change in jury instructions, its ultimate justification must be that it is desirable that a jury should not be compelled to follow the law. If indeed this is a desirable state of affairs, then the jury should be told of its power. Counsel should be told that they may address nullification in summation, and be able to argue to the jury that it should not apply the law given by the court, but rather follow its own conscience. Moreover, juries should only include those people who are capable of exercising their nullification power. There is no mystery about the power of nullification. It is the power to act against the law. In its immediate application, it would confuse any conscientious citizen serving on a jury, by advising the person that after all is said and done, he can do whatever he pleases. Jury nullification is an unfortunate but unavoidable power. It should not be advertised, and to the extent constitutionally permissible it should be limited. Efforts to protect and expand it are inconsistent with the real values of our system of criminal justice and therefore it is not desirable. We conclude that the power of jury nullification is not a precious attribute of a right to trial by jury. The power of the jury to acquit despite overwhelming proof guilt and the juries belief of guilt beyond a reasonable doubt, is not a right that the jury must be informed of. It is nothing more than a power. Reversed on other grounds.

Analysis:

This opinion raises the issue of the jury's role and power in criminal trials. Specifically, this court strongly favors the role of the jury as the fact-finding body, leaving the judge as the law-finding entity. More importantly, it strongly disfavors the power a jury has to disregard the law. Reasons that jury nullification power exists include protection against governmental oppression, and allowing the jury to send a message about some social issue, that is more important than a particular case. Moreover, as the "conscience of the community," the jury may use this power to protect against socially undesirable convictions. However, the court strongly opines and sets forth many reasons why the power of jury nullification does more harm then good. Most importantly, it finds that it should be ultimately up to the elected representatives to determine what is a crime and what is not. It is the legislature's responsibility, and not twelve people picked at random, to revise law that is found to be unfair or imprecise. Though there are both advocates and critics on the issue of jury nullification, this court's opinion follows the overwhelming rule that jury nullification instructions to the jury are not permissible.

Chapter 2

To punish is to inflict pain upon a person by taking their life, liberty, or property. Since these attributes are inalienable rights granted to every individual, any system that intentionally causes such suffering, must have a justification. There are two types of moral justification. The first view, the consequentialist view, focuses on actions as means to good ends. The second view, deontology, focuses on actions as ends in themselves.

The primary consequentialist theory of punishment is utilitarianism. According to this view, the purpose of laws is to maximize the net happiness of society. Therefore, punishment is imposed in order to reduce antisocial behavior. Utilitarianism as applied to the criminal law takes different forms. One form is general deterrence. It states that a person is punished in order to convince the general community to forego criminal conduct.

A second form is specific deterrence. This approach states that the goal of punishment is to deter future misconduct by the individual who is punished. Accordingly, imprisonment prevents a person from committing crimes in the outside society during the period of segregation. Finally, a non-classical variety of utilitarianism is rehabilitation. Though the goal of this form is also to reduce future crime, it prefers to use punishment to reform the wrongdoer, rather than to secure compliance through fear of punishment.

The non-consequentialist, or deontological moral theory of punishment is retributivism. According to this view, punishment is imposed because an individual is deserving of it. Retributivist differ among themselves regarding the best way to defend their philosophy. According to one form, assaultive retribution, it is morally right to hate criminals. The desire to punish or hate, is morally desirable because it demonstrates that the crime victim respects himself. A second form, protective retributivism, justifies punishment as a means of securing moral balance in society. According to this view, those who embark in antisocial behavior, renounce the burdens others have assumed, reap the benefits of the system, and destroy the equilibrium. It is fair, therefore, to require payment of debt, through punishment that is equal to the debt owed, in order to restore equilibrium. Indeed, according to this view, the wrongdoer has a right to be punished.

Lastly, a third form of retributivism, victim vindication, defends punishment as a way to right a wrong. According to this view, by committing a crime, a criminal elevates himself with respect to others, making a false moral claim about his worth. Punishment corrects this claim, by allowing the victim to reaffirm his worth as a human being. It therefore represents the defeat of the wrong doer, making him even, once again, to the victim.

Critics of utilitarianism approach contend, first, that the general deterrence theory justifies using a person solely as a means to an end. That, utilitarianism may justify the punishment of one known to be innocent of wrongdoing, as long as this serves a greater societal purpose. Thus, it ignores the dignity and human rights of the wrongdoer. Although utilitarians do not deny the possibility that punishment of an innocent person could be justified, they insist that the factual circumstances supporting such a result would never come into play. Furthermore, they argue that the persecution of an innocent man would lead to wider consequences, not consistent with the utilitarian view of punishment.

Second, critics of rehabilitation argue that criminals cannot be reformed. In essence, they argue that since family, school, and religion have failed, then why should any other form of treatment succeed. However, advocates of rehabilitation believe that reformation is preferable to punishment based on fear, or the "just deserts" attitude of retribution. They point out that the rehabilitative model preserves the concept of redemption, evident in Judeo-Christian values.

Critics of retributivism contend that the infliction of pain is senseless and even cruel, if it does no good to society. Moreover, critics contend that retributivism glorifies anger and legitimizes hatred. Lastly, critics claim that retributivism is irrational, because it is founded on emotions. Retributivist believe however, that emotion can have a moral content. Anger demonstrates our awareness that the criminal has violated our rights, has acted unjustly and therefore, deserves to be punished. It is morally good when it demonstrates that we value ourselves and the rights of other crime victims.

Neither theory has won the ultimate debate, as both theories have proven to attract law makers. Therefore, the law of crimes that has developed is not philosophically consistent. Some laws are primarily retributive in nature, while others are dominantly utilitarian in character. At a minimum, many scholars believe in a hybrid system. Thus, like retributivist, they would not punish an innocent person, even if it would do some greater societal good. On the other hand, they would not punish a guilty person unless it would lead to a greater societal benefit.

Chapter 2

NOTE: THE PURPOSE OF THIS OUTLINE IS TO ORGANIZE THE CASES SO THAT ONE CAN QUICKLY UNDERSTAND THE RELEVANCE OF EACH CASE TO THE COURSE. NO ATTEMPT IS MADE IN THIS OVERVIEW TO ADDRESS EVERY CONCEPT THAT MUST BE STUDIED. BE SURE TO READ THE ENTIRE CASEBOOK AND/OR OTHER MATERIALS TO GAIN A FULL UNDERSTANDING OF ALL CONCEPTS.

I. Introduction: Statistics and Concerns
   A. This chapter focuses on the justifications for punishment, sentencing decisions, and the goal of proportionality of punishment. Although there are many other forms of punishment, incarceration is presently the typical form of punishment for serious crimes.
   B. There are important moral and public policy questions about our punishment system.
      1. The most important are the following:
         a. Who should be punished, and
         b. How much punishment is appropriate?
      2. Another question is whether we under-use non-incarcerative methods of punishment. In order to answer these and other penological questions, it is first necessary to decide why we punish at all.

II. Theories of Punishment
   A. *Utilitarian Justification of Punishment* approves or disapproves of every tendency to augment or diminish the happiness of a particular party.
      1. The general object which all laws have, or ought to have, in common, is to augment total happiness of the community, and to exclude mischief. However, since punishment is mischief it should only be used to exclude some greater evil.
      2. Therefore, punishment should not be imposed where there is no mischief for it to prevent, where it cannot prevent the mischief, where the mischief it would produce would be greater than the mischief it prevents, and where the mischief may be prevented without it. *Jeremy Bentham.*
   B. Utilitarian theories of when punishment can have beneficial purposes have varied but the following are the most important.
      1. *General deterrence.* Knowledge that punishment will follow deters people from committing crimes.
         a. The person who has already committed the crime cannot, of course, be deterred from committing that crime. However, his punishment may help deter others. Seeing others punished for certain behavior can create in people a sense of association between punishment and the act, that may constrain them even when they are sure they will not get caught.
         b. In a properly developed penal code, the benefits to be gained by committing crimes, would be outweighed by the harms of punishment. Accordingly, the smaller the chance of detection, the more severe the penalty should be.
      2. *Individual deterrence.* The imposition of punishment creates fear in the offender that if he repeats his act, he will be punished again.
         a. To deter an offender from repeating his actions, a penalty should be severe enough to outweigh, in his mind, the benefits of the crime.
         b. More severe punishment of repeat offenders is warranted, because the first penalty has proven to be an ineffective individual deterrent.
      3. *Incapacitation.* These punishments, such as imprisonment, physically prevent persons of dangerous disposition from acting upon their destructive tendencies.
      4. *Reform.* Punishment may help to reform the criminal so that his wish to commit crimes will be lessened, and perhaps so that he can be a happier, more useful person. Penalties may contribute to reform. However, reform is usually conceived as involving more positive steps, such as educational training programs. Their primary purpose is to alter the options that the released convict will face. *Kent Greenawalt.*
   C. Retributive Justifications of Punishment
      1. Juridical punishment can never be imposed merely as a means for promoting another good either with regard to the individual or to society, but must in all cases be imposed only because the individual on whom it is imposed has committed a crime.
         a. A person should never be dealt with merely as a means subservient to the purpose of another, nor be mixed up with the subjects of real right.
         b. Furthermore, a person must be found guilty and punishable before there can be any thought of drawing from his punishment any benefit for himself or his fellow citizens.
         c. The penal law is a categorical imperative, and woe to the person who uses the theories of utilitarianism to discover some advantage that may discharge that person from the justice of punishment. For if justice and righteousness perish, human life would no longer have any value in the world.
         d. Even if a civil society agreed to dissolve itself with the consent of all its members, the last murderer lying in the prison ought to be executed before the resolution was carried out. This ought to be done so that everyone may realize the desert of his deeds. *Immanuel Kant.*
      2. Despite the differences which exist as to the nature of morals, no one regards murder, rape, arson,

robbery, theft, or the like, with any feeling but detestation.

   a. The infliction of punishment by laws, gives definite expression and a solemn justification to the hatred which is excited by the commission of the offense.

   b. Thus, criminal law proceeds upon the principle that it is morally right to hate criminals, and it confirms and justifies that sentiment by inflicting upon criminals punishments which express it. I think it highly desirable that criminals should be hated, and that the punishment imposed upon them should be so contrived as to give expression to that hatred. *2 James Fitzjames Stephen.*

3. Retributivism is divisible into "negative" and "positive" variants.

   a. Negative retributivism, accepted by many or most scholars, holds that it is morally wrong to punish an innocent person even if society might benefit from the action.

   b. Positive retributivism is more controversial, and holds that not only must an innocent person never be punished, one who is guilty must be punished. It is divisible into two categories, "assaultive" and "protective" retribution.

     (1) Assaultive retribution holds that it is morally right to hate criminals. Punishment is justified without any consideration of the criminal's rights. The difficulty with this thesis is that it is based in significant part on re venge- utilitarianism rather than on retribution. It justifies punishment of criminals because it deters private vengeance, and sends a useful message to would-be offenders that such conduct is wrongful.

     (2) Protective retribution is based on the proposition that not only does a just society have a right to punish, but that criminals also have a right to be punished. *Joshua Dressler.*

4. If a total case is made against hatred, it must be made against examples where the hatred appears at its best. For instance, where a person has in fact been treated very immorally, reasonably believes that the wrongdoer is totally unrepentant of the wrongdoing, and hates the wrongdoer and desires that the wrongdoer suffers. This kind of case must be made central in any comprehensive attack on the nature and justification of hatred that is retributive in nature. *Jeffrie G. Murphy & Jean Hampton.*

   a. I have previously argued that resentment is essentially tied to self-respect, as an emotional defense against attack on self esteem. Even supposing this is true, it may seem that it will not help very much in justifying hatred.

   b. The hater, unlike the resenter, is not simply engaged in protest and self-assertion, but also desires that the object of his hate be hurt. The desire to hurt another then, must sometimes be justified.

   c. If there is any truth at all in retributive theories of punishment, then it is sometimes permissible that persons be hurt, in response to their wrongdoing. Therefore, it is sometimes permissible to desire to hurt people for retributive reasons.

   d. We may say that retributive hatred is a strategy designed to see that people get their just deserts. The wrongdoer gets what is deserved, and the victim gets some personal satisfaction from seeing the justice done.

   e. Retributive hatred is thus in principle vindicated as a permissible, if not mandatory, response of a victim to wrongdoing.

5. Connecting punishment with the violation of rules, and making public the provision for punishment, is both reasonable and just.

   a. First, it is only reasonable that those who comply with the rules, are given some assurance that they will not be assuming burdens that others will not.

   b. Second, fairness dictates that a system, in which benefits and burdens are equally distributed, has a mechanism designed to prevent an unequal distribution of the benefits and burdens.

   c. Third it is just to punish those who have violated the rules and caused unfair distribution of benefits and burdens.

   d. These individuals have acquired an unfair advantage by reaping benefits, without assuming the burdens. Therefore, they owe something to others. Punishing such individuals restores the equilibrium of benefits and burden by taking from the individual what is owed.

   e. Finally, there are also a variety of operative principles which provide some guarantee that the system of punishment does not promote unfair distribution of benefits and burdens.

     (1) For one thing, provision is made for a variety of defenses, each of which diminishes the chances of taking a benefit from a person who has not derived an unfair advantage.

     (2) For instance, when someone has an epileptic seizure and strikes another, that person is excused, because punishment in this case is punishment of the innocent. It is punishment of a person who did not voluntarily renounce a burden others have assumed. Therefore it would not restore equilibrium, but instead cause the unequal distribution of benefits and burdens. *Hebert Morris.*

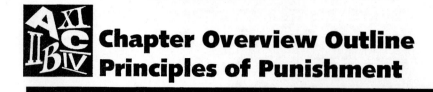

Chapter Overview Outline
Principles of Punishment

6. A retributivist commitment to punishment is not merely a commitment to taking hubristic wrongdoers down a peg or two. It is also a commitment to asserting moral truth in the face of its denial.

    a. If I have value equal to my assailant, then that must be made manifest after I have been victimized. By victimizing me, the wrongdoer has declared himself elevated with respect to me.

    b. If I cause the wrongdoer to suffer in proportion to my suffering , his elevation over me is denied, and moral reality is reaffirmed.

    c. Therefore retribution is the defeat of the wrongdoer at the hands of the victim. It is a symbol that is conceptually required to reaffirm the victim's equal worth in the face of a challenge to it. Punishment makes this assertion by inflicting on a wrongdoer, something comparable to what he inflicted on the victim. To master him in the way he mastered the victim. *Jeffrie G. Murphy & Jean Hampton.*

III. The Penal Theories in Action

  A. A person may be punished and convicted of murder, despite having killed   out of necessity. *The Queen v. Dudley and Stephens.*

    1. However, the amount of punishment imposed, depends on the facts of each case. *People v. Superior Court (Du).*

  B. Thus, even a sentence of probation is permissible for voluntary manslaughter, due to the unusual facts of the case. *People v. Du.*

  C. On the other hand, life imprisonment is permissible punishment for other situations, such as those involving career criminals. *United States v. Jackson.*

IV. Proportionality of Punishment

  A. General Principles

    1. The principle and standard of punishment is quality, by which the pointer of the scale of justice is made to incline no more to one side than the other.

    a. It may be rendered by saying that the undeserved evil which any one commits on another is to be regarded as perpetrated on himself. Thus, it may be said that if you slander another, you slander yourself; if you strike another you strike yourself.

    b. This is the right of retaliation, and properly understood, it is the only principle which in regulating a public court, as distinguished from a private judgment, can definitely assign both the quality and the quantity of a just penalty. *Immanuel Kant.*

    2. The general object of all laws is to prevent mischief. When it is worthwhile to use punishment as a means to prevent mischief, there are four objects, governed by the principle of utility, to keep in mind. Further-

more, there are rules to these four objects, by which the proportion of punishment is to be governed.

    3. The first object is to prevent all offences whatsoever.

    a. Rule 1. Since the object is to prevent mischief, the value of the punishment must not be less than what is sufficient to outweigh the profit of the offence.

    b. Rule 2. The greater the mischief, the greater the punishment.

    4. The second object is, if an offence is to be committed, to induce the wrongdoer into committing a less mischievous offence.

    a. Rule 3. The punishment for the greater offence must be sufficient to induce a man to prefer the lesser penalty.

    5. The third object is, when a man has resolved upon a particular offence, to dispose him to do no more mischief than is necessary for his purpose.

    a. Rule 4. The punishment should be adjusted in such a manner to each particular offense, that for every part of the mischief, there may be a motive to restrain the offender from giving birth to it.

    6. The last object is to prevent the mischief at as cheap a rate as possible.

    a. Rule 5. The punishment should not be more than what is necessary to bring it into conformity with the rules here given. *Jeremy Bentham.*

  B. Constitutional Principles

    1. The Eighth Amendment to the United States Constitution provides that, "Excessive bail shall not be required, nor excessive fines imposed, nor cruel and unusual punishment inflicted."

    2. In 1910, the Supreme Court ruled that this clause also prevented punishments that, by their excessive length or severity, were "grossly disproportionate to the offense charged.

    3. However, the Supreme Court has struggled with the question of what constitutes "grossly disproportional" punishment, and has been deeply divided on whether the federal judiciary should become involved at all in the proportionality overview.

    a. The Supreme Court has undergone a proportionality review in the past, and held that the death penalty is a grossly disproportionate and excessive punishment for the crime of raping an adult woman. *Coker v. Georgia.*

    b. More recently however, the Supreme Court has debated on whether to undergo any proportionality review at all, or at least limit it to cases of when the harshest penalty, the death penalty, is imposed. *Harmelin v. Michigan.*

The Queen v. Dudley and Stephens

(Society) v. (Cannibals)
14 Q.B.D. 273 (1884)

M E M O R Y   G R A P H I C

Instant Facts
Two English seamen are convicted of murder for killing and eating a young crew member.

Black Letter Rule
A person may be punished and convicted of murder, despite killing out of necessity.

Case Vocabulary

GENERAL DETERRENCE: A form of utilitarianism, which states that the goal of punishing a person is to convince the general community to forego similar misconduct.

RETRIBUTIVISM: A principle that justifies punishment, by stating that misconduct is deserving of it.

SPECIFIC DETERRENCE: A form of utilitarianism, which states that the goal of punishing a person is to convince that person to forego similar misconduct.

UTILITARIANISM: A principle that justifies punishment as a potential pain and deterrent to anti-social behavior.

Procedural Basis: Appeal to the Queen's Bench Division, of a conviction for felony and murder.

Facts: On July 5th, 1884, Thomas Dudley (Dudley) (D1), Edward Stephens (Stephens) (D2), Brooks, and Richard Parker (Parker) (a young seventeen- or eighteen-year-old English boy) set out to sea on the Mignonette, a yacht. Subsequently, they were cast away in a storm at sea, 1600 miles away from the Cape of Good Hope, and were compelled to put into an open boat belonging to the Mignonette. For three days, the four individuals only had two 1-lb. tins of turnips and no water to subsist upon. On the fourth day, they caught a small turtle, which was entirely consumed after twelve days. For eight days after, they had nothing to eat, and no fresh water, except for rain water they were able to catch. On July 24th, Dudley (D1) proposed to Stephen (D2) and Brooks, but not to Parker, that lots should be cast to see who should be put to death and used for food to save the rest. Brooks refused and there was no drawing of lots. The next day, July 25th, when no vessel appeared to save them, Dudley (D1) and Stephens (D2) agreed to kill Parker, despite Brooks dissent. Dudley (D1) offered a prayer asking for forgiveness should any of them be tempted to commit a rash act, and then approached the young boy. The young boy, lying helpless at the bottom of the boat, weakened by famine and by drinking sea water, unable to resist, and never assenting to be killed, was cut in the throat and killed by Dudley (D1). The men fed upon the young boy, and then were rescued by a passing vessel. Dudley (D1) and Stephen (D2) were tried and convicted of murder.

Issue: Should a person be punished and convicted of murder, for killing out of necessity?

Decision and Rationale: (Coleridge, C.J.) Assuming any necessity to kill anybody, there was no greater necessity than here. If the men had not fed upon the young boy, they probably would have not survived to be rescued. The young boy, being in a much weaker condition, was likely to have died before them. However, if upon the whole matter the court should find that the killing of Richard Parker be felony and murder, then the jurors say that Dudley (D1) and Stephens (D2) were each guilty of felony and murder as alleged in the indictment.

Analysis:

This case raises the issue of who is deserving of punishment. Specifically, it asks the reader to decide whether Dudley (D1) and Stephens (D2) are deserving of punishment for their conduct, and why. Is your answer based on utilitarian principles of general and specific deterrence? More precisely, will punishment convince the general community to forego similar conduct, or deter future misconduct by the offenders. Or is your answer based on the retributive principle, that this conduct is deserving of punishment? It may be a combination of both principles. The answer may turn upon whether the murder was really a necessity, seen as a necessity in the eyes of Dudley (D1) and Stephens (D2), or whether necessity can justify the taking of an innocent boy's life. The answer may also turn upon the feelings of remorse, if any, felt by the murderers. All in all, the purpose of this case is to introduce the reader to reasons for punishment.

People v. Superior Court (Du)

(Society) v. (Judge)
5 Cal. App. 4th 822, 7 Cal. Rptr. 2d 177 (1992)

M E M O R Y   G R A P H I C

Instant Facts

A liquor store owner is convicted of voluntary manslaughter, after shooting and killing a young customer, believed to be a shoplifter, in the back of the head while the customer was leaving.

Black Letter Rule

The amount of punishment imposed for voluntary manslaughter depends on the facts of each case.

Case Vocabulary

VOLUNTARY MANSLAUGHTER: The intentional killing of another human being without malice aforethought.

Procedural Basis: Appeal to the California Court of Appeals, of a judgment by the trial court, giving probation for voluntary manslaughter.

Facts: Empire Liquor Market (Empire) is one of two liquor stores owned and operated by Billy Du and wife Soon Ja Du (Du) (D). It is located in a bad area where shoplifting was a usual occurrence. On March 16, 1991, Du (D) worked at Empire, while Du's (D) husband, slept in the family van outside. While Du (D) was with two other customers, she observed fifteen-year-old Latasha Harlins (Latasha) enter the store, take a bottle of orange juice from the refrigerator, place it in her back pack, and proceed to the counter with the juice partially visible. Du (D) had observed many shoplifters in the store, and it was her experience that people who shoplifted would take merchandise, hide it, then approach the counter, pay for a smaller item, then leave. Witnesses testified that when Latasha approached the counter with about two or three dollars in her hand, she was confronted by Du (D), who called Latasha a "bitch" and accused her of stealing. After Du (D) asked Latasha to pay for the juice, Latasha replied "what juice?" A struggle ensued when Du (D) began to pull on Latasha's sweater trying to retrieve the juice, which fell out of the bag and onto the floor. Latasha then hit Du (D) with her fist, twice in the eye, causing Du (D) to fall behind the counter. Du (D), believing that if she was hit one more time she would die, then through a stool from behind the counter that missed Latasha. Subsequently Du (D) reached behind the counter and pulled out a .38-caliber revolver. Latasha then placed the orange juice on the counter, turned to leave and was shot in the back of the head by Du (D). Latasha was killed instantly with two dollars in her hand. At trial, Du (D) testified that she had never held a gun before, nor knew how it worked. Moreover, Du (D) testified that she did not remember firing and that she did not intend to kill Latasha. The gun was purchased in 1981 by Du's (D) husband, but was never fired. In 1988 the gun was stolen from the other liquor store Du (D) owned, but was returned by police in 1990. At trial a ballistics expert testified that the gun had been altered, and that the trigger pull necessary to fire the gun had been drastically reduced, and that the gun could be fired without putting much pressure on the trigger. Furthermore, the safety mechanism did not function properly. The Jury found Du (D) guilty of voluntary manslaughter, which implied that Du (D) had the intent to kill and that the killing was unlawful. Thus the jury rejected the defenses that the killing was unintentional and that Du (D) killed in self-defense. After the conviction, a probation report was prepared. It revealed that Du (D) was a 51-year-old Korean-born naturalized American citizen, who arrived in the United States in 1976. After saving enough money, Du (D) and her husband purchased Empire, despite warnings that it was in a "bad area." The store was plagued with problems from the beginning. The area surrounding the store was frequented by narcotics dealers and gang members. The store itself was burglarized over 30 times and shoplifting occurred 40 times per week. Furthermore, Joseph Du, Du's (D) son, had been threatened over 30 times, and more than 20 times people came into the store and threatened to burn it down. The report also revealed that Latasha had suffered many painful experiences in her life, including the death of her mother. She lived with her extended family in South Central Los Angeles. Latasha had just graduated Junior High where she was an honor student the previous spring. She was involved in activities at a youth center as an assistant cheerleader, member of the drill team, and summer junior camp counselor. She was a good athlete and church member. The probation officer concluded in his report that Du (D) would be most unlikely to repeat this or any crime if she were allowed to remain free, and that Du (D) would not seek to harm another. However, although Du (D) expressed concern for the victim and her family, this remorse was centered largely on the effect the incident had on Du (D) and her own family. Ultimately, the probation officer concluded and recommended that probation be denied, and that the defendant be sentenced to state prison.

Issue: How much punishment should be imposed upon a person unlikely to repeat similar misconduct?

Decision and Rationale: (Ashby, J.) OMITTED.

Analysis:

This case raises the concern about the amount of punishment to impose upon an individual. The decision and rationale of the appellate court is purposely omitted, in order to allow the reader to develop his or her own opinion of how much punishment Du (D) is deserving of. Specifically, the reader must decide based on these facts, whether Du (D) should be given probation or sent to prison. In answering, the reader should first consider the surrounding circumstances, keeping in mind the history of problems that plagued Du (D) and the liquor store. Second, the reader should also keep in mind that 51-year-old Du (D) was assaulted, albeit by a young woman fifteen years of age. Third, the gun was unknowingly altered with a hair pin trigger, giving the contention that the murder was accidental, greater strength. Fourth, the reader should consider whether Du (D) overreacted, and if so, whether the overreaction was understandable. Fifth, the reader should consider Latasha's background, and her actions during the incident. Finally, the reader should consider which form of punishment would better serve a societal purpose, based on theories of utilitarianism and retributivism. From a utilitarian standpoint, the reader should keep in mind that, according to the probation report, Du (D) was unlikely to commit this crime or similar crimes in the future. Moreover, if the killing was accidental (though the jury found it intentional), is it possible to deter society from accidental misconduct? From a retributivist standpoint, the reader should ask which punishment is Du (D) more deserving of? This may turn upon whether she overreacted to the situation, and whether this overreaction was understandable. It may also turn upon Du's (D) feeling of remorse, which is centered largely on herself and her family, and not Latasha. The question is not an easy one to answer. Luckily, the following trial court opinion does go through an analysis, justifying the imposition of probation upon Du (D).

People v. Du

(Society) v. (Store Owner)
No. BA037738

M E M O R Y   G R A P H I C

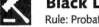

Instant Facts

A liquor store owner is convicted of voluntary manslaughter, after shooting and killing a young customer, and is given probation, even though originally sentenced to ten years in state prison.

Black Letter Rule

Rule: Probation is a permissible punishment for voluntary manslaughter in unusual cases.

Case Vocabulary

PROBATION: A sentence or punishment that allows a convicted person to return to the community, instead of serving time in prison.

Procedural Basis: Sentence hearing after a trial convicting a liquor store owner of voluntary manslaughter.

Facts: (More detailed facts are presented in *People v. Superior Court (Du)*,, the preceding case.) After being convicted of voluntary manslaughter for killing Latasha Harlins (Latasha), Soon Ja Du (Du) (D) was sentenced to ten years in state prison. However, the sentence was then suspended and Du (D) was placed on probation.

Issue: Is a sentence of probation for voluntary manslaughter permissible in unusual cases?

Decision and Rationale: (Karlin, J.) Yes. [Trial Court Opinion] Probation is a permissible punishment for voluntary manslaughter in unusual cases. The district attorney suggest that imposing less than the maximum sentence will send a message that a black child's life is not worthy of protection. This is dangerous rhetoric, which serves no purpose other than to pour gasoline on a fire. It is not my job to exact revenge for those who demand it. Justice is never served when public opinion, prejudice, revenge, or unwarranted sympathy are considered by a sentencing court. In imposing a sentence, I must consider the objectives of sentencing: 1) to protect society, 2) to punish the defendant for committing a crime, 3) to encourage the defendant to lead a law-abiding life, 4) to deter others, 5) to isolate the defendant so she can't commit other crimes, 6) to secure restitution for the victim, and 7) to seek uniformity in sentencing. First, because of the unique nature of each crime of voluntary manslaughter, uniformity in sentencing is virtually impossible. Statistics show that sentences imposed upon defendants convicted of voluntary manslaughter range from probation with no jail time to incarceration in state prison. Second, I do not believe that Du (D) needs to be incarcerated in order to protect society. Moreover, I do not believe that state prison is needed in order to encourage Du (D) to lead a law-abiding life, or to isolate her so that she cannot commit other crimes. However, state prison may be needed to punish Du (D). In the instant case, there is a presumption against probation because a firearm was used, as set forth in California Penal Code 1203(e) [which provides that except in unusual cases, probation shall not be granted to any person who used a deadly weapon upon a human being]. Therefore in order to overcome that presumption, the court must find this case to be unusual. There are three reasons that I find this case unusual. First, the statute is aimed at criminals who arm themselves when they go out and commit crimes. It is not aimed at shopkeepers who lawfully possess firearms for protection. Second, Du (D) has no past criminal record. Third, Du (D) participated in the crime under circumstances of great provocation, coercion, and duress. Thus, this case is an unusual case that overcomes the statutory presumption against probation. Finally, Du (D) should be placed on probation. First, the crime was committed because of unusual circumstances, such as great provocation. Second, although Latasha was not armed with a weapon at the time of her death, she had used her fists as weapons just seconds before she was shot. The district attorney argues that Latasha was justified in her assault on Du (D). However, had Latasha not been shot and had the incident which preceded the shooting been reported, it is my opinion that the district attorney would have relied on the store videotape and Du's (D) testimony to make a determination of whether to file charges against Latasha. Third, having observed Du (D), I cannot conclude that there was any degree of criminal sophistication in her offense. Nor can I conclude that she is a danger to others if not incarcerated. Furthermore, I do not believe that Du (D) would be here today if the gun she had grabbed had not been altered. This was a gun that had been stolen and returned to the Du family shortly before the shooting. There is no reason to believe Du (D) knew the gun had been altered in such a way as to, in effect, make it an automatic weapon with a hairpin trigger.

Finally, I cannot ignore the very real terror experienced by the Du family before the shooting, and the fear Du (D) experienced as she worked the day of the shooting. On the day of the shooting Du (D) volunteered to cover for her son to save him one day of fear. She may have reacted inappropriately to Latasha, but her over-reaction was understandable.

Analysis:

This trial court opinion provides the reader with an answer and analysis to the question posed in the previous case. In imposing a sentence, the court first states seven objectives to sentencing. It then states that uniformity in sentencing is virtually impossible because of the unique nature of each crime of voluntary manslaughter, but that probation is not an uncommon sentence. The court then goes on to conclude that imprisoning Du (D) serves no utilitarian purpose. Specifically, the court concludes that prison is not a necessary punishment to protect society, to encourage Du (D) to lead a law-abiding life, to isolate Du (D) so that she cannot commit other crimes, and to deter others. Finally, the court concludes that imprisoning Du (D) serves no retributivist purpose for punishment, because the court believed that Du's (D) overreaction to Latasha was understandable, given Du's (D) past experiences. It also saw no "criminal sophistication" in Du's (D) criminal act, and stated that Du (D) had no way of knowing that the gun was altered. Furthermore, it found that Latasha was not completely blameless in the incident. Therefore, although there may have been a statutory presumption against probation, the unusual circumstances that surrounded this case were strong enough to overcome that presumption. Thus, Du (D) was not deserving of a prison sentence. This case is a good example of the many considerations taken into account when determining how much punishment to impose upon a convicted person.

United States v. Jackson

(Society) vs. (Bank Robber)
835 F.2d 1195 (7th Cir. 1987)

M E M O R Y   G R A P H I C

Instant Facts

A convicted criminal is given a life sentence, after committing armed robbery of a bank the day of his release from prison, under a statute forbidding possession of weapons by career criminals.

Black Letter Rule

The imposition of life in prison is a permissible punishment for career criminals.

Case Vocabulary

POUR ENCOURAGER LES AUTRES: "To encourage others."

Procedural Basis: Appeal to the United States Court of Appeals, of a sentence of life in prison for possession of a weapon by a career criminal.

Facts: On May 30, 1986, Dwight Jackson (Jackson) (D), after being sent to prison on two bank robbery convictions, was released as part of a "work release program." Thirty minutes after being let out, Jackson (D), who had been previously convicted of four armed bank robberies and one armed robbery, brandished his revolver, and robbed the Continental Bank of Oakbrook in Terrace, Illinois. A passer-by witnessed a suspicious person flee the bank and noted the license plate of the car. Subsequently, Jackson (D) was back in prison before the sun set on the day of his release. Jackson (D) was sentenced to life in prison under 18 U.S.C App. S1202 [which provides that anyone who possesses any firearm and who has three previous felony convictions for robbery and/or burglary, shall be imprisoned not less than fifteen years, and shall not be eligible for parole]. Jackson (D) appealed.

Issue: Is the imposition of a life sentence a permissible punishment for a career criminal?

Decision and Rationale: (Easterbrook, J) Yes. Jackson (D) contends that the statute permits only a determinate number of years, and not a life sentence. However, when parole is forbidden, a judge may give either sentence to reach the same result. Jackson (D) was 35 when he committed the crime. Unless there are startling advances in geriatric medicine, a long term of imprisonment and life sentence are the same sentence. Therefore, it is silly to read the statute as authorizing one but not the other. The selection of a sentence within the statutory range is essentially free of appellate review. Jackson (D) is a career criminal and specific deterrence had failed. The court was entitled to consider general deterrence and incapacitation. Although life without possibility of parole is the upper end of the scale of sanctions, the imposition of life in prison is a permissible punishment for career criminals. The statute reflects a judgment that career criminals who persist in possessing weapons should be dealt with most severely. Affirmed.

Concurrence: (Posner, J.) Though I join the opinion and judgement of the court, I believe the sentence that Jackson (D) received is too harsh. He is unquestionably a dangerous and hardened criminal, who has been convicted of armed robbery four times. However, though I do not mean to denigrate the gravity of his offenses, the fact that he has never inflicted physical injury is relevant to deciding whether the sheer enormity of his conduct warrants life imprisonment. Few murderers, traitors, or rapists are punished so severely. The ground for the sentence in this case must be sought elsewhere. One ground for his sentence, as articulated by the district judge, is the need to prevent Jackson (D) from committing further crimes. However, it is extremely unlikely that if Jackson (D) were released 25 or 30 years from now, he would resume his career as a bank robber. Criminal careers taper off with age. Crimes that involve a risk of physical injury to the criminal are especially a young man's game. In 1986 only 3.4 percent of persons arrested for robbery were 60 years old. To suppose that, if Jackson (D) is fortunate enough to live on in prison into his seventies or eighties, it would still be necessary to detain him lest he resume his life of crime after almost a lifetime in prison, is too speculative to warrant imprisoning him till he dies of old age. The probation officer who conducted a complete investigation of Jackson (D), recommended a ten-year sentence. This may be too short, but it is some indication that imprisonment for the rest of Jackson's (D) life is too long, if the only concern is with the crimes he might commit if he were ever released. The remaining possibility is that this savage sentence is proper *pour encourager les autres*. Even if one were sure that Jackson (D) would be harmless in the last 10 to 20 years of his life, his sentence might be justified if the example of it were likely to deter other people similarly situated, from committing such crimes. This is possible, but speculative, for it was not mentioned by the district judge. We should ask how many 35-year-olds would rob a bank if they knew that if they were caught it would mean 20 years in prison without possibility of parole, compared to the number who would do so if it meant life in prison. Bank robbery is a crime of acquisition, not passion. The net gains, when the expected cost of punishment is figured in, is very small. It's a loser's game at best. Persons who would go ahead and rob a bank in the face of my hypothetical 20-year sentence, are unlikely to be deterred by tightening the punishment screws still further. A civilized society locks up such people until age makes them harmless, but it does not keep them in prison until they die.

Analysis:

This opinion continues the concern over the amount of punishment that should imposed upon convicted criminals. It is another good example of the many concerns that are taken into account when imposing punishment upon a convicted person. The court first determines that a life sentence is statutorily permitted. It then affirms the imposed life sentence, justifying the decision under utilitarian, general deterrence principals. Specifically, the court uses the decision as a warning, that career criminals who insist on possessing weapons will be dealt with severely. Although the concurring judge agrees with the judgment, he believes that a life sentence is too harsh because Jackson (D) never inflicted physical injury. Therefore, based on retributivist principals, he is not deserving of such a severe punishment. Second, because criminal careers taper off with age, the imposition of a 25 to 30 year sentence would serve the principal of specific deterrence, just as much as life in prison. Lastly, either a sentence for a term of years or a life sentence, would have an equal general deterrent effect. All in all, the severity of the punishment in this case, turns upon whether sentencing Jackson (D) to life in prison will have a strong "general deterrent" effect. As stated, the majority believes that this sentence will serve as an example to others, and deter them from similar misconduct. On the other hand, the concurring judge believes that a less severe penalty will serve the same purpose equally. This is a good transition into the next case, which deals with the proportionality principle of crime and punishment.

Coker v. Georgia

(Rapist) v. (Community)
433 U.S. 584, 97 S.Ct. 2861, 53 L.Ed.2d 982 (1977)

M E M O R Y   G R A P H I C

Instant Facts

A convicted felon is sentenced to death, after escaping from prison, breaking into a house where he robbed a couple, raping and kidnapping the wife, and driving off in the couple's car.

Black Letter Rule

The death penalty is a grossly disproportionate and excessive punishment for the crime of raping an adult woman, prohibited by the Eighth Amendment.

Case Vocabulary

CRUEL AND UNUSUAL PUNISHMENT: Punishment that inflicts torture, or by its excessive length or severity, is greatly disproportionate to the crime committed.
RAPE: Unlawful sexual intercourse with a non-consenting person, sometimes requiring the use of force.

Procedural Basis: Certification to the Supreme Court of the United States, of a sentence of death for rape.

Facts: On September 2, 1974, while serving various sentences for murder, rape, kidnapping, and aggravated assault, Coker (D) escaped from the Ware Correctional Institution near Waycross, Georgia. At 11 o'clock that night, Coker (D) entered into the house of Allen and Elnita Carver through an unlocked kitchen door. After threatening the couple with a "board," Coker (D) tied Mr. Carver in the bathroom, obtained a knife from the kitchen, and took Mr. Carver's money and the keys to the family car. Brandishing the knife, Coker (D) then raped Mrs. Carver and drove away in the family car, taking Mrs. Carver with him. Soon after, Mr. Carver freed himself and notified police. Coker (D) was apprehended and Mrs. Carver was unharmed. Coker (D) was charged with escape, armed robbery, motor vehicle theft, kidnapping, and rape. The jury found Coker (D) guilty, rejecting his plea of insanity, and a sentencing hearing was conducted. The jury was instructed that it could consider as aggravating circumstances, whether the rape had been committed by a person with a prior record of conviction for a capital felony. It could also consider whether the rape had been committed in the course of committing another capital felony, namely, the armed robbery of Allen Carver. Although at least one aggravating circumstance must be found before the death penalty may be imposed, the jury was also instructed that even if aggravating circumstances were present, the death penalty need not be imposed if there were circumstances that may be considered as reducing the degree of moral culpability. The jury, finding both of the aggravating circumstances on which they were instructed, sentenced Coker (D) to death by electrocution. Both the conviction and the sentence were affirmed by the Georgia Supreme Court. Coker (D) appealed to the United States Supreme Court.

Issue: Is the death penalty for the rape of an adult woman, a grossly disproportionate punishment prohibited by the Eighth Amendment as "cruel and unusual"?

Decision and Rationale: (White, J.) Yes. It is now settled that the death penalty is not invariably cruel and unusual punishment within the meaning of the Eighth Amendment. However, the court firmly embraces the holdings and dicta from prior cases to the effect that the Eighth Amendment bars not only those punishments that are "barbaric," but also those that are "excessive" in relation to the crime committed. A punishment is "excessive" and unconstitutional if it either, 1) makes no measurable contribution to acceptable goals of punishment and hence, is nothing more than the purposeless and needless imposition of pain and suffering, or 2) is grossly out of proportion to the severity of the crime. Furthermore, these Eighth Amendment judgements should not be merely the subjective views of individual Justices. Attention must be given to the public attitudes concerning a particular sentence-history and precedent, legislative attitudes, and the response of juries reflected in their sentencing decisions. By 1977, even though numerous states and the federal government had authorized capital punishment for rape, Georgia was the sole jurisdiction authorizing death for rape of an adult woman. Only two other states allowed capital punishment for the rape of a child. Moreover, since 1973 Georgia juries had sentenced rapist to death only six times in 63 rape convictions. Therefore, we conclude that a sentence of death for the rape of an adult woman, is grossly disproportionate and excessive, and is therefore forbidden by the Eighth Amendment. These recent events evidencing the attitude of state legislatures and sentencing juries do not wholly determine this controversy. However, the legislative rejection of capital punishment for rape confirms our own judgment, that death is indeed a disproportionate penalty for the crime of raping and adult woman. We do not discount the seriousness of rape as a crime. Short of homicide, it is the "ultimate violation of self." Rape, without a doubt, is deserving of serious punishment, but does not compare with murder. Although it may be accompanied by another crime, rape by definition does not include the death or even the serious injury to another person. Life is over for the victim of murder. However, life for the rape victim, though it may not be nearly as happy, is not over or normally beyond repair. Although the jury found that two aggravating circumstances existed, which is necessary under Georgia law for the imposition of the death penalty, this does not change our conclusion. Coker (D) may have had prior convictions for capital offenses, but that does not change the fact that the instant crime being punished is a rape not involving the taking of life. Reversed

Concurrence and Dissent: (Powell, J.) I concur with the judgment of the court and the plurality's reasoning, supporting the view that ordinarily death is disproportionate punishment for the crime of raping an adult woman. There is no indication that Coker's (D) offense was committed with excessive brutality or that the victim sustained serious or lasting injury. However the plurality does not limit its holding to the case before us or similar cases. Instead, it holds that capital punishment is always a disproportionate penalty for rape. It is unnecessary for the plurality to write in terms so sweeping as to foreclose each of the 50 state legislatures from creating a narrowly defined substantive crime of aggravated rape punishable by death. It is not this court's function to formulate the relevant criteria that might distinguish aggravated rape from the more usual case, but perhaps a workable test would embrace the factors identified by Georgia. A test that includes the cruelty and viciousness of the offender, the manner in which the crime was committed, and the consequences suffered by the victim.

Dissent: (Burger, J.) The "cruel and unusual punishment" clause does not give members of this court license to engraft their conceptions of proper public policy onto the considered legislative judgment of the states. Unlike the plurality, I would narrow the inquiry in this case to the question actually presented. Whether or not the Eighth Amendment prohibits Georgia from executing a person, who in three years raped three women, killing one and attempted to kill another, who is serving prison terms exceeding his probable lifetime, and who did not hesitate to escape at the first available opportunity. In my view, the Eighth Amendment does not prevent the state from taking an individual's "well demonstrated propensity for life-endangering behavior," into account in devising punishment. Although the plurality acknowledges the gross nature of rape, it takes too little account of the profound suffering the crime imposes upon the victims and their loved ones. The plurality's conclusion is based upon the bare fact that murder ends the life of the victim, but rape does not. However, it is not irrational, nor constitutionally impermissible for a legislature to make the penalty more severe than the crime, in order to deter wrongdoers. The test cannot have the primitive simplicity of "life for life, eye for eye, tooth for tooth." The state must be permitted to engage in a more sophisticated weighing of values in dealing with criminal activity, which consistently poses serious danger of grave bodily harm. I see no constitutional barrier in punishing by death all who engage in such activity, regardless of whether the risk comes to fruition in any particular instance.

Analysis:

This opinion raises the concern of proportionality in punishing criminals. The Eighth Amendment of the United States Constitution, prohibits the imposition of "cruel and unusual" punishments. The Supreme Court of the United State has determined that "cruel and unusual," includes punishments that are grossly disproportionate or excessive, when compared to the crime committed. Therefore, although it has been established that the death penalty itself is not "cruel and unusual," it may be a punishment grossly disproportionate to the crime of rape. In the instant case the majority argues that while rape is a serious crime, it does not deprive the victims of their lives. In taking into account other sentences given for rape, the majority concludes that the death penalty, is an excessively disproportionate punishment for rape, and is therefore prohibited by the Eighth Amendment. The dissent on the other hand, believes that the death penalty for rape is not prohibited by the Eighth Amendment. The dissent argues that Georgia should be allowed to formulate its own punishment, taking into account Coker's (D) criminal history. Moreover, the dissent argues that while the punishment may be disproportionate to the crime, it is not so grossly disproportionate, that it is prohibited by the Eighth Amendment. This case turns upon the seriousness given to the crime of rape, the consideration given to other penalties that have been imposed for rape, and the consideration given to past offenses. All in all, the opinion provides a good example of the difficulty of determining what constitutes "grossly disproportionate" punishment.

Harmelin v. Michigan

(Drug Dealer) v. (United States)

501 U.S. 957, 111 S.Ct. 2680, 115 L.Ed. 2d 836 (1991)

M E M O R Y   G R A P H I C

 Instant Facts

A criminal, convicted of possession of 672 grams of cocaine, is sentenced to life in prison, the harshest penalty given for that offense.

Black Letter Rule

Imposition of a mandatory sentence of life in prison without possibility of parole, for a conviction of possessing more than 650 grams of cocaine, is not "cruel and unusual" punishment.

Case Vocabulary

STARE DECISIS: The doctrine of precedent which requires a court, assuming the issue is the same, to follow its own previous decision, or the previous decision of a higher court in the same jurisdiction.

Procedural Basis: Certification to the United States Supreme Court, of a mandatory sentence of life in prison without the possibility of parole, for possession of 650 grams of cocaine.

Facts: Harmelin (D) was convicted of possessing 672 grams of cocaine and was sentenced to a mandatory term of life in prison without the possibility of parole. The Michigan Court of Appeals, rejected Harmelin's (D) contention that the sentence was "cruel and unusual" within the meaning of the Eighth Amendment, and affirmed the trial court's sentence. Harmelin (D) appeals to the United States Supreme Court.

Issue: Is the imposition of a mandatory sentence of life in prison without possibility of parole, for a conviction of possessing more than 650 grams of cocaine, "cruel and unusual" punishment?

Decision and Rationale: (Scalia, J.) No. We have previously held that it did not constitute "cruel and unusual punishment" to impose a life sentence, under a recidivist statute, upon a defendant who had been convicted successively of fraudulent use of a credit card to obtain $80 worth of goods, passing a forged check in the amount of $28.36, and obtaining $120.75 by false pretenses. We have also held, that the length of the sentence actually imposed is purely a matter of legislative prerogative. Moreover, we have also rejected an Eighth Amendment challenge to a prison term of 40 years and a fine of $20,000 for possession and distribution of nine ounces of marijuana. However, we set aside a life imprisonment sentence, without the possibility of parole in the our last decision on this subject to date, *Solem v Helm* (*Solem*) [finding that life imprisonment for three convictions of third degree burglaries, one of obtaining money by false pretenses, one of grand larceny, one of third-offense driving while intoxicated, and one of writing a "no account" check with intent to defraud, was a disproportionate penalty under the Eighth Amendment]. This decision based its conclusion principally upon the proposition that a right to be free from disproportionate punishment was embodied within the "cruel and unusual punishment" provision of the Eighth Amendment. However, we think it enough that those who framed and approved the federal constitution choose, for whatever reason, not to include within it the guarantee against disproportionate sentences that some state constitutions contained. Neither congress nor any state legislature has ever set out with the objective of crafting a penalty that is "disproportionate, though many penalties may seem so because they were made for other times or other places, with different social attitudes, different criminal epidemics, different public fears, and different prevailing theories of penology. There are extreme examples that no rational person could accept. But for the same reason these examples are easy to decide, they are certain never to occur. If the constitutional proportionality principle exists, its real function is to enable judges to evaluate a penalty that some assemblage of men and women has considered proportionate and to say that it is not. The standards seem so inadequate that the proportionality principle becomes an invitation to imposition of subjective values. This becomes so clear from a consideration of the three factors test that *Solem* found relevant to the proportionality determination. The test takes into consideration, 1) the inherent gravity of the offense, 2) the sentence imposed for similarly grave offenses in the same jurisdiction, and 3) sentences imposed for the same crime in other jurisdictions. First, assessing the gravity of an offense can be very difficult, as different communities and different states vary in their penalties of certain offenses. In the instant case, who are we to say what is excessive, when the Michigan Legislature, and not we, know the situation on the streets of Detroit. The second factor fails for the same reason. One cannot compare the sentences imposed by the jurisdiction for "similarly grave" offenses if there is no objective standard of gravity. Furthermore, even if "similarly grave" crimes could be identified, the penalties for them would not necessarily be comparable, since there are many other justifications for a difference. For example, crimes that are more difficult to detect, warrant a substantially higher penalty, in order to have a deterrent effect. The third factor may be easy to apply, but has no conceivable relevance to the Eighth Amendment. States may criminalize an act that other states do not criminalize at all. We have held that because of disproportionality, it was a violation of the Cruel and Unusual Punishment Clause to impose capital punishment for rape. Proportionality review is one of several respects in which we have held that death is different, and have imposed protections that the Constitution nowhere else provides. We would leave it there, but will not extend it further. Affirmed.

Concurrence: (Kennedy, J.)   While I concur in the judgment, my approach to the Eighth Amendment analysis differs from Scalia's. Regardless of the argument, stare decisis counsels our adherence to the narrow proportionality principle. Despite the conflicting analysis, our past decisions do yield some common principles. The first principle is that the fixing of prison terms is properly within the province of the legislatures and not the courts. The efficacy of any sentencing system cannot be assessed absent agreement on the purposes and objectives of the penal system. The legislatures are the ones responsible for making these fundamental choices and implementing them. The second principle is that the Eighth Amendment does not mandate adoption of any one penological theory. Third, differences in the underlying theories of sentencing and in the length of prison terms, are the inevitable and often beneficial result of the federal structure. Even assuming identical philosophies, differing attitudes of local condition, may yield different, yet rational, prison terms for particular crimes. Thus, just because a state has the most severe penalty for a particular crime, does not render the punishment grossly disproportionate. Fourth, proportionality review by federal courts, should be informed by objective factors to the maximum possible extent. Taking into account all these principles, the conclusion reached is that the Eighth Amendment does not require strict proportionality between crime and sentence. Rather, it forbids only extreme sentences that are "grossly disproportionate" to the crime. In the instant case, Harmelin's (D) life sentence is the second most severe sentence permitted by law. Harmelin (D) was convicted of possession of more than 650 grams of cocaine. Enough to yield between 32,500 and 65,000 doses. Although Harmelin (D) suggests that his crime was nonviolent and victimless, this argument is absurd. To the contrary, this crime threatened to cause grave harm to society. Harmelin (D) also contends that our proportionality decision requires a comparative analysis to other penalties imposed for other crimes in Michigan, and sentences for the same crime in other jurisdictions. However, a reading of our cases leads to the conclusion that intra- and inter-jurisdictional analyses are only appropriate in rare cases where a threshold comparison of the crime committed and the sentence imposed leads to an inference of gross disproportionality. The proper role for comparative analysis is to validate an initial judgment that a sentence is grossly disproportionate. Because of the gravity of Harmelin's (D)offense, the comparison of his crime with his punishment, does not raise the inference of gross disproportionality. Therefore, no comparative analysis of his sentence to others in Michigan and across the nation is warranted.

Dissent: (White, J.) The Eighth Amendment does not refer specifically to proportionality, but does forbid "excessive" fines, a restraint that suggests that a determination of excessiveness should be based at least in part on whether the fine imposed is disproportionate to the crime committed. Although Scalia argues that those who drafted and approved the Amendment chose not to include a guarantee against disproportionality, had there been an intention to exclude it, the Members of the First Congress would have said so. In any event, there can be no doubt that prior decisions of this Court have construed the Amendment to include the proportionality principle. Scalia provides no mechanism for addressing extreme situations of disproportionality. Though he states that these situations are easy to decide and are sure to never arise he provides no basis for deciding such cases should they arise. As for Kennedy, abandonment of the second and third factors set forth in *Solem*, makes any attempt at an objective proportionality analysis futile. By taking into account only two factors, the gravity of the offense and the severity of the crime, the court has no basis for the determination of gross disproportionality, other than the subjective views of the judges. This is the very sort of analysis shunned by the Eighth Amendment. Because there is no justification for overruling or limiting *Solem*, its proportionality analysis applies. The first factor requires an assessment of the gravity of the offense and the harshness of the penalty. Drugs are without a doubt a serious societal problem. However, to justify such a harsh mandatory penalty as that imposed here, the offense should be one which will always warrant that punishment. Mere possession of drugs even in such a large quantity is not so serious an offense that it is punished by life imprisonment. Moreover, unlike other crimes directed against particular persons, possession of drugs affects the criminal who uses the drugs most directly. The ripple effect on society caused by possession of drugs is often not the direct consequence of possession, but of the resulting addiction. The second prong of the analysis is the examination of sentences imposed on other criminals in the same jurisdiction. Life without parole, is the harshest penalty available in this jurisdiction. Crimes directed against the persons and property of others such as second-degree murder, and rape, do not carry such a harsh mandatory sentence. Harmelin (D) has been treated in the same manner as, or more severely than, criminals who have committed far more serious crimes. The third factor examines sentences imposed for the same crime in other jurisdictions. No other jurisdiction imposes a punishment nearly as severe as this one for the same crime.

Analysis:

As illustrated, the Supreme Court not only struggles with the concept of "grossly disproportionate" punishment, it is also deeply divided, especially when the death penalty is not involved, on whether to undertake a proportionality determination at all. Scalia first contends that there is no proportionality guarantee in the Eighth Amendment. Then he goes on to argue, that the three-factor test used in *Solem*, offers no solution to the question of disproportionality. He concludes, by limiting the need for determining proportionality, to cases, like Choker, where the death penalty is involved. The concurring opinion reaches the same judgement, but argues that the a proportionality review is only required when the punishment would lead to an inference of "gross disproportionality." It concludes that the Eight Amendment does not prohibit disproportional sentences, only grossly disproportionate sentences. And finally, the dissent argues first, that finding disproportionality is the first step in answering the question of excessiveness, or cruel and unusual punishment. It then contends that the *Solem* factors should not be overruled, but instead still provide the best method for answering the question. The opinion may leave you with a "proportionality" test, but does not determine whether a proportionality review is required at all. Inferentially, it leaves decisions on a case by case basis, that may give the court too much power to make a subjective analysis. Also, it may lead to instability in the law, by allowing conflicting judgments in every case.

Chapter 3

If you were convicted of and punished for a criminal offense, would you prefer that the law defined your conduct as criminal before you committed the act or afterwards? You probably would prefer the former. When reading the law that defines your offense, you would probably want the law to state clearly and precisely the conduct required to constitute the offense. Further, you would probably like to know how a court would interpret the criminal statute that defines your conduct as criminal. [If you disagree, just walk down to your local jail and ask for voluntary incarceration.]

The legality principle is fundamental to American criminal law jurisprudence. The principle is "no crime without law, no punishment without law." This principle prohibits punishing a person for his acts if the law had not defined the acts as criminal at the time the person engaged in them. The legality principle is important because it prevents vindictive after-the-fact criminal punishment and ensures that people have fair notice of the conduct that constitutes a criminal offense.

Since legislative bodies have the authority to enact laws, the authority of the courts is limited to interpreting laws. Therefore, it is a violation of the legality principle and the Fifth or Fourteenth Amendment Due Process Clause if a court construes a criminal statute in a manner that enlarges its scope and then applies the expanded definition retroactively to a criminal defendant.

Central to the legality principle is statutory clarity. If individuals are to have fair notice of the conduct that constitutes a criminal offense, then the criminal statute that defines the offense must not be so vague that persons of common intelligence must necessarily guess at its meaning and differ as to its application. A criminal statute that lacks clarity does not provide fair notice. Convicting and punishing a person pursuant to a statute that lacks clarity is a violation of due process of law. Further, criminal statutes that encourage arbitrary arrests are unconstitutionally vague.

When deciding legality principles and statutory clarity issues, courts often interpret criminal statutes. For example, a court may use the common law to determine if an unborn, but viable, fetus is a human being. It may use numerous statutory interpretation techniques to determine the meaning of a simple English word such as "carry." The primary goal of statutory construction is to ascertain the intent of the legislative body that enacted a statute; however, this is not necessarily an easy task to accomplish. Interpreting a statute in a manner that is consistent with a legislative body's intent may require a great deal of ingenuity. Nonetheless, courts and attorneys spend a significant amount of time interpreting criminal statutes. Furthermore, the manner in which a court frames a statutory interpretation issue is just as important as the variety of interpretation techniques that it uses to interpret criminal statutes.

Chapter 3

NOTE: THE PURPOSE OF THIS OUTLINE IS TO ORGANIZE THE CASES SO THAT ONE CAN QUICKLY UNDERSTAND THE RELEVANCE OF EACH CASE TO THE COURSE. NO ATTEMPT IS MADE IN THIS OVERVIEW TO ADDRESS EVERY CONCEPT THAT MUST BE STUDIED. BE SURE TO READ THE ENTIRE CASEBOOK AND/OR OTHER MATERIALS TO GAIN A FULL UNDERSTANDING OF ALL CONCEPTS.

I.   The Principle of Legality
   A. No crime without law, no punishment without law.
      1. The legality principle prohibits convicting and punishing an individual for a criminal offense if the law does not define his conduct as criminal when he engaged in the conduct.
      2. The legality principle serves two purposes.
         a. It prevents after-the-fact vindictive punishment.
         b. A criminal statute gives society fair notice of its effect and permits society to rely on its meaning.
      3. When alleged criminal conduct is not expressly prohibited by a criminal statute, a violation of the legality principle does not exist if the alleged criminal conduct is a common law offense and a general criminal statutory provision permits the punishment of common law offenses. *Commonwealth v. Mochan*.
      4. Due process is an important part of the legality principle.
         a. The Fifth and Fourteenth Amendments' Due Process Clauses require that citizens receive fair notice of conduct deemed criminal.
         b. There is a violation of due process when a court's construction of a criminal statute enlarges its scope, and the court applies the expanded definition of the statute retroactively. *Keeler v. Superior Court*.
   B. Statutory clarity insures fair notice to the citizenry.
      1. Conviction and punishment for violating a criminal statute that lacks clarity is a violation of due process of law.
      2. A criminal statute must not be so vague that persons of common intelligence must necessarily guess at its meaning and differ as to its applications.
      3. Prior judicial interpretation of the terms of a statute challenged for unconstitutional vagueness can defeat the challenge. *In Re Banks*.
         a. A criminal statute is not unconstitutionally vague if prior court opinions have construed the statute.
         b. A criminal statute that is vague on its face is not unconstitutionally vague as law-abiding citizens have a responsibility to read the statute, prior court opinions that construe the statute and law treatises in order to understand the statute's meaning.
      4. There is a due process violation when a criminal statute lacks clarity such that it is susceptible of enforcement in an arbitrary or discriminatory manner.
      5. Criminal statutes that fail to give ordinary people notice that their conduct is illegal and that encourage arbitrary arrests are unconstitutionally vague. *Papachristou v. City of Jacksonville*.

II. Statutory Interpretation
   A. Courts interpret criminal statutes to ascertain legislative intent.
   B. A simple English word such as "carry" can require statutory interpretation to determine legislative intent. *United States v. Foster*.
   C. To determine legislative intent, courts use a number of techniques to interpret a criminal statute, including but not limited to, looking at the purposes appearing from the statute taken as a whole, a statute's words and history, the common law, and the circumstances surrounding the statute's adoption.

Commonwealth v. Mochan

(People of Pennsylvania) v. (Man Suggesting Sodomy to a Married Woman that Is Not His Wife)

(1955) 177 Pa. Super. 454, 110 A.2d 788

M E M O R Y   G R A P H I C

Instant Facts

The trial court convicted Mr. Mochan (D) for a common law misdemeanor not codified expressly as a statutory offense for telephoning Mrs. Zivkovich several time per week and making lewd and obscene comments to her.

Black Letter Rule

When the conduct alleged is not prohibited expressly by criminal statute, a violation of the legality principle does not exist if a statutory provision permits punishment of common law offenses.

Case Vocabulary

NULLEM CRIMEN SINE LEGE; NULLA POENA SINE LEGE: A Latin phrase that states no crime without pre-existent law and no punishment without pre-existent law.

Procedural Basis: Appeal from misdemeanor conviction for lewd and obscene conduct not codified in criminal statute but classified as a misdemeanor at common law.

Facts: The People of Pennsylvania (P) indicted Mr. Mochan (D) for intending to debauch, corrupt, embarrass, and vilify Mrs. Zivkovich, a married woman with an outstanding character in the community. Mr. Mochan (D) was a stranger to Mrs. Zivkovich. Several times during each week, Mr. Mochan (D) telephoned Mrs. Zivkovich and made lewd, immoral, and obscene remarks to her. His comments included suggestions of intercourse and sodomy with Mrs. Zivkovich. The Pennsylvania trial court convicted Mr. Mochan for his conduct, and he appealed alleging that his conduct was neither punishable pursuant to statutory or common law.

Issue: When the conduct alleged is not prohibited expressly by a criminal statute, may the conduct nevertheless be found to be illegal if a criminal statutory provision permits punishment of common law offenses?

Decision and Rationale: (Hirt) No. When the conduct alleged is not prohibited expressly by a criminal statute, conduct may nevertheless be found to be illegal if a criminal statutory provision permits punishment of common law offenses. Mr. Mochan (D) received a trial before a judge. The trial court convicted him of intending to debauch, corrupt, harass, embarrass, and vilify Mrs. Zivkovich, because he telephoned her numerous times. During the telephone conversations, Mr. Mochan (D) made lewd and obscene statements that included suggesting that Mrs. Zivkovich engage in adultery and sodomy. Case precedent that decides whether Mr. Mochan's (D) conduct is criminal does not exist. Notwithstanding, Section 1101 of the Pennsylvania Penal code of 1939 permits punishment of common law offenses. The controlling principles of this court state that the common law is sufficient to punish as a misdemeanor acts that injure or intend to injure the public, affect public morality, and obstruct or pervert public justice. Additionally, conduct that openly outrages decency and is injurious to public morals is a misdemeanor at common law. If conduct is scandalous and affects the morals or health of the community, it is indictable at common law. Even to maliciously vilify the Christian religion is an indictable offense pursuant to the common law. Precedent sustains that an endeavor to persuade a married women to commit adultery is not indictable under the common law of Pennsylvania. However, Mr. Mochan's (D) conduct exceeds mere oral solicitation to commit adultery. His statements, accompanied by lewd, immoral, and filthy language, suggested sodomy. Therefore, his conduct exceeds solicitation of adultery. Not only were his statements injurious to Mrs. Zivkovich, they were potentially injurious to members of the public which include telephone operators, individuals who share Mr. Mochan's (D) four-party telephone line, and two persons in Mrs. Zivkovich's household who heard Mr. Mochan's (D) statements. Mr. Mochan's conduct establishes a common law misdemeanor. Judgment affirmed.

Dissent: (Woodside) The Pennsylvania Legislature determines the conduct that injures or tends to injure the public, because one of its most important functions is to determine the conduct that the State will punish. The majority's delegation to itself the power to apply general principles to conduct that it finds offensive or injurious to the public vitiates the constitutional power of the legislature. The common law is a part of the law of Pennsylvania, and Pennsylvania may punish conduct that violates it. Notwithstanding, the legislature decides the acts that are punishable, even acts that are an offense under the common law. Mr. Mochan's (D) conduct is reprehensible. Nonetheless, it is not conduct punishable under a law of Pennsylvania, as the majority failed to cite such a law.

Analysis:

Under the principle of legality, conduct is not punishable unless the law defines it as criminal before it occurs. Further, the Due Process Clause of the Fifth Amendment, applicable to the states through the Fourteenth Amendment, prohibits courts from creating offenses by enlarging statutes. Additionally, the Due Process Clause requires criminal statutory clarity. The clause prohibits conviction and punishment of persons pursuant to a statute that is vague so as to require them to differ as to its application and guess at its meaning. Individuals have the responsibility to research the law to determine criminal conduct, even if they must hire an attorney to do so. This research must include prior court opinions that construe a statute as well as legal treaties. If these research sources clarify the meaning of the statute, there is no violation of the Due Process Clause for statutory vagueness. In the instant case, Section 1101 of the Pennsylvania Penal Code authorizes punishing common law offenses that are not codified expressly in the penal code. The Superior Court of Pennsylvania affirms Mr. Mochan's (D) conviction for solicitation of sodomy and filthy language while acknowledging that case law precedent for its decision does not exist. This situation presents perplexing questions. Since the Pennsylvania Legislature did not define expressly Mr. Mochan's (D) conduct as criminal and the Pennsylvania courts had not previously found his conduct to be criminal, was Mr. Mochan (D) convicted for conduct that lacks a criminal definition in violation of the legality principle? Did the Superior Court of Pennsylvania violate the Due Process Clause by enlarging Section 1101 of Pennsylvania Penal Code by creating a criminal offense by stating that the common law, in the absence of judicial precedent, is sufficiently broad to punish conduct that directly injures or tends to injure the public? Does section 1101 of the penal code lack statutory clarity, or could Mr. Mochan (D) have researched the common law or legal treaties and found that his conduct would be punishable under the common law? The fact that Pennsylvania abolished common law offenses is evidence of the perplexity of these questions. [By the way, why is solicitation of sodomy a criminal offense and solicitation of adultery is not a criminal offense? Surely you will use your active mind to ponder this question into the wee hours of the morning.]

Keeler v. Superior Court

(Murderer of Unborn Fetus) v. (Court Alleged to Lack Jurisdiction Over the Murder Charge)

(1970) 2 Cal. 3d 619, 87 Cal. Rptr. 481, 470 P.2d 617

M E M O R Y   G R A P H I C

Instant Facts

Mr. Keeler (D) allegedly murdered an unborn but viable fetus by kicking his pregnant wife in the stomach.

Black Letter Rule

There is a violation of the Due Process Clause when a court construes a criminal statute contrary to the legislative intent and applies its expanded definition of the statute retroactively to a person's conduct.

Procedural Basis: A writ of prohibition to arrest murder proceedings.

Facts: Mrs. Keeler became pregnant by a man who was not her husband before receiving a divorce from Mr. Keeler (D). After Mr. Keeler (D) learned of the pregnancy, he met Mrs. Keeler while she was driving down a mountain road, blocked the road with his car, and impeded Mrs. Keeler's progress. He then walked over to Mrs. Keeler's car and confronted her about the pregnancy. When Mrs. Keeler did not respond, he assisted her out of her car. Mr. Keeler (D) then looked at Mrs. Keeler's stomach and became extremely upset. He pushed her against the car, shoved his knee into her abdomen, and struck her in the face. The blow to Mrs. Keeler's abdomen caused extensive bruising of the abdomen wall. Medical personnel performed a Caesarian section on Mrs. Keeler. They discovered that the head of the fetus was severely fractured and delivered it stillborn. A pathologist opined that the death was immediate and caused by the skull fracture. He also opined that the injury could have been the result of Mr. Keeler (D) shoving his knee into Mrs. Keeler's stomach. Mrs. Keeler's obstetrician provided evidence that the fetus had developed to a stage of viability prior to its death. The district attorney filed an information that charged Mr. Keeler (D) with murder of the viable but unborn fetus and infliction of traumatic injury and assault upon his wife. Mr. Keeler (D) then filed a writ of prohibition to arrest the murder proceeding against him, and the Supreme Court of California granted review.

Issue: Is there is a violation of the Due Process Clause when a court construes a criminal statute contrary to the legislative intent and applies its expanded definition of the statute retroactively to a person's conduct?

Decision and Rationale: (Mosk) Yes. There is a violation of the Due Process Clause when a court construes a criminal statute contrary to the legislative intent and applies its expanded definition of the statute retroactively to a person's conduct. Section 187 of California's Penal Code defines murder as the unlawful killing of a human being with malice aforethought. The legislature of 1872 enacted section 187. It took the language for this section from an 1850 enactment. An important question is whether the fetus that Mr. Keeler (D) is alleged to have murdered is a human being under California law. The inquiry begins by examining the intent of the 1850 legislature. This court presumes that the legislature was familiar with the common law in 1850. It further presumes that a legislature intends to continue common law rules in statutory form when it uses common law language in its enactments. Pursuant to the common law of 1850, a child must be born alive to support a charge of murder. Additionally, an infant could not be the subject of homicide at common law unless it had been born alive. The legislature of 1850 used common law language to define murder as the unlawful killing of a human being, and the common law at that time required a person to be born alive to support a charge of murder. Therefore, the legislature of 1850 intended that the term *human being* refer to a person that is born alive. We further find that there is nothing in the legislative history that demonstrates the legislature of 1872 had a different intention when in enacted section 187. It is the policy of California to construe a penal statute as favorably to the defendant as its language and the circumstances of its application permit. Since Mr. Keeler (D) is entitled to the benefit of reasonable doubt as to the true interpretation of section 187, we hold, for the aforementioned reasons, that the legislature did not intend to include the killing of an unborn fetus under the purview of section 187. The People of California (P) argue that science now facilitates the survival of a viable fetus born prematurely. They then conclude that this fact supports the finding that the killing of such a fetus is punishable under section 187. Their argument is unpersuasive. First, the authority to define punishable crimes rest entirely with the legislature. While a court may construe a statute according to a fair import of its terms to promote justice, it lacks authority to create offenses by enlarging a statute. The fair import of the terms in section 187 compels this court to reject enlarging the statute by construing its terms to cover an unborn but viable fetus. Second, even if we enlarge the statute to cover an unborn but viable fetus, the enlargement would not be applicable to Mr. Keeler (D) because the Due Process Clause guarantees him fair notice of punishable acts. California case law does not hold that killing an unborn but viable fetus supports a charge of murder, nor does the case law of our sister states. To apply a new definition of section 187 to Mr. Keeler (D) is not fair notice; it is an application without any notice. The Ex Post Facto Clause's prohibition against retroactive penal legislation supports this reasoning. The People's (P) suggested enlargement as applied to Mr. Keeler (D) violates the Due Process Clause. Therefore, this court refuses to engage in such unconstitutional folly.

Dissent: (Burke) The majority incorrectly suggests that it must confine its reasoning to common law concepts and the common law definition of murder. The California Penal Code defines homicide as the unlawful killing of a human being. The interpretation of the term human being need not remain static or fixed in time. The duty of this court is to render a fair and reasonable interpretation of the term in accordance with present conditions to promote justice and carry out the evident purpose of the legislature when enacting section 187.

Human existence is a spectrum that stretches from birth to death. Damaging a corpse is not homicide, because a corpse is not a human being. Nonetheless, medical life revival, restoration, and resuscitation advancements have modified society's understanding of what constitutes a corpse. If the majority would not ignore these advancements nor exonerate a killer of an apparently drowned child simply because the child would have been considered dead in 1850, why does it ignore medical advances that promote the survivability of a fetus? In this case, the issue before the court should have been determined with medical testimony about the survivability of the fetus prior to Mr. Keeler's (D) conduct. The majority states its lack of authority to create new offenses, however, murder is not a new offense. The legislature used the broad term human being and directed the courts to construe the term according to its fair import to promote justice. Do we serve justice by excluding an unborn viable fetus from the definition of a human being given the present conditions of our time? Further, Mr. Keeler (D) knew or should have known that his conduct could cause a homicide. Therefore, contrary to the majority, the potential for a Due Process Clause violation for lack of fair notice that his conduct could constitute a murder does not exist.

Analysis:

Even though most states have abolished common law offenses, this case provides an excellent example of the importance of common law doctrine as it relates to criminal offenses. A dispositive question in this case is whether a viable but unborn fetus is a human being pursuant to California law. As courts are to interpret the law rather than create it, they must determine the intent of their legislatures when construing statutes. Courts use various techniques to ascertain the intent of their legislatures. They include the legislative history of an act and the circumstances surrounding its enactment, earlier statutes on the same subject, the common law as understood at the time of the act's adoption, and interpretation of the same or similar statutes. In this case, the Supreme Court of California primarily used the common law to ascertain the intent of the 1850 and 1872 legislatures. It is interesting to note that the court presumes that the legislatures were familiar with the relevant common law. The court also presumes that common law language in statutory form means that the legislature intended a common law interpretation. These two presumptions are critical as they take the court directly where it wants to go. Armed with these presumptions, the court states that under the common law in 1850 an infant could not be the subject of a homicide unless it had been born alive. [The California Legislature must have known this]. The statute employs common law language. As a result, the case is resolved. This raises two interesting questions. Is a presumption of common law knowledge by a legislature a good one, or is the presumption simply a technique used to make a finding of legislative intent when the a court cannot truly ascertain the intent? Since it is found that a viable fetus is not a human being, the remainder of the opinion is academic. Clearly, a court that speaks eloquently about its limited judicial authority and duty to ascertain legislative intent will not contradict itself with judicial enlargement of a statute. Further, it is reasonable to presume that the Supreme Court of California is not interested in a tongue thrashing by The United States Supreme Court for violating the Due Process Clause. Perhaps this case is of interest because of the secondary implications the ruling has on the issue of the legality of abortion. If the court had ruled that the fetus was a human being, what would this mean for a person seeking an abortion?

In Re Banks

(State of North Carolina) v. (Peeping Tom)
(1978) 295 N.C. 236, 244 S.E.2d 386

M E M O R Y   G R A P H I C

Instant Facts

Banks (D) was charged with violating a Peeping Tom statute.

Black Letter Rule

Prior judicial interpretation of the terms of a statute challenged for unconstitutional vagueness can vitiate the challenge.

Case Vocabulary

INDICIA: Signs, indications, or circumstances that point to the existence of a given fact as probable but not certain.

IN PARI MATERIA: A rule of statutory construction that holds that statutes that relate to the same subject matter should be read, construed, and applied together so that the legislative intention can be gathered from the whole of the enactments.

Procedural Basis: State (P) appeals of trial court ruling holding Peeping Tom statute unconstitutionally vague.

Facts: The State of North Carolina (P) charged Mr. Banks (D) with violating its Peeping Tom statute. The statute states that any person who secretly peeps into a room occupied by a female person shall be guilty of a misdemeanor. The trial court found the statute to be unconstitutionally vague, and the State (P) appealed its ruling.

Issue: Can prior judicial interpretation of the terms of a statute challenged for unconstitutional vagueness vitiate the challenge?

Decision and Rationale: (Moore) Yes. Prior judicial interpretation of the terms of a statute challenged for unconstitutional vagueness can vitiate the challenge. Pursuant to the principle of statutory clarity, a criminal statute must not be so vague that people of common intelligence must necessarily guess at its meaning and differ as to its application. Conviction and punishment under statutes that lack clarity are a violation of the Due Process Clause. The definiteness requirement insures fair notice of prohibited conduct and a reasonably ascertainable standard of guilt. Mr. Banks (D) alleges that the intended scope of the State's (P) Peeping Tom statute is indefinite and reasonable persons could differ as to its application. He argues that the statute, if taken literally, prohibits conduct the State (P) did not intend to punish. Essentially, he argues that the statute cannot mean that which it states. In North Carolina, if a statute is susceptible to a constitutional and an unconstitutional interpretation, this court should adopt the interpretation that yields a finding of constitutionality. However, courts must strictly construe a criminal statute with regard to the conduct it is supposed to suppress. The intent of the legislature is controlling. Where a statute is ambiguous, courts resort to judicial construction to ascertain the legislative intent. Means and indicia courts use to determine legislative intent include the purposes appearing from a statute taken as a whole, a statutes phraseology and words, the law as it prevailed before the statute, the remedy and the harm to be remedied, the end to be accomplished, statutes in pari materia, and a statute's preamble or title. Legislative history of an act and the circumstances surrounding its enactment, earlier statutes on the subject, the common law at the time of the enactment and previous interpretations of the same or similar statutes provide other indicia to determine legislative intent. In *Wainwright v. Stone* [a case upholding Florida's Crime Against Nature statute against a challenge of vagueness] the United States Supreme Court stated that the judgment of federal courts as to the vagueness of a state statute must be made in the light of prior state constructions of the statute. This language suggests that judging a statute challenged on the ground of unconstitutional vagueness in light of its common law meaning, its statutory history, or prior judicial interpretation of its particular terms is an appropriate course of action. North Carolina derived its Peeping Tom statute from the common law crimes of nuisance and eavesdropping. The commonly understood meaning of Peeping Tom in this country is a person who sneaks up to a window and peeps for the purpose of spying and invading the privacy of others. North Carolina's Peeping Tom statute makes it a crime to peep secretly. In a prior case, this court dealt with the Peeping Tom statute and conduct within the purview of the common law usage of the term Peeping Tom. It interpreted the word peep in a manner that conveys the idea of a Peeping Tom. The court stated that peep means to look cautiously or slyly - as if through a crevice - from chinks and knotholes. In another case, it stated that the word secretly, as used in the Peeping Tom statute, conveys the idea of spying upon another with the intention of invading a female's privacy. These judicial interpretations give the language of the statute meaning. They sufficiently inform a person of ordinary intelligence, with reasonable precision, that the Peeping Tom statute prohibits wrongful spying into

In Re Banks (Continued)

a room inhabited by a female with the intent of violating her legitimate expectation of privacy. Therefore, the statute is not unconstitutionally vague as to violate the state constitution or the Due Process Clause. Additionally, Mr. Banks (D) challenges the statute on the ground that it is overbroad because it prohibits innocent conduct. In *Zwickler v. Koota*, the United States Supreme Court stated that the doctrine of overbreadth has not and will not be invoked when a limited construction has been or could be placed on a challenged statute. In *Lemon v. State* [a case upholding Georgia's Peeping Tom Statute], the Supreme Court of Georgia stated that Georgia's statute was narrowed by the requirement of wrongful intent. North Carolina's Peeping Tom statute is narrowed by the judicial interpretation requiring that the act condemned must be a spying for the wrongful purpose of invading the privacy of a female occupant of a room. The interpretation does not condemn innocent conduct. The statute is not unconstitutionally overbroad.

Analysis:

This case illustrates how prior judicial interpretation of the terms of a statute facing constitutional attack can save the statute. If a statute lacks clarity, it violates the Due Process Clause because it fails to give notice of the conduct the statute intends to punish. Mr. Banks (D) challenged the Peeping Tom statute on the ground of unconstitutional vagueness. Using its prior judicial interpretations of the terms of the statute, the Supreme Court of North Carolina held that the statute is not unconstitutionally vague. Before using its prior judicial interpretation of the statute terms, the court notes that North Carolina derived its Peeping Tom statute from the common law crimes of nuisance and eavesdropping. Additionally, it notes that the commonly understood the meaning of the term Peeping Tom as a person that peeps through a window for the purpose of spying on and invading the privacy of a female occupant. It then states that in a *prior* case involving the Peeping Tom statute the court *interpreted* the word "peep" to mean to look cautiously or slyly - as if through a crevice - out from chinks and knotholes. This meaning conveys the idea of a Peeping Tom. Addressing the meaning of the word "secretly" in the Peeping Tom statute, the Supreme Court of North Carolina states that in a prior case it indicated the word conveys the idea of spying upon a female with the intention of invading her privacy. Armed with these prior interpretations, the court finds that the statute prohibits the wrongful spying into a room upon a female with the intent of violating her legitimate expectation of privacy. Since the statute prohibits definite wrongful conduct, spying into a room upon a female with the intent of violating her legitimate expectation of privacy, the statute gives fair notice of the conduct it prohibits. Therefore, persons of common intelligence need not guess at the meaning of the Peeping Tom statute nor differ as to its application. Consequently, the statute is not unconstitutionally vague. On its face, the statute remains vague; however, this fact is of no consequence. Since the law requires a person to know the conduct that society prohibits, even if he must research prior opinions or legal treatises, the statute is not vague. Further, prior judicial interpretation of the terms of a statute challenged for overbreadth can save the statute. A statute is unconstitutionally overbroad if it punishes innocent conduct. The Supreme Court of North Carolina interpretations of peep and secretly narrow the scope of the statute to wrongful conduct. Innocent conduct is not in the statutes purview; therefore the Peeping Tom statute is not unconstitutionally overbroad.

Papachristou v. City of Jacksonville

(Prowler by Auto) v. (People)
(1972) 405 U.S. 156; 92 S.Ct. 839; 31 L.Ed.2d 110

M E M O R Y   G R A P H I C

 Instant Facts

Papachristou (D) and seven others were convicted of violating a Jacksonville, Florida vagrancy ordinance.

Black Letter Rule

Laws that fail to give ordinary people notice that their conduct is illegal and that encourage arbitrary arrests are unconstitutionally vague.

Case Vocabulary

ARBITRARY: Not administered consistently in accordance with a fixed set of rules.
DISCRETION: Personal freedom to make a decision.
NOLLED: Nullified; voided.
STIPULATED: Agreed upon by the parties in advance.

Procedural Basis: Appeal from conviction for vagrancy.

Facts: Papachristou (D) and seven others were convicted of violating a Jacksonville, Florida vagrancy ordinance. The ordinance made it a crime to be a vagrant, and defined vagrant broadly so as to include such groups as common drunkards, night walkers, thieves, habitual loafers [you know who you are!], and those able to work but living off of their wives and children. Papachristou (D), a white woman, and her companions, another white woman and two black men, were convicted of vagrancy - prowling by auto. At the time they were detained, Papachristou (D) and her companions were driving down a main street in Jacksonville, but police claimed they were arrested because their car had been stopped near a used-car lot that had been broken into repeatedly. Police denied that the racial mixture in the car influenced their decision to make the arrests. Smith (D) and Henry (D) were convicted of vagrancy - vagabonds after they aroused suspicion by walking up and down a street one morning looking for a friend they were to meet there. Heath (D) was arrested for "common thief" and his companion for "loitering" when they encountered police in Heath's (D) girlfriend's driveway. Heath's (D) arrest was based upon his reputation as a thief. Campbell (D) was charged with "common thief" after police stopped him for speeding, although [oddly enough] no speeding ticket was issued. Brown (D), who had a reputation as a thief and drug dealer, was convicted of "disorderly loitering on the street" and "disorderly conduct - resisting arrest with violence." Police had stopped Brown (D) coming out of a hotel, searched him, and found heroin, at which point Brown (D) began to resist the officers. The defendants challenged the vagrancy ordinance on the grounds that it was unconstitutionally vague.

Issue: Is a law that fails to give ordinary people notice that their conduct is illegal and encourages arbitrary arrests constitutional?

Decision and Rationale: (Douglas) No. A law that fails to give ordinary people notice that their conduct is illegal and encourages arbitrary arrests is unconstitutionally vague. The ordinance here makes criminal a range of conduct, such as nightwalking, that is normally innocent and is often engaged in by ordinary, law-abiding citizens. People of ordinary intelligence, even had they read the law, would not be aware which conduct was forbidden or how the law was meant to be applied. The vagrancy law also lacks any requirement that a suspect have a specific criminal intent. Instead, the Jacksonville police are given broad discretion to determine who seems suspicious, presumably in an effort to nip crime in the bud. Arresting people suspected of future criminality, however, is not allowed in this country. The Fourth and Fourteenth Amendments require police to have probable cause before they make arrests. Laws are meant to be equal and just in their application, and the vagrancy ordinance here gives police too much discretion for even-handed administration to be possible. The ordinance is plainly unconstitutional. Judgment reversed.

Analysis:

This decision was the final judgment on vagrancy statutes and was no great surprise to many legal scholars who had deemed such laws unconstitutional well before 1972. Debate continues [as it always does in the legal world], however, over just how much power law enforcement should have in dealing with people who arouse suspicion but have yet to commit an illegal act. The conflict is between the rights of citizens not to have to wait until something truly bad happens and the desire of society to have uniform laws that do not encroach on the rights of the innocent. The problem with the statute in this case was that it gave police too much power and discretion to decide who seemed suspicious. In such a situation, outside factors such as race, gender, or social class may come into play in decisions about whether to make an arrest. Additional guidance as to which specific conduct is prohibited presumably makes a statute more objective, giving police less room to insert personal biases or subjective beliefs into the performance of their duties. In *Terry v. Ohio*, the Supreme Court upheld the power of police to briefly stop and frisk a person on the street who reasonably seems suspicious for a short period without probable cause. This eliminated much of the need for vagrancy and loitering statutes of the type here, which were most often used as a means to investigate more serious crimes.

United States v. Foster

(Drug Trafficking Law Enforcer) v. (Drug Trafficker With A Gun)
(1998) 133 F.3d 704

M E M O R Y   G R A P H I C

Instant Facts

Foster (D), a drug trafficker, was convicted of carrying a firearm in relation to a drug trafficking crime.

Black Letter Rule

A simple English word such as *carry* can require statutory interpretation to ascertain legislative intent.

Case Vocabulary

IN PARI MATERIA: A rule of statutory construction that holds that statutes that relate to the same subject matter should be read, construed, and applied together so that the legislative intention can be gathered from the whole of the enactments.

Procedural Basis: Appeal from conviction of carrying a firearm in relation to a drug trafficking crime.

Facts: Leon Foster (D) manufactured methamphetamine. When the police became aware of his illegal activity, they pulled him over while he was driving his pickup truck and arrested him. Under his truck bed's snap-down tarp, the police found a loaded 9mm semiautomatic firearm and a bucket. A scale, plastic baggies, and handwritten notes with prices were inside the bucket. Mr. Foster was convicted of possessing methamphetamine, in violation of 21 U.S.C. § 844, and "carrying" a firearm during and in relation to a drug trafficking crime, in violation of 18 U.S.C. § 924(c)(1). Mr. Foster (D) appealed the conviction for "carrying" a firearm.

Issue: Can a simple English word such as "carry" require statutory interpretation to ascertain legislative intent?

Decision and Rationale: (Kozinski) Yes. A simple English word such as "carry" can require statutory interpretation to ascertain legislative intent. Section 924(c)(1) states that whoever during and in relation to any crime of violence or drug trafficking crime uses or *carries* a firearm shall in addition to the punishment provided for such crime of violence or drug trafficking crime, be sentenced to imprisonment for five years. The issue before this court is whether Mr. Foster (D) carried a firearm when he drove with it in his truck bed. "Carry" appears to be a simple word, but it has differing relevant uses. It may mean to transport or to arrange for the transportation of an object. It may also mean to hold an object while moving from place to place. The common understanding of the phrase 'someone is carrying a firearm' is a person has a firearm on his person. In *United States v. Barber* [a case interpreting the predecessor of § 924(c)(1)], the court gave the verb "carry" a broad definition when it stated that in ordinary usage, "carry" includes transportation or arranging for transportation. In *United States v. Hernandez* [a case interpreting the word "carry" when a vehicle is not involved], the court narrowed its interpretation of the verb by stating that a person must transport a firearm on or about his person to carry it. This interpretation means that the firearm must be immediately available for use. In Black's Law Dictionary, broad and narrow definitions of the verb exist. Additionally, it defines carrying arms and weapons as to wear, bear, or carry them upon the person or in the clothing or a pocket for the purpose of use. This particular narrow definition is more relevant to the issue at hand. There are those who criticize the narrow definition when applied to a defendant who has a firearm readily assessable within the passenger compartment of a moving car rather than on his person because it seems to exonerate the defendant. The critics fail to understand that the essence of the narrow definition is the ease of accessibility of the weapon while it is in motion rather than its location on a person. Therefore, a weapon in a moving car that is within reach can be said to be carried. In *Bailey v. United States* [the leading case on § 924(c)(1)], the United States Supreme Court began its analysis of the verb "use" by considering its ordinary dictionary meaning. Faced with several different interpretations, the Court considered the verb's placement and purpose in the statute. The Court emphasized that since the statute contains two distinct terms, "uses" and "carries," the Court must define them narrowly enough that neither engulfs the other. Since a person may use a firearm without carrying it and carry a firearm without using it, the Bailey Court narrowly defined "use" as active employment. Construing the terms in pari materia, there is no basis to define "carry" broadly when "use" has a narrow definition. Considering "use" in the context within the broader statute, the Bailey Court examined its employment in § 924(d) and argued that the term should have the same meaning in § 924(c)(1). Unfortunately, "carry" does not appear elsewhere within § 924. However, the Bailey Court warned that if the term "use" is defined too broadly, it would become synonymous with "possess," a term appearing elsewhere in the statute. If "carry" is defined broadly, there is a risk that it will become synonymous with "transport", a term appearing in many places in the gun statutes. This court refuses to take this risk. Since there is minimal legislative history on "carry," it is reasonable to speculate about the purpose a prohibition on carrying a firearm during and in relation to a violent or drug trafficking crime serves. Using or carrying a firearm makes those crimes more dangerous and can lead to injury or violence. However, a gun in a bag under the tarp in a truck bed presents substantially less risk. The previous arguments suggest a narrow definition for "carry." Further, where a criminal law is ambiguous, this court is wary of imposing criminal liability for conduct that the law does not clearly prohibit. This cautiousness supports the rule of lenity. Given the narrow definition of "carry," this court finds that Mr. Foster's (D) firearm was not immediately available to him. To use the firearm, he would have to stop and exit his truck, walk to its rear, open a snap-down tarp, and unzip the bag containing the gun. He could access his gun more quickly if it was within easy hand's reach. Judgment of conviction for carrying a firearm reversed and remanded for resentencing.

Dissent: (Trott) Rather than attack in a straightforward and analytical way the meaning of "carry" in a context of a motor vehicle, the majority casts the proposition as a duel between two interpretations of the word. The common word "carry" takes on metaphysical proportions that require the majority to throw the rule of lenity as a life raft to sinking drug traffickers. This court decided United States v. Barber, a case that reaches the correct result with respect to the word "carry" in a vehicle case. Barber was arrested with a gun in a locked glove compartment, and the court decided whether the gun was "carried" under the predecessor to § 924(c)(1). That opinion states that Congress never specifically addressed the question whether the term "carries" encompasses "transport" or "possesses," but the ordinary meaning of the term embraces Barber's transportation of the weapon. In ordinary usage, the verb "carry" includes transportation or causing to be transported. This court further stated that there is nothing in the legislative history indicating that Congress intended any hyper-technical or narrow reading of the word "carries." The transportation test announced in that holding is applicable today. The word "carry" derives from a Latin word that means cart or vehicle. The majority cites *Hernandez* to support the narrow definition of "carry;" however, *Hernandez* is not on point because a vehicle was not in issue. Regarding Congress's intend purpose prohibiting carrying guns during drug trafficking crimes, it is doubtful Congress would recognize the broad versus narrow distinction as espousing its purpose. Further, the distinction gives drug traffickers the least exposure to the law's reach when they are more vulnerable to detection by law enforcement. After reading the majority's opinion, drug traffickers will delight in knowing they can carry their guns in the trunk or under the hood of their car's during and in relation to drug trafficking crimes and remain beyond the reach of § 924(c)(1).

Analysis:

This case illustrates how courts use statutory interpretation techniques and strategies to ascertain legislative intent. The majority's strategy consists of looking in Black's Law Dictionary for the meaning of "carry." It finds broad and narrow definitions but finds the narrow definition of carrying a weapon on or about a person more appealing. It then seeks interpretation guidance from the Bailey case since Bailey interpreted the term "uses" in § 924(c)(1). The Bailey Court gave "use" a narrow definition. Construing "use" and "carry" in pari materia, the majority believes that a narrow definition of "carry" is appropriate. Next, the majority looks to the context within the broader statute to find a definition that matches the term "carry" or suggests a definition of it. "Carry" does not appear elsewhere in the statute. However, the majority notes that the Bailey Court was concerned about "use" becoming synonymous with "possess." Following Bailey's lead, the majority, having rejected the dictionary's transportation meaning of "carry," favors the narrow definition of "carry" so that the word will not become synonymous with transportation. Additionally the majority examined the minimal legislative history to ascertain the intended purpose for "carry." Finding little assistance there, it reasons that a gun carried in the manner as Mr. Foster (D) carried his creates substantially less risk than carrying a gun in hand's reach. By contrast, the dissent uses the ordinary usage of the word "carry" to argue for the broad transportation definition. Additionally, it uses *Barber*, a case involving a gun in a locked glove compartment and decided by this court to support its broad definition position. While statutory interpretation techniques are important, the manner in which one frames a statutory interpretation issue is more important. The dissent frames the interpretation issue of "carry" in the context of a motor vehicle. Framed in this fashion, it is able to argue for the broad transportation definition of "carry" in a straightforward and well reasoned manner. The majority frames the issues as a duel between different interpretations of "carry." It bootstraps its argument for a narrow definition by selecting a narrow definition from the dictionary. It then uses its ingenuity to employ other techniques to support its dictionary choice.

Perspective
Actus Reus

Chapter 4

Now, you are in the custody of the United States Board of Prisons. [What did you do, and what were you thinking?] Generally, a crime requires the concurrence of a physical act and a mental state that causes harm. If the prosecution cannot prove beyond a reasonable doubt that harm resulted from this concurrence, criminal liability does not attach. Actus reus is the physical act of a criminal offense. The mental state is mens rea.

So, what is a physical act? If there is a criminal assault with a deadly weapon statute, and an automobile mechanic who has an automatic response to certain stimuli strikes another person with a wrench, did the mechanic commit the physical act required by the assault statute? If a criminal statute prohibits appearing in a public place and manifesting an intoxicated condition, and someone brings a person to a public place and that person manifests an intoxicated condition, did the person commit the physical act of appearing in a public place?

The essence of actus reus is a voluntary act that causes harm. The physical component of the act is bodily movement or a muscular contraction that may or may not be visible. A voluntary act is a willed act. For example, reflexive actions, epileptic seizures, and spasms are not voluntary acts. You may think of them as involuntary acts, but an involuntary act is not actus reus. At first, the concept of a willed act may seem confusing since all acts, even involuntary acts, involve brain activity. However, the concept is very simple as the following exercise demonstrates. Tap your fingers on your desk. [Tap as you do when you are bored in class.] Now, assume that your fingers are tapping on the desk and you are observing the tapping but you cannot stop it. The case in which you controlled the tapping was a voluntary act. A voluntary act requires a sophisticated mental process that leads to a decision to perform a muscular contraction. The second scenario, uncontrollable tapping, is an event [notice that we did not say act] that simply requires physiological brain activity. Therefore, a voluntary act requires the use of the mind. An event (involuntary act) only requires the use of the brain. Criminal liability attaches only when there is a voluntary act.

In certain circumstances, an omission to act, rather than a voluntary act, may support criminal liability. For criminal liability to attach in these circumstances, the defendant must have committed an act of omission when he had a legal duty to act. Further, he must have had knowledge of the facts giving rise to the duty, and it must have been possible for the defendant to act.

The status of parties may give rise to a legal duty. For example, parents have a legal duty to protect their minor children from physical harm. Statutes may define legal duties. An example is a duty to pay taxes on earned income. Legal duties may arise from contractual obligations. Doctors have a contractual legal duty to provide ordinary medical care to their patients. A legal duty may arise from a voluntary undertaking. If an individual voluntarily gives aid to a person in peril, that individual must use reasonable care and continue the assumption of care so as not to leave the person in a condition that is worse than the condition he was in before receiving aid. If an individual creates a peril, he has a legal duty to come to the aid of a person in the position of danger.

A defendant may be liable for an offense if he commits an act of omission, but only if there is a legal duty to act. Therefore, it is extremely important to remember that mere moral obligation does not create a duty to act.

Chapter 4

NOTE: THE PURPOSE OF THIS OUTLINE IS TO ORGANIZE THE CASES SO THAT ONE CAN QUICKLY UNDERSTAND THE RELEVANCE OF EACH CASE TO THE COURSE. NO ATTEMPT IS MADE IN THIS OVERVIEW TO ADDRESS EVERY CONCEPT THAT MUST BE STUDIED. BE SURE TO READ THE ENTIRE CASEBOOK AND/OR OTHER MATERIALS TO GAIN A FULL UNDERSTANDING OF ALL CONCEPTS.

I. Actus Reus: The Physical Component of A Crime
  A. Actus reus is a physical act.
    1. A physical act is bodily movement or muscular contraction that may or may not be visible.
    2. For criminal liability to attach, the physical act must cause harm.
  B. Actus reus requires voluntary physical movement.
    1. A voluntary act is a willed act. *State v. Utter*.
      a. A willed act requires a sophisticated mental process that leads to a decision to perform bodily movement or a muscular contraction.
      b. An involuntary act, an act that does not support criminal liability, only requires physiological brain activity. It does not require the use of the mind.
    2. The defendant, rather than a third person, must perform the voluntary act if criminal liability is to attach. *Martin v. State*.
  C. In certain circumstances, an omission to act, rather than a voluntary act, may support criminal liability.
    1. A person may be criminally liable if he fails to perform a legal duty and his omission causes harm; however, mere moral obligation does not create a legal duty. *People v. Beardsley*.
    2. Commonly recognized legal duties include:
      a. Statutorily imposed duties: A person has a duty to pay taxes on earned income.
      b. Duties arising from a status relationship: Parents have a duty to protect their minor children from physical harm.
      c. Duties arising from contractual obligations: A doctor has a duty to provide ordinary medical care to his patients.
      d. Duties based on creation of a risk: An individual who wrongfully places another person in a dangerous position has a duty to come to the aid of that person.
      e. Duties arising from voluntary assistance: An individual who voluntarily renders aid to a person has a duty to use reasonable care and continue to provide assistance if withdrawal of

assistance would place the person in a worse position than if no assistance was rendered.
  D. It is important to distinguish affirmative acts from omissions to act.
    1. Removal by a medical doctor of life support equipment from a comatose patient that is unlikely to recover is an act of omission rather than an affirmative act. *Barber v. Superior Court*.
      a. The cessation of heroic life support measures is a withdrawal or omission of treatment rather than an affirmative act. *Barber v. Superior Court*.
      b. A medical doctor does not have a legal duty to continue treatment once it has proved to be ineffective. *Barber v. Superior Court*.
  E. Result crimes and conduct crimes: the role of social harm.
    1. When the law punishes a person for an unwanted outcome, that person committed a result crime (e.g., Death is the unwanted outcome of a criminal homicide.). The unwanted outcome is social harm because a crime is an offense against society.
    2. Laws that prohibit specific behavior define conduct crimes.
      a. An example of a conduct crime is driving under the influence of drugs or alcohol.
      b. Conduct crimes attempt to prevent the tangible harm associated with an unwanted outcome.
      c. When a person commits a conduct crime, there is social harm because the conduct tends to destroy individuals and valuable society interests.
  F. An attendant circumstance may be an element of a crime.
    1. An attendant circumstance element of a crime is a condition that must exist in conjunction with a result or prohibited conduct if criminal liability is to attach.
    2. An attendant circumstance element is a component of actus reus.
      a. If it is an offense to drive an automobile in an intoxicated condition, the words "in an intoxicated condition" represent an attendant circumstance, and the conduct is driving an automobile.
      b. Actus reus is absent if the conduct of driving does not occur when a person is in an intoxicated condition.

Martin v. State

(Intoxicated Man) v. (People of Alabama)
(1944) 31 Ala. App. 334, 17 So. 2d 427

M E M O R Y   G R A P H I C

Instant Facts

Police officers arrest an intoxicated man at his home, take him onto a highway, and arrested him for public drunkenness.

Black Letter Rule

A defendant must perform the physical act for each element of a crime that has an actus reus component.

Procedural Basis: Appeal from conviction of being drunk in a public place and engaging in conduct manifesting drunkenness.

Facts: Police officers arrested Mr. Martin (D) at his home and took him onto a public highway. While on the highway, Mr. Martin (D) used loud and profane language in a manner that suggested that he was intoxicated. Mr. Martin (D) was convicted for violating a statute that prohibited appearing in a public place in an intoxicated condition and manifesting that condition with indecent conduct or loud and profane language. Mr. Martin (D) appealed the conviction.

Issue: Must a defendant perform the physical act for each element of a crime that has an actus reus component?

Decision and Rationale: (Simpson) Yes. A defendant must perform the physical act for each element of a crime that has an actus reus component. Mr. Martin (D) was convicted for violating a statute that provides that an individual in an intoxicated condition who appears in a public place where one or more persons are present and manifest his intoxication by boisterous or indecent conduct, or loud and profane language shall be fined upon conviction. On its face, the statute requires voluntary appearance in a public place. The State (P) cannot prove an accusation of public drunkenness by establishing that the arresting officer, while the defendant was in an intoxicated condition, involuntarily and forcibly carried him to a public place. Reversed and rendered.

Analysis:

Alabama's public drunkenness statute has two elements. First, the accused must appear in a public place. Appearance requires a voluntary physical act. Mr. Martin (D) appeared in a public place; however, he did not perform any physical act, voluntary or involuntary, that led to his appearance, since the police officers *took* him onto the public highway. Therefore, the required actus reus for this element does not exist. Second, the accused must manifest his drunken condition at the public place he appeared. Since Mr. Martin (D) voluntarily used loud and profane language while he was on the highway in an intoxicated condition, the required actus reus for this element exists. Notwithstanding, a crime did not occur, because the statute requires a coincidence of voluntarily appearing in public and manifesting an intoxicated condition through certain conduct.

A PERSON WHO ACTS UNCONSCIOUSLY MAY NOT HAVE THE REQUISITE ACTUS REUS

State v. Utter

(People of Washington) v. (Stabber)
(1971) 4 Wash. App. 137, 479 P.2d 946

M E M O R Y   G R A P H I C

Instant Facts
Intoxicated father with an alleged conditioned response condition fatally stabs his son in the chest.

Black Letter Rule
A voluntary act requires the consent of the actor's will.

Procedural Basis: Appeal from conviction of manslaughter.

Facts: One afternoon, Mr. Utter's (D) son entered the apartment he shared with his father. Shortly thereafter, the son said, "Dad don't." The son, having been stab in the chest, stumbled into the hallway of the apartment building and collapsed. The son stated that his father stabbed him and then died. On the day of the incident, Mr. Utter (D) drank just under a quart of port wine during the morning hours. In the afternoon, he drank whiskey with a friend. Mr. Utter (D) remembers drinking whiskey with his friend and being in jail subsequent to his son's death, but he does not remember the intervening events. Mr. Utter (D) entered the armed services in 1942. He served as a combat infantryman and received an honorable discharge in 1946. During trial, Mr. Utter (D) introduced, through a psychiatrist, evidence on conditioned response, an act or pattern of activity occurring so rapidly and uniformly as to be an automatic response to certain stimulus. Mr. Utter (D) testified that he received jungle warfare training while he was in the armed services. He further testified that on two occasions in the 1950's he reacted violently towards people approaching him unexpectedly from the rear. The trial court ruled that conditioned response was not a defense and instructed the jury to disregard the evidence on the subject. Mr. Utter (D) was convicted of manslaughter, and he appealed.

Issue: Does a voluntary act require the consent of the actor's will?

Decision and Rationale: (Farris) Yes. A voluntary act requires the consent of the actor's will. The major issue is whether it was error for the trial court to instruct the jury to disregard the evidence on conditioned response. The actus reus for manslaughter is homicide. The statutory definition of homicide is the killing of a human being by the act, procurement, or omission of another. Mr. Utter (D) asserts that he presented the conditioned response evidence during his trial to determine if he committed a homicide. He contends that his evidence, if believed, establishes that he did not commit a homicidal act. It is sometimes said that a crime does not exist unless a voluntary act causes harm. The phrase "voluntary act" is synonymous with the word "act." An act is a willed movement or the omission of a possible and legally required performance. A spasm is not an act. Mr. Utter (D) contends that any alleged acts he committed did not involve mental processes. Instead, they were learned physical reactions to external stimuli that operated automatically on his autonomic nervous system. Further, he contends that a person in an automatistic or unconscious state is incapable of committing a culpable homicidal act. It is important to realize that this is not a question of mental incapacity; rather, it is recognition that the law judges criminal responsibility at the level of conscious. There is authority that supports Mr. Utter's (D) contentions. Criminal liability does not attach in the absence of a voluntary act. The absence of consciousness excludes the possibility of a voluntary act as well as any specific mental state. Without the consent of the will, human actions are not culpable. If there is no will to commit an offense, is there a just reason for a party to receive the punishment designated for the offense? An act committed while a person is unconscious is not really an act. Rather, it is a physical event or occurrence for which there can be no criminal liability. Notwithstanding, unconsciousness does not, in all cases, provide a defense to a crime. Voluntary intoxication that induces unconsciousness is not a complete defense. In a case where there is evidence that the accused has consumed alcohol or drugs, a trial court should give a cautionary instruction with respect to voluntarily induced unconsciousness. Whether, Mr. Utter (D) was in an unconscious or automatistic state at the time he allegedly committed criminal acts is a question of fact. However, the evidence presented at trial was insufficient to present this issue to the jury.

State v. Utter (Continued)

Analysis:

Actus reus is a voluntary act that causes harm. Mr. Utter stabbed his son and his son died. The harm is the death of the son. The issue in this case is whether Mr. Utter's (D) stabbing of his son was a mere physical event or an act. If Mr. Utter (D) was conscious at the time of the fatal stabbing, there was a voluntary act because there was a coincidence of physical movement and an exercise of the will; otherwise, there is no act. No act, no criminal liability. Assume Mr. Utter (D) does not suffer from conditioned response and someone drugs him without his consent. Now, assume that the effect of the drug makes him unconscious (i.e., no consent of the will). Further, assume that in this unconscious state he fatally stabs his son. Did Mr. Utter (D) commit a homicide? No. Now, make the same assumptions, except rather than someone drugging Mr. Utter (D), he voluntarily ingests the drugs. Is there a homicide? What answer does the opinion suggest? The opinion states that there are times when unconsciousness is not a defense to a crime. This language is misleading. Actus reus is an element of a crime. If the prosecution cannot prove this element beyond a reasonable doubt, the law holds that a crime did not occur. If a crime does not occur, there is no reason to offer an affirmative defense.

HIGH COURT CASE SUMMARIES

©2002 West Group. All Rights Reserved. Do not duplicate.

People v. Beardsley

(People of Michigan) v. (Non-actor)
(1907) 150 Mich. 206, 113 N.W. 1128

WELL, THERE'S NOTHING I CAN DO TO STOP HER!!

M E M O R Y   G R A P H I C

Instant Facts
Intoxicated male fails to assist his female friend who was in a stupor from drinking alcohol and ingesting morphine.

Black Letter Rule
A person may be criminally liable if he fails to perform a legal duty and his omission causes harm.

Procedural Basis: Appeal from conviction of manslaughter.

Facts: Mr. Beardsley (D) was a married man who lived in a tenant house. Ms. Burns was his close female friend. Frequently, Mr. Beardsley (D) and Ms. Burns drank together, and on two occasions, they had met at a house that facilitates rendezvous for lovers. Ms. Burns met Mr. Beardsley (D) at his residence on a Saturday evening while Mr. Beardsley's (D) wife was out of town. The couple immediately began to drink alcohol together. Except for a portion of Sunday afternoon when Mr. Beardsley (D) was at work, the couple continually drank together until Monday. A young man that worked at Mr. Beardsley (D) place of employment delivered alcohol to Mr. Beardsley's (D) residence. On Monday afternoon, the young man went to Mr. Beardsley's (D) home to determine if he required anything. While there, Mr. Beardsley (D) said they must fix up the rooms and Ms. Burns could not be found at his residence by his wife who would return at any time. Ms. Burns then sent the young man to the drug store to purchase some camphor and morphine tablets. When the young man returned with the requested items, Ms. Burns concealed the morphine tables from Mr. Beardsley (D). Upon returning from a room, Mr. Beardsley (D) and the young man noticed that she was putting morphine tablets in her mouth. Mr. Beardsley (D) struck the box of morphine tablets from her hand and crushed some of the tablets that fell on the floor with his foot. Ms. Burns picked up two of the tablets and swallowed them. Her total consumption of morphine was approximately three or four grains. An hour later, Ms. Burns was in a stupor and failed to respond when Mr. Beardsley (D) spoke to her. Mr. Beardsley (D) telephoned the young man and asked him to return to his home and help him move Ms. Burns to a tenant's basement room. The young man returned and proceeded to take Ms. Burns to the basement room. Mr. Beardsley (D) was too intoxicated to be of any assistance. The basement tenant arrived at the house and helped the young man move Ms. Burns to his basement room. Mr. Beardsley (D) asked the tenant to look after Ms. Burns and have her leave through the back when she awoke. Between 9 and 10 o'clock that Monday evening, the tenant became alarmed about Ms. Burns's condition. He called the city marshal and a doctor. The marshal and doctor examined Ms. Burns and determined that she was dead. Mr. Beardsley (D) was convicted of manslaughter. The prosecution's theory of the case was Mr. Beardsley (D) omitted to perform his duty to care for and protect Ms. Burns. Mr. Beardsley (D) appealed his conviction.

Issue: May a person be criminally liable if he fails to perform a legal duty and his omission causes harm?

Decision and Rationale: (McAlvay) Yes. A person may be criminally liable if he fails to perform a legal duty and his omission causes harm. The People (P) do not contend that Mr. Beardsley (D) was an active agent of Ms. Burns's death. Instead, the contention is Mr. Beardsley (D) owed Ms. Burns a duty that he failed to perform, thereby causing Ms. Burns's death. Under some circumstances, a person is chargeable with manslaughter if he omits to perform a duty that he owes to another and the omission results in the death of that person. However, the duty neglected must be a legal duty rather than a mere moral obligation. Further, it must be a duty imposed by law or contract, and the omission to perform the duty must be an immediate and direct cause of death. The authorities are in harmony as to the relationships that must exist between the parties to create a legal duty, the omission of which establishes legal responsibility. These relationships include, but are not limited to, husband and wife, parent and child, and master and seaman. If a person in such a relationship knows the other party to the relationship is in peril of life and willfully or negligently fails to take reasonable steps to rescue the party, the person is guilty of manslaughter if his omission to act is the cause of death. Therefore, an individual who from domestic relationship, public duty, voluntary choice, or otherwise has the custody and care of a person who is in a helpless condition must execute his responsibilities with proper diligence or be found guilty of manslaughter if his culpable negligence causes the death of the helpless person. Given the aforementioned principles, consideration of mere moral obligation cannot influence the outcome of the case at bar. The questions are whether Mr. Beardsley (D) owed a duty to Ms. Burns at the time of her death, and if so, whether his omission to perform this duty caused her death. The facts of this case disclose that Ms. Burns was a woman past 30 years of age. She had married twice and was accustomed to visiting saloons and using intoxicants. She had been intimate with Mr. Beardsley at least twice. There is no evidence or claim in the record that Ms. Burns was a victim of fraud or duress. The prosecution contends that at the time of Ms. Burns' death, Mr. Beardsley (D) stood in the shoes of her natural guardian and protector. In this capacity, it alleges that Mr. Beardsley (D) owed Ms. Burns a legal duty that he failed to perform. However, the aforementioned principles establish that a mere moral obligation does not create a legal duty. The fact that Ms. Burns was in Mr. Beardsley's (D) home does not create a legal duty as exists between a husband and wife. Mr. Beardsley had not assumed care or control over Ms. Burns. If two men became intoxicated under similar circumstances and one of them committed suicide, no one would claim that a legal duty existed that could make the other man criminally liable for omitting to make an effort to rescue his companion. The fact that Ms. Burns was a woman does not change the law. Conviction set aside, and Mr. Beardsley is ordered discharged.

Analysis:

This case demonstrates that, in certain circumstances, criminal liability may be predicated on an omission to act when there is a duty to act. The duty to act may be statutorily imposed, or it may result from a status relationship such as husband and wife, parent and child, and master and servant. In the instant case, the prosecution contended that a status relationship existed between Mr. Beardsley (D) and Ms. Burns. It alleged that Mr. Beardsley (D) had the status of a natural guardian and protector. The Supreme Court of Michigan rejected this contention because it was not supported by precedent. A duty to act may arise from an express or implied contract. For example, a doctor has a duty to provide ordinary medical care to his patient. Additionally, a person has a duty to act when he places another person in peril. A person also has a duty to act once he has volunteered his assistance. Once an individual offers assistance to a person in peril, he as a duty to continue to provide aid if a failure to do so places the person in a worst condition.

THERE IS A DISTINCTION BETWEEN REMOVAL OF LIFE SUPPORT FROM A COMATOSE PATIENT (WHICH IS NOT A CRIME) AND EUTHANASIA

Barber v. Superior Court

(Physician) v. (Trial Court)
(1983) 147 Cal.App.3d 1066, 195 Cal.Rptr. 484

M E M O R Y   G R A P H I C

Instant Facts

Barber (D), a physician, removed Herbert (a comatose patient with little chance of recovery) from life support at his family's request.

Black Letter Rule

Removal of life support equipment from a comatose patient who is unlikely to recover is not an affirmative act, but an act of omission, that, if in accord with the patient's or surrogate's wishes, does not give rise to criminal liability.

Case Vocabulary

BRAIN DEATH: A condition where the body shows no response to stimuli, shows no bodily function such as breathing or movement, and shows no brain activity.

Procedural Basis: Appeal from reinstatement of complaint for murder and conspiracy to commit murder.

Facts: Shortly after surgery, Clarence Herbert suffered a cardiac arrest. He was revived and placed on life support. After a few days, Barber (D) and other physicians determined that Herbert was in a deep coma from which he would probably not recover. Herbert had severe brain damage, leaving him in a vegetative state, although there remained some brain activity. Barber (D), Herbert's internist, informed Herbert's family of his opinion and chances for recovery. The family drafted a written request to the hospital, stating that they wished to take Herbert off life support. When they took him off, Herbert continued to breathe without the equipment. After two more days, the family ordered the removal of Herbert's intravenous tubes [just what was in Herbert's will?]. Herbert died some time later.

Issue: Does removal of life support from a vegetative, but not brain dead, person constitute murder?

Decision and Rationale: (Compton) No. If Barber (D) lawfully and intentionally killed Herbert, malice is presumed regardless of motive. Euthanasia is neither excusable nor justifiable in California. It is conceded by all that Herbert was not dead by either statutory or historical standards, since there was still minimal brain activity. If Herbert were "brain dead," this prosecution could not have been instituted. We conclude that cessation of "heroic" life support measures is not an affirmative act, but a withdrawal of treatment. Although the treatments are self-propelled to a degree, each pulsation of the respirator or each drop of fluid from the IV device is comparable to a manually administered injection or medication. The authority cited by the Government (P) holds that a murder charge may be supported by the failure to feed a child. This case is easily distinguishable. The parent in that case had a clear duty to feed an otherwise healthy child. Here, faced with a vegetative patient with little chance of recovery, the duty of a physician is markedly different. Where it is not possible to ascertain the choice the patient himself would have made when in such a state, the surrogate [usually the family] ought to be guided by their knowledge of the patient's feelings and desires. If the patient's feelings and desires are not known, the surrogate should be guided by the patient's best interests, and the impact on those closest to the patient. There is evidence that Mr. Herbert did not want to be kept alive by machines. Herbert's wife and children decided that Herbert should receive no further treatment—we find no legal requirement that prior judicial approval was necessary. Writ prohibiting prosecution issued.

Analysis:

Barber may be profitably compared to *Gilbert* [husband shot his sick wife who complained that she wanted to die]. *Gilbert* was clearly a euthanasia case, and *Barber* was clearly a case of omission—not an affirmative act like *Gilbert*, right? The court in *Barber* seems to get around the issue of euthanasia by an act/omission analysis, but some scholars are not convinced by the court's reasoning. Herbert was still alive after the respirator was turned off—what killed Herbert was the denial of food and water. Thus, some commentators argue that the physicians caused Herbert's death, just as if Herbert's wife starved her comatose husband at home. Is there a real moral difference between Mr. Gilbert and Mrs. Herbert and the doctors? In *Barber*, the court brings up the issue of omission—a solution to a *Gilbert*-type holding—and the doctor's duty to the comatose patient, asserting that burdens of treatment outweighed the benefits, so that it was not worth continuing treatment. The family made the decision after consulting with the physicians. Clearly, the physician is faced with a difficult task that presents many moral concerns that must be carefully balanced. Operating in a medical system largely under control by HMO's that must maintain profitability [as an assurance to those who love their HMO, this is asserted as a market fact and not as a condemnation], one hopes that physicians are able to weigh the benefits and burdens without interference, and are able to consult the family having as their sole concern the patient's and family's well-being.

Perspective
Mens Rea

Chapter 5

We've all seen the part on television shows where the jury files in after a long and volatile trial to give its much-anticipated verdict. Everyone waits with bated breath to find out if the defendant is "Guilty" or "Not Guilty." But perhaps you've never thought about just what it means to say a person is guilty or is not guilty of committing a crime.

Modern criminal codes usually proscribe certain conduct—they designate specific acts which our society deems injurious, harmful or bad. If an act is considered dangerous or unsafe, or if performing the act would have a deleterious effect on society in general, we have in many cases deemed the act to be criminal. However, our criminal laws have evolved such that, as a society, we have recognized that it is not usually appropriate to punish a person for committing an act if the person did not have a culpable state of mind when he performed the act. Generally, just having committed the act is not enough. The vast majority of modern crimes require both a proscribed act *and* a sufficiently blameworthy or guilty state of mind to support a criminal conviction.

That's where mens rea comes in. Mens rea is a Latin term that literally means "guilty mind." It is one of two essential elements of every crime—the other being the actus reus. It is almost always the case that a person cannot be punished for having committed a crime unless it is shown that he performed a proscribed act (actus reus) while possessed of a particular mental state of mind (mens rea).

That being said, it is not always easy to determine whether an actor had a particular state of mind when he committed an act. For example, if a statute makes it a crime to intentionally start a fire that causes damage to property—what result if the actor started the fire by accident? What if there is some evidence that could lead the jury to believe that he intentionally started the fire, and some evidence that points toward the fire being wholly accidental? What if starting the fire was accidental, but it started after he intentionally broke into and entered another person's property? Exactly what was the actor's frame of mind in each of these three situations? You can see, of course, that the answer to the last question will determine whether the jury comes back with a "Guilty" or "Not Guilty" verdict.

Additionally, we all know that our society does not only criminalize acts that are done intentionally. Sometimes our criminal codes make it a crime if a person does something he knows is wrong, or something he should know is wrong. Sometimes we punish people criminally for doing things they think are wrong when they go ahead and do them anyway. And sometimes we punish people for being too careless with regard to whether something is wrong or not—people who act recklessly or negligently.

It is clear, then, that the requirement of a mens rea is relatively simple. The determination of which mental state is required and whether the actor in fact possessed it is another story, however. Sometimes the statutes define the particular mental state that is required, but sometimes there is no mention of a mens rea in the wording of an offense. To complicate things further, there are a very few crimes that do not require a mens rea at all (strict liability). The cases in this chapter describe the nature of mens rea and point out some of the difficulties associated with the requirement that a person have a "guilty mind" in addition to having committed a proscribed act in order to be convicted. They should give you a new appreciation for the thorny task that faces every jury in a criminal case.

Chapter 5

NOTE: THE PURPOSE OF THIS OUTLINE IS TO ORGANIZE THE CASES SO THAT ONE CAN QUICKLY UNDERSTAND THE RELEVANCE OF EACH CASE TO THE COURSE. NO ATTEMPT IS MADE IN THIS OVERVIEW TO ADDRESS EVERY CONCEPT THAT MUST BE STUDIED. BE SURE TO READ THE ENTIRE CASEBOOK AND/OR OTHER MATERIALS TO GAIN A FULL UNDERSTANDING OF ALL CONCEPTS.

I. Nature of Mens Rea
    A. "Mens rea" means literally, guilty mind.
    B. In modern criminal law, we examine the actor's state of mind to determine both the propriety and grading of punishment.
        1. It is the criminal law's mantra that an "act does not make the doer of it guilty, unless the mind be guilty; that is, unless the intent be criminal." *United States v. Cordoba-Hincapie.*
        2. Modern criminal law has evolved so as to require a guilty state of mind in order to punish a person who commits a proscribed act.
    C. The term "mens rea" is commonly understood as having either of two meanings—the "culpability" meaning or the "elemental" meaning.
        1. The culpability approach to mens rea is one that broadly interprets the term. If a court is applying the culpability meaning, it will find that an actor is guilty of an offense if he performed the act with a morally blameworthy state of mind.
        2. The elemental approach to mens rea is one that interprets the term narrowly. Using this approach, mens rea means that particular state of mind that is expressly required by the definition of the offense, i.e. intentionally, knowingly or recklessly.
    D. A statute that requires an actor to act "maliciously" is satisfied if it is shown that the person acted intentionally or recklessly, but will not be satisfied by a showing that the person acted "wickedly." *Regina v. Cunningham.*

II. Issues of Proof regarding Mens Rea
    A. A person acts with "intent" if he consciously desires to bring about specific harm or knows that such harm is practically certain to result from his actions. *People v. Conley.*
        1. The "natural and probable consequences doctrine" is sometimes used to help the prosecution prove intent. The doctrine permits an inference that a person usually intends the foreseeable consequences of his actions.
        2. The natural and probable consequences doctrine cannot be used as a presumption. The Supreme Court held that it was unconstitutional for a judge to instruct a jury that "the law presumes that a person intends the ordinary consequences of his voluntary acts" because the prosecution has the burden of proving *every* element of a crime beyond a reasonable doubt. If the presumption applied, the prosecutor would be relieved of his burden to prove intent, and could instead rely on the presumption. The Court said this kind of presumption was an unconstitutional denial of due process.
        3. The doctrine of "transferred intent" sometimes applies when a person intends to cause a particular social harm to one person but ends up causing the same harm to another.
            a. The doctrine usually only applies to transfered intent from onevictim to another. The doctrine does not apply to a transfer of an intent to cause one particular type of social harm to a different type of social harm.
            b. Some courts apply the doctrine of transferred intent to situations where an actor intends to cause a particular harm to one person and does so, and at the same time causes the same harm to second person.
        4. Courts frequently refer to crimes as being either "specific intent" offenses or "general intent" offenses.
            a. A specific intent offense is one in which a particular mental state is expressly provided for in the definition of the crime. Specific intent crimes are analogous to the "elemental" approach to mens rea.
            b. A general intent offense is one that does not specify a particular mental state. It is usually sufficient for the prosecutor to prove that the act was committed with a morally blameworthy state of mind. The definition of a general intent crime complements the "culpability" approach as defined above.
        5. The Model Penal Code Approach
            a. The MPC consistently applies the elemental approach to mens rea; that is, the prosecution must prove that the actor committed each element of the crime with the particular state of mind required by the wording of the offense.
            b. The MPC abandons all common law definitions of mental states and substitutes instead "purposefully, knowingly, recklessly, or negligently."
                (1) A person acts purposefully if it is his conscious intent to bring about a particular social harm.
                (2) A person acts knowingly if he knows that his conduct will result in a particular social harm.
                (3) A person acts recklessly if he persists in acting in the face of a substantial and unjustifiable risk.
                (4) A person acts negligently if he inadvertently creates a risk of which he ought to be aware.
    B. Knowledge of attendant circumstances.
        1. Some offenses require as an element of the crime that the actor have knowledge as to the existence of a particular fact when he or she commits an act.
        2. Unless the applicable criminal code states otherwise, a requirement that a person commit a certain act "knowingly" with respect to a particular fact (attendant circumstance) will not be satisfied unless the person had actual knowledge of the existence of the particular fact. *State v. Nations.*
            a. The MPC recognizes the common law "willful blindness doctrine," which charges a person with acting "knowingly" with respect to an existing fact when the person deliberately closes his eyes to what would have otherwise been obvious to him. *United States v. Caminos.*
            b. In essence, then, the common law and the MPC

impose knowledge of an attendant circumstance on a person when there is a high probability of its existence.

C. Problems in Statutory Interpretation.

1. Some statutes are ambiguous with respect to the mens rea required for conviction.

2. If a statute is ambiguous regarding whether a mens rea term applies to all or only some of the elements of a crime, the court should examine the legislative intent to determine the correct interpretation. *United States v. Morris.*

3. The rules of punctuation and grammar are also used by courts in interpreting ambiguous statutes.

4. The modern view espoused by Section 2.02(4) of the Model Penal Code is that a single mens rea term in a statute modifies each actus reus element of the offense, unless the legislature plainly indicates a contrary purpose.

III. Strict Liability

A. Offenses that do not possess any mental element are defined as strict liability offenses.

1. Strict liability is commonly seen in offenses characterized as "public welfare offenses." These offenses typically are created by statute, are part of a regulatory scheme and carry relatively minor punishments or fines. Liability for these offenses attaches without regard for the actor's intent or state of mind. *United States v. Cordoba-Hincapie.*

2. When a statute is silent as to the required mens rea, the determination of the necessary mental state is made by construing the statute itself and by examining the intent of the legislature. *Staples v. United States.* Silence in a statute regarding the necessary mental state does not automatically imply that the offense is a strict liability crime.

3. Strict liability offenses are generally disfavored. *United States v. United States Gypsum Co.*

B. In general, a mistake of fact or a mistake of law is no defense to a strict liability offense. *Garnett v. State.*

1. In some cases, though, a mistake of age is a defense to the strict liability offense of statutory rape.

2. The MPC generally rejects strict liability offenses, and accepts them only when the grade of the offense can be reduced to a violation and is punishable only by a fine or other civil penalty. *MPC § 2.05.*

3. Defenders of strict liability claim that such offenses have a deterrent effect on large classes of people. Critics say that punishing people without taking into account whether they possessed a culpable state of mind is inconsistent with our moral and social values. *Wasserstrom, Strict liability in the Criminal Law.*

IV. Mistake

A. The general rule is that a mistake of fact is no defense to a crime. An exception exists when the mistake negates the mental state required for conviction of the crime.

1. A mistake of fact, either reasonable or unreasonable, is a defense to a specific intent crime if it negates the specific mental state required by the wording of the offense. *People v. Navarro.*

2. At common law, a reasonable mistake of fact is a defense to a general intent crime. An unreasonable mistake will not provide an excuse and is not a defense to a general intent crime.

3. Mistake is almost never a defense to a strict liability crime.

B. Regarding a mistake of law, the common law rule and the rule recognized generally is that a mistake of law does not relieve a person of criminal liability. *People v. Marrero.* In other words, ignorance of the law is no excuse.

1. The MPC generally codifies the common law approach in that it maintains that "neither knowledge, recklessness or even negligence as to the existence, meaning or application of the law is an element of an offense" unless the definition of the offense states otherwise. Therefore, under the MPC, ignorance of the law is no defense because it does not negate an element of the crime.

2. The MPC and some state codes recognize a limited exception, though, and provide for a narrow mistake of law defense. The defense applies only when a person acts in "reasonable reliance upon an official statement of the law, afterward determined to be invalid or erroneous, contained in a statute or other enactment." *MPC § 2.04.* In other words, a mistake of law defense applies when a person acts in accordance with a present statute, which statute is later determined to be invalid. The operative fact is that the statute as written has to condone the behavior. If a person therefore acts within the statutory limits, he will not be held accountable if the statute is later changed.

3. When a defendant reasonably relies upon an official statement of the law that is later deemed erroneous, he is entitled to an estoppel defense. *Commonwealth v. Twitchell.*

4. The Supreme Court recognized an ignorance of the law defense in a case where the defendant, a prior felon, did not register in Los Angeles when she moved there. The Court focused on the fact that her mere presence in Los Angeles without registering made her subject to criminal liability. In such a case, the Court held that actual knowledge of the duty to register was necessary and recognized an ignorance of law defense because the defendant claimed she did not know about the registration ordinance. *Lambert v. California.*

5. Another very narrow exception is that a mistake of law, either reasonable or unreasonable, will be a defense to a crime if it relates to the mental state necessary and it negates the specific intent required for conviction. *Cheek v. United States.*

   a. A mistaken belief that a law is unconstitutional as written will not be a defense if the person holding the belief violates the law. *Cheek v. United States.*

United States v. Cordoba-Hincapie

(Government) v. (Accused)
(1993) 825 F. Supp 485 (E.D.N.Y.)

M E M O R Y   G R A P H I C

Instant Facts
None Stated

Black Letter Rule
To be guilty of a crime which has as one of its elements, "mens rea," the criminal must have a guilty state of mind.

Case Vocabulary

ACTUS REUS: The physical element of a crime; that is, the voluntary, conscious or volitional movement or action that, when combined with the requisite mental frame of mind, makes the actor punishable for having committed a crime.

MENS REA: The mental element of a crime, which encompasses performing the proscribed act with a guilty or morally blameworthy state of mind.

Procedural Basis: None Stated

Facts: None Stated

Issue: What is mens rea?

Decision and Rationale: (Weinstein, D.J.) A guilty mind, a guilty or vengeful purpose; a criminal intent.

Analysis:

This short excerpt serves as an introduction to the concept of mens rea and the function that it has historically served in the administration of criminal law. You are by now [hopefully!] aware that there are two broad components to every crime: the actus reus (a voluntary physical act, or sometimes, the lack of a physical act) and the mens rea (the requisite mental state of mind). By now the student should have explored some of the issues that surround the actus reus, including some of the difficulties associated with identifying the act which is proscribed by law. You probably found that it is not always as easy as one might think to identify a voluntary, conscious or volitional movement that is sufficient to satisfy the actus reus requirement. However difficult the concept of actus reus may be, though, it is [regrettably] the more straightforward and simplistic of the two components. The concept of mens rea is traditionally much more difficult for law students to grasp, largely because the term itself is amorphous and is subject to a variety of different definitions. It has become axiomatic in modern criminal law systems that for an act to be punishable, it must be committed with a culpable state of mind. This case alerts the student to the fact that mens rea was not always required in order to be held accountable for criminal acts. As you are probably already aware from discussions in other classes, the English system started out as one based in strict liability. With reference to criminal law, then, at one time it was only necessary to show that the actor had performed the proscribed act (the actus reus). The law was not concerned with the actor's state of mind. Accidental or intentional, blameless or blameworthy, the actor could be convicted if he committed the act, regardless of his state of mind when doing so. Over time though, punishment for crimes became wrapped up in societal views of guilt as encompassing some kind of moral blameworthiness or culpability. As the case points out, the degree of culpability has changed over time, gradually becoming more narrow and clearly defined. We have begun to identify those states of mind that we as a society feel *should be punished* (when combined with some proscribed act, that is). And although it is rare for modern courts to invoke punishment for an actor's having merely a "morally blameworthy" state of mind when he performed an act, it is important to recognize that courts often differ in their interpretation of the meaning of the mens rea requirement. In reading opinions, keep in mind that the court may be speaking of mens rea in a broad sense—meaning a morally blameworthy state of mind, or in a more narrow sense—meaning the precise state of mind required by the law in order to make the actor punishable for having committed the offense.

Regina v. Cunningham

(English Government) v. (Thief)

(1957) 41 Crim. App. 155, 2 Q.B. 396, 2 All. Eng. Rep. 412

M E M O R Y   G R A P H I C

 ## Instant Facts

A thief stole a gas meter from the basement of a house, which caused the gas to leak into an adjoining house and partially asphyxiate an elderly woman who lived there.

 ## Black Letter Rule

The mens rea requirement is satisfied by a showing of either intentional or reckless conduct; a showing of malice or wickedness will not suffice.

Case Vocabulary

INTENTIONALLY: A state of mind indicating that a person performed an act purposefully or willfully, and not accidentally.

MALICE: A state of mind showing an evil intent, or one that causes a person to purposely or willfully commit an act with no regard for its effect on others.

RECKLESSNESS: A state of mind indicating a callous disregard for the foreseeable consequences of performing an act.

Procedural Basis: Appeal after a conviction for unlawfully and maliciously poisoning a person.

Facts: Cunningham (D) was engaged to Mrs. Wade's daughter. Mrs. Wade owned a house that had been divided into two individual homes. Mrs. Wade lived on one side with her husband and Cunningham (D) was to live on the other side after his marriage to the Wades' daughter. Cunningham (D) was out of work and needed money, so he went into the basement of the unoccupied portion of the house and stole the gas meter. In a statement to the police, Cunningham (D) admitted that he wrenched the gas meter from the wall, stole the money from within (8 shillings) and discarded the meter. Although there was a shut off valve about 2 feet from the meter, Cunningham (D) did not turn off the gas. As a result, gas leaked through the basement wall and into Mrs. Wade's house, where it partially asphyxiated her while she was sleeping in her bedroom. Cunningham (D) was indicted for violating Section 23 of the Offenses against the Person Act [making it a felony to unlawfully and maliciously administer poison to a person, or cause poison to be administered to a person, so as to endanger the person's life]. The trial judge instructed the jury that the term "malicious" in the statute meant "wicked." The jury convicted Cunningham (D) and he appealed, claiming that the judge erroneously instructed the jury as to the meaning of the word "malicious."

Issue: Will a mens rea requirement of "maliciousness" be satisfied by a finding that the actor acted "wickedly" when he performed the proscribed acts?

Decision and Rationale: (Byrne, J.) No. In order to satisfy the mens rea requirement of maliciousness, the actor must either intentionally set out to cause the harm that resulted, or he must have been reckless with regard to whether the harm would in fact result. If the actor did not intend to bring about the harm, he must at least have been able to foresee that the harm could occur if he persisted in his actions. He would be acting recklessly if he chose to disregard the foreseeable risk of harm and to act anyway. In the instant case, it does not appear that Cunningham (D) intentionally released the gas to poison Mrs. Wade. [The notion is open to debate, however, as Mrs. Wade was his mother-in-law to be, after all.] The trial judge instructed the jury that the statutory concept of "malicious" meant wicked; that is, they could convict if they found that Cunningham (D) was doing something he knew he should not have been doing, something that was wrong. We think that definition was too broad. In the context of this statute, an act is "malicious" if it is done intentionally or recklessly. The jury should have been instructed that Cunningham (D) could have been convicted if he acted "maliciously" in that he intended to cause an injury to Mrs. Wade, or he foresaw that *someone* might be injured by the escaping gas, but recklessly persisted in stealing the meter anyway. Because the jury was erroneously instructed as to the meaning of "malicious," we cannot be sure beyond a reasonable doubt that they found that Cunningham (D) acted with the requisite state of mind. Appeal allowed and conviction quashed.

Analysis:

As this case demonstrates, the concept of mens rea is a tricky one—even for judges. As you have already seen, the concept of mens rea evolved over time from a general notion of moral blameworthiness i.e. being possessed of "evil intent" or an immoral motive, to a more narrowly defined state of mind—often one that is specifically required by the wording of the offense. This case shows that evolution because, quite clearly, the trial court and the appellate court applied two different definitions of mens rea. The trial court followed the "culpability" approach to mens rea, which would support a finding of guilt based on more general immoral or improper motives. In this case, the offense required that an actor "maliciously" cause poison to be administered to a person. The trial court's instruction suggested that Cunningham (D) could be convicted if he acted wickedly; that is, if he was morally blameworthy in a general sense for stealing the gas meter, or if he knew he was doing something wrong. But Cunningham (D) certainly knew he was doing something wrong when he stole the meter. The crucial question becomes whether his knowledge that he was doing something wrong when he stole the meter was enough to constitute the maliciousness that was required to hold him accountable for the much greater offense of endangering a person's life. The appellate court's concern was that the jury may have convicted Cunningham (D) because his act of stealing the meter indicated that he was a "bad" or "immoral" man. Although such a finding may have been sufficient under the "culpability" approach to mens rea, the appellate court clearly found that more was required to constitute the "malice" required by the statute. The appellate court applied the "elemental" approach to mens rea, under which the proper inquiry was whether Cunningham (D) acted intentionally or recklessly to cause the gas to escape and poison someone. It is important to recognize that the appellate court *did not* quash the conviction because the evidence indicated that Cunningham (D) lacked the requisite mens rea. It could be argued that Cunningham (D) foresaw when he wrenched the meter from the pipes that someone might be injured by the gas. The jury might have found that he was reckless by disregarding a very real risk. The appellate court quashed the conviction because, as the jury was instructed, it may have (and probably did) convict Cunningham (D) because his act of stealing the meter was wrong, rather than inquiring as to whether he possessed the necessary level of intent or recklessness mandated by the statute.

People v. Conley

Government) v. (Accused Batterer)
(1989) 187 Ill. App. 3d 234, 134 Ill. Dec. 855, 543 N.E. 2d 138

M E M O R Y   G R A P H I C

Instant Facts

After an altercation at a high school party, two boys got into a fight where one boy hit the other in the face with a wine bottle, which caused extensive injuries to the other boy's mouth and teeth.

Black Letter Rule

A person acts with intent if it is his conscious object to cause a social harm or he knows that such harm is almost certain to occur as a result of his conduct.

 ## Case Vocabulary

AGGRAVATED BATTERY: A battery committed with a heightened level of violence—usually with a deadly weapon or other extreme circumstances surrounding the act.
BATTERY: An intentional harmful or offensive touching of a person without his or her consent.

Procedural Basis: Appeal following a conviction for aggravated battery.

Facts: About 200 high school kids attended a party where they paid admission to drink unlimited beer. Sean O'Connell attended the party with several of his friends, including Marty Carrol. At one point during the party, Sean and his friends were approached by a group of about 20 boys, who accused Sean's group of making derogatory comments. Sean's group denied making the comments, said they wanted no trouble and left the party. On their way to the car, someone across the street yelled "there's those guys from the party." Sean and Marty were approached by a boy who demanded that Marty give him a beer from the six pack Marty was carrying. Marty refused and the boy took a swing at Marty with a wine bottle. Marty ducked and the wine bottle hit Sean in the face. As a result of the blow, Sean's upper and lower jaw were broken, along with four other bones in his face. At trial, Marty identified Conley (D) as the boy who hit Sean. Conley (D) was charged with aggravated battery based on permanent disability and great bodily harm. An expert testified that Sean sustained a permanent condition called "mucosal mouth" and permanent partial numbness in one lip as a result of the blow. Conley (D) was convicted of aggravated battery based on permanent disability. On appeal, Conley contended that the State (P) failed to prove a permanent disability, and alternatively, that the State (P) failed to prove that he intended to inflict a permanent disability. The court addressed the issue whether the injuries inflicted constituted a permanent disability and found that they did.

Issue: In order to satisfy the requirement of intent, is it necessary to find that the actor consciously desired to bring about a particular harm?

Decision and Rationale: (Cerda, J.) No. Intent is satisfied if it can be shown either that a person consciously desires to bring about a particular harm or that he knows that his conduct is practically certain to cause the harm. Conley (D) argues that it is not enough for the State (P) to prove that he intended to cause some harm. Rather, for his conviction to stand, Conley (D) maintains that the State (P) must have proven that he intended to cause a *permanent disability*. The State (P) contends that such a showing was not necessary; that it had only to prove that Conley (D) intended to strike Sean. We agree that the State (P) was required to show that Conley (D) intended to cause a permanent disability, because that is the standard that is enunciated in the statute. [The statute provides that a person who intentionally or knowingly causes great bodily harm or permanent disability while committing a battery has committed an aggravated battery.] Whether the State (P) has met its burden of proving intent, then, turns on the statutory meaning of the words "intentionally" and "knowingly." The statute provides that a person acts intentionally if it is his conscious desire or purpose to bring about a result. He acts knowingly if he is consciously aware that the result is practically certain to occur from his conduct. Here, the State (P) was required to prove beyond a reasonable doubt that Conley (D) either consciously desired to bring about a permanent disability when he struck Sean with the bottle, or that he knew that his conduct was practically certain to result in such permanent disability. Of course, the jury was permitted to infer intent from the evidence provided and from the surrounding circumstances. Conley (D) introduced no evidence to negate a finding of intent. A jury confronted with the circumstances, such as the force of the blow, the weapon used, and the absence of a warning, could have inferred that Conley (D) either intended to cause a permanent disability or knew that a permanent disability could certainly result. The evidence was therefore sufficient to support a finding of intent beyond a reasonable doubt. Affirmed.

Analysis:

Many crimes have as a prerequisite to punishment or conviction that the accused intentionally have committed some proscribed act. At common law, an actor was considered to have acted intentionally if he desired to bring about a certain social harm or he knew that such harm was virtually certain to result from his actions. In the instant case, the statute used the terms "intentionally" and "knowingly" in the same manner as the common law used the term "intentionally." Conley (D) was arguing that, while the State (P) may have proven that he struck Sean intentionally, it did not prove that he *intended to cause a permanent disability*. [In other words, he was arguing that he may have wanted to hurt Sean, and hurt him bad, but the State didn't prove that he wanted to hurt him *that* bad!] The court didn't buy the argument, probably because even if Conley (D) did not intend to cause a permanent disability, he certainly knew (or should have known) that hitting someone in the face with a wine bottle [hard!] could potentially result in a permanent disability. The court alludes in the opinion to the fact that the jury was permitted to infer intent because of the presumption that one intends the natural and probable consequences of his actions. This is called the "natural and probable consequences" doctrine, and it is problematic when used in conjunction with proving causation or intent in criminal cases. The Supreme Court has ruled that a *presumption* that a person intends the natural and probable consequences of his actions unconstitutionally alleviates the prosecution's burden of proving every element of a crime and is therefore violative of the due process clause. A judge is not constitutionally permitted to instruct the jury that it may presume intent from the resulting outcome. Instead, the jury is permitted to *infer* intent from the surrounding circumstances and from the evidence that is presented. In all probability, the jury is doing the same thing whether you call it a "presumption" or an "inference." The members of the jury are simply using their common sense and collective experiences to decide if it is likely that the actor intended the consequences that resulted from his actions.

State v. Nations

(Government) v. (Nightclub Owner)

(1984) 676 S.W.2d 282 (Missouri Court of Appeals, Eastern District)

M E M O R Y   G R A P H I C

Instant Facts

A nightclub owner was charged with endangering the welfare of a child less than seventeen years old when she hired a sixteen-year-old to dance in her club. She claimed that she had asked the girl for identification and that she thought the girl was eighteen.

Black Letter Rule

Unless the applicable criminal code states otherwise, a requirement that a person commit a certain act "knowingly" with respect to a particular fact will not be satisfied unless the person had actual knowledge of the existence of the particular fact.

 ## Case Vocabulary

ATTENDING CIRCUMSTANCES: Facts that surround a particular event; in the criminal sense, it is a required element of some offenses that an actor has knowledge of a particular fact, but chooses to act anyway.

Procedural Basis: Appeal from a conviction for endangering the welfare of a child less than seventeen years old.

Facts: Nations (D) owned a nightclub called "Main Street Disco." Police officers entered the disco and observed a scantily clad girl dancing with another female on a stage for tips. After watching the girl for a few minutes, the police approached Nations (D) and questioned her about the girl's age. Nations (D) told the police that both of the girls on the stage were of legal age and that she had checked their identification when she hired them. The police then questioned the young-looking girl about her age. She told them first that she was eighteen but later admitted to being sixteen. She had no identification with her [but then she didn't have any clothes on]. At trial, the girl testified that Nations (D) had asked her for her identification that night and that she was crossing the stage to get her ID when the police arrived. Nations (D) testified that she had asked the girl for identification that night (the first night she hired the girl) and the girl told her that she would "show it to her in a minute." Nations (D) was convicted of endangering the welfare of a child under seventeen years old. Nations (D) appealed, claiming that the State (P) did not prove that she knew the girl was under seventeen and therefore did not prove that she had the intent to endanger the welfare of a child under seventeen.

Issue: If a statute requires a person to act "knowingly" with regard to a certain fact, can she be convicted if she does not have actual knowledge of the fact?

Decision and Rationale: (Satz, J.) No. If a statute requires that a person act "knowingly" with respect to an attending circumstance as an element of the offense, the State (P) must prove that the accused had actual knowledge of the circumstance in order to meet its evidentiary burden. Our Criminal Code defines "knowingly" as actual knowledge. A person acts knowingly with respect to attendant circumstances when he is aware that those circumstances exist. Although our Criminal Code is based upon the Model Penal Code ("MPC"), our legislature did not define the term "knowingly" as broadly as does the MPC. Under the MPC, a person acts knowingly with respect to a particular fact if he has actual knowledge of the existence of the fact *or he is aware of a high probability of the existence of the fact.* Therefore, the MPC contemplates knowledge in cases where the actor willfully blinds himself to the existence of the fact, or when he deliberately chooses to remain ignorant of the fact. We feel that this latter definition of "knowledge" is identical to "recklessness." Under the MPC, then, an accused who recklessly and willfully fails to investigate the existence of a fact is charged with the knowledge of that fact. That is not the case with our Code, however. Our Code restricts the definition of "knowingly" or "knowledge" to those instances where the actor has actual knowledge of the existence of a particular fact. In this case, the State (P) did not prove that Nations (D) knew that the girl was under seventeen years old. As this was a required element of the offense, and the State did not meet its burden of proof, the conviction can not stand. Judgment reversed.

Analysis:

Knowledge of an attending circumstance is a different element of the crime than is intent. If knowledge of an attending circumstance is a required element of a crime, then the prosecution must prove *both* elements in order to obtain a conviction. Perhaps the most important impression to take away from this case is that there is a conceptual difference between knowledge as intent (as was discussed previously in *People v. Conley*) and knowledge with respect to attending circumstances. In the former case, the accused is considered to have acted intentionally if it was his conscious desire to bring about a certain harm, or he *knew* that the harm would be virtually certain to result. In other words, with respect to whether a person had the requisite intent to cause harm, he will be charged with acting intentionally if he did in fact act intentionally or if he acted knowingly. Contrast that definition of knowingly with the one used in the instant case—where Nations (D) could only be convicted if the State (P) proved she actually knew that the girl was underage. The latter definition is the more precise and, certainly, the more difficult to prove from a prosecutorial point of view. With respect to knowledge as intent, the prosecution must prove only that the accused knew that the harm was *practically certain* to result. If knowledge of an attending circumstance is an element of the crime, though, the prosecution must prove that the accused *did in fact know of the attending circumstance*, but chose to act anyway. Of course, in the latter instance, the prosecution must first prove that the actor had the requisite intent, and additionally must prove that the actor actually knew of the particular fact that constitutes the attending circumstance. Keep in mind, though, that different criminal codes have different definitions of knowledge with respect to attending circumstances. In a jurisdiction that follows the MPC, the prosecution's burden is somewhat lightened because it has to prove either that the accused actually knew of the attending circumstance or that she was aware of a high probability of its existence and deliberately chose *not* to know about it i.e. to purposefully avoid learning something that she did not want to know. [The old deaf, dumb and blind routine.] If the criminal code in *Nations* had followed the MPC, it is arguable that the conviction might have been upheld because whether Nations (D) actually knew or she was aware of a high probability that the girl was underage would have been a question of fact for the finder of fact. The finder of fact is in the best position to assess the credibility of the witnesses at trial, and if the fact-finding body (either the jury or the judge, if it was a bench trial) did not believe Nation's testimony, it might well have found that she possessed the requisite knowledge.

United States v. Morris

(Government) v. (Hacker)
(1991) 928 F. 2d 504 (2d Cir.)

M E M O R Y   G R A P H I C

Instant Facts

A computer hacker intentionally unleashed a worm virus onto the Internet while it was in its nascent stages. Although he did not mean to cause any damage, he underestimated the copy rate of the worm and subsequently caused the crash of several high level government computer systems.

Black Letter Rule

If a statute is ambiguous regarding whether a mens rea term applies to all or only some of the elements of a crime, the court should examine the legislative intent to determine the correct interpretation.

Case Vocabulary

SCIENTER: Literally, scienter means "knowingly." It is a general mens rea term that sometimes means intent, but more often simply means guilty knowledge.

Procedural Basis: Appeal of conviction for violating the Computer Fraud and Abuse Act of 1986 [adopted by Congress to protect against computer crimes].

Facts: Morris (D) was a graduate student in a Ph.D. program in computer science at Cornell University. He had extensive experience with computers from undergraduate study at Harvard and from various jobs. Morris (D) spoke to some of his fellow students about the ease with which he could infiltrate the security of certain computer networks. In October of 1988, Morris created a virus, or worm, to release on the Internet. At that point, the Internet consisted of a group of national computer networks that connected various governmental agencies, universities, medical research facilities and military operations. Morris (D) created the worm to demonstrate the inadequacies of the security systems on the Internet. He programmed the worm to infect computers quietly and unobtrusively. However, Morris (D) was concerned that computer operators would be able to detect the worm and disable it, so he deliberately made it difficult to kill. In order to ensure that the worm only infected a previously uninfected computer, Morris (D) programmed the worm to ask each computer if it already had a copy of the worm. If the computer answered "no," then the worm would infect it. Morris (D) became concerned that programmers could outsmart the worm by programming their computers to say "yes" automatically, so he placed an override in the program that would automatically re-infect a computer after the worm had received seven consecutive "no" answers. Unfortunately, Morris (D) underestimated the rate of re-infection. After he released the worm onto the Internet on November 2, 1988, many computer systems around the country crashed. At that point, Morris (D) tried to send a message detailing how to kill the worm, but the systems were not functioning properly and could not receive the message. The estimated cost of dealing with the worm ranged from $200 to $53,000 in different facilities. Morris (D) was charged with violating 18 U.S.C. § 1030(a)(5)(A) [making criminally liable anyone who intentionally accesses a federal computer without authorization and damages or destroys information therein and thereby causes damage in excess of $1,000 in one year]. Morris (D) was convicted and appealed, claiming that the statutory language indicated that the government had to prove both that he intended the unauthorized use of a federal interest computer and that he intended to cause a loss. The government (P) contended that the language of the statute was clear and unambiguous, that the adverb "intentionally" modified only the access portion of the statute and that a resort to legislative history was unnecessary.

Issue: Is a court required to determine the legislative intent behind a criminal statute if it is ambiguous as to whether a mens rea term modifies all or only some of the elements of the offense?

Decision and Rationale: (Newman, C.J.) Yes. In a case such as this one, where the wording of the offense is ambiguous as to the mens rea requirement, resort to the legislative history to determine legislative intent is appropriate. It is true that there is no hard and fast rule here. Some courts have interpreted similar statutes by taking into account sentence structure and the rules of grammar. We are not convinced, however, that punctuation should be the only consideration. Nor are we convinced, as the government (P) would have us be, that the placement of the comma in this statute renders the text so clear as to preclude a review of legislative history. Congress amended the Computer Fraud and Abuse Act of 1986 in 1988 to better reflect its intent. At that point, Congress added the Section now at issue. The old version covered anyone who knowingly accessed a computer without authorization and who knowingly used, modified or destroyed information, thereby causing damage or loss. The 1988 amendment changed the mental state requirement from "knowingly" to "intentionally."

Additionally, the 1988 amendment used the scienter requirement only once. The new Section covers anyone who intentionally accesses a government computer without authorization and alters, damages or destroys information, thereby causing damage or loss. The new section does not repeat the scienter requirement after the access phrase. We think the legislative history indicates that Congress intended the mens rea requirement of "intentionally" to modify only the access phrase, and not to apply also to the damages phrase. Judgment of conviction affirmed.

Analysis:

The issue in this case is one that frequently arises with respect to criminal statutes. The modern view is that a mens rea term placed at the beginning of the statute modifies all of the phrases in the statute. That is the view that the Model Penal Code espouses in Section 2.02(4). According to the Model Penal Code, a single mens rea term in a statute modifies each actus reus element of the offense, unless the legislature plainly indicates a contrary purpose. However, courts occasionally come to different conclusions. One common exception occurs when the actus reus term is an attending circumstance. In this case, courts do not always view the mens rea term as modifying the attending circumstance. Thus, a statute that makes it a felony for intentionally breaking and entering the dwelling house of another would probably be construed as requiring that the defendant intended to break into and enter, but not that he intended the structure to be a dwelling house. Another common exception is when, like in the instant case, the phrase containing the mens rea requirement is set off from the rest of the statute by punctuation. In that case, it may be evident that the mens rea term was intended only to modify the actus reus provision within the set off phrase.

United States v. Cordoba-Hincapie

(Government) v. (Accused)
825 F.Supp 485 (EDNY 1993)

M E M O R Y   G R A P H I C

Instant Facts
Not Stated.

Black Letter Rule
In some limited circumstances, criminal liability can exist absent any mens rea.

Procedural Basis: Not Stated.

Facts: Not Stated.

Issue: Not Stated.

Decision and Rationale: (Weinstein, D.J.) In almost every instance, mens rea is a required element for criminal liability to exist. Although the rule used to be that no criminal liability could attach absent mens rea, this rule has undergone significant changes over time. The law now recognizes that a man can be convicted of some kinds of crimes even without a guilty frame of mind--without a mens rea. Probably the most common examples of crimes that do not require a mens rea for conviction are those crimes categorized as "public welfare offenses." Historically, the law has permitted criminal liability to attach without regard to fault with respect to violations of liquor laws, traffic laws, sanitary laws and the like. These so-called "strict liability" crimes generally arise from the need to protect the public welfare through the orderly administration of laws promulgated for the collective good of society. Strict liability crimes permit the wrongdoer to be convicted of the crime regardless of whether he had a guilty mind when he acted. In general, the law has tolerated strict liability crimes that involve fairly light penalties, i.e. fines. When the penalties begin to get more harsh, i.e. imprisonment or hefty fines or forfeitures, our criminal justice system generally requires mens rea for criminal liability to exist. One exception to these general rules is the crime of statutory rape. Historically, statutory rape has been a strict liability crime, despite the fact that conviction for statutory rape carries with it significant penalties and the potential for long-term imprisonment.

Analysis:

You've just spent the better part of a Chapter learning that the law has evolved in such a way as to mandate a mens rea requirement in conjunction with an actus reus in order to impose criminal liability on a person. One common exception to the requirement of a mens rea is the "strict liability" offense. Although strict liability is a disfavored doctrine in the criminal law, it survives with respect to certain "public-welfare" or regulatory offenses. A common example [and one of which we are all, unfortunately, too well aware] is the traffic code. Traffic laws, liquor laws, sanitary and building laws are all examples of the kinds of regulations for which there can be strict liability for violations. These regulatory offenses generally have in common light penalties or fines, and do not usually involve a direct infringement on the rights of others. In addition, they are usually part of a broad regulatory scheme implemented to protect the collective interests of society. And they are relatively new offenses, rather than crimes that stem from the common law. A general rule of thumb is that the more severe the penalty involved, the more likely that the court will find that the government must prove the necessary mens rea. If penalties are relatively minor, though, and the offense is part of a broad regulatory scheme or is intended to regulate harmful or injurious substances for the public welfare, a court is more likely to find that no mens rea need be proven.

Staples v. United States

(Gun Owner) v. (Government)

(1994) 511 U.S. 600, 114 S.Ct. 1793, 128 L. Ed. 2d 608

M E M O R Y   G R A P H I C

Instant Facts

A man was charged with violating a federal statute that required registration of automatic weapons because police found a modified AR-15 civilian rifle (similar to the M-16 military machine gun) in his home.

Black Letter Rule

If a federal crime does not expressly state a mens rea requirement, the determination of the necessary mental state is made by construing the statute itself and by examining the intent of Congress.

Case Vocabulary

STRICT LIABILITY: A category of criminal offense that does not require a mens rea; only an actus reus is required for conviction.

Procedural Basis: Appeal to United States Supreme Court of conviction for violating a federal registration statute.

Facts: Local police and federal agents executed a search warrant at Staples' (D) home where they found a modified AR-15 rifle. The rifle is a civilian version of the military's M-16, except that the AR-15 is a semi-automatic weapon. The M-16 is a selective fire rifle that allows the operator to switch between automatic fire and semi-automatic fire with the flip of a switch. The parts of an M-16 are interchangeable with the parts of an AR-15 and can be used to convert the AR-15 into an automatic weapon. The federal agents observed that Staples' (D) gun had been modified with M-16 parts and that a metal stop that would ordinarily have been on the AR-15 to prevent its being modified into an automatic weapon had either been filed or worn away. The federal agents tested the gun and found that it was capable of fully automatic fire. Staples (D) was charged with violating the National Firearms Act ("Act"), which requires that all statutorily defined "firearms" be registered in the National Firearms Registration and Transfer Record. The Act defines "firearm" as a gun that shoots or can readily be made to shoot more than one shot automatically with one pull of the trigger, without having to manually reload. Violations of the Act are punishable by up to ten years in prison. Staples' (D) weapon was not registered. He insisted that the gun had never been fired automatically when he possessed it. Staples (D) contended that the weapon had only fired semi-automatically—and even then he said that it had sometimes been problematic. Staples (D) requested the trial judge to instruct the jury that the government had to prove that he knew that the gun would fire automatically in order to establish a violation of the Act. The trial court rejected the proposed instruction and Staples (D) was convicted. He was sentenced to five years of probation and a $5,000.00 fine. The Court of Appeals affirmed and Staples (D) petitioned the United States Supreme Court for certiorari.

Issue: If a federal criminal statute is silent as to the mens rea requirement, will it be construed as a strict liability offense?

Decision and Rationale: (Thomas, J.) No. The requirement of mens rea is firmly embedded within our system of justice. A statute that is silent as to the mens rea requirement should not be construed as dispensing with mens rea absent a clear indication of congressional intent to dispense with the requirement. It is true that we have recognized that mens rea is not always a required element of some crimes. Those offenses that we have labeled "public welfare" or regulatory offenses sometimes do not require a showing of mens rea. Instead, they are typically referred to as "strict liability" offenses. In most cases, we have recognized such offenses only when they involve the regulation of potentially dangerous or harmful items. In those cases, we have charged the possessor of such an item with the knowledge that the item is dangerous and that the responsibility is his to determine whether the law regulates his conduct. But we have not traditionally done away with the requirement of mens rea with regard to statutes that regulate otherwise lawful and innocent conduct. We are confronted with such a statute here. Citizens of our country have traditionally owned guns; within certain boundaries it is perfectly lawful for them to do so. Although guns are potentially dangerous items, the prevalence of gun ownership in this country militates against dispensing with a mens rea requirement that a person know the characteristics of his gun make it illegal. We do not believe that Congress, by remaining silent on the point, intended that there be no requirement of mens rea with respect to this statute. Additionally, the Act imposes a penalty of up to ten years imprisonment. We have historically examined the nature of the penalty provided for by the statute when determining whether the statute subjected the violator to strict liability. Generally, the small penalties that attach to public welfare offenses justify dispensing with the mens rea requirement.

Although we do not adopt an absolute rule, we note here that the provision of such a harsh penalty in the statute is inconsistent with a finding that this is a public welfare offense that dispenses with the mens rea requirement. Judgment of conviction reversed.

Dissent: (Stevens, J.) The Act does indicate the express intent of Congress to dispense with a mens rea requirement because it does not contain a knowledge requirement at all. Nor does the statute describe a common law offense. Public welfare offenses are those offenses that have been statutorily created and regulate dangerous items. They heighten the duties of those who possess or use them and they do not depend on the existence of a particular mental state. This Act is silent as to a knowledge requirement, and silence on the part of Congress indicates that it intended to alleviate the burden of proving that the defendant knew that his conduct was unlawful. I would find that this Act fits the description of a public welfare statute.

Analysis:

This case exemplifies some of the problems associated with construing a statute as imposing strict liability. Of course, it is axiomatic in our jurisprudence that an act committed without an attendant wrongful mental state is not criminally punishable. That is the rule in the overwhelming majority of cases. Our criminal justice system has evolved in such a way as to require a mens rea: strict liability offenses are highly disfavored. [Except sometimes.] There are policy factors in favor of recognizing strict liability offenses as well as those opposing the recognition. As the case indicates, one of the reasons that the mens rea requirement is dispensed of in some offenses is to ease the prosecution's burden of proof. That is, while the prosecution usually has to prove every element of the crime beyond a reasonable doubt to obtain a conviction, categorizing an offense as a strict liability crime alleviates the prosecution's burden of having to prove intent or knowledge. With respect to regulatory offenses, doing away with the prosecution's duty to prove the mental element lessens the burden on our court systems and promotes social compliance with regulatory schemes. On the other hand, imposing strict liability sometimes means that people who had no intention of violating the law or did not even know that their conduct was illegal are convicted of crimes. Conviction in such a case seems to undermine the notion that our criminal justice system only punishes those who perform proscribed acts with a sufficiently culpable state of mind. It is important to recognize, however, that most commentators agree that strict liability is appropriate and can be imposed when the statute regulates items that are particularly harmful or dangerous.

Garnett v. State

(Mentally Disabled Man) v. (Government)
(1993) 332 Md. 571, 632 A.2d 797

M E M O R Y   G R A P H I C

Instant Facts

A 20-year-old man with an I.Q. of 52 has sexual intercourse with a 13-year-old whom he believed was 16.

Black Letter Rule

Mistake of age is not a defense to the strict liability crime of statutory rape.

Case Vocabulary

MALUM PROHIBITUM: Typically refers to offenses that are not wicked per se, such as regulatory offenses.
MORAL WRONG THEORY: Holds that an actor should be held responsible despite mistake where, if the facts were as the accused believed them to be, the accused's conduct would still be immoral.
STRICT LIABILITY: Refers to offenses that do not require any mens rea, but hold an actor responsible regardless of intent.

Procedural Basis: Appeal from conviction for statutory rape.

Facts: Raymond Garnett (D) is a 20-year-old, mentally disabled man. He has an I.Q. of 52, and interacts socially at the level of an 11- or 12-year-old. In November or December of 1990, a friend introduced Garnett (D) to Erica Frazier, a 13-year-old girl. On February 28, 1991, Erica invited Raymond into her room, and the two had sexual intercourse. Nine months later, Erica gave birth to a child, of which Raymond is the biological father. Raymond was convicted of one count of second degree rape under Maryland Code § 463, which reads in part, "A person is guilty of rape in the second degree if the person engages in vaginal intercourse with another person . . . [w]ho is under 14 years of age and the person performing the act is at least four years older than the victim." Garnett (D) attempted to offer evidence of his belief that Erica Frazier was 16, but the court explained that a even a good faith mistake as to age was no defense. Maryland Code § 463 does not set a particular mens rea requirement. The Government (P) insists that the statute was designed to impose strict liability. Garnett (D) replies that criminal law exists to punish the morally culpable, and such culpability was absent in his case.

Issue: Is statutory rape a strict liability offense to which mistake of age is no defense?

Decision and Rationale: (Murphy) Yes. The requirement that an accused must have acted with a culpable mental state is an axiom of criminal jurisprudence. Legislatures have created strict liability statutes dealing with public health and welfare issues, usually imposing fines for misconduct. Statutory rape, on the other hand, imposes a sentence of up to 20 years in prison. Strict liability is a somewhat disfavored doctrine. The Model Penal Code [MPC], for example, requires that a person act with some degree of mens rea to be held criminally liable. The MPC recognizes strict liability solely for offenses deemed "violations," defined as wrongs subject to fines, forfeitures, or other civil penalty. Likewise, commentators disapprove of statutory rape as a strict liability crime, noting that statutory rape prosecutions proceed even when there is evidence supporting the defendant's belief that the complainant was of age. Strict liability for the offense is not justified by the "moral wrong theory," which would hold that Garnett (D), acting without mens rea, nonetheless deserves punishment for having violated moral teachings that prohibit sex outside marriage. Maryland has no law against fornication. Also, the criminality of an act performed without a guilty mind rests uneasily on the subjective, shifting moral norms of some members of the community. Seventeen states have allowed the mistake of age defense in some form. However, Maryland's statute does not require the Government (P) to prove mens rea, and makes no allowance for a mistake of age defense. The silence as to mens rea results from legislative design in drafting the statute. The legislative history also reveals that the statute was viewed as imposing strict liability. Even among states with an available mistake of age defense, most do not allow the defense where the complainant is aged 14 years or less. Any new provision in Maryland law that introduces a mistake of age defense must result from legislative amendment. Judgment Affirmed.

Dissent: (Bell) Despite the legislative history and the majority's interpretation of the statute, I do not believe that the General Assembly can subject a defendant to strict liability in every case. To hold that the Government (P) need not prove mens rea with respect to the age of the complainant, or that Garnett (D) may not offer a defense, offends fundamental principles of justice and is inconsistent with due process. I would hold that Garnett (D) should be allowed the opportunity to produce evidence supporting his claim of mistake of age. If he is able to produce such evidence, the Government (P) must then show beyond a reasonable doubt that the act was committed without any mistake of fact.

Analysis:

The majority walks the reader through various reasons why statutory rape should not be a strict liability defense. Suddenly, the court yanks the rug out from underneath the reader's feet [a favorite judicial trick to frustrate law students]. Before pulling out the rug, the majority mentions the moral wrong theory. The moral wrong theory holds that an actor should be held responsible despite mistake where, if the facts were as the accused believed them to be, the accused's conduct would still be immoral. In the famous case of *Regina v. Prince*, the defendant Prince was found guilty of "taking . . . [an] unmarried girl . . . under the age of sixteen . . . out of the possession . . . of her father." The girl was 13, but Prince believed her to be 18. Out of seventeen judges deciding the case [not a typo], ten held that the offense was a strict liability crime. Six others held that mens rea had to be proven. But then wouldn't the mistake of age defense apply, so that Prince should be acquitted? The judges avoided this result by relying on the moral wrong theory. Assuming that Prince reasonably believed that the girl was 13, he would still be culpable. Although the girl was not 13, she was still of "tender years," and Prince knew that he was taking the girl from her father, which is an immoral act. The implication is that Prince knew the act was immoral. Yet as the majority in Garnett observes, it is sometimes difficult to ascertain what constitutes moral behavior in a diverse society.

People v. Navarro

(Government) v. (Accused Thief)

(1979) 99 Cal.App.3d Supp. 1, 160 Cal. Rptr. 692

M E M O R Y   G R A P H I C

Instant Facts

A man was charged with theft for taking four wooden beams from a construction site and, but argued that he had no intent to steal the beams because he thought they had been abandoned.

Black Letter Rule

With regard to a specific intent crime. a mistake of fact is a defense if the mistake negates the specific intent required in the definition of the crime.

Case Vocabulary

FELONIOUSLY: Done with a deliberate intent to commit a felony or a crime.

THEFT: The taking of another's property without his consent with the intent to permanently deprive the person of the property.

Procedural Basis: Appeal of a conviction for petty theft.

Facts: Navarro (D) entered a construction site and removed four wooden beams from the site. He was charged with grand theft. The statute provided that any person who feloniously steals the property of another is guilty of theft. The statute was a codification of the common law offense of larceny, which is the "trespassory taking and carrying away of the personal property of another with the intent to steal the property." Navarro (D) presented evidence that he did not intend to steal the beams, but that he thought they had been abandoned and the owner would have no objection to his taking them. Navarro (D) requested a jury instruction to the effect that if he took the beams with a good faith belief that they had been abandoned he could not be convicted, even if the belief was objectively unreasonable. The judge modified the requested instruction, and instead instructed the jury that if Navarro (D) took the beams with a reasonable and good faith belief that they had been abandoned, he could not be convicted. Navarro (D) was convicted of petty theft and appealed. He contended that the judged erred in his instruction of the jury.

Issue: Does a mistake have to be reasonable in order to negate the mental state required by a specific intent crime?

Decision and Rationale: (Dowds, J.) No. Even an unreasonable mistake will be a defense to a specific intent crime if it negates the specific mens rea requirement. Navarro (D) was charged with theft, which is a specific intent crime. The offense requires that a person feloniously steal the property of another to be convicted; that is, a person must *intend* to steal the property. Navarro (D) presented evidence that tended to show that he lacked the specific intent required by the wording of the offense, i.e. that he thought the beams had been abandoned. The Supreme Court has stated that "where a felonious intent must be proven it can be done only by proving what the accused knew." We understand the Supreme Court's words to mean that it is not enough to show that a reasonable man would have known the true nature of the facts. Instead, where a specific intent is required to convict a person of a crime, the prosecution must show that the accused actually possessed the requisite intent. In these circumstances, it does not matter if the alleged mistake is objectively reasonable or unreasonable. If a mistake as to the facts or law negates the specific intent required by the statute, the accused is entitled to a defense. The trial court erred when it instructed the jury that Navarro (D) could be acquitted only if the jury found that he entertained a reasonable and good faith belief that he had a right to take the beams. Judgment of conviction reversed.

Analysis:

This case demonstrates the common law approach to mistake as a defense to a crime. The common law makes a distinction between specific and general intent crimes with regard to mistakes. If the offense is a general intent crime, only a reasonable mistake of fact or law will provide a defense for the accused. This is so because at common law, general intent crimes required only a morally blameworthy state of mind rather than a specific mental state. Recall that the culpability approach to mens rea usually coincided with common law general intent crimes. Therefore, if common law rules are applied, the first step in analyzing a mistake defense is to determine whether the crime is a specific intent or a general intent offense. If it is a general intent offense and the mistake is reasonable, the actor will not have acted with a morally blameworthy state of mind and so should be entitled to a defense. If the mistake is unreasonable, it has no bearing on the blameworthiness of the individual and he will not be entitled to a defense. On the other hand, if the offense is a specific intent crime, any mistake, reasonable or unreasonable, that both relates to the specific intent required and negates the mental state necessary for conviction will entitle the accused to a defense. This result is in keeping with the elemental approach to mens rea. Using the elemental approach, if a mistake means that the accused did not have the specific intent required to commit the crime, then he is not guilty.

People v. Marrero

(Government) v. (Federal Corrections Officer)

(1987) 69 N.Y.2d 382, 515 N.Y.S.2d 212, 507 N.E.2d 1068

M E M O R Y   G R A P H I C

Instant Facts

Marrero (D), a federal corrections officer, was convicted for violating a statute which he believed gave him the right to carry a gun.

Black Letter Rule

An erroneous interpretation of the law does not excuse violation of the law, even where the interpretation is reasonable.

Case Vocabulary

ACTING IN RELIANCE: Actions based on trust in another person's words or actions.

MISTAKE OF LAW: An incorrect interpretation of the legal effect of a given law or set of facts.

Procedural Basis: Appeal after conviction for unlawful possession of a pistol.

Facts: Marrero (D), a federal corrections officer, was convicted of unlawful possession of a pistol under a statute containing an exemption for "peace officers." The statutory definition of "peace officers" included "correction officers of any state correction facility or of any penal correctional institution." The trial court dismissed the charge, but the Appellate Division ruled by a 3-2 vote that only state and not federal officers were covered by the provision. At the ensuing criminal trial, the court refused to instruct the jury that it should acquit Marrero (D) if he reasonably believed himself to be a peace officer under the statutory definition. Marrero (D) claimed that he relied on interpretations of fellow officers and teachers, as well as the language of the statute itself, in forming his belief that he could carry a pistol.

Issue: Does misinterpretation of a statute excuse its violation, where the statute does not have a mens rea requirement?

Decision and Rationale: (Bellacosa) No. A mistake of law does not excuse the commission of prohibited acts. Contrasted with kidnapping, which allows a showing of good-faith belief in the legality of the conduct to negate intent, a weapons statute violation imposes criminal liability regardless of intent. The mistake of law defense is available to defendants who have relied on an "official statement" of the law, either expressed in a statute or by a public servant or agency charged with administering, enforcing, or interpreting the law. Marrero (D) claims that his conduct was based on an official statement of the law contained in the statute itself. In view of the ambiguous wording, Marrero (D) argues that his "reasonable" interpretation falls under this exception. However, allowing Marrero (D) this exception would make mistake of law a generally applied or available defense, rather than an unusual exception. The Government (P) analogizes New York's *official statement* defense to the Model Penal Code. The Model Penal Code provides that the *official statement* defense only applies when the accused acts in reliance on a statute that actually authorizes his conduct. If the *official statement* of the law is afterward determined to be invalid or erroneous, the *official statement* defense protects those who mistakenly acted in reliance. Reviewing the legislative history, it is evident that the legislature intended the New York official statement defense statute to be similarly construed. Marrero's (D) conduct was never authorized by statute; he only thought that it was. If Marrero's (D) arguments were accepted, the exception would swallow the rule. Mistakes of law would be encouraged. Wrong-minded individuals would use the defense to avoid conviction. To avoid these consequences, the conviction is affirmed.

Dissent: (Hancock) In interpreting a statute, a court should look first to the particular words of the statute in question. Here, there is but one natural and obvious meaning: If a defendant founded his interpretation on an official interpretation of the statute, he should have a defense. The precise phrase from the Model Penal Code limiting the defense to reliance on a statute "afterward determined to be invalid or erroneous" was omitted from New York's penal code. How can the legislature be assumed to have enacted the very language that it specifically rejected? Also, the majority suggests that the Legislature intended the defense to be available solely in acts involving mala in se offenses, such as kidnapping. On the contrary, it is with mala prohibita (regulatory) offenses that reasons of policy and fairness call for a relaxation of the rule limiting the mistake of law defense.

Analysis:

The majority is concerned that if Marrero (D) is acquitted, people might get the message that the law is subjective, that the law is whatever the individual believes it to be. Marrero (D) does not argue, however, that he should be able to interpret the statute however he likes, but that the statute is so ambiguous that his interpretation is completely reasonable, and that a reasonable interpretation should be covered under the defense. The majority possibly exaggerates the effect an acquittal would have. For most statutes, the window of "reasonable" interpretation is fairly narrow, and judges and juries could be trusted to spot the occasional "unreasonable" interpretation. A positive effect of allowing a broader mistake of law defense would be that, where a law allows a wide array of reasonable interpretations, legislators might make a better effort to ensure that legislation is clear and understandable. Also, individualists might be pleased with an interpretation of the mistake of law defense that does not sacrifice the individual for the sake of society at large.

Cheek v. United States

(Delinquent Taxpayer) v. (Government)
(1991) 498 U.S. 192, 111 S. Ct. 604, 112 L.Ed.2d 617

M E M O R Y   G R A P H I C

Instant Facts

A pilot who had previously filed tax returns stopped filing them because he became influenced by a group who believed that the income tax system was unconstitutional. The IRS charged him with willful tax evasion.

Black Letter Rule

A mistake of law, either reasonable or un-reasonable, will be a defense to a crime if it negates the specific intent required for conviction.

Procedural Basis: Appeal to United States Supreme Court of conviction for tax evasion.

Facts: Cheek (D) was a pilot for American Airlines. He duly filed his tax returns through the year 1979, but thereafter ceased to file his returns. Beginning in 1980, he began claiming excessive withholding deductions—eventually claiming 60 [not a typo!] allowances on his W-2—and also claimed he was exempt from federal income taxes. Cheek (D) did so because he had become associated with and influenced by a group that believed that the federal income tax system was unconstitutional. He was charged with tax evasion under a statute that provided, "any person who willfully attempts . . . to evade or defeat any tax imposed by this title . . . shall be guilty of a felony." Evidence was presented at trial that Cheek (D) was involved in a number of civil lawsuits challenging the constitutionality of the federal income tax between 1982 and 1986. At each of those trials, Cheek (D) and the other plaintiffs were told that their claims were frivolous or had been repeatedly rejected by the courts. At trial, Cheek (D) represented himself and testified that because he had been attending seminars and listening to lectures sponsored by this anti-tax group he believed that the federal income tax laws were invalid. He also believed that his wages were not income under the federal statute. Cheek (D) presented evidence of a letter from an attorney stating that the Sixteenth Amendment did not authorize a tax on wages as income—only profits and gain. [It's probably safe to assume that this attorney is no longer practicing.] His defense was that he sincerely believed that the tax laws were being unconstitutionally applied and that his failure to file income tax returns was therefore lawful. He argued that, based on his belief that he was acting lawfully, he did not possess the willfulness necessary to convict him of tax evasion. The trial court instructed the jury that if it found that Cheek (D) "honestly and reasonably believed he was not required to pay income taxes" then he could be acquitted. When the jury could not make this decision, the trial judge further instructed them that an honest but unreasonable belief is not a defense and does not negate willfulness. The jury convicted Cheek (D). His argument on appeal was that the judge erred by instructing the jury that only a reasonable mistake about the law negated willfulness.

Issue: Is a mistake of law that relates to the specific intent of a crime a defense to criminal prosecution?

Decision and Rationale: (White, J.) Yes. The general rule is that a mistake of law is no excuse. A limited exception applies when a mistake of law negates the specific mental state required for conviction. The statute makes it a criminal violation to willfully evade federal income tax obligations. Because of the extreme complexity of the modern tax code, our cases have repeatedly interpreted the term "willfully" to mean a voluntary, intentional violation of a *known legal duty*. In order for a mistake of law to negate willfulness, then, the mistake must relate to whether the accused *knows* of a legal duty. If, because of the complexity of the tax laws, an individual does not know of a legal duty, the mistake affords him a defense because it negates the requirement that he voluntarily and intentionally violate a known legal duty. We do not agree with the Court of Appeals that such a mistake must be reasonable. Even an unreasonable mistake would negate a finding that the individual knew of a legal duty. In this case, if the jury believed Cheek's (D) assertion that he did not think the federal tax code treated wages as income, then it could find that he did not know he had a legal duty to pay income taxes on his wages. His mistaken belief as to his duty to pay taxes on his wages would negate any finding that he intentionally violated a known legal duty. With respect to Cheek's (D) constitutional claims, however, the general rule that mistake is no defense applies. Unlike his belief about wages, Cheek's (D) constitutional claims do not arise from a mistaken belief derived from the complexity of the tax code. Instead, his claims indicate that he was intimately familiar with the applicable provisions of the federal income tax code. Cheek (D) claims mistake in that he believed that the tax laws were unconstitutional as applied to him. In other words, he was aware that the law imposed upon him a duty to pay taxes, but mistakenly believed that the law itself was unconstitutional. Because of his mistaken belief as to constitutionality, Cheek (D) voluntarily and intentionally did not pay his taxes. We believe that Cheek's (D) views about the constitutionality of the tax code in general would not preclude a finding that he willfully attempted to evade the tax laws. The District Judge did not err by instructing the jury not to consider Cheek's views about constitutionality. Remanded for a new trial.

Dissent: (Blackmun, J.) It is simply unbelievable to me that in this day and age an individual could try to defend the fact that he did not file a tax return by claiming that he mistakenly believed that his wages were not income. Our cases have defined "willfulness" with respect to the tax code as a voluntary and intentional violation of a known legal duty. Cheek (D) undoubtedly knew he had a legal duty to pay taxes on his income. He should not have been allowed to assert his "mistaken" belief that his wages were not income as a defense to "willfulness."

Analysis:

This is a difficult case to follow. The Court begins by acknowledging that the term "willfulness" in the tax code has a particularized meaning. The common law rule is that ignorance of the law or a mistake of the law is no defense. Because the tax code has grown so complex, though, the courts have had to soften the common law rule with respect to tax offenses. The government is not interested in punishing those individuals who genuinely did not know they were subject to a particular provision of the code. Instead, the government seeks to punish those who know they have a legal duty to pay taxes but purposefully and intentionally do not do so. Thus, the courts have interpreted the statutory requirement of "willfulness" in the tax code as meaning the individual voluntarily and intentionally violated a known legal duty. It is because of this definition of willfulness that the Court finds that the lower courts erred by instructing the jury that only a reasonable mistake on Cheek's (D) part would constitute a defense. Cheek (D) was essentially claiming that he did not know of his statutory duty to pay taxes on his wages. As is the case with a mistake of fact, when a crime is a specific intent offense and a mistake negates the existence of the specific intent, the accused is entitled to a defense. As applied to this case, if Cheek (D) mistakenly believed his wages were not income, he would not have known he had a legal duty to pay income taxes on his wages. If he did not know he had a legal duty under the tax code, he could not have voluntarily and intentionally set out to violate that duty. It does not matter whether his belief was objectively unreasonable. If the jury believed his claim, then he was entitled to an acquittal. The same is not necessarily true of his claim of mistake as to the constitutionality of the tax laws. There, Cheek (D) did not claim he was unaware of his statutory duty. Instead, the gravamen of his claim was that he knew he had a duty to pay taxes but mistakenly thought that the law itself was unconstitutional. Therefore, his mistake claim had nothing to do with negating the mental element of the crime—it was simply a mistake as to whether the law was applicable. In other words, Cheek (D) mistakenly thought the law did not apply to him. This is the kind of mistake that fits squarely within the common law rule that a mistake of law does not excuse its violation.

Chapter 6

Imagine that D points a gun at V, intending to kill V. A few seconds before D pulls the trigger, X independently shoots and instantly kills V, and D's bullet hits an already dead V. In this hypothetical, D seems to have satisfied everything necessary to be convicted of murder. D has satisfied the actus reus of the crime by the voluntary act of pulling the trigger, and the killing of another human being occurred. Furthermore, D has satisfied the mens rea of the crime, by intending to kill V. However, common sense tells us that D is guilty of attempted murder, and not murder. Common sense is confirmed by another prerequisite to criminal liability, causation.

Analytically, causation is an ingredient of a crime's actus reus, providing a link between the voluntary act or omission and the social harm. It is justified in retributive concepts of just deserts, ensuring that criminal responsibility is personal. Moreover, it serves as a mechanism for determining how much the wrongdoer owes to society. Under retributive principles, punishment for undesired behavior should not exceed the harm caused. Thus, for example, attempted murder is punished less severely than murder.

The causation analysis is divisible into two parts: 1) actual cause, and 2) proximate cause. The first prong of the causation analysis, "actual cause" or "cause-in-fact", is used to exclude forces from responsibility for an ensuing harm. In other words it narrows the choices of individuals that may be held accountable for a social harm.

Traditionally courts use the "but for" test in determining the "actual cause" of a prohibited result. That is, a person is the "actual cause" of a prohibited result, if the prohibited result would not have happened when it did, "but for" the voluntary acts or omissions of that person.

Accordingly, acceleration of bringing about a prohibited result has been equated with actual causation. The words "when it did," in the "but for" analysis, are essential to the correct application of the test. Therefore, if a person's conduct contributes to bringing about the prohibited result earlier, even if the result would have happened regardless, that person is still the actual cause of the prohibited result.

In rare instances where the "but for" test fails, for example when two independent forces simultaneously cause a prohibited result, each of which was alone sufficient to cause the prohibited result, courts have used the "substantial factor" test. That is, a person is the "actual cause" of a social harm, if that person was a substantial factor in bringing about that harm.

The second prong of the causation analysis, "proximate cause" or "legal cause", is used to determine which among the "but for" causes, should be held criminally liable for a prohibited result. Generally, an act is the proximate cause of an ensuing harm, unless there is a sufficiently independent or supervening cause of the ensuing harm. For instance, in the hypothetical previously posed, imagine that before V was hit by a bullet, he was struck and killed by lightning. This would be a sufficient intervening cause that would relieve X or D of liability for murder.

According to some courts, foreseeability is the main factor in determining proximate causation. Thus, if the intervening act was reasonably foreseeable to the original actor, the original actor is still the proximate cause for an ensuing harm.

The Model Penal Code, unlike common law, treats the "but for" analysis as exclusive to the determination of causation. It replaces the determination of "proximate cause", with issues relating instead to the actor's culpability. Specifically, section 2.03 deals with situations in which the actual result of the defendant's conduct diverges from that which was designed, contemplated, or risked. Thus, a person has not acted with the requisite culpability, unless the actual result, including the way in which it occurred, was not too different from what was intended or reasonably expected.

Chapter 6

NOTE: THE PURPOSE OF THIS OUTLINE IS TO ORGANIZE THE CASES SO THAT ONE CAN QUICKLY UNDER-STAND THE RELEVANCE OF EACH CASE TO THE COURSE. NO ATTEMPT IS MADE IN THIS OVER-VIEW TO ADDRESS EVERY CONCEPT THAT MUST BE STUDIED. BE SURE TO READ THE ENTIRE CASE-BOOK AND/OR OTHER MATERIALS TO GAIN A FULL UNDERSTANDING OF ALL CONCEPTS.

I. Introduction
   A. "Causation" is a prerequisite to criminal liability, which acts as the link between the actus reus (voluntary act or omission) and the social harm.
      1. The causation analysis is divisible into two parts called, "cause-in-fact" and "proximate cause", both of which are necessary prerequisites to the imposition of criminal liability. *Velazquez v. State.*

II. Actual Cause or Cause-In-Fact
   A. Actual cause constitutes the first prong of the causation analysis, used to eliminate those forces and individuals that cannot be held criminally responsible for a social harm.
      1. The prosecution must prove beyond a reasonable doubt, that a defendant is the "actual cause" of a prohibited result, in order to impose criminal responsibility upon that defendant. *Oxendine v. State.*
      2. Traditionally, courts apply the "but for" test in order to make a determination of "actual cause". Thus, if the social harm would not have occurred, but for a person's voluntary act or omission, then that person is the actual cause of the social harm. *Velazquez v. State.*
      3. In rare instances when the "but for" test fails, for example when two defendant's commit two separate acts, each of which is sufficient to bring about the prohibited result, courts have followed a "substantial factor" test in determining the "actual cause." *Valazquez v. State.*
         a. Thus, if a person's voluntary act or omis-sion is a substantial factor in bringing about a prohibited result, then that person is the actual cause of the prohibited result.
   B. Courts also equate "acceleration" with "actual cause." *Oxendine v. State.*
      1. A careful application of the "but for" test, with the addition of the three words "when it did," supports this.
      2. The test asked whether the prohibited result would have happened *when it did*, but for the voluntary acts of the defendant.
      3. Thus, if a person's voluntary act or omission accelerated the process of a prohibited result, such as death, then that person is the actual cause of the prohibited result.

III. Proximate Cause or Legal Cause
   A. Proximate cause constitutes the second prong of the causation analysis, used to determine who among the "but for" causes, should be held criminally responsible for a prohibited result.
      1. The prosecution must prove beyond a reasonable doubt, that a defendant is the proximate cause of a prohibited result, in order to impose criminal responsibility upon that defendant. *Kibbe v. Henderson.*
      2. Courts have held that, if after a person's voluntary act or omission, the prohibited result is produced by a sufficiently independent or intervening cause, then the original actor is not the proximate cause of the prohibited result.
   B. An "intervening cause" is an independent force that produces harm after the defendant's voluntary act or omission has been committed.
   C. Some courts provide that the determination of "proximate cause" depends on whether the ultimate result was foreseeable to the original actor, or whether the victim failed to do some-thing easily within the victim's grasp, that would have extricated him from danger. *Kibbe v. Henderson.*
   D. Omission, Intended Consequence, Apparent Safety, Voluntary Act

1. An omission may never function as a superseding, intervening cause of a prohibited result. In other words, no matter how unforeseeable an omission may be, this "negative act" will not cut off liability of an earlier "positive act."

2. One scholar has opined, that any *intended consequence* of an act is proximately caused by that act. *Rollin M. Perkins.*

   a. In other words, a person may be held criminally responsible for a prohibited result, if the result was an intended consequence of that person's voluntary act or omission.

   b. Thus, although the prohibited result may not have occurred precisely as the wrongdoer expected, the wrongdoer will not escape criminal liability.

3. The "Apparent safety" doctrine states, that when a person reaches a position of safety, the original wrongdoer is no longer responsible for the ensuing harm.

4. According to some professors, the criminal law does not hold a person responsible for resulting harm, if there is an intervening cause that springs from "free, deliberate and informed" human action. Thus, once a voluntary human act is discovered, the law will not trace back the casual chain any further. *H.L.A Hart & Tony Honore.*

E. The Model Penal Code Section 2.03, subsection 2 and 3 are based on the theory that "but for" causation is the only causal requirement needed, and the remaining issue is the proper scope of liability in light of the actor's culpability.

1. Subsection 2 addresses the culpability requirement with respect to purpose and knowledge. Thus if the actual result is not within the purpose or contemplation of the actor, the culpability requirement is not satisfied unless:

   a. The actual result differs from the desired result only in that a different person or property was injured, or in that the actual injury was not as serious as the desired injury.

   b. The actual result involves the same kind of injury or harm as that designed or contemplated, but in which the precise injury inflicted was different or occurred in a different way.

2. Though the governing principles are the same as subsection 2, subsection 3 deals with offenses in which recklessness or negligence is the required culpability.

   a. Specifically, where the actual result is not within the risk of which the actor was aware, or in the case of negligence, of which he should have been aware.

IV. Concurrence of the Elements

A. Elements of a crime must occur concurrently in order to impose criminal liability. *State v. Rose.*

1. Thus, for example, in order to be held liable for [negligent] manslaughter, the elements of culpable negligence and killing must occur concurrently, or the negligence must cause the death. It is not enough that both elements were satisfied at different instances. *State v. Rose.*

Velazquez v. State

(Drag Racer) v. (Community)
561 So.2d 347 (FL 1990)

M E M O R Y   G R A P H I C

Instant Facts

A "drag racer" is prosecuted for vehicular homicide, after participating in a race on a public road, where the other racer lost control of his car, drove through a guardrail, and died.

Black Letter Rule

Causation is a necessary prerequisite to the imposition of criminal liability.

Case Vocabulary

CAUSATION: The producing of a prohibited result, which is required for the imposition of criminal liability.
SINE QUA NON: A necessary element or ingredient.

Procedural Basis: Appeal to the Florida Court of Appeals, of a conviction for vehicular manslaughter.

Facts: Velazquez (D) and the victim, participated in a "drag race" on a public road. After finishing the course of the race, the victim unexpectedly turned his car around and drove at a speed estimated at 123 m.p.h. toward the starting line, with Velazquez (D) following behind at a similar speed. As both reached the starting point at the end of the road, the victim, unable to stop his car, died when his car hurdled through a guardrail. Velazquez (D) was convicted of vehicular homicide under Florida's vehicular homicide statute, §82.071 [which defines vehicular homicide as the killing of a human being by the operation of a motor vehicle by another in a reckless manner likely to cause the death of, or great bodily harm to, another]. Velazquez (D) appeals.

Issue: Is causation a necessary element to the imposition of criminal liability?

Decision and Rationale: (Hubbart, J.) Yes. Causation is a necessary prerequisite to the imposition of criminal liability. There are two statutory elements to vehicular homicide: 1) the defendant must operate a motor vehicle in a reckless manner likely to cause the death of, or great bodily harm to, another, and 2) this reckless operation of a motor vehicle must be the proximate cause of the death of a human being. It seems clear that the proximate cause element requires, at the very least, a causation-in-fact test. In other words the defendant must be the cause-in-fact of the death of a human being. In this respect, vehicular homicide is no different than any other criminal offense in which the occurrence of a specified result, caused by a defendant's conduct, is an essential element of the offense. Clearly, there can be no criminal liability for such result-type offenses unless it can be shown that the defendant's conduct was a cause-in-fact of the prohibited result. Although a showing of this cause-in-fact is insufficient in itself to establish the aforesaid "proximate cause" element, it is clearly a sine qua non ingredient thereof. Courts throughout the country have uniformly followed the traditional "but for" test in determining whether the defendant's conduct was a cause-in-fact of a prohibited consequence. Under this test, a defendant's conduct is a cause-in-fact of a prohibited result if the said result would not have occurred "but for" the defendant's conduct. Thus, a defendant's reckless operation of a motor vehicle is cause-in-fact of the death of a human being, if the subject death would not have occurred but for the defendant's reckless driving, or would not have happened in the absence of such driving. In rare cases, the "but for" test fails. This anomaly occurs when two defendants, acting independently and not in concert with one another, commit two separate acts, each of which alone is sufficient to bring about the prohibited result. It also occurs when two defendants concurrently inflict mortal wounds upon a human being, each of which is sufficient to cause death. In such cases, each defendant's action was not a "but for" cause of death because the deceased would have died even in the absence of either defendant's conduct, although obviously not in the absence of both defendant's conduct considered together. In these rare cases, the courts have followed a "substantial factor" test. Specifically, the defendant's conduct is a cause-in-fact of a prohibited result if the subject conduct was a "substantial factor" in bringing about the said result. Thus, each defendant's conduct in independently and concurrently inflicting mortal wounds on a deceased clearly constitutes a "substantial factor" in bringing about the deceased's death, and consequently, is a cause-in-fact of the deceased's death. The "proximate cause" element embraces more however than the aforesaid "but for" and "substantial factor" causation-in-fact analysis. Even where a defendant's conduct is a cause-in-fact of a prohibited result, courts throughout the country have for good reason declined to impose criminal liability, 1) where the prohibited result of the defendant's conduct is beyond the scope of any fair assessment of the danger created by the defendant's conduct, or 2) where it would otherwise be unjust, based on fairness and policy consideration, to hold the defendant criminally responsible for the prohibited result.

Analysis:

The purpose of this case is to introduce the reader to the concept of causation in criminal law. Similar to torts, causation is a necessary element to the imposition of criminal liability. Specifically, a person must be the cause-in-fact and proximate cause of a specific result. In the instant opinion, the court first states that proximate causation is a necessary element to the imposition of criminal liability. It then recognizes that the starting point of this analysis begins with the determination of "actual cause" or "cause-in-fact." The position of the opinion provided in the casebook does not apply the facts to the case. Rather, such analysis is left for classroom discussion. Courts generally use the "but for" test in determining a defendant's status as the "cause-in-fact" of a prohibited result. That is, a person is a cause in fact of a prohibited result, if the prohibited result would not have happened, "but for" the actions of the person. In rare cases, where the "but for" test fails, courts will use the "substantial factor" test in their determination of cause-in-fact. In such cases, a person is a cause-in-fact of a prohibited result, if the person's conduct clearly constitutes a "substantial factor" in bringing about the prohibited result. However, as the court mentions, being the cause-in-fact of a prohibited result is not enough, by itself, to establish proximate causation. The cause-in-fact analysis is used only to narrow the choices of persons that may be held accountable. In order to impose liability, a person must also be the proximate cause of the prohibited result. Although this opinion does not delve deeply into the determination of proximate causation, it does recognize that courts have declined the imposition of criminal liability upon those determined to be the cause-in-fact of a prohibited result, 1) where the prohibited result of the defendant's conduct is beyond the scope of any fair assessment of the danger created by the defendant's conduct, or 2) where it would be unjust or unfair to hold the defendant criminally responsible for the prohibited result. Thus, a question the reader may ask is whether it is fair to hold Velazquez (D) criminally liable for vehicular homicide, despite the independent actions of the victim.

Oxendine v. State

(Child Abuser v. Community)

528 A.2d 870 (1987)

M E M O R Y   G R A P H I C

Instant Facts

A father is convicted of manslaughter, after beating his six-year-old child who had been earlier pushed into a bathtub (causing injuries) by the father's girlfriend.

Black Letter Rule

Actual causation or causation-in-fact is a necessary prerequisite to the imposition of criminal liability.

Case Vocabulary

ACCELERATION: The bringing about of a prohibited result at an earlier time than it would be expected to occur, which is sufficient to satisfy "but for" determination of causation.

ACTUAL CAUSE (CAUSE-IN-FACT): The first prong of the causation analysis, determined traditionally by the application of the "but for" test.

MANSLAUGHTER: The intentional killing of a human being without malice aforethought.

Procedural Basis: Certification to the Supreme Court of Delaware of a conviction for manslaughter.

Facts: On January 18, 1984, Leotha Tyree (Tyree), Jeffery Oxendine's (Oxendine) (D) girlfriend, pushed Jeffrey Oxendine, Jr. (Jeffrey), Oxendine's (D) six-year-old son, into the bathtub causing microscopic tears in his intestines which led to peritonitis. During a break from work that evening, Oxendine (D) telephoned Jeffery, who complained of stomach pains. When Oxendine (D) returned home he saw bruises on Jeffrey and knew that Tyree had beaten the child earlier that day. The next morning, at 7:30 a.m., Oxendine (D) went into Jeffrey's bedroom and began screaming at him to get up. A neighbor testified to hearing sounds coming from Jeffrey's room, of blows being struck, obscenities being uttered by a male voice, and cries from a child saying, "Please stop, daddy, it hurts." After the sounds continued for five to ten minutes, the witness heard a final noise consisting of a loud thump, as if someone had been kicked or punched "with a great blow." Later that day, Jeffrey's abdomen became swollen. When Oxendine (D) arrived home from work around 5:00 p.m., Tyree urged Oxendine (D) to take Jeffrey to the hospital. Oxendine (D), apparently believing that Jeffrey was exaggerating his discomfort, went out, bought a newspaper, and returned home to read it. Upon his return Tyree had prepared to take Jeffrey to the hospital. On the way to the hospital, Jeffrey stopped breathing, and was pronounced dead shortly after his arrival at the hospital. During trial, the State called medical examiners Dr. Inguito and Dr. Hameli, who both testified that Jeffrey's death was caused by intra-abdominal hemorrhage and acute peritonitis, occurring as a result of blunt force trauma to the front of the abdomen. Similarly, each pathologist identified two distinct injuries, one caused more than twenty-four hours before death, and one inflicted less than twenty-four hours before death. Dr. Inguito could not place any quantitative value on, nor tell which of the hemorrhages caused the death. Moreover, Dr. Inguito was not asked, nor did he express any opinion as to whether the second hemorrhage accelerated Jeffrey's death. Dr. Hameli, on the other hand, was of the opinion that the earlier injury was the plain underlying cause of death, although the second hemorrhage was an aggravating circumstance. Furthermore, Dr. Hameli could not give an opinion as to whether the second hemorrhage accelerated Jeffrey's death. As part of her case, co-defendant Tyree called Dr. Hoffman, a medical examiner, who only perceived one injury, inflicted twelve hours before death. However, in answering a hypothetical posed by the prosecutor, Dr. Hoffman opined that, given Jeffrey's weakened state as a result of the significant trauma to his abdominal cavity, another blunt force trauma to the same area, would accelerate death. At the end of trial Oxendine (D) moved for judgment of acquittal. The motion was denied and the jury was instructed on the elements of recklessness, causation, and on various lesser offenses. The ultimate and only theory of causation that the jury was instructed on, was based on acceleration. Specifically, the trial court was instructed that a defendant who causes the death of another is not relieved of responsibility for causing the death if another later injury accelerates the death of the other person. Contribution without acceleration is not sufficient. Oxendine (D) was convicted of manslaughter, and sentenced to twelve years' imprisonment. Oxendine (D) appealed, arguing that the Trial Court committed reversible error by denying his motion for a judgment of acquittal on the issue of causation. Specifically, Oxendine (D) argued that the State's medical testimony, relating to which of the codefendant's admittedly repeated beating of Jeffrey was the cause of death, was so vague and uncertain as to preclude his conviction of any criminal offense.

Issue: Is actual causation necessary to the imposition of criminal liability for manslaughter?

Decision and Rationale: (Horsey, J) Yes. Actual causation or causation-in-fact is necessary for the imposition of criminal liability. In order to convict Oxendine (D) of manslaughter, the State had to show that his conduct caused Jeffrey's death. In the instant case, the evidence established that Oxendine (D) inflicted a non-lethal injury upon Jeffrey after his son had, twenty-four hours earlier, sustained a lethal injury from a previous beating by Tyree. Thus, in order to convict Oxendine (D) of manslaughter, the State was required to show, for the purposes of causation, that Oxendine's conduct accelerated the child's death. The Superior Court correctly instructed the jury that contribution without acceleration is insufficient to establish causation. Although it is possible to make the victim's pain more intense, we do not equate aggravation with acceleration. Thus, the relevant inquiry is, but for Oxendine's infliction of the second injury, would Jeffrey have died when he died? If the second injury caused Jeffrey to die any sooner, Oxendine would be deemed to have caused his son's death. A finding of medical causation, may not be based on speculation or conjecture. Almost anything is possible, and it is improper to allow a jury to consider and base a verdict upon a possible cause of death. Therefore, a doctor's testimony can only be considered evidence when his conclusions are based on reasonable medical certainty that a fact is true or untrue. The State's expert medical testimony, even when viewed in the light most favorable to the State, was insufficient

to sustain the State's ultimate theory of causation on which the court instructed the jury. Both Dr. Inguito and Dr. Hameli, were unable to state with any degree of medical certainty that the second injury contributed to the death of the child. Dr. Inguito could only testify that it was possible that the second injury contributed to death. Dr. Hameli testified that the second injury could have, but probably would not cause death. Moreover, he could not give an opinion as to whether the second injury accelerated Jeffrey's death. Similarly, Dr. Inguito was not asked, nor did he offer an opinion about acceleration. The record establishes that the only theory of causation under which the State submitted the case to the jury was the acceleration theory. Although those responsible must be punished, there must be proof as to who, if anyone, inflicted the injuries that resulted in death. However, because there was sufficient evidence for a rational trier of fact to conclude beyond a reasonable doubt that Oxendine (D) was guilty of a lesser included offense, assault in the second degree, the trial court properly denied Oxendine's (D) motion for judgment of acquittal. Therefore, we reverse the conviction of manslaughter, and remand the case to the Superior Court for entry of a judgment of conviction and resentence.

Analysis:

This case is a good example of the first part of the causation analysis, called the "actual cause" or "cause-in-fact". Courts make this determination in order to narrow the choices of those that can be held criminally liable for a prohibited result. As stated in the previous case, courts traditionally use the "but for" test in determining actual cause. In the instant case, the court equated "actual cause" with "acceleration". More specifically, Oxendine (D) would be found the actual cause of Jeffrey's death, if his contribution to Jeffrey's injuries accelerated Jeffrey's death. Accordingly, contribution without acceleration, would not be sufficient to convict Oxendine (D) of manslaughter. Therefore, as the court states, the relevant inquiry is, but for Oxendine's (D) infliction of the second injury, would Jeffrey have died *when he did*? The last three words, "when he did" in the courts "but for" analysis, supports the conclusion that "acceleration" equals "actual cause". Because the only theory of causation, under which the State submitted the case to the jury was the acceleration theory, the State had the burden of proving beyond a reasonable doubt, that Oxendine (D) accelerated Jeffrey's death. However, the State's two expert medical witnesses, were unable to conclude with reasonable medical certainty, that Oxendine's (D) acts accelerated Jeffrey's death in anyway. Therefore, although there was sufficient evidence to sustain a conviction for a lesser offense, there was insufficient proof for manslaughter.

Kibbe v. Henderson

(Thief v. Not Stated)
534 F.2d 493 (1976)

M E M O R Y   G R A P H I C

Instant Facts

A person is convicted of second degree murder, after robbing, undressing, and abandoning a highly intoxicated individual on a two-lane highway, who was run over by pickup truck.

Black Letter Rule

Proximate or legal causation is a necessary prerequisite to the imposition of criminal liability.

Case Vocabulary

PROXIMATE CAUSE (LEGAL CAUSE): The determination of who, among those that satisfy the "but for" cause, should be held criminally liable or accountable for a prohibited result.

Procedural Basis: Appeal to the United States Court of Appeal, of a conviction for second degree murder.

Facts: On December 30, 1970, Barren Warren Kibbe (Kibbe) (D), and his codefendant, Roy Krall (Krall), met George Stafford (Stafford) at a bar in Rochester, New York. Stafford had been drinking so heavily and was so intoxicated, that by 9:00 p.m. the bartender refused to serve him further, despite Stafford's offer to pay with a hundred dollar bill. At some point that evening, Stafford began soliciting a ride to Canandaigua from the other patrons at the bar. Kibbe (D) and Krall, who confessed to having already decided to rob Stafford, offered a ride. They first stopped at a second bar, where Stafford was again refused any drinks by the bartender because of his inebriated condition. Then the three proceeded to a third bar, where each were served additional drinks. At about 9:30 p.m. that evening, the three left for Canandaigua in Kibbe's (D) car. According to the statements of Kibbe (D) and Krall, as Krall was driving, Kibbe (D) demanded Stafford's money, and upon receiving it, forced Stafford to lower his trousers and remove his boots to prove that he had no more. At some time between 9:30 and 9:40 p.m., Stafford was abandoned on the side of an unlit, rural two-lane highway. His boots and jacket were also placed on the shoulder of the highway, but his eyeglasses remained in the car. There was testimony that it was "very cold" that night, and that there was an open and lighted service station in the general vicinity, no more than one-quarter of a mile away. About half an hour after Stafford was abandoned, Michael Blake (Blake), a college student, was driving his pickup truck northbound on the highway at 50 miles an hour. This was ten miles over the posted speed limit. A car passed Blake on a southbound direction and the driver flashed his headlights at Blake. Immediately thereafter, Blake saw Stafford sitting in the middle of the northbound lane with his hands in the air. Blake testified that he "went into a kind of shock" as soon as he saw Stafford, and did not apply his brakes, nor attempt to avoid hitting Stafford, because he "didn't have time to react." After the collision, Blake stopped his truck and returned to assist Stafford, whereupon he found that the decedent's trousers were around his ankles, and that his shirt was up to his chest. Stafford was wearing neither his jacket nor his boots. Stafford suffered massive head and body injuries as a result of the collision and died shortly after. The Medical Examiner testified that these injuries were the direct cause of death, and an autopsy revealed a high alcohol concentration of .25% in his blood. Among other things, Kibbe (D) was found guilty of murder in the second degree under New York Penal Law S125.25(2) [which provides that a person is guilty of murder in the second degree when he recklessly engages in conduct which creates a grave risk of death to another, and thereby causes the death of another]. The Appellate Division affirmed the conviction on finding that there was sufficient evidence that Stafford's death was caused by Kibbe's (D) acts. Kibbe (D) appeals to the United States Court of Appeals, contending that the question of causation was a pivotal issue at trial, and that the judge's failure to instruct the jury with respect to that issue, allowed the jury to convict without finding that every element of the crime had been proven beyond a reasonable doubt.

Issue: Is proximate or legal causation, a necessary element of a criminal conviction?

Decision and Rationale: (Lumbard, J.) Yes. Proximate or legal causation is a necessary prerequisite to the imposition of criminal liability. In the instant case, the judge failed to define or explain the issue of causation, as the term is used in the New York statute, in his charge to the jury. Nor did the judge mention the legal effect of intervening or supervening cause. The omission of any definition of causation, permitted the jury to conclude that the issue was not before them, or that causation could be inferred merely from the fact that

Stafford's death succeeded his abandonment by Kibbe (D) and Krall. Even if the jury was aware of the need to determine causation, the court's instruction did not provide the tools necessary to that task. The complexity of the definition of legal causation, requires an explanation of intervening and supervening cause, as essential to the jury's determination. It has been held that where death is produced by an intervening force, such as Blake's operation of his truck, the liability of one who put an antecedent force into action will depend on the difficult determination of whether the intervening force was a sufficiently independent or supervening cause of death. Given the proper standard of causation, the jury could have found that Blake had been so reckless as to absolve Kibbe (D) of legal responsibility for Stafford's death. Similar cases provide that the controlling questions are whether the ultimate result was foreseeable to the original actor and whether the victim failed to do something easily within his grasp that would have extricated him from danger. We conclude that the trial judge's incomplete instructions took a necessary determination of causation of death from the jury and thereby violated Kibbe's (D) constitutional right to have every element of the crime with which he was charged, proven beyond a reasonable doubt.

Analysis:

This well-written opinion provides a good example of the necessity and difficulty of determining "proximate" or "legal causation", the second prong of the causation analysis. Courts make this determination in order to decide who among the "but for" causes, should be held liable for a prohibited result. Here, the trial judge did not provide jury instructions with respect to causation. As the appellate court analyzes, this issue's complexity requires that the jury be given instructions. The appellate court recognizes that, when not given the proper "tools", the jury may be overreaching in their decision to impose criminal liability. As the court states, criminal liability for a prohibited result may be absolved, if there is a sufficient independent or supervening cause for the prohibited result. The determination may also depend on the foreseeability of the intervening cause of the prohibited result. Therefore, this case may turn upon the amount of negligence, if any, of Blake, and whether this is a sufficient intervening cause. It may also turn upon the foreseeability of Stafford's action of sitting in the middle of the road, or upon Stafford's failure to go to the service station close by. In any case, the jury was not given the tools necessary to make a proper determination of the proximate cause of Stafford's death.

State v. Rose

(Society v. Pedestrian Killer)

112 R.I. 402, 311 A.2d 281 (R.I. 1973)

M E M O R Y   G R A P H I C

 Instant Facts

An automobile driver is convicted of negligent manslaughter, after hitting a pedestrian, and dragging the pedestrian who was lodged underneath the vehicle.

 Black Letter Rule

Elements of a crime must occur concurrently in order to impose criminal liability for that crime.

Case Vocabulary

CULPABLE NEGLIGENCE: Extreme or gross negligence, sufficient for the imposition of criminal liability.

INVOLUNTARY MANSLAUGHTER: An unlawful killing, committed without intent, by an act of criminal or culpable negligence.

NEGLIGENCE: Failure to act as a reasonably prudent person.

Procedural Basis: Certification to the Supreme Court of Rhode Island of a conviction for leaving the scene of an accident and manslaughter.

Facts: On April 1, 1970, at about 6:30 p.m., David J. McEnery (McEnery) was struck by the vehicle of Henry Rose (Rose) (D), at the intersection of Broad and Summer Streets in Providence. According to the testimony of a bus driver, who was traveling north on Broad, and stopped at a traffic light at the intersection of Summer Street, McEnery was starting to cross Broad Street. As he reached the middle of the southbound lane, he was stuck by a "dirty white station wagon," that was proceeding southerly on Broad Street. McEnery was thrown up on the hood of the car. The station wagon stopped momentarily while the body of McEnery rolled off the hood, and then immediately drove off along Broad Street. The bus driver exited the bus in order to help McEnery, but was unable to locate the body. At about 6:40, a police officer located a white station wagon on Haskins Street, 610 feet from the scene of the accident. The body of McEnery was discovered wedged beneath the vehicle, when it was found that the vehicle had been registered to Rose (D). Rose (D) was indicted, and found guilty of, 1) leaving the scene of an accident resulting in death, and 2) with negligent manslaughter. Rose (D) moved for a new trial arguing that he could only be convicted if the prosecution could show that McEnery was killed when Rose (D) drove away, not if he was killed from the initial impact. Rose's (D) motion for a new trial was denied. Rose (D) appeals.

Issue: Must the elements of a crime all occur at the same time in order to impose criminal liability?

Decision and Rationale: (Roberts, J.) Yes. Elements of a crime must occur concurrently in order to impose criminal liability. We first turn to Rose's (D) contention that the trial court erred in denying his motion for a directed verdict. In a criminal case, where the evidence adduced by the state and the reasonable inferences to be drawn therefrom, even when viewed in a light most favorable to the state, are insufficient to establish guilt beyond a reasonable doubt, the court must grant the defendant's motion for a directed verdict. Here, Rose (D) argues that the evidence didn't exclude any reasonable hypotheses or theory of innocence. Concerning the indictment for manslaughter, Rose (D) directs our attention to the fact that the court charged the jury that there was no evidence in the case of culpable negligence on the part of Rose (D), up to and including the time at which McEnery was struck by the station wagon. The court further charged the jury that, in order to find Rose (D) guilty of manslaughter, it would be necessary to find that McEnerey was alive immediately after the impact (driving away) and that the conduct of defendant following the impact constituted culpable negligence. Rose (D) is contending that if the evidence is susceptible of a finding that McEnery was killed upon impact, he was not alive at the time he was being dragged under Rose's (D) vehicle and Rose (D) could not be found guilty of manslaughter. An examination of the testimony of the medical witness makes it clear that, in his opinion, death could have resulted upon the initial impact, because of a massive fracture of the skull. The medical witness also testified that death could have resulted a few minutes after the impact, but conceded that he was not sure when it did occur. We agree with Rose's (D) contention. The evidence is such that death could have occurred after Rose (D) had driven away with McEnery's body lodged under his car and, therefore, consistent with guilt. On the other hand, the medical testimony is equally consistent with a finding that McEnery could have died instantly upon impact and, therefore, be consistent with a reasonable conclusion other than guilt. It is clear then, that the testimony of the medical examiner lacking any reasonable medical certainty as to the time of the death of McEnery, we are unable to conclude that on such evidence, defendant was guilty of manslaughter beyond a reasonable doubt. We conclude that it was error to deny Rose's (D) motion for a directed verdict. However, we do not reach the same conclusion with respect to Rose's (D) indictment for leaving the scene of an accident.

Analysis:

As the heading to this section states, this opinion deals with concurrence of the elements. Elements of a specific crime must occur concurrently in order to impose criminal liability for that crime. In the instant case, Rose (D) was charged with manslaughter. For the purposes of this fact situation, the elements of negligent or involuntary manslaughter that needed to be proven beyond a reasonable doubt included culpable negligence and, of course, death. However, it was also necessary to prove that these elements occurred simultaneously, or more specifically, that Rose's (D) culpable negligence was the cause of the ensuing death. What is important to understand in this case is that both elements of manslaughter existed. There was a killing, and Rose (D), more likely than not, was culpably negligent by leaving the scene of the accident, especially with McEnery wedged underneath the vehicle. However, it can not be proven beyond a reasonable doubt that Rose's (D) culpable negligence was the cause of death. If McEnery died immediately after the initial impact, then Rose (D) cannot be guilty of manslaughter, because of the lack of proof of culpable criminal negligence up to that point. If McEnery died because he was dragged underneath the car, however, Rose (D) would be guilty, because his culpable negligence in leaving the scene of the accident, was the cause of the ensuing death. Since both situations were equally possible, the trier of fact could not reasonably believe beyond a reasonable doubt, that Rose (D) was guilty of manslaughter. This case turns, therefore, upon the time of McEnery's death. Without sufficient proof that the elements of the crime of manslaughter were satisfied concurrently, Rose (D) could not be held criminally liable for manslaughter.

Chapter 7

Homicide is defined as when one person kills another. It has no moral connotations on its own. Homicide covers all killings whether or not they are legal or justified. The most horrific murder is a homicide, as is the clearest case of self-defense, or even a state execution. Whether a homicide is criminal is dependent on the circumstances that surround it, and the mental state of the killer.

Murder is defined in common law as the killing of a person with malice aforethought. Malice aforethought is really just a confusing way of saying that the killing was intentional, the result of a felony, or the product of recklessness that shows a complete disregard for human life.

Murder is divided into degrees, usually murder in the first degree and murder in the second degree. Basically murder first is the category that is meant to contain all of the worst crimes, those worthy of the greatest penalty. The primary difference between murder first, and murder second is the question of whether the crime was premeditated. A crime that was planned has been thought to be more evil than one that occurs on the spur of the moment. Most states have also encoded a list of violent felonies, which, if they result in death, make the felon guilty of felony-murder in the first degree.
Murder in the second degree is a catchall category, which covers all the homicides that qualify as murder but are not murder in the first degree. Non-intentional murders that show a reckless disregard of human life fall into this category. So do murders that were not premeditated but which do not qualify for mitigation as manslaughter. Felony-murders that are based on the commission of a felony that is not on the list for murder first are also murder in the second degree.

Manslaughter is illegal homicide that does not show malice aforethought. It is divided into two basic categories: voluntary and involuntary manslaughter. Voluntary manslaughter at common law is defined as killing in the heat of passion that was caused by adequate provocation. Under the model penal code it is defined as extreme emotional disturbance for which there is a reasonable explanation or excuse. The basic idea that underlies both of these rules is that when someone is out of control because of the intensity of their emotional reaction to some provocation which came from outside of themselves that is enough to justify a mitigation of their charge and their sentence.
Involuntary manslaughter occurs when a death is the result of criminal negligence. In this case the person who caused the death did not intend to kill, and had no awareness of the risk to life that he was creating. However he took an action which created a grave risk of death, and he should have been aware of it even though he was not. Criminal Negligence is the least culpable of the mental states but still involves a level of carelessness with human life that creates criminal liability.

The felony murder rule, which was mentioned several times above, deserves some further explanation. Basically, if a person commits a felony and in committing that felony causes the death of another person, no matter how unintentionally, the person committing the felony is guilty of murder. This has been a controversial idea because it can result in a person who commits a non-violent felony, with no idea that he is placing anyone in danger of death, being guilty of murder.

One of the central themes of criminal homicide law is the question of how to identify, codify and punish the different levels of culpability that can be present in different homicides. The formulas above are an overview of approximately how most states decide which are the most serious crimes. But there are substantial variations in different state's statutes. The question of what the most serious crimes are becomes particularly important when looking at what penalty is appropriate for these crimes. Punishment for homicide ranges from probation to the death penalty. The death penalty is such a serious penalty that it has created a set of law unto itself. The Supreme Court has debated whether it is even per se constitutional. The current decision is that it is, but that may depend on society's changing standards of decency. The Supreme Court has imposed special requirements in order to ensure it is not applied in an arbitrary or capricious manner. There must be a trial followed by a separate sentencing hearing. At the sentencing hearing the defendant must be provided with an opportunity to present any mitigating evidence and the jury must consider the individual defendant and the specific circumstances of the crime. Even with these standards cases challenging whether our judicial system can ever find an adequate system to administer the death penalty in a constitutional way are being both debated and litigated.

Chapter 7

NOTE: THE PURPOSE OF THIS OUTLINE IS TO ORGANIZE THE CASES SO THAT ONE CAN QUICKLY UNDERSTAND THE RELEVANCE OF EACH CASE TO THE COURSE. NO ATTEMPT IS MADE IN THIS OVERVIEW TO ADDRESS EVERY CONCEPT THAT MUST BE STUDIED. BE SURE TO READ THE ENTIRE CASEBOOK AND/OR OTHER MATERIALS TO GAIN A FULL UNDERSTANDING OF ALL CONCEPTS.

I. Overview
   A. Statistics: in 1996 there were 19,645 murders reported in the United States.
   B. Murder
       1. At common law murder is the killing of one person by another with malice aforethought.
           a. Malice can be found when there was an intent to kill, when there was an intent to cause grievous bodily harm, when the murderer acted with an abandoned and malignant heart, or when the killing happened as a result of a felony that was intentionally committed.
       2. Early statutory law modified this common law understanding of murder by dividing murder into degrees.
           a. By 1794 Pennsylvania defined murder first as murder committed by lying in wait, poison, or murder that was deliberate, willful and premeditated.
           b. This division into degrees was done so that the worst murders could face the harshest consequences.
   C. Manslaughter
       1. Originally all criminal homicide under common law was murder. The division of criminal homicides into murder and manslaughter evolved over time in recognition that some homicides were more culpable than others.
       2. Common law defines man slaughter as a killing that is the result of a sudden heart of passion in the killer that causes him to lose self control, and for which there was adequate provocation.
           a. Manslaughter under common law also included negligent homicide: unintentional killings where the killer did not show a depraved heart, but did show more than ordinary civil negligence.
           b. There is also the misdemeanor-murder rule, where an unintended death caused by the commission of an illegal act, which is not a felony, is manslaughter.
       3. Most states recognized manslaughter, as it existed in common law, in their early statutory schemes.
           a. The main change found in early statutes, if any, was a differentiation for purposes of punishment between involuntary and voluntary manslaughter.
   D. Modern Statutory Variation
       1. *California* statutory law is basically consistent with common law definitions of murder and manslaughter, but there are some specific modifications.
           a. While under common law a homicide required the killing of individual human beings, California specifically recognized fetuses capable of being murdered.
           b. California, as do most states, includes a specific list of felonies, which elevate any death caused by their commission to murder in the first degree.
       2. *Illinois* statutory law is much more of a departure from common law. Illinois requires no premeditation in order to find Murder first.
           a. There is no distinction between Murder 2nd and Voluntary Manslaughter.
           b. This means that Illinois only recognized a difference of degree for killings done in the heat of passion if that passion was adequately provoked.
           c. In addition, Illinois has a special provision that makes someone who supplies illegal drugs which when taken by the victim resulted in the victim's death guilty of a newly created division of homicide called Drug Induced Homicide.
       3. *Michigan's* statutory scheme basically follows common law.
           a. The killing of a law enforcement officer is added to the list of factors that make a murder into a murder in the first degree.
           b. Also there is a provision under manslaughter that provides that if someone kills a fetus while attempting to kill its mother, is guilty of manslaughter.
       4. *New York* statutes include any fetus over 24 weeks as a protected interest.
           a. They divide manslaughter into degrees.
           b. They add illegal abortion and aiding a suicide

Chapter Overview Outline
Criminal Homicide

to the definition of manslaughter in the second degree.

  c. And in New York killing with intent to cause serious injury is manslaughter and not murder.

  d. The difference between Murder first and Murder second in New York is whether the person is eligible for the death penalty.

    (1) Thus the factors that make a murder, murder in the first degree are the aggravating factors of the crime, for example: killing a police officer or being cruel and wanton.

5. *Pennsylvania* statutes divide murder into three degrees.

  a. Murder first is intentional killing that is willful, deliberate and premeditated.

  b. Murder second is felony-murder.

  c. Murder in the third degree is all other murders.

  d. Manslaughter in Pennsylvania basically follows common law but there are a few additional provisions.

    (1) A person who kills and believes the killing to be legal under justification, where that belief is unreasonable, is guilty of manslaughter.

    (2) And a person who supplies illegal drugs which when used by the victim cause the victim's death is also guilty of manslaughter.

E. Protected Interest

1. The interest protected by the law against criminal homicide is a living human being. Fetuses are only included in this category when it is provided for under statute. It is also impossible to commit homicide against someone who is already dead.

2. *People v. Eulo*:

  a. When person "A" commits an action that results in person "B" becoming brain dead, causing that brain death is enough to make person "A" criminally liable for the homicide, even if life support is keeping person "B's" heart beating and lungs breathing.

  b. When hospital workers turn off the life support on a person who is brain dead so that the breathing stops, this does not create criminal liability, because a brain dead person, being dead, is not a legally protected interest.

II. Intentional Killings

A. Degrees of Murder

1. Within intentional killings the difference between murder in the first degree and murder in the second is whether the killing was deliberate, willful and premeditated.

  a. In this formula to be deliberate, an action must have been deliberated over, to be willful it must have the force of the person's will behind it, and to be premeditated it must have been considered beforehand.

  b. However the courts' application of this formula is subject to great variation.

2. While premeditation seems to suggest some plan or thought in advance of the action taken to kill, courts have ruled that it can take place within the same instant in which the killing takes place. *State v. Schrader*

3. Evidence of long term abuse and neglect is not enough to show that the death that resulted from the final beating was willful, deliberate and premeditated. *Midgett v. State*

4. When a loving son watches his father suffer and carefully considers what will be necessary to end his suffering, and then brings to the hospital the means to kill his father and then carefully does kill his father, that is a deliberate, willful and premeditated crime. The son's charitable motive is not relevant and he is guilty of murder in the first degree. *State v. Forrest.*

B. Manslaughter: "Heat of Passion" Killings. The Intentional killings that qualify as manslaughter are killings that take place after the killer has lost control of himself due to a very strong emotional reaction caused by an outside provocation deemed adequate.

1. Common Law Principles

  a. Common Law developed a very limited set of circumstances that were recognized as adequate provocation. *Giroud v. State.*

    (1) They were basically a physical attack on the killer, the assault of a family member, or the sight of the killer's spouse in the act of sex with someone else.

    (2) While there was some recognition that there could be room for expanding manslaughter beyond these situations.

    (3) There was a strong line against recogniz-

ing any provocation that was only verbal could be adequate.

   b. Courts have used both justification and excuse as the rationale for mitigating a crime from murder to manslaughter, and sometimes they have combined the two. *Rethinking Heat of Passion: A Defense in Search of a Rationale*, Dressler.

     (1) The excuse rationale acknowledges that the killing was very bad but uses the killers impaired state due to the provoked passion to reason that a reduction in the penalty for the killing is appropriate.

     (2) One can see the excuse justification at work in cases that emphasize the level of emotional disturbance.

     (3) The justification rationale suggests that because the person killed is the person who provided the provocation that caused the passion that resulted in the killing, their death is partially justified, providing a reason for a reduced consequence.

     (4) The justification rationale is particularly apparent when the court refuses to accept any transfer of provocation, such as when one person provokes the killer and the killer mistakenly kills someone else.

  2. The Objective Standard: Who is the "Reasonable Man": For a provocation to be adequate a provocation must be such as would provoke a "reasonable man."

   a. The question then becomes what characteristics of the killer one may consider in deciding whether he acted as a reasonable man would.

   b. When applying the reasonable man standard, the jury can consider the age and gender of the killer and any specific characteristics of the defendant which would make the provocation more grave to him.

     (1) For example: when the provocation is the taunting of a man by questioning his sexual ability, the jury may consider the fact that he was impotent. *Director of Public Prosecutions v. Camplin*.

  3. Model Penal Code

   a. The Model Penal Code defines manslaughter as killing under the influence of extreme emotional disturbance for which there is a reasonable explanation or excuse.

   b. There must be an objective basis for the extreme emotional disturbance that exists outside of the killer's own mental condition. *People v. Casassa*.

     (1) Thus the claim by a mentally ill man that he was provoked into extreme emotional disturbance by the reasonable rejection by a woman was too particular to the man's own mental condition to be a reasonable explanation or excuse, though no one doubted that the man acted under extreme emotional disturbance.

III. Unintentional Killings When Someone Takes an Unjustified Risk

  A. Unintentional Murder in the Second Degree

   1. Even when a killing is completely unintentional it can still qualify as murder if malice can be implied. *Berry v. Superior Court.*

   a. It is implied when the person who caused the death acted with an abandoned and malignant heart.

   b. A person acts with an abandoned and malignant heart when they are aware that their actions create a high probability of death, and when the action they are taking serves an anti-social purpose or a wanton disregard of life.

   c. When this kind of risk taking results in a person's death it is murder in the second degree.

  B. Involuntary Manslaughter

   1. The difference between unintended murder second, and involuntary manslaughter is basically the awareness of the risk.

   2. Involuntary manslaughter is when the killer was unaware that his actions created a high probability of death but they none the less took a risk that a reasonable person would have known it was wrong to take. Thus when the charge is involuntary manslaughter evidence of the killer's awareness of the risk is irrelevant. *State v. Hernandez.*

  C. Statutory Variation

   1. States can pass statutes to make those who cause a death through ordinary negligence guilty of involuntary manslaughter even though normally criminal negligence would be necessary for a criminal charge.

   2. The difference between ordinary negligence

and criminal negligence is that while criminal negligence does not require an awareness of the risk, it does require that it is the sort of risk that one should be aware could cause death. *State v. Williams.*

IV. Unintentional Killings, The Felony-Murder and Misdemeanor-Manslaughter Rules
  A. The Felony-Murder Rule, Simple Form
    1. In its simple version, the felony-murder rule means that if a person causes the death of another person during the commission of a felony, the person causing the death is guilty of murder.
      a. If the felony the person was committing is included as one of the listed felonies in that states murder first statute then they are guilty of murder in the first degree, otherwise they are guilty of murder second.
    2. Even when the person committing the felony takes no actions that would foreseeably lead to someone's death if a death results from a felony the felony-murder rule applies. Thus when one of the victims died of a heart attack caused by fear after the robber had left the scene the robber was guilty of murder. *People v. Stamp.*
    3. The death from a car accident that happened after a high speed chase as the felons were attempting to avoid arrest for the felony of breaking into cars on a closed car sales lot is murder because of the felony-murder rule, even though the court actually disapproves of this result considering that the underlying felony was not violent. *People v. Fuller.*
  B. The Policy Debate
    1. The case against the rule:
      a. The rationale for the felony-murder rule under the common law is not clear because when it originated all felonies were punishable by death. Modern courts have rationalized the application of rule in three basic ways:
        (1) The rule serves as a deterrent;
        (2) Intent to commit a felony can be transferred into intent to kill; and
        (3) People who cause death are generally liable and need to face retribution.
      b. All of these justifications are flawed. It is hard to see how this rule can effectively

deter deaths that the felons did not anticipate or intend. *The Felony-Murder Rule - A Doctrine at a Constitutional Crossroads.*
        (1) The intent to commit a felony is very different from the intent to kill, and thus the two intents are not really transferable.
        (2) And the idea of a general liability and retribution for all deaths flies in the face of all of the divisions of homicide into murder, manslaughter and their various degrees.
        (3) The United States is the only western country that still applies the rule.
    2. The case for the rule (*In Defense of the Felony Murder Doctrine*)
      a. Crimes have two required parts, the mens rea (required mental state) and the actus rea (the act and all its factual consequences).
      b. The actual result of the actus rea has always been figured into the charge and the penalty that is faced by the criminal. No reasonable legal system punishes attempted murder and murder in the same way, even though the mens rea and the actions of the criminal could be identical.
      c. Thus it is reasonable to have a special consequence for felonies that result in death. Such consequences reaffirm the sanctity of human life.
      d. Also while it may seem that deaths that are not intended can not be deterred, deterrence is a complicated thing, and it may cause felons to be a bit more careful about putting lives in danger.
      e. In addition the felony-murder rule focuses judicial resources on crimes that have had the most impact on human life. And finally it makes the law unambiguous and by making mens rea irrelevant decreases the likelihood of self-serving perjury.
  C. Limitations on the rule
    1. The felony-murder rule persists in most jurisdictions, but it does not generally persist in its traditional form. *The Endurance of the Felony-Murder Rule.*
      a. In most cases its impact has been limited through legislation or court precedent.
      b. These limitations are in large part due to a general hostility towards the rule and its consequences, but in fact they may be re-

sponsible for its continued existence.

c. The limitations have prevented society from having to face the most egregious consequences of the rule and thus have prevented it from being wholly abolished.

2. The Inherently Dangerous Felony Limitation (*People v. Burroughs*)

   a. In order for a death resulting from the commission of a felony to be murder the felony must be inherently dangerous to human life.

   b. Thus because it is possible to commit the felony of medical practice without a license without endangering human life, a man who practiced medicine without a license causing the death of his patient is not guilty of felony-murder.

3. The "Independent Felony" or Merger Limitation: When the underlying felony which is providing the basis for a felony-murder would normally merge with some form of homicide charge, that felony can not provide a basis for a felony murder charge. Thus felony child abuse, which caused a death that would normally be charged as manslaughter, can not form the basis of a felony-murder charge. *People v. Smith*.

4. Killings "in Furtherance" of the Felony

   a. The felony-murder rule only applies when the death is caused by an act done in furtherance of the felony. An airplane crash while transporting marijuana that caused the death of one of the felons can't be the basis of a felony-murder charge for the other, because the crash was caused by pilot inexperience and bad weather and not by any attempt to further the felony. *King v. Commonwealth*.

   b. The killing of an accomplice by someone opposing the commission of the felony is not done in furtherance of the felony and therefore can not support a felony-murder charge. *State v. Bonner*.

V. Capital Murder

A. The Constitutional and Policy Debate

   1. The death penalty is not a violation of the cruel and unusual punishment clause of the Eight Amendment as long as the death penalty remains acceptable to society, is not applied when it is grossly disproportionate to the crime

being punished, and is not administered in an arbitrary and capricious manner.

B. The Quest for a Reliable Procedure

   1. The lingering question of racial discrimination: While a careful statistical study of the way Georgia applied the death penalty indicates that there is a racial disparity in the way it is applied, that is not enough evidence that a particular defendant was the victim of racial discrimination and thus is not enough to overturn a death sentence. *McClesky v. Kemp*.

   2. In order for the death penalty to be applied in a constitutional manner the jury must consider the circumstances of the crime and the defendant as an individual. *Payne v. Tennessee*.

      a. It has been argued that the presentation of victim impact evidence can prevent the reasoned consideration of such evidence and create a situation where emotion rather than reason is the basis for the sentencing decision.

      b. Despite this the Supreme Court finds that victim impact evidence is not unconstitutional in capital sentencing hearings.

C. Substantive Limitations on the Death Penalty

   1. In order to be constitutional the death penalty must be proportional to the crime it is used to punish. This has resulted in the Supreme Court ruling that imposing the death penalty for rape is unconstitutional. It has also placed some limits on the application of the death penalty in cases that involve felony-murder and accomplice liability.

   2. The mere participation in a felony that results in a death, even if that death is properly charged as murder first under the felony-murder rule is not enough to allow for a constitutional application of the death penalty. *Tison v. Arizona*.

      a. This is because the death penalty must be based on the individual's personal culpability.

      b. However, when the individual substantially participates in a felony which has a high likelihood of resulting in the death of others, is present at the time of the killing, and does nothing to prevent the death, that will provide enough personal culpability to justify the death sentence.

People v. Eulo

(Prosecutor) v. (Shooter)
(1984) 63 N.Y.2d 341, 482 N.Y.S. 436, 472 N.E.2d 286

MEMORY GRAPHIC

Instant Facts

Shooter shot the victim who was pronounced brain dead. The hospital then harvested the victim's organs and turned off life support. Shooter claims hospital killed victim, not he.

Black Letter Rule

When a person is brain dead, he is dead for purposes of assigning criminal liability for homicide.

Case Vocabulary

BRAIN DEATH: Usually, some version of the test: 1) no response to painful stimuli, 2) no spontaneous movement, 3) no reflex reaction and finally 4) a flat EEG reading after a 24 hour period has passed. However, several states have adopted statutory definitions and it is important to check the specific definition for the jurisdiction.
HOMICIDE: A legally neutral term for one person killing another. While homicide clearly includes cases of murder and manslaughter, it also includes post-trail execution by the state, killing in self-defense and other legally sanctioned forms of killing.
STATUTORY CONSTRUCTION: Generally, the interpretation of laws enacted by the legislature. Also a judicial function identifying the correct interpretation of a statute when different interpretations are being argued.

Procedural Basis: Two separate defendants appeal to overturn two separate convictions for manslaughter under similar facts.

Facts: Eulo (D) and Bonilla (D) were separately prosecuted and convicted of manslaughter. Eulo (D) shot his victim in the head. The victim was then taken to the hospital where he was placed on life support. Later the hospital evaluated the victim's condition and determined that his brain was no longer functioning and that he was therefore brain dead. The victim's heart and lungs were still functioning, but only because they were hooked up to machines that kept them that way. With the consent of the victim's family the victim was declared dead. His organs were harvested for donation and life support was terminated. Bonilla's (D) case has substantially the same facts. Both Eulo (D), and Bonilla (D) contend that their actions did not cause the victims' deaths. They argue that in New York death has always been considered to have occurred only when breathing and heartbeat have irreversibly ceased, and that the jury was not properly instructed as to this. This is important, as criminal liability for homicide does not attach until the point of the victim's death. There was extensive testimony at both trials about the victims' having been diagnosed as brain dead. Based on this Eulo (D) and Bonilla (D) contend that the jury may have wrongly concluded that they were guilty of homicide if they were guilty of causing brain death.

Issue: Is a person criminally liable for homicide if he is criminally liable for causing brain death?

Decision and Rationale: (Cooke) Yes. A person bears responsibility for causing a death, if that person's actions result in brain death, even if it was only after the hospital removed life support that the heartbeat and breathing stopped. To fully address the contentions of Eulo (D) and Bonilla (D) we must examine the correct interpretation of the term "." The term has not been expressly defined by the New York State legislature. When a term in a statute is not defined, the court will generally use the ordinary and accepted meaning, and will follow definitions established by judicial precedence. However, definitions may change over time based on changed circumstances, and the court must do its best to support the apparent purpose of the statute. Traditionally death has been defined under common law as the irreversible cessation of breathing and heart rate and the court agrees with that definition as far as it goes. However, circumstances have changed. It is now possible for breathing and heartbeat to be maintained by machines. When these signs are maintained in this way, they are no longer a clear indication of life. Because of this the medical community now considers the cessation of brain activity (brain death) to be a measure of death. This has been recognized by statute in several states. It is considered an extension of the traditional criteria. Though the New York legislature has not yet recognized such an extension, we do not feel that it meant to prevent the court from doing so. Thus a person is dead either when their breathing and heart beat stop irreversibly, or when there is no further brain function (brain death). This interpretation is also consistent with the apparent purpose of the homicide statutes of this state that a person be held responsible for homicide when their actions have caused the victim's total loss of brain function. In these particular cases our affirmation of the convictions is further supported by the fact that even if only the traditional meaning of death was used, and it was found that death did not occur until the machines were turned off, Eulo (D) and Bonilla (D) would still be responsible for the cause of death. Because of the brain death diagnosis, it was medically appropriate to turn the machines off. Thus turning the machines off would not be sufficient intervening cause to interrupt the defendants' liability. Based on all of this there was sufficient evidence for a reasonable juror to find beyond a reasonable doubt that the defendants caused the victims' deaths. Affirmed.

Analysis:

It is not that uncommon these days to hear stories of people having been dead for a number of minutes before eventually being revived. Of course, they were not actually dead; whatever our various beliefs about what happens to our souls when we die, as a physical process death is irreversible. What people tend to mean when they talk of having been dead is that their heart had stopped and they weren't breathing. Our definition of death is changing. Even the so-called traditional definition of death mentioned in this case marks an evolution, from: a person is dead when his heart stops and he isn't breathing; to: a person is dead when his heart stops and he isn't breathing, and we can't revive him. That change reflects an advancement in medicine, as does the expansion of that definition to include brain death. The definition may change again in the future as we gain a greater understanding of how the body works. However, this is a criminal law class, and not bioethics, so why is it important to be aware of the evolving definition of death? The first reason is that understanding what death is, is a part of understanding of what homicide is. Generally homicide is defined as the killing of one person by another person. Implicit in that statement is the assumption that the victim is a living person. If X cuts off Y's head and puts it on a pike in his garden, and Y was alive when X cut of his head, then X has committed homicide. If Y was dead when X cut off his head, then X has not. [X may well have other legal problems. He could probably be prosecuted for dismembering a corpse, illegal disposal of human remains, and various health code violations; not to mention being sued by the homeowners association of his subdivision for violation of the covenant regarding garden ornaments, but he didn't commit homicide.] In both cases X performs the same action, cutting off Y's head, but the results of the action are different. Homicide requires not only the action of the perpetrator, but also the specific result that the victim changes from being alive to being dead. This brings us to the second reason that we are considering the definition of death, causation. To meet their burden, prosecutors must show that a defendant caused the death of the victim beyond a reasonable doubt. In Eulo (D) and Bonilla's (D) case, the court found causation fairly easily. Clearly Eulo (D) and Bonilla (D) caused the victims' brain death by shooting the victims in the head. Even if one disagreed with the court's expanded definition of death, which includes brain death, Eulo (D) and Bonilla (D) actions still caused the death, because the only reason the life support was turned off, and the organs harvested, is that this is the medically appropriate action once brain death has been diagnosed. The definition of death could have a much greater impact on a slightly different sort of case. Say X shoots Y, and Y ends up in an ICU in critical condition, but not brain dead, if Y then dies it is reasonable to argue that X caused Y's death. However, if Z who has always hated Y finds out that Y is in the ICU and sneaks in and disables the life support, then it was Z who caused Y's death. Z would be liable for the homicide, and X would not. [Don't worry there would still be plenty of other ways to prosecute X.] On the other hand, if Y is brain dead when Z disconnects the life support, then the court's expansion of the definition of death becomes crucial. If the court follows the "traditional" definition for death, Z is still guilty, because Z stopped the breathing and heartbeat and therefore caused the death. Z is different from the doctors above because Z actions arise out of his own intervening malice and are not a result of X's actions. However, under the definition adopted by this court: that brain dead is the same as dead, then X is guilty of homicide because he caused brain death, and Z is not because his actions were performed against a dead body. [See Hitchcock's "The Trouble with Harry."]

State v. Schrader

(Prosecutor) v. (Guy Who Stabbed Victim)
(1982) 172 W.Va. 1, 302 S.E.2d 70

M E M O R Y   G R A P H I C

Instant Facts
A guy in a gun store got into a heated argument with the owner and stabbed him 51 times.

Black Letter Rule
A killing can be willful, deliberate and premeditated even if the intent to kill did not arise until the instant in which the killing took place.

Case Vocabulary

CULPABILITY: The extent to which an action or person is worthy of blame.
DEGREES OF CRIME: The division of a crime into levels based on the circumstances and moral judgment of the legislature.
JURY INSTRUCTIONS: Instructions given by the judge to the jury concerning the law to be applied in the case. Often, proposed instructions are submitted to the judge by both the prosecution and the defense. Many jurisdictions have standardized instructions that the judge is required to use.

Procedural Basis: Appeal to the Supreme Court of West Virginia to overturn a conviction for murder in the First Degree.

Facts: William Schrader, Jr. (Schrader) (D) went to a gun store owned by Frank Millione (Millione). Schrader was there to see if he could buy or sell some war souvenirs. Schrader (D) states that he and Millione got into an argument when he questioned the authenticity of a sword Millione had previously sold to him. It was during this argument that Schrader (D) stabbed Millione 51 times with a hunting knife. Schrader (D) claimed at trial that he stabbed Millione in self-defense. Schrader (D) stated that he knew that Millione had carried weapons in the past. And that he believed that when Millione reached into his pocket Millione was about to shoot him. Schrader (D) acknowledged that Millione never did produce a gun from his pocket during the fight. Millione had stab wounds on his face, head, neck back and chest. [Apparently Schrader (D) had a bad aim.] At the trial the jury was instructed that in order for them to find that the killing was premeditated it was not necessary for them to find that any intent to kill existed before the time of the killing itself. Schrader (D) contends that this was an improper jury instruction, because it eliminates the "pre" in "premeditated."

Issue: For a killing to be premeditated, deliberate, and willful, must the intent to kill have been formed at some period of time before the killing itself took place?

Decision and Rationale: (Neely) No. There is no requirement that the intent to kill be formed at some period of time before the killing itself, for the killing to be premeditated, deliberate and willful. It may seem that to say that is to ignore the meaning of what it is to premeditate. However, words in statutes are not always defined in the same way as they would be in a dictionary. In this case we examine the meaning the legislature was likely to have intended and the way the term has been previously defined in case law. There is no definition for the word within the statute itself. However the wording of this statute has a long history. A statute dividing Murder into degrees using the language "willful, deliberate and premeditated" was adopted by the Pennsylvania assembly in 1794. [That's right, just 18 years after the signing of the Declaration of Independence.] In 1795, a Pennsylvanian case, *Commonwealth v. Mulatto Bob* (holding that premeditation can exist in the time it takes one man to hit another with an axe) was decided. [Wouldn't you just love the job of trying to defend a guy officially known to the court as Mulatto Bob?] Thus premeditation was already interpreted as something that could happen in an instant. The state of Virginia adopted a statute with similar language in 1796. As no attempt was made to change the definition of premeditated as it had been previously interpreted in Pennsylvania we can assume that the Pennsylvanian interpretation was what was intended. Further there is a Virginia case *King v. Commonwealth* (no time is too short for a wicked man to frame in his mind a scheme for murder), which makes the same interpretation and which specifically approved the holding in *Mulatto Bob*. West Virginia then adopted Virginia's murder statute and its interpretation in 1868 [Just in case you've forgotten your American history, this is basically the point when West Virginia broke off from Virginia for various reasons related to the Civil War.] Since the adoption of the statute West Virginia courts have interpreted the concept of premeditation as something that could be accomplished in the "blink of an eye" and that is the way we will interpret it here. In addition, in murder trials the jury is usually given a range of instructions allowing jurors to choose the level of culpability they feel is appropriate. It is very difficult to neatly and simply explain all of these levels of culpability in standard jury instructions. Yet, we do feel that it is important that the jury be given the opportunity to find the lesser degree when they feel circumstances call for it. We agree that the jury instruction given in this case does not do the job perfectly. However, it is the jury instruction that has been traditionally given and we have upheld it before. It seems to be as good as any other. Therefore we find the jury instruction correctly given and uphold the conviction; appeal denied.

Analysis:

In the early recognition under common law that murder was a crime there was no separation of degrees and the universal penalty was execution. Over time it was felt that there should be some differentiation between the levels of culpability in murder. [They still planned to execute everyone but they had to decide should one be allowed to confess to a priest before they died.] Two of the types of murder that was seen as particularly heinous were murder by poison and murder by lying in wait. Both of these types of murder seemed to involve a level of treachery and deceit that was felt to display an evil intent which was not present in a direct attack under the influence of strong passion or rage. This evolved into the concept of the premeditated murder that is one of the ways we distinguish Murder in the First Degree. As can be seen in this case, the interpretation of what is involved in premeditation becomes very important, and can also become very subjective. Under the ruling here, the jury is free to find Murder First, but would still be allowed to find Murder Second, if they found the impulsiveness of the action to be worthy of mercy. The court acknowledges that it is difficult to explain in terms of objective standards how the jury should differentiate between the degree of culpability. This combined with the court's apparently feeling that the jury should decide, can be criticized as leaving the case open to whatever subjective standards the jury wishes to apply. Possibly, this is what the court intends. It may be that the court has a point that there are limits to the objectivity possible in the real world. However, this does present problems. Subjective judgments may be based on criteria we no longer feel is appropriate. Certainly juries in the past, and arguably in the present, have been shown to be more willing to convict an African American man than a white one. Is it right to allow a jury to find a person of color guilty of Murder First because of a possibly unconscious feeling that they are more culpable? The amount of premeditation necessary for a finding of Murder in the First Degree varies from state to state. Michigan, for example, defines premeditate as to think about beforehand. In some cases it has even been found in Michigan that this thinking needs to happen in a reasonably cool state of mind. In 1995, when the Supreme Court of Appeals in West Virginia had a second chance to look at this issue *State v. Guthrie* (premeditation does not take a specific period of time, but there must be some time between the formation of the intent to kill and the actual act; there must be an opportunity to reflect.), the result was that they effectively overruled the case here. The fact that West Virginia has had second thoughts does not mean, however, that the reasoning found in this case is no longer relevant. There are many states where premeditation is still seen as something that can occur in an instant and the controversy lives on.

Midgett v. State

(Child Abuser) v. (Prosecutor)
(1987) 292 Ark. 278, 729 S.W.2d 410

M E M O R Y   G R A P H I C

Instant Facts

A father who had been in the habit of physically abusing and neglecting his son, got drunk and beat him again resulting in the child's death. The father was found guilty of murder 1st by the trial court.

Black Letter Rule

Evidence of intentional child abuse, which eventually resulted in the child's death, is not sufficient by itself to show the premeditated intent to kill necessary to sustain a conviction for murder in the first degree.

 ### Case Vocabulary

DELIBERATE: (As used in the context of willful, deliberate and premeditated) Decided after careful, cool consideration.

Procedural Basis: Appeal to the Supreme Court of Arkansas of a conviction for murder in the first degree.

Facts: Midgett (D) was the father of several children including Ronnie Midgett, Jr (Ronnie Jr.), who were living with him. Ronnie Jr.'s mother was not living in the home. Midgett, (D) had been beating Ronnie Jr. for some time. This was established both by the fact that bruises had been noticed on Ronnie Jr. at school, and from partially healed injuries discovered during the autopsy. On the day that Ronnie Jr. died, Midgett (D) brought him to the hospital, stating that something was wrong with his child. The autopsy revealed evidence of substantial bruising, rib fractures, undernourishment and poor development. The medical examiner concluded that Ronnie Jr. died from blunt force trauma consistent with having been struck by a large human fist. Ronnie Jr.'s sister testified at the trial that on the day in question Midgett (D) had gotten very drunk and had been hitting Ronnie Jr. all day. Midgett (D) contends that despite the evidence of child abuse, there is no evidence that he had an intent to kill which was premeditated.

Issue: Is evidence of the intent to abuse a child sufficient to show the premeditated intent to kill that would sustain a conviction for murder in the first degree?

Decision and Rationale: (Newbern) No. The evidence in this case does not show that Midgett (D) intended to kill Ronnie Jr. He had abused the child before without the child dying. There is no evidence showing that this occasion was different. Thus the evidence does not support a leap from an intent to abuse to an intent to kill. In addition, if at sometime during the abuse Midgett (D) did conceive the intent to kill, the evidence shows that he was drunk and enraged at the time. This evidence does not support a finding of premeditation. Therefore, there is no evidence in this case of a premeditated intent to kill, and the conviction for first degree murder can't be sustained. However, there is clearly sufficient evidence here to uphold a verdict of murder in the second. It is understandable that society might seek to punish this kind of child abuse more severely. In some states they have changed the law so that aggravated battery is one of the felonies that can raise a charge of first degree murder. But that is not the case in this state. Because we must follow the laws as they exist at this time, we can not let the jury's verdict stand. There is insufficient evidence to support it. Conviction modified to murder in the second degree and as modified, sustained.

Dissent: (Hickman) This is the case of a child who died as a result of being subjected to deliberate, methodical, intentional and severe abuse. In finding that there is not enough evidence here to sustain a conviction for murder in the first degree, the majority is substituting its judgment for that of the jury. The majority assumes that the father did not intend to kill the child, but simply to subject him to further abuse. It would be just as reasonable for the jury to decide, based on the evidence of Midgett's (D) past behavior, choking, starving and beating the boy, that Midgett had intended to kill him for months. Thus, the jury did have sufficient evidence for murder in the first degree and we should support their verdict.

Analysis:

On its most straight forward level this case considers the question of what evidence is necessary to show that a murder is willful, deliberate and premeditated. The majority ruled that evidence of intentional abuse was not enough. The dissent disagrees. This is relevant because it is the deciding factor between a conviction for first and second-degree murder. Murder is divided into degrees because of the feeling that different kinds of murder are more culpable than others. Thus, this case also raises the question of whether the current criteria that separate these two degrees of murder correctly identifies the more culpable party. Is a father who effectively turns his child's life into a living hell, and who kills the child in the process, less culpable for his child's murder just because he didn't actually intend for the child to die? Some state legislatures apparently don't think so. Noting that murder is also murder in the first degree if the death is the result of the perpetrator's commission of certain listed felonies, Illinois has added aggravated battery to that list. (Aggravated battery is the way this kind of child abuse would be likely to be charged.) California passed a torture murder statute that would make this father guilty of Murder first, without considering what his intent was. What these solutions do not do is answer the question of whether the fact that the murderer had a premeditated intent to kill is ever a good way of determining culpability. This question will be further considered in the next case: *State v. Forrest*.

State v. Forrest

(Prosecutor) v. (Loving Son)
(1987) 321 N.C. 186, 362 S.E.2d 252

M E M O R Y   G R A P H I C

Instant Facts

Forrest's (D) father was terminally ill and in the hospital with a do-not-resuscitate order. Forest (D) killed his father by shooting him, stating he did not want his father to suffer any longer.

Black Letter Rule

Killing someone to prevent his further suffering is still murder in the first degree, if it is willful, deliberate, and premeditated.

 ### Case Vocabulary

DIRECTED VERDICT: When the side which carries the burden of proof fails to make a prima facie case the judge may direct that a verdict to be entered without submitting the issue to a jury. The judge may do this because in such a case there is only one verdict that is possible under the law. The verdict that results from this process is a directed verdict.

TERMINAL: In the context of an illness, the stage of the illness that is going to result in death. In some states this is a legally defined term which can be relevant to the consideration of what kinds of treatment can be withdrawn from a dying patient.

Procedural Basis: Appeal to the Supreme Court of North Carolina of a conviction for first degree murder.

Facts: John Forrest (Forrest) (D) brought his father into the hospital on the 22nd of December. Forrest's (D) father was suffering from several severe medical complaints. It was determined that his condition could not be treated and that he was going to die. The hospital agreed that no extreme measures should be taken to prolong his life. On Christmas Eve Forrest (D) went to see his father. A nurses aid was tending to the father, and Forrest asked her to stop, stating that his father was dying. The nurse's aid told him she thought his father was getting better. She noticed that Forrest (D) seemed very upset and was about to cry. She went to get a nurse. The nurse attempted to comfort Forrest (D) by telling him she thought his father was getting better. At this point Forrest (D) became very angry and told her that he had been taking care of his father for years and he would take care of him. The nurse and nurse's aid left. Forrest (D) began to cry, told his father how much he loved him and then shot him four times in the head. He dropped the gun on the floor of the room and then went into the hall and announced that he had "killed his daddy". He stated, "You can't do anything to him now. He's out of his suffering." He also said, "I know they can burn me for it, but my dad will not have to suffer anymore." The gun used was a 22-caliber, and had to be cocked separately for each shot. The jury were provided with four possible verdicts, murder first, murder second, voluntary manslaughter, and not guilty. They found Forrest (D) guilty of murder first. On appeal Forrest (D) contents that the trial court was incorrect in not granting his motion for a directed verdict on the charge of murder in the first-degree. He argues there was insufficient evidence of premeditation and deliberation to support the charge.

Issue: Is there sufficient evidence of premeditation and deliberation to support a charge of murder in the first degree, if the killing was done to prevent suffering and the perpetrator was clearly upset at the time of the offense.

Decision and Rationale: (Meyer) Yes. Murder in the first degree is the intentional and unlawful killing of a human being with malice and with premeditation and deliberation. In this case there is substantial evidence that the killing was premeditated and deliberate. We previously decided a case where we found that for a killing to have been premeditated there are definable circumstances that should be considered. First, did the victim provoke the killer? Second, how did the killer act during the killing and what did he say. Third, did the killer threaten the victim? Fourth, was there ill will between the parties? Fifth, did the killer continue to attack the victim after he was incapacitated? And sixth, was the killing done in a brutal manner. Clearly Forrest's (D) terminally ill father did nothing to provoke Forrest (D) to kill him. In addition Forrest's (D) father was helpless before Forrest (D) took any action against him. Forrest (D) shot his father four times, cocking the gun separately each time. Forrest (D) took the gun to the hospital. And finally, Forrest's (D) own statements support the idea that he had carefully considered his actions before taking them. He stated that he was aware that he could be "burned" for his actions in killing his father. He stated that he wanted to end his father's suffering. He stated that he had promised his father he would not allow him to continue suffering. All of this points to the fact that he had premeditated his actions. And that he had had time to deliberate about the consequences and benefits of this act. Because premeditation and deliberation are clear in this case, the trial court did not err in submitting the issue of murder first to the jury. Conviction upheld.

Analysis:

Most people disagree with the outcome of this case, especially when it is compared with the outcome of the previous case in the book: *Midgett v. State* (which held that intentional child abuse was not sufficient evidence of premeditation). And yet, both of these decisions are based on a straightforward application of the law to the facts. The law states that murder, which is willful, deliberate and premeditated, is murder in the first degree. As discussed in the decision section above, in this case the court found that the facts clearly provided sufficient evidence of premeditation. In *Midgett*, the court decided that as the father was in a drunken rage, and had beaten the child before without killing him, that there wasn't sufficient evidence of premeditation. The interpretation of the meaning of the law is also very straightforward. Premeditated is defined the same way it would be in the dictionary. Thus, it seems unlikely that what people are disagreeing with in these cases is the application or the interpretation of the law. What people disagree with here is the law itself, and the results it produces. And, as discussed in the analysis of *Midgett*, that raises the question of whether premeditation is the correct way to identify what makes one murder worse than another. What is legal is often confused with what is moral. And it is true that one of the things that the law is attempting to achieve is the codification of what is morally acceptable behavior in society. However, it is much more difficult to legislate morality than it might seem at first. It is very difficult to come up with laws that are comprehensible, flexible enough to cover all the possible circumstances, and yet ridged enough to provide objective standards for everyone. What society considers to be morally acceptable behavior changes over time. As medical care has advanced, our attitude towards the prolonged process of dying with a terminal illness has changed. Because of this we are more likely to sympathize with Forrest's (D) motives in this case. But, society's changing views of what is acceptable are not always a good guide to what is right. After all there were many laws, deemed morally acceptable in their time, which condoned actions such as slavery. Could changing our laws to accommodate euthanasia turn out to be that same kind of moral lapse that slavery was? If one wants to change the law, so as to change the outcome of this case, these are the types of questions that must be considered.

Girouard v. State

(Husband) v. (Prosecutor)
(1991) 321 Md. 532, 583 A.2d 718

M E M O R Y   G R A P H I C

 ## Instant Facts

A husband killed his wife by stabbing her 19 times after she said horrible things, threatened to leave him and told him he would be court-marshaled.

Black Letter Rule

Words alone are not adequate provocation to provoke a reasonable person to kill in the heat of passion, thus they are not enough to mitigate murder to manslaughter.

Case Vocabulary

ADEQUATE PROVOCATION: Provocation that is so upsetting that it would make a reasonable person so angry that they are no longer capable of reasoned deliberation or premeditation.

MITIGATE: To reduce in severity. Circumstances may mitigate a crime by indicating that the person committing the crime is less culpable. Judges can also mitigate a sentence by making it shorter or otherwise less harsh because of remorse, cooperation with police or other such factors.

MUTUAL COMBAT: A fight that both parties enter into voluntarily, not a case where one party unexpectedly attacks and the other merely defends himself. It is similar to a duel but without formal rules or protocol. Sometimes referred to as a mutual affray.

Procedural Basis: Appeal to the Court of Appeals of Maryland of a conviction for murder.

Facts: Steven S. Girouard (D) (Steven) and Joyce M Girouard (Joyce) got married in August of 1987. Both of them were in the army. The marriage was very tense, and there was some indication that Joyce had been unfaithful. Two months into the marriage Steven (D) overheard Joyce talking on the phone about leaving him. He asked her what that was about and she refused to answer him. He knocked over the food she was eating and left the room. She followed him, hit him on his back and pulled his hair. [The honeymoon is over.] She told him that he was a terrible husband, and that she had never wanted to marry him. She said several other things, which were very insulting. This included telling him she had reported him to the JAG for spousal abuse and that he would probably be court-marshaled. Through all of this she continually asked him what he was going to do about it. Steven (D) then went into the kitchen and got a knife which he held under a pillow. He then went back to talk to Joyce and she continued to harangue him. Steven (D) claims that he kept waiting for her to say that she was joking and that when she did not, he stabbed her 19 times. Steven (D) was 6'2" tall, and weighed over 200 pounds. Joyce was 5'1" and weighed 115 pounds. After the killing, Steven (D) dropped the knife and took a shower. He attempted to slash his wrists but was unsuccessful. He then called the police and told them he had murdered his wife. He was found wandering, distraught, talking about how much he loved his wife and could not believe what he had done. At his trial a psychiatrist testified that Steven's (D) personality was very fragile, and that he had suffered an extreme explosion of rage combined with intense panic. He was convicted of murder in the second degree. Steven (D) contends that manslaughter should include all criminal homicides that lack the malice essential for murder. And, that the court should thus extend the definition of what constitutes adequate provocation to include cases like his. The prosecutor contends that the court should not extend adequate provocation to any case that involves provocation by words alone because doing so would mean that any domestic argument that ends in murder would be mitigated to manslaughter.

Issue: Are words alone enough to provoke a reasonable person to kill in the heat of passion and thus constitute adequate provocation to mitigate the charge of murder down to manslaughter?

Decision and Rationale: (Cole) No. The difference between murder and manslaughter is that manslaughter lacks the malice that is present in a murder. This malice is shown to be missing because the killing is done in a sudden heat of passion caused by adequate provocation before there has been a reasonable opportunity for the passion to cool. There are four situations which have been traditionally recognized as adequate provocation: 1) discovering your spouse having sex with someone else, 2) being engaged in mutual combat, 3) having been subjected to assault and batter by the victim, and finally, 4) discovering injury to a family relative or third party. It seems reasonable to suggest that these situations do not cover all the cases that could legitimately be called manslaughter. We are willing to consider expanding the criteria to other situations that fit the Rule of Provocation. The Rule of Provocation requires: 1) adequate provocation, 2) that the killing be the result of a sudden heat of passion, 3) there has been no opportunity to cool off and 4) there must be a causal connection between the provocation and the fatal act. We will assume all of these requirements have been met except for adequate provocation, which is the issue in this case. In order for provocation to be adequate it must be capable of causing a reasonable man to act from passion rather than reason. Maryland case law indicates that words alone are not enough to reach this standard. The only time words have been held to be adequate provocation was when they indicated an immediate intention to inflict injury and were accompanied by a clear ability to carry out the intention. We recognize that the words Joyce used were a significant provocation. However, they do not rise to the level of an adequate provocation. It is not reasonable to suggest that Joyce was threatening Steven (D) with physical harm she had the ability to immediately carry out. She was considerably smaller than Steven (D). She was not armed. Through the testimony at trial an attempt was made to suggest that because of Steven's (D) particular psychology he was particularly vulnerable to Joyce's words, making them adequate provocation. However the standard is what would adequately provoke a reasonable person, it does not take the particular vulnerabilities of the killer into account. Words alone are not enough to provoke a reasonable man to kill in the heat of passion and are thus not an adequate provocation to mitigate murder down to manslaughter. We affirm.

Analysis:

To put this case into context it is useful to look at why this is not a case of murder in the first degree. Murder in the first is willful, deliberate and premeditated. He did intend to kill her. He went and got a knife, came back into the room, waited a while and then stabbed her 19 separate times. If these were the only facts considered this would look like a case of murder first. The main factor that prevents that verdict is the level of emotional involvement in this case. Steven does seem to have loved Joyce. [In a seriously sick, needs mental health involvement, kind of way.] And the argument touched on several highly emotional issues. It is pretty clear that this killing happened in the heat of passion, and that there was thus no cool deliberation or thoughtful premeditation. Murder second and manslaughter have the heat of passion in common. The difference between them is the provocation by the victim. Someone who commits murder second is considered less culpable than someone who commits murder first because killing in the heat of passion is seen as more understandable and less evil than someone who would use coolly considered treachery. Following the same reasoning manslaughter is even less culpable because with provocation the killer had a good reason for the passion. This reasoning would be the excuse defense to manslaughter. Basically the killer is here admitting that he or she did something wrong, but is arguing that they should not be punished so severely because he lost control for a good reason. Another way to consider the reasoning behind manslaughter is found in the justification defense. Here the killer is arguing that because the provocation of the victim was so outrageous the act of killing is not as bad as it would be normally. This defense examines the conduct of the victim and asks society to approve to some degree of the killer's conduct. Both defenses have been recognized by the courts and used as an explanation of why a finding of manslaughter is appropriate. Both defenses can be criticized as sending inappropriate messages to society as a whole. The excuse defense is questionable because it is not clear if losing control to the point where one kills is excusable. Most domestic violence and child abuse involves anger and a loss of control. Many of the abusers in these cases honestly believe that they were provoked by their victims. When a therapist works with an abuser to try and stop the abuse there are two central ideas that they try to get the abuser to accept. The first is that they must take responsibility for their own emotions. And the second is that they must control their behavior no matter how much emotion they are feeling. When the law sends the message that strong emotion is an excuse that makes actions less culpable it undermines this effort. The justification defense has also been criticized. It focuses attention on the victim and not on the actions of the killer. This creates a situation where the trial of the killer becomes a trial of the victim. This becomes particularly distasteful in the long line of cases where a husband kills his wife after discovering her being unfaithful. While society does not approve of adultery, it is not something for which a criminal penalty is assessed. Thus it seems strange that the law should continue to consider it any kind of justification for killing someone. The outcome of this case, a refusal to recognize words alone as an adequate excuse for losing control and killing, or as a justification of killing, is very reasonable in light of these considerations.

Director of Public Prosecutions v. Camplin

(English Prosecutor) v. (15-Year-Old)
(1978) 2 All Eng. Rep. . 168, 2 W.L.R. 679

M E M O R Y   G R A P H I C

Instant Facts

A 15-year-old boy killed a middle-aged man after that man had forcibly sodomized him and laughed about it. His defense was that it was manslaughter because of provocation.

Black Letter Rule

When applying the reasonable man standard in manslaughter cases the jury can consider the gender and age of the killer as well as other characteristics which would increase the provocative nature of a particular insult.

Case Vocabulary

PUGNACIOUS: Being disposed to get into fights. (PUGNACITY: The dispositional trait that makes one want to get into fights.)

RATIOCINATION: The act of reasoning logically and systematically. [Actually an overly long word used to show a level of pompousness appropriate to the House of Lords.]

Procedural Basis: Appeal to the House of Lords of an Appeals Court ruling overturning a conviction for murder.

Facts: Camplin (D) was 15 years old when he killed Mohammed Lal Khan (Khan), a middle-aged man. Camplin (D) killed Kahn by splitting his skull with a chapatti pan [mama mia!], while the two of them were alone in Khan's flat. Camplin (D) admits to the killing, and his only defense is that this is a case of manslaughter rather than murder because of severe provocation. Camplin (D) states that Khan had forcibly sodomized him despite his resistance and that Khan then laughed at him. Camplin (D) claims that this is when he lost control and attacked Khan. Camplin's (D) defense attorney suggested to the jury that they should take Camplin's (D) age into account when considering whether he had been provoked under the reasonable man standard. The Judge in the trial court felt that this was wrong as a matter of law and specifically instructed the jury not to consider Camplin's (D) age. Camplin (D) was found guilty of murder. The conviction was overturned on appeal, and the director of public prosecutions appealed the case to the House of Lords.

Issue: Should the jury be allowed to consider the characteristics of the killer when deciding the question of whether the provocation in the case was sufficient to make a reasonable man take the same actions the killer did?

Decision and Rationale: (Diplock) Yes. The Homicide Act of 1957 was passed in order to soften the harsh way the common law of manslaughter had developed in our courts. Under this act if there is any evidence on which the jury could find that the killer was provoked, by the words or actions of the victim, then the question of whether this provocation was adequate to make a reasonable man do as the killer did is left to the jury. This statute removes all the previous rules of what is or is not provocation. Words alone can now be considered as adequate provocation. In addition, it specifically makes the question of what would be adequate provocation to make a reasonable man lose control a question for the jury and not the judge. Originally the reasonable man standard was introduced in order to prevent a person from relying on his own bad-temper or tendency towards violence as an excuse for his lack of self-control. The application of the term has never been limited to adult males. In fact many courts use "person" instead of "man," and "ordinary, average, or normal" instead of "reasonable". Further, the understanding of what provokes a reasonable man changes over time with the changing values of society. In the 17th century a reasonable man would respond with a sword to the provocation of being pulled on the nose. Now, well into the 20th century, courts have ruled that even when punched in the face, the reasonable man does not respond with a weapon. The response of different people to different insults also varies. A racial slur is more offensive if the person to whom it is addressed is a member of the race being insulted. Thus the jury must be allowed to consider the characteristics of the person being provoked in order to assess the level of provocation. The characteristic at issue in this case is the killer's age. While he was not being taunted about his age, his age is relevant to the level of self-control he can be expected to have. Failing to take it into account would be to ignore the awareness of human weakness that is built into the whole doctrine of provocation. Therefore in order to properly apply the law the judge should instruct the jury that the reasonable man referred to in the question is that of a person of the same age and sex as the accused, who also shares the accused's other characteristics in as far as they are relevant to the nature of the provocation. And the jury should then take the killer's characteristics into consideration in deciding whether the provocation was adequate. Vote to dismiss the appeal. (This upholds the Appeal Court ruling overturning the conviction.)

Concurrence: (Simon of Glaisdale) It would be unjust to allow a person to mitigate his actions in killing because he was a drunkard, bad-tempered or prone to violence while a sober and restrained person is held fully responsibly. [We do not like to provide perverse incentives in the law for those who just can't get their lives together.] Thus we have the doctrine of the reasonable man. But to avoid injustice it is not necessary for the reasonable man to have no individual characteristics. On the contrary the individual characteristics must be considered in order to understand theimportance of a provocation. The impact of saying that a man's character is as crooked as his back is completely dependent on whether the man is known for his perfect posture, or his spinal deformities. Thus the reasonable man standard should be read as meaning a man of ordinary self-control in the circumstances. To apply that standard it is necessary for the jury to consider the entire factual situation, which includes the characteristics of the person accused. Vote to dismiss the appeal.

Analysis:

There are three different stages where the killer's characteristics could be considered in deciding a case of manslaughter. The first would be when deciding whether or not the killer was actually so provoked that he lost his self-control. The second is in deciding if the provocation would be especially provoking to the killer. And then the third would be in determining the amount of self-control that could be reasonably expected from the killer. The first stage can only be judged from the point of view of the killer, and is thus totally subjective. The second and third stages have been more controversial. Both of the Lords whose opinions are included in this case argue that the characteristics of the killer must be considered when one decides whether something was provocative to him. They point out that racial epithets are more provoking to a member of the race that is being demeaned, as well as several other examples. Lord Simon of Glaisdale in his opinion, does not seem to draw a distinction between considering the characteristics of the killer for purposes of stages two and three. Instead he feels that you must consider all of the facts of the killer's situation in considering what a person who shared all the killer's characteristics but who had reasonable self-control would have done in his place. Lord Diplock on the other hand does recognize that there is a difference between stages two and three. He is aware that there is a distinction between considering the medical condition of a man who has been insulted for being a cripple and considering the age of the defendant in deciding what level of self-control he should be expected to exercise. In general he restricts consideration of the characteristics of the defendant to the second stage, but he does make an exception for the gender and age of killer, which he feels are relevant to the third stage. He does not give us a good explanation for why the gender and age of a killer should be considered in deciding the level of self-control society can expect while other characteristics should not. He merely states that to require old heads on young shoulders would be a violation of the spirit of the law. Are age and gender such totally defining characteristics for all individuals that this approach is justified? Admittedly people do not have control over age or gender so it seems unjust not to consider them if they truly prevent the exercise of self-control. But several other characteristics are also beyond our control. No one can control how tall he is. Alcoholism is now considered a disease; should it be considered something that an individual can control? Scientists are currently making compelling arguments that an individual's disposition is almost totally decided by genetics and early environment. Considering this, doesn't a person with a pugnacious disposition have a right to at least make his case? As has been clear earlier in this chapter it is very hard to draw consistent standards to identify what makes one homicide more or less culpable than another.

People v. Casassa

(Prosecutor) v. (Killer)
(1980) 49 N.Y.2d 668, 427 N.Y.S.2d 769, 404 N.E.2d 1310

M E M O R Y   G R A P H I C

Instant Facts
After dating Casassa (D) the victim told him that she was not interested. He obsessed about her, stalked her, and killed her. His only defense is that he was acting under extreme emotional disturbance caused by her rejection.

Black Letter Rule
The test of whether the extreme emotional disturbance of the killer had a reasonable explanation or excuse depends on a reasonable evaluation of the external circumstances that the killer believed he was facing and not on the killer's personal point of view.

Case Vocabulary

AFFIRMATIVE DEFENSE: A defense that must be raised by the defendant. Some other affirmative defenses in criminal law include self-defense, insanity, alibi, coercion, and duress.

EXTREME EMOTIONAL DISTURBANCE: The phrase, found in the Model Penal Code, used to describe the state of someone who has temporarily lost their self-control because of something external which had a severe emotional effect on them.

FINDER OF FACT: The party charged with determining, when at least some facts are in contention during a trial, what facts are true. In a jury trial the finder of fact is the jury. In a bench trial the judge combines this role with his role as arbitrator of the law.

Procedural Basis: Appeal of a conviction for murder in the second degree to The Court of Appeals of New York.

Facts: Victor Casassa (D) (Casassa) met Victoria Lo Consolo (Lo Consolo) because they lived in the same apartment complex. They dated a few times casually. Lo Consolo informed Casassa (D) that she was not falling in love with him. Casassa (D) says that this rejection devastated him. After this initial rejection Casassa (D) started doing some odd things. He broke into the apartment below Lo Consolo's so that he could eavesdrop on her while she pursued other relationships. He claims the things he heard further devastated him. He broke into her apartment and lay naked in her bed. He reports having had a knife with him at that time of the break-in. He said he knew he was going to either kill himself or her. Finally on February 28, 1977 he brought several bottles of wine and liquor to her as a gift. When she did not accept this gift he pulled out a steak knife and stabbed her in the throat, after which he pulled her to the bathroom and submerged her body in the tub to make sure she was dead. Casassa (D) does not dispute these facts. He waived a jury trial and had a bench trial before a judge. The defense presented only one witness, a psychiatrist. The psychiatrist testified that Casassa (D) had become obsessed with Lo Consolo and that her rejection combined with his peculiar personality attributes had placed him under the influence of an extreme emotional disturbance at the time of the killing. The state presented several witnesses, among them another psychiatrist. He testified that while Casassa (D) was emotionally disturbed, this should not qualify as an extreme emotional disturbance because his disturbed state was the result of his own twisted mind and not external factors. The trial court found Casassa (D) guilty of murder in the second degree. Casassa (D) appeals arguing that the statute requires the court to examine the case from his point of view and that from his point of view he was suffering from extreme emotional disturbance caused by what he believed was a reasonable explanation or excuse.

Issue: Is the test of whether an extreme emotional disturbance of the killer was caused by a reasonable explanation or excuse determined from the subjective point of view of the killer?

Decision and Rationale: (Jasen) No. This case is to be decided under section 125.25 of the New York Penal Code, which provides that if the killer can show that he acted under the influence of an extreme emotional disturbance for which there was a reasonable explanation or excuse, he qualifies for an affirmative defense reducing murder in the second degree to manslaughter. Section 125.5 was basically adopted from the Model Penal Code. The "extreme emotional disturbance" defense in the Model Penal Code is an outgrowth of the "heat of passion" defense found in the common law, but it is considerably broader. It eliminates entirely the provision which required that there be no cooling off period between the provocation and the actions which caused the death. It also eliminates the rigid rules concerning what is and what is not adequate provocation. Several incidents can be combined to form the reasonable explanation of the killer's extreme emotional disturbance. The arguments presented by individual defendants can be considered on their own merits. However, it is not a wholly subjective test. It has two separate components. The first component, that the act must have actually been done in a state of "extreme emotional disturbance," is considered subjectively from the killer's point of view. The second component, whether there was a reasonable explanation or excuse for that emotional disturbance, is meant to be more objective. It takes the point of view of a person facing the same circumstances, as the killer believed he was facing, but without any of the particular quirks the killer may have had. [Yes, this is another reworking of the "reasonable man" idea; you didn't really think we were going to escape that, did you?] In this case Casassa (D) has no problem meeting the first component. He was acting out of extreme emotional disturbance. However, the judge, acting here as the finder of fact, reached the conclusion that this emotional disturbance was based on factors peculiar to Casassa (D). And that because these factors were peculiar to him, there was no reasonable explanation or excuse. This conclusion is consistent with the correct application of the law. The definition of manslaughter from the Model Penal Code intentionally leaves the finder of fact with the discretion to make judgmental evaluations of what is reasonable. Here the judge, as finder of fact, has made his decision. Overturning his finding in this case would be inconsistent with the intention of the act. We affirm.

Analysis:

In *Giroud* the court, following common law, was very limited in what it could consider as provocation. Certainly words alone could never be enough to mitigate murder down to manslaughter. Then *Camplin* presents a 1957 statute that specifically overturns those limitations, and the debate turns to how to define a "reasonable man." Further on in *Camplin* the definition of a reasonable man is expanded by taking into account at least some of the characteristics of the killer. Now in *Casassa* the Model Penal Code goes even farther by removing the causal nature of the provocation all together. The killer doesn't even have to be provoked, just extremely emotionally disturbed for some acceptable external reason. In this case, there is no justification defense at all; the victim has done nothing of which society disapproves. It seems rather as if the law on manslaughter is sliding down a slippery slope, giving more and more discretion to the jury. What all of these cases have in common is that it is very difficult to define the point where we should have compassion for a person who kills after being pushed too far. It has been argued that manslaughter no longer makes sense. The loss of control is not necessarily a good way to identify someone who should spend less time in prison. The fact that a person can lose control and kill someone because of external circumstances does not tend to lessen a person's dangerousness to society. Feminists have long objected to manslaughter on the basis that it is used as an excuse when abusive men murder their wives. On the other hand is there really anyone who can honestly say that they can't imagine any situation in which he or she might be pushed to kill? What if someone is forced to watch the rape and murder of his mother? What if a person came face to face with some modern-day version of Hitler? If a person kills under those circumstances don't we owe him compassion? Perhaps manslaughter is like pornography, and we have to depend on the jury to "know it when they see it."

Berry v. Superior Court

(Pit Bull Owner) v. (Government)
(1987) 208 Cal.App.3d 783, 256 Cal.Rptr.344

M E M O R Y   G R A P H I C

Instant Facts
Berry's (D) pit bull attacked and killed a two-year old child.

Black Letter Rule
The keeping of a dangerous animal used to safeguard an illegal operation constitutes sufficient basis from which a trier of fact could derive implied malice.

Case Vocabulary

WRIT OF PROHIBITION: A writ issued by an appellate court to prevent a lower court from overrunning or exceeding its jurisdiction.

Procedural Basis: Petition for a writ of prohibition seeking dismissal of murder charges.

Facts: Berry (D) and the Soto family shared a common driveway. Berry (D) had his pit bull "Willy" tied up on his lot. James Soto, aged two-and-a-half, went near the dog and was mauled. Berry (D) got the dog off the boy, but the child died before the emergency crew arrived on the scene. There was no evidence that Willy had ever attacked a human being before. However, there was considerable evidence that he had been trained as a fighting dog and that he posed a known threat to people. Berry (D) bought Willy from a trainer who informed Berry (D) of Willy's aggressiveness and his exceptionally hard bite. Police found many manuals on dog training and fighting in Berry's (D) possession. Berry (D) had told Mrs. Soto that she needn't be concerned with his other dogs, but that the children should keep away from "the one that he had on the side of the house" which was behind a six-foot fence. Willy was tethered onto a fence on the west side of the house, but was not enclosed. Police found some 243 marijuana plants growing behind defendant's house, and Willy was tethered in such a location that anyone wanting access to the plants would first have to pass by the dog. An animal control expert testified that pit bulls are selectively bred to be aggressive to other animals, and that animal control officers consider a pit bull to be dangerous unless proved otherwise. By petition for a writ of prohibition, Berry (D) seeks dismissal of the murder charges.

Issue: Could the keeping of a dangerous animal, accessible to the public, support a belief of implied malice?

Decision and Rationale: (Yes) *People v. Watson* (case involving reckless speeding while intoxicated) states that the test of implied malice in an unintentional killing is the actual appreciation of a high degree of risk that is objectively present. There must be a high probability that the act done will result in death, and that it be done with an antisocial motive and a wanton disregard for life. Willy's owner may have been actually aware of the dog's danger to people. He kept the dog chained, spoke of it as dangerous, and warned the Sotos of the dog's danger to children [not to mention he had the dog guarding the pot—the dog wasn't just for show]. Berry (D) also had extensive knowledge of the breed, which supports the inference that he knew that such dogs are dangerous. Additionally, there is arguably some evidence of an antisocial purpose in keeping the dog, because owning a fighting dog is illegal, and because the dog was kept to guard Berry's (D) marijuana. Illegality of the underlying conduct is not an element of the charge, but may be relevant in establishing intent. We do not know the actual probability that a death could result from Berry's (D) conduct in keeping such a dog. Presumably, that is a question of fact to be submitted to the jury, requiring instructions that a high probability of death would result from the circumstances before it can convict of murder. The petition for writ of prohibition is denied. [Berry (D) was convicted of involuntary manslaughter at trial, and sentenced to three years eight months.]

Analysis:

State v. Hernandez

(Prosecutor) v. (Drunk Driver)
(1991) 815 S.W.2d 67

M E M O R Y G R A P H I C

Instant Facts

Hernandez (D), while drunk, drove his van into a truck killing one person and injuring two others. At trial the drinking slogans that Hernandez used to decorate his van were admitted into evidence over defense objection.

Black Letter Rule

Evidence to show that the accused was aware of the risks of his behavior is not admissible to show mental state when the charge is involuntary manslaughter.

Case Vocabulary

CRIMINAL NEGLIGENCE: Negligence that is a gross deviation from a reasonable standard of behavior and is thus culpable. Criminal negligence expands the liability for any damages so that it includes criminal liability as well as civil.

PER CURIAM: Indicates a decision by the whole court instead of just one judge. Sometimes used for opinions from the chief justice.

Procedural Basis: Appeal of a conviction for involuntary manslaughter to the Missouri Court of Appeals.

Facts: On September 12, 1988 Robert Butcher (Butcher) was driving a truck in which Kevin Butcher, his son and Cecil Barrymore were passengers. They were traveling southbound. Pedro M. Hernandez (D) (Hernandez) was driving a van in the opposite direction on the same highway. When Butcher first saw the van it was coming around a curve, on two wheels, and had crossed over into on-coming traffic. Butcher made an effort to avoid the van, which returned to its own side of the line. The van then lurched back across the line and collided with Butcher's truck. As a result of the collision Cecil Barrymore was killed and both Butcher and his son were injured. When Sherry Howard, an employee of the ambulance service tended to Hernandez (D) at the scene of the accident she asked him if he had been drinking. He told her he had had a twelve pack and some whiskey. Hernandez's van was decorated with pins, stickers and signs containing drinking slogans such as: "The more I drink the better you look"; and "Reality is for those who can't stay drunk." [Why not just get one that says "Please pull me over, I really enjoy field sobriety tests"?] Hernandez (D) was charged with involuntary manslaughter. His sun visor, which was covered with the stickers, was admitted into evidence over a defense objection. Hernandez contends that this evidence should not have been admitted because it was not relevant to the charge and was used to show that he was a "bad person" and seeks to overturn his conviction. The state argues that it submitted the evidence to show that Hernandez (D) was aware of the risks of his behavior and approved of excessive drinking.

Issue: Should evidence which is offered to show that the defendant was aware of the risks of his behavior but which is also prejudicial to his character be admissible when the charge is involuntary manslaughter?

Decision and Rationale: (Per Curiam) No. For evidence to be admissible it must be more relevant than prejudicial. To be relevant it must tend to support or establish a fact or issue between the parties. To prove involuntary manslaughter the prosecutor has to prove 1) that Hernandez (D) acted with criminal negligence and 2) that Cecil Barrymore died as a result of that negligence. Criminal negligence is the least culpable of the mental states that are an element in the commission of a crime. It does not require that Hernandez (D) be aware of the risk he was creating towards others, but only that he did create such a risk and was criminally negligent in doing so. As a result evidence of his awareness of the risk is not relevant and the prosecution can't put the drinking slogans into evidence. In addition, to admit this evidence to show that the defendant approved of excessive drinking would be to admit character evidence. As Hernandez (D) did not place his character into issue in the case, character evidence from the prosecution is not admissible. Hernandez's (D) conviction for involuntary manslaughter is overturned.

Dissent: (Shrum) The majority argues that it is not necessary to show an awareness of the risk to others, when proving criminal negligence. This is true. However, it is still necessary to prove that the negligence shown by Hernandez (D) in this case rises to a criminal level. In order to do so it is necessary to prove that his conduct was a gross deviation from the standard of care that a reasonable person would show. It must be shown that there is real culpability in Hernandez's (D) failure to be aware of the risk his behavior posed to others. To find Hernandez (D) guilty of involuntary manslaughter, the jury must find 1) that Hernandez (D) created a substantial and unjustifiable risk to the lives of others by driving while intoxicated, 2) that even if he was not aware that by driving while he was intoxicated created this risk he should have been, and 3) that by creating this risk he killed Cecil Barrymore. Some of the stickers with the drinking slogans were relevant to show the second of these elements. The slogan: "The more I drink th[e

State v. Hernandez (Continued)

better you look" indicates that he knew that drinking affected his perception. "Reality is for those who can't stay drunk," indicates that he was aware that drinking prevented him from being in touch with the world around him. He should have known that these affects of alcohol would prevent him from being able to drive responsibly and that this might place the lives of others at risk. Thus while I agree that this evidence could not be admitted, under this charge, to show that Hernandez was aware of the risk he posed to others, it should be admissible to show that Hernandez's negligent failure to be aware of that risk was criminal.

Analysis:

The basic question raised by reading this case after reading *Berry* is what exactly is the difference between an unintended murder in the second degree and involuntary manslaughter. [In the real world the difference is a good plea bargain, but knowing the technicalities of the law can come in handy when you are trying to squeeze out a deal at 4:30 on a Friday afternoon.] The legal answer is that murder second requires a different mental state, "an abandoned and malignant heart" under common law or "recklessness" under the Model Penal Code while involuntary manslaughter requires only criminal negligence. So, what does the prosecutor have to do to get a conviction under each of these mental states? For murder in the second degree, the prosecutor must prove that 1) the accused was actually aware that his conduct created a substantial risk of death to others by driving while intoxicated, 2) there was no justification or excuse for that risk and 3) the risk resulted in the death of the victim. For involuntary manslaughter he must prove 1) the accused created a substantial and unjustifiable risk, 2) that even if the accused was unaware of this risk he should have been and 3) that this risk resulted in the death of the victim. The practical difference then comes down to proving whether or not the accused was actually aware that his conduct was creating an unacceptable risk of death. Various kinds of evidence can be used to show this state of mind. In *Berry* there was evidence that the dog owner knew about the risk because of statements he made, literature found in his house, the way he treated the dog, and testimony that he knew there were small children next door. However, when that case went to trial, all he was actually found guilty of was involuntary manslaughter. In this case, *Hernandez*, the evidence of the drinking slogans would have been admissible if the charge had been murder in the second degree, because then they would have been relevant to show actual awareness of the risk [not to mention a certain level of depraved indifference]. Why then, were these two cases charged differently? Charges often depend on the discretion of the prosecutor. Arguably the prosecutor in *Hernandez* made a strategic error in charging. If the charge had been murder, then he could have admitted all of this evidence, and even if the jury had not felt that his case was strong enough to sustain the murder charge the jury could have found involuntary manslaughter as a lesser-included offense. However, the full circumstances are rarely apparent in reading the case after an appeal.

HIGH COURT CASE SUMMARIES
95

©2002 West Group. All Rights Reserved. Do not duplicate.

State v. Williams

(Government) v. (Negligent Parents)
(1971) 4 Wash.App. 908, 484 P.2d 1167

M E M O R Y   G R A P H I C

Instant Facts

The Williams (D), parents of a 17-month-old child with an abscessed tooth, did not supply necessary medical care, and the child died as a result.

Black Letter Rule

A showing of ordinary negligence may be sufficient to support a conviction for manslaughter.

Case Vocabulary

ORDINARY NEGLIGENCE: Ordinary or simple negligence is the failure to exercise the caution or care that a reasonably prudent person would have exercised in similar circumstances.

Procedural Basis: Appeal from conviction for manslaughter due to ordinary negligence.

Facts: Walter Williams (D) is a 24-year-old Sheshont Indian with a 6th grade education. His wife, Bernice Williams (D), is a 20-year-old part-Indian with an 11th grade education. At the time of the marriage, Bernice had two children, the younger of whom was a 14-month-old son. Both Walter and Bernice had a great deal of love for the child. The child became ill on September 1. Both defendants were aware that the child was ill. However, Bernice and Walter "were ignorant," and did not realize how sick he was. They thought he had a toothache, which they did not believe to be life-threatening. They gave the child aspirin in hopes of improving his condition. They did not take the child to a doctor for fear that the Welfare Department would take the baby from them. The abscessed tooth developed into an infection of the mouth and cheeks, eventually becoming gangrenous. This condition, accompanied by the child's inability to eat, brought on malnutrition, which lowered the child's resistance and eventually produced pneumonia, causing death on September 12. The infection lasted about two weeks. A pathologist testified that the infection would have to have been treated within the first 5 days in order to save the child. The Williams (D) were convicted of manslaughter due to their negligence in not seeking medical treatment for the child.

Issue: May simple negligence support a conviction for manslaughter?

Decision and Rationale: (Horowitz) Yes. There is a parental duty to provide medical care to a dependent, minor child. To prove involuntary manslaughter, the common law requires that a breach of this duty had to amount to more than mere ordinary or simple negligence—a showing of gross negligence was required. In Washington, however, the statutes defining manslaughter require only a showing of simple or ordinary negligence. The concept of ordinary negligence requires a failure to exercise the "ordinary caution" necessary to make out the defense of excusable homicide. Ordinary caution is the kind of caution that a man of reasonable prudence would exercise under the same or similar conditions. If the conduct of a defendant, regardless of his ignorance, good faith, or good intentions, fails to measure up to this standard, he is guilty of ordinary negligence. If such negligence proximately causes the death of the victim, the defendant is guilty of manslaughter. Timeliness in the furnishing of medical care must be considered in terms of ordinary caution. The law does not require that a parent call a doctor at the first sign of illness. However, testimony from the defendants indicates that they noticed the child was ill 10 to 14 days before the child died. In the five critical days in which it would have been possible to save the child's life, the parents noticed that the child was fussy, could not keep food down, and that his cheek turned a "bluish color like." The defendants thought that dentists would not pull a tooth "when it's all swollen up like that." Also, both parents feared that the child would be taken away from them if they took him to a doctor. Thus, there is sufficient evidence that the defendants were put on notice of the symptoms of the illness, and failed to exercise ordinary caution. Judgment affirmed.

Analysis:

This is a tragic case where the offender "should have known." This standard has troubled some commentators who wonder whether criminal liability should ever be based on an objective standard. Some suggest that the threat of criminal liability does not serve as a deterrent to negligent conduct. The negligent person is unaware of the risk, and cannot be deterred by a thought of possible punishment for taking an unreasonable risk that, in fact, he does not know he is taking. The competing argument contends that the threat of punishment makes people think harder about their conduct generally. When people consider the risks of their conduct, they tend to reduce the risks of their conduct, and thus create a safer society. Another issue that arises in *Williams* is the cultural issue, though the court does not make much of it. There is a great deal of scholarship on the problem of the reasonable person definition, which is primarily informed by a world view that is white, male, and middleclass. To some extent, a trial by jury consisting of one's peers [if this is indeed possible—since many citizens take pride in their ability to avoid jury duty, the choice may be somewhat limited] may counteract some of the potential for injustice in application of the predominant reasonable person standard.

People v. Stamp

(Prosecutor) v. (Robber)

(1969) 2 Cal.App.3d 203, 82 Cal.Rptr. 598

M E M O R Y   G R A P H I C

Instant Facts

After being robbed at gunpoint, the victim, who had heart disease, suffered a fatal heart attack brought on by his fear during the robbery.

Black Letter Rule

The commission of a felony makes the felon strictly liable for any death caused by the felony, even if the death was not intended or foreseeable and the victim's medical condition contributed to the death.

Case Vocabulary

PRECIPITATE: To make an event happen more quickly. To cause things to come to a crisis before they were supposed to.

Procedural Basis: Appeal to the Court of Appeals, Second District, of a conviction for murder in the first degree under the felony-murder rule.

Facts: Stamp (D) robbed a business, armed with a gun and a blackjack. Stamp (D) ordered everyone to lie on the floor and remain there for five minutes while he and his accomplice fled. The victim, who was present and had severe heart disease, then suffered heart palpitations and died. Three different doctors testified at the trial that the victim's heart attack was brought on by his fear during the robbery. Stamp (D) contends that the felony-murder rule does not apply to cases like this.

Issue: Is a person who committed a felony criminally liable for a death caused during the felony even if the person had no intention of killing anyone and could not have foreseen that the victim had a heart condition such that fear could cause him to die?

Decision and Rationale: (Cobey) Yes. The law in California is that a killing during the commission of robbery in the first degree is murder in the first degree. It does not matter whether the robbers planned to kill anyone, whether they intended to kill anyone or if the death was a mere accident. No intentional act is necessary beyond the intent to commit the robbery. Nor is it necessary that the victim's death be a foreseeable result of the robbery. As long as the robbery has a causal relationship with the death nothing else need be shown. In this case Stamp (D) committed a robbery in the first degree. In doing this he threatened the victim with a gun causing him to feel great fear. This fear, as testified to by the doctors, precipitated the victim's death. The felony-murder rule does apply to this case. Appeal denied.

Analysis:

Being convicted of murder in the first degree makes a person eligible to the harshest sentences available under our justice system. It is the same level of conviction Stamp (D) would face if he had entered the building and deliberately shot the victim in the head. This doesn't seem to make sense. One of the arguments made in support of the felony murder rule is that it will deter serious felonies that could result in the victim's death. But would consideration of the felony-murder rule have been likely to deter Stamp (D) in this case? Probably not, because Stamp (D) didn't think that anyone was going to die. It has also been suggested that the felony-murder rule encourages felons to be more careful to protect human life in the commission of their crimes. This also does not seem to make sense in this case. Assuming that he was going to commit armed robbery what could Stamp (D) have done that would have prevented this guy's death? [Perhaps the "prudent" armed robber gets a full medical history of his victim's beforehand?] The incentive the felony-murder rule provides in this case seems to point the other way. If a person is going to commit a robbery arguably they would be better off shooting their victim immediately. After all if the victim dies later for some unforeseen reason, that person would be found guilty of murder first anyway, and if they kill the victim, the victim won't be able to call the police, identify them, or cause them any other trouble while they are trying to rob the place and get away.

People v. Fuller

(Prosecutor) v. (Tire Thieves)
(1978) 86 Cal.App.3d 618, 150 Cal.Rptr. 515

M E M O R Y   G R A P H I C

Instant Facts

Two guys who were attempting to escape a police officer who had observed them stealing tires got into a high speed chase which resulted in an accident that killed the driver of another car.

Black Letter Rule

The felony-murder rule imposes strict liability for deaths caused by the commission of one of the enumerated felonies, which include burglary, even when the death is accidental.

Procedural Basis: Appeal to the Court of Appeal, Fifth District, of the trial court's striking of a murder charge based on the felony-murder rule.

Facts: Two men (the tire thieves) (D) were stealing tires off of cars from a dealer's lot early one Sunday morning. A police officer noticed them acting in a suspicious manner. The police officer made a U-turn to return to the lot at which point the tire thieves (D) got into their car and drove off. A chase followed that covered about seven miles and lasted from 10 to 12 minutes. The chase came to an end when the tire thieves' (D) car ran a red light and struck another car in the middle of an intersection. The driver of the other car was killed. The prosecutor charged the tire thieves with burglary, because they had been breaking into locked cars, and with murder under the felony-murder rule. The trial court struck down the murder charge. The prosecutor appealed that ruling.

Issue: Can an accidental death caused by a high-speed chase during the commission of a burglary be charged as murder in the first degree under the felony-murder rule?

Decision and Rationale: (Franson) Yes. We are bound by precedent to find that the felony-murder rule applies in this case. Californian law specifically enumerates burglary as one of the felonies that makes a death caused during the commission or attempted commission of the enumerated felonies chargeable as murder in the first degree. The tire thieves (D) committed burglary when they broke into locked vehicles for the purpose of theft. Then they caused the death of the victim by crashing into his car during a high-speed chase. The felony-murder rule imposes strict liability for this death and it does not matter that it was accidental. We do not believe that this is the appropriate outcome, and if we were not bound by precedent we would hold that the tire thieves (D) should not be prosecuted for felony murder because the crime which they intended to commit, car burglary, does not usually pose a danger to human life. However, under current law, the trial court erred in striking the murder charge, and we hold that the tire thieves (D) can be charged with murder.

Analysis:

If the doors to the vehicles in this case had been unlocked so that the tire thieves (D) did not have to break into the cars, then they could only have been charged with theft (probably a misdemeanor) and the felony-murder rule would not have applied. Of course, the reckless behavior involved in engaging in a high speed chase with a police officer might be found to be enough to support murder in the second degree. Considering that breaking into cars on a deserted dealer's lot early Sunday morning, with no weapons, is not something that one would expect to involve violence, and further considering that we have other ways to address reckless driving, does it make sense to apply a rule which makes this conduct equivalent to cold-blooded premeditated murder? When the felony-murder rule first emerged all felonies were punishable by death; thus the distinction was possibly not that important. England, the country where the rule originated, dropped it in 1957. Germany and France apparently never had such a doctrine. The United States the only major western country that still recognizes the rule. Two states, Hawaii and Kentucky have done away with it, and many others have limited its application. This case is a good example of why they have done so.

"HEALER" NOT GUILTY OF FELONY-MURDER WHEN HIS UNLICENSED PRACTICE OF MEDICINE KILLS THE PATIENT

People v. Burroughs

(Prosecutor) v. ("Healer")
(1984) 35 Cal.3d 824, 201 Cal.Rptr. 319, 678 P.2d 894.

M E M O R Y   G R A P H I C

Instant Facts
A healer who practiced unlicensed medicine killed a patient, who had come to him with terminal leukemia, by massaging his stomach, which caused a fatal hemorrhage.

Black Letter Rule
The felony unlicensed practice of medicine can not sustain a murder conviction of felony-murder because it is not a felony which is in the abstract inherently dangerous to human life.

Case Vocabulary

ANACHRONISTIC: Something that has continued beyond the time for which it was appropriate.
DISJUNCTIVE: The form that is used to set up a choice. One thing or another but not both, as in: "great bodily harm, serious mental or physical illness, or death."
MALEVOLENCE: Spite, ill will or malice. (Note: The judge in this case talks about finding malevolence in every felony that has been found to be inherently dangerous to human life. Malevolence is a synonym for malice. Malice is specifically not required in felony-murder cases.)

Procedural Basis: An appeal to the Supreme Court of California of a conviction for felony practice of medicine without a license and felony-murder in the second degree.

Facts: The victim, Lee Swatsenbarg (Lee) was diagnosed with terminal leukemia. He unsuccessfully sought treatment from a variety of traditional medical sources. Then he went to Burroughs (D) who called himself a "healer". He claimed to have cured thousands of people. His method of treatment involved drinking a special lemonade, being exposed to colored lights and vigorous massage which he administered himself. Lee agreed to undergo this treatment, which was supposed to last 30 days. During that time Lee was to consume nothing but the special lemonade, salt water and herb tea. He was also to bathe himself in colored lights and Burroughs (D) would come and massage him. Lee was to avoid contact with his doctor during this period. Within two weeks Lee's condition had begun to rapidly deteriorate. Burroughs (D) told Lee he was progressing according to schedule and told him not to get a bone marrow test his doctor wanted. Over the next week Lee became even more ill. He was in severe pain and vomiting frequently. Burroughs (D) administered several deep abdominal massages. Three and a half weeks into treatment Lee died at Burroughs' house. The death was a result of a hemorrhage in Lee's abdomen caused by Burroughs' (D) deep abdominal massage. The trial court ruled that an underlying felony of unlicensed practice of medicine could support a felony murder charge because such practice was inherently dangerous to human life, and instructed the jury that if Lee's death resulted from the felony they should find murder in the second degree. Burroughs contends that this instruction was incorrect.

Issue: Was the trial court incorrect when it ruled that the felony of unlicensed practice of medicine could support a felony-murder conviction because it is a felony that is inherently dangerous to human life?

Decision and Rationale: (Grodin) Yes. As a court we have repeatedly ruled that the felony-murder rule is a highly artificial anachronism. We do not wish to extend it in any way beyond the application required by the statute. Therefore we have created a standard that for the felony-murder rule to apply, the underlying felony must be inherently dangerous to human life. We did this because we believe the purpose of the felony-murder rule to be the deterrence of unnecessary violence during the commission of felonies which might result in a homicide. Felonies that are not inherently dangerous to human life are not likely to be deterred by the felony-murder rule because their perpetrators are not likely to perceive the risk of death involved. In the inherently dangerous to human life standard we look at the felony charge in the abstract. We do not apply the facts of the case, because in any case where the prosecution seeks to apply the felony-murder rule there has been a death and therefore reviewing the facts which lead to that death could make the felony seem more dangerous than it is. Our first step is to look at the primary element of the charge, and then we look at the elements that elevate the charge to a felony. In this case Burroughs (D) was practicing medicine with out a license. The primary element there is the care of sick or injured people without a license. In and of itself this is not an act that is inherently dangerous to human life, but could include such innocent activities as the application of a bandage or the provision of cold medicine. What elevates this to a felony is when it is done in circumstances or conditions which cause or create a risk of great bodily harm, serious mental or physical illness or death. This statute enumerates two kinds of risk that do not involve death. Great bodily harm could include a broken limb or disfigurement which does not pose a risk to the patient's life. And a risk of serious mental illness while it can cause a need for additional medical treatment does not have to endanger the person's life in any way. Thus it would be possible to commit the felony of practicing medicine without a license without endangering a person's life, and therefore this felony is not inherently dangerous. In addition, in the past when we have found that a felony was inherently dangerous to human life, there has always been a certain level of malevolence involved. For example we have found that poisoning food, drink or medicine with an intent to injure was inherently dangerous to human life. However there is no indication in this case that Burroughs (D) wanted to do anything other than cure the patient and then collect his fee. The second-degree murder conviction is reversed.

Analysis:

On a common sense level it seems odd to find that the practice of medicine without a license in circumstances or conditions which cause or create a risk of great bodily harm, serious mental and physical illness or death is not an activity which is inherently dangerous to human life. Admittedly it would be possible to do it without killing anyone, but are there any felonies besides the various forms of homicide that can not be done without killing someone. An armed robber can commit a robbery without killing anyone. Even a person committing assault could limit themselves to assaulting parts of the body that are not likely to cause death. The court based its decision in this case in part on it previous decision in *People v. Henderson* [false imprisonment is not a felony that is inherently dangerous to human life]. In that case, the defendant accused another person of stealing his television, when that person denied it the defendant forced him into his car at gunpoint drove to another location where a second person was supposed to confirm the theft. When they reached the second person's house the gun went off accidentally killing the second person. Again it does not seem to make sense that a crime that involved forcing a person around at gunpoint is not inherently dangerous to human life. The basis for this decision was that the false imprisonment statute also made it a felony to imprison someone by fraud or deceit, which the court felt was not inherently dangerous. Thus the matter of whether the felony will be considered inherently dangerous to human life ends up depending on whether the legislature randomly combined in one statute the possibly lethal methods of committing a crime with the "safer" methods, or whether the two methods were separated out. If false imprisonment by use of a weapon were a separate charge, the court's ruling would have been likely to be different. Several states outside of California recognize the inherently dangerous to human life standard but apply it to the facts of the case instead of the abstract felony in order to avoid this problem. The answer to why the California court decided not to do this can most likely be found in the fact that the court, by its own admission, does not like the felony murder rule and basically refuses to apply it in any situation where it is not specifically required by statute.

People v. Smith

(Government) v. (Child Abuser)
(1984) 35 Cal.3d 798, 201 Cal.Rptr. 311, 678 P.2d 886

M E M O R Y   G R A P H I C

Instant Facts

Smith (D) and her boyfriend beat Smith's two-year-old to death; Smith (D) was charged with second-degree felony murder.

Black Letter Rule

Felony child abuse which results in death is held to merge with the homicide so as to preclude a conviction of second degree murder on a felony murder theory.

Procedural Basis: Appeal from conviction of felony child abuse and second-degree murder on the felony murder rule.

Facts: Smith (D) and her two daughters, three-and-a-half-year-old Beth and two-year-old Amy, lived with David Foster. On the day Amy died, she refused to sit on the couch instead of the floor to eat a snack. Smith (D) became angry, and took Amy to her room where she spanked and slapped her. Smith (D) hit her repeatedly, knocking her to the floor. Foster then joined Smith (D) to "assist" in Amy's discipline. Beth testified that Foster and Smith (D) were striking Amy and were also biting her. Beth also testified that Foster put a wastebasket on Amy's head and hit her on the head with his fist. Smith (D) knocked Amy backwards, and Amy hit her head on the closet door. Amy went into respiratory arrest. She was taken to the hospital, but died later that evening. Smith (D) originally took all responsibility for the incident because of concern about the possible effect on Foster's probation status. Later, however, Smith (D) testified that she only spanked Amy, and that Foster had bitten and hit Amy while she was out of the room. Smith (D) testified that she told Foster that she would continue the discipline, and yelled at Amy for 15-20 minutes so that Foster would have time to "cool off." Foster returned to the room and began slapping Amy because she would not look at him. Smith (D) stated that although she realized Amy was being abused she did not think that her life was in danger. Smith (D) finally intervened, at which point Amy stiffened and fainted. Smith (D) was charged with felony child abuse and second-degree murder under the second-degree felony murder doctrine. The second-degree felony murder instruction informed the jury that an unlawful killing is second-degree murder if it occurs during the commission of a felony inherently dangerous to human life, and that felony child abuse is such a crime. Smith (D) contends that the crime of felony child abuse was an integral part of and included with the homicide, and hence it was merged into the homicide.

Issue: May felony child abuse serve as the underlying felony to support a conviction of second-degree murder on a felony-murder theory?

Decision and Rationale: (Mosk) No. Our opinions have repeatedly emphasized that felony murder is a disfavored doctrine. Although felony murder is the law in this state, we have sought to ensure that the doctrine be given the narrowest possible application consistent with its purpose—to deter those engaged in felonies from killing negligently or accidentally. We have restricted the scope of the felony murder rule by holding it inapplicable to felonies that are an integral part of and included in fact with the homicide. However, the felony-murder doctrine may still apply if the underlying offense was committed with an independent felonious purpose. Felony murder jury instructions have the effect of relieving the jury of the necessity of finding one of the elements of the crime of murder—malice aforethought. To allow such use of the felony murder doctrine would effectively preclude the jury from considering the issue of malice in all cases wherein homicide has been committed as a result of a felonious assault—a category which includes the great majority of all homicides. The offenses of assault with a deadly weapon, burglary with intent to assault, and discharging a firearm at an inhabited dwelling [a favorite California pastime] have all been held to merge into a resulting homicide. Cases in which the merger doctrine did not apply include those involving armed robbery, poisoning food, drink, or medicine, kidnapping, and felony child abuse by malnutrition. To violate the felony child abuse statute, the conduct must be willful, and must be committed under circumstances or conditions likely to produce great bodily harm or death. Application of the felony murder rule is barred where "the purpose of the conduct was the very assault which resulted in death." The purpose of the child abuse in this case was plainly the very assault that resulted in death. Thus, the underlying felony was unquestionably an integral part of the homicide. It was therefore error to give a felony-murder instruction in this case. The error must be deemed prejudicial. The judgment is reversed insofar as it convicts Smith (D) of second-degree murder; in all other respects, the judgment is affirmed.

Analysis:

The court claims that "[I]t would be wholly illogical to allow this kind of assaultive child abuse to be bootstrapped into felony murder merely because the victim was a child rather than an adult." Dismissing the propriety of felony child abuse as a basis for felony murder seems somewhat problematic, however. The court seems to be claiming that since the purpose of the conduct was the very assault that resulted in death, it does not matter if the target of the assault is a child or an adult. But the law already distinguishes between assault on an adult and assault on a child, and distinguishes between the two in sentencing. It does not seem wholly illogical [maybe partly illogical, if the idea even makes sense] to argue that this difference supports a finding that felony child abuse may be sufficiently different in seriousness as to support felony-murder. For the court, though, this would represent an expansion of the felony murder doctrine, which they take pains to avoid.

King v. Commonwealth

(Drug Distributor) v. (Prosecutor)

(1988) 6 Va.App. 351, 368 S.E.2d 704.

M E M O R Y   G R A P H I C

Instant Facts

Two guys were flying an airplane containing 500 pounds of marijuana when they crashed and one of them died. The survivor was charged with felony-murder.

Black Letter Rule

The felony-murder rule only applies when the death is caused by an act done in furtherance of the felony.

Case Vocabulary

IN FURTHERANCE OF: In order to make possible or easier.

RES GESTEA: In simple translation means things that are done; so to say that the homicide is committed in the *res gestea* of the initial felony, is to say the homicide is committed in the course of the things done to commit the felony.

Procedural Basis: Appeal to the Court of Appeals of Virginia of a conviction for felony-murder based on felony possession with intent to distribute.

Facts: King (D) and Bailey were flying an airplane containing 500 pounds of marijuana. They were heading for a Virginia airport. They encountered fog, got lost and crashed into a mountain. Bailey was killed instantly. King was charged with felony-murder of Bailey based on their felony possession of marijuana.

Issue: Does the felony-murder rule apply to a death that occurred during the commission of a felony but which was not caused by an act done in furtherance of the felony.

Decision and Rationale: No. A person who commits a felony is not liable for any death that randomly occurs while that felony is being committed. There must be a causal relationship between the death and the underlying felony. It is only when the homicide emanates from the things that are done to commit that felony that the court finds that it was committed in the perpetration of that felony. The felony in this case was possession of marijuana with intent to distribute. The fact that King (D) and Bailey had possession of a large amount of marijuana did not cause Bailey's death. The death was caused by inexperienced piloting in bad weather conditions. That piloting was not affected by the perpetration of the felony. The crash would not have been any different if they had been flying to a Virginia airport on vacation. Therefore there was no causal relationship between the felony and the death, and the death did not emanate from the felony. Thus the felony-murder clause does not apply to this case. The situation would be different if they had been flying the plane particularly low to avoid detection and that had caused the crash. [Does this mean that the court thinks the two were "high"?] However, as things stand we reverse the conviction for felony-murder.

Analysis:

A homicide exists when one person causes the death of another. The causation part of that formula is very important, and it is even more important when society is going to hold someone criminally liable for a death. A just society can not randomly seek someone to blame and punish for every death, no matter how emotionally appealing that idea might be. Feeling anger is a normal part of the grieving process. When a death occurs suddenly and is related in time to a felony, the felon seems an obvious target for that anger. A felon is an attractive scapegoat, why should anyone care if they face an overly harsh application of the law. They asked for it by committing the felony in the first place. The problem with this is that for criminal law to have any meaning it must bear some relationship to what is just. It is not just to charge a person who is coincidentally connected with a death through the commission of a felony with the same crime as a person who intentionally kills. If the accused did not cause the person's death then there isn't even a homicide to be considered. And in order for the accused to face criminal liability for that homicide there must be something culpable within the causation. In felony-murder the culpability comes from the commission of the felony, because otherwise no malice is required. Thus limiting the application of the felony-murder rule to cases where the death is caused by an act done in furtherance of the felony is really only a recognition of justice.

State v. Bonner

(Prosecutor) v. (Robber)

(1992) 330 N.C. 536, 411 S.E.2d 598.

M E M O R Y   G R A P H I C

Instant Facts

Four men attempted to rob a restaurant, they were stopped by a policeman, who shot two of them. The survivors were charged with felony-murder for the death of the co-defendants.

Black Letter Rule

A conviction for felony-murder cannot be based on the killings of accomplices to the defendant who were killed by someone acting in opposition to the crime.

Case Vocabulary

ACCOMPLICE LIABILITY: The criminal liability of one who aids, advises or encourages another in the commission of a crime. Being an accomplice to a crime creates an agency relationship for the purposes of that crime.

AGENCY: When one party acts for another and the other is bound by the first party's actions.

Procedural Basis: Appeal to the Supreme Court of North Carolina of two convictions for felony-murder with armed-robbery as the underlying felony.

Facts: Bonner (D) and Witherspoon (D) attempted to rob a restaurant along with two other accomplices. The restaurant employed Dallas Pruitt, who was an off-duty police officer, as a security guard. He prevented the robbery by shooting and killing Bonner (D) and Witherspoon's (D) accomplices. Bonner (D) and Witherspoon (D) were then charged with felony-murder for the deaths of those accomplices.

Issue: Does the common law theory of felony-murder extend to make felon's liable for the deaths of their accomplices who are killed by someone attempting to prevent the felony?

Decision and Rationale: (Whichard) No. The resolution of this issue is contained within the finding in *State v. Oxendine*. In this case Walter Oxendine (Oxendine) and two others attacked Proctor Lockelear (Proctor). A gunfight was started. Robert Wilkins (Wilkins), a bystander was killed by Proctor. The jury was instructed that it could find Oxendine guilty of felony murder even if Proctor fired the fatal shot. The court overturned his conviction. The court first stated the rule of accomplice liability, which would make Oxendine liable if he or one of his accomplices had shot Wilkins. And then explained why this rule did not apply to this situation. Proctor was not an accomplice of Oxendine, nor were they working in concert. In fact Proctor was working to prevent Oxendine's purpose. For criminal liability for a death to be assigned to someone, it is necessary to prove that that person, or his agent, did the killing. Further the court went on to say that if Proctor had shot one of Oxendine's accomplices instead of a bystander, it would be even more clear that Oxendine could not be held to be liable. Oxendine's accomplices had agreed to face their own risks in the enterprise, and again Oxendine would not have been working in concert with Proctor to bring about their deaths. Thus *State v. Oxendine* stands for the rule that felons cannot be found guilty of felony-murder when their adversary kills an accomplice. This is the rule followed by the majority of jurisdictions. In *State v. Canola*, (which held that felony-murder could not be applied when a victim shot one of the accomplices to a robbery) the court specifically noted that it was following the majority view in the country and that it did not know of any court that opposed it. [As a matter of fact, the court in Canola was incorrect, Missouri, Florida, and Illinois hold a different theory where the death of an accomplice at the hand of someone opposing the crime can be felony-murder based on a proximate cause theory. But that is not part of the court's opinion in this case.] Another reason that courts have supported the fact that the death of an accomplice at the hand of someone attempting to stop the crime is not a basis for felony-murder is that, when a killing is done to prevent a felony, then it is generally justifiable and thus not an unlawful act. It would be unreasonable to be able to transfer to a felon the guilt for a killing that was not a crime. Therefore in this case, Bonner (D) and Witherspoon (D) are not guilty of felony-murder in this case. They did not shoot their accomplices, so they are not actually responsible for their deaths. They were not acting in common purpose with Dallas Pruitt, so they were not constructively responsible for the deaths. And finally Dallas Pruitt, was a police officer acting to stop a dangerous felony. What he did was his duty; it was not an illegal act. Thus the killing of the accomplices in this case was not criminal and criminal liability can't be transferred from it. We overturn the convictions for felony-murder.

Analysis:

To understand this case it is helpful to understand the idea of accomplice liability. This is covered in far greater detail later in the course. However the basic concept is fairly easy. It holds that anyone who aids, advises, or encourages someone in the commission of a crime is also criminally liable for that crime. This means that if a group decides to commit a robbery, then everyone in the group is criminally liable for any criminal actions taken by a member of that group during the commission of the robbery. Thus if A, B and C are trying to rob D and A shoots

V, who just happens to be there, then B and C are also criminally liable for the shooting of V. Part of the theory of this is that A is B and C's agent in the shooting. In *Oxendine*, this is turned around. A, B and C are attacking D, and then D shoots V. Here A, B and C are working in concert with each other, but they are not working in concert with D, so D is not an agent of A, B and C, and A, B and C do not share liability with D. Then in *Bonner* B, W, X, and Y are trying to rob a restaurant when P shoots X and Y. B and W are not working in concert with P. P is not their agent. Further X and Y were working with B and W, they could be said to have agreed to the risk that working with B and W entailed. And further since P was doing his duty in shooting X and Y, there is no criminal liability that he could share with B and W even if he had been acting as their agent. Therefore B and W are not criminally liable for the death of X and Y. The analysis above does represent the majority view in the country at the moment, but there are some states that see it differently. They examine the idea of liability in these cases from a proximate cause point of view. If A, B and C attempt to rob D and D shoots C, then instead of looking at the problem of agency, they examine whose actions were the proximate cause of C's death. As D's actions in shooting C are justifiable he is not seen as the cause. Instead A and B who initiated the criminal action which resulted in D's need to defend himself are held to be the proximate cause of C's death and thus they are liable, and can be found guilty of felony-murder. [You now have the ABCs of felony-murder.]

Gregg v. Georgia

(Condemned Man) v. (State)

(1976) 428 U.S. 153, 96 S.Ct. 2909, 49 L.Ed.2d 859

M E M O R Y   G R A P H I C

Instant Facts

Gregg (D) was found guilty of murder and sentenced to death under a new Georgia statute which was designed to reform the state's imposition of the death penalty so that it would be constitutional.

Black Letter Rule

The death penalty as imposed on murderers by the Georgia statute is constitutional because the death penalty is consistent with societal standards, is not an excessive punishment, and the statute provides sufficient safeguards to prevent it from being imposed in an arbitrary or capricious manner.

Case Vocabulary

GRATUITOUS INFLICTION OF SUFFERING: To make someone suffer pain or other distress beyond what is necessary or warranted by the situation.

PENOLOGICAL JUSTIFICATION: Justification based on the theory and practice of criminal rehabilitation.

PLURALITY: An opinion issued by an appellate court that does not represent the majority of the justices but which has more justices joined to it than any concurring opinion.

Procedural Basis: Appeal to the United States Supreme Court of a capital sentence imposed by a court in Georgia.

Facts: Gregg (D) was convicted of murder with intent to kill and armed robbery. At the post-conviction sentencing hearing the jury imposed the death penalty. This was done in accordance with Georgia's new statutory scheme for the imposition of the death penalty. The new Georgia statute requires a bifurcated trial. Guilt is determined in the traditional manner during the first stage, then if the defendant's guilt is established a presentence hearing is held. The defendant is accorded wide latitude in presenting evidence at this hearing. The evidence submitted in the earlier trial is also considered. In order to return a sentence of death the jury must find beyond a reasonable doubt that at least one of 10 listed aggravating factors is present in the crime. Gregg (D) is appealing his sentence.

Issue: Is the death penalty as imposed by the Georgia Statute constitutional?

Decision and Rationale: (Stewart) Yes. The meaning of the 8th Amendment changes as the standards of what society considers decent evolve. However, this is not a subjective standard. It is necessary to find an objective measure of what society currently considers decent. And beyond current standards of public decency, in order to satisfy the requirements of the 8th Amendment a penalty must accord with the recognition of the dignity of a human being, which is the basic concept, underlying the amendment. This means that the penalty must not be excessive. It must not involve the unnecessary and wanton infliction of pain. And the severity of the punishment must not be grossly out of proportion with the crime. The imposition of the death penalty against murderers has a long history in both the United States and England. The framers accepted it, and it was practiced in every state at the time that the 8th Amendment was included in the Constitution. This court has recognized for nearly 200 years that the death penalty itself is not unconstitutional per se. Since *Furman v. Georgia* [earlier Supreme Court case which found the death penalty as then practiced in Georgia to be unconstitutional] 35 states have enacted new death penalty statutes, and Congress has passed a law authorizing the death penalty for air piracy. In addition, the involvement of juries in these cases directly connects the sentence to the contemporary values of society. Thus the death penalty as imposed here is clearly within society's standards. There must also be penological justification so that it doesn't result in the gratuitous infliction of suffering. The death penalty serves two such purposes, retribution and deterrence. While retribution is no longer the dominant objective of criminal law it is still a legitimate objective. The death penalty serves as an expression of society's moral outrage at particularly heinous crimes. This is somewhat necessary in a civilized society where we deny a victim's family the right to take their own revenge. Statistical studies have been inconclusive on the question of whether the death penalty serves as a deterrent. We feel that the question of deterrence is best left to legislatures who can consider the particular applicability of the studies to their locality and have more creative solutions available to them. As to the death penalty being a disproportionate penalty, we can not believe that that is the case where it is imposed for the crime of murder. Based on all of this we conclude that the death penalty is not unconstitutional per se. The question thus becomes can Georgia impose the death penalty in this case. In *Furman* we recognized that the death penalty is unlike any other punishment and that it must not be inflicted in an arbitrary or capricious manner. However the statutory system Georgia now uses to impose the death penalty successfully addresses those concerns. Georgia now requires a bifurcated proceeding, which ensures that the sentencing authority gets the information relevant to the imposition of the sentence and provides standards for the use of that information in making the sentencing decision. Based on this we uphold the imposition of the death penalty in this case.

Concurrence: (White) In effect what Gregg (D) is arguing is that there is an unconstitutional amount of discretion in our entire system of justice. He is arguing that no matter how effective the death penalty may be as a punishment, government created and run by human beings is inevitably too flawed to administer it. We can not accept this as a part of constitutional law. Administering the death penalty is a very serious responsibility and mistakes will be made. However one of society's greatest responsibilities is that of protecting the lives of its citizens from murder, and I will not interfere in Georgia's attempt to meet that responsibility.

Dissent: (Brennan) The cruel and unusual punishment clause must draw its meaning from the evolving standards of decency that mark the progress of a maturing society. In *Furman* I concluded that our civilization and the law had progressed to the point where the punishment of death for whatever crime and under whatever circumstances is cruel and unusual. I won't repeat the whole of my argument in that case here, however I will say that inherent in the clause is the primary moral principle that the state, even as it punishes, must treat its citizens in a manner consistent with their intrinsic worth as human beings. A punishment must not be so severe as to be degrading to human dignity.

Dissent: (Marshall) It is true that 35 states have passed laws providing for imposition of the death penalty since *Furman*, however I do not believe that this is a true indication of the standards of society. I believe, and this has been backed up by recent studies on the subject, that an informed citizenry would find the death penalty

as practiced morally offensive. In addition, even if favored by the public the death penalty would remain unconstitutional because it is excessive. The true question here is whether the death penalty is necessary to accomplish a legitimate legislative purpose in punishment when a less severe penalty, life imprisonment, would do as well. The death penalty has not been shown by any study to be an effective deterrent. There is no correlation between capital punishment and lower rates of capital crime. This leaves us with retribution as the only possible justification for capital punishment. The plurality has argued that the death penalty as retribution may be necessary to prevent people from resorting to self-help to get their revenge. But this is not a valid argument; we have other methods for requiring citizens to confine themselves to civilized behavior. Besides this is more of an argument of expediency than a justification of the value of retribution itself. If retribution is to be a justification it must be based on the idea that the death of the murderer is a moral good in itself. This argument is a direct rejection of the 8th Amendment's requirement that we must treat even wrong doers in a manner that is consistent with their intrinsic worth as human beings. Therefore the death penalty is excessive as it fails to advance any legitimate legislative purpose beyond what could be achieved through the less severe punishment of life imprisonment.

Analysis:

In order to fully understand this case it is necessary to have some knowledge of the case that came before it: *Furman v. Georgia*. *Furman* was decided in 1972. It overturned four death sentences from Georgia. All nine justices wrote opinions in the case, which totaled over 200 pages. Only two of the justices, Brennan and Marshall, the same justices who dissent in *Gregg*, argued that the death penalty was unconstitutional *per se*. They were joined by three other justices, Douglas, Steward and White, in the judgment overturning the Georgia death sentences, but these justices did not agree that the death penalty itself was unconstitutional. Their concern was that Georgia seemed to be imposing the death penalty in a way that was arbitrary, capricious, or discriminatory. The other four justices, C.J. Burger, Blackmun, Powell and Rehnquist, all dissented, rejecting both the procedural and *per se* attacks on the death penalty. The effect of Furman was to invalidate the death penalty in all states because while the judgment had not found the death penalty unconstitutional per se, none of the statutes currently enacted met the standards required to show they were not arbitrary or capricious. As stated within *Gregg*, thirty-five states then went on to adopt new statutes based on the model penal code, so that they could impose the death penalty in a way that would survive a constitutional challenge. The judgment in *Gregg* then held that the death penalty imposed under these new statutes had in fact reached its goal and the death penalty was constitutional once again. Gregg is also a good outline of what is necessary for a penalty to be constitutional under the 8th Amendment. The penalty must conform to contemporary societal standards of decency. The penalty must also accord with the dignity of a human being, which is the underlying principle of the 8th Amendment. In order to do this it must not be excessive. To avoid being excessive it must achieve a legitimate purpose of punishment and it must not be grossly out of proportion with the crime. The plurality and the dissent disagree as to what would truly indicate society's true standards of decency, but more centrally they disagree as to what would make a punishment excessive. The dissent argues that a punishment is excessive unless it is the least severe punishment that will meet the legitimate goals of punishment. The plurality argues that a punishment is not excessive unless it exceeds the legitimate goals of punishment. It is this disagreement that lets them take the same fact - that it has not been proven that the death penalty does or does not have a deterrent effect and both use it as an argument to support their case. This is a philosophical disagreement and is a good illustration of how the personal beliefs of those serving on the court will inevitably shape their opinions.

U.S. SUPREME COURT SAYS DEATH SENTENCE IS CONSTITUTIONAL, EVEN WHEN STUDY SHOWS BLACKS WHO KILL WHITES ARE DISPROPORTIONATELY SENTENCED TO DEATH

McCleskey v. Kemp

(Black Man) v. (Person Holding McCleskey in Custody)

(1987) 481 U.S. 279, 17 S.Ct. 1756, 95 L.Ed.2d 262

M E M O R Y   G R A P H I C

 Instant Facts

A black man found guilty of killing a white man challenges his sentence based on a study that shows that blacks who kill whites get the death more than whites who kill whites, or those who kill blacks.

Black Letter Rule

A statistical study that shows a risk that capital sentencing is influenced by race does not prove that a specific sentence violates the 8th or 14th Amendment.

Case Vocabulary

EQUAL PROTECTION VIOLATION: A violation of the 14th amendment guarantee that no member of one class will be denied the same protection under the law, which is enjoyed by members of other classes.

INVIDIOUS: Stirs up envy and resentment. Used in law to describe discrimination, which is arbitrary, irrational, and not reasonably related to a legitimate purpose.

JURY VENIRE: The group of people, summoned to the court, from which a jury is chosen.

WRIT OF HABEAS CORPUS: In criminal cases a writ to produce the prisoner, which is directed to the party keeping a prisoner in custody. It is used to test the legality of the imprisonment.

Procedural Basis: Appeal to the Supreme Court of the United States of the denial of a writ of habeas corpus.

Facts: Warren McCleskey (McCleskey) (D), a black man, was convicted of murdering a white police officer during the course of a robbery. The jury recommended the death penalty and the judge sentenced him to death. McCleskey's (D) sentence was upheld through all state appeals. McCleskey (D) then filed a writ of habeas corpus in federal court. Among other claims this writ raised a claim that in Georgia the death penalty is administered in a racially discriminatory manner in violation of the 14th and 8th Amendments. In support of this claim McCleskey (D) proffered a statistical study by Professors Baldus, Pulaski, and Woodworth. The results of the study are as follows: People (of any race) charged with killing whites got death in 11% of the cases. People (of any race) charged with killing blacks got death in 1% of the cases. Another statistic showed that black defendants got the death penalty 4% of the time, and white defendants got the death penalty 7% of the time. When the race of the victim and defendant are combined, 22% of cases where blacks killed whites resulted in the death penalty. Also, only 8% of whites who killed whites got the death penalty. Only 1% of blacks who killed blacks got death. And, 3% of whites who killed blacks got the death penalty. This data was further analyzed to take account of other variables which resulted in one model that showed that those who kill whites were 4.3 times more likely to get the death penalty than those who kill blacks, and that black defendants were 1.1 times more likely to get the death penalty than other defendants.

Issue: Can a statistical study that shows a risk that capital sentencing is influenced by race prove that a specific death sentence is unconstitutional under the 8th or 14th amendments?

Decision and Rationale: (Powell) No. McCleskey (D) is arguing, on the basis of the study, that his sentence was influenced by racial discrimination and that this was a violation of his right to equal protection under the 14th amendment and his right not to be subjected to cruel and unusual punishment under the 8th amendment. We first consider his equal protection claim. A successful equal protection claim comes in two parts. First it must be shown that there was purposeful discrimination; then, it must be shown that the discrimination had a discriminatory effect on the person bringing the claim. McCleskey (D) has not offered any specific evidence of discrimination in his case, instead he has offered a general statistical study. The court has accepted statistics as proof of discrimination in some equal protection cases. However, those cases involved the selection of a jury venire in a particular district, and Title VII employment discrimination cases, that are different from the situation here. A capital sentence must be recommended by a properly selected jury. Each of the juries that recommend such a sentence is unique. Each jury is required to consider several factors, which include specific characteristics of the defendant and the facts of the individual case. The cases where we have found statistical studies sufficient have involved fewer entities with fewer variables. In addition because our criminal justice system depends on juries exercising their discretion we would require a higher standard of evidence before we would find that that discretion had been abused. Therefore we find that there is not enough evidence here to support the charge of an equal protection violation. We then turn to McCleskey's (D) 8th amendment claim. A sentence that was definitely based on racial consideration would be a violation of the 8th amendment. However there is no proof here that this particular sentence was racially based. All the statistical study offered here can show is that there is a risk that racial considerations were involved. This risk cannot be completely eliminated because the jury has discretion in reaching its decision. The discretion of the jury is a necessary part of giving each case the individual attention that is an important part of a just system. This discretion also benefits the defendant, because if the jury decides against the death penalty that decision can not be appealed, but a decision for the death penalty is still open to appellate review. Any system that involves human judgment will show some discrepancies; thus the test of constitutionality can't require perfection. Instead we require that the system be surrounded by as many safeguards as possible, a requirement which has been met in this case. In addition, there are two other considerations that influence us against accepting McCleskey's (D) claim. The first is that if McCleskey's (D) argument were to be taken to its logical conclusion it could undermine the entire criminal justice system. The 8th amendment is not limited to capital cases, and as we stated above no realistic system is going to be completely free of discrepancies. Second, we feel that this sort of issue is better addressed by the local legislature as they have a better understanding of how the statistics reflect their local conditions as well as more flexibility to address the problems presented.

Dissent: (Brennan) At some time during the planning of his defense McCleskey (D) must have asked his lawyer about his chances. To answer this question honestly his lawyer would have to tell him that his chances were going to be significantly and negatively influenced by his race and the race of the victim. The majority finds that this is acceptable. This finding is at odds with our consistent concern for rationality in capital sentencing. Rationality in sentencing requires consideration of each individual as a unique human being. Decisions that are influenced by race do not meet this requirement. The greater likelihood that a black defendant will be sentenced to death, and the likelihood that the murder of a black victim will result in less punishment, is a devaluation of the lives of black people. The majority argues that this risk must be greater than what has been shown in this case before we interfere in the discretion of the jury. But the reason the discretion of the jury exists is so that the required individual consideration can happen, and this is just what racist decisions undermine. It is true that a justice system administered by people will always be imperfect. However, that means that we will always be faced with the task of drawing the line at the point where those imperfections become unacceptable. The slippery slope argument used by the majority in refusing to find the imperfections demonstrated by this study unacceptable ignores the special nature of capital punishment and the special repugnance of racial discrimination.

Analysis:

In reading this case it is important to take note of the findings of the study and in doing so to understand that race still plays a significant role within the system. If you walk into any criminal court in a major city in the United States you will see that minority groups are seriously over represented as defendants, while they are seriously under represented as judges, lawyers, clerks and bailiffs. (Admittedly some progress has been made with court personnel, but the majority remain white.) [If you really want to get honest, take a look at the racial mix of the classroom when you take this class and consider whether race made a difference in getting you here.] All of the justices in this case acknowledge that the system is inevitably imperfect, that discrepancies will exist. This is a tacit admission that race will always play a role. The question thus becomes is this an acceptable way to administer the death penalty. Some level of imperfection will have to be accepted in the criminal justice system as a whole because we have to have a criminal justice system, and it has to be run by fallible human beings. We do not have to have a death penalty. The court split five to four on this case. After his retirement Justice Powell indicated that he regretted his vote and his opinion in this case. If he had changed his vote at the time, what is currently the dissent would have been the law of the land. This is still a very relevant issue.

Payne v. Tennessee

(Killer) v. (State)

(1991) 501U.S. 808, 111 S.Ct. 2597, 115 L.Ed.2d 720.

M E M O R Y   G R A P H I C

 ## Instant Facts

Three-year-old survived his wounds when his mother and sister were killed. At the sentencing hearing for the killer his grandmother testified about how this had affected him. The killer was sentenced to death.

Black Letter Rule

The 8th amendment does not prohibit the introduction of victim impact evidence at the sentencing phase of a capital trial.

Case Vocabulary

GUILT PHASE / PENALTY PHASE: A capital trial is divided into two phases. The first, the guilty phase, is the trial where it is decided whether or not the defendant is guilty of the capital offense. If the defendant is found guilty then the trial moves on to the penalty phase, where the sentence is considered.

NON SEQUITUR: A statement, within the context of a conversation, argument or writing, which does not follow the logic of the things that were said before it.

STARE DECISIS: A doctrine that holds that once a matter of law has been carefully considered and decided it will be followed in all future cases. This promotes security and certainty in the law. The decision of a point of law should be strictly followed unless departure is really necessary to vindicate plain and obvious injustice.

Procedural Basis: Appeal to the United States Supreme Court of an earlier ruling on a motion for habeas corpus.

Facts: Pervis Tyrone Payne (D) (Payne) lived in the apartment across the hall from Charisse Christopher (Charisse) and her two children, 2-year-old Lacie and 3-year-old Nicholas. One Saturday, after drinking all morning and injecting cocaine, Payne (D) went to Charisse's apartment and started making sexual advances towards her. She rejected him. Payne (D) became violent. He stabbed Charisse and her daughter Lacie to death. He also attacked Nicholas who only survived after seven hours of surgery. A neighbor called the police after hearing the screams. Payne (D) was found by the first police officer on the scene covered with blood. The scene inside the apartment was very bloody. Charisse had received 84 wounds, none of which was fatal and had most likely bled to death. Payne's (D) defense presented four mitigation witnesses, his mother and father and his girlfriend as well as a psychologist at the sentencing hearing. The psychologist testified that Payne (D) had a low IQ and was mentally handicapped. Charisse's mother also testified at the sentencing hearing. She was asked about how her grandson Nicholas was affected by the murders of his mother and sister. She described him as crying for his mother and being very worried about his little sister. In his closing argument during the sentencing hearing the prosecutor talked about the effect all this was having on Nicholas. He told the jury that Nicholas was conscious throughout the attack and that he was in the same room when his mother and sister were killed. The prosecutor argued that giving Payne (D) the death penalty would be a comfort to Nicholas when he grew up and was able to understand what had happened. The jury sentenced Payne to death.

Issue: Does the 8th amendment prohibit the introduction of victim impact evidence at the sentencing phase of a capital trial?

Decision and Rationale: (Rehnquist, C.J) No. We granted certiorari in this case in order to reconsider our holdings in *Booth* and *Gathers* that the 8th Amendment prohibits the presentation of victim impact testimony during the sentencing hearing in a capital case. In Booth we held that victim impact testimony could not be considered because for the death penalty to be constitutional the defendant must be considered as a unique and individual human being. And, the sentencing hearing must thus center around the blameworthiness of the defendant's conduct so that the jury can focus on whether this defendant should receive the death penalty. The blameworthiness in this context is based on the defendant's character and his actions. Factors of which the defendant was not aware, such as the way certain victims would be impacted, or special qualities of the victim, are not relevant to that blameworthiness. We are now reconsidering that decision. The blameworthiness of the defendant is no longer the only thing we feel should be considered at the sentencing hearing. The amount of harm done by an offense has always been relevant under criminal law. Two defendants who performed exactly the same actions in committing a crime would be punished differently if one of those crimes resulted in a death and the other did not. Judges have always considered the amount of harm done in a capital case when they have been given discretion over the sentence. There has been some concern that considering victim impact evidence will lead to the comparison of victims with some being considered less valuable than others. We do not feel that this will actually be the result. We feel that this evidence is instead used to show the unique value of each victim as an individual human being. As it is unconstitutional to prevent the defendant from putting on any evidence that might tend to mitigate his crime in a capital sentencing hearing, mitigation for the defendant can always be heard. It is thus unfair that the prosecutor be prevented from balancing this evidence with evidence about the victim. Therefore we rule that victim impact evidence in capital sentencing hearings is not prohibited by the 8th Amendment and we uphold the sentences in this case.

Concurrence: (Souter) Because all victims are unique individuals with family and other human connections, the defendant should be able to foresee the kind of impact his actions will have on victims of his crime. That there would be such impact is inevitable. Because it is inevitable it has moral relevance to the defendant's conduct. Therefore victim impact evidence is relevant to assessing the defendant's blameworthiness and is relevant and appropriate at a capital sentencing hearing.

Dissent: (Marhshall) The ruling of the majority in this case is a direct overruling of our previous ruling in *Booth*. There has been no change in the law governing this situation or the factual situation, thus the ruling here is a violation of *stare decisis*.

Dissent: (Stevens) Not only is Marshall correct about this ruling being a violation of *stare decisis*. However, even if we had never decided *Booth* and *Gathers* the ruling of the majority would represent a sharp break with our previous reasoning regarding capital sentencing. There is no support in our previous cases for the presentation at sentencing of evidence that sheds no light on the defendant's moral culpability but rather serves to encourage juror's to make their decision out of emotion rather than sound reasoning. It would clearly be inappropriate to allow the defendant in a capital case to enter evidence that his victim was engaged in immoral behavior of which the defendant was unaware at the time of the killing. The state should be bound by the same limitation and be prohibited from offering positive information about the victim of which the defendant was unaware. In *Locket v. Ohio* we found that those who would be responsible for making the decision to sentence a defendant to death must not be prevented from considering any factor that mitigated the defendant's crime. Victim impact evidence can have the effect of emotionally blinding the jury to the legitimate mitigation offered by the defense. To consider details of the impact of the crime on the victims does not simply balance the mitigation offered by the defendant. The victim is not on trial and is not facing the awesome power of the state. It is true that the consideration of the harm a crime causes is relevant in criminal law, but that is only when that harm is foreseeable. To the extent that the defendant should have known that any such crime would have a foreseeable impact on victims, the jury is also completely capable of comprehending this kind of generic harm with out any specific evidentiary support. In the end specific evidence presented to show special harm suffered by the victim can only serve to support the idea that some victim's lives were more valuable than others. This is as offensive as the idea that prosecutors should seek the death penalty in cases with a white victim, but offer plea bargains in cases where a black person was killed. I recognize that the majority's decision today is likely to be very popular politically, and that it will please many very thoughtful people. However, the court is the one place in a democracy where public opinion should not be the deciding factor. This is the place where the voice of the many should not be able to eliminate the rights of the few.

Analysis:

How would hearing the victim's mother describing the crying of her grandson for his mother affect you if you were on the jury in this case? You would have already heard evidence of what exactly happened during the crime during the guilt phase. The grandmother's testimony would not add to your understanding of the factual harm caused. But it would inevitably have a very emotional impact on you. Many people would have a very difficult time listening to such evidence without crying. The basic rule about the admission of evidence is that it must be more relevant than prejudicial. Defense attorneys' often argue that especially gory crime scene photos should not be admitted because they are too likely to inflame the jury's emotions and thus be more prejudicial than informative. Of course, the prosecution argues to admit the photos for their informative nature, but also wants this emotional impact. One way this conflict has been resolved is by only allowing the prosecution to submit the evidence in black and white, which avoids some of the emotional impact of the blood. What kind of informational value does the grandmother's testimony have? The jury already knew that Nicholas has seen his mother and sister murdered and that he had been very seriously wounded himself. Did they have to be told that he was grieving for his mother or sister? Surely that was something they already knew. The emotionally inflammatory nature of this evidence balanced against its informative value would then seem to argue against its admission. The court, however, rules the other way. And it overrules its own previous decisions in order to do so. Why does it do that? One argument the dissent puts forward is that the majority was influenced by public opinion. Clearly defending "victim's rights" is much more popular with the public than defending the rights of those facing capital murder charges. Arguably however, it is defending the rights of the unpopular that is the Supreme Court's most important job.

Tison v. Arizona

(Felony-murderers) v. (State)
(1987) 481 U.S. 137, 107 S.Ct. 1676, 95 L.Ed.2d 127

M E M O R Y   G R A P H I C

⚡ Instant Facts

The Tison brothers decided to break their father and his cell-mate out of prison, during the escape the father and cell-mate killed a family while the Tison brothers were present.

⚖ Black Letter Rule

Major participation in the felony committed combined with reckless indifference to human life is enough to supply the culpability necessary to constitutionally impose the death penalty.

📖 Case Vocabulary

ATTENUATED: Describes something that has been drawn out to the point it has been made thin and weak.
DETERRENT: Anything that prevents, or tends to prevent a person from doing something.
FELONY-MURDER SIMPLICITER: The felony-murder doctrine makes a person guilty of murder because a death resulted from their commission of a felony. Simpliciter is a Latin term for simple, or simplicity. Together in this context they express the idea of the level of a person's culpability created by mere participation, particularly as an accomplice, in an underlying felony which caused a death, as opposed to the greater culpability of someone who actually pulled the trigger or directly killed the victim.
RETRIBUTIVE PURPOSE: A justification of a punishment based on the theory that every crime should be paid for with some kind of equivalent punishment.
TANGENTIAL: Describes relationship that is limited by only connecting at one point, a weak and non-relevant connection.

Procedural Basis: Appeal of two death sentences to the United States Supreme Court.

Facts: Gary Tison (Gary) was sentenced to life imprisonment for murder. His family decided to break him out of jail. He insisted that his cellmate Randy Greenawalt (Greenawalt) also be included in the escape. Three of Gary's sons went to the prison with a large number of weapons. They armed their father, Gary, and his cellmate Greenawalt, and then the five men brandishing weapons were able to flee the prison without any shots being fired. After leaving the prison, the car they were traveling in had a flat tire near an isolated house. The group decided to flag down a passing motorist and steal a car. Raymond Tison (Raymond) (D) stood in front of their disabled car while the others were armed and waiting out of sight. A Mazda being driven by John Lyons (Lyons) pulled over to offer assistance. In the car with Lyons were his wife, his 15-year-old niece and his 2-year-old son. Ricky Tison (D) and Raymond (D) went to fill a water jug some distance away. Gary and Greenawalt killed all of the Lyonses. Both Ricky and Raymond expressed surprise at the killings. They made no effort to aid the victims and continued on with Gary and Greenawalt. They also participated in the final gun battle with the police that ended with all of them being taken into custody. The state tried Ricky (D) and Raymond (D) separately. They were each charged with capital murder of the four victims as well as with armed robbery, kidnapping, and car theft. The capital murder charges were based on Arizona felony-murder law providing that a killing occurring during the perpetration of robbery or kidnapping is capital murder, and that each person participating is legally liable for the acts of his accomplices. Both Ricky (D) and Raymond (D) were found guilty and sentenced to death. The case was appealed to the Arizona Supreme Court and affirmed. United States Supreme Court accepted certiorari.

Issue: Is it constitutional to impose the death penalty on two major participants in a felony, which resulted in the death of four non-participants, even when they did not personally inflict the fatal injury and did not intend the death?

Decision and Rationale: (O'Conner) Yes. We took certiorari in this case to consider how our previous decision in *Enmund v. Florida* [a getaway driver not eligible for death penalty for the unplanned murders committed by his accomplices while he was waiting in the car] applies to these facts. Only nine states allow the death penalty for accomplices not directly involved in the killing. Studies have shown that juries very rarely find for the death penalty under these situations. We agree that limited participation in a crime, which in itself is not a capital offense and where the death of a non-participant is not expected, is not capital material. Such an offense is unlikely to be deterred by application of the death penalty, as the outcome is not anticipated. Also that is the kind of behavior that does not show a sufficient personal culpability to justify the state in seeking the death penalty for purposes of retribution. In Enmund we found that in order to be eligible for the death penalty the individual defendant must show a high level of personal culpability, and that the state had failed to meet that standard. However, the facts of this case differ significantly from the situation in *Enmund*. We accept that Ricky (D) and Raymond (D) had no intention to kill the victims in this case. Yet, their actions show a much greater involvement in the underlying felony than was the case in *Enmund*. They took lethal weapons into a prison. They then armed two men who had previously been convicted of murder with those weapons and aided them in using the weapons to escape. They were aware that one of these men had killed a prison guard in a previous escape attempt. Raymond (D) flagged down the car containing the victims knowing that they would face an armed ambush when they stopped. Ricky (D) was armed and waiting with the others when the car stopped. They were both at the scene while the murders took place and took no steps to aid the victims. They also participated in the final shootout with the police. While having an intent to kill is obviously relevant to the question of personal culpability it is not the only consideration. A person who kills in self-defense may do so very intentionally but with no culpability. Alternatively someone engaged in the torture of another person who doesn't care whether or not his victim lives or dies is extremely culpable. The mental state displayed in that kind of act would be a reckless indifference to human life, and that is also what is present in the case we are considering here. Ricky (D) and Raymond (D) must have been aware that their actions were very likely to result in someone's death, and they were centrally involved in the events that lead to the deaths. Based on this we find that the capital sentences imposed on Ricky (D) and Raymond (D) are constitutional.

Dissent: (Brennan) The felony-murder doctrine is a holdover from a time when a person could be executed for committing any felony. This made the mental state related to the killing irrelevant, as the intent to commit the underlying felony provided sufficient culpability to justify a death sentence. In most American jurisdictions and practically all European and Commonwealth countries a felon can not be executed for a murder that he or she did not specifically intend

to commit. The majority argues that the intent to kill is not a good way to identify the most culpable of murders. They suggest the example of one who tortures someone to death without a care as to whether they lived or died or the robber who shoots indiscriminately during the robbery not caring who might be hit. But there is a crucial element in those cases, which is missing here. In both of those examples the culpability is found in the actions that the perpetrators personally took that caused the death, committing the torture, or firing the gun. Reckless indifference to human life can only rise to the highest level of culpability if there is intentional reckless action. Intent is a central part of what makes an action culpable. Ricky (D) and Raymond (D) did not intend the death of the victims in this case, they were surprised by it. They did not take the actions that resulted in the victim's death. We believe that culpability arises out of the results of a choice made out of an individual's free will. Death, the state's ultimate sanction must be reserved for those whose culpability is greatest.

Analysis:

This case is yet another 5-4 decision. The court is very closely divided here. What is really interesting however is what they agree about. Both the majority and the dissent argue that in order to be eligible for the death penalty the defendant must have a high level of personal culpability and not simply culpability that is transferred to him from an accomplice. Thus *Enmund* is not over-ruled. While being an accomplice, and participating in a named felony on any level can make a person guilty of murder first it takes more than that to provide a constitutional basis for a death sentence. The debate is over what specifically makes a defendant sufficiently personally culpable. Being the getaway driver for a robbery where no one is supposed to be killed is not sufficient. The dissent would require either an intent to kill or reckless indifference to human life combined with direct action to cause the death. The actual ruling in this case is even less definite requiring major involvement in an underlying felony, which has a high likelihood of causing the death of a non-participant. The armed robbery in *Enmund* would apparently not be considered to have posed a high likelihood of causing the death of a non-participant. While the armed robbery by hijacking the car in this case does. Clearly the majority is using a very fact specific standard. This then becomes the heart of what a lawyer does in the sentencing hearing in this type of case. The prosecutor will work to show the defendants involvement in the case was as serious as possible, and to show that the felony posed an obvious risk to the lives of others. Meanwhile the defense will work to minimize the defendant's involvement and emphasize the unexpected nature of the death.

Chapter 8

Though rape has often been characterized as the most heinous of crimes next to murder, rape law often amounted to an unfair hurdle for actual victims. Rape law delved deeply into gender stereotypes, making it unfair for those whose actions deviated from the "norm." Though in modern times courts wish to reform the injustices inherent in rape trials, there is a big concern about defendants' rights. While law reforms may allow higher conviction and reporting rates for crimes of rape and sexual offense, they may also allow an increase in the number of innocent individuals being reported and convicted of rape.

At its beginnings, raping a woman was seen not as a crime against the victim, but against the male "owner" of the victim. More currently, many laws require a showing of force, in order to convict an assailant of rape. Accordingly traditional rape law required women to put up the utmost resistance to their assailants, as evidence that the assailant used force to overcome the victim's resistance. Courts used a "male standard," requiring female victims to follow the instincts of every proud female and fight back, despite the physical dangers and unfairness that may arise from this standard. One big problem with the "resistance" requirement was that courts would confuse this element with consent. In other words, if the victim did not physically resist, it was found hard to believe that she did not consent. Furthermore, although victims were not required to resist if there was a sufficient threat of force, victim's fear would have to be reasonable in order to convict perpetrators of rape. For instance, courts have held that a general fear, based on past experience with an assailant, is not sufficient to convict the assailant of rape. The threat of force, and the fear generated from that threat, would have to occur at the time of the rape, and had to have been specific to that crime.

In trying to equalize the law of rape, reformers have attempted to dispense with the resistance requirement. However, because the element of force still existed, it was difficult to determine exactly how much force or threat of force was required. On the one hand some courts have held that, although a female is not required to physically resist, verbal resistance alone is not sufficient evidence of forcible rape. On the other hand, some courts have held that the force element of rape is satisfied merely by the act of penetration, and that a rape is committed if there is no consent by words or actions. Decisions such as these, leave the task of rape law reform open for more change.

Traditional rape law also allowed a female rape victim to implicitly go on trial for her sexual history, despite exposure of the victim's private life. Today, most state rape laws contain rape-shield statutes, which restrict or prohibit evidence and cross-examination about a victim's prior sexual conduct and reputation. On the one hand, evidence such as this is rightfully excluded from trial, because of the embarrassment it causes a complainant, and because of the prejudice it might have on juries. On the other hand, excluding this evidence may impede a defendant's constitutional right to confrontation and cross-examination, or may exclude evidence that is relevant to the issues being adjudicated. Again, both the victims' and defendants' rights and interest must be weighed in considering what evidence rape-shield statutes may exclude from trial.

Another "rape law" issue deals with securing a victim's consent to sexual intercourse through the use of deception. Generally, courts have held that fraud-in-the-factum, will vitiate consent. For instance, if a patient consents to having medical treatment done to her, and allows the insertion of a medical instrument into her private area, but the doctor misleading replaces the surgical instrument with his penis, the doctor will be convicted of rape. Fraud-in-the-inducement, however will not vitiate consent. Thus, a person who voluntarily engages in the act of intercourse, but does so because she was deceived, will receive no redress from the law of rape. Arguably, obtaining consent by deception should be handled as they are now. Though "seducers" and liars may be despicable for obtaining consent through deception, these crimes should be held to a lesser degree than forcible rape.

Yet another issue of rape law deals with the mens rea or intent aspect of the crime. Rape is considered a general intent offense, meaning that a defendant can be found guilty, if the defendant had a morally blameworthy state of mind. Therefore, a mistake-of-fact as to the victims consent, may be used as a defense, if it is based on a reasonable and good faith standard.

Mens rea however, is not generally an element of statutory rape, which is sexual intercourse with a person under the age of consent as defined in the statute. According to this "strict criminal liability" law, rape is committed by completing the act of sexual intercourse, regardless of whether the minor consented to the act. Statutory rape is defended on grounds that the "immature" cannot understand the consequences and implications of the act of sexual intercourse, and must therefore be protected from the influences of the more mature. The perpetrator, must suffer the consequences if he is to invade this strong public policy of protecting the young. However, opponents of statutory rape laws believe that it is unfair to give criminal punishments on a strict liability basis, as people may be convicted despite having a good faith belief that the other person is old enough to give consent to sexual intercourse. Although both sides give compelling arguments, the Model Penal Code provides a good example of balancing both sides' interest, providing a mens rea element for statutory rape, only if the victim is over a certain age.

A final issue deals with the procedural aspect of rape trials. Specifically, it was traditionally required that juries in rape trials were given cautionary jury instructions, requiring the jury to treat a complainant's testimony with special care. This followed beliefs that false accusations of rape were easily made, but hard to defend. This would be especially true for the many cases where only the complainant and the accused had personal knowledge of the incident. Many courts today have dispensed with this requirement, finding no reason to assume that a victim's testimony in a rape trial, is less trustworthy than the victim's of other crimes. However this raises concerns about defending false accusations of rape. Following either method, just like all other issues in rape law, may tip scales of justice too far to one side.

Chapter Overview Outline
Rape

Chapter 8

NOTE: THE PURPOSE OF THIS OUTLINE IS TO ORGANIZE THE CASES SO THAT ONE CAN QUICKLY UNDERSTAND THE RELEVANCE OF EACH CASE TO THE COURSE. NO ATTEMPT IS MADE IN THIS OVERVIEW TO ADDRESS EVERY CONCEPT THAT MUST BE STUDIED. BE SURE TO READ THE ENTIRE CASEBOOK AND/OR OTHER MATERIALS TO GAIN A FULL UNDERSTANDING OF ALL CONCEPTS.

I.   Statistics and Social Context
  A.   "Rape" is forced sexual intercourse with a male or female without consent, by an offender of the same or different sex.
  B.   "Sexual Assault" includes a wide spectrum of victimizations including attacks or threats of unwanted sexual contact. U.S. Dept. of Justice, Bureau of Justice statistics:
    1.   Between 1993 and 1995, the number of rapes and sexual assault victims has dropped 30%. The 1993 rate translated into about 1 rape/ sexual assault for every 435 persons age 12 or older. The 1995 rate was about 1 offense for every 625 persons age 12 or older.
    2.   Rates of rape/sexual assault were highest among residents age 16 to 19, low-income residents, and urban residents, with no significant difference among racial groups.
    3.   Overall, about 91% of victims were female, and 99% of offenders were male.
    4.   A majority of rapes/sexual assaults were found to occur between 6 p.m. and 6 a.m., in or near the victim's home, without the presence of a firearm.
    5.   While most rapes/sexual assaults involved one offender with whom the victim was acquainted with, a majority of multiple-offender offenses involved strangers.
    6.   While a majority of victims took some form of self-protective action during the crime, such as resistance by struggling, just over half felt that their action helped. 1 out of 5 victims felt that resisting made the situation worse.
    7.   In 1995, 87% of recorded forcible rapes were completed crimes and the remainder were classified as attempts. Only about half of all reported forcible rapes were cleared by an arrest.
  C.   There is overwhelming sexism in the law of rape, revealed only when rape is examined relative to other crimes.
    1.   The criminal law reflects male views and male standards, imposing its judgement on men who have injured other men. This standard is applied to crimes committed against women in judging the conduct of women victims.
    2.   The law of rape inevitably treads on the explosive ground of sex roles, of male aggression and female passivity, of our understanding of sexuality, and areas where differences between a male and female perspective may be most pronounced. *Susan Estrich-Rape.*
  D.   While traditional rules for proving rape, which make it necessary for a victim to resist the assailant, may provide too difficult a task for a victim, it is necessary to ensure that modern law reform does not make it too easy for any individual to charge another with the crime of rape. *Roundtree v. United States.*

II.   Actus Reus and "Force"
  A.   General Principles of Traditional Forcible Rape:
    1.   Rape is the carnal knowledge of a woman, forcibly (traditionally necessitating that the victim physically resist) and against her will.
    2.   Actual force, sufficient to overcome the victim's physical resistance, or a reasonable threat of force, making it unnecessary for the victim to resist, is a necessary element of rape. *Rusk v. State.*
    3.   An implied threat of force, may be found sufficient to satisfy the "force" element of rape, and is a question solely within the jurisdiction of the jury. *State v. Rusk.*

a.   *However*, a general fear of force is not sufficient for a conviction of rape. The element of force or threat of force must occur at the time of the alleged rape, and must be used to obtain sexual intercourse. *State v. Alston.*

B.   Verbal resistance as Evidence of "Force"

1.   At one end of the spectrum the traditional view of rape is a scenario where a stranger puts a gun to the head of the victim, threatens to kill her or beats her, and then engages in sexual intercourse. But cases of rape are never this clear cut.

   a.   When less force is used, no injury is inflicted, when threats are inarticulate, or where the woman merely says no and does not fight, the understanding is different.

   b.   The law should evaluate the conduct of "reasonable" men, not according to a Playboy-macho philosophy that says "no means yes," but by according respect to a woman's words. *Susan Estrich-Rape.*

2.   Although resistance may no longer be required for a conviction for rape, verbal resistance alone is not sufficient to prove rape, absent a showing of forcible compulsion. *Commonwealth v. Berkowitz.*

   a.   However, transitions in rape law, which eliminate the element of resistance, have made it possible to satisfy the element of "force" by the mere act of completing sexual penetration, and have made it possible to prove rape where there is absence of affirmative consent by words or actions. *State of New Jersey in the Interest of M.T.S.*

C.   Deceptions and Non-physical Threats

1.   Using deceptions to obtain consent to intercourse will only vitiate a victim's consent to intercourse, if the deception used is fraud-in-the-factum and not fraud-in-the-inducement. *Boro v. Superior Court.*

2.   To say that those who use deceptions to obtain consent to sexual intercourse should not be considered in the same category as those who obtain consent through threats of bodily harm is one thing. To say that these persons have committed no crime at all is another.

   a.   What is most striking about these types of cases is the fact that had these men been seeking money instead of sex, their actions would plainly violate traditional state criminal prohibitions. Yet lying to secure sex is old-fashioned seduction, not considered a crime in most jurisdictions. *Susan Estrich-Rape.*

   b.   However, while this insight may be true as far as it goes, what bearing does it have on rape law? What would be the limits of liability for rape by fraud? Although in cases where fraud is used to obtain intercourse, the man is a despicable predator, labeling him a rapist may go too far. There has to be a distinction between coercion and the loss of bodily integrity due to the gravest of threats, which merit thegreater punishment of being called a rapist. *Vivian Berger-Not So Simple Rape.*

III.   Criminal Intent or Mens Rea

A.   Rape is a general-intent offense, requiring that a perpetrator possess a morally blameworthy state of mind regarding the female's lack of consent.

B.   A mistake-of-fact defense, negating a defendant's mens rea in the case of rape, as in other general intent offenses, must be based on a reasonable good faith standard. *Commonwealth v. Sherry.*

C.   Courts have held that a "reasonable mistake" may be a defense to the crime of rape, and that jury instructions should be given as to mistake-of-fact, unless there is no substantial evidence of equivocal conduct on the part of the female. *People v. Williams.*

IV.   Proving Rape

A.   Rape Shield laws and statutes prohibit or restrict evidence or cross-examination, concerning a victim's prior sexual conduct or reputation.

1. In determining the admissibility of evidence in rape trials, the interests of "rape shield" laws in protecting the victim, must be weighed against the defendant's constitutional rights of cross-examination and confrontation. *State v. Herdon.*

2. Evidence that is irrelevant to the issue of consent between the complainant and the defendant, such as the complainant's sexual conduct with third parties, should be excluded from trial by "rape shield" statutes. *People v. Wilhelm.*

B. Cautionary jury instructions require a jury to consider a witnesses' or complainant's testimony with special care because of the emotional involvement of the witness or complainant, and the difficulty of determining the truth of the allegations made by the witness or complainant.

1. Having no reason to continue the institutional assumption that alleged rape victims are less trustworthy witnesses than other victims of crime, courts have held that cautionary jury instructions are no longer required in rape trials. *State v. Bashaw.*

2. There are dramatic differences in the position of the criminal accused in the United States today from one so accused in the past, making cautionary jury instruction unnecessary, since defendants today have other protection from wrongful conviction. *People v. Ricon-Pineda.*

C. *The Model Penal Code Section 213.6(5)* justifications for requiring:

1. Cautionary jury instruction and

2. Corroboration of the complainant's testimony

D. Although it is a matter of speculation, many observers believe that false accusations are common in the context of rape.

E. There may be likely prejudice to defendants, merely arising from the emotional hostility generated from an accusation of rape.

F. It is difficult to defend a false accusation of a sexual offense, when the issues often boil down to attitudes, conflicting accounts, and confrontation.

V. Statutory Rape

A. Statutory Rape is committed when a person engages in sexual intercourse with another who is under age, as defined by the state's statute.

1. Generally, statutory rape has no mens rea or intent element, is committed merely by the act of having sexual intercourse with a person who is underage, and therefore does not allow for a mistake-of-fact as to the age of the other person as a defense. *Garnett v. State.*

B. The "strict liability" aspect of statutory rape is defended by the public policy objective, that protection of society, of the family, and of the infant demand that perpetrators be punished merely because of the act itself. *People v. Ratz.*

1. It is believed that persons who are under the statutorily defined age of consent, lack the capacity to give consent because they are too naïve and innocent to understand the implications and the nature of the act, and that therefore they need protection from mature influences. *People v. Hernandez.*

Roundtree v. United States

(Not Stated) v. (Not Stated)

581 A.2d 315 (1990)

M E M O R Y   G R A P H I C

Instant Facts

Concurrence in part and dissent in part, noting the unfairness of traditional rape trials, and the need to treat both parties equally in shaping law reforms.

Black Letter Rule

Improving rape law to redress the unfairness victims face at trial, must not dilute the determination that all defendants receive a fair trial.

Case Vocabulary

RAPE / SEXUAL ASSAULT: Sexual intercourse with another person, without the other person's consent, traditionally requiring the use of physical force or a sufficient threat of the use of force.

Procedural Basis: Appeal to the District of Columbia Court of Appeals.

Facts: Not Stated.

Issue: Do courts have a dual commitment to rape victims and criminal defendants?

Decision and Rationale: Not Stated.

Concurrence and Dissent: (Schwelb, J.) Yes. Improving rape law to redress the unfairness victims face at trial, must not dilute the determination that all defendants receive a fair trial. Under a legal tradition established by men, female victims of rape and sexual abuse were treated unfairly pursuant to a pervasive double standard of sexual morality. In a revealing passage in the Bible, rape was treated as an offense against the unmarried woman's father rather than against her. The rapist's punishment included payment to the "owner," and forced marriage to the victim, obviously giving the woman no choice about becoming the perpetrator's wife. Some two millennia later, Sigmund Freud, the father of psychoanalysis, still viewed the "exclusive right of possession of a woman," as the "essence of monogamy." This right demanded that the girl bring into marriage, no memory of past sexual relations. Until quite recently, the complaining witness in a sexual assault case was presumed to be so lacking in credibility that special rules of corroboration, unheard of in other crimes, were deemed necessary and appropriate. The defendant charged with a sexual offense could effectively put the victim on trial for her entire sexual history and reputation, in relation to the issue of consent. Thus, the most private facts of a woman's life were exposed to the world. Moreover, despite their perceived natural timidity and delicacy, victims of rape were required to put up the utmost resistance to their assailants before a guilty verdict would be sustained. Women that did resist vigorously were often treated as deriving sexual pleasure from being overcome. Therefore, it is hardly surprising that only a small percentage of rape cases and sexual abuse were reported, and that fewer still resulted in conviction. In reaction to these palpable injustices, the courts in this and other jurisdictions, took a number of measures to redress the balance. However, the end does not justify the means. Our commitment to eradicating past and present wrongs by improving rape laws, may not be permitted to dilute our determination that all defendants, including those charged with sexual offenses, receive their constitutional right to a fair trial.

Analysis:

This case serves as an introduction to the issue of rape, mentioning many of the topics that will be presented in detail in the following articles and cases. It starts by noting that the traditional view of rape, was seen as a crime against the male "owner" of the female victim, rather than a crime against the female herself. It moves on to illustrate the difficulties women had to face in attempting to convict a rapists, and what was at stake. More specifically, it notes that according to traditional rape law, women were required to put up the utmost resistance to their assailants. In other words, courts used a "male standard", requiring women to "fight back", despite the physical dangers and unfairness that may arise from this standard. Moreover, traditional law allowed a female rape victim to implicitly go on trial for her sexual history, despite exposure of the victim's private life. Though, in modern times, courts wish to reform the injustices inherent in rape trials, there is concern about the defendant's rights. As the opinion notes, the law has a conflicting dual commitment to rape victims and criminal defendants. While law reforms may allow higher conviction and reporting rates for crimes of rape and sexual abuse, they may also allow an increase in the number of innocent individuals being reported and convicted of rape. Thus inherent in the crime of rape, is the difficulty of determining the true victim in the trial. While traditional rules for proving rape may prove too difficult of a task for a victim, it is necessary to ensure that modern law reforms do not make it too easy for any individual to charge another with the crime of rape.

Rusk v. State

(Light Choker) v. (Community)
43 MD.App. 476, 406 A.2d 624 (M.D. 1979)

M E M O R Y   G R A P H I C

Instant Facts

A man is convicted of second degree rape, after meeting a twenty-one year old mother of two at a bar, bringing her up to his house, and having sexual intercourse her, despite the lack of force.

Black Letter Rule

Actual force or threat of force is a necessary element of rape.

Case Vocabulary

FORCE: A traditional element of rape requiring physical acts sufficient to overcome a victim's resistance.
THREAT OF FORCE: An explicit threat, which would render a victim unable to resist.

Procedural Basis: Appeal to the Court of Special Appeals of Maryland, of a conviction for second degree rape.

Facts: The victim was a twenty-one-year-old mother of a two-year-old son, separated but not divorced from her husband. After leaving her son with her mother, the victim attended a high school reunion, after which she and a female friend went bar hopping in the Fells Point Area of Baltimore, taking separate cars. At the third bar, the victim met Edward Salvatore Rusk (Rusk) (D). After conversing for about five or ten minutes, the victim agreed to give Rusk (D) a ride home. When they arrived at Rusk's home, the victim parked at the curb on the side of the street opposite from Rusk's (D) rooming house, but did not turn off the ignition. Rusk (D) asked the victim numerous times to come up to his apartment, which, as the victim testified, made her afraid. While the victim tried to convince Rusk (D) that she didn't want to go up to his apartment, stating that she was separated and that it might cause her marital problems especially if she was followed by a detective, Rusk (D) took the keys out of the car and walked over to her side of the car. Rusk (D) then opened the door and said, "Now will you come up?" The victim agreed, testifying that at that point, she was scared because she did not know where she was, whether to run, and could not think of anything else to do. After following Rusk (D) to the room, the victim was left alone while Rusk (D) went to the bathroom. However, the victim made no attempt to leave, and while there was evidence that there was a phone inside the room, the victim testified that she did not notice one. When Rusk (D) came back, he sat on the bed and pulled the victim onto the bed. The victim stated that she then removed her slacks and removed his clothes because Rusk (D) asked her to. After undressing, the victim testified that she was still begging Rusk (D) to let her leave, but that Rusk (D) continued to say, "no." At which point the victim stated that she was really scared, more from the look in his eyes. Not knowing what to say, the victim asked Rusk (D), "If I do what you want, will you let me go without killing me?" The victim then began to cry, and Rusk (D) putting his hands on the victim's throat, began to lightly choke her. At this point the victim asked, "If I do what you want, will you let me go?" After Rusk (D) said yes, the victim proceeded in doing what Rusk (D) desired. After the victim performed oral sex on Rusk (D), they had sexual intercourse. After the incident and upon arriving at home, the victim sat in her car and wondered about what Rusk (D) would have done if she did not assent to his wishes. Believing that the right thing to do was to report the incident, she immediately proceeded to Hillendale to find a police car. Rusk (D) was convicted of rape in the second degree and of assault. Rusk (D) did not challenge the conviction for assault, but appeals the conviction for rape.

Issue: Is actual force or the threat of force, an essential element to the crime of rape?

Decision and Rationale: (Thompson, J.) Yes. Actual force or the threat of force, is an essential element to the crime of rape. Evidence must warrant a conclusion that the victim resisted and that her resistance was overcome by force, or that she was prevented from resisting by threats to her safety. The victim's testimony offers no evidence of resistance to sex acts, nor any fear that would overcome her attempt to resist or escape. The possession of her keys may have deterred her vehicular escape, but not her departure seeking help in the rooming house or in the street. Furthermore, "the way he looked," fails utterly to support the requirement of fear. The victim argues that the issue of whether or not intercourse was accompanied by force or threats of force is one of credibility to be resolved by the triers of the fact. We cannot follow this argument. The trial judge on ruling on a motion to acquit, must first determine that there is legally sufficient evidence for the jury to find the victim was reasonably in fear. Cases from other jurisdictions have followed the rule that the victim's fear which overcomes her will to resist must be a reasonable fear. We find the evidence legally insufficient to warrant a conclusion that Rusk's (D) actions created in the mind of the victim a reasonable fear, that if she resisted, he would have harmed, or that faced with such resistance, he would have used force to overcome it. Although Rusk (D) lightly choked the victim, we do not believe that "lightly choking" along with all the facts and circumstances in the case, were sufficient to cause a reasonable fear which overcame the victim's ability to resist. At oral argument it was brought out that, "lightly choking," could have been a heavy caress. In the absence of any other evidence showing use of force by Rusk (D), we find that the evidence was insufficient to convict Rusk (D) of rape. Reversed.

Dissent: (Wilner, J.) The majority has effectively substituted their own view of the evidence for that of the judge and jury. In so doing, they have not only improperly invaded the province allotted to those tribunals, but has also perpetuated and given new life to myths about the crime of rape that have no place in our law today. There is clear evidence to show that Rusk (D) had vaginal intercourse with the victim, and that the act was against the victim's will. The point at issue is whether it was accomplished by force or threat of force. Courts often tend to confuse the two elements of force and lack of consent. The cause of this confusion is the notion that the victim must actively resist the attack upon her. Failure to do so entitles a court, as it seems, to find that there was no force or threat of force, that the act was not against the victim's will, or that the victim consented, leading ultimately to the conclusion that the victim was not raped. Thus, the focus is almost entirely on the extent of resistance, or the victim's acts, rather than those of her assailant, in the victim's reaction to the wrongful stimulus. Submission is not the

equivalent of consent, and I believe the real test is whether the assault was committed without the consent and against the will of the victim. In the instant case we know nothing about the victim and Rusk (D). We don't know how big they are, what they look like, whether one is bigger and stronger than the other, or what their past life experiences have been. Moreover, we do not know what the inflection was in Rusk's (D) voice as he dangled the car keys in front the victim, or what Rusk's (D) mannerisms were. However, the trial judge and the jury could discern some of these things, by observing the two people in court. If Rusk (D) had desired, and the victim had given, her wallet instead of her body, there would be no question about Rusk's (D) guilt of robbery. Taking the car keys under those circumstances would have certainly supplied the requisite threat of force and negated the element of consent. No one would seriously contend that because she failed to raise a hue and cry she had consented to the theft of her money. Why then is such life-threatening action necessary when it is her personal dignity that is being stolen? A judge and jury observing the witness and hearing the testimony, concluded without dissent that there was sufficient evidence to find beyond a reasonable doubt that Rusk (D) had sexual intercourse with the victim by force or threat of force against her will and without her consent. In other words, they found the extent of her resistance and the reasons for her failure to resist further were reasonable. Furthermore, there is no claim that the jury was misinstructed. Yet the majority of this Court, has simply concluded that the victim's fear was not a reasonable one, brushing aside the judgment of the trial court and jury.

Analysis:

This case serves as a good example of the traditional definition of rape, which requires the use of force or the threat of force upon the victim. First, in the instant case, the facts presented only illustrated a limited amount of actual force. Specifically, light choking was a use of force, but not sufficient to satisfy this element of rape. As stated in this opinion, "actual force" obligates the victim to provide some resistance, in order to show that the victim was overcome. A problem arises however, when more force is used by the perpetrator because of the victim's resistance, which places the victim in a much greater risk of danger. Although resistance leads to a clear cut case of "sufficient force", it places the victim in a position vulnerable to serious bodily injury. As the dissent points out, resistance in other crimes such as robbery, is not required nor advised, yet is an essential element when personal dignity, instead of property, is at stake. This is due to the fact, as the dissent states, that courts often confuse the elements of force and consent. Therefore, on the one hand, the consensual aspect of other crimes such as robbery, are often more distinguishable than in cases of rape or sexual abuse. Thus resistance provides evidence that the victim was not consenting. On the other hand however, there are many other ways to prove that the victim did not consent, making the elements of "actual force" and resistance unnecessary for that determination. Second, in the instant case, because the use of actual force was not illustrated by the facts, it was essential to a finding of rape that there was a sufficient threat of force. One can infer from the majorities opinion, that "fear of force" and "threat of force" are not the same. Though the victim may fear that the perpetrator may use force, this fear must be "reasonable". Thus the perpetrator must actually make an affirmative threat. The victim in this case may have believed that she was being threatened, and even asked Rusk (D), "If I do what you want, will you let me go without killing me?" However, this court found that although Rusk answered this question with a "yes," which may be taken as an "implied threat", this was insufficient to satisfy the "threat of force" element of rape. Therefore, it may be inferred that if there is no explicit threat towards the victim, then the victim's fear was not reasonable. As the dissent points out, despite the lack of an explicit threat, the "threat of force" may be implicitly based on, among other things, the size of the parties, their history, and the inflection of their voices. Therefore, since these were factors available only to the trial court, perhaps the "threat of force" issue should have been left for the trial court to decide.

State v. Rusk

(Community) v. (Light Choker)
289 Md. 230, 424 A.2d 720 (M.D. 1981)

M E M O R Y   G R A P H I C

Instant Facts

The Court of Appeals of Maryland affirms the trial courts conviction of second degree rape, finding that the reasonableness of the victim's apprehension of fear was a question of fact for the jury to determine.

Black Letter Rule

An implied threat is sufficient to satisfy the element of force for rape.

Case Vocabulary

IMPLIED THREAT OF FORCE: A reasonable threat of force that places a victim in apprehension of bodily harm, inferred by the circumstances, which renders the victim unable to resist.

Procedural Basis: Appeal to the Court of Appeals of Maryland, of a reversal by the Court of Special Appeals, of a conviction of second degree rape.

Facts: (See prior opinion for *Rusk v. State*.)

Issue: Is an implied threat sufficient to satisfy the element of force for rape?

Decision and Rationale: (Murphy, J.) Yes. An implied threat is sufficient to satisfy the element of force for rape. The reversal by the Court of Special Appeals was in error for the fundamental reason so well expressed in the dissenting opinion. The reasonableness of the victim's apprehension of fear was plainly a question of fact for the jury to determine. Reversed and remanded to the Court of Special Appeals with direction that it affirm the judgment of the Criminal Court of Baltimore.

Dissent: (Cole, J.) I agree with the Court of Special Appeals. Although we no longer require a female to resist to the utmost or resist where resistance would be fool hardy, we do require the victim's submission to stem from fear generated by something of substance. Submission by force is required, as a seducer does not equate with a rapist. The victim must follow the natural instinct of every proud female to resist, by more than mere words. She must make it plain that she regards such sexual acts as abhorrent and repugnant to her natural sense of pride, unless the defendant has objectively manifested his intent to use physical force to accomplish his purpose. In the absence of any verbal threat to do her grievous bodily harm or the display of any weapon and threat to use it, I find it difficult to understand how a victim could participate in these sexual activities and not be willing.

Analysis:

Though the court in this opinion correctly reversed the Court of Special Appeals, it did so based on the determination that questions of fact are rightly within the jurisdiction of the jury. However, this still serves as a good example of the traditional rule of forcible rape. Though the rule does not explicitly require resistance, it seems that resistance is essential to proving "force", specifically when no explicit "threat of force" is made. Again, although resistance may provide clear evidence of "actual force", it places the victim in a position susceptible to physical harm. As stated by the dissent, a woman is required to "follow the natural instinct of every proud female," and "resist" her assailant. However, this may not be realistic, or at the very least, fair. This implicit requirement of resistance requires a woman to take an active role in fighting back. Though many are capable of this, those that are passive are left with no redress for their injuries. Moreover, the dissent finds it incredible, that in the absence of any actual or constructive use of force, a person engaging in sexual acts does not consent. This illustrates how easy it is to confuse the elements of consent and force, though the two mean and require different things. Specifically, because resistance is seen as a necessary prerequisite to the finding of actual force, it is easy to mistake lack of resistance as implied consent. Second, it seems to the dissent that only explicit threats would make resistance unnecessary, and consent evidentiary. However, if a victim is in reasonable apprehension of bodily harm, the victim need not resist, despite the lack of an explicit threat. Therefore, as held by the majority, an implied or implicit threat of force may be sufficient to satisfy the "force" element of rape.

State v. Alston

(Community) v. (Ex-boyfriend)
310 N.C. 399, 312 S.E.2d 470 (N.C. 1984)

M E M O R Y   G R A P H I C

⚡ Instant Facts

An ex-boyfriend is convicted of the second rape of his ex-girlfriend, after having intercourse with her at his friends house, despite not using force on the day of the alleged rape.

⚖ Black Letter Rule

The element of force of threat of force must occur at the time of the alleged rape, and must be used to obtain sexual intercourse.

Case Vocabulary

FORCE / THREAT OF FORCE: Elements, either of which are necessary to a finding of rape, that must occur at the time of the rape, and used to obtain sexual intercourse.

Procedural Basis: Certification to the Supreme Court of North Carolina of a conviction for second degree rape.

Facts: At the time of the incident Cottie Brown (Brown) and Alston (D) had been in a consensual sexual relationship for six months. Brown testified that although she sometimes enjoyed their consensual sexual relations, she often had sex with Alston (D) just to accommodate him. On those occasions, she would stand still and remain entirely passive while Alston (D) undressed her and had intercourse with her. Furthermore, during the six months, the two had conflicts which, at times, involved some violence. Alston (D) had struck Brown several times during the relationship when she refused to give him money, or refused to do what he wanted. Around May 15, 1981, Alston (D) struck Brown after Brown refused to give Alston (D) money. Brown left the apartment she shared with Alston (D) and moved in with her mother. After Brown left, Alston (D) called her several times and visited her at Durham Technical Institute (DTI) where she was enrolled in classes. When he visited her they talked about their relationship, but Brown never broke off the relationship with Alston (D), because she was afraid that Alston (D) would be angry. She did not have intercourse with Alston (D) after May 15 until the alleged rape on June 15. On June 15, Alston (D) arrived at DTI by taxicab to find Brown standing close to the school door. After blocking Brown's path as she walked toward the door, Alston (D) asked Brown where she had moved. After refusing to tell him, Alston (D) grabbed Brown's arm and told her that she was going with him. Brown testified that it would have taken some effort to pull away. The two walked toward the parking lot and Brown told defendant she would walk with him if he let her go. Alston (D) then released her. Brown testified that she did not run away because she was afraid of him, although other students were nearby. Both began a casually paced walk around the neighborhood of the school while talking about their relationship. Alston talked about Brown's "dogging" him and making him seem a fool and about Brown's mother's interference in the relationship. When the two left the parking lot, Alston (D) threatened to "fix" Brown's face so that her mother could see he was not playing. While walking out of the parking lot, Brown told Alston (D) that she wished to go to class, but Alston (D) replied that she was going to miss class that day. Passing several people, the two walked along several streets and went down a path close to a wooded area where they stopped and talked. Alston (D) again asked where she had moved. Brown asked Alston (D) whether he would let her go if she told him. Alston (D) then asked whether the relationship was over and Brown told him that it was. Alston (D) then said that he had a right to make love to her again, to which Brown did not respond. The two turned around at that point and began walking towards a street they had walked down previously. Although Alston (D) did not say where they where going, when he said to Brown that he wanted to make love, she knew they were going to the house of a Alston's (D) friend Lawrence Taylor (Taylor), where they have gone on prior occasions to have sex. On the way there the two passed the group of men they had passed previously. However, Brown did not ask for assistance because some of the men were friends of Alston (D), and she assumed that they would not help. When they entered the house, Taylor was inside. Brown sat in the living room while Alston (D) and Taylor went to the back of the house and talked. When asked why she didn't leave at that point, Brown replied, "It was nowhere to go. I don't know. I just didn't." Alston (D) returned and began talking to Brown about another man she had been seeing. By that time, Taylor had left the room and perhaps the house. Alston (D) asked Brown if she was "ready." Brown replied by saying, "no," and informing Alston (D) that she did not consent to going to bed with him. Alston (D) began kissing her, then pulled her from the chair in which she had been sitting and started undressing her. He told her to lie down on the bed which was in the living room. She complied and Alston (D) pushed apart her legs and had sexual intercourse with her. Although Brown cried during the intercourse, she did not attempt to push Alston (D) away. Afterwards, they talked. Brown made a complaint to the police the same day. Alston (D) continued to call Brown after June 15, but she refused to see him. One evening Alston (D) called from a telephone both and told her that he had to talk. When he got to her apartment he threatened to kick her door down and Brown let him inside. Once inside, Alston (D) said that he had intended merely to talk to her, but that he wanted to make love again after seeing her. After Brown sat down and looked at Alston (D), he began kissing her, then picked her up and carried her to the bedroom. He performed oral sex on her and she testified that she did not try to fight him off because she found she enjoyed it. The two stayed together until morning and had sexual intercourse several times that night. Alston (D) was convicted of second degree rape. Alston (D) appeals.

Issue: Must force or the threat of force occur at the time of the offense and be used to obtain sexual intercourse?

Decision and Rationale: (Mitchell, J.) Yes. The element of force of threat or force must occur at the time of the alleged rape, and must be used to obtain sexual intercourse. Second degree rape involves vaginal intercourse with the victim both by force and against the victim's will. Consent by the victim is a complete defense, unless the consent was induced by fear of violence. If the particular acts of intercourse for which the defendant is charged were both by force and against the victim's will, the offense is rape without regard to the victim's consent given to the defendant for prior acts of intercourse. Here, Brown and Alston (D) have engaged in a prior continuing consensual relationship, making the determination of Brown's state of mind at the time of the alleged rape more difficult. The State ordinarily will be able to show Brown's lack of consent to the specific act charged, only by evidence of statements or actions by the victim which were clearly communicated to Alston (D) and which expressly indicated Brown's withdrawal of any prior consent and lack of consent to the particular act of intercourse. The State did introduce evidence that Brown did not consent to sexual intercourse with the defendant on June 15. Brown's testimony provided substantial evidence that the act of sexual intercourse was against her will. However, the State did not offer substantial evidence of the element of force. Actual physical force need not be shown in order to establish force sufficient to constitute an element of the crime of rape. Threats of serious bodily harm which reasonably induce fear thereof are sufficient. In the present case, there was no substantial evidence of either actual or constructive force. There is evidence that when the two walked out of the parking lot, Alston (D) told Brown he was going to "fix" her face so that her mother could see he was not "playing." However, although this threat and Alston's (D) act of grabbing Brown by the arm at the school may have induced fear, it appears to have been unrelated to the act of sexual intercourse. More important, the record is devoid of evidence that Brown was in any way intimidated into having sexual intercourse with Alston (D) by that threat or any other act on June 15. We note that the absence of an explicit threat is not determinative in considering whether there was sufficient force in whatever form to overcome the will of the victim. It is enough if the totality of circumstances gives rise to a reasonable inference that the unspoken purpose of the threat was to force the victim to submit to unwanted sexual intercourse. Here, although Brown's general fear of Alston (D) may have been justified by his conduct on prior occasions, there was no evidence that Alston (D) used force or threats to overcome the will of Brown. Therefore Brown's general fear was not sufficient to show that Alston (D) used force to support a conviction of rape. Reversed.

Analysis:

This case serves as another example of the traditional rule that rape requires the elements of lack of consent and use of force. The beginning of the opinion states that the victim clearly communicated to Alston (D), by her statements and actions, that she did not consent to sexual intercourse on June 15. However, the court does not find substantial evidence of actual force or threats of force, sufficient for a finding of rape. As the reader can plainly see from the facts, Alston (D) did make explicit threats to Brown. However, because these threats were not specifically made to obtain sexual intercourse, they were not sufficient to satisfy the element of force. Moreover, although the court states that they recognize the sometimes violent history of Brown and Alston's (D) relationship, they opine that Brown's general fear is not enough, absent force, or threats of force, to find that Brown's will was overcome into having sexual intercourse on June 15. Though it may seem that this case presents nothing new in comparison to the previous cases, it is important for two reasons. First, it does a very good job of illustrating that consent and force are two separate elements. Thus it shows that lack of consent alone, is not enough to support a conviction for rape. Second this opinion adds new concepts in findings of force. Specifically, the opinion requires that the use of force or threats of force, must be found to have occurred at the time of the offense, and must be specifically used to obtain sexual intercourse. Therefore, although the court states that it recognizes and understands Brown's "general fear," in consideration of her relationship to Alston (D), this fear is not sufficient absent an explicit threat used to obtain sexual intercourse. This occurrence is an example of how a victim of prior beatings and mistreatment, may be broken down to the point where nonconsensual intercourse may be obtained without the use or threatened use of immediate force. Thus, despite what the court states, it seems to ignore the fact that Brown had been the victim of violence in the past, and may have too narrowly focused their attentions to the absence of threats of force on June 15.

Commonwealth v. Berkowitz

(State) v. (College Student)

415 Pa. Super. 505, 609 A.2d 1338 (P.A. 1992)

M E M O R Y   G R A P H I C

Instant Facts

A college student is convicted of raping his girl friend in his dorm room, after the friend voluntarily entered his dorm room and repeatedly said "no" to his sexual advances, although she did not physically resist.

Black Letter Rule

Verbal resistance alone, is not sufficient evidence of rape.

Case Vocabulary

RESISTANCE: An implicit requirement to the finding of the element of force in rape convictions.

Procedural Basis: Appeal to the Superior Court of Pennsylvania, of a conviction for rape and indecent assault.

Facts: In the spring of 1988, Berkowitz (D) and the victim were both college sophomores at East Stroudsburg State University, ages twenty and nineteen years old respectively. At about 2:00 pm on April 19, 1988, the victim returned to her room after class and drank a martini to "loosen up a bit" before going to meet her boyfriend, with whom she had argued with the night before. Ten mintes later she walked to her boyfriend's dormitory lounge to meet him, but he had not yet arrived. Having nothing else to do, she walked up to Berkowitz's (D) room to look for Earl Hassel (Earl), Berkowitz's (D) roomate. Although the victim knocked on the door several times, there was no answer. After writing a note to Earl, the victim knocked again, and upon finding the door unlocked, walked in. She saw someone lying on the bed with a pillow over his head, whom she thought to be Earl. After lifting the pillow from his head, the victim realized it was Berkowitz (D). The victim asked Berkowitz (D) which dresser was his roommate's, and left the note. Before the victim could leave Berkowitz (D) asked the victim to stay and "hang out." She complied because "she had time to kill" and because she didn't really know appellant but wanted to "give him a fair chance." Berkowitz (D) asked her to give him a back rub but she declined, explaining that she did not trust him. Berkowitz (D) then asked the victim to have a seat on his bed, but instead, the victim sat on the floor, and the two conversed about a mutual friend and about the victim's problems with her boyfriend. Thereafter, Berkowitz (D) moved off the bed and down on the floor, and "kind of pushed [the victim] back with his body. It wasn't a shove, it was just kind of a leaning-type thing." Next Berkowitz (D) straddled and began kissing the victim. After the victim responded, "Look I gotta go. I'm going to meet [my boyfriend]," Berkowitz (D) lifted up her shirt and bra and began fondling her. The victim then said "no." After about thirty seconds of kissing and fondling, Berkowitz "undid his pants and moved his body up a little bit." Though the victim kept saying "no," she was unable to move. Berkowitz (D) then tried to put his penis in the victim's mouth. The victim did not physically resist, but continued to verbally protest in a scolding manner. Ten or fifteen seconds later, the two rose to their feet, and Berkowitz (D), ignoring the victim's complaints, locked the door so that no one could enter from outside. However, this lock, as the victim knew, could not lock people inside the room. Berkowitz (D) then put, but did not force the victim onto the bed, removed her sweatpants and underwear from one of her legs, and guided his penis into her vagina. The victim did not physically resist in any way while on the bed, nor did she scream, but testified that she "couldn't like go anywhere," and that, "it was like a dream was happening or something." After Berkowitz (D) was inside the victim, the victim began saying "no, no to him softly in a moaning kind of way…because it was just so scary." After about thirty seconds, Berkowtiz (D) pulled out his penis and ejaculated onto the victim's stomach. Immediately thereafter, Berkowitz (D) got off the victim, and said, "Wow, I guess we got carried away." To this the victim retorted, "No, we didn't get carried away, you got carried away." The victim then quickly got dressed, raced downstairs to her boyfriend who was by then waiting for her in the lounge, and began crying. After the victim and her boyfriend went up to his dorm room and cleaned the seamen off the victim's stomach, the boyfriend called the police. During trial, it was found by defense counsel on cross-examination, that two weeks prior to the incident, the victim attended a school seminar entitled, "Does 'no' sometimes means means 'yes'?" Among other things, the lecturer at this seminar had discussed the average length and circumference of human penises. After the seminar, the victim and several of her friends discussed the subject matter of the seminar over a speaker-telephone with Berkowitz (D) and his roommate Earl. The victim testified that during the conversation, she had spoken to Berkowitz (D) about the size of his penis, to which Berkowitz (D) suggested to the victim that the she "come over and find out." She declined. Furthemore, the victim testified that on two other occasions, she had stopped by

Berkowitz's (D) room while intoxicated. During one of those times, she laid down on his bed, but she testified that she did not remember if she asked Berkowitz (D) about his penis size again at that time. According to Berkowitz (D), the victim began communications after the seminar by asking him the size of his penis and whether he would show it to her. Berkowitz (D) suspected that the victim wished to pursue a sexual relationship with him because she had stopped by his room twice after the phone call while intoxicated, laying down on his bed with her legs spread and again asking to see his penis. He believed that his suspicions were confirmed when she initiated the April 19th encounter by stopping by his room, again after drinking, and waking him up. Berkowitz (D) testified that although he did initiate the first physical contact, the victim warmly responded to his advances by passionately returning his kisses. He conceded that she was continually whispering "no," but claimed that she did so while passionately moaning. Thus Berkowitz (D) took such protests to be thinly veiled acts of encouragement, and locked the door so that no one would walk in on them. The two then laid down on the bed, the victim helped him take her clothing off, and he entered her. Berkowitz (D) agreed that the victim continued to say "no" while on the bed, but carefully qualified his agreement, explaining that the statements were "moaned passionately." After hearing both accounts, the jury convicted Berkowitz (D) of rape and indecent assault, and Berkowitz (D) was sentenced to imprisonment of one to four years for rape, and a concurrent term of six to twelve months for indecent assault. Berkowitz (D) appeals his rape conviction.

Issue: Is verbal resistance alone, sufficient to prove that force was used?

Decision and Rationale: (Per Curiam) No. We contend that upon review, the facts show nothing more than what legal scholars refer as "reluctant submission." The victim herself admits that she was neither hurt nor threatened at any time during the encounter. She never screamed nor attempted to summon help, though the incident occurred in a college dormitory in the middle of the afternoon. There has never been an affirmed conviction for forcible rape under similar circumstances, and the evidence here fails to establish forcible compulsion. The Commonwealth's position is that the jury's conclusion that Berkowitz's (D) forcible conduct overcame the victim's will is reasonable. The victim was acquainted with Berkowitz (D) and had no reason to be fearful or suspicious of him, and her resorting to verbal resistance only is understandable. More importantly, perhaps, it is only her lack of consent that is truly relevant. It is entirely reasonable that Berkowitz (D) sat on the victim, pushed her on the bed and penetrated her before she had time to fully realize her plight and raise a hue or a cry. If the law required active resistance, rather than the simple absence of consent, speedy penetration would immunize the most violent attacks. But, contrary to Berkowitz's (D) argument Pennsylvania law says she can "just say no," which is what the victim said repeatedly. The trial court agreed with the commonwealth's position, but we cannot. If the jury could have reasonably determined from the evidence adduced that all of the necessary elements of the crime were established, then the evidence will be deemed sufficient to support the verdict. In Pennsylvania, the crime of rape in the first degree is defined as engaging in sexual intercourse with another person not his spouse, 1) by forcible compulsion, 2) by threat of forcible compulsion that would prevent resistance by a person of reasonable resolution, 3) who is unconscious, or 4) who is so mentally deranged or deficient that such a person is incapable of consent. The alleged victim need not resist.

The determination of whether there is sufficient evidence to demonstrate beyond a reasonable doubt that an accused engaged in sexual intercourse by forcible compulsion (which we have defined to include not only force or violence, but also moral, psychological or intellectual force used to compel a person to engage in sexual intercourse against that person's will) or by threat of such forcible compulsion that would prevent resistance by a person of reasonable resolution is, of course, a determination that will be made in each case based upon the totality of the circumstances that have been presented to the fact finder. Significant factors to consider include the ages of the victim and the accused, the respective mental and physical conditions of the victim and the accused, the atmosphere and physical setting in which the incident was alleged to have taken place, the extent to which the accused may have been in a position of authority, domination or custodial control over the victim, and whether the victim was under duress. There existed no significant disparity between the ages of the victim and Berkowitz (D), no physical or mental condition of one party differed from the other in any material way, nor was the atmosphere in any way coercive, as the victim freely walked into Berkowitz's (D) room and voluntarily stayed there. Furthermore, there was no evidence to suggest that Berkowitz (D) was in any position of authority or domination over the victim, nor that the victim was under duress. Indeed, nothing in the record manifests any intent of Berkowitz (D) to impose moral, psychological or intellectual coercion upon the victim. Nor is this a case of a threat of forcible compulsion. The victim herself has admitted during trial that Berkowitz (D) did not threaten her in any manner, and the record fails to reveal any express or even implied threat that would prevent resistance by a person of reasonable resolution. The commonwealth contends that since the victim did not consent to engage in the intercourse, any force used to complete the act of intercourse thereafter constituted "forcible compulsion." The precise degree of actual physical force necessary to prove "forcible compulsion" is a determination that will be made in each case based on the totality of the circumstances. Even in the light most favorable to the Commonwealth, the victim's testimony as to the physical aspects of the encounter cannot serve as a basis for "forcible compulsion." The record is devoid of any evidence regarding the respective sizes of the parties. Therefore we can only speculate as to the coercive effects of "leaning" against the victim or placing the "weight of his body" or top of her. Moreover, even if the record indicated some disparity in the respective weights or strength of the parties, such acts are not inconsistent with consensual relations. Thus, there is no evidence that the victim could not have at any time, removed herself from Berkowitz's (D) bed and left the room without any risk of harm or danger to herself whatsoever. These circumstances simply cannot be bootstrapped into sexual intercourse by forcible compulsion. Similarly inconclusive is the fact that the victim testified that the act occurred in a relatively brief period of time. At most, the physical aspects of the encounter establish that appellant's sexual advances may have been unusually rapid. However inappropriate such conduct may be seen to be, it does not, standing alone, prove that the victim was "forced to engage in sexual intercourse against her will." Lastly, we must consider the fact that during the encounter, the victim repeatedly and continually said "no." Unfortunately for the Commonwealth, this evidence alone cannot suffice to support a finding of "forcible compulsion." Although evidence of verbal resistance is unquestionably relevant in a determination of "forcible compulsion," it is not dispositive or sufficient evidence of "forcible compulsion". If the legislature had intended to define rape as nonconsensual intercourse, it would have done so. However, they defined rape as sexual intercourse by "forcible compulsion," and there is no evidence of such, nor mental coercion or threat in the instant case. Though it may seem that this reasoning is at odds with the "no resistance requirement," this requirement must be applied only to prevent any adverse inference to be drawn against the person who, while being "forcibly compelled" to engage in intercourse, chooses not to physically resist. Since there is no evidence that the victim was at any time "forcibly compelled" to engage in sexual intercourse, our conclusion is not at odds with the "no resistance requirement." We discharge Berkowitz (D) as to the rape conviction, and remand on the case for the indecent assault charge.

Analysis:

This case provides yet another example of the traditional rule of rape, where both the elements "non-consent" and "force" are necessary for criminal liability. Here, the court finds that although the victim did not consent to the intercourse, there was no force, threat of force, or some mental coercion which is necessary for rape. What is important to note about this case is the use of the word "no," which was consistently repeated by the victim. It is obvious from the decision that in order to prove force, the use of verbal resistance alone, is not sufficient. Although the court purports to follow a "no resistance requirement," in their determination of "force," physical resistance is still required unless the perpetrator uses or threatens the use of force. Thus, as the court states, although verbal protest is relevant evidence in proving that the intercourse was against the victim's will, it is not enough evidence for "forcible compulsion." Once again, the female victim is required to fight back whenever she can.

State Of New Jersey In The Interest Of M.T.S.

(Community) v. (Seventeen-Year-Old)

129 N.J. 422, 609 A.2d 1266 (N.J. 1992)

M E M O R Y   G R A P H I C

Instant Facts

A seventeen-year-old is convicted of the rape of a fifteen-year-old who was asleep at the time of penetration.

Black Letter Rule

Resistance is not a required element of rape.

Case Vocabulary

FORCE: An element of rape satisfied by the use of sufficient physical action needed to complete the act of sexual intercourse.

Procedural Basis: Certification to the Supreme Court of New Jersey of a conviction for acquaintance rape.

Facts: On May 21, 1990 fifteen-year-old C.G. was living in a town home with her mother, her three siblings, and several others including M.T.S. (D) and his girlfriend. M.T.S. (D), then age seventeen, was temporarily living at the home with the permission of C.G.'s mother. He slept downstairs on the couch, while C.G. had her own room on the second floor. At approximately 11:30 p.m. C.G. went upstairs after watching television with her mother, M.T.S. (D), and M.T.S.'s (D) girlfriend. According to C.G., earlier that day M.T.S. (D) had told her three or four times that he "was going to make a surprise visit up in [her] bedroom," but she did not take him seriously. She also testified that M.T.S. (D) had attempted to kiss her on numerous other occasions and at least once had attempted to put his hands inside of her pants, but that she had rejected all of his previous advances. On May 22, at approximately 1:30 am, C.G. awoke to use the bathroom. As she got out of bed, she found M.T.S. (D) standing in the doorway fully clothed. C.G. testified that M.T.S. (D) stated that, "he was going to tease [her] a little bit," but that she thought nothing of it. She then walked past him, used the bathroom, and then returned to bed, falling into a "heavy" sleep within fifteen minutes. The next thing C.G. recalled was waking up with M.T.S. (D) on top of her, her underpants and shorts removed, with his penis into her vagina. She immediately slapped M.T.S. (D) in the face and then, "told him to get off [her], and get out." She did not scream or cry out, and M.T.S. (D) complied in less than one minute after being struck. She said she did not know how long M.T.S. (D) had been inside of her before she awoke. C.G. said that after M.T.S. (D) left the room, she "fell asleep crying" because "[she] couldn't believe that he did what he did to [her]." She did not immediately tell anyone of the events that morning because she was "scared and in shock." C.G. was not otherwise harmed. According to M.T.S. (D), he and C.G. had been good friends for a long time, and their relationship "kept leading on to more and more." He testified that three days preceding the incident they had been "kissing and necking," and had discussed sexual intercourse. M.T.S. (D) also stated that C.G. encouraged him to "make a surprise visit up in her room." At exactly 1:15 am on May 22, he entered C.G.'s bedroom as she was walking to the bathroom. When she returned the two began kissing and eventually moved to the bed. After continuing to kiss and touch for about five minutes, the two proceeded to engage in sexual intercourse. According to M.T.S. (D), he "stuck it in" and "did it [thrust] three times, and then the fourth time," C.G. pushed him off and told him "stop, get off," and M.T.S. (D) "hopped off right away." After about one minute, M.T.S. (D) asked C.G. what was wrong and she replied with a slap to his face. He recalled asking her what was wrong a second time, and her replying, "How can you take advantage of me or something like that." The trial court found M.T.S. (D) guilty of second-degree sexual assault. The Appellate Division reversed determining that the absence of force beyond that involved in the act of sexual penetration precluded a finding of second-degree sexual assault. The State appeals.

Issue: Is resistance a necessary element of rape?

Decision and Rationale: (Handler, J.) No. Resistance is not a required element of rape. The New Jersey Code defines "sexual assault" as the commission "of sexual penetration....with another person" with the use of "physical force or coercion." An unconstrained reading of the statutory language indicates that both the act of "sexual penetration" and the use of "physical force or coercion" are separate and distinct elements of the offense. However, the Code does not provide assistance in interpreting the words, "physical force." Therefore the initial inquiry is whether the statutory words are unambiguous on their face and can be understood and applied in accordance with their plain meaning. The state asserts that "physical force" entails any amount of sexual touching brought about involuntarily. The Public Defender asserts that "physical force" entails a use of force sufficient to overcome lack of consent. Thus, sexual assault requires the application of some amount of force in addition to the act of penetration. Current judicial practice suggests that "physical force" entails "any degree of physical power of strength used against the victim, even though it entails no injury and leaves no mark." Common experience or understanding does not yield a conclusive result. The dictionary provides several definitions of force, including: 1) power, violence, compulsion, or constraint exerted on or against a person or thing, 2) a general term for exercise of strength or power to overcome resistance, or 3) strength or power of any degree that is exercised without justification or contrary to law upon a person or thing. Thus, because of the conflicting interpretations of "physical force," we must turn to the legislative intent, relying on legislative history and the contemporary context of the statute. The origin of the rape statute that the current statutory offense of sexual assault replaced can be traced back to English common law. Under the common law, rape was defined as "carnal knowledge of a woman against her will." Although American jurisdiction generally adopted the English view, over time they added the requirement that the knowledge have been forcible, apparently in order to prove that the act was against the victim's will. As of 1796, New Jersey statutory law defined rape as "carnal knowledge of a woman, forcibly, and against her will. Under traditional rape law, in order to prove that a rape had occurred, the state had to show both that force had been used and that the penetration had been against the woman's will. The presence or absence of consent often turned on credibility. To demonstrate that the victim had not consented to the intercourse, and also that sufficient force had been used to accomplish the rape, the state had to prove that the victim had resisted. Courts and commentators historically distrusted the testimony of victims. Evidence of resistance was viewed as a solution to the credibility problem, because it was an outward manifestation of nonconsent. The judicial interpretation of the pre-reform rape law in New Jersey, with its reliance on resistance by the victim, greatly minimized the importance of the forcible and assaultive aspect of the defendant's conduct, turning the focus to the victim's response. Reformers have emphasized empirical research indicating that women who resisted forcible intercourse often suffered far more serious injury as a result. That research discredited the assumption that resistance to the utmost was the most reasonable or rational response to a rape. Critics of rape agreed that the focus of the crime should be shifted from the victim's behavior to the defendant's conduct, and particularly to its forceful and assaultive, rather than sexual, character. There were, however, differences over the best way to redefine the crime. Some advocated a standard that defined rape as nonconsensual sexual intercourse, while others urged the elimination of any reference to consent from the definition of rape. Nonetheless all proponents of reform shared a central premise, that the burden of showing non-consent should not fall on the victim of the crime. In dealing with the problem of consent, the reform goal was to eliminate the burden that had been placed on victims to prove they had not consented. Similarly, with regard to force, rape law reform sought to give independent significance to the forceful or assaultive conduct of the defendant and to avoid a definition of force that depended on the reaction of the victim. In urging that the "resistance" requirement be abandoned, reformers sought to break the connection between force and resistance. The circumstances surrounding the actual passage of the current law reveal that it was conceived as a reform measure reconstituting the law to address a widely-sensed evil and to effectuate an important public policy. Those circumstances are highly relevant in understanding intent. We are thus satisfied that an interpretation of the statutory crime of sexual assault to require physical force in addition to that entailed in the act of involuntary or unwanted sexual penetration would be fundamentally inconsistent with the legislative purpose to eliminate any consideration of whether the victim resisted or expressed non-consent. Because the statute eschews any reference to the victim's will or resistance, the standard defining the role of force in sexual penetration must prevent the possibility that the establishment of the crime will turn on the alleged victim's state of mind or responsive behavior. We conclude, therefore, that any act of sexual penetration engaged in by the defendant without the affirmative and freely-given permission of the victim to the specific act of penetration constitutes the offense of sexual assault. Therefore, physical force in excess of that inherent in the act of sexual penetration is not required for such penetration to be unlawful. Persons need not expressly announce their consent to engage in intercourse for there to be affirmative permission. Permission to engage in an act of sexual penetration can be and indeed often is indicated through physical action rather than words. It is enough that a reasonable person would have believed that the alleged victim had affirmatively and freely given authorization to the act. We emphasize as well that what is now referred to as "acquaintance rape" is not a new phenomenon. The vast majority of sexual assaults are perpetrated by someone known to the victim. Similarly, contrary to common myths, perpetrators generally do not use guns or knives and victims generally do not suffer eternal bruises or cuts. This more realistic view of rape was a central concern of the proponents of reform in the 1970's. In a case such as this one, in which the State does not allege violence or force extrinsic to the act of penetration, the factfinder must decide whether the defendant's act of penetration was undertaken in circumstances that led the defendant to reasonably believe that the alleged victim had freely given affirmative permission to the specific act of sexual penetration. Such permission can be indicated through words or actions that, when viewed in the light of all the surrounding circumstances, would demonstrate to a reasonable person affirmative authorization for the specific act of sexual penetration. The focus must be on the nature of the defendant's actions. The role of the factfinder is to decide whether the defendant's belief that the alleged victim had freely given affirmative permission was reasonable. In these cases neither the alleged victim's subjective state of mind nor the reasonableness of the alleged victim's actions can be deemed relevant to the offense. In sum, in order to convict under the sexual assault statute in cases such as these, the State must prove beyond a reasonable doubt that there was sexual penetration and that it was accomplished without the affirmative and freely-given permission of the alleged victim. If there is evidence that the defendant reasonably believed that such permission had been given, the State must demonstrate either that defendant did not actually believe that affirmative permission had been freely-given or that such a belief was unreasonable under all of the circumstances. The trial court concluded that the victim had not expressed consent to the act of intercourse, either through her words or actions. We conclude that the record provides reasonable support for the trial court's disposition. Reversed.

Analysis:

This case exemplifies a transition in rape law. Specifically, the opinion in effect does away with the requirement of resistance. Although the element of "force" still expressly exists, the amount of force required amounts to as much force needed to complete the act of sexual penetration. Therefore, a male commits forcible rape, as long as he has intercourse without securing a consent or a "yes," either by words or actions. The female is not required to resist, nor required to say "no." The underlying reasoning of this case seems to be that a female should not be required to object to the male's sexual advances in order to render a subsequent act of penetration impermissible. It goes beyond the idea that "no means no," to the concept that "silence means no." Thus, the courts analysis raises a concern. What conduct short of an express "yes," is sufficient to constitute permission? The court states that actions may assert permission. However, the facts of the instant case tend to show that C.G. was willing to engage in consensual kissing and heavy petting, but that this permission did not extend to intercourse. Therefore, again, if there is no express consent or "yes" and no express "no", what actions will suffice short of express permission to have sexual intercourse? All in all this case leaves the jury to decide whether the evidence presented leads to the conclusion that the defendant was reasonable in his belief of the victim's consent. This case can be criticized for the court's decision to effectively ignore a statutory element of the crime that was specifically enacted by the legislature. It is rare to see a court assert that the plain and clear language of a criminal statute was not meant to be.

Boro v. Superior Court

(Donor) v. (State)

163 Cal. App. 3d 1224, 210 Cal. Rptr. 122 (1985)

M E M O R Y   G R A P H I C

Instant Facts

A man is charged with rape after fraudulently inducing a woman to have sex with him in order to cure her illness, and his motion to dismiss denied, despite the woman's consent to the intercourse.

Black Letter Rule

Fraud-in-the-factum, not fraud in the inducement, will vitiate consent to intercourse.

Case Vocabulary

FRAUD-IN-THE-FACTUM: Misrepresentation or concealment of the actual act about to occur or occurring.

FRAUD-IN-THE-INDUCEMENT: Misrepresentation or concealment which leads another to enter into a transaction with false or mistaken beliefs.

Procedural Basis: Appeal to the California Court of Appeal of a denial of a motion to dismiss a charge of rape.

Facts: The rape victim, Ms. R, received a telephone call from a person who identified himself as "Dr. Stevens" and said that he worked at Peninsula Hospital. "Dr. Stevens" told Ms. R. that he had the results of her blood test and that she had contracted a dangerous, highly infectious and perhaps fatal disease, from the use of public toilets. He further explained that there were only two ways to treat the disease. The first was a painful surgical procedure costing $9,000 and requiring uninsured hospitalization for six weeks. The second alternative was to have sexual intercourse with an anonymous donor who had been injected with a serum which would cure the disease. This would cost $4500. When Ms. R. stated that she lacked sufficient funds, "Dr. Stevens" suggested that $1000 would suffice as a down payment. Ms. R. then consented to intercourse with the anonymous donor, believing it was the only choice she had. [Perhaps the victim had an IQ equal to her age!] After discussing her intentions with her work supervisor, Ms. R proceeded to the Hyatt Hotel in Burlingame as instructed, and telephoned "Dr. Stevens." Dr. Stevens became furious when he learned Ms. R. had informed her employer of the plan and threatened to terminate his treatment, finally instructing her to inform her employer she had not decided to go through with the treatment. Ms. R. did so. She then went to her bank, withdrew $1000, and as instructed, checked into another hotel and called "Dr. Stevens" to give him her room number. About a half hour later, Boro (D) the "donor" arrived at her room and the two had sexual intercourse. Boro filed a motion to dismiss Count II, charging him with a violation of Penal Code 261 [which defines rape as an act of sexual intercourse with a person who is at the time unconscious of the nature of the act, and this is known to the accused]. The motion was denied. Boro (D) appeals.

Issue: Will fraud-in-the-inducement vitiate a victim's consent to intercourse?

Decision and Rationale: (Newsom, J.) No. Fraud-in-the-factum, not fraud in the inducement, will vitiate consent to intercourse. At the time of penetration, it was Ms. R.'s belief that she would die unless she consented to sexual intercourse with the defendant. The People contend that Ms. R. was "unconscious of the nature of the act" because Boro's (D) misrepresentation caused Ms. R. to believe that the intercourse was in the nature of a medical treatment, and not simply an ordinary act of intercourse. Boro (D) contends that Ms. R. was plainly aware of the nature of the act in which she voluntarily engaged, so that her motivation in doing so is irrelevant. There is sparse California authority on this subject. In one case, the defendant was a physician who "treated" several victims for menstrual cramps. Each victim testified that they were treated in a position with their back to the doctor, bent over a table, with feet apart, in a dressing gown. The treatment consisted of the defendant first inserting a metal instrument, then substituting an instrument which "felt different". The victim did not realize that the second instrument was in fact the doctor's penis. This case is useful to this analysis, because it exactly illustrates certain traditional rules in the area of our inquiry. Thus, as a leading authority has written, if deception causes a misunderstanding as to the fact itself, there is no legally-recognized consent because what happened is not that for which consent was given. This is fraud in the factum. Whereas consent induced by fraud is as effective as any other consent, if the deception relates not to the thing done but merely to some collateral matter. This is fraud in the inducement. The victim in this case consented, not to sexual intercourse, but to penetration by a medical instrument. The consent was to a pathological, and not a carnal, act, and the mistake was therefore in the inducement and not in the factum. The language of our statute could not be plainer. Courts of this state have previously confronted the general rule that fraud in the inducement does not vitiate consent. We can not entertain the slightest doubt that the legislature well understood how to draft a statute to specify fraud in the inducement as vitiating consent. If the legislature had desired to, it could certainly have done so. To so conclude is not to vitiate the heartless cruelty of Boro's (D) scheme, but that it comprised crimes of a different order.

Analysis:

This case brings up the issue of deceptions and non-physical threats in rape law. Specifically, its purpose is to lay out the common law distinction between consent that is obtained by fraud-in-the-factum vs. fraud-in-the-inducement. The Court does a good job of explaining, using a prior case as an illustration, that fraud in the factum vitiates consent. In general, fraud in the factum exists when the act consented to, differs from the act that actually took place. In the instant case, the fraud existed in a matter collateral to the act of sexual intercourse. Specifically, fraud was used to obtain consent to the act of sexual intercourse, but the victim knew that she had consented to the sexual intercourse. The Court here expressed that if the legislature wished to, it could have included fraud-in-the-inducement in the rape statute. The legislature understood that doing so would pose serious concerns about where to draw the line in rape cases. On the one hand, if fraud converted every act of sexual intercourse into rape, a male would be prosecuted every time he falsely claimed love or made promises that he did not intend to keep, in order to secure the female's consent to intercourse. In other words every "seducer" would be chargeable as a rapist. On the other hand, for example, what if a man fraudulently claimed that he did not have a sexually transmitted disease in order to obtain a female's consent. Arguably, cases involving fraud-in-the-inducement should be handled as they are now. As the court states, the perpetrator is not without blame, and falls into a lesser category than "rapist." He should be punished to a lesser degree than someone who used force to obtain sexual intercourse.

Commonwealth v. Sherry

(State) v. (Doctor)
386 Mass. 682, 437 N.E.2d 224 (1982)

M E M O R Y   G R A P H I C

Instant Facts

Three doctors are convicted of rape after taking a nurse to a house and separately having intercourse with her, despite the doctors' mistake-of-fact as to the nurse's consent.

Black Letter Rule

A defense of mistake-of-fact must be based on a reasonable good faith standard.

Case Vocabulary

MISTAKE-OF-FACT: A reasonable or good faith mistake, concerning the existence of an essential element of a crime.

Procedural Basis: Certification to the Supreme judicial court of Massachusetts of a conviction for rape.

Facts: The victim, a registered nurse, and defendants, all doctors, were employed at the same hospital in Boston. On September 5, 1980, Sherry (D1), along with another doctor, was a host at a party for some hospital staff. At this party, the victim had a conversation with Hussain (D2), during which he made sexual advances toward her. Later in the evening, Hussain (D2) and Sherry (D1) pushed her and Lefkowitz (D3) into a bathroom together, shut the door, and turned off the light. They did not open the door until Lefkowitz (D3) asked them to leave her in peace. At various times, the victim danced with both Hussain (D2) and Sherry (D1). Some time later, Hussain (D2) and Sherry (D1) grabbed the victim by her arms and pulled her out of the apartment, as Lefkowitz (D3) said, "We're going up to Rockport." The victim verbally protested but did not physically resist the men because she thought that they were just "horsing around." Nor was she physically restrained as they rode down an elevator with an unknown fifth person, or as they walked through the lobby of the apartment building. The victim testified that once outside, Hussain (D2) carried her over his shoulder to Sherry's car and held her in the front seat as the four drove to Rockport. En route she engaged in superficial conversation with the three defendants. She testified that she was not in fear at this time. When they arrived at Lefkowitz's (D3) home in Rockport, she asked to be taken home. Instead Hussain (D2) carried her into the house. Once in the house, the victim and two of the men smoked marijuana, and all of them toured the house. After being invited by Lefkowitz (D3) to view an antique bureau in a bedroom, all of them entered and the men began to disrobe. Although the victim was frightened and began to verbally protest, the three men proceeded to undress her and maneuver her onto the bed. One of the defendants attempted to have the victim perform fellatio while another attempted intercourse. After the victim told them to stop, two of the defendants left the room temporarily, and each defendant separately had intercourse with the victim in the bedroom. The victim testified, that she felt physically numbed, humiliated, and disgusted and could not fight. After this sequence of events, the victim claimed that she was further sexually harassed and forced to take a bath. Some time later, Lefkowitz (D3) told the victim that they were returning to Boston because Hussain (D2) was on call at the hospital. On their way back, the group stopped to view a beach, eat breakfast, and get gasoline. The victim was taken back to where she left her car and drove herself home. The defendants testified to a similar sequence of events, although details of the episode varied significantly. According to their testimony, Lefkowitz (D3) invited Sherry (D1) to accompany him from the party to a home that his parents owned in Rockport. The victim, upon hearing this, inquired as to whether she could go along. As the three were leaving, Sherry (D1) extended the invitation to Hussain (D2). At no time did the victim indicate her unwillingness to accompany the defendants. Upon arrival in Rockport, the victim wandered into the bedroom where she inquired about the antique bureau. She sat down on the bed and kicked off her shoes, whereupon Sherry (D1) entered the room, dressed only in his underwear. Sherry (D1) helped the victim get undressed, and she proceeded to have intercourse with all three men separately in turn. Each defendant testified that the victim consented to the acts of intercourse. Sherry (D1), Hussain (D2), and Lefkowitz (D3) were convicted of rape without aggravation. Sherry (D1), Hussain (D2), and Lefkowitz (D3) appeal.

Issue: Must a defense of mistake-of-fact as to whether consent was given be based on a reasonable good faith standard?

Decision and Rationale: (Liacos, J.) Yes. Sherry (D1), Hussain (D2), and Lefkowitz (D3) contend that the judge's jury charge was inadequate and the cause of prejudicial error. However the instructions given by the trial judge placed before the jury the essential elements of the crime required to be proved.

The judge instructed the jury that intercourse must be accomplished with force sufficient to overcome the woman's will, or by threats of bodily harm, inferred or expressed, which engendered sufficient fear so that it was reasonable for her not to resist. These instructions correctly stated the elements of proof required for a rape conviction. Sherry (D1), Hussain (D2), and Lefkowitz (D3), appear to have been seeking to raise a defense of good faith mistake on the issue of consent. They would require the jury to "find beyond a reasonable doubt that the accused had actual knowledge of [the victim's] lack of consent." In doing so, they argue that mistake-of-fact negating criminal intent is a defense to the crime of rape. A defense of mistake-of-fact must be based on a reasonable good faith standard. Whether a reasonable good faith mistake-of-fact as to consent is a defense to the crime of rape has never to our knowledge, been decided in this Commonwealth. We do not reach the issue whether a reasonable and honest mistake to the fact of consent would be a defense, for even if we assume it to be, the defendants did not request a jury instruction based on a reasonable good faith standard. We are aware of no American Court of last resort that recognizes mistake-of-fact, without consideration of its reasonableness as a defense, nor do the defendants cite such authority. Affirmed.

Analysis:

This case raises the issue of the mens rea or intent aspect of the crime of rape. Rape is a general-intent offense. Therefore a defendant is guilty of rape if he possessed a morally blameworthy state of mind regarding the female's lack of consent. Thus, as a general rule, a person is not guilty of rape if he entertained a genuine and reasonable belief that the female voluntarily consented to intercourse with him. As you can see, this rule conforms with ordinary common law mistake-of-fact doctrine relating to general-intent offenses. As illustrated by the opinion, the issue of mens rea rarely arises in rape prosecutions. Most likely, the reason for this is because in traditional rape prosecutions, the element of force required to secure intercourse, would effectively invalidate a claim that the perpetrator was mistaken with regards to consent. However, the issue of mens rea is more significant in acquaintance-rape prosecutions, in jurisdictions where the resistance rule has been eliminated, and in jurisdictions where a conviction may be obtained in the absence of force beyond that which is necessary for intercourse. Moreover, the analysis of this issue is the same in rape cases, as it is in other general-intent offenses. All in all, the main purpose of this case is to show the reader that, although the issue of mens rea and the defense of mistake-of-fact is rare in rape cases, it is worth attention.

State v. Herndon

(Not Stated) v. (Not Stated)

145 Wis.2d 91, 426 N.W.2d 347

M E M O R Y   G R A P H I C

Instant Facts

Opinion by the Court of Appeals of Wisconsin discussing the process of weighing a defendant's Sixth Amendment rights against the interest of rape-shield laws, when determining the admissibility of evidence.

Black Letter Rule

The interest of rape-shield laws (which prohibit the cross-examination of rape victims) and a defendant's Sixth Amendment rights must be weighed in order to determine whether certain evidence should be admissible.

Case Vocabulary

RAPE-SHIELD LAW: A statute which prohibits or restricts evidence or cross-examination concerning a victim's prior sexual conduct or reputation.

Procedural Basis: Opinion by the Court of Appeals of Wisconsin discussing rape shield legislation.

Facts: Not Stated.

Issue: Should the interests of "rape shield" laws be weighed against a defendants constitutional rights in determining the admissibility of evidence?

Decision and Rationale: (Morse, J.) Yes. The Sixth Amendment to the United States Constitution guarantees a defendant a fair trial by providing him with the right to cross-examine all witnesses against him. It also guarantees a defendant the right to compulsory process of witnesses to testify on his behalf. The United States Supreme Court, when addressing a state statute that impinges on these confrontation and compulsory rights, has resorted to a balancing test in which the state's interest in enacting a statute is weighed against the defendants constitutional interests. Rape shield laws have been enacted by almost every state. In general, they deny a defendant in a sexual assault case the opportunity to examine the complainant concerning her prior sexual conduct or reputation. They also deny the defendant the opportunity to offer extrinsic evidence of the prior sexual conduct, or reputation for sexual conduct or practices of the complainant. Rape shield laws were implemented to overcome the invidious and outrageous common law evidentiary rule allowing complainants to be asked in depth about their prior sexual experiences for the purpose of humiliation and harassment and to show unchastity. These statutes reflect the judgment that most evidence about chastity has far too little probative value on the issue of consent to justify extensive inquiry into the victim's sexual history. According to Professor Harriett R. Galvin, rape shield laws can be categorized into four approaches. The Michigan approach are general prohibitions on prior sexual conduct or reputation evidence, but have highly specific exceptions allowing for this evidence in those circumstances in which it is highly relevant and material to the presentation of a defense and therefore constitutionally required. For example, under the Massachusetts rape shield law, exceptions are made for prior consensual acts with the defendant or recent conduct of the complainant which would explain her physical features, characteristics, or conditions. The evidence is first submitted to the trial court in an in camera hearing so that the court may weigh the relevancy of the evidence against its prejudicial effect on the victim. Policies for this type of rape shield law include: 1) preventing the harassment and humiliation of the complainant, 2) keeping out evidence that has no bearing on the issue of consent at the time in question, 3) excluding evidence in order to keep the jury focused on issues relevant to the case at hand, and 4) promoting effective law enforcement because a victim will more readily report and testify in sexual assault cases if she does not fear that her prior sexual conduct will be brought before the public. Laws written under the Texas approach are purely procedural in nature and often involve "untrammeled judicial discretion." For example, Arkansas' rape shield law provides that, notwithstanding a general prohibition of opinion, reputation or specific sexual conduct evidence, evidence of the complainant's prior sexual conduct with the defendant or any other person, may be used provided certain procedures are followed, and the trial court determines that the probativeness of the evidence outweighs its prejudicial nature. Oregon's rape shield law is a good example of the federal approach. Its key features include: 1) a general prohibition of sexual conduct or reputation evidence, 2) exceptions allowing for this evidence in circumstances where the evidence is undeniably relevant to an effective defense, and 3) a general "catch-basin" provision allowing for the introduction of relevant evidence on a case by case basis. The key feature of the California approach is that the sexual conduct or reputation evidence is separated into two categories. Evidence offered to prove consent is generally inadmissible unless the evidence concerns prior sexual conduct between the complainant and the defendant.

However, any sexual conduct or reputation evidence may be used to attack the complainant's credibility as long as the trial court determines that it is relevant to the issue. Since their creation, rape shield laws have generally passed constitutional muster. Because the probativeness of the evidence is so minuscule when compared the potential prejudice, the Sixth Amendment rights must bend to protect the innocent victims. On the other hand, the courts have also universally held that both cross-examination and witnesses brought on behalf of the defendant may show prior consensual sex if that evidence shows a complainant's unique pattern of conduct similar to the pattern of the case at hand, or shows that the complainant may be biased or have motives to fabricate the charges. In such cases, the issues of a witness' bias and credibility are not collateral, and the rape shield laws must give way to the Sixth Amendment.

Analysis:

This case serves as an introduction to what is known as "rape-shield" laws. As this case states, rape-shield statutes have been enacted in virtually every state. Although, as you can see from the different approaches noted in the opinion, these laws vary, they generally deny the defendant in a rape trial the opportunity to cross-examine the complainant, or to offer extrinsic evidence, concerning her prior sexual conduct or reputation absent good cause. On the other hand, while protecting the victim's interests, these laws may also increase the risk that an accused person might be denied the opportunity to introduce evidence that would demonstrate his innocence. Furthermore, rape-shield laws may conflict with the defendants Sixth Amendment right to confront and cross-examine his accusers. This opinion does a good job of illustrating that these constitutional rights are not absolute, and that the interest of the rape-shield laws must be weighed against the defendant's needs, in determining which evidence should be admissible. All in all, the main purpose of this case is to give background information into rape-shield laws.

PUBLIC SEXUAL CONDUCT WITH OTHERS HELD NOT RELEVANT TO THE ISSUE OF CONSENT

People v. Wilhelm

(Society) v. (Observer)
190 Mich. App. 574, 476 N.W.2d 753 (M.I. 1991)

M E M O R Y   G R A P H I C

Instant Facts

A man is convicted of third-degree criminal sexual conduct, after not being allowed to introduce evidence that he and his friend observed the complainant expose her breasts to others at a tavern.

Black Letter Rule

Evidence of a victim's sexual conduct with a third party is irrelevant to the issue of consent with the defendant.

Procedural Basis: Appeal to the Michigan Court of Appeals of a conviction for third-degree criminal sexual conduct.

Facts: Wilhelm (D) was convicted of third-degree criminal sexual conduct, and sentenced to a three to nine month prison term. Wilhelm (D) appeals claiming that the trial court abused its discretion when it prohibited him from introducing certain testimony concerning alleged prior acts of the victim. Both the victim and Wilhelm (D) were at a bar, but not together. Wilhelm (D) and another witness observed the victim lift up her shirt and expose her breast to two men who were sitting at her table. During trial the prosecutor argued that the rape-shield statute [which provides evidence of specific instances of the victim's sexual conduct and reputation shall not be admitted unless the judge finds that the evidence is material to a fact at issue in the case] prohibited evidence of the victim's conduct at the bar. Wilhelm (D) moved to have this evidence admitted as relevant to the issue of whether the victim had consented to intercourse with him later that evening. In support of his argument Wilhelm (D) turned to *State v. Colbath*, a New Hampshire case, claiming that the two states have similar rape-shield statutes. In *Colbath*, the victim and defendant engaged in public sexual relations in a tavern, then proceeded to the defendants trailer where they had intercourse. The defendant's live-in companion after discovering the two, violently assaulted the victim. The New Hampshire Supreme Court held that the defendant's right of confrontation required that the defendant be allowed to demonstrate that the probative value of the inadmissible evidence outweighed its prejudicial effect on the victim. The court noted that the public character of the complainant's behavior was significant. On the one hand, her open and sexually suggestive conduct has far less potential for damaging the sensibilities than revealing what the same person may have done behind closed doors. On the other hand, evidence of public displays can be taken to indicate a contemporaneous receptiveness to sexual advances that cannot be inferred from evidence of private behavior with chosen sex partners. It would understate the importance of such evidence to hold it as merely relevant.

Issue: Is evidence of sexual conduct with third parties relevant to the issue of consent?

Decision and Rationale: (Per Curiam) No. Evidence of a victim's sexual conduct with a third party is irrelevant to the issue of consent with the defendant. Wilhelm (D) treats the statute's purpose of protecting the victim's privacy as though it extends only to private acts. However, one of the purposes of the law is to encourage victims to report and testify without fear that the trail court's proceeding would veer from an impartial examination of the accused's conduct on the date in question, and instead take on the aspects of an inquisition during which the victim would be required to acknowledge and justify her sexual past. Furthermore, we fail to see how a woman's consensual sexual conduct with another in public indicates to third parties that the woman would engage in similar behavior with them. Finally, Wilhelm (D) contends that the preclusion of the evidence under the rape-shield law deprived him of his right of confrontation. Moreover, evidence of a victim's sexual conduct with a third party is irrelevant to the issue of whether she consented to sexual relations with him. We believe *Colbath* is distinguishable. There the victim's behavior constituted a public display of general interest in sexual activity with which the defendant was directly involved. Moreover, the victim in *Colbath* had left the bar with various men several times during the afternoon, and the beating she had received from the defendant's live-in companion in that case provided a motive for fabrication.

Analysis:

This case serves as an illustration of the balancing test, weighing the defendants rights against victim's and rape-shield statute's interest, in determining the admissibility of evidence. Specifically, it's purpose is to get the reader thinking about whether evidence of a victim's sexual conduct should be inadmissible because it is irrelevant, or should it be inadmissible because it is prejudicial. Here, it is important to mention that evidence may not be admissible because it is irrelevant. That is, it does not pertain to the particular issue being decided in a trial. However, evidence may also be inadmissible, because it is highly prejudicial to a party. That is, the evidence may be relevant in deciding the issue at hand, but would cause a jury to concentrate less on the real issue, and more on the evidence which was presented. Therefore, the probative value of the evidence, may be outweighed by its prejudicial effect on the opposing party. For example, in the instant case, if evidence was introduced concerning the victim's prior sexual conduct with others at the tavern, a jury may concentrate highly on the character of the witness and her actions with others while at the tavern, and give too little thought to the main issue in the case, the victims consent to Wilhelm(D). If so, then this evidence is inadmissible because it is highly prejudicial to the victim's case. In the opinion, however, the court determined that this evidence was inadmissible because it was irrelevant. It distinguished *Colbath* by finding that the victim's actions with others were irrelevant to the issue of consent with Wilhelm. It must be remembered however, that the defendant let other men fondle her uncovered breast in a public tavern, and then went home with Wilhelm (D). It seems that because there were no witnesses to corroborate either parties stories, this does not seem wholly irrelevant to the issue of consent. At the least, it could create a reasonable doubt regarding Wilhelm's (D) mens rea. However, it would be highly prejudicial to the victim.

State v. Bashaw

(Society) v. (Cautionary Instruction Rapist)
296 Or. 50, 672 P.2d 48

M E M O R Y   G R A P H I C

Instant Facts
A man is convicted of first degree rape, and appeals contending that the trial court erred by reusing to give a cautionary jury instruction.

Black Letter Rule
Cautionary jury instructions are not mandatory in rape trials.

Case Vocabulary

CAUTIONARY JURY INSTRUCTIONS: Jury instructions which require a jury to consider a witnesses' or complainant's testimony with special care because of the emotional involvement of the witness or complainant, and the difficulty of determining the truth of the allegations made by the witness or complainant.

Procedural Basis: Certification to the Supreme Court of Oregon for a conviction for first degree rape.

Facts: During a rape trial, the court refused to give Bashaw's (D) requested jury instruction. The instruction read, " A charge such as that made against the defendant in this case one which is easily made and once made difficult to defend against even if the person accused is innocent. Therefore, the law requires that you examine the testimony of the female person named in the Information with caution." Bashaw (D) was convicted of first degree rape and attempted rape in the first degree. Bashaw (D) appeals contending that the trial court erred by refusing to give his requested instruction.

Issue: Are cautionary jury instructions mandatory in rape trials?

Decision and Rationale: (Jones, J.) No. Cautionary jury instructions are not mandatory in rape trials. Bashaw's (D) instruction should never be given in any rape case. A jury may imply form this instruction that the court is expressing reservations about the credibility of the alleged victim. The jury has the duty of weighing and evaluating the credibility of all witnesses. This instruction was spawned over 70 years ago by Lord Chief Justice Mathew Hale. His comment does not reflect contemporary thought or experience. This instruction assumes that the charge of rape is easily made. In fact, quite the opposite is true. The crime is one of degradation as well as violence, fear of reprisal and embarrassment contributes to the victim's hesitation to report it. Those who do report it must confront the trauma of the encounter with the police, the investigation of the crime and the ordeal of trial. The instruction also incorrectly states that the charge of rape is more difficult to defend against than other crimes. Of adults arrested, only sixty percent were charged, and almost half were acquitted or had the case dismissed. In thirty-five percent of these cases, the defendant was convicted of rape, and in sixteen percent, of some lesser offense. As compared to other crimes, these charging and conviction figures rank very low. Thus, we find no reason to continue the institutional assumption that alleged rape victims are less trustworthy witnesses than other victims of crime. We do not say a trial court may never approve a cautionary instruction involving a witness. The interest of justice may require an appropriate instruction in a special situation. But, this is not such a case.

Analysis:

This case continues the analysis concerning the weighing of a victim's and defendant's rights in sexual offense trails. Specifically it brings up the issue of cautionary jury instructions, which were often used and not uncommonly mandatory in many jurisdictions. Cautionary jury instructions, such as the one in this case, required the jury to treat a complainant's testimony with special care, because of the difficulty of determining the truth of alleged sexual activity that occurred in private. As stated in the opinion, the practice of giving cautionary jury instructions in rape trials came about for many reasons. These reasons include the assumptions that accusations of a sexual offense are easily made, hard to defend, and that maybe a jury would be likely prejudiced from the start, because of the emotional hostility created by the crime of rape, that they would be quick to convict someone accused. The opinion in this case provides the other side of the coin, arguing that these cautionary instructions have no place in today's rape cases. It argues, specifically, that victim's hesitate to report occurrences of sexual offenses, and that statistics prove the difficulty of convicting those charged. The question of whether cautionary jury instructions should be given in rape prosecutions, or for that matter should be made mandatory, is not easy to answer. As with other issues presented in this chapter, decisions such as this one may necessarily tip the balance too far to one side when weighing the interests of both parties. For this reason, this court correctly does not extend their holding to every rape case, but instead allows other courts to make a case by case, witness by witness, determination of whether to give a cautionary jury instruction.

Garnett v. State

(Mentally Disabled Man) v. (Society)
332 Md. 571, 632 A.2d 797

M E M O R Y   G R A P H I C

Instant Facts

A mentally disabled twenty-year-old man is convicted of statutory rape, after engaging in sexual relations with a thirteen-year-old girl friend, despite the lack of criminal intent.

Black Letter Rule

Criminal intent or mens rea, is not an element of statutory rape.

 ## Case Vocabulary

STATUTORY RAPE: Sexual intercourse with another, who is under the statutorily defined age of consent.

Procedural Basis: Appeal to the Court of Appeals of Maryland of a conviction for second degree rape.

Facts: At the time of the incident, Raymond Lennard Garnett (Garnett) (D) was a twenty-year-old, mentally disabled man, with an I.Q. of 52. According to his guidance counselor, Garnett (D) interacted with others socially at school at the level of someone 11 or 12 years of age. Garnett (D) attended special education classes, and for at least one period of time, was educated at home when he was afraid to return to school due to his classmates taunting. He was unable to complete vocational assignments, or pass any State's functional tests required for graduation. Garnett (D) eventually received only a certificate of attendance rather than a high-school diploma. In November or December 1990, a friend introduced Garnett (D) to Erica Frazier (Erica), then aged 13. The two then subsequently talked occasionally by telephone. On February 28, 1991, Garnett (D), apparently wishing to call for a ride home approached Erica's house at about nine o'clock in the evening. Erica opened her bedroom window, and Garnett (D) took a ladder and climbed up. The two talked and later engaged in sexual intercourse. On November 19, 1991, Erica gave birth to Garnett's (D) baby. Garnett was subsequently convicted of second degree rape under § 463(a)(3) of Maryland's rape statute [which provided that a person is guilty of second degree rape if the person engages in vaginal intercourse with another person who is under 14 years of age, and the person performing the act is at least four years older]. At trial Garnett (D) proffered evidence to the effect that Erica herself and her friends had previously told Raymond that she was 16 years old, and that Garnett (D) acted with that belief. The trial court excluded the evidence as immaterial, opining that the violation was a strict liability offense. Garnett (D) was sentenced to five years probation and ordered to pay restitution. Garnett (D) appeals.

Issue: Is criminal intent or mens rea a necessary element for a conviction of statutory rape?

Decision and Rationale: (Murphy, J.) No. Criminal intent or mens rea, is not an element of statutory rape. The Maryland statute does not expressly set forth a requirement that the accused have acted with a criminal state of mind, or mens rea. Garnett (D) contends that criminal law exists to assess and punish morally culpable behavior, and essentially asks us to engraft an implicit mens rea requirement to the statute. Modern scholars generally reject the concept of strict criminal liability as unjust, because the actor is subjected to the stigma of a criminal conviction without being morally blameworthy. Thus, criminal sanctions are inappropriate in the absence of a mens rea, whether based on preventive or retributive principles. Dean Singer has articulated some weaknesses of strict criminal liability theory, and has concluded that, "the predicate for all criminal liability is blameworthiness: it is the social stigma which a finding of guilt carries that distinguishes the criminal [penalty] from all other sanctions." If the predicate is removed, the criminal law is set adrift." Accordingly, the Model Penal Code (MPC), conscious of the disfavor of strict criminal liability, requires at a minimum that criminal culpability be followed by acting purposefully, knowingly, recklessly, or negligently, i.e., with some degree of mens rea. In regards to statutory rape, the MPC strikes a compromise with its general policy against strict liability crimes, prohibiting defenses of ignorance or reasonable mistake of age when the victim is below the age of ten, but allowing these defenses when the critical age stipulated in the offense is higher than ten. In addition to these arguments, commentators also observe that statutory rape prosecutions often proceed even when the defendant's judgment as to the age of the victim is warranted by her appearance, her sexual sophistication, her verbal misrepresentations, and the defendant's careful attempts to ascertain her true age. We acknowledge here that it is uncertain to what extent Garnett's (D) intellectual and social retardation may have impaired his ability to comprehend imperatives of sexual morality in any case. We understand that the legislature of 17 states have enacted laws permitting a mistake of age defense in some form in cases of sexual offenses with underage persons. However we think it sufficiently clear that Maryland's second degree rape statute defines a strict liability offense that does not require the State to prove mens rea. It makes no allowance for a mistake-of-age defense, nor any reference to the actor's knowledge, belief, or other state of mind. As we see it, this silence as to mens rea results from legislative design. First, the subsection stands in stark contrast to the provision immediately before it, which expressly provides an element that the actor know or should reasonably know that the victim is mentally defective, mentally incapacitated, or physically helpless. Second, an examination of the drafting history of this statute, reveals that the statute was viewed as one of strict liability from its inception and throughout the amendment process. The legislature explicitly raised, considered, and then explicitly jettisoned any notion of a mens rea element with respect to the complainant's age in enacting the statute. Therefore, we must conclude that the current law imposes strict liability on its violators. This interpretation is consistent with the traditional view of statutory rape as a strict liability crime designed to protect young persons from the dangers of sexual exploitation by adults. The majority of states retain statutes which impose strict liability for sexual acts with under age complainants. Any new provision introducing an element of mens rea should properly result from an act of the Legislature itself, rather than judicial fiat. Affirmed.

Dissent: (Eldridge, J.) Although I agree with the majority that an ordinary defendant's mistake about the age of his or her sexual partner is not a defense to a prosecution under §463(a)(3) of the Maryland rape statute, I do not believe that the statute contains no mens rea requirement at all. There are pure strict liability offenses that have the purpose of regulation rather than punishment. Also there are other strict liability offenses where the legislature has dispensed with a knowledge requirement, but has not intended to impose criminal liability regardless of the defendant's state of mind. Neither the statutory language nor the legislative history of this subsection of the statute indicate that the General Assembly intended to define a pure strict liability offense. Making the offense punishable by a maximum of 20 years imprisonment, is strong evidence that the General Assembly did not intend to create a pure strict liability offense. In the typical situation, involving older person's engaging in consensual sexual activities with a teenager below the age of consent, which the General Assembly likely contemplated when it enacted this statute, the defendant knows and intends that he or she is engaging in sexual activity with a young person. As the majority points out, the traditional view is that those who engage in sex with young persons do so at their peril, assuming the risk that their partners are underage. It seems to me that the above-mentioned knowledge factors, and particularly the mental ability to appreciate that one is taking a risk, constitute the mens rea of the offense. The General Assembly assumed that a defendant is able to appreciate the risk involved by intentionally and knowingly engaging in sexual activities with a young person. There is no indication that the General Assembly intended to attach criminal liability to a person who is unable to appreciate that risk because of a mental impairment.

Dissent: (Bell, J.) I do not dispute that the legislative history of section 463 may be read to support the majority's interpretation that subsection (a)(3) was intended to be a strict liability statute. Nor do I disagree that it is in public interest to protect the sexually naïve child from the adverse effects of sexual relations. I do not believe, however, that the General Assembly, in every case, can subject a defendant to strict criminal liability. To hold, as a matter of law that section 463 (a)(3) does not require that the State prove that a defendant possessed the necessary mental state to commit the crime, or that the defendant may not litigate that issue in defense, "offends a principle of justice so rooted in the traditions of the conscience of our people as to be ranked as fundamental," and is therefore, inconsistent with due process.

Analysis:

The purpose of this case is to allow the reader to decide whether they agree or disagree with the strict liability aspect of statutory rape. As the dissent in this case mentions, strict liability offenses, such as traffic tickets, are reserved for crimes where the purpose of punishment is to regulate violators. Also, they are reserved for crimes where punishments are less severe than in cases of rape. On the one hand, protection of society and of the family and the infant, support statutory rape. Lack of consent is not an element, because it is thought that age alone will bring an understanding of the sexual act to a young person. In this sense, the law concludes that a young person is incapable of giving consent to undertake sexual acts. However, on the other hand, is it fair to convict a perpetrator, and subject him to the same criminal stigma as a person convicted of forcible rape, based on a theory of strict liability. In the instant case, the majority acknowledged that it was uncertain as to what extent Garnett's (D) intellectual and social retardation may have impaired his ability to comprehend imperatives of sexual morality. However they did not feel the need to delve into the issue, because there was no need to prove any mental aspect of this crime. A good question to ask is whether the legislature, in drafting the statute in this case, contemplated a situation such as this. Based on utilitarian principles, how would this reform those who are mentally incapacitated? Furthermore, based on retributivist principles, why is Garnett (D) deserving of punishment, when he is possibly incapable of understanding the severity of his crime? Lastly, in balancing the interest of both the defendants and victims in shaping laws pertaining to the crime of rape, do legal assumptions about age and maturity tip the scales too far in the direction of the victim? Or does public policy require that young victims be protected at all cost? Lastly, is it fair that many, if not most of these statutes contain gender-specific provisions, protecting only young females from mature male sexual influences? This discussion is nothing new. While some statutes are gender-neutral, and do provide a mens rea element, a majority of states and courts still hold statutory rape as a strict liability criminal offense.

Perspective
General Defenses to Crimes

Chapter 9

Why do we allow some crimes to go unpunished? Perhaps the better question is why do we punish some people for their criminal behavior and not others. Is there such a thing as a "good" crime?

What happens when a person harms another person, but we think he was fully within his rights to harm the other person? Do we ever really have the right to harm another? Remember when you were a kid and some kid at school hit you, and you told your mom, "Bobby hit me!" She would check to make sure you were okay, but then ask, "What did you do?" Mom knew, generally speaking, that people didn't go around hitting other people just for the fun of it. What she was really asking was, "Did you deserve it?" The law of defenses is not so much a "did he deserve it" law, because it is morally and legally difficult to say that someone deserves to be harmed (or to die), but that there are circumstances under which we understand why a person might harm another. If Bob is walking down the street, in a bad mood, and he bumps into Frank which (because of his bad mood) makes him think Frank ran into him on purpose, he might just throw a punch at Frank. Frank is not too pleased, and a little taken-aback by the extreme reaction to bumping into someone, so in order to protect himself from Bob's tirade, he throws a punch at Bob. Now add to this scenario, a host of other "what ifs."

What if Bob was drunk? What if Bob had just seen Frank kissing Bob's wife? What if Frank indeed just kissed Bob's wife, but did so just to tick off Bob because, well, Bob's an idiot and its fun to watch him get mad? What if Frank is Francine, and Bob (6' 5" tall and 280 pounds) bumps into Francine (5' and 110 pounds) late at night and knocks her packages to the ground and calls her an impolite name? What if Francine is scared-out-of-her-wits and shoots Bob with the .22 pistol she carries to protect herself on her way home each evening? What if she has been mugged in her neighborhood before? What if Bob and Francine are married and every single night when she comes home from work, he hits her? What if, one night she comes home from work early and when she sees Bob coming through the front door, she decides to (and does) shoot him dead? When we are aware of the different circumstances that surround a crime, we can then decide whether what is technically a criminal act (killing) is also a legal wrong (murder).

Consider Bob again, now he is just a regular guy, driving along in his car and sees another car run over a child and then drive away. Bob jumps out of his car, picks up the severely injured (lips are turning blue) child and puts him in his car. He rushes the child to the hospital, and on the way he runs through a stop sign. Should Bob be given a ticket just because he was trying to get the child to the hospital as quickly as possible? Sometimes violations of the law are justified, such as the case where Bob can obey the traffic rules, or he can get the child to safety as soon as possible. He has to choose between breaking a traffic violation, or suffer the greater harm of having the injured child die.

There are times when a criminal actor will be excused because the actor is incapable of knowing right from wrong, or that his particular conduct is considered to be wrong. It is not always difficult to know when a person is "crazy" (God told me to shoot the first person who walked out of the local McDonald's carrying a backpack). However, we might have a difficult time deciding whether such a person should be found legally guilty of harming another person, because we believe that he did not have the capacity to know it was wrong to murder (God told him to, so it must be all right) or that because he was "crazy" he couldn't control his own actions.

All the "what ifs" revolve around the social, moral, and legal question of when is a person worthy of blame, and what social, moral, and legal purposes does punishing the wrongdoer serve?

Chapter 9

NOTE: THE PURPOSE OF THIS OUTLINE IS TO ORGANIZE THE CASES SO THAT ONE CAN QUICKLY UNDERSTAND THE RELEVANCE OF EACH CASE TO THE COURSE. NO ATTEMPT IS MADE IN THIS OVERVIEW TO ADDRESS EVERY CONCEPT THAT MUST BE STUDIED. BE SURE TO READ THE ENTIRE CASEBOOK AND/OR OTHER MATERIALS TO GAIN A FULL UNDERSTANDING OF ALL CONCEPTS.

I. Categories of Defenses
    A. Failure of Proof — Instances where one or more of the necessary elements of crime are missing.
    B. Offense Modifications — Although an actor may have technically fulfilled the necessary elements of a crime, his conduct is not what lead to the harm that the law is trying to prevent.
    C. Justifications — All elements of the crime have been committed, and the resulting harm is the type of harm the statute was designed to prevent and punish. However, the actor will have a defense if the harm he committed was done to prevent an even greater harm (usually committed in order to protect a greater social interest).
    D. Excuses — All elements of the crime have been committed, but the circumstances are such that the actor was not acting under his own free will.
    E. Nonexculpatory Public Policy Defenses — When an actor's conduct satisfies all the elements of the crime, but so much time has passed between the commission and the discovery of that crime that society has determined to not pursue it. The time limit is embodied in a Statute of Limitation. *Criminal Law Defenses*.

II. Burden of Proof (The Fourteenth Amendment's Due Process Clause requires that a factfinder must be convinced "beyond a reasonable doubt of every fact necessary to constitute the crime charged." The burden of proof is upon the prosecution. *In re Winship*.)
    A. A state statute that sets forth the elements to a crime may not, as written, require a defendant to bear the burden of rebutting the statute's presumption supporting any element of the crime. *Mullaney v. Wilbur*.
    B. However, it is not a due process violation for a state to require a defendant to bear the burden of proof in establishing an affirmative defense. *Patterson v. New York*.

III. Principles of Justification
    A. Self-Defense: General Principles
        1. A person is justified in taking another's life when it can be shown it was necessary to take another's life in order to save his own.
            a. In order to invoke the right to self-defense a person must show the threat to him was real and apparent, unlawful and immediate; that he honestly believed that he was in immediate peril of death or serious bodily harm, and that his response was necessary to save himself.
            b. The belief must be objectively reasonable in light of the surrounding circumstances.
            c. The force used against an attacker must be necessary, i.e., proportional to the threat imposed. Deadly force may not be used against non-deadly force.
            d. The person who instigates a conflict (or the one at fault for the situation) is the aggressor and does not have a right to claim self-defense. *United States v. Peterson*.
                (1) An aggressor has a right to self-defense only if he announces his intent to retreat and makes a good faith effort to retreat.
                (2) Under the majority rule, one is permitted to stand and use deadly force whenever it seems reasonably necessary to save himself.
                (3) Under the minority rule, one must "retreat to the wall," i.e., if there is a known avenue of safe retreat it must be taken to avoid taking the life of another.
        2. Self Defense: Justification Theories
            a. Public Good
                (1) The common law allowed the killing of another if it was for the benefit of society. For example, a public official would be allowed to take a life, if necessary to prevent prison escapes, or an individual might be allowed to kill another to prevent an "atrocious crime" that would harm society.
                (2) It does not necessarily follow that *saving oneself* protects society.
            b. Moral Rights
                (1) If an aggressor attempts to take another's life he has devalued his own life and for-

feited his right to life.

 (2) If the aggressor dies in his attempt to kill another, his killer may claim his own right to life to justify his actions and his actions are morally justified.

 c. Personal Autonomy

  (1) An individual in society has a right to innocently (legally) live his life without illegal interference by others.

  (2) When a wrongdoer illegally intrudes upon an innocent person, that person has the right to defend himself.

 d. Unlawful Aggression

  (1) When an individual lives in a society that recognizes an individual's right to life, he has a right to defend his life against an aggressor when the government fails to do so.

  (2) This right is upheld against the government, thus the right to claim self-defense when the government charges murder. *Applying the Theories of Justifiable Homicide to Conflicts in the Doctrine of Self-Defense.*

B. Self Defense: Reasonable Belief

 1. In General

  a. A reasonable belief requirement is an objective standard, i.e., "what would a reasonable man do in the same situation as the defendant." *People v. Goetz.*

  (1) In order to use deadly force, a defendant must not only believe the force he is about to encounter is deadly, but that a deadly force is necessary to repeal it.

  (2) The reasonable man standard can take into consideration the surrounding circumstances of the incident, including the defendant's past experiences which might cause him to believe he was in danger, and the amount of force necessary to repell that danger.

 2. Model Penal Code (MPC)

  a. Under the MPC, if a defendant has a mistaken belief in the need to use deadly force, he may still argue and perhaps prevail on a self-defense claim.

  b. However, if it is a negligently or recklessly formed belief, the defendant may be convicted of a crime which requires a negligent or reckless intent.

 3. Objective/Subjective/Mixed Standard

  a. "Reasonable man" standard evolves into "reasonable person" standard to take into account the gender of persons involved in the incident. *State v. Wanrow.*

  b. This includes the defendant's point of view, properly formed by all facts and circumstances known to defendant including those known prior to the incident. This means the incident is to be viewed from the defendant's (subjective) point of view.

 4. Battered Woman Syndrome

  a. Battered women syndrome testimony may provide relevant information relating to the defendant's subjective belief of harm and to the reasonableness of her actions.

  (1) An expert witness may explain to a jury the pattern of abuse, and why women don't leave their abusers.

  (2) Testimony may also demonstrate how a battered wife is able to predict her husband's abusive behavior.

  b. However, the threat to defendant must be imminent, before the defendant is allowed to argue self-defense. *State v. Norman.*

C. Defense of Others

 1. A person is justified in intervening in an unlawful attack if he reasonably believes that the victim (third-party) of that attack would be justified in using force to protect himself, and the intervening person reasonably believes his intervention is necessary to protect the third-party from the unlawful attack. *Commonwealth v. Martin.*

 2. The intervening person must only use proportional force, i.e., the amount of force necessary to protect the victim.

D. Defense of Property, Habitation, and Law Enforcement Defenses

 1. Generally, a person is *not* justified in using deadly force to protect personal property.

 2. The common law (and many States) do have laws which allow the use of deadly force against an unlawful intruder in one's home. Some States only justify the use of deadly force if, in addition to the unlawful entry, it is reasonable to believe that the intruder intended to commit a felony once inside the home.

 3. However, a deadly mechanical device (e.g., a spring gun) may not be used to protect property. *People v. Ceballos.*

4. Law Enforcement Defenses
    a. Whenever an officer restrains a person from walking away, he has seized that person under the Fourth Amendment.
    b. Under the Fourth Amendment's reasonableness requirement, a police officer may not use deadly force to effect the arrest of a fleeing felon unless it is necessary to prevent the escape and the officer has probable cause to believe that the suspect poses a significant threat of death or serious physical injury to the officer or others. *Tennessee v. Garner*.

E. Necessity
    1. Generally
        a. A defendant must reasonably believe his unlawful actions are necessary to avoid a greater evil. This is an objective test.
        b. The defense of necessity is limited to the following circumstances (*Commonwealth v. Leno*):
            (1) The defendant must be faced with a clear and imminent danger
            (2) The defendant can reasonably expect that his conduct will be the direct cause of stopping the danger
            (3) There is no legal alternative which will stop the danger
            (4) The Legislature has not precluded the use of the defense of necessity in the situation at hand.
    2. Civil Disobedience
        a. Indirect protests of congressional policies do not meet the requirements of the defense of necessity. *United States v. Schoon*.
        b. Under general civil disobedience theory, if a person chooses to violate a law in order to demonstrate the injustice of such a harm, one must also submit to the punishment. Asking to be released from such punishment (through the defense of necessity) undermines the underlying moral, ethical, and legal significance of the civil disobedience.
        c. Within the Political Necessity Doctrine, individuals are empowered to protest, and juries might acquit such a defendant in order to overcome an unpopular law. On the other hand, jury nullification has the effect of juries making policy decisions instead of legislatures. *The State Made Me Do It*.

3. Defense to Murder
    a. The defense of necessity as a defense to murder can be loosely thought of in terms of "self-defense."
        (1) The idea being that if one is threatened with imminent unlawful violence, it may be necessary to respond with violence in order to protect oneself.
        (2) A broader application would be where a person might claim it was necessary to divert flood waters which flooded and thus, killed the occupants, of a farmhouse in order to save a whole town.
    b. However, a person may not claim the defense of necessity if he killed an *innocent* person in order to save himself even from what appears to be dire circumstances. There are times when one must sacrifice oneself rather than to take innocent lives. *The Queen v. Dudley and Stephens*.

IV. Principles of Excuse
    A. There are different theories upon which the idea that although a person's actions cause harm to society, he should not be punished for such actions.
        1. Causation theory suggests that if a person is not morally to blame, but acts under the compulsion of mental illness or coercive threat he should be excused from punishment. However, if the person was intoxicated and caused harm, then he is not excused and is held responsible for his actions.
        2. Character theory suggests that a person of moral bad character will be punished for his bad acts.
            a. The moral character is inferred from the bad acts.
            b. Generally, if a person robs a liquor store we infer he only cares about the cash or liquor he can acquire and does not care what harm he causes.
            c. However, our opinion may change if we were to learn that he stole the money because someone threatened to kill his brother if he did not.
            d. We assume that people of good moral character [like us] might violate the law by robbing a liquor store under such coercion, and we excuse the robber's actions.

Chapter Overview Outline
General Defenses to Crimes

3. Free Choice theory suggests that a person should only be punished for his unlawful actions if he had the capacity and fair opportunity to freely choose whether to violate the law. *Understanding Criminal Law.*

B. Duress
1. Elements of the Defense of Duress (*United States v. Contento-Pachon*) are:
   a. An immediate threat of death or serious bodily injury
   b. A well-grounded fear that the threat will be carried out
   c. No reasonable opportunity to escape the threatened harm.
2. Necessity or Duress?
   a. Under the defense of duress the defendant is usually coerced (threat of imminent physical harm) by another person to do the very act for which he is being prosecuted.
      (1) He is not acting under his own free will.
      (2) The defense of *duress* provides an *excuse* for the unlawful action.
   b. Under the defense of necessity the defendant is usually in a situation, not of his own making, under which he chooses the lessor of two evils. The defense of *necessity* is said to *justify* the unlawful action taken.
   c. An escaped prisoner who found himself in the situation of remaining on a prison honor farm and being sexually attacked, or escaping to avoid such attack is entitled to assert the defense of necessity. *People v. Unger.*
3. Duress — Not a Defense to Murder
   a. A defendant can be charged with murder even though he was only an accomplice to the killing, such as, only driving the get-away car. Duress can be a defense to such a defendant.
   b. However, duress is not a permitted defense to a defendant who is the person who actually kills another (innocent) person. *Regina v. Howe.*
   c. Recall in *Dudley and Stephens* that necessity was also not permitted as a defense to a defendant who took an innocent life.

C. Intoxication
1. Voluntary
   a. Voluntary intoxication is relevant to the extent that it shows that the defendant was so inebriated he was not capable of forming the necessary intent to commit the crime charged. It does not provide the basis to excuse the crime. *Commonwealth v. Graves.*
   b. Note that Pennsylvania's legislature, following the *Graves* decision, amended its statutes to not allow voluntary intoxication as a defense and not allow evidence of such in order to negate an element of a crime.
      (1) However, it continued to allow such evidence whenever it was relevant to reduce murder from a higher degree to a lower degree of murder.
2. Involuntary (Four Kinds)
   a. Coerced Intoxication is involuntarily induced by reason of duress or coercion.
   b. Pathological Intoxication produces a grossly excessive response compared to the amount consumed to which the defendant did not know he is susceptible.
   c. Intoxication by Mistake occurs when the defendant is unaware that the substance he is ingesting is an intoxicant.
   d. Unexpected Intoxication occurs when the defendant is unexpectedly intoxicated due to the ingestion of a medically prescribed drug. This defense requires:
      (1) That the defendant must not know, or have reason to know, that the prescribed drug is likely to have an intoxicating effect (If he knows, or has reason to know, that the prescribed drug is likely to have an intoxicating effect, then he is voluntarily intoxicated);
      (2) The prescribed drug, and not some other intoxicant, is in fact the cause of the defendant's intoxication at the time of his alleged criminal conduct;
      (3) The defendant, due to involuntary intoxication, is temporarily insane. *City of Minneapolis v. Altimus.*
   e. Some jurisdictions that recognize any or all of the four kinds of involuntary intoxication require that the condition result in temporary insanity before they allow the defense.

D. Insanity
1. Competency
   a. A defendant must be competent to stand trial. He must be able to communicate with his attorney and have a rational and factual

understanding of the proceedings.

b. If a defendant claims incompetency (which may be raised at the outset or even during trial), he must prove his incompetence by a preponderance of the evidence. Any higher standard would violate due process.

c. If a defendant is judged incompetent, he is committed to a mental health facility (the criminal proceedings do not continue). The commitment period may exceed any criminal sentence he might have received had he been convicted of the crime charged.

d. If a defendant is permanently incompetent (e.g., a person who has never, and will never, age beyond pre-school years) he may only be committed for a reasonable time to determine his incompetency, and whether there is a substantial probability that he will attain competency in the foreseeable future.

   (1) If a defendant will never attain competency, a State must either begin civil commitment proceedings or release the defendant.

e. There are substantial due process and personal integrity issues concerning whether a defendant who is, without medication, incompetent to stand trial should be forced to take medications that will make him competent to stand trial.

2. Pre-Trial Procedure

a. Some jurisdictions require the defendant to issue a "not guilty by reason of insanity" plea (as opposed to just "not guilty").

b. The prosecution must be notified of any expert witnesses who will testify regarding the defendant's mental condition at the time of the incident. The defendant must submit to a court-ordered psychiatric evaluation.

c. A highly controversial verdict of "guilty but mentally ill" has been adopted by a growing number of states.

   (1) This is not a defense; it comes into play during sentencing.

   (2) If mental health care is indicated, the defendant receives such care either in prison or a mental health facility.

   (3) He must still serve the entire sentence imposed.

3. Burden of Proof at Trial

a. The burden used to be on the prosecution to

show the defendant's sanity.

b. Now, insanity is an affirmative defense.

   (1) The prosecution must still set forth and prove the elements of the crime.

   (2) The defense's evidence of insanity, in addition to the general nature of the defense, may create reasonable doubt regarding the elements of the crime charged, e.g., whether the defendant had (at the time of the incident) the requisite mental state.

4. Post-Trial

a. Defendants who are found not guilty by reason of insanity are not customarily immediately released.

b. The procedures differ by state, e.g., in some states, defendants are automatically committed to psychiatric facilities for treatment; in other states, defendants can be detained to determine their current status of mental illness.

c. A defendant may be held as long as he is both mentally ill and dangerous.

   (1) However, a State violates due process if it holds a defendant against his will if he is no longer suffering from mental illness.

   (2) This is so even if the defendant is dangerous to himself or others.

   (3) An inclination toward violence is not a sufficient reason to commit (or detain) a sane person against their will.

d. Some States have adopted controversial commitment laws which allow for the prosecutor to file a petition to have a "sexual predator" involuntarily civilly (as opposed to criminally) committed.

5. Insanity as an Excuse

a. In our society there are three asserted purposes of the criminal law: rehabilitation, deterrence and retribution. None of these is satisfied when we punish the truly irresponsible (the insane). *United States v. Freeman.*

b. *United States v. Johnson* sets forth the background of the insanity defense.

   (1) The M'Naghten rule is a two-pronged test which requires that:

      (a) At the time of the incident the defendant was "laboring under such a defect of reason, from disease of the mind, as not to know the nature and quality of the act he was doing, *or*

    (b) If he did know, that he did not know that what he was doing was wrong."

  (2) The Irresistible Impulse test adds a volitional requirement to the M'Naghten rule.

    (a) It requires that because of the defendant's disease of the mind, he could not resist the impulse to commit the unlawful act.

    (b) The idea is the impulse completely destroyed the defendant's mind such that he couldn't exercise his own will.

  (3) The now-abandoned "Durham" test provided that "an accused is not criminally liable if his unlawful act was the *product* of mental disease or mental defect."

  (4) The MPC relieves a defendant of criminal responsibility when because of a mental disease or defect, the defendant lacks the substantial capacity to appreciate the wrongfulness of his conduct, and he lacks the substantial capacity to conform his conduct to the requirements of law.

  c. After the Hinckley insanity acquittal, several states reverted to the M'Naghten rule. Congress adopted a federal definition of insanity which places upon the defendant a high burden of proof (clear and convincing evidence) such that he must show that at the time of the incident he was unable to appreciate the nature and quality or the wrongfulness of his acts.

  d. "Wrongfulness" incorporates a legal and a moral element.

  (1) The legal element requires that a defendant appreciate that his conduct violates the law. The moral element requires that a defendant appreciate that his conduct also violates society's moral standards.

  (2) If a defendant, because of his mental disease or defect, honestly believes that society would approve of his conduct if it shared his understanding of the circumstances underlying his actions, he would be entitled to prevail on an insanity defense. *State v. Wilson.*

  (3) If a person appreciates both that his conduct violates the law and society's moral standard he is not allowed the defense of insanity just because of his personal, albeit delusional, moral standard.

  e. Convincing the Jury

  (1) Once a defendant has introduced evidence of insanity, the burden is on the prosecution to prove beyond a reasonable doubt a defendant's sanity. *State v. Green.*

  (2) One commentator suggests that "crazy" happens on a continuum and juries can determine "crazy" without the help of expert testimony. The idea is that because the medical definition of what constitutes a mental disorder changes over time, such expert testimony is inappropriately relied upon by courts and juries in determining who should be held legally responsible for their criminal conduct. *Crazy Behavior, Morals, and Science.*

  f. Should the Defense of Insanity be Abolished?

  (1) There is a concern that the defense is abused by many people to escape punishment.

  (2) There is an argument that any psychiatric diagnosis should be relevant only after trial to determine what kind of confinement or treatment is appropriate, not to determine criminal responsibility. *Model Penal Code and Commentaries Comment to § 4.01.*

  (3) There are substantial arguments on both sides of this debate often centered around whether the actor should be held blameless (morally and legally) for his admittedly criminal act.

E. Diminished Capacity

  1. Diminished capacity doctrine has two basic *theories,*

  a. That the defendant did not have the requisite mental intent to commit the crime charged, *or*

  b. "Partial responsibility" which holds that even if the technical elements of the crime charged are satisfied, the defendant who is operating under a mental abnormality which renders him unable to control himself should be convicted of a lessor crime or receive a lessor punishment. *Undiminished Confusion in Diminished Capacity.*

  2. The diminished capacity defense is not uniformly accepted. Some jurisdictions find the subjectivity, open-ended, and non-uniform

terminology of the diminished capacity test inconsistent and unreliable. *State v. Wilcox.*

    a.   The sometimes rejected rule is that expert testimony as to a defendant's abnormal mental condition may be received and considered, as tending to show, in a responsible way, that the defendant did not have the specific mental state required for a particular crime or degree of crime — even though he was aware that his act was wrongful and was able to control it, and hence not entitled to complete exoneration.

    b.   Jurisdictions that prohibit the diminished capacity defense, do not necessarily prohibit the insanity defense which they claim is a more bright line test.

F.   Infancy

    1.   At common law the conclusive presumption was that a child under the age of seven was incapable of criminal intent, that a child of fourteen was fully responsible, and for those in-between there was a rebuttable presumption of criminal incapacity.

    2.   When a child is within the "in-between" years, the burden of production and persuasion of rebutting the presumption of incapacity (proving capacity) is on the prosecution. *In re Devon T.*

V.   The Latest Trends in Defenses — Addiction/Alcoholism, Rotten Social Background, and the Cultural Defense.

A.   A criminal law which punishes an individual for the "status" of being a drug addict violates the constitutional prohibition against cruel and unusual punishment. *Robinson v. California.*

    1.   Before punishment is imposed there must be some kind of act which violates the law and social morals. Appearing in public while intoxicated is an "act" which a state may punish without violating constitutional principles. *Powell v. Texas.*

    2.   Alcoholism is an insufficiently defined term (illness) which does not meet the level of a defense which would excuse a criminal act.

B.   One argument of "Rotten Social Background" is that an individual who is raised in an environment in which he is socially and economically deprived should be excused from responsibility for his criminal conduct (an African-American man shot a white Marine who called him a "dirty nigger bastard") because his particular experiences impaired his ability to control his behavior due to his rotten social background. *United States v. Alexander.*

C.   An individual's cultural background is a relevant factor in determining whether the defendant's admittedly criminal behavior is to be excused under the principle that because the defendant's technical violation of the law may not, under the circumstances of the case, involve any moral turpitude. *State v. Kargar.*

D.   An argument for allowing the cultural defense is that one of the basic goals of the criminal justice system is to ensure justice for the individual defendant. In simplest terms, does the punishment fit the crime? In a country that purports to embrace pluralism, the law must allow for preserving different moral and social values.

    1.   The argument notes that immigrants to this country may not have the knowledge of our laws or that their conduct violates our laws. This may not completely excuse the criminal conduct, but it might be taken into consideration in lessening the degree of responsibility or in lessening the punishment. *The Cultural Defense in Criminal Law.*

    2.   One of the problems with this theory, is that in practice the customs or "norms" of other cultures (that are defined as criminal conduct under federal and state laws) almost always involve conduct that violently harms women and children.

STATUTE THAT REQUIRES DEFENDANT TO PROVE AFFIRMATIVE DEFENSE DOES NOT VIOLATE DUE PROCESS

Patterson v. New York

(Jealous Estranged Husband) v. (State)
(1977) 432 U.S. 197

M E M O R Y   G R A P H I C

Instant Facts

The Supreme Court upheld the second-degree murder conviction (of an estranged husband who killed his (soon-to-be) ex-wife's boyfriend) stating that it did not violate due process for defendant to have to affirmatively show he acted under extreme emotional disturbance [which the jury didn't buy].

Black Letter Rule

A state may require a defendant to bear the burden of proving to a jury that he should not be found guilty of the crime charged because he has a valid affirmative defense.

Case Vocabulary

AFFIRMATIVE DEFENSE: A legal defense that, when proved, relieves the accused from the responsibility for his otherwise criminal conduct.
MITIGATING CIRCUMSTANCES: The extenuating circumstances which surround illegal conduct which may lessen the severity of the punishment.

Procedural Basis: The Supreme Court upheld New York Court of Appeals judgment finding state statute constitutional and convicting defendant.

Facts: Patterson (D) was estranged from his wife (Roberta) after a short and unstable marriage. Roberta resumed a relationship with John Northrup (Northrup) to whom she was at one time engaged. Patterson (D) borrowed a rifle, went to his father-in-law's house, and through a window saw Roberta (partially undressed) and Northrup together. He entered the house and shot Northrup in the head twice which [of course] killed him. Patterson (D) was charged with second degree murder. There are two elements to New York's (P) statute, 1.) Intent to cause the death of another person, and 2.) Causing the death of such person or of a third person. New York (P) also has a manslaughter statute under which "a person is guilty of manslaughter if he intentionally kills another person under circumstances which do no constitute murder because he acts under the influence of extreme emotional disturbance for which there was a reasonable explanation or excuse." Extreme emotional disturbance is an affirmative defense in New York. Although Patterson (D) confessed to the killing, at trial he raised this defense. The jury was instructed that if it found beyond a reasonable doubt Patterson (D) intentionally killed Northrup but that Patterson (D) had demonstrated by a preponderance of the evidence that he had acted under the influence of extreme emotional disturbance, it had to find Patterson (D) guilty of manslaughter instead of murder. The jury found Patterson (D) guilty of second degree murder. On appeal Patterson (D) argued that New York's (P) statute unconstitutionally shifted the burden of proof. The Court of Appeals did not find the statute unconstitutional and upheld the conviction as did the Supreme Court.

Issue: Does it violate a defendant's 14th amendment due process rights if a state requires him to bear the burden of proof regarding an affirmative defense?

Decision and Rationale: (White) No. Patterson (D) argues that New York's statute is the same kind of statute that we recently found to be unconstitutional because it improperly placed the burden of proof upon a defendant to disprove an element of the crime charged. In *Mullaney v. Wilbur*, the charge was murder under a Maine statute which included an element of malice aforethought, whether express or implied. Maine's manslaughter statute provided a lesser punishment for "whoever unlawfully kills a human being in the heat of passion, on sudden provocation, without express or implied malice aforethought . . . ." In *Mullaney*, the jury was instructed that malice could be implied from "any deliberate, cruel act committed by one person against another suddenly or without a considerable provocation," in which event an intentional killing was murder unless by a preponderance of the evidence it was shown that the act was committed "in the heat of passion, on sudden provocation." We held that Maine's statute unconstitutionally shifted the burden of proof from the prosecution to the defendant in that it required the defendant to prove that the killing had occurred in the heat of passion on sudden provocation. While we did hold that under the due process clause the prosecution had the burden of proving *each element* of the crime charged beyond a reasonable doubt, we did not find and do not now find that the prosecution has the burden of proving the nonexistence of all available affirmative defenses. The case here differs from *Mullaney*. In *Mullaney*, the statutory *presumption* was of malice aforethought. Maine's statute required the defendant to prove that he acted without malice. A defendant is not required to disprove any of the elements that constitute the crime for which he is charged. New York's (P) statute does not shift the burden of proving an essential element of the crime charged. New York's (P) statue only requires that the prosecution show that Patterson (D) intended to kill another person, and did kill such person. There is no malice aforethought element. If an intentional killing is shown it is murder. The affirmative defense of extreme emotional disturbance does not negai any of the elements of the crime. It is a separate issue regarding mitigating circumstances. It is the defendant's burden to demonstrate any mitigating circumstances. Just because New York (P) recognizes mitigating circumstances it is not constitutionally required to prove their nonexistence in each case in which the fact is put in issue. The New York Court of Appeals is affirmed.

Dissent: (Powell) The effect of Maine's unconstitutional statute is no different from the effect of New York's (P) statute. The Court is upholding New York's (P) law which requires the defendant to prove extreme emotional disturbance. The Court struck down Maine's law because the defendant was required to show that he acted in the heat of passion, in order to negate the element of malice. We held that this shifting of the burden of proof was unconstitutional. The Court states that because the burden showing extreme emotional disturbance is written as an affirmative defense, it passes constitutional scrutiny. We struck down the statute in *Mullaney* because it required a defendant to disprove an element of the crime charged. Maine's statute was invalid, the Court reasoned, because it defined murder as the unlawful killing of a human being with malice aforethought, either express or implied. Malice, the Court reiterates, in the sense of the absence of provocation, was part of the definition of the crime. The fact of malice was presumed unless the defendant persuaded the jury otherwise by showing that he acted in the heat of passion. Under New York's (P) statute, there is no mention of the element of, or the fact of malice. The absence of malice is written into its statute entitled as an affirmative defense. The defendant is required to show by preponderance of the evidence that he acted under extreme emotional disturbance. The burden in *Mullaney*, which we found unconstitutional, is the same burden here and should be found unconstitutional. The unstated presumption in New York's (P) law is the same presumption we held unconstitutional in Maine's law. Historically, the prosecution bore the burden of proving factors that made a substantial difference in punishment or stigma attached to the defendant's actions. Heat of passion (of which extreme emotional disturbance is a direct descendent) was an important element distinguishing both punishment and stigma. The presence or absence of extreme emotional disturbance makes a critical difference in being convicted of murder or manslaughter. The prosecution should bear the burden in order to gain a conviction. A legislature's ability to "write around" the requisite elements should not provide constitutional protection to this statute.

Analysis:

Is the presumption in the statute(s) as written and enforced that a defendant is guilty unless he can prove otherwise, or is it that he is innocent until proven guilty? If a statute states, "a person who causes the death of another human being is guilty of murder *unless* he can show that he did not kill with malice aforethought or that he acted in self-defense," it reads as if a person is guilty unless proven innocent. If a defendant claims that he acted in self-defense in killing another person, should the prosecution, in order to get a conviction, have to prove (beyond a reasonable doubt) the defendant did not act in self-defense, or should the defendant have to prove by a lesser standard (preponderance of the evidence) that he acted in self-defense? According to the reasoning in *Patterson*, it depends on how the statute is written. If written "guilty unless defendant can prove otherwise," it is unconstitutional. However, if just the basic elements are set forth in defining the crime ("a person who causes the death of another human being is guilty of murder"), and the rest of the sentence is written separately ("a person is only guilty of manslaughter, not murder, if he can show that he acted in self-defense") and entitled an affirmative defense, the court states it is constitutionally permissible under the due process clause. There are different burdens of proof in a criminal trial. There is the burden of production, e.g., when the prosecution must have enough evidence to bring the charges in the first place, or a defendant claims he acted in self-defense. If the court finds enough evidence to support the claim, it is allowed to be argued in front of a jury. The next issue is who bears the burden of persuasion, that is, who bears the burden of proving the issue to the jury. The burden of persuasion is what is at issue in Patterson.

United States v. Peterson

(Federal Prosecutor) v. (Windshield Wiper Protector)
(1973) 483 F.2d 1222

M E M O R Y   G R A P H I C

Instant Facts

Peterson (D) was convicted of manslaughter (over his argument of self-defense) for shooting and killing Keitt whom he caught stealing the windshield wipers off of his wrecked car.

Black Letter Rule

The aggressor in a conflict that results in another's death cannot justify his actions under the right of self-defense.

Case Vocabulary

CURTILAGE: The area and any buildings immediately surrounding a residence usually enclosed by some kind of fence.
DEADLY FORCE: A force which if taken will cause death or is likely to create a substantial risk of causing death or serious bodily harm.

Procedural Basis: On appeal to the U.S. Court of Appeals, D.C. Circuit, upholding conviction.

Facts: Peterson (D) came out of his house into his backyard to protest the fact that Keitt (accompanied by two friends) was taking the windshield wipers off of his wrecked car. After a verbal exchange, Peterson (D) went into his house to get a pistol, which he loaded while standing in his back yard yelling at Keitt not to move. At this point Keitt was already in his car about to leave. Peterson (D) walked to the gate holding his pistol and said, "If you come in here I will kill you." Keitt got out of his car, walked to Peterson (D) and said, "What the hell do you think you are going to do with that?" He then walked back to his car and got a lug wrench. With the wrench in a raised position, he advanced toward Peterson (D) who stood with the pistol pointed at him. Peterson (D) warned Keitt not to "take another step," which Keitt did, and Peterson (D) shot him in the face from a distance of about ten feet. Death was apparently instantaneous. Peterson (D) was charged with second-degree murder, but convicted of the lesser included offense of manslaughter. Peterson (D) appeals, arguing that a jury instruction which allowed the jury to consider whether he was the aggressor in the altercation that immediately preceded the homicide was improper. He also argues as improper the jury instruction which allowed the jury to take into consideration when deciding the necessity of his actions, the undisputed fact that at no time did he retreat from Keitt's approach with the lug wrench.

Issue: Does the instigator of a conflict have the right to claim it was necessary to take a life in order to preserve his own?

Decision and Rationale: (Robinson) No. From the time of English common law *justified* murder has existed in the form of self-defense. Self-defense is a law of necessity. If circumstances exist that require a defensive action, the defensive action must be realistically necessary to alleviate the threat imposed. [The reaction to a threat must be proportional to the threat. You are not justified in killing someone because they hit your backpack while passing you in the hallway.] The only time deadly force is necessary is when one is met with deadly force, i.e., there must be no other way to survive the circumstances than to take a life. The threat must be real and apparent, unlawful and immediate. The defender [this is the defendant, the other guy is dead] must have honestly believed that he was in immediate peril of death or serious bodily harm, and that his response was necessary to save himself. The defender's beliefs must also be objectively reasonable in light of the surrounding circumstances. If a person incites, encourages, or otherwise promotes the circumstances that lead up to his killing another, that person is the aggressor and is not entitled to the claim of self-defense. Only if the aggressor communicates to his opponent his intent to withdraw [walk-away] and in good faith attempts to do so may he claim self-defense. In the majority of jurisdictions one may stand his ground and use deadly force whenever it seems reasonably necessary to save himself. We do not follow the majority rule. Our law is closer to the common law rule requiring "retreat to the wall." This rule forbids the use of deadly force when it is possible to make a safe retreat. Although in modern times there may be exceptions to the concept of walking away from a fight, no such exception applies here. The circumstances that are relevant here begin after Peterson (D) returned to the yard with a pistol as Keitt was about to leave the scene. At this point Keitt was not the aggressor, if he ever had been. Before that only verbal threats had ensued (mere words do not constitute aggression) and a misdemeanor was in progress (the law does not tolerate the use of deadly force in protection of property). After Peterson (D) returned to the yard, he loaded his pistol, walked toward Keitt, dared him to come in, and threatened to kill him if he did. Peterson (D) may not assert self-defense under these circumstances because he is the person who created them. In addition, as noted by the minority rule, Peterson (D) is required to walk-away from the conflict (if he can do so safely). He could have, yet he did not. Peterson (D.

argues he was not required to retreat as he was standing in his own yard when Keitt advanced on him. The right of self-defense is not available to the party who provokes or stimulates the conflict. Under the facts, the jury instructions were proper. Judgement of the trial court for conviction affirmed.

Analysis:

Peterson (D) argued that under the "castle doctrine" (a man's home is his castle) he was not required to retreat. The idea is that one is already in one's home (the suggested place of safety) and it is unreasonable to require more of someone. The court noted that this exception has been extended by some courts to include the occupant's presence within the curtilage outside his dwelling. The court noted that the status of this doctrine was undecided in the District of Columbia (which is the jurisdiction here). It was, however, unnecessary to determine the status because it was irrelevant here because Peterson (D) instigated the conflict in his backyard. The person at fault in creating the conflict cannot assert it was necessary to take a life. The court noted Peterson's (D) aggressive action was the same type of aggressive action taken by similarly situated defendants who were not allowed the right to self-defense because they put themselves into a fight after they had already reached safety. The defendant in *Laney v. U.S.*, escaped from an ensuing mob, then checked a gun he was carrying and returned to the area and shot into the mob (killing one of them). Similarly, in *Rowe v. U.S.*, the defendant left a friend's home where a fight had ensued outside, went to his own apartment, got his gun, and returned to the fight where he was advanced upon by several men at whom he shot, killing two of them. Remember that there must be an honest and *reasonable belief* that someone is about to cause you immediate, unlawful seriously bodily harm or death before you are justified in using deadly force to repel them. Are you required to avoid threatening people in order to claim self-defense? If it means you have to walk home from work by a different route? Although you have a "right" to carry on your daily routine without unlawful interference, the law does not permit you to use unlawful means (killing someone) when you could have avoided the confrontation in the first place. On-the-other-hand, just because your conduct angers or even harms another, this does not necessarily give him the right to kill you. There are often less violent ways to express your displeasure with someone and/or defend yourself.

OBJECTIVE "REASONABLE MAN" STANDARD IS THE PROPER STANDARD FOR DETERMINING STATUTORY "REASONABLE BELIEF" REQUIREMENT

People v. Goetz

(State of New York) v. (Subway Gunman)
(1986) 68 N.Y.2d 96

M E M O R Y   G R A P H I C

Instant Facts

A frightened (or perhaps angry) man carrying an unlicensed pistol shot and wounded four youths after they approached him on a New York subway train and told him to give them $5.00.

Black Letter Rule

Before a defendant can prevail on a self-defense argument, it must be shown that his "reasonable belief" regarding the necessity to use deadly force comports with a "reasonable man" objective standard.

Case Vocabulary

GRAND JURY: A panel of individuals who after hearing the prosecution charges and prosecution witness's testimony determines whether there is probable cause to make a defendant stand trial.

INDICTMENT: The written means by which a defendant is charged with alleged offenses for which he cannot be found guilty unless proven beyond a reasonable doubt.

Procedural Basis: Lower appellate court's dismissal of charges reversed by the Court of Appeals of New York.

Facts: On December 22, 1984, Bernhard Goetz (D) boarded a subway car in Manhattan on which there were, among others, four youths from The Bronx. Two of the youths had screwdrivers inside their coats. One of the youths asked Goetz (D) "how are you," to which Goez (D) responded "fine." One or two of the youths walked over to Goetz (D) (possibly putting Goetz (D) in-between themselves and the other two youths) and stated to Goetz (D) "give me five dollars." Goetz (D) responded by taking out his unlicensed .38 caliber pistol and shooting in rapid succession one youth in the chest, another in the back, a third in the arm. According to Goetz's (D) statement, he shot at, but missed, one of the youths who was by now sitting on a bench. He said to him, "you seem to be all right, here's another," and fired a shot into the youth's side which severed his spinal chord. According to Goetz's (D) statement, "if I was in a little more under self-control . . . I would have put the barrel against his forehead and fired." Goetz (D) also stated that he purchased the gun in 1981 after he had been hurt in a mugging. He stated he subsequently prevented two other assailants simply by displaying the gun. He stated that he knew from the smile on the face of the youth that approached him, they were trying to "play with me." Although he was certain none of them had guns, he was afraid they were going to "maim" him. The lower court held that the objective test submitted to the grand jury to determine the defense of justification was in error; a subjective test should have been utilized. It dismissed the charges of attempted murder, assault, and weapons possession. The Court of Appeals of New York reversed the lower court's dismissal holding that the correct test of reasonableness under New York's (P) law is an objective test, and reinstated the charges against defendant.

Issue: Before a jury can find that a defendant's use of deadly force was necessity must it determine that not only did defendant reasonably believe his use of deadly force was necessary, but that a "reasonable man" in his situation would find the use of deadly force necessary?

Decision and Rationale: (Wachtler) Yes. New York (P) recognizes the defense of justification. Penal Law § 35.15(1) sets forth the general principles: "[a] person may . . . use physical force upon another person when and to the extent he reasonably believes such to be necessary to defend himself or a third person from what he reasonably believes to be the use or imminent use of unlawful physical force by such other person." A limitation is found in Penal Law § 35.15(2): "A person may not use deadly physical force upon another person under circumstances specified in subdivision one unless (a) He reasonably believes that such other person is using or about to use deadly physical force . . . or (b) He reasonably believes that such other person is committing or attempting to commit a kidnapping, forcible rape, forcible sodomy or robbery." The issue turns on the definition of the repeated phrase "reasonably believes." The prosecutor instructed the grand jury that the objective test was to be used in determining whether Goetz (D) reasonably believed he was under one of the triggering conditions set forth above (the youths were using or about to use deadly force or were committing or about to commit one of the stated felonies). The prosecutor told the grand jury they were to consider the circumstances of the incident and determine "whether the defendant's conduct was that of a reasonable man in the defendant's situation." (This is the objective test). The lower court held that because the law is written as "*he* reasonably believes," the correct test is a subjective test, i.e., whether the defendant's beliefs and reactions were reasonable to *him*. The lower court is incorrect. Under the lower court's subjective test any jury would have to acquit a man who claimed he felt his actions were warranted and reasonable. The objective test provided by the prosecutor is the correct test under New York's (P) law. The Model Penal Code which only requires that a defendant show that "he believed that the use of deadly force was necessary" is not New York's (P) law. New York (P) requires that a defendant "reasonably believe" his actions are necessary to defend himself from a force he "reasonably believes" another is committing or about to commit against him. This objective standard does not foreclose a jury from considering the circumstances facing a defendant. The circumstances include, e.g., the action taken by the alleged assailant, the physical characteristics of all persons involved, and defendant's relevant knowledge about the assailant. In addition, the jury may consider any prior experiences of the defendant which would provide a reasonable basis for a belief that another's intentions were to harm or rob him or that the use of deadly force was necessary under the circumstances. The Appellate Division is reversed and the dismissed charges of the indictment reinstated.

Analysis:

Goetz (D) was acquitted of all charges except for possession of a concealed weapon by a jury composed of eight men, two women (ten white and two African-American). He served eight months of his one year jail sentence. He was ordered by a six-member civil jury to pay $18 million in compensatory damages and $25 million in punitive damages to the young man who was paralyzed. Whether Goetz (D) was out-of-control or calculating after he drew his gun depends on one's interpretation of the facts. There was much debate about the racial overtones of the case because Goetz (D) was a middle-aged white male, and the young men were African-American. What is the practical difference between what Goetz (D) believed and what a reasonable man in the same situation would have believed? Goetz's (D) fear may have been reasonable, but it is difficult to define his reaction as reasonable. Under the New York law both aspects must be reasonable before a defendant can prevail on self-defense. The case points out that under the Model Penal Code if someone kills another based upon his mistaken belief it was necessary to do so to protect himself against death, he may prevail on a self-defense claim. However, if the defendant's belief was not only wrong, but his belief was negligently or recklessly formed, he may be convicted of a type of homicide which requires only a negligent or reckless criminal intent (perhaps manslaughter instead of murder).

State v. Wanrow

(State of Washington) v. (Killer Mom)

88 Wash.2d 221

M E M O R Y   G R A P H I C

Instant Facts

Ms. Wanrow (D) shot and killed a neighborhood man in a confrontation after neighbors asserted that the man (who had previously tried to take Ms. Wanrow's son off his bike and into the man's house) was a child molester.

Black Letter Rule

All the facts and circumstances known to a defendant, including those known prior to the incident and the genders of the persons involved, must be taken into consideration when deciding if a defendant's belief of danger was reasonable.

Procedural Basis: On appeal to state supreme court which overturned the lower court's jury's finding for second-degree murder.

Facts: Ms. Wanrow's (D) two children were staying with Ms. Hooper and her seven-year-old daughter. Some months prior to the incident here, Ms. Hooper's daughter had been molested but had not told her mother who had done the molesting. After playing in the neighborhood, Ms. Wanrow's (D) son told Ms. Hooper that a man had tried to pull him off of his bike and drag him into the man's house. Soon thereafter this man, William Wesler (decedent) (Wesler), showed up on Ms. Hooper's front porch saying "I didn't touch the kid, I didn't touch the kid." Upon seeing Wesler, Ms. Hooper's daughter indicated to her mother that he was the man who had molested her. Ms. Hooper's landlord saw Wesler and told Ms. Hooper that Wesler had tried to molest another young boy who had previously lived there and that Wesler had at one time been committed to a state mental hospital. A couple of nights earlier someone had slashed Ms. Hooper's bedroom window and she suspected it was Wesler. The police were called and Ms. Hooper requested they arrest Wesler. She was told they could not arrest him until Monday and she should go to the station on Monday and swear out a warrant. Ms. Hooper's landlord suggested she keep a baseball bat near the door in order to hit Wesler over the head if he should try to enter the house. The police stated, "Yes, but wait until he gets in the house." Being frightened, Ms. Hooper called Ms. Wanrow (D) and asked her to spend the night. Ms. Wanrow (D), being frightened, called her sister and brother-in-law (Chuck Michel) and asked them to spend the night also. The adults stayed up all night. Around 5:00 a.m., and unknown to the others, Chuck Michel took the baseball bat and went to Wesler's house. When Chuck Michel arrived at Wesler's home, Wesler suggested they go to Ms. Hooper's and clear up the whole thing. Upon arriving at Ms. Hooper's, only Wesler entered the house. Wesler was 6' 2" tall, and was visibly intoxicated. He was asked to leave but refused to do so. Much confusion and yelling ensued. Wesler made a comment that one of the boys sleeping on a couch was cute. This, of course, made matters much worse. Ms. Wanrow (D), who is 5' 4" tall, and at the time had a broken leg in a cast and was using a crutch, went to the door to call Chuck Michel into the house. Wesler was directly in front of her when she turned around. Ms. Wanrow (D) testified that she was gravely startled by this situation and shot Wesler in a reflex action.

Issue: Are (1) the genders of the persons involved, and (2) the facts and circumstances learned prior to an altercation, relevant factors that a jury must consider when deciding if a defendant's belief of danger was reasonable?

Decision and Rationale: (Utter) Yes. There are serious errors in the jury instructions defining the justification of self-defense. First, the jury was instructed to consider only the acts and circumstances which occurred "at or immediately before the killing." This is not Washington's (P) law on self-defense. The justification of self-defense is to be evaluated in light of *all the facts and circumstances known to the defendant*, including those known substantially before the killing. In *State v. Ellis* [first-degree murder conviction overturned when trial court instructed the jury that prior threats made by the decedent were insufficient justification for defendant's belief of danger] we stated that the vital question is the reasonableness of the defendant's apprehension of danger. The jury should try to understand the situation from the defendant's point-of-view. It is quite proper for prior experiences to come into play when determining the validity of a claim of self-defense. Second, the instructions are filled with masculine pronouns. The instructions were not only presented as an objective standard, but as a masculine standard. The incident here was not an altercation between two men. The instruction states that a person may not resort to the use of a deadly weapon if *his* assailant has threatened *him* "with naked hands." Even though other instructions note that the relative size and strengths of the persons involved are to be considered, these instructions are not sufficient to inform a jury that Ms. Wanrow's (D) actions are to be judged against her own subjective impressions. In today's society women are rarely provided the means to acquire the skills necessary to protect themselves against attack without using a deadly weapon. The instructions require the jury to compare Ms. Wanrow's (D) point of view with that of a reasonable male finding himself in the same situation. In the context of this case, the instructions violate Ms. Wanrow's (D) right to equal protection of the law. The instructions are improper because they set forth an objective standard of reasonableness, and as written suggest that Ms. Wanrow's (D) conduct should be judged against that of a reasonable man in the same situation. Ms. Wanrow's conviction is reversed.

Analysis:

What would a reasonable man do in this scenario? How about a reasonable man who is 5' 4" tall with his leg in a cast and using a crutch? How about a man whose child had been threatened by the 6' 2" tall man? What about a man who is suddenly confronted by the 6' 2" tall, intoxicated man who had previously physically removed his child from his bike? How much do your stereotypes of women and men (mothers and fathers) play into your definition of reasonable? Remember, even with an objective standard, the definition of "reasonable" includes the circumstances in which the defendant finds herself. The facts known to the defendant and the circumstances that led to and incorporate any altercation necessarily include an element of subjectivity. The jury is to step into the shoes of the defendant and view the altercation from her point of view. Think of it as watching a detective television show. The detectives are chasing a bad guy into a warehouse. The bad guy has led the detective there to ensnare him in a trap. The bad guy is hiding behind some boxes. We are watching the scene through the eye of a camera, and we see the whole scene -- the detective coming in the doorway, the bad guy hiding behind the boxes. We can watch objectively, and can say to the detective [not that any of us would actually talk to a television set], "Don't go in there, it's a trap!" However, the detective and the bad guy are viewing the scene only from their point of view which is subjective. The court is saying a jury must view the scene from the point of view of the people (the defendant) involved, not from an outside, objective point of view. The test is not just what would a reasonable person do, but what would a reasonable person do if she knew what defendant knew and was standing in her shoes at the time of the incident. Was Ms. Wanrow (D) supposed to wait for the landlord to do something, or the police, or [the ever helpful] Chuck Michel? The facts state she was frightened enough to bring along a pistol. The facts do not tell us why or how the pistol made its way from her purse to her hands. Facts are often either missing or contested leaving it up to the jury to fill in the facts and judge the credibility of the witnesses providing the testimony. The decision here does *not* set forth a broad rule that women are allowed to use deadly force when confronted with less than a deadly threat. It does set forth the idea that gender, as well as other facts, such as prior threats and physical size, may be relevant in determining whether a defendant's perception of danger is reasonable.

State v. Norman

(North Carolina) v. (Abused Killer)
89 N.C.App. 384

M E M O R Y   G R A P H I C

Instant Facts

Judy Norman (D) shot and killed her sleeping, intoxicated husband after enduring ever-increasing bouts of his abusive behavior.

Black Letter Rule

The fact that an abusive aggressor was passive at the moment of his killing does not necessarily preclude a defendant from claiming self-defense.

Procedural Basis: On appeal to the Court of Appeals of North Carolina ordering new trial.

Facts: Judy (D) and John Thomas "J.T." Norman (decedent) (Norman) were married for 25 years and had four living children. Starting five years into the marriage, Norman began to drink and beat his wife. When Judy (D) was pregnant with their youngest child, Norman kicked her down a flight of stairs, causing the baby to be born prematurely the next day. Norman required Judy (D) to prostitute herself in order to support him. Norman often threatened to kill Judy, cut off her breasts, and cut her heart out. He often referred to Judy (D) as "dogs," "whores," and "bitches." He often required her to eat cat or dog food from dog bowls, and to sleep on the concrete floor. He often beat Judy (D) with whatever was in his hand, an ashtray, a flyswatter, a beer bottle. He threw food at Judy (D), refused to let her eat, put cigarettes out on her skin, and required her to bark like a dog. All of these activities were accompanied by regular beatings at Norman's whim and sometimes to "show off" for other people. On June 10, 1985, Norman forced Judy (D) to prostitute herself at a truck stop on Interstate 85. Later that day he arrived intoxicated at the truck stop and began to hit Judy (D), slammed the car door into her, and threw hot coffee on her. On the way home he was stopped by police and arrested for driving under the influence. The next morning, Norman was extremely angry after being released from jail and beat Judy (D) throughout the day. Twice, he told her to make him a sandwich. When she brought him the sandwiches, he threw them to the floor. She made the third sandwich using paper towels to cover her hands because he didn't want her to touch the bread. He smeared the third sandwich on her face. That evening police responded to a domestic quarrel reported at the Norman residence. Judy (D) was bruised and crying, but refused to take out a warrant on her husband as advised by the officers because she was afraid if she did, Norman would kill her. Later that evening, the police were dispatched to the Norman residence again. Norman was interfering with emergency personnel who had been called because Judy (D) took an overdose of "nerve pills." Norman, intoxicated, stated they should "let the bitch die." Norman threatened to kill Judy (D), her mother, and her grandmother. After being treated at the hospital, Judy (D) spent the night at her grandmother's house as advised by the therapist at the hospital. The next day, June 12, a friend of Norman's asked him to drive with him to a nearby town to pick up his paycheck. Norman went to his friend's house and Judy (D) drove them. During the trip, Norman slapped Judy (D) for following a truck too closely, poured a beer over her head, and kicked her in the side of the head while she was driving. He told her he would "cut her breast off and shove it up her rear end." Later that day, one of their children informed Judy's (D) mother that Norman was beating Judy (D) again. Judy's (D) mother called the sheriff's department, but no one arrived at that time. Norman again threatened to kill Judy (D). He smashed a doughnut on her face and put out a cigarette on her chest. In the afternoon, Norman laid down on the larger of two beds in the bedroom to take a nap. Judy (D) tried to lie down on the smaller bed, but Norman told her that she couldn't and that dogs should sleep on the floor. One of their children came into the room and asked if Judy (D) could babysit one of their grandchildren. Norman said Judy (D) could do so. When the baby began to cry, Judy (D) took the baby to her mother's house because she was afraid the crying would wake Norman. She found a .25 automatic pistol at her mother's house. She took the pistol back to her house, loaded it, and shot Norman twice in the head while he slept. [What took her so long?]

Issue: If a consistently abusive spouse is passive at the moment a battered defendant spouse kills him, is defendant still entitled to claim self-defense?

Decision and Rationale: (Parker) Yes. Judy (D) testified that she could no longer stand things at home. She explained she could not leave Norman because he would find her and kill her. She had left him before and he always found her and beat her. Several witnesses testified to the facts presented here.

Two expert witnesses in the field of forensic psychology testified regarding battered spouse syndrome. Dr. Tyson testified that Judy's (D) case had progressed beyond the standard case and had escalated into the kinds of torture and degradation associated with prisoner-of-war camps. Judy (D) was behaving at a basic survival level. When asked if Judy (D) believed it was reasonably necessary to kill Norman, Dr. Tyson stated that Judy (D) believed she had no other choice, that in order to protect herself and her family she had to use deadly force against Norman. Dr. Rollins, who performed the psychiatric evaluation, similarly testified. He stated that Judy (D) believed that Norman was in complete control. That Judy had suffered Norman's abuse for so long she felt worthless and could not see a way to escape. Dr. Rollins testified that Judy's (D) action appeared necessary to her. He did not find any evidence of any psychotic disorder. Judy (D) was not allowed to put forth an argument of self-defense. The basic issue is whether Norman's passivity at the time of the killing *precludes* Judy (D) from asserting self-defense. We hold that the facts presented are sufficient to allow Judy (D) to argue the defense of self-defense to the jury. Self-defense incorporates an objective and subjective standard. The subjective standard relates to what the defendant perceived at the time of the shooting. The question is did the defendant believe it was necessary to kill the deceased in order to save herself from death or great bodily harm. The objective standard relates to what a reasonable person would believe if they were in defendant's circumstances. The record has more than sufficient testimony to support the argument that Judy (D) believed that she would have to kill Norman in order to save her self from death or great bodily harm. In addition, both experts testified that the abusive pattern reduced Judy (D) to a level of "learned helplessness." A defendant's inability to withdraw from the hostile situation and her vulnerability in relation to her abuser are factors to be considered in determining the reasonableness of a defendant's belief in the necessity to kill the abuser. Battered spouse syndrome usually has three phases — the tension-building phase, the violent phase, and the quiet or loving phase [apparently Norman skipped the quiet, loving phase]. During the violent phase, when the traditional concept of self-defense would permit a defendant to protect herself, she is least able to do so because she is immobilized by fear, if not actually physically restrained. Given the expert testimony provided here, it is our opinion that there may be circumstances under which the killing of a passive victim does not preclude the defense of self-defense. Based on the evidence a jury *could* find that Judy (D) believed it necessary to kill Norman to save herself, and that her belief was reasonable under the circumstances. The jury could find that Norman's sleep was but a momentary hiatus in a continuous reign of terror, that Judy (D) merely took advantage of her first opportunity to protect herself, and that there was the kind of provocation required for self-defense. The trial court erred in failing to instruct the jury on self-defense. A new trial is granted.

Analysis:

[The defense Judy (D) should have asserted is the "he needed killing" defense.] Recall that there are two burdens of proof. The first burden of proof relates to whether the prosecution has sufficient evidence to bring the charges in the first place, and whether the defendant has presented sufficient evidence to claim an affirmative defense. Here, Judy (D) was not allowed to argue self-defense to the jury. The reason the trial court didn't allow the argument is that Norman was asleep [passed out?] when Judy (D) shot him. Her action didn't fit within the traditional notion of self-defense. The idea is that the threat to Judy (D) wasn't *imminent enough* or that she could have walked-away. The appeals court stated, "we do not believe that a battered person must wait until a deadly attack occurs or that a victim [decedent] must in all cases be actually attacking or threatening to attack at the very moment defendant commits the unlawful act [killing] for the battered person to act in self-defense. Such a standard, in our view, would ignore the realities of the condition [battered spouse syndrome]." The appellate court believed that a jury could determine whether, and to what extent, to accept the expert testimony and determine whether Judy (D) was justified in killing Norman. Think back to the *Omichinski* article. Which justification theory applies to the facts here? It is reasonable to argue that Judy (D) had a right to defend herself against Norman's unlawful interference with her life. It can also be reasonably argued that Norman's violent actions threatened Judy's (D) life and thereby Norman forfeited his right to life.

State v. Norman

(North Carolina) v. (Abused Killer)
324 N.C. 253

M E M O R Y   G R A P H I C

Instant Facts

Trial court did not allow an abused wife to argue self-defense after she killed her sleeping, abusive husband; although the Court of Appeals held she could argue self-defense, it was overturned by the state supreme court, which agreed with the trial court.

Black Letter Rule

A defendant must have a reasonable fear of *imminent* death or great bodily harm before she is entitled to a jury instruction on self-defense.

Procedural Basis: North Carolina Supreme Court held that defendant could not argue self defense and overturned appellate court holding in favor of defendant's ability to so argue.

Facts: The facts are set forth in the Court of Appeal decision for *State v. Norman* (the previous case).

Issue: Did the defendant produce sufficient evidence such that the trial court was required to instruct on self-defense?

Decision and Rationale: (Mitchell) No. Before a defendant is entitled to a jury instruction on self-defense, the evidence must show that the defendant killed due to a reasonable fear of *imminent* death or great bodily harm. We conclude that the evidence here would not support such a finding. The trial court properly declined to allow such an instruction. The court of appeals is reversed. Only if defendants are required to show that they killed due to a reasonable belief that death or great bodily harm was *imminent* can the justification for homicide remain clearly and firmly rooted in necessity. A threat is imminent when it must be instantly met and cannot be avoided by calling others for help, including the protection of the law. *All* the evidence tended to show that Judy (D) had plenty of time and opportunity to find other ways to prevent future abuse by Norman. The expert testimony simply showed that Judy (D) felt generally threatened and that she believed her life would, at some point, end because of her abuse. It did not show that Judy (D) killed in the belief that Norman presented a threat of *imminent* death or great bodily harm. To stretch the law of self-defense to fit this case would require changing the imminent requirement. This change would tend to allow the opportune killing of abusive husbands by their wives solely on the basis of the wives' testimony based only on their speculation as to the probability of future assaults by their husbands.

Dissent: (Martin) It must first be noted that the problems of fabricated evidence are not unique to trials of battered wives who kill. The possibility of fabricated evidence arises in all cases in which a defendant seeks the benefit of self-defense. Here, there were several witnesses who substantiated the facts and circumstances supporting a claim of self-defense. There is no reasonable basis to attack the credibility of evidence for the defendant here. This is not an attempt to expand the requirements of self-defense. The proper issue for this court is to determine whether the evidence, viewed in the light most favorable to the defendant, was sufficient to require the trial court to instruct on the law of self-defense. I conclude that it was. Imminence must be viewed from the defendant's point of view. The question is not whether the threat was *in fact* imminent, but whether Judy's (D) belief in the impending nature of the threat, given the circumstances as she saw them, was reasonable. Judy (D) was incarcerated by fear. For the battered wife, if there is no escape, no momentary sense of safety, then the next attack, which could be a fatal one, is imminent. Witnesses' testified as to Judy's (D) intense fear and the events of the last three days of Norman's life which could have led a juror to conclude that Judy (D) reasonably perceived a threat to her life as "imminent," even while her husband slept. Norman had reduced the quality of Judy's (D) life to such an abysmal state that, given the opportunity to do so, the jury might well have found that she was justified in acting in self-defense for the preservation of her tragic life.

Analysis:

Judy's (D) conviction for involuntary manslaughter was commuted by the Governor of North Carolina only two months after she began her six-year sentence. Why involuntary manslaughter and not murder? Some states allow an imperfect defense when the defendant has a genuine, but unreasonable belief it was necessary to kill in order to save herself. The imminence requirement has historically meant something is about to happen immediately, as in, right now. Because the court finds that the threat of harm was not imminent, it never gets to the issue of whether it was necessary for Judy (D) to kill Norman to avoid death or great bodily harm. The majority of the cases (75%) that involve a battered spouse killing the abusive spouse meet the imminence requirement and the defendant is allowed a self-defense instruction. These cases involve some sort of confrontation between the spouses that results in the abuser's death. In nonconfrontational cases, like the case here, some jurisdictions allow the self-defense instructions and some do not. No jurisdiction allows such an instruction when the battered spouse hires a third party to kill her spouse. What purpose does the expert testimony serve in the cases where a battered spouse kills? Such testimony can be instrumental in a case where a battered spouse kills her spouse when he is asleep or there is a momentary lull from abuse. It demonstrates a defendant's subjective point of view and allows a jury to understand why she believed it was necessary to take such an action in order to avoid imminent death or great bodily harm. Expert testimony provides an explanation regarding the cycle of abuse in battered wife syndrome and explains to the jury why the wife didn't "just leave" her abuser. Recall that the deceased's prior behavior may be relevant in determining the reasonableness of the defendant's perception of harm. Whether the case is a confrontational case or nonconfrontational, decedent's prior behavior demonstrates why a defendant's perception of harm on the occasion of the killing required her to respond with deadly force. One commentator has noted that battered women are often "hypervigilant" regarding their abuser's behavior. Behavior that others may not think of as threatening, the battered wife knows is a signal that her husband is about to attack her.

Martin v. State

(Intoxicated Man) v. (People of Alabama)

(1944) 31 Ala. App. 334, 17 So. 2d 427

M E M O R Y   G R A P H I C

Instant Facts

Police officers arrest an intoxicated man at his home, take him onto a highway, and arrested him for public drunkenness.

Black Letter Rule

A defendant must perform the physical act for each element of a crime that has an actus reus component.

Procedural Basis: Appeal from conviction of being drunk in a public place and engaging in conduct manifesting drunkenness.

Facts: Police officers arrested Mr. Martin (D) at his home and took him onto a public highway. While on the highway, Mr. Martin (D) used loud and profane language in a manner that suggested that he was intoxicated. Mr. Martin (D) was convicted for violating a statute that prohibited appearing in a public place in an intoxicated condition and manifesting that condition with indecent conduct or loud and profane language. Mr. Martin (D) appealed the conviction.

Issue: Must a defendant perform the physical act for each element of a crime that has an actus reus component?

Decision and Rationale: (Simpson) Yes. A defendant must perform the physical act for each element of a crime that has an actus reus component. Mr. Martin (D) was convicted for violating a statute that provides that an individual in an intoxicated condition who appears in a public place where one or more persons are present and manifest his intoxication by boisterous or indecent conduct, or loud and profane language shall be fined upon conviction. On its face, the statute requires voluntary appearance in a public place. The State (P) cannot prove an accusation of public drunkenness by establishing that the arresting officer, while the defendant was in an intoxicated condition, involuntarily and forcibly carried him to a public place. Reversed and rendered.

Analysis:

Alabama's public drunkenness statute has two elements. First, the accused must appear in a public place. Appearance requires a voluntary physical act. Mr. Martin (D) appeared in a public place; however, he did not perform any physical act, voluntary or involuntary, that led to his appearance, since the police officers *took* him onto the public highway. Therefore, the required actus reus for this element does not exist. Second, the accused must manifest his drunken condition at the public place he appeared. Since Mr. Martin (D) voluntarily used loud and profane language while he was on the highway in an intoxicated condition, the required actus reus for this element exists. Notwithstanding, a crime did not occur, because the statute requires a coincidence of voluntarily appearing in public and manifesting an intoxicated condition through certain conduct.

SPRING GUNS MAY NOT BE USED TO PROTECT PROPERTY, EVEN IF THE OWNER COULD USE THE SAME FORCE WERE HE PRESENT

People v. Ceballos

(Government) v. (Garage Gun-Trap Setter)
(1974) 12 Cal.3d 470, 116 Cal.Rptr. 233, 526 P.2d 241

M E M O R Y   G R A P H I C

Instant Facts

Ceballos (D) set a gun to shoot at anyone who attempted to enter his garage.

Black Letter Rule

An injury or killing by the use of a deadly mechanical device is not justified where the device injures in response to a non-violent burglary.

Case Vocabulary

DISPOSSESSION: Ejectment or deprivation of a dwelling or other property.

Procedural Basis: Appeal from conviction of assault with a deadly weapon.

Facts: Don Ceballos (D) lived in a small home with the living quarters above the garage, though Ceballos (D) sometimes slept in the garage. In the garage Ceballos (D) had about $2,000 worth of property. In March of 1970, Ceballos (D) noted that some tools had been stolen from his home. In May he noticed that the lock on his garage door was bent and that there were pry marks on the door. The next day he mounted a .22 pistol in the garage. The pistol was aimed at the center of the garage doors and was connected by a wire to one of the doors so that the pistol would discharge if the door were opened several inches. Two boys, Stephen, aged 16, and Robert, aged 15 came to Ceballos' (D) house while he was away. Both were unarmed with a knife or a gun. Stephen removed the lock with a crowbar, and as he pulled the door outward, was hit in the face with a bullet. Stephen testified that he was not sure if he was going to steal anything, but wanted to go in the garage and look. Ceballos (D) testified that he felt he should set some kind of trap to protect himself and his property. When initially questioned by police, Ceballos (D) stated that he did not have much, and wanted to protect what he did have. The jury found Ceballos (D) guilty of assault with a deadly weapon. Ceballos (D) appealed, contending that under Penal Code section 197, had he been present, he would have been justified in shooting Stephen.

Issue: Is the use of a deadly mechanical device justified to protect against a non-violent burglary?

Decision and Rationale: (Burke) No. Courts have concluded that a person may be held criminally liable for injuries or death resulting from a deadly mechanical device that he sets on his premises. However, an exception to the rule is recognized where the defendant would have been justified in taking the life or inflicting the injury with his bare hands. However, allowing persons to employ deadly mechanical devices imperils fireman, police officers, and children. When the actor is present, he may realize that deadly force is not necessary, but deadly mechanical devices are without mercy or discretion. Furthermore, even if the rule justifying the use of deadly mechanical devices were applied here, Ceballos (D) would not be justified in shooting Stephen. A killing in defense of property is justified, inter alia, when committed against one who manifestly intends to commit a felony. Furthermore, the felony intended to be committed must be a forcible and atrocious crime, such as murder, mayhem, rape and robbery. Burglary is sometimes included as a forcible and atrocious crime, but only where the burglary creates a reasonable fear of great bodily harm. The burglary in this case did not threaten death or serious bodily harm. Ceballos (D) also contends that another subsection of Penal Code section 197 justifies the homicide since he committed the homicide while attempting to apprehend a felon. However, his testimony indicates that the purpose of the killing was not to apprehend a felon, but to prevent a burglary. Under the common law, extreme force could be used to prevent dispossession of a dwelling house, or against burning of a dwelling. Here we are not concerned with dispossession or burning, but a burglary that did not justify the use of deadly force. We conclude as a matter of law that the exception to the rule of liability for injuries inflicted by a deadly mechanical device does not apply here. Judgment affirmed.

Analysis:

The common law regarding the use of spring guns or trap guns to protect property is changing. Under the old common law rules, a deadly mechanical device could be used where the intrusion was such that the person, if he were present, would be justified in taking the life or inflicting the harm with his own hands. Now many states hold that a resident may not justifiably use a spring gun to repel an intruder, even if he would be justified in inflicting the same harm with his bare hands. As the court in *Ceballos* noted, spring guns kill indiscriminately. Under the old common law rules, the two kids who entered Ceballos' (D) garage committed larceny, not burglary, since they entered during the daytime, and in a typical common law jurisdiction, Ceballos (D) would not have been allowed to use deadly force [California considers a daytime entry to be burglary]. Had they entered at night, their act likely would have constituted burglary, and Ceballos (D) would have been justified in using deadly force.

Tennessee v. Garner

(State) v. (Dead Suspect's Father)

(1985) 471 U.S. 1, 105 S.Ct. 1694, 85 L.Ed.2d 1

M E M O R Y   G R A P H I C

Instant Facts

Unarmed 15-year-old burglar was shot dead by police after he attempted to scale a fence in order to flee the scene of the crime.

Black Letter Rule

Fourth Amendment reasonableness requirement prohibits officers from using deadly force to effect the arrest of a fleeing felon unless it is necessary to prevent the escape and the officer has probable cause to believe that the suspect poses a significant threat of death or serious physical injury to the officer or others.

Case Vocabulary

42 U.S.C. § 1983: A federal civil rights action brought against a person or entity in which it is alleged that the person or entity, acting under authority of state law, deprived an individual of their Federal Constitutional rights.

Procedural Basis: On appeal to the Supreme Court upholding the court of appeals' finding that an officer was not justified in using deadly force against an unarmed, nondangerous, fleeing felon.

Facts: Police Officers Wright and Hymon (D2) responded to a "prowler inside call" placed by a neighbor. Upon arrival, the neighbor was on her porch and indicated to police she heard glass breaking and that someone was inside her neighbor's house. Wright called-in to report they were at the scene while Hymon (D2) went behind the house. After hearing a door slam and seeing someone run across the yard, Hymon (D2) saw, with the aid of his flashlight, Edward Garner (Edward) who appeared to be 5'5" or 5'7" and about 17 or 18 years old, crouched at the base of a 6-foot-high chain link fence at the edge of the yard. Hymon (D2) could see Edward's face and hands and saw no weapon. Hymon (D2) called out, "police, halt" and took a few steps toward Edward. Edward began to climb over the fence. Hymon (D2) was convinced that if Edward made it over the fence he would elude capture. Hymon (D2) shot at Edward, hitting him in the back of the head. Edward subsequently died on the operating table. Ten dollars and a purse taken from the house were found on his body. Tennessee's (D1) statute provides, " if, after notice of the intention to arrest the defendant, he either flees or forcibly resists, the officer may use all the necessary means to effect the arrest." The police department policy was slightly more restrictive, but still allowed the use of deadly force in cases of burglary. Although investigated by the Memphis Police Firearm's Review Board and presented to a grand jury, neither took any action. Edward's father (Garner) (P) brought a 42 U.S.C. § 1983 action [violation of civil rights] in federal court against Hymon (D2) , the police department, the department's Director, the Mayor and the city of Memphis. After a 3-day bench trial the District Court found in favor of the defendants, concluding that Hymon's (D2) actions were authorized by state law and the law was constitutional. The District Court reasoned that Hymon (D2) had used the only reasonable and practicable means of preventing Edward's escape, and that Edward had "recklessly and needlessly attempted to vault over the fence to escape, thereby assuming the risk of being fired upon." The Court of Appeals reversed and remanded. It reasoned that the killing of a fleeing suspect is a "seizure" under the Fourth Amendment, and is constitutional only if reasonable. It also found that the state law failed as applied here because it did not adequately distinguish between felonies of different magnitudes; the facts presented did not justify the use of deadly force. Tennessee (D1) appealed.

Issue: Is it reasonable under the Fourteenth Amendment to use deadly force against a nondangerous, fleeing felon?

Decision and Rationale: (White) No. We conclude that such force may not be used unless it is necessary to prevent the escape and the officer has probable cause to believe that the suspect poses a significant threat of death or serious physical injury to the officer or others. Whenever an officer restrains the freedom of a person to walk away, he has seized that person. Although it may not be clear when minimal interference by an officer becomes a seizure, there can be no question that apprehension by the use of deadly force is a seizure subject to the reasonableness requirement of the Fourth Amendment. Tennessee (D1) argues that if the requirement of probable cause is met (an officer may arrest a person if he has probable cause to believe that person committed a crime) then there is no Fourth Amendment issue as to how that seizure is made. We do not agree. There are many cases in which this Court, by balancing the extent of the interference by an officer against the need for it, has examined the reasonableness of the manner in which a search or seizure is conducted. Even with probable cause an officer may not always seize a suspect by killing him. The suspect's fundamental interest in his own life and society's interest in a judicial determination of guilt and punishment are up against the government's interest in effective law enforcement. The argument for force is that overall violence will be reduced by encouraging peaceful submission of suspects who know that they may be shot if they flee. Although effective law enforcement and overall reduction of violence are admittedly important goals, we are not convinced that the use of deadly force is a sufficiently productive means of accomplishing these goals to justify the killing of nonviolent suspects. The majority of police departments in this country have forbidden the use of deadly force against nonviolent suspects. In addition, the majority of police department regulations in large cities allow the firing of a weapon only when a felon presents a threat of death or serious bodily harm. Tennessee (D1) has failed to convince us that shooting nondangerous fleeing suspects is so vital as to outweigh the suspect's interest in his own life. Where the suspect poses no immediate threat to the officer or to others, the harm resulting from failing to apprehend him does not justify the use of deadly force to do so. An officer may not seize an unarmed, nondangerous suspect by shooting him dead. The Tennessee (D1) statute is unconstitutional to the extent it authorizes the use of deadly force against such fleeing suspects. However, the statute is not unconstitutional on its face. Where the officer has probable cause to believe that the suspect poses a threat of serious bodily harm, either to the officer or to others, (or the officer has probable cause to believe the suspect has committed a crime involving the infliction or threatened infliction of serious physical harm) it is not constitutionally unreasonable to prevent escape by using deadly force. Our interpretation of the Fourth Amendment in modern times is not limited by the common law rule which allowed for the use of whatever means necessary to arrest a fleeing felon (although most jurisdictions flatly prohibit the use of deadly force to stop a fleeing misdemeanant). When the common law rule was first imposed virtually all felonies were punishable by death. Courts justified the rule by emphasizing the dangerousness of felons. Today, almost none of the crimes previously punishable by death remain so. In addition, numerous misdemeanors involve conduct more dangerous than many felonies (e.g., drunken driving is more physically threatening than white-collar crimes). In addition, handguns were not carried by officers until the latter part of the Nineteenth Century. When the common law rule developed, deadly force meant hand-to-hand struggle during which the safety of the officer was obviously at risk. The changes in technology and legislation mean the common law rule is distorted beyond recognition when literally applied. The District Court concluded that Hymon (D2) was justified in shooting Edward because state law allows, and the Federal Constitution does not forbid, the use of deadly force to prevent the escape of a fleeing felony suspect if no alternative means of apprehension is available. In reversing, the Court of Appeals accepted the District Court's factual conclusions (one of which is that Edward was not armed) and held that "the facts, as found, did not justify the use of deadly force." We agree with the Court of Appeals. Hymon (D2) never attempted to justify his actions on any basis other than the need to prevent escape. Hymon (D2) did not have probable cause to believe that Edward, whom he correctly believed to be unarmed, posed any physical danger to himself or others. We hold that Tennessee's (D1) statute is invalid insofar as it purported to give Hymon (D2) the authority to act as he did.

Dissent: (O'Connor) Household burglaries are serious crimes. According to Department of Justice statistics, 3/5 of all rapes in the home, 3/5 of all home robberies, and 1/3 of home aggravated and simple assaults are committed by burglars. Even if a particular burglary, when viewed in retrospect, does not involve physical harm to others, the harsh potentialities for violence inherent in the forced entry into a home preclude characterization of the crime as "innocuous, inconsequential, minor or nonviolent." Because burglary is a serious and dangerous felony, the public interest in the prevention and detection of the crime is of compelling interest. The legitimate interests of the suspect are adequately accommodated by the Tennessee (D1) statute: to avoid the use of deadly force and consequent risk to his life, the suspect need merely obey the valid order to halt. A proper balancing of the interest involved suggest that use of deadly force as a last resort to apprehend a criminal suspect fleeing from the scene of a nighttime burglary is not unreasonable within the meaning of the Fourth Amendment. The reasonableness of this action for purposes of the Fourth Amendment is not determined by the unfortunate nature of this particular case; instead, the question is whether it is constitutionally impermissible for police officers, as a last resort, to shoot a burglary suspect fleeing the scene of a crime.

Analysis:

Garner's (P) complaint alleged that the shooting violated the Fourth, Fifth, Sixth, Eighth, and Fourteenth Amendments of the U.S. Constitution. The case as presented here only deals with the Fourth Amendment right to be free from unreasonable searches and seizures. Why isn't the scope of what constitutes "deadly force" discussed in this case? ['Cause the suspect was shot dead. Pay attention.] There are other methods of detaining a suspect that although not resulting in death, might fall within the scope of the use of deadly force. Dogs (used to find, bite and/or hold suspects), pepper spray, and threats of violence are used by various police departments to detain suspects. The validity of the method used and the surrounding facts make it difficult to guess at what would and would not constitute reasonable force by an officer. However, because an officer's actions have the authority of law, it is his burden to act within its bounds. The age of the suspect, that it was night, and that the suspect appeared unarmed were all factors used in determining whether the officer's use of deadly force was reasonable. The majority appears to view many of the facts in retrospect, e.g., the suspect was 15-years-old, that he was unarmed, that he only stole a minimum amount from the house. But the main issue appears to be that because the suspect appeared nonthreatening at the time the officer fired on him, that the officer's use of deadly force was unreasonable. It appears from the lack of any official reprimand that the officer was acting within department policy. However, the point is that under the facts presented the state law (underlying the policy) was not constitutionally reasonable. To support its finding of unreasonableness, the majority notes that some police departments and the FBI have adopted policies to not use deadly force in similar circumstances. The dissent notes that as regrettable as the circumstances are, the reasonableness of the officer's conduct cannot be viewed after the fact. The dissent points out repeatedly that the officer fired his weapon as a last resort. There was no way for the officer to know, at the time of the crime, whether the suspect stole ten dollars, or had murdered the occupants of the house. The dissent claims that the majority has created a Fourth Amendment right for burglary suspects to flee from officers. This simply goes beyond a realistic reading of the majority opinion. The majority simply holds that officer's do not have a blanket constitutional right to kill fleeing burglary suspects.

Commonwealth v. Leno

(Massachusetts) v. (Needle Exchange Organizer)
415 Mass. 835, 616 N.E.2d 453

M E M O R Y   G R A P H I C

Instant Facts

Conviction upheld for man who distributed free, clean needles (in violation of state law) in exchange for dirty needles in his attempt to curb the spread of AIDS.

Black Letter Rule

Evidence which would trigger a reasonable doubt about whether a defendant's unlawful actions were justified as a choice between evils must be presented before a defense of necessity is proper.

 ## Case Vocabulary

JURY NULLIFICATION: When a jury, although it may believe that a defendant has violated the law, finds the defendant "not guilty," perhaps because it believes the law is incorrect.

MOTION IN LIMINE: A motion submitted to a court prior to trial to have certain evidence excluded from trial because it is (arguably) irrelevant and/or highly prejudicial to one of the parties.

Procedural Basis: On appeal to the Supreme Judicial Court of Massachusetts affirming the conviction of Leno (D).

Facts: A former drug addict who had been sober for several years started a needle-exchange program in Lynn, Massachusetts with the intent to help prevent the spread of AIDS. Massachusetts ip
s one of ten states that prohibits distribution of hypodermic needles without a prescription. Leno (D) (one of two defendants; Ingalls is the second defendant) was charged with and convicted of unauthorized possession of instruments to administer controlled substances, and unlawful distribution of an instrument to administer controlled substances in violation of law. Leno (D) purchased the needles in Vermont. Then, at a specific location at a specific time every Wednesday night in 1991 (until arrested in June) he exchanged dirty needles for clean ones without charging for doing so. Leno (D) offered significant testimony from experts on AIDS, and needles exchange programs, who asserted that needle exchange programs resulted in helping reduce the risk of spreading AIDS. A research director for the Massachusetts Legislature testified that although the Legislature had considered repeal of the prescription requirement at various times, the Legislature had not repealed the requirement prior to trial. At trial, Leno (D) requested and was refused a jury instruction on the defense of necessity.

Issue: Before a defense of necessity may be asserted must a defendant show that the danger motivating his unlawful conduct was imminent, and that he acted out of necessity at all times that he engaged in the unlawful conduct?

Decision and Rationale: (Abrams) Yes. Leno (D) does not deny that he violated the law. He contends the trial court erred when it refused to instruct the jury on the defense of necessity. The trial court did not err. The conviction is affirmed. Leno's (D) request for the jury instruction was properly denied by the trial court. The defense of necessity is limited to the following circumstances: (1) the defendant is faced with a clear and imminent danger, not one which is debatable or speculative; (2) the defendant can reasonably expect that his action will be effective as the direct cause of abating the danger; (3) there is no legal alternative which will be effective in abating the danger; and (4) the Legislature has not acted to preclude the defense by a clear and deliberate choice regarding the values at issue. The circumstances requiring such an instruction are not met. The defense is not applicable unless a person is "faced with a clear and imminent danger, not one which is debatable or speculative. In addition, there must be no legal alternative which will be effective in abating (to lesson or to stop) the danger. The prevention of possible future harm does not excuse a current systematic violation of law in anticipation of the eventual overall benefit to the public. Leno (D) asserts that the current law is ineffective and dangerous. The effectiveness or wisdom of a statute is not for this court to determine. We defer to the legislature's decision (as set forth in the statute) of how the distribution of drug-related paraphernalia is controlled. Leno (D) and other citizens may utilize Massachusetts' (P) popular initiative to show their disagreement with the Legislature's policies. Leno's (D) argument that the increasing number of AIDS cases constitutes a societal problem of great proportions, and that the needle exchange program is an effective way to produce the over-all reduction in the spread of HIV, and future incidence of AIDS, does not make out an argument for necessity, but for jury nullification. Leno (D) is not entitled to the jury instruction on necessity which would only serve as a disguise for an argument for jury nullification.

Concurrence: (Liacos) First, I reiterate a concern, although it is not at issue here, that evidence of necessity not be excluded by a motion in limine once a defendant has made a sufficient offer of proof. Even though a defendant may not be entitled to an instruction on the defense of necessity, the presentation of evidence regarding necessity allows the jury to fulfil their vital function to temper the enforcement of strict rules of laws by applying their common sense to the case and thus act as a check on the arbitrary enforcement of the law. Second, I hope the Legislature will take careful note of the extensive and uncontroverted evidence presented on the effectiveness of needle exchange programs and join the vast majority of jurisdictions that have decriminalized possession and distribution of hypodermic syringes.

Analysis:

Under *Leno*, a defendant must have a *reasonable* belief that his conduct is necessary. The Model Penal Code only requires a subjective test, i.e., that the defendant actually believe his actions were necessary to avoid an evil. A sympathetic jury might well have agreed with Leno (D) that he should not be punished for distributing free, clean needles even if there was a law that stated to distribute syringes without a prescription was illegal. This is why the majority was concerned that the arguments were really to sway a jury into a "not guilty" decision, despite the evidence that the Leno (D) admitted to violating the statute. The jury might have various reasons for deciding that Leno (D) should not be convicted of violating the statute. A jury's various reasons might include that they believe there is a big problem with AIDS in our society and if someone wants to spend his time and money to combat it, that is better than spending tax dollars to deal with the problem. A jury might feel that Leno (D) was unfairly targeted by police, or believe that the law was not one which should be enforced in general. The defense of necessity is usually invoked in cases where, e.g., a driver runs a stop sign in order to rush his deathly ill child to the hospital, or a driver runs into an unoccupied vehicle in order to avoid hitting a person crossing the street. The idea is that although a defendant violated the law, it was necessary for the defendant to violate a lesser law (property damage) in order to avoid a greater harm (death of an individual). The issues in *Leno* do not appear to rise to the same level. Leno (D) was not personally faced with what he claimed was a "societal problem of great proportion," nor was he faced with a "clear and imminent danger."

United States v. Schoon

(Government) v. (Indirect Civil Protestor)

(1991) 939 F.2d 826

M E M O R Y   G R A P H I C

Instant Facts

Schoon (D) and others protested congressional policies at an IRS office, and claimed the necessity defense as a justification for their actions.

Black Letter Rule

Indirect protests of congressional policies can never meet all the requirements of the necessity doctrine, and the necessity defense is therefore unavailable in such cases.

Case Vocabulary

INDIRECT CIVIL DISOBEDIENCE: A protest in which the participants violate a law which is not itself the object of protest, as opposed to direct civil disobedience, where the participants violate the very law they mean to protest.

POLITICAL NECESSITY DEFENSE: A defense where the protestors attempt to assert a defense based on a need to effect political change or to bring an issue political recognition.

Procedural Basis: Appeal from trial court's denial of necessity defense in indirect civil disobedience case.

Facts: Thirty people, including Schoon (D), entered an IRS office in Tucson, where they chanted "Keep America's tax dollars out of El Salvador" [couldn't they come up with a rhyme, or a shorter chant?], splashed simulated blood on the walls [ketchup?], counters, and carpeting, and obstructed the office's operation. Schoon (D) offered evidence of the conditions in El Salvador as the motivation for their conduct. Schoon (D) attempted to assert a necessity defense, arguing that acts in protest of American involvement in El Salvador were necessary to avoid further bloodshed in that country. The district court precluded the necessity defense based on Ninth Circuit precedent. Specifically, the court noted that (1) the requisite immediacy was lacking; (2) the actions taken would not abate the evil; and (3) other legal alternatives existed.

Issue: Is the necessity doctrine available as a defense to charges stemming from indirect protests of congressional policies?

Decision and Rationale: (Boochever) No. This is a case of indirect civil disobedience, since the protestors were violating a law which is not itself the object of protest. We conclude that the elements of the necessity defense are lacking in indirect civil disobedience cases. Necessity is a utilitarian defense. It justifies criminal acts taken to avert a greater harm, maximizing social welfare. In instances of acceptable necessity defenses, the "crime" averted the occurrence of an even greater "harm." Analyzing the actions of the protestors, we see that there can be no aversion of harm by the protest, since the El Salvador policy cannot be deemed a cognizable harm. The policy does not violate the Constitution, and it was adopted according to appropriate congressional procedure. Also, in political necessity cases involving indirect civil disobedience, the act alone is unlikely to abate the evil precisely because the action is indirect. The IRS obstruction is unlikely to abate the killings in El Salvador, or immediately change Congress' policy. Thus, there is no substantial causal relationship between the criminal conduct and the harm to be averted. Finally, in indirect civil disobedience cases the legal alternatives will never be deemed exhausted when the harm can be mitigated by congressional action. Cases involving protest of congressional policy have implicitly decided that, because Congress can change its mind at any time in response to citizen protest, petitioning Congress is always an adequate legal alternative. Thus, there can never be an absence of legal alternatives where congressional action is the protest's aim. What these cases are really about is gaining notoriety for a cause. Indirect protests of congressional policies can never meet all the requirements of the necessity doctrine. Judgment affirmed.

Analysis:

In *Schoon* the court blocked the necessity defense in all indirect civil disobedience cases. Some advocates of a "political necessity" defense argue that protestors should have the right to such a defense because it allows stifled or unheeded viewpoints to be heard in a public forum. Also, the defense allows the jury to voice its opinion on a controversial subject. However, some believe that allowing the defense would, as Joshua Dressler says, "undesirably erode the principle of traditional civil disobedience, which is that people who are compelled by conscience to violate the law, but who also believe in the democratic system, should accept their punishment (as Gandhi and Martin Luther King did) as part of their protest."

The Queen v. Dudley and Stephens

(English Prosecutor) v. (Hungry Sailors)

(1884) 14 Q.B.D. 273

M E M O R Y   G R A P H I C

Instant Facts

English sailors at sea for 20 days (the last 9 days without food or water) killed and consumed a cabin boy for which they were found guilty of murder.

Black Letter Rule

A defendant's actions are not justified under the defense of necessity if he deliberately kills an innocent person in order to save his own life.

Case Vocabulary

THE CROWN: This is the British equivalent of the United States bringing the criminal prosecution on behalf of the people.

QUEEN'S BENCH DIVISION: Modern term for court of common law in England, so named because the sovereign used to preside; when there is a King, it is referred to as the King's Bench.

SPECIAL VERDICT: A jury's finding of the facts submitted to a court upon which a court will determine the application of the law; this is usually done by submitting specific questions to a jury which often can be answered with a "yes" or "no."

Procedural Basis: On appeal to the Queen's Bench Division finding from a jury's special verdict for conviction of murder.

Facts: After a storm, three English seaman (sailors) and one, 17-year-old cabin boy (boy) were cast away in an open boat that belonged to the yacht on which they had served. Initially, they had two-one pound tins of turnips which they ate over three days. On the fourth day, they caught and ate a small turtle. They had no fresh water, except occasional rain water they caught in their oilskin caps. After eighteen days at sea, Dudley (D1) and Stephens (D2) began to discuss with the third sailor, Brooks, what should be done if they were not soon rescued. Dudley (D1) suggested one should be sacrificed to save the others, indicating that the boy should be sacrificed. Brooks dissented. No one asked the boy. The next day, Dudley (D1) proposed that lots should be cast to decide who would be put to death to save the rest. Again, Brooks refused to consent, and no one asked the cabin boy. They did not draw lots. Dudley (D1) and Stephens (D2) talked about how they had families and suggested it would be better to kill the boy so that their lives could be saved. They decided that if there was no vessel in sight by the next morning, the boy should be killed. The next day (twentieth day at sea) [the last food was the turtle] Dudley (D1) told Brooks to "have a sleep," and made signs to Stephens (D2) and Brooks that the boy should be killed. Stephens (D2) agreed, but Brooks again dissented. The boy was lying on the bottom of the boat, weak and helpless, and did not assent to be killed. Dudley (D1) offered a prayer asking forgiveness if any of them should be tempted to commit a rash act and that their souls might be saved. He went to the boy, and telling him that his time had come, put a knife into his throat and killed him. The sailors fed upon the body and blood of the boy for four days. On the fourth day they were rescued by a passing vessel. It was set forth in the special verdict that it was likely that the boy, being the weakest, would die before the others; that if the sailors had not fed upon the boy, they probably would not have survived to be rescued; that there was no rescue in sight; that if they did not feed upon the boy or one of themselves soon, they would die of starvation; that there was no appreciable chance of saving life except by killing someone for the others to eat; that assuming any necessity to kill anybody, there was no greater necessity for killing the boy than any of the men. The jury could not determine whether under the circumstances the law would consider Dudley (D) and Stephens (D) guilty of murder and asked the advice of the court.

Issue: May a person who takes an innocent life in order to save his own claim the defense of necessity?

Decision and Rationale: (Lord Coleridge) No. Under the facts, the jury states that it is unable to determine whether Dudley (D1) and Stephens (D2) are guilty of murder and referred it to this court to determine what are the legal consequences of the facts. In every passage that speaks to necessity the reference is in the ordinary sense, that is, the repelling by violence which is justified so far as it was necessary to repel an unlawful violence against oneself. To quote Lord Hale, "If a man be desperately assaulted and in peril of death, and cannot otherwise escape unless, to satisfy his assailant's fury, he will kill an innocent person then present, the fear and actual force will not acquit him of the crime and punishment of murder, if he commit the fact, for he ought rather to die than kill an innocent." There is no current authority for the proposition of necessity under the circumstances. Now it is admitted that the deliberate killing of this unoffending and unresisting boy was clearly murder, unless the killing can be justified by some well-recognized excuse under the law. It is also admitted that there is no excuse unless the killing was justified by what has been called "necessity." But the temptation to act which existed here was not what the law has ever called necessity. To preserve one's life is generally speaking a duty, but it may be the plainest and highest duty to sacrifice it. War is full of instances in which it is a man's duty not to live, but to die. The duty, in case of shipwreck, of

The Queen v. Dudley and Stephens (Continued)

a captain to his crew, of the crew to passengers, of soldiers to women and children; these duties impose on men the moral necessity, not of the preservation, but of sacrifice of their lives for others. It is not correct, therefore, to say that there is any absolute or unqualified necessity to preserve one's life. There is an awful danger of allowing the principle that has been argued. Who is to be the judge of this sort of necessity? By what measure is the comparative value of lives to be measured? Is it to be strength, or intellect, or some other standard?

Although we are mindful of the dire circumstances here, a man has no right to declare temptation to be an excuse, nor allow compassion for the criminal to change or weaken in any manner the legal definition of the crime. It is therefore our duty to declare that the act in this case was wilful murder, that the facts as stated in the verdict are no legal justification of the homicide. In our unanimous opinion Dudley (D1) and Stephens (D2) are guilty of murder, and sentence of death is imposed.

Analysis:

The boy's name was Richard Parker. The cite here is to the Queen's Bench Division [England]. Note that the date is 1884. After this decision, the Crown commuted the sentence of death to six months. If this happened today, there would certainly be a lot of public opinion on the matter, but the legal result wouldn't necessarily change. It is no wonder that the jury couldn't decide whether the actions of the sailors were justified by the circumstances. It is difficult to convict a person when you understand and perhaps even agree with the actions they have taken, or if you think that because they were in such unique circumstances you should not pass judgment upon them. The Crown certainly thought, for whatever reason, that the punishment was too severe under the circumstances. People often justify their actions with the thought that "it was him or me." However, the Court points out that there are circumstances under which one is supposed to sacrifice one's own life for the greater good of society. The Court refers to several legal authorities without finding an easy answer to the issue before it. Although a public opinion poll on the matter might show that many people would forgive the sailors, this does not impact on the legality of their actions. The sailors were not under an immediate threat of death and certainly under no threat from the boy. It would be one thing [morally, legally] to allow the boy to die and then consume him, but it is altogether another thing to kill him in order to consume him. ["To consume:" which is not unlike consummé, i.e., boy soup.] Keep in mind that the facts make all the difference when a jury is determining whether a defendant is justified when he has taken another's life.

A THREAT OF FUTURE HARM WILL NOT JUSTIFY A DEFENSE OF DURESS, EXCEPT WHERE THE HARM IS SO LIKELY TO OCCUR THAT THE ACTOR CANNOT ESCAPE THE SITUATION

United States v. Contento-Pachon

(Government) v. (Unwilling Drug-Runner)
(1984) 723 F.2d 691

M E M O R Y   G R A P H I C

Instant Facts

Contento-Pachon (D), a Colombian national acting under duress, swallows balloons filled with cocaine for transport to the U.S. and is arrested at customs.

Black Letter Rule

A defendant may assert the defense of duress when he acts under a threat of future harm only when the harm is likely to occur so quickly that the defendant cannot escape the situation.

Case Vocabulary

NECESSITY DEFENSE: A justification defense where a defendant's actions result from an emergency not of his own creation, and where he commits a harm that is less severe than what would have occurred had he not taken action.

Procedural Basis: Appeal from conviction for narcotics transport after motion for exclusion of duress defense is granted.

Facts: Contento-Pachon (D) is a native of Bogota, Colombia, and is employed as a cab driver. One of Contento-Pachon's (D) passengers, Jorge, offered him a job working as a chauffeur. When later he contacted Jorge, however, he was told that the job would consist of swallowing cocaine-filled balloons and transporting them to the United States. Contento-Pachon (D) agreed to consider the job. About a week later, Contento-Pachon (D) told Jorge that he would not accept the job. Jorge responded by telling Contento-Pachon (D) details about his personal life, and informing him that failure to cooperate would result in the death of his wife and his three-year-old child. The pair met again the following day, and Contento-Pachon's (D) life and his family's lives were again threatened. At this point, Contento-Pachon (D) agreed to take the cocaine into the United States. Contento-Pachon (D) swallowed 129 balloons of cocaine [a Guinness World Record, as seen on FOX]. He was informed that he would be watched at all times during the trip, and that if he failed to follow Jorge's instructions he and his family would be killed. When Contento-Pachon (D) arrived in the United States, he consented to have his stomach x-rayed. The x-rays revealed the cocaine. At Contento-Pachon's (D) trial, the Government (P) moved to exclude the defenses of duress and necessity. The motion was granted. Contento-Pachon (D) was convicted of unlawful possession of a narcotic with intent to distribute.

Issue: May a defendant assert the defense of duress when he acts under a threat of future harm likely to occur so quickly that the defendant cannot escape the situation?

Decision and Rationale: (Boochever) Yes. There are three elements to a duress defense: (1) an immediate threat of death or serious bodily injury; (2) a well-grounded fear that the threat will be carried out; (3) no reasonable opportunity to escape the threatened harm. Factfinding is usually a jury function, and the trial court rarely rules on a defense as a matter of law. Where the trial court finds the evidence insufficient as a matter of law to support a defense, the court may exclude the evidence. The trial court found Contento-Pachon's (D) evidence insufficient. However, the threat of danger was immediate because Contento-Pachon (D) had reason to believe that Jorge would carry out his threats. Jorge knew where the family lived, and Contento-Pachon (D) contends that he was being watched the entire trip. If Contento-Pachon (D) failed to cooperate, the consequences would have been immediate and harsh. Contento-Pachon (D) had no real opportunity to escape the danger by going to the authorities, since he believed the Bogota police were corrupt and were linked to the drug traffickers. His only other alternative to escape the danger was to flee. To flee, Contento-Pachon (D) would have had to pack all his belongings, leave his job, and take his family beyond the reach of the drug traffickers. Thus, Contento-Pachon (D) presented a triable issue on escapability. The Government (P) argues that the defense of duress also requires that a defendant offer evidence that he attempted to turn himself in to authorities upon reaching a position of safety. However, this element seems to apply only to prison escape cases. In cases not involving prison escape, there seems to be no real difference between this element and the third element as listed above. At the first opportunity to cooperate with authorities without alerting the observer, he consented to an x-ray. We hold that a defendant who has acted under a well-grounded fear of immediate harm with no opportunity to escape may assert the duress defense, if there is a triable issue of fact whether he took the opportunity to escape by submitting to authorities at the first reasonable opportunity. The trial court correctly disallowed Contento-Pachon's (D) use of the necessity defense, because his actions were coerced by human, not physical forces. In addition, he did not act to "promote the general welfare," another instance where the defense of necessity is properly invoked. Because the trier of fact should be allowed to consider the credibility of the proffered evidence as to duress, we reverse. The court correctly excluded Contento-Pachon's (D) necessity defense. Reversed and remanded.

Analysis:

The court distinguishes the duress-defense from a defense of necessity as the one resulting from human coercion, the other resulting from coercion by "physical forces." "Physical forces" refers to events of nature, such as storms or privations. In some modern cases, however, the distinction is lost—some modern codifications of duress and necessity combine the two doctrines into an overarching "choice of evils" doctrine. The defense of necessity is promoted on utilitarian grounds, upholding the principle that the law ought to encourage the fruition of the greater good at the expense of the lesser. However, the defense is not absolute. In a famous English case, *Regina v. Dudley*, three sailors and a cabin boy were adrift in an open lifeboat. After seven days without water and nine without food, two of the sailors killed the cabin boy, and all three sailors drank his blood and fed on his body. The court found the two sailors guilty of murder, though there was a net preservation of life, since all four likely would have died had the crime not been committed. In an American case, nine sailors and thirty-two passengers were stranded on a lifeboat after a shipwreck. A storm threatened to sink the lifeboat, and the sailors decided that they must lighten the boat's load to weather the storm. Some of the sailors began throwing unmarried male passengers off the boat, and the boat arrived safely at port. At the trial of one of the sailors, where he was convicted of manslaughter, the court held that the surplus sailors should have sacrificed themselves before the passengers, and that between people in equal situation, those to be sacrificed should be determined by lot.

People v. Unger

(Illinois) v. (Escaped Inmate)
(1977) 66 Ill. 2d 333, 5 Ill. Dec. 848, 362 N.E.2d 319

M E M O R Y   G R A P H I C

 Instant Facts

Unger (D) escaped from an honor farm (prison) in Illinois and claimed it was necessary for him to do so as he was forced to choose between the lessor of two evils (escaping or being subjected to homosexual attacks and possibly death).

Black Letter Rule

An escaped prisoner may assert the defense of necessary if he can set forth facts that would tend to show that his choice to escape was the lessor of two evils — to escape or to remain and be subjected to repeated sexual assault.

Case Vocabulary

DURESS: To place another person under duress is to unlawfully coerce that person to commit an unlawful act which that person would not otherwise commit.

Procedural Basis: On appeal to the Illinois Supreme Court affirming the judgment of the appellate court to reverse the conviction.

Facts: Francis Unger (D) was serving a one-to three-year term for auto theft. On March 7, 1972, Unger (D) walked off of an honor farm after receiving death threats and threats of homosexual attacks by other inmates. He was caught two days later in a motel room. Unger (D) testified that on the day he walked off the honor farm he received an institutional telephone call in which an unidentified person threatened him with death because the caller believed Unger (D) had reported the assaults to prison officials. Unger (D) had previously been sexually attacked at the honor farm by three inmates whom he named at trial. Prior to his transfer to the honor farm Unger (D) testified that a fellow inmate had brandished a six-inch knife in an attempt to force him to engage in homosexual activities. Unger (D) was 22 years old, 155 pounds, and testified that he was not a particularly good fighter. At no time did Unger (D) report any of the incidences to the proper authorities. Unger (D) said he left the honor farm to save his life and that he planned to return once he found someone who could help him. He stated he was attempting to get enough money from friends to hire an attorney, and after obtaining legal advice, intended to return to the prison. [Sure he was.]

Issue: If an escaped inmate asserts that the conditions under which he found himself forced him to choose between escaping or being sexually assaulted is he entitled to assert the defense of necessity?

Decision and Rationale: (Ryan) Yes. The trial court submitted the following jury instruction (People's Instruction No. 9) over the objection of Unger (D): "The reasons, if any, given for the alleged escape are immaterial and not to be considered by you as in any way justifying or excusing, if there were in fact such reasons." The trial court refused to submit jury instructions that provided that for the affirmative defenses of (1) necessity, and (2) compulsion (duress). Illinois (P) contends that as a matter of law neither defense is available to Unger (D). We agree with the appellate court finding that the giving of People's Instruction No. 9 was reversible error. We also hold that it was reversible error for the trial court to not instruct on the defense of necessity. The defenses of duress and necessity have both been allowed in prison escape situations. In *People v. Harmon*, the defense of duress was held to apply in a case where the defendant alleged that he escaped in order to avoid repeated homosexual attacks by fellow inmates. In *People v. Lovercamp*, a limited defense of necessity was held to be available to two defendants whose escapes were allegedly motivated by fear of homosexual attacks. If Unger's (D) testimony is believed, he was forced to choose between two admitted evils by the situation which arose from actual or threatened homosexual assaults and fears of reprisal. Unger's (D) testimony (of previous attacks, and threatened further attacks, and of death threats) was sufficient to justify the giving of a necessity instruction. Illinois (P) insists that the following test from *Lovercamp* is the appropriate test to follow in order to decide if a necessity instruction is proper: (1) The prisoner is faced with a specific threat of death, forcible sexual attack or substantial bodily injury in the immediate future; (2) There is no time for a complaint to the authorities or there exists a history of futile complaints which make any result from such complaints illusory; (3) There is no time or opportunity to resort to the courts; (4) There is no evidence of force or violence used towards prison personnel or other 'innocent' persons in the escape; and (5) The prisoner immediately reports to the proper authorities when he has attained a position of safety from the immediate threat. These conditions are relevant factors to be considered in assessing a claim of necessity. However, we do not hold that each condition is, as a matter of law, necessary to establish a meritorious necessity defense. These conditions go to the weight and credibility of a defendant's testimony. The absence of one or more of the conditions listed would not necessarily mandate a finding that a defendant could not assert the defense of necessity. The absence of one condition does not alone disprove the claim of necessity and should not, therefore, automatically preclude an instruction on the defense.

Analysis:

The court sets forth various theories (asserted by various commentators) on duress and necessity. The court notes it has been suggested that a major distinction between duress and necessity is that the source of the coercive power in cases of compulsion (duress) is from human beings, whereas in situations of necessity the pressure on the defendant arises from the forces of nature. Also, compulsion generally requires an impending, imminent threat of great bodily harm together with a demand that the person perform the specific criminal act for which he is eventually charged. Where the defense of compulsion is successfully asserted, the coercing party is guilty of the crime. Another commentator suggests that the relevant consideration should be whether the defendant chose the lesser of two evils (necessity), or whether he was unable to exercise free choice at all (compulsion/duress). The court notes that the circumstances presented do not neatly fit into either defense. However, the court does decide that necessity is an appropriate defense here because (1) Unger (D) was not deprived of his free will by the threat of imminent physical harm (compulsion/duress), and (2) Unger's (D) testimony was sufficient to raise the affirmative defense of necessity. The credibility of Unger's (D) testimony, of course, is left to the jury to determine. The court was not saying that Unger's (D) testimony was believable. Only that his testimony was sufficient to raise the defense of necessity and entitle him to a jury instruction. The court noted that a defense of compulsion would be applicable in the unlikely event that a prisoner was coerced by the threat of imminent physical harm to perform the specific act of escape. Necessity is a justification defense. Duress is an excuse defense.

A PERPETRATOR OF A MURDER IS NOT ENTITLED TO ASSERT THE DEFENSE OF DURESS

Regina v. Howe

(English Prosecutor) v. (Coerced Murderer)
(1987) 1 App.Cas. 417, 1 All E.R. 771

M E M O R Y   G R A P H I C

Instant Facts
Howe (D), in the midst of beating a young man, complied with an order given by one of his cohorts to strangle the young man, later claiming he acted under duress from threat of death to himself; as a matter of law, Howe's (D) claim of duress is not permitted.

Black Letter Rule
The defense of duress is not available to the perpetrator of a murder.

Case Vocabulary

BLACKSTONE: (1723-80) Sir William Blackstone was a famous English judge and writer on law; he wrote what is referred to as "Blackstone's Commentaries," a commentary on the common law of England often referred to in Anglo-American courts.
CO-CONSPIRATOR: One of at least two persons who joins in agreement to do an unlawful act.
HOUSE OF LORDS: The upper house of British Parliament.
LORD HALE: (1609-76) (English) Lord Chief Justice from 1671-76.
PERPETRATOR: This is the guy who actually commits the crime charged.
REGINA: The Latin (and official) reference to the Queen of England.

Procedural Basis: The court of appeals certified a question of law of general importance to the House of Lords.

Facts: Howe (D) and three others were prosecuted for, among other things, the murder of a 19-year-old young man. Howe (D) [and friends] took the victim to a secluded spot and kicked and punched him. Howe (D) strangled the victim after being so ordered by one of his co-conspirators (Murray). Howe (D) claimed Murray would have beaten him (Howe (D)) to death if he had not complied with the order to kill the young man.

Issue: Is the defense of duress available to the person who actually commits a murder?

Decision and Rationale: (Hailsham) No. We may look back to the time of Lord Hale and Blackstone and note from their writings that a man under duress "ought rather to die himself than escape by murder of an innocent. I accept, of course, that duress is held to be a complete defense to almost all other crimes. It is not available to a defendant accused of murder. In a case such as *Director of Public Prosecutions for Northern Ireland v. Lynch*, the defendant [who drove the car utilized in the murder of a police officer and was allowed the defense of duress as he claimed coercion by members of the Irish Republican Army to participate as an accomplice] was not the actual perpetrator of the murder. However, in *Abbot v. The Queen*, the defendant [who, among others, dug a pit into which they threw the victim, stabbed and beat her to death, then buried her alive] as an actual participant in the murder was denied the defense of duress. Any academic who does not understand the difference between these two cases has parted company with a full sense of reality. *Dudley and Stephens* is the authority on the availability on the supposed defense of necessity. If we were to decide (which we do not) that duress was available for the perpetrator of a murder, then we would also have to say that *Dudley and Stephens* is no longer good law. Duress arises from the wrongful threats or violence of another human being and necessity arises from any other objective dangers threatening the defendant. This, however, is a distinction without a difference, since on this view duress is only that species of the genus of necessity [how did we get to biology analogies?] which is caused by wrongful threats. I consider the right course to deny the defense of duress to a person charged with murder when he is the actual killer. It is neither good morals, good policy or good law to suggest, as did the majority in *Lynch* and the minority in *Abbott* that the ordinary man of reasonable fortitude is not supposed to be capable of heroism if he is asked to take an innocent life rather than sacrifice his own. Many will succumb as in *Dudley and Stephens*, but many will not. The law should not cast the cloak of its protection upon the coward in the name of a "concession to human frailty." It has been suggested that we might treat duress as analogous to provocation, or diminished responsibility, and say that in indictments for murder, duress might reduce the crime to manslaughter. I am quite unable to accept this. Unlike the doctrine of provocation, which is based on emotional loss of control, the defense of duress is put forward as a "concession to human frailty" whereby a conscious decision is coolly undertaken, to sacrifice an innocent human life.

Analysis:

The court of appeals certified three questions of law to the House of Lords. The casebook only provides the first question regarding the availability of duress. The "decision" here is from an excerpt of a speech given by one member of the House of Lords (Hailsham) on the question presented. The issue of whether the defense of duress is available to the perpetrator of the actual killing is relevant in that sometimes a person who does not actually commit the murder, can be nevertheless, charged with murder. For example, some criminal statutes allow for the charge of murder against all those involved in a crime that results in a killing, even for the poor slob who drove the get-a-way car. The opinion here distinguishes such a case, *Lynch*, in which the defense of duress was allowed to the defendant who was the accomplice (drove the car) in the

©2002 West Group. All Rights Reserved. Do not duplicate.

murder. Notice that those who are faced with deciding what exactly is a justification defense (necessity) and an excuse defense (duress) often do not quite agree as to which is which. In *Dudley and Stephens*, the court attempts to distinguish necessity from duress, and here, duress is considered to be a mere subset of the greater whole [math analogy] of necessity. Under duress, we might consider a perpetrator excused from his conduct if we are assured that he committed the crime because someone else held a gun to his head and coerced him to so act. Under duress, we understand that the perpetrator is not necessarily acting by his own free will. However, under necessity, the coercive circumstances involve not another person, but other forces which compel the choice between evils. When Hailsham links the defense of duress with the defense of necessity, he is basically saying that Howe (D) was not justified in his actions. Necessity is the justification defense, that is, that one is justified in choosing the lessor of two evils. Hailsham suggests that a person who would take an innocent life in order to save his own is rationalizing that one innocent life (the victim) is at least as valuable as another innocent life (the perpetrator). Hailsham states that, "in such a case a man cannot claim that he is choosing the lessor of two evils. Instead, he is embracing the cognate but morally disreputable principle that the ends justify the means." Hailsham is saying that the perpetrator ought to sacrifice his own life, that is, that he is not justified in his actions. [Think: *Dudley and Stephens*.] This does not really address the issue of the defense of duress where we excuse the actor.

Commonwealth v. Graves

(Pennsylvania) v. (Drunk, High, and Forgetful Robber)

(1975) 461 Pa. 118, 334 A.2d 661

M E M O R Y   G R A P H I C

Instant Facts

Graves (D), while intoxicated and high, burglarized, robbed, and injured an old man who subsequently died from his injuries; Graves' (D) conviction for murder was reversed (and a new trial awarded) by the state supreme court.

Black Letter Rule

Although voluntary intoxication is not an excuse for unlawful actions, evidence thereof may be introduced to negate the intent requirement of the crime charged.

Case Vocabulary

COMMONWEALTH: Used in the sense of a "State," i.e., a group of people choosing self-government, and which is local in nature, but also a necessary part of a nation.
SODIUM AMYTAL TEST: An hypnotic, sedative drug used to elicit feelings and/or memories; it is commonly, but incorrectly, referred to as a truth serum.

Procedural Basis: On appeal to the Pennsylvania Supreme Court which reversed the conviction for murder and ordered a new trial.

Facts: Pursuant to a prior conceived plan, Daniel Graves (D) (Graves) and his cousins Thomas and Edward Mathis burglarized the home of 75-year-old Sebastiano Patiri, and robbed him. Mr. Patiri later died from injuries sustained in the robbery. Graves (D) testified that on the day of the incident he drank a quart or more of wine and took a pill which was LSD. He testified that this caused him to hallucinate (seeing such things as cars jumping over each other), and that he became unconscious and suffered limited amnesia. He contended that he had no recollection of the occurrence at Mr. Patiri's home. A professional psychiatrist (doctor) testified that he gave Graves (D) a polygraph and a sodium amytal test which confirmed that Graves (D) was telling the truth about ingesting the wine and LSD. The doctor testified that in his opinion, because Graves (D) was under the influence of these intoxicants that "he wasn't able to form the proper conscious intent to take a life, to assault." Graves' (D) counsel than asked the doctor his opinion as to whether Graves (D) could, at the time of the incident, form the specific intent to take or steal from a person. The court sustained Pennsylvania's (P) objection to this question. The court rejected Graves' (D) request for a jury instruction that set forth that if they found Graves (D) incapable of forming the intent to commit burglary or robbery because of the consumption of wine or the ingestion of the drug, or both, he could not be guilty of these offenses.

Issue: Can evidence of voluntary intoxication be admitted to negate an element of the crime charged?

Decision and Rationale: (Nix) Yes. The trial court erred in denying Graves (D) the opportunity to introduce evidence of the effect of intoxication on his ability to form the requisite intent of the crimes of burglary and robbery. The trial court relied on a previous opinion of this court which we now reverse to the extent that it suggests that evidence of intoxication offered for the purpose of negating the presence of specific intent may not be used in cases other than felonious homicide. The trial court incorrectly held that the evidence of intoxication was irrelevant as to the robbery and burglary charges. For many years we have admitted testimony of intoxication in the most serious crime in this Commonwealth, i.e., murder in the first degree. To now contend that it would be less reliable in lesser offenses would be the height of absurdity. We also find that the trial court committed reversible error when it refused to permit evidence and to charge the jury as to the possible effect of Graves' (D) consumption of alcohol and ingestion of drugs upon his capacity to form the requisite intent required in the charges of robbery and burglary. In addition, in view of the fact that the jury was given the option to consider the case under a theory of felony-murder, the finding of murder in the first degree is overturned. The sentence is reversed and a new trial awarded. It is fundamental law in this jurisdiction that voluntary intoxication neither exonerates nor excuses criminal conduct. The only permissible probative value evidence of intoxication may have in criminal proceedings is where it is relevant to the question of the capacity of the defendant to have possessed the requisite intent of the crime charged. Evidence of intoxication becomes relevant if the degree of inebriation has reached that point where the mind was incapable of attaining the state of mind required. It must be emphasized that although evidence of intoxication never provides a basis for exoneration or excuse, it may in some instances be relevant to establish that the crime charged in fact did not occur. When the legislature has included within the definition of a crime, specific intent or deliberation and premeditation, then this element must be proved beyond a reasonable doubt. The defendant must be allowed to produce relevant evidence to contest the issue.

Dissent: In the instances where an individual has voluntarily placed

Commonwealth v. Graves (Continued)

himselfin a state of intoxication so as to be incapable of conceiving any intent, we have permitted evidence of such intoxication to lower the degree of guilt within a crime, but only where the legislature has specifically provided for varying degrees of guilt within a crime. Thus, murder in the first degree may be reduced to murder in the second degree. There exist no analogous degrees of robbery. The majority has adopted a new position which, in effect, will allow voluntary intoxication to serve as an excuse for criminal responsibility. An individual who places himself in a position to have no control over his actions must be held to intend the consequences. It matters little that the majority regards such evidence as only bearing upon an element of the crime, the specific intent of the perpetrator, rather than serving as a defense to the crime. The end result is the same and no amount of legal jargon will make it otherwise.

Analysis:

The felony-murder option given to the jury goes to the question of Graves' (D) ability to form the specific intent to take or steal from a person. That is why his attorney asked the doctor if, in his opinion, Graves (D) could form the intent necessary to steal from a person. Pennsylvania (P) objected to the question because it didn't want the doctor to answer in the negative. The court did not allow the doctor to answer. The idea here is that because Mr. Patiri died as a result of the felony robbery and burglary, Pennsylvania (P) can still charge Graves (D) with murder. Pennsylvania (P) just needed to prove the intent for the felony robbery and burglary to get its conviction for murder, which it did. Upon retrial, the testimony of intoxication will be allowed so that Graves (D) can argue he did not have the *intent* to commit the crimes which he *in fact* committed. Of course, Mr. Patiri is still dead whether Graves (D) "meant to" harm him or not. With necessity, or duress, the motivating factors are outside the control of the perpetrator, and the defenses are not permitted. Here, the court is allowing a person who voluntarily placed himself in the situation that caused the harm to argue he was not responsible for the harm because he was too drunk. [This argument wouldn't work with your parents, but it works with this court.] After this case, the legislature quickly amended the law to overturn the result in *Graves*. This is an instance where it is easy to find Graves (D) morally responsible, but if the law sets forth an element of specific intent and an intoxicated Graves (D) was incapable of forming that intent he is not legally responsible. The dissent extends the time frame of responsibility to include Graves' (D) decision to become intoxicated and would hold him legally responsible for his actions while under the influence.

City of Minneapolis v. Altimus

(City) v. (Valium-taking, hit-and-run Driver)
(1976) 306 Minn. 462, 238 N.W.2d 851

M E M O R Y G R A P H I C

Instant Facts
Minnesota Supreme Court allows Valium-taking hit-and-run driver a jury instruction on the unexpected intoxicant theory of involuntary intoxication.

Black Letter Rule
The circumstances under which it is appropriate to allow a defense of involuntary intoxication due to unexpected intoxication are: (1) the defendant did not know of the intoxicant's effect, (2) the intoxicant (and not something else) cause the intoxication, and (3) the intoxicant caused temporary insanity.

Procedural Basis: On appeal to the Supreme Court of Minnesota overturning the trial court's conviction.

Facts: On September 25, 1973, Robert Altimus (D) (Altimus) went to see his doctor at the Veterans Administration Hospital for treatment of a back problem and the flu. His doctor prescribed Valium (a skeletal muscle relaxant). Three days later, Altimus (D) was driving south on Hiawatha Avenue when he made an illegal left turn from a right-hand lane and crashed into a garbage truck proceeding northward on Hiawatha. He immediately backed up and drove easterly on Lake Street at a slow speed (slow because his car was badly damaged from the collision). Policemen, who observed the accident, followed Altimus (D) and stopped him after about one block. Altimus (D) stated he did not have his driver's license with him, but did produce a transfer of title from Robert Altimus to William Jones. Altimus (D) told the officers his name was William Jones. At trial, he did not dispute the facts, but introduced evidence designed to show that he did not have the requisite state of mind to be guilty of the traffic charges. His doctor testified that he had prescribed the Valium and that its normal side effects included drowsiness, fatigue, ataxia (involuntary muscle movements) and confusion. The doctor also testified that hyperexcitability, although more rare, was also a possible side effect. Altimus (D) testified that the Valium had a strange effect on him, making it impossible for him to control himself and that he did not know who owned the automobile which he had driven, and he remembered nothing about the accident or the events that followed. The court denied Altimus' (D) request for a jury instruction on the defense of involuntary intoxication.

Issue: Is a defendant entitled to assert the defense of involuntary intoxication if due to such intoxication he unintentionally and nonnegligently did the act for which he is charged?

Decision and Rationale: (Kelly) Yes. Generally, *voluntary* intoxication does not apply to traffic offenses because these offenses do not require that a specific intent to do a prohibited act. While general offenses do not require the wrongdoer specifically intend to commit the crime for which he is charged, we have held that before criminal liability can attach it is essential that the defendant intentionally or negligently do the act which constitutes the crime. The common law rule was that voluntary intoxication was never a defense to a criminal charge. The common law distinguished *involuntarily* from voluntary intoxication, however, and found involuntary intoxication to be a defense to criminal liability if it caused the defendant to become temporarily insane. Four different kinds of involuntary intoxication have been recognized: (1) *Coerced* intoxication, (2) *Pathological* intoxication, (3) intoxication by *Mistake*, and (4) *Unexpected* intoxication resulting from the ingestion of a medically prescribed drug. Coerced intoxication [is what you think it is] is induced by reason of duress or coercion. Some courts find this a complete defense to all criminal liability. Pathological intoxication occurs when a person takes an intoxicant which normally wouldn't result in intoxication, but which results in a grossly excessive response in the taker. Some jurisdictions have held such defendants not criminally liable; others require that the defendant must be deprived of mental capacity to the degree necessary for an insanity defense. Intoxication by mistake occurs when the defendant is unaware that the substance he is taking is an intoxicant, such as when he is tricked by another into taking the substance. In one instance, a defendant killed a third party after someone gave him "breath purifiers" which were in fact cocaine tablets. Unexpected intoxication occurs when the defendant is unexpectedly intoxicated due to the ingestion of a medically prescribed drug. [Bingo!] Altimus (D) claims that due to the ingestion of a prescribed drug he was unexpectedly intoxicated to the point of unconsciousness, incapable of controlling his actions, and thus not criminally responsible for his actions. A defense of involuntary intoxication due to unexpected intoxication requires: (1) that the defendant must not know, or have reason to know, that the prescribed drug is likely to have an intoxicating effect. If the defendant knows, or has reason to know, that the prescribed drug will have an intoxicating effect, then he is *voluntarily* intoxicated; (2) the prescribed drug, and not some other intoxicant, is in fact the cause of the defendant's intoxication at the time of his alleged criminal conduct; (3) the defendant, due to involuntary intoxication, is temporarily insane. The circumstances that would allow such a defense are rare. We hold, nevertheless, that in the instant case such an instruction was necessary because Altimus (D) introduced evidence sufficient to raise the defense of temporary insanity due to involuntary intoxication. We reverse the conviction.

Analysis:

The court is requiring more than just evidence that Altimus (D) was involuntarily intoxicated due to an unexpected intoxication from taking prescribed drugs. It is requiring that the effect of the drug be so severe as to cause temporary insanity. (Insanity is the next section.) If the jury believes that Altimus (D) and/or the circumstances meet the three-part test, then he neither intentionally nor negligently ran into the garbage truck. What if Altimus (D) took more medication than was prescribed? It would seem to fall outside the requirement that the medication be "prescribed." What if he regularly took more than prescribed because that is the only way he had relief from pain, and (until this accident) never caused him any mental instability? If he was not aware of the intoxicating effect and was not warned by his doctor of the intoxicating effect this issue would be a question of fact for the jury. Under this scenario he still gets the jury instruction. All four categories of involuntary intoxication have been applied in some jurisdictions as requiring that the involuntary intoxication be such "that [the actor] did not understand and appreciate the consequences of his act," or that it render the actor temporarily insane.

United States v. Freeman

(Government) v. (Chronic Drug Abuser)

(1966) 357 F.2d 606

M E M O R Y   G R A P H I C

 Instant Facts

Freeman (D), a chronic drug abuser and alcoholic, was convicted of the sale of narcotics using the *M'Naghten* Rules to determine his criminal liability.

Black Letter Rule

Model Penal Code Section 4.01, which emphasizes "appreciation" of conduct, rather than simply knowing whether it is right or wrong, should be used in place of the narrow *M'Naghten* Rules to determine whether a defendant lacks criminal responsibility due to mental impairment or defect.

Case Vocabulary

PHRENOLOGY: A rejected science that believed character could be determined by the shape and contours of the skull.

RECIDIVISM: A chronic relapse into crime; repeatedly offending.

Procedural Basis: Appeal from a conviction for two counts of selling narcotics.

Facts: Charles Freeman (D) was tried and found guilty on two counts of selling narcotics, and he was sentenced to concurrent five year terms for each count. At trial Freeman (D) alleged that, at the time of sale of the narcotics, he did not possess sufficient capacity and will to be held responsible for the criminality of his acts. The District Court rejected this contention and relied on the *M'Naghten* Rules which allow acquittal only when it is proved that "at the time of committing the act, the party accused was laboring under such a defect of reason, from disease of the mind as not to know the nature and quality of the act he was doing, or, if he did know it, that he did not know he was doing what was wrong." Freeman (D) consumed large amounts of heroin over a fourteen-year period, and was in the habit of consuming one or two bottles of wine per day to increase the effect of the drugs. Freeman (D) also drank six to nine shots of whiskey each day. A psychiatrist, Dr. Denber, observed that Freeman (D) displayed no variation in his emotional reactions, speaking in a flat monotone. As a result of taking impure narcotics for so long, Freeman (D) suffered from frequent episodes of toxic psychosis, characterized by an inability to know what he was doing or where he was. Freeman (D) also boxed for a period of time, and suffered three knock-outs, which led to a general vagueness about details [details like where he was, or what his name is]. Denber noted that Freeman (D) had suffered innumerable brain traumata, which over time resulted in the destruction of brain tissue. Denber initially testified that Freeman (D) was incapable of knowing right from wrong. Later, he acknowledged that Freeman (D) had an awareness of what he was doing in the sense that he knew that he was selling heroin. A psychiatrist called by the Government (P), Dr. Carson, testified that Freeman (D) was able to distinguish between right and wrong within the meaning of the *M'Naghten* test despite his heavy use of narcotics and alcohol. He noted that Freeman (D) possessed the capacity to enter into purposeful conduct and recognized that it was wrong, as evidenced by the fact that Freeman (D) was fearful of being apprehended and sought to conduct the sale in a private location [the men's room]. Carson acknowledged that Freeman (D) had some limitations on his ability to distinguish right from wrong, but not to the degree required by the *M'Naghten* test. The court held that Freeman's (D) condition did not satisfy the requirements of this test, and he was found guilty as charged.

Issue: Should the trial court have applied a less rigid test than the *M'Naghten* rules, so that psychiatric testimony could have been directed towards the defendant's capacity to appreciate the wrongfulness of his conduct, rather than being confined to *M'Naghten's* narrow "right-wrong" inquiry?

Decision and Rationale: (Kaufman) Yes. Before the *M'Naghten* test was established, the concepts of phrenology and monomania were being developed, and had significant influence on *M'Naghten's* right and wrong test. The rule of *M'Naghten's* case froze these concepts into the common law just as they were becoming obsolete. *M'Naghten* focuses on the ability to know right from wrong, so it does not permit the jury to identify those who can distinguish between right and wrong but cannot control their behavior. The test is also unrealistic because it does not recognize degrees of incapacity. Our mental institutions are filled with people who to some extent can differentiate between right and wrong, but lack the capacity to control their actions. A fatal defect in the *M'Naghten* rules stems from the excessive limitations placed on expert psychiatric testimony—the expert is compelled to test guilt or innocence by a concept which bears little relation to reality. The "irresistible impulse" test was created as a substitute to the *M'Naghten* rules. However, the irresistible impulse rule is inherently inadequate and unsatisfactory. The irresistible impulse test is unduly restrictive because it excludes the far more numerous instances of crimes committed after excessive brooding and melancholy by a person who is unable to control his conduct. The *Durham* test, articulated in 1954, stated that a defendant is not criminally responsible "if his unlawful act was the product of mental disease or mental defect." *Durham* eliminated the *M'Naghten* "right-wrong" dichotomy. However, the *Durham* rule also fails to give the fact-finder any standard by which to measure the competency of the defendant. As a result, psychiatrists testifying that the defendant suffered from a mental disorder effectively usurped the jury's function as the fact-finder. In 1962, the American Law Institute adopted Section 4.01 of the Model Penal Code. Unlike the *M'Naghten* rules, the Model Penal Code formulation is in harmony with modern medical science, since it views the mind as a unified entity and recognizes that mental disease may impair its functioning in numerous ways. The use of the word "substantial" to modify "incapacity" emphasizes that "any" capacity is not sufficient to avoid criminal responsibility but that "total" incapacity is also unnecessary. The choice of the word "appreciate," rather than "know," is significant because mere intellectual awareness that conduct is wrongful, when separated from understanding of the moral import of the behavior, can have little significance. Since Freeman's (D) responsibility was determined under the rigid standards of the *M'Naghten* Rules, we are compelled to reverse his conviction and remand the case for a new trial using Model Penal Code Section 4.01 to determine his responsibility. We wish to emphasize, however, that mere recidivism or narcotics addiction will not justify acquittal under Section 4.01. We also emphasize that those suffering from mental disease or defect, while relieved from criminal responsibility, should not be set free to continue to pose a threat to life and property. Those adjudged criminally irresponsible should be turned over to state officials for commitment to a mental hospital pursuant to state procedures. Conviction reversed and remanded.

Concurrence: (Waterman) We have now been persuaded that we should be dissatisfied with the *M'Naghten* Rules because of the discoveries which have, over the course of the 120 years since *M'Naghten*, changed our concepts of mental disease. It is nevertheless true that the scope of serious expert inquiry into the control of conduct has not halted. Tomorrow we may find that Section 4.01 needs further judicial adjustment in light of tomorrow's further discoveries.

Analysis:

Soon after the Model Penal Code formulation appeared it was adopted by all of the U.S. Courts of Appeals. However, it was repudiated in 1984 in favor of a right-wrong, *M'Naghten*-style test. Nevertheless, a number of states have accepted the Model Penal Code test, some by statute, and some by court decision. The "substantial capacity" test, though appreciated by the court in *Freeman*, has been criticized as refurbishing the *M'Naghten* and irresistible impulse rules. Generally, the words "substantial capacity" and "appreciate" have been criticized because they do not have a stable meaning, and jurors and experts are bound to have various competing interpretations. Overall, the Model Penal Code formulation has been praised by commentators as achieving two important goals of a test of responsibility: the formulation gives expression to an intelligible principle, and it fully discloses that principle to the jury.

State v. Johnson

(Rhode Island) v. (Not Stated)
121 R.I. 254, 399 A.2d 469

M E M O R Y   G R A P H I C

Instant Facts
Johnson sets forth the development of the insanity test.

Black Letter Rule
A new standard that allows a jury to consider volitional as well as cognitive impairments before imposing criminal responsibility supercedes the restrictive M'Naghten rule.

Case Vocabulary

KEN: [Barbie's significant other, a.k.a., boy toy] Within the range of what one knows; knowledge or consciousness.

MONOMANIA: A mental state characterized by an obsessive interest in a particular idea.

PHRENOLOGY: A theory that the brain was divided up into various sections, each section impacted a different mental function.

VOLITION: The willful exercise of choosing or deciding to act.

Procedural Basis: Not Stated.

Facts: Not Stated.

Issue: Should the M'Naghten test be abandoned in favor of a new standard for determining the criminal responsibility of those who claim they are blameless by reason of mental illness?

Decision and Rationale: (Doris) Yes. Any legal standard designed to determine criminal responsibility must satisfy several objectives, among which are the following: It must accurately reflect the underlying principles of substantive law and community values; it must comport with the realities of scientific understanding and the scientific information must be articulated in such a way that the experts, lawyers, and jury understand it; the definition of such standard must preserve to the trier of fact its full authority to render a final decision on the issue of criminal responsibility. The time has arrived to modernize our rule. We set forth below a brief evolution of criminal responsibility and its criticisms, and adopt [a version] of the Model Penal Code (MPC) which has received widespread and evergrowing acceptance. We believe it represents a significant, positive improvement over our existing rule. It acknowledges that volitional as well as cognitive impairments must be considered by the jury in its resolution of the responsibility issue. Additionally, the test employs vocabulary sufficiently in the common ken that its use at trial will permit a reasonable three-way dialogue between the law-trained judges and lawyers, the medical-trained experts, and the jury. The "knowledge of good and evil" test of criminal responsibility had its inception in England in the 1500's with an emphasis on the "good and evil" part. It shifted in the 1700's to emphasize the "knowing" part. These tests were evolving during a time when beliefs in demonology and witchcraft were widespread; a time when psychiatry was hardly a profession, let alone a science. The psychological theories of phrenology and monomania thrived and influenced the development of the "right and wrong" test. Both of these compartmentalized concepts have been soundly rejected by modern medical science which views the human personality as a fully integrated system. The celebrated and controversial case of Daniel M'Naghten (tried in 1843) froze these concepts into the common law just at the time they were beginning to come into disrepute. The M'Naghten rule (M'Naghten) is the following two-pronged test: "To establish a defense on the ground of insanity it must be clearly proved that, at the time of committing the act, the party accused was laboring under such a defect of reason, from disease of the mind, as not to know the nature and quality of the act he was doing, or if he did know it, that he did not know that what he was doing was wrong." The test's emphasis upon knowledge of right and wrong refuses to recognize volitional or emotional impairments, viewing the cognitive element as the singular cause of conduct. This requires the psychiatrist to testify in terms of unrealistic concepts having no medical meaning. The rule calls for the psychiatrist to render a moral or ethical judgment, not a scientific opinion, and takes away the jury's function as the decision maker. The M'Naghten rule was supplemented by the "irresistible impulse" test. It adds a volitional component to the cognitive component of M'Naghten, but still in absolute terms. The irresistible impulse is considered in terms of a complete destruction of the governing power of the mind. It misleadingly suggests that such impulses only happen in sudden bursts, and ignores the more common instances of crimes committed after excessive brooding and melancholy by one who is unable to resist sustained physic compulsion. The "Durham" test, although subsequently abandoned, was a significant break with M'Naghten. The Durham test was designed to allow full and complete testimony and allow the jury to consider all relevant evidence. The basic idea of the Durham test is that "an accused is not criminally responsible if his unlawful act was the product of mental disease or mental defect." The undefined scope of "product" of mental disease did not give enough guidance to the jury, and the expert testimony infringed upon the jury's role. Although the test created a great deal of commentary and helped recast the law of criminal responsibility, it was unworkable in practice. After years of criticism of these tests, a new test of criminal responsibility which we have adopted [a version of] today, was provided by the MPC.

Analysis:

The court sets forth the following information about the M'Naghten case. M'Naghten attempted to assassinate Sir Robert Peel, Prime Minister of England, but shot Peel's private secretary instead. There had been several previous assassination attempts on the royal family. The jury was instructed with a test which was heavily influenced by an expert witness who was critical of the "right and wrong" test. M'Naghten was acquitted. The public outcry was lead by the Queen. The Judges of England were summoned before the House of Lords to justify their actions, and reversed the charge used at trial and provided what is now the M'Naghten rule (set forth in the Decision and Rationale). The commentary to § 4.01 of the MPC sets forth a standard which "relieves the defendant of responsibility under two circumstances: (1) when, as a result of mental disease or defect, the defendant lacked substantial capacity to appreciate the criminality [wrongfulness] of his conduct; (2) when, as a result of mental disease or defect, the defendant lacked substantial capacity to conform his conduct to the requirements of law." Notice the use of the word "appreciate" as opposed to "know" in part 1 of the MPC standard. The capacity to conform one's conduct is the volitional aspect of the standard. The MPC standard was adopted by a majority of the states. After John Hinckley's attempted assassination of President Reagan (1981), and his subsequent insanity acquittal, at least four states eliminated the defense of insanity. Several states reverted to M'Naghten. In 1984, Congress adopted the Insanity Defense Reform Act which allows the affirmative defense of insanity when "as a result of a severe mental disease or defect [the defendant] was unable to appreciate the nature and quality or the wrongfulness of his acts. Mental disease or defect does not otherwise constitute a defense." The defendant has the burden of proof which is the high [difficult, not loopy] standard of "by clear and convincing evidence." This test uses "appreciate" which is broader than M'Naghten's "know." It uses "severe" with mental disease or defect, which is a new requirement.

State v. Wilson

(Connecticut) v. (Delusional ["gonna save the world"] Shooter)
(1997) 242 Conn. 605, 700 A.2d 633

M E M O R Y   G R A P H I C

 Instant Facts

Wilson (D) shot to death a friend's father (Jack) because he thought Jack was the mastermind of a huge conspiracy to control everyone's mind, particularly Wilson's (D) mind.

Black Letter Rule

Even if a defendant appreciates that his actions were illegal, if he believes, due to his mental disease or defect, that his actions were morally justified (society would condone his actions if it understood the situation like the defendant understands the situation) then he will not be criminally responsible for his actions.

Case Vocabulary

DEIFIC: Making divine; a deific command is an instruction from God.
DELUSIONAL: To hold a steadfast belief in an idea that is contrary to facts and logic.
ENIGMATIC: Puzzling or mysterious.
JUXTAPOSITION: Words or things which are next to each other, or placed side by side in order to compare them.
TRANSGRESS: To violate the law; to go beyond the established boundaries.

Procedural Basis: On appeal to the Supreme Court of Connecticut reversing the conviction and remanding for a new trial.

Facts: Wilson (D) and Jack Peter's (Jack) son, Dirk Peters (Dirk) had attended high school together. On August 5, 1993, Wilson (D) went to Jack's home, argued with him, then shot Jack numerous times with a semiautomatic revolver which he had purchased two days prior. Jack died. Wilson (D) went to the police after the shooting and gave a sworn statement which included the following: (1) his life had been ruined by Dirk, who had drugged, hypnotized and brainwashed him; (2) Jack had assisted Dirk in these activities; (3) Dirk and Jack were responsible for his schizophrenia; (4) the conduct of Dirk and Jack required "drastic action" and "drastic retribution"; and (5) he had shot Jack repeatedly at Jack's home earlier that day. Wilson (D) believed that Jack was the mastermind of a large organization bent on controlling the minds of others and was responsible for Wilson's (D) pathetic life (mom dead, pets dead, girlfriend gone, unemployed, sexually inadequate, physically weak, and drug addicted). Wilson (D) had, during the first half of 1993, repeatedly called police to inform them of Jack's evil plans, but the police told Wilson (D) that it was impossible for them to investigate his allegations. At trial, Wilson (D) requested (and was denied) a jury instruction which incorporates a moral element into the definition of "wrongfulness" such that "an accused is not criminally responsible for his offending act if, because of mental disease or defect, he believes that he is morally justified in his conduct — even though he may appreciate that his act is criminal." The jury rejected Wilson's (D) claim of insanity and convicted him for murder. He was sentenced to sixty years imprisonment. Upon appeal, Wilson (D) argues that the trial court's denial to instruct the jury on the moral component of the insanity defense is reversible error. Wilson (D) argues that the morality element of "wrongfulness" must be defined in purely personal terms. Connecticut (P) argues that morality must be defined by an objective societal standard.

Issue: Is a defendant criminally responsible for his illegal actions if, because of his mental disease or defect, he believes that he is morally justified in his conduct, although he may appreciate that his actions are legally criminal?

Decision and Rationale: (Palmer) No. Our statute, § 53a-1(a), which is modeled after the Model Penal Code (MPC) allows for the affirmative defense of insanity. It states that "in any prosecution for an offense, it shall be an affirmative defense that the defendant, at the time he committed the proscribed act or acts, lacked substantial capacity, as a result of mental disease or defect, either to appreciate the wrongfulness of his conduct or to control his conduct within the requirements of the law." Three features of the MPC are noteworthy. First, similar to, but not exactly like, our prior common law standard, this test incorporates both a cognitive (to appreciate the wrongfulness of his conduct) and volitional (to control his conduct within the requirements of the law) prong. Second, the test focuses on the defendant's actual appreciation of, not merely his knowledge of, the wrongfulness of his conduct. To *appreciate* the wrongfulness of one's conduct is to understand beyond the bare abstraction of the fact that a certain action is wrong, but to grasp the importance and reality of the conduct. Third, and most important here, is the juxtaposition in the MPC of the word "criminality" with the bracketed word "wrongfulness." The drafters of the MPC did this in order to allow the individual states to decide which of these two standards to adopt to describe the nature of the conduct that a defendant must be unable to appreciate in order to qualify as legally insane. The history of the MPC indicates that "wrongfulness" incorporates a moral element. It is without dispute Connecticut's (P) legislature intended to include this moral element in its insanity statute. We do not agree with Wilson (D) that the standard is completely personal, and although we do agree with Connecticut (P) that there is a societal moral standard involved in the statute, it is not as narrow as Connecticut (P) insists. (Connecticut (P) argued for an objective standard which would mean that "criminality" and "wrongfulness" would be interpreted the same way, which would render meaningless the legislature's choice of the term "wrongfulness.") We need to point out that Wilson's (D) attempt to define morality in purely personal terms are inconsistent with the MPC, judicial precedent, and the assumptions underlying our criminal law. The text accompanying the MPC indicates that a person who appreciates *both* that his conduct violates the criminal law and society's moral standards, should not be allowed the defense of insanity just because of his personal, albeit delusional, moral code. In addition, the large majority of jurisdictions that have considered this cognitive prong of the defense, follow a societal, rather than a personal, standard. Finally, defining the moral element of wrongfulness according to a purely personal standard would undermine the moral culture on which our societal norms of behavior are based. We conclude that a defendant may establish that he lacked substantial capacity to appreciate the "wrongfulness" of his conduct if he can prove that, at the time of his criminal act, as a result of mental disease or defect, he substantially misperceived reality and harbored a delusional belief that society, *under the circumstances as the defendant honestly but mistakenly understood them*, would not have morally condemned his actions. [Highlight the sentence you just read; it is the court's rule for the definition of "wrongfulness."] If a defendant appreciated that his conduct violated the criminal law, yet sincerely believed (due to his mental disease or defect) that society *would* approve of his conduct *if* it shared his understanding of the circumstances underlying his actions, he would be entitled to prevail on the defense. Connecticut (P) argues that Wilson (D) did not provide sufficient evidence to support an instruction on the definition of "wrongfulness." Connecticut (P) claims that Wilson's (D) evidence only tended to show that he followed his own purely personal moral standard. Three expert witnesses who all examined Wilson (D) testified to the effect that he actually believed that by killing Jack he was saving the world from Jack's evil plans. On the basis of this testimony, we conclude that Wilson (D) presented sufficient evidence to support the instruction because a jury reasonably could have found, by a preponderance of the evidence, that Wilson (D) misperceived reality and acting on the basis of that misperception, did not substantially appreciate that his actions were contrary to societal norms. The judgment for conviction is reversed and the case is remanded for a new trial.

Concurrence: (Katz) I concur in the result reached by the majority. I am concerned, nonetheless, that the test as interpreted by the majority may exclude certain defendants who are obviously impaired and for whom the interests of justice would not be served by a criminal conviction; specifically, those defendants who, *because of their mental illness*, adhere to a personal code of morality. In declaring that a defendant who, despite his mental illness, has the substantial capacity to appreciate social boundaries, yet nonetheless, chooses to transgress those boundaries must be held criminally responsible, the majority seeks to exclude those otherwise sane individuals who would use the insanity defense as a shield when seeking to satisfy personal grudges, or impose personal political beliefs. I wholeheartedly agree with this goal. I disagree with the majority, however, that the defense should not apply to an individual who is mentally ill and *because of that illness* believes that society's rules do not apply to his or her actions. It is my belief that such a person is not *capable of appreciating* the legal and social import of his or her acts, and therefore, should not be held criminally responsible.

Dissent: (McDonald) The majority approves a jury instruction that provides a definition of wrong as something against societal morality, but not objectively so. Under this formula, a person who knows murder is wrong in the eyes of society and knows that society does not share his perception that the victim needs to be killed may be excused if he believes, because of mental illness, that society would condone the killing if it, too, saw the need. This should not be written into our law. If a defendant recognizes his conduct is both criminal and wrong in the eyes of society, as murder clearly is, public safety demands that he be held responsible for his actions. It is hoped that we can still rely on the common sense of jurors, coping with these enigmatic instructions, to safeguard us.

Analysis:

The court uses "society's morals" in two different ways. One way is the legal expression of society's morals as expressed in the criminal statutes; the other is the more general societal moral standard that we [those of us who are sane] understand to be what other people think is right and wrong. The latter is best summed up with that phrase your mother used to use on you to try to get you to conform your conduct to societal norms — "What will the neighbor's think?" There is a third way to define the "moral standard," that is the purely personal moral standard. This is a subjective standard which appears to have made its way into the majority's definition despite the majority saying that it rejected it. The majority includes the phrase, *"under the circumstances as the defendant honestly but mistakenly understood them"* within its rule. This certainly reads like a subjective, personal standard. How would you like to be on the jury that gets this court's instruction defining "wrongfulness?" One study of juror behavior has shown that juries come to the same conclusion regardless of the instruction given. Another study indicates that juries use their own sense of justice to evaluate the testimony and determine if the defendant is not guilty by reason of insanity. The majority notes that a person who was following a delusional "deific command" might fall within a category of cases in which a person's delusional personal beliefs so clouded his cognition as to render him incapable of recognizing the broader moral implications of his actions. This person, the majority states, would be entitled to be acquitted under the cognitive prong of the insanity defense. Can a person who believes that he is *morally justified* in his actions, despite appreciating the illegality of his actions, be deterred (this time or next) by the prospect of criminal punishment? Will criminal punishment rehabilitate such a person? A person who is incapable of understanding that his delusion is in fact a delusion is probably not going to be deterred from his actions. Such a person believes he is morally justified, that is, once he explains the situation as he sees it, others will approve of his actions and certainly not punish, but thank him. It is also highly unlikely that criminal confinement will have a rehabilitative effect on such a person.

ONCE A DEFENDANT PRODUCES EVIDENCE OF INSANITY, PROSECUTION MUST PROVE SANITY BEYOND A REASONABLE DOUBT

State v. Green

(Tennessee) v. (Unbathed, Ousiograph-hunting Cop Killer)
(1982) 643 S.W.2d 902

M E M O R Y   G R A P H I C

 ### Instant Facts
Eighteen year old Steven Green's (D) conviction for murder of a police officer was set aside because Tennessee's (P) rebuttal evidence was not sufficient to refute the overwhelming proof of Green's insanity.

Black Letter Rule
Prosecution has the burden to prove beyond a reasonable doubt a defendant's sanity in order to rebut a defendant's evidence of his insanity.

Case Vocabulary

COMPLICITY: To participate (as the actual actor or with another person) in a criminal plan or act.
DELUSIONS OF GRANDEUR: A fixed false belief that you are exalted above all other people or things (e.g., that you are royalty or a god.)
DELUSIONS OF PERSECUTION: A fixed false belief that someone or something is persistently pursuing, harassing, and/or oppressing you [like your civil procedure professor or the financial aid officer].
FORENSIC PSYCHOLOGIST: That branch of psychiatry dealing with mental disorders as they relate to legal principles.
LAY TESTIMONY: [Not expert testimony.] Given by a witness who is not an expert on the matter at hand, but generally, is testimony which is "first-hand knowledge" of the witness.

Procedural Basis: On appeal to the Court of Criminal Appeals of Tennessee setting aside the conviction for murder because of Green's insanity.

Facts: Steven Green (D) (Green), beginning at the age of seven years, had sudden outbursts of anger and violence, both institutionalized and out-patient psychiatric treatment, and a need to find a machine he called an "oustograph" or "ousiograph" which he believed could detect who was attempting to send messages to his brain and "direct" him. He refused to bathe, stayed in bed during the days, and walked the streets at night. He carried a bag around with him which he told his parents kept him company. He laughed at inappropriate times and would stare into space and move his mouth without saying anything. He complained that the television talked back to him. By the age of sixteen he dropped out of school, but then enrolled in a Navy reserve program, returned to school and managed to graduate in June 1978. He reported to Navy training but a few weeks later he was discharged for failure to adapt to regulations. Between this time and January 1979, his whereabouts were often unknown. He did stay with various relatives during part of this time (he stayed with an uncle for six to seven weeks, and an aunt for two weeks) who testified to Green's (D) bizarre behavior. On January 18, 1979, Chattanooga police found the body of Officer Harry Wilcox (Wilcox) lying face down in a pool of blood in a restroom at Warner Park. He had been shot twice in the head, and his police revolver was missing. On his back, officer's found a plastic bag containing a note. The note, addressed to Agent Ray Hanrahan (Hanrahan) of the FBI, contained a meaningless string of words and phrases, including reference to an "ousiograph." Police were led to Green (D) by contacting Hanrahan who Green (D) had previously contacted about finding an "ousiograph" to help detect who was sending messages to his brain. At trial, Green (D) offered both lay and expert testimony to establish that he was insane at the time he committed the offense. Tennessee (P) disputed the fact that Green (D) suffered from a mental disease or disorder. Upon appeal, Tennessee (P) argues that Green (D) had the capacity to know right from wrong and to control his behavior at will.

Issue: To rebut a defendant's evidence of insanity, must the prosecution (here, Tennessee) prove beyond a reasonable doubt that the defendant is sane?

Decision and Rationale: (Daughtrey) Yes. Green (D) was arrested on January 20, 1979, and charged with the murder of Wilcox. In March 1979, John Littleton was hired as local counsel for Green (D). After attempting to talk with Green (D), he immediately asked for a psychiatric evaluation which the court ordered. Dr. Speal, a forensic psychologist diagnosed Green (D) as paranoid schizophrenic, a condition which is characterized by irrational thinking, feelings inappropriate to the situation, an overly suspicious nature, hostility, and delusions of grandeur and of persecution. Dr. Speal's test of Green (D) in March 1979, showed that Green (D) was psychotic at the time and suffering from auditory hallucinations. He saw Green (D) over a period of 18 months. By May 1979, it was necessary to hospitalize Green (D). He was found incompetent to stand trial. Six months later, he was found to be "greatly improved." Both Dr. Pieper and a clinical nurse who evaluated Green (D) testified that at the time Green (D) killed Wilcox he was acting under the control of delusions or hallucinations or both, that he therefore did not understand that his act was wrong and could not conform his conduct to the requirements of law. Tennessee's (P) rebuttal evidence offered to establish Green's (D) sanity at the time of the offense, consisted of testimony by five Chattanooga police officers and a former county employee. The arresting officer, who spent about two hours with Green (D), testified he was "cooperative," "coherent," and "intelligent," but did not want to talk about the shooting. The other officers (one of whom had been Wilcox's friend), who either took Green (D) to a rescue mission or arrested him for vagrancy, both before and after the killing, testified that Green (D) was cooperative, coherent, and not operating under any delusions, but was unkept and that he smelled. A former county employee gave Green (D) a ride in his van the day Wilcox was shot. He testified that he and Green (D) engaged in small talk for about 45 minutes and that he noticed nothing out of the ordinary about him. From this testimony, Tennessee (P) took the position that Green (D) was "not insane and crazy and bizarre at the time the killing happened," but was just a "little bit different." However, the testimony that described him as normal is not inconsistent with a determination that Green (D) was insane at the time of the offense. The medical experts unrefuted testimony is that a paranoid schizophrenic can operate in a seemingly normal way. Dr. Pieper testified that such a person could appear quite normal, until someone says something, or something happens which the person regards as threatening and it can set them off. Given the nature of the evidence offered by Green (D), the burden of proof in this case squarely fell upon Tennessee (P) to establish Green's (D) sanity beyond a reasonable doubt. Tennessee (P) argues that the nature of Green's (D) condition was not sufficient to meet the two prong test for insanity. It argues that evidence that Green (D) fled the scene and hid the weapon proves he knew the wrongfulness of his acts. The most obvious response to this argument is that the record shows only that Green (D) left the scene at some point and the revolver was never recovered; neither of these facts establishes beyond a reasonable doubt that Green (D) was attempting to conceal his identity nor complicity from the police, or that he otherwise was able to appreciate the wrongfulness of what he had done. Even if we conceded that this behavior evidenced some appreciation of the wrongfulness of his conduct, the record is wholly devoid of any evidence that at the time he shot Wilcox, Green (D) was able to conform his conduct to the dictates of law. Tennessee's (P) only argument in response to overwhelming evidence of Green's (D) incapacity in this respect is that he failed to react violently to the other officers he came into contact with showing his ability to conform his conduct to the law with respect to Wilcox. This argument, of course, not only begs the question (that is, whether under this analysis any initial violent behavior could ever be the product of insanity), but it also ignores the nature of paranoid schizophrenia, as described by experts in this case. Tennessee (P) points out that the jury is not bound by expert testimony. However, the Tennessee Supreme Court has clearly delineated what proof the State must produce to meet and overcome evidence of insanity. The test basically sets forth that the State can introduce evidence by expert testimony on insanity, or relevant lay testimony, or through the showing of acts or statements of the defendant, at or near the time of the commission of the crime, which are consistent with sanity and inconsistent with insanity. In this case, although the acts of Green (D) at or near the time of the killing were arguably "consistent with sanity," quite obviously they were not also "inconsistent with insanity." We have no choice but to set aside Green's (D) conviction.

Analysis:

Notice that Tennessee (P) did not offer any expert testimony to rebut Green's (D) expert testimony. Expert testimony is not required and lay testimony seemed to satisfy the jury. The expert's role is to provide information to the jury about the defendant's medical condition. It is the jury's role to determine whether the defendant in his condition should be held responsible for his actions. It is possible that the jury was more concerned for the public safety, or that because the victim was a police officer, Green (D) should be punished regardless of his mental capacity. The appeals court noted that a reviewing court should be most wary of disturbing a jury verdict. However, it also quotes from a Supreme Court case that notes that there are rare cases "where the facts adduced as to the existence and impact of an accused's mental condition may be so overwhelming as to require a judge to conclude that no reasonable juror could entertain a reasonable doubt." One commentator believes that we (society, jurors) can determine whether an individual is "crazy" without expert medical testimony, and that the decision of whether to punish a "crazy" person is a social and moral judgment, not one that should be determined by an expert's opinion. His point is that medical opinions change over time as to what is a mental disorder, and that experts are often given too much authority in the courtroom, i.e., they usurp the function of the jury. However, without some kind of guideline or opinions it would be pure guessing on our part. Weirdness occurs on a sliding scale. How weird does a person have to be to be excused for his criminal conduct? Think about what kinds of information you would want/need to know about a defendant that would cause you to consider that his actions were a result of his inability (because of his mental disease or defect) to know or appreciate the wrongfulness of his actions, or to control his conduct. One view that the defense of insanity should be abolished is provided in the commentaries to the Model Penal Code which states that any psychiatric diagnosis should be relevant only after trial to determine what kind of confinement or treatment is appropriate, not to determine criminal responsibility.

State v. Wilcox

(Government) v. (Diminished Capacity Hopeful)
(1982) 70 Ohio St.2d 182, 436 N.E.2d 523

M E M O R Y   G R A P H I C

Instant Facts

Wilcox (D), borderline retarded and schizophrenic, commits murder and burglary, and seeks to assert the diminished capacity defense.

Black Letter Rule

The diminished capacity defense, in which a defendant presents expert psychiatric testimony that relates to his alleged incapacity to form the requisite intent for his crimes, is an inconsistent, unpredictable, and disfavored doctrine.

Case Vocabulary

DIMINISHED CAPACITY: An impaired mental state, short of insanity, that may be caused by disease or intoxication, that prevents the actor from having the requisite mens rea to be held criminally liable.
SCHIZOPHRENIA: A mental disorder that is characterized by a separation of rational thought from emotions, and is often accompanied by delusions.

Procedural Basis: Appeal from a conviction for murder and burglary.

Facts: Wilcox (D) participated in a burglary in which the victim was shot and killed. A psychiatrist found that Wilcox (D) was borderline retarded, schizophrenic, dyslexic, and suffering from organic brain syndrome. After a few months of treatment, Wilcox (D) was found competent to stand trial. He introduced psychiatric testimony in support of his plea of not guilty by reason of insanity, but the trial court refused on the theory that Wilcox's (D) mental condition precluded him from forming the specific intent to commit aggravated murder and burglary. In Ohio, aggravated murder requires an intent to kill, and aggravated burglary requires a purpose to commit theft or a felony. The jury returned a verdict of guilty and the trial court imposed a life sentence on the murder count and an additional term on the burglary count.

Issue: May a defendant present expert psychiatric testimony, though not showing that he was legally insane, yet relating to his alleged incapacity to form the requisite intent for his crimes?

Decision and Rationale: (Sweeney) No. There are a number of variations on the diminished capacity theme. According to federal case law, "expert testimony as to a defendant's abnormal mental condition may be received and considered, as tending to show, in a responsible way, that defendant did not have the specific mental state required for a particular crime or degree of crime—even though he was aware that his act was wrongful and was able to control it, and hence was not entitled to complete exoneration." However, our review of history and policies underlying the diminished capacity concept weigh against adoption of this rule in Ohio. The diminished capacity concept originated in Scotland more than a century ago. It was used to reduce the punishment of the "partially insane." Most American jurisdictions, with the exception of California, have been slow to adopt it [it comes as no surprise to many other states that California adopted to the rule first, since they consider California to be almost exclusively peopled with partially insane individuals]. Justifications for the doctrine are that (1) it ameliorates defects in a jurisdiction's insanity test criteria; (2) it permits the jury to avoid imposing death sentences on criminally responsible yet mentally disabled killers; and (3) it permits the jury to make more accurate individualized culpability judgments; and (4) it logically fits next to the settled rule that evidence of voluntary intoxication may be considered in determining whether the accused acted with the requisite intent. We find none of these justifications sufficiently compelling. The diminished capacity defense does serve to ameliorate the strict *M'Naghten* standard. However, Ohio does not adhere to the *M'Naghten* standard, opting for a more flexible standard. Ohio's test for criminal responsibility adequately safeguards the rights of the insane. The insanity concept operates as a bright line test, separating the criminally responsible from the criminally irresponsible. The diminished capacity test posits a series of blurry lines of gradual culpability. Also, although analogizing diminished capacity to voluntary intoxication has some appeal, we find the concepts to be quite disparate. It takes much more expertise for jurors to apply finely differentiated psychiatric concepts associated with diminished capacity, than to determine whether a defendant was so intoxicated as to be mentally unable to intend anything. The subjectivity, open-endedness, and non-uniform terminology make the diminished capacity test inconsistent and unpredictable. We hold, therefore, that the partial defense of diminished capacity is not recognized in Ohio. Wilcox (D) was rightly barred from offering expert psychiatric evidence, unrelated to the insanity defense, to show that he lacked the mental capacity to form the specific intent required for his crimes. Conviction affirmed.

Analysis:

There are many arguments against recognition of the diminished capacity defense. The first argument is that there is no need for the defense if psychiatrists testify accurately. It should be much easier to show that a defendant is insane than to show that he lacks the required mens rea due to mental illness or defect. Also, some juries may not be able to understand the "finely differentiated" concepts which might separate premeditation and deliberation from an intent to kill. Some courts question the reliability of psychiatric testimony—indeed, we have seen how the Supreme Court noted that the discipline is not fully developed, and so care must be taken in accepting psychiatric testimony. Another concern is that the doctrine will allow for compromise verdicts, where the jury that is divided on the issue of whether or not the defendant is insane may decide to take the middle ground. Finally, some have expressed concern that the diminished capacity doctrine does not adequately protect the public. Individuals who would have been convicted and sentenced to a longer prison term may have their terms shortened by a successful defense, or those found not guilty by reason of insanity may serve shorter sentences than they would have had in prison.

EVIDENCE OF KNOWLEDGE OF RIGHT AND WRONG OVERCOMES REBUTTABLE PRESUMPTION OF INFANT'S INCAPACITY

In Re Devon T.

(Maryland) v. (13-Year-Old Heroin Dealer)
(1991) 85 Md.App. 674, 584 A.2d 1287

M E M O R Y   G R A P H I C

Instant Facts

Devon (D) (almost 14 years old) was caught at school with twenty zip-lock bags of heroin and was convicted with the equivalent of possession with intent to distribute, despite his claim of incapacity due to infancy.

Black Letter Rule

Rebuttable Presumption of incapacity due to infancy may be overcome with sufficient evidence of a defendant's capacity to distinguish right from wrong.

Case Vocabulary

DELINQUENT: A child (under a specific age)who has violated a law.
INCRIMINATION: To be exposed to criminal charges or sanctions.
MASTER: A person who is appointed by a court to carry out certain duties on behalf of the court, such as discover evidence or take testimony, and file a report of his findings with the court.

Procedural Basis: On appeal to the Court of Special Appeals of Maryland affirming juvenile court's finding for delinquency (conviction).

Facts: Devon T. (D) (Devon) was 13 years, 10 months, and 2 weeks of age the day a security guard at his middle school directed him to empty his pockets (the Assistant Principal was there too) which revealed a brown bag containing twenty zip-lock plastic bags which contained heroin. [The contents of a brown-bag lunch have changed since we were in junior high.] Devon (D) was charged with an act which, if committed by an adult, would have constituted the crime of possession of heroin with intent to distribute. He was found to be delinquent by the juvenile court. Devon (D) timely raised the defense of infancy.

Issue: Does the prosecution's evidence that the defendant knew the difference between right and wrong and knew, moreover, that what he was doing was wrong overcome the rebuttable presumption of incapacity due to infancy?

Decision and Rationale: (Moylan) Yes. Our defense of infancy follows from the traditional M'Naghten test, from which the relevant question here relates to the cognitive question of whether Devon (D), at the time of the offense, had the cognitive capacity to distinguish right from wrong. At common law the conclusive presumption was that a child under the age of seven was incapable of criminal intent, at age fourteen was fully responsible, and for those in-between there was a rebuttable presumption of criminal incapacity. It is generally considered that the criminal law only imposes sanctions upon those who are blameworthy — those who know they are doing wrong but nonetheless persist in their wrongdoing. Our juvenile courts began as a place where rehabilitation intervention could begin. Over time, the juvenile courts took on the appearance, sanctions, and defenses of criminal courts. A finding of delinquency, unlike other proceedings in juvenile court, unmistakably exposes the delinquent to the possibility of unpleasant sanctions. Clearly, the juvenile would have the available defenses of insanity, mental retardation, and involuntary intoxication. It would be inconceivable that he could be found blameworthy and suffer sanctions, notwithstanding precisely the same lack of understanding and absence of moral accountability, simply because the cognitive defect was caused by infancy rather than by one of the other incapacitating mechanisms. The defense of infancy in a juvenile delinquency adjudication is thus available just as it would be in a criminal trial. Initially, Devon (D) had the benefit of presumptive incapacity. Maryland (P) had the burdens (of both production and persuasion) of rebutting that presumption. It had to produce evidence permitting the reasonable inference that Devon (D) at the time of doing the act knew the difference between right and wrong. In short, when Devon (D) walked around school with twenty zip-lock bags of heroin, apparently for sale or other distribution, could he pass the M'Naghten test? Was there legally sufficient data before the judge to infer that Devon (D) knew the difference between right and wrong and knew, moreover, that what he was doing was wrong? The applicable common law on doli incapax (a mind doli incapaz is incapable of malice or criminal intent, as opposed to a mind doli capax which is capable of malice and criminal intent) with relation to the infancy defense establishes that on the day before their seventh birthday, no persons possess cognitive capacity. (0 per cent). It also establishes that on the day of their fourteenth birthday, all persons possess cognitive capacity. (100 per cent). This places Devon (D) at 98.2 per cent of the way along that continuum. Statistically, this places Devon (D) with other people of his age group wherein 98.2 per cent would be expected to posses cognitive capacity. [Remember your LSAT score?] The fact that the quantum of proof necessary to overcome presumptive incapacity diminishes in substantially the same ratio as the infant's age increases only serves to lesson Maryland's (P) burden, not to eliminate it. We hold that Maryland (P) successfully carried its burden. The report of the juvenile master shows that Devon

(D) was within his age group for his grade level (although he had flunked the sixth grade twice due to truancy and lack of motivation), that he acknowledged he understood his attorney's advice and the significance of the fact that if he testified he could be asked about his offense. Devon (D) indicated he wished to remain silent. The exchange between Devon (D) and his attorney suggests that an observer could infer some knowledge on Devon's (D) part of the significance of incrimination. After he had been adjudicated and no further risk of incrimination was possible, the juvenile master asked Devon (D) (and a companion who had also been adjudicated delinquent) if they had any statement to make. Neither responded. The permitted inference was that the two were not mere babes caught up in a web they did not understand, but were following a well-established "Code of Silence" and were fully conscious of the ongoing war between lawful authority and those who flout it and had

deliberately chosen to adhere to the latter camp. The circumstances here are significant to Devon's (D) knowledge of right and wrong. The case broke when a grandmother (who had to have her own live-in grandson institutionalized) complained to the school that several of her grandson's classmates used her home (while she was at work) as a "hide out" from which to sell drugs. Children who are unaware that what they are doing is wrong have no need to hide out or to conceal their activities. There were no needle marks or other indications of personal use on Devon's (D) body. Devon's (D) charge was not mere possession, it was possession with intent to distribute. This was the finding of the court and it was supported by the evidence. We hold that the surrounding circumstances here were legally sufficient to overcome the slight residual weight of the presumption of incapacity due to infancy. The conviction if affirmed.

Analysis:

The court's inference of knowledge from Devon's (D) choice to remain silent is bothersome. In adult criminal trials a jury can be instructed that it may not infer guilt (or anything else for that matter) from the fact that the defendant did not testify. However, all the procedural and evidentiary rules of adult criminal trials are not the same in juvenile proceedings. In addition, a court's review of the full record (the juvenile master's report, and the transcript from the hearing, not to mention the zip-lock bags) and its experience with criminal matters often creates a rather savvy judge who can get to the relevant point rather succinctly. There is no volitional element here, only the cognitive element. Because the court is only looking to the cognitive element, the focus is on the circumstances surrounding the criminal or delinquent act itself. If there were also an issue with the volitional element, other information could be relevant, such as social maturity, his scholastic attainments, and other aspects of Devon's mental and psychological make-up. But that is not the case under Maryland's (P) infancy defense. The court notes that the common law principle underlying the defense of infancy is an unwillingness to punish someone who is not capable of forming criminal intent. And that in order to form criminal intent, a person has to know the difference between right and wrong. This is all linked to the idea of blameworthiness of the criminal actor. The court notes that Maryland (P) has adopted the Model Penal Code for the insanity defense, but that the language of the M'Naghten test had traditionally been the common denominator for a whole category of defenses based upon mental incapacity including infancy.

Robinson v. California

(Needle-Marked Narcotic Addict) v. (California)

(1962) 370 U.S. 660, 82 S. Ct. 1417, 8 L. Ed.2d 758

M E M O R Y   G R A P H I C

Instant Facts

Robinson's (D) misdemeanor conviction and imprisonment for being addicted to narcotics was overturned by the United States Supreme Court.

Black Letter Rule

To the extent that a state law which requires imprisonment for the use of, or addiction to, narcotics is interpreted to allow imprisonment for addiction alone, such law inflicts cruel and unusual punishment in violation of the Fourteenth Amendment.

Case Vocabulary

EIGHTH AMENDMENT: "Excessive bail shall not be required, nor excessive fines imposed, nor cruel and unusual punishments inflicted."

NEW TESTAMENT: A part of the Christian Bible consisting of several books.

Procedural Basis: On appeal to the United States Supreme Court overturning conviction.

Facts: Robinson (D) was convicted by a jury of violating a California (P) health and safety statute which states (in relevant part) that "no person shall use, or be under the influence of, or be addicted to the use of narcotics," unless administered under the supervision of a person licensed by the State to prescribe and administer narcotics. The statute imposes a sentence of not less 90 days and no more than one year in the county jail for those convicted of violating the statute. The judge instructed the jury that Robinson (D) could be convicted under a general verdict if the jury agreed *either* that he was of the "status" *or* had committed the "act" denounced by the statute, and that the prosecution only had to show *either* that Robinson (D) used a narcotic in Los Angeles County, *or* that while in the City of Los Angeles he was addicted to the use of narcotics. Officer Brown testified that he had occasion to examine Robinson's (D) arms one evening on a street in Los Angeles some four months before the trial and had observed scar tissue and discoloration on Robinson's (D) right arm, and numerous needle marks and scabs approximately three inches below the crook of the elbow on his left arm. He also testified that, upon questioning, Robinson (D) admitted to occasional use of narcotics.

Issue: Does it constitute cruel and unusual punishment to imprison a person solely because of their narcotic addiction?

Decision and Rationale: (Stewart) Yes. The broad power of a State to regulate the narcotic drugs traffic within its borders is undoubtedly a broad one, and is not at issue. The issue here is whether the statute as construed by the California court in this case is repugnant to the Fourteenth Amendment to the Constitution. The courts could have, but did not, construe the statute as requiring actual drug use within the State's jurisdiction. Although there is evidence that Robinson (D) had used narcotics in Los Angeles, the jury was instructed that they could convict him even if they did not believe that evidence. It is impossible to know from the jury's verdict that Robinson (D) was not convicted solely for his "status" of being "addicted to the use of narcotics." This statute is not one which punished for the use of narcotics, for their purchase, sale or possession, or for antisocial or disorderly behavior resulting from their use. Rather, we deal with a statute which makes the "status" of narcotic addiction a criminal offense for which the offender may be prosecuted at any time. It is unlikely that any State at this time in history would make it a criminal offense for a person to be mentally ill, or a leper, or to be afflicted with a venereal disease. Although a State may find it necessary to require such a victim be dealt with by compulsory treatment, or involuntary quarantine, a law which made a criminal offense of such a disease would doubtless be universally thought to be an infliction of cruel and unusual punishment in violation of the Eighth and Fourteenth Amendments. California's (P) statute is such a statute. Even counsel for California (P) recognizes that narcotic addition is an illness which it is possible to be contracted innocently (use of prescribed drugs) or involuntarily (addicted from the moment of birth). We hold that a state law which imprisons a person thus afflicted as a criminal, even though he has never touched any narcotic drug within the State or been guilty of any irregular behavior there, inflicts a cruel and unusual punishment in violation of the Fourteenth Amendment. Even one day in prison would be cruel and unusual punishment for the "crime" of having a common cold. The conviction is reversed.

Concurrence: (Douglas) I wish to make more explicit the reasons why I think it is cruel and unusual punishment in the sense of the Eighth Amendment to treat as criminal a person who is a drug addict. We [as in, humanity] have a long history, going at least back to the New Testament, of believing and treating those who are afflicted with a disease, mental or physical, of being punished for some sin. Various horrid treatments, such as bleeding, water cures (dunking a person under water for long periods of time), and early forms of electric shock, were imposed to drive from the body the evil spirit or toxin. This attitude continues in respect to drug addicts. The impact of addicts on a community causes alarm and often leads to punishment. Cruel and unusual punishment results not from confinement, but from convicting the addict of a crime. The stigma and irreparable damage that attaches to a conviction for addiction cannot be justified as a means of protecting society, where civil commitment would do as well.

Concurrence: (Harlan) Insofar as addiction is identified with the use or possession of narcotics within a State's jurisdiction, it may be reached by the State's criminal law. But in this case the trial court's instructions permitted the jury to find Robinson (D) guilty on no more proof than that he was present in California while he was addicted to narcotics. Since addiction alone cannot reasonably be thought to amount to more than a compelling propensity to use narcotics, the effect of this instruction was to authorize criminal punishment for a bare desire to commit a criminal act.

Dissent: (White) I do not consider Robinson's (D) conviction to be a punishment for having an illness or for simply being in some status or condition, but rather a conviction for the regular, repeated or habitual use of narcotics immediately prior to his arrest and in violation of the California law. The evidence was that Robinson (D) lived and worked in Los Angeles. He admitted before trial that he had used narcotics for three or four months, three or four times a week, usually at his place with his friends. He stated to police that he had last used narcotics in the City of Los Angeles 8 days before his arrest. [How high do you have to be to admit to an officer the last time you shot-up?]

Analysis:

The jury was given a general verdict form as opposed to a special verdict form. With a special verdict they could have been asked point by point what they found to be the facts, or for specific violations of the statute. For example, a special verdict could have presented a series of questions, e.g., "do you find that Robinson (D) used narcotics within the City of Los Angeles," and/or "do you find that Robinson (D) was in possession of narcotics," and/or "do you find that Robinson was addicted to narcotics." Instead the jury was given a general verdict from which they could answer "yes or no" to only one question asked in the alternative, that is, "do you find that *either* Robinson (D) had the "status" of being addicted, *or* committed the "act" of using [which seems to imply possession] narcotics?" Since it is unknown under which theory Robinson (D) was convicted, the Supreme Court is holding that because it could have been that Robinson (D) was convicted only because of his status of being addicted, the resulting imprisonment constituted cruel and unusual punishment. The Eighth Amendment prohibits the infliction of cruel and unusual punishment. The Fourteenth Amendment prohibits *the states* from inflicting cruel and unusual punishment. Read the next case, *Powell v. Texas,* for a narrow interpretation of *Robinson v. California.*

Powell v. Texas

(Publically Intoxicated Alcoholic) v. (Texas)
(1968) 392 U.S. 514, 88 S. Ct. 2145, 20 L. Ed.2d 1254

M E M O R Y   G R A P H I C

Instant Facts
Powell's (D) conviction for being drunk in public upheld by the Supreme Court.

Black Letter Rule
The Eighth Amendment prohibition against cruel and unusual punishment is not violated when a state imposes sanctions for public behavior (public intoxication) which violates its law.

Procedural Basis: On appeal to the United State Supreme Court affirming conviction.

Facts: Leroy Powell (D) (Powell) was arrested, charged, convicted, and fined $50.00 for being found in a state of intoxication in a public place. A psychiatrist (Dr. Wade), after examining Powell (D), testified that Powell (D) is a "chronic alcoholic," who by the time he is intoxicated is not able to control his behavior, and who has reached this point because he has an uncontrollable compulsion to drink. When asked, on cross-examination, whether Powell's (D) act in taking the first drink when he was sober was a "voluntary exercise of his will," Dr. Wade answered yes. He qualified his answer, however, by stating that "these individuals have a compulsion, and this compulsion, while not completely overpowering, is a very strong influence, an exceedingly strong influence, and this compulsion coupled with the firm belief in their mind that they are going to be able to handle it from now on causes their judgment to be somewhat clouded." He admitted that when Powell (D) is sober he knows the difference between right and wrong. Powell (D) testified regarding the history of his drinking problem, his many arrests for drunkenness, that he was unable to stop drinking, that when he was intoxicated he could not control his behavior, and that he did not remember his arrest on the occasion for which he was being tried. He admitted, on cross-examination, that he had one drink on the morning of the trial and had been able to discontinue drinking. Texas (P) made no attempt to obtain expert psychiatric testimony of its own. It did nothing to examine the scope of Dr. Wade's reference to "compulsion" which was "not completely overpowering," but which was "an exceedingly strong influence," or to inquire into the question of the proper role of such a "compulsion" in constitutional adjudication. The trial judge disallowed the claimed defense, finding as a matter of law that chronic alcoholism was not a defense to the charge. Powell's (D) counsel submitted, and the trial court entered, the following "findings of fact": (1) That chronic alcoholism is a disease which destroys a person's will power to resist the constant, excessive consumption of alcohol; (2) That a chronic alcoholic does not appear in public by his own volition but under a compulsion symptomatic of the disease; (3) That Powell (D) is a chronic alcoholic.

Issue: May a state court interpreting a state law find as a matter of law that chronic alcoholism (even if it is a disease) is not a defense to the crime of public intoxication?

Decision and Rationale: (Marshall) Yes. The "findings of fact" are not findings of fact in any recognizable, traditional sense in which that term has been used in a court of law. They are nothing more than disguised premises designed to bring this case within the scope of this court's decision in *Robinson v. California*. There is no agreement in the medical community for a definition of alcoholism. We will not extend our decision in *Robinson* which only dealt with the addiction or sickness of a person, to this situation where the conviction is for the act of being in public while intoxicated. In *Robinson*, this court held as unconstitutional a state law which imposed jail time on a defendant solely based upon his "status" of being a drug addict. On its face the present case does not fall within that holding, since Powell (D) was convicted, not for being a chronic alcoholic, but for being in public while drunk on a particular occasion. The criminal sanction is imposed on public behavior which may create substantial health and safety hazards, both for Powell (D) and the public, and which offends the moral and esthetic sensibilities of a large segment of the community. The dissent suggests that *Robinson* stands for the principle that "criminal penalties may not be inflicted upon a person for being in a condition he is powerless to change." However, the entire point of *Robinson* is that criminal penalties may be inflicted only if the defendant has committed some act, has engaged in some behavior, which society has an interest in preventing. It does not deal with the question of whether certain conduct cannot constitutionally be punished because it is, in some

Powell v. Texas (Continued)

sense, "involuntary" or "occasioned by compulsion." The record from below is woefully inadequate to support the contention that Powell (D) was unable at the time of the incident to control either his drinking or his being in public when drunk. It is easily admitted that a system which provided for the adequate treatment of alcoholics would be good for society, not to mention the alcoholic, however, such a system does not exist on the necessary scale. The criminal system of jail time and/or fines for petty offenses such as public drunkenness is minimal. The criminal system in place, although an unpleasant reality, cannot be said to be irrational. Without a better rehabilitation system in place, it is difficult to say that the criminal process is utterly lacking in social value. The doctrines of criminal law that are utilized to assess the moral accountability of an individual for his antisocial needs cannot be set aside here. The elements of a crime, (e.g., the intent, the act) and the defenses (e.g., insanity, mistake, justification, duress) work together and are adjusted over time to reflect the evolving goals of criminal law and the changing religious, moral, philosophical, and medical views of the nature of man. This process has always been thought to be the province of the States. Conviction affirmed.

Concurrence: (Black) Texas (P) law serves many state purposes, e.g., it gets alcoholics off the street and into a jail where they are provide food, clothing, and shelter long enough to sober up, thus keeping the public and themselves safe. A State should not be held constitutionally required to make the inquiry as to what part of a defendant's personality is responsible for his actions and to excuse anyone whose action was, in some complex, psychologic sense, the result of "compulsion." We are asked to apply *Robinson*, but it is not applicable here because it involved punishment for the mere propensity, or the desire to commit an offense, evidence of which is considered relatively unreliable and difficult for a defendant to rebut. Laws which require the State to prove that the defendant actually committed some proscribed act involve none of the problems encountered in *Robinson*, and the requirement of a specific act

provides some protection against false charges. The question of whether an act is "involuntary" is an inherently elusive question, and one which Texas (P) may treat as irrelevant.

Concurrence: (White) The chronic alcoholic with an irresistible urge to consume alcohol should not be punished for drinking or for being drunk. Powell's (D) conviction was for the different crime of being drunk in a public place. Many alcoholics do make it a point to begin and end their drinking binges in private. It is possible that such an alcoholic will lose his power to control his movement and appear in public. The Eighth Amendment might forbid conviction in such a circumstance, but only on a record satisfactorily showing that is was not feasible for him to have made arrangements to prevent him being in public when drunk and that his extreme drunkenness sufficiently deprived him of his faculties on that occasion. Alcoholics without homes [sounds like a support group, doesn't it] are not only unable to resist drinking, but are then necessarily drunk in public. If such facts were sufficiently proved, punishment would be for the single act of unresistible drunkenness for which punishment would violate the Eighth Amendment.

Dissent: (Fortas) Criminal penalties may not be inflicted upon a person for being in a condition he is powerless to change. In this case, Powell (D) is charged with a crime composed of two elements — being intoxicated and being found in a public place while in that condition. The crime, so defined, differs from that in *Robinson*. The statute covers more than a mere status. But the essential constitutional defect here is the same as in *Robinson*, for in both cases the particular defendant was accused of being in a condition which he had no capacity to change or avoid. A person may not be punished if the condition essential to constitute the defined crime is part of the pattern of his disease and is brought about by a compulsion symptomatic of the disease. Such punishment violates the Eighth Amendment prohibition against cruel and unusual punishment.

Analysis:

Powell (D) was asking the court to apply the rule in *Robinson*, that is, to find the sanctions for being intoxicated in public inflicted cruel and unusual punishment. The Court refused to extend the rule to the facts presented here. It did not consider the "status" of "being addicted" to be the same thing as the "act" of "being drunk in public." It had no [none, nada] problem finding that Texas (P) had the right to determine the extent to which it would define and penalize a person's offensive actions. Justice White, although attempting to provide constitutional protection to at least some chronic alcoholics also seems to think that while they are drunk they should be more responsible. This simply doesn't seem to be a practical possibility. Justice Stewart who penned *Robinson* joined the dissent. There are various views on the usefulness of punishing alcoholics/addicts. One view is that to punish alcoholics deters others from drinking in the first place. It also brings to the individual alcoholics attention that society considers his drinking and resulting behavior to be unacceptable. Another view is that once a person is addicted and out-of-control that the desire for vengeance (retribution) does not justify treating such a person as a criminal.

State v. Kargar

(Maine) v. (Overly Affectionate [!] Dad)
(1996) 679 A.2d 81

M E M O R Y   G R A P H I C

⚡ Instant Facts

In accordance with Afghani custom, Kargar's (D) kissed his young son's penis as a sign of love for his child which was considered by his neighbor, the police, the prosecution, and the trial court to violate Maine's statute prohibiting sexual acts with a child under the age of 14 years.

⚖ Black Letter Rule

When a state has a *de minimis* statute, the court *must* consider the full range of relevant factors and circumstances surrounding the defendant's admittedly criminal conduct before ruling on his motion to dismiss.

📖 Case Vocabulary

DE MINIMIS STATUTE: Based upon the concept that the law does not pay attention to trivial matters.
EXTENUATIONS: Circumstances which make the criminal conduct less offensive, less loathsome; "extenuating circumstances" may also reduce the punishment.
VACATE: To void or rescind a judgment.

Procedural Basis: On appeal to the Supreme Judicial Court of Maine vacating the conviction for gross sexual assault.

Facts: Mohammand Kargar (D) (Kargar) and his family were Afghani refugees who had been in this country for approximately three years. They were babysitting a neighbor's daughter who saw Kargar (D) kiss his 18-month-old son's penis and also saw a picture of the same. She told her mother this and her mother contacted the police. The police legally searched Kargar's (D) apartment and found the picture. Kargar (D) admitted to kissing his son's penis and told the officer that it is accepted as common practice in his culture. He was arrested. At the court trial Kargar (D) moved for a dismissal of the case pursuant to Maine's (P) *de minimis* statute. By agreement, the trial phase was held first, followed by the *de minimis* hearing. Kargar (D) and other Afghani people who were familiar with Afghani practice and custom testified that kissing a young boy (up to the age of three, four or five) on all parts of the body was to show love for the child. Kargar (D) testified that his culture views the penis of a child as not the holiest or cleanest part of the body because it is from where the child urinates. He stated that kissing his son there shows how much he loves his child precisely because it is not the holiest or cleanest part of his body. The witnesses testified that under Islamic law any sexual activity between an adult and a child results in the death penalty for the adult. Kargar (D) also submitted statements from a professor of Near Eastern Studies at the University of Arizona who was also a religious teacher and Director of Afghan Mujahideen Information Bureau in New York which supported the testimony of the other witnesses. Maine (P) did not present any witnesses at the *de minimis* hearing. The court denied Kargar's (D) motion and found him guilty of two counts of gross sexual assault.

Issue: Are culture, lack of harm, and innocent state of mind relevant factors that must be considered by a court before ruling on a defendant's motion to dismiss?

Decision and Rationale: (Dana) Yes. Maine's (P) *de minimis* statute allows the court to dismiss a prosecution if it finds that the defendant's conduct, among other things, did not actually cause the harm sought to be prevented or did so in only a way too trivial to warrant condemnation, or is not the type of conduct envisioned by the Legislature in defining the crime. In determining whether the prosecution should be dismissed, the court is required to view the defendant's conduct "having regard to the nature of the conduct alleged and the nature of the attendant circumstances." This analysis is, by necessity, case-specific. The purpose of the statute is to allow a court to dismiss charges which although they amount to a criminal act, do not under the circumstances involve any moral turpitude. An objective consideration of the surrounding circumstances is authorized and include such issues as (1) the defendant's background, experience and character; the defendant's knowledge of the existence of the crime; (2) the consequences to him, the victim, and society of the crime; (3) the possible mitigating circumstances which might lesson the punishment; (4) and any other data which might reveal the nature and degree of culpability in the offense. Our review of the record reveals that the court denied Kargar's (D) motion without considering the full range of relevant factors. The court focused on whether the conduct met the definition of gross sexual assault which nullified the effect of the *de minimis* statute. The focus is on whether the admittedly criminal conduct was envisioned by the Legislature when it defined the crime. Because the statute allows for the presentation of other "extenuations" that cannot be regarded as envisioned by the Legislature, the trial court was required to consider the possibility that the result of a conviction *in this case* could not have been anticipated by the Legislature when it defined the crime of gross sexual assault. Prior to 1985, this type of act (genital-mouth contact) included an element requiring that the act be done to satisfy sexual gratification. The Legislature amended the statute by removing this element. The Legislature stated at the time that there was not a concern that the definition would exclude "innocent" touching. This illuminates the fact that an "innocent" touching such as occurred in this case has not always been recognized as inherently criminal under our law. The Legislature's inability to comprehend "innocent" touching is highlighted by reference to another criminal sexual act (the touching of genitals involving direct contact with an instrument or devise manipulated by another). The Legislature kept the requirement that in order for this act to be criminal, it must be done to satisfy sexual gratification or to cause bodily injury or offense contact. The Legislature's stated reason for such requirement was to exclude "innocent" contacts, such as for a proper medical purpose or "other valid reason." All of the evidence presented at the hearing supports the conclusion that there was nothing "sexual" about Kargar's (D) conduct. There is no real dispute that what Kargar (D) did is accepted practice in his culture. Although the court entirely suspended Kargar's (D) sentence, the two convictions expose him to severe consequences including his required registration as a sex offender and the possibility of deportation. We agree with Kargar (D) that the court erred as a matter of law because it found culture, lack of harm, and his innocent state of mind irrelevant to its *de minimis* analysis. The convictions are vacated.

Analysis:

The court refers to the fact that the Legislature amended the gross sexual assault statute to eliminate the element of sexual gratification. Before the amendment, it was possible to have an "innocent" genital-mouth touching. The amendment served to make genital-mouth touching illegal whether it was innocent or purposeful. The idea here is that the Legislature deleted the sexual gratification requirement because it was an extraneous requirement; they couldn't envision such an act that wouldn't be sexual in nature. The court's point is that the *de minimis* statute is provided for situations like the case here -- that there was an "innocent" touching that the Legislature hadn't considered when it wrote the law. Maine (P) was concerned with the potential harm caused by courts using the factors of this case to allow even more exceptions to the criminal statutes. It thought the Legislature was better suited to collect data, and debate the social costs and benefits, and clearly define what conduct constitutes criminal activity. The court noted that the crime here was already clearly defined, but that the Legislature had also allowed for the adjustment of criminal statutes by courts in extraordinary cases. You can count on a lively debate about the extent to which culture should be considered in excusing admittedly criminal conduct. There is an argument that a newly arrived immigrant will not know all the laws of this country that someone raised here would know. While this may not completely excuse the crime, it might be a mitigating factor in culpability or punishment. Also, a person raised in a foreign culture will have religious and moral norms which he or she might feel compelled to follow even if it violates the law. The biggest problem with this is that such "norms" almost always involve conduct that violently harms women and children.

Chapter 10

Inchoate, or anticipatory, offenses are defined as crimes which are imperfect or uncompleted. That is, the underlying substantive crime has not actually been committed. Inchoate crimes are nevertheless important, for they often do lead to other crimes. For example, an individual who is thwarted in an attempted robbery may try again – and succeed. But even the failures are threats to society, as well as to potential victims.

Criminal solicitation permits punishing people who are the instigators of crimes but who do not actually commit those crimes. The solicitor may be the prime reason the crime eventually is committed. Because of the potential seriousness of solicitation, some states have very strict requirements for a successful abandonment or renunciation defense.

It is not always easy to distinguish solicitation, which involves preparation, and attempt, which involves perpetration along with the required criminal state of mind. The facts of each case must be analyzed carefully to determine whether there is any direct movement toward committing a crime – in other words, whether there is an attempt.

Abandonment and legal impossibility are two defenses that may be permitted in criminal attempt cases. Both require careful consideration of the facts. Frequently it is difficult to determine whether the alleged criminal really abandoned the attempt or just failed to achieve the goal of successfully committing a crime. Likewise, it may be difficult to determine the difference between factual impossibility, which usually is not a defense, and legal impossibility, which may be a valid defense.

Criminal conspiracy is a crime that is frequently utilized by prosecutors. Because some jurisdictions permit prosecution and conviction for a substantive crime (such as murder) *and* conspiracy (such as conspiracy to commit murder), conspiracy is a very important tool for prosecutors. Conspiracy is important, too, because this crime may be successfully prosecuted even when the predicate crime did not occur. For example, a person may be found guilty of conspiracy to commit burglary even though the burglary was not committed. Conspiracy is favored by prosecutors because it is so broadly defined. Conspiracy statutes generally are sufficiently precise to pass constitutional scrutiny but sufficiently broad to encompass a wide range of acts. Another reason that conspiracy is a popular crime with prosecutors is that it permits punishment of individuals for crimes committed by others. Some of these crimes may even go beyond the original agreement. Some jurisdictions, however, limit the criminal liability of a person for the criminal acts of a co-conspirator only if those acts are reasonably foreseeable.

Chapter 10

NOTE: THE PURPOSE OF THIS OUTLINE IS TO ORGANIZE THE CASES SO THAT ONE CAN QUICKLY UNDERSTAND THE RELEVANCE OF EACH CASE TO THE COURSE. NO ATTEMPT IS MADE IN THIS OVERVIEW TO ADDRESS EVERY CONCEPT THAT MUST BE STUDIED. BE SURE TO READ THE ENTIRE CASEBOOK AND/OR OTHER MATERIALS TO GAIN A FULL UNDERSTANDING OF ALL CONCEPTS.

I. Overview: General deterrence is at most a minor function to be served in fashioning provisions of the penal law addressed to inchoate crimes; that burden is discharged on the whole by the law dealing with substantive offenses. *American Law Institute-Model Penal Code and Commentaries, Comment to Article 5.*

II. Attempt
   A. General Principles
   1. The primary function of the crime of attempt is to provide a basis for law-enforcement officers to intervene before an individual can commit a completed offense. *Double Inchoate Crimes.*
   2. Both incomplete and complete attempts may support, although to a different extent, similar predictions about the defendant's propensities to do harm, as may the substantive offense. *Criminal Attempts and the Role of Resulting Harm Under the Code, and in the Common Law.*
   B. Grading Criminal Attempts
   1. It is doubtful that the threat of punishment for an inchoate crime can add significantly to the net deterrent efficacy of the sanction threatened for the substantive offense that is the actor's object. Hence, there is a basis for economizing in use of the heaviest and most afflictive sanctions by removing them from the inchoate crimes. *American Law Institute-Model Penal Code and Commentaries, Comment to Section 5.05.*
   C. Mens Rea
   1. Only the specific intent to kill satisfies the intent element of the crime of attempted murder. *People v. Gentry.*

   2. Attempted felony murder is not a crime in Maryland. *Bruce v. State.*
   3. Even if a party unambiguously intends to commit an offense, it is sometimes difficult to identify the target offense. *People v. Terrell.*
   D. Actus Reus
   1. General Principles: Preparation alone is not enough, there must be some appreciable fragment of the crime committed. *United States v. Mandujano.*
   2. Distinguishing Preparation from Perpetration: The Tests at Work
      a. Collection and preparation of materials in a room for the purpose of setting fire to them, accompanied with a solicitation of another to set the fire, is near enough to the accomplishment of the substantive offense to be punishable. *Commonwealth v. Peaslee.*
      b. For an act to constitute an attempt it must come very near to the accomplishment of the crime. *People v. Rizzo.*
      c. Whenever the design of a person to commit crime is clearly shown, slight acts done in furtherance of this design will constitute an attempt. *People v. Miller.*
      d. When an actor possesses materials to be used in the commission of a crime, at or near the scene of the crime, and where the possession of those materials can serve no lawful purpose of the actor under the circumstances, the jury is entitled, but not required, to find that the actor has taken a "substantial step" toward the commission of the crime if such action is strongly corroborative of the actor's overall purpose. *State v. Reeves.*
   E. Punishing Pre-Attempt Conduct
   1. To constitute "a communication containing a threat" under 18 U.S.C. Sec. 875(c), a communication must be such that a reasonable person (1) would take the statement as

©2002 West Group. All Rights Reserved. Do not duplicate.

Chapter Overview Outline
Inchoatte Offenses

a serious expression of an intention to inflict bodily harm (the mens rea), and (2) would perceive such expression as being communicated to effect some change or achieve some goal through intimidation (the actus reus). *United States v. Alkhabaz.*

F. Special Defenses
1. Impossibility: The fact that a female, upon whom the sexual acts were performed, was already dead at the time of their commission, is no bar to conviction for attempted rape. *United States v. Thomas.*
2. Abandonment: A prisoner contemplating a prison breach, but still within a prison having not yet attempted the act, is in a position to abandon the criminal act voluntarily, thereby exonerating himself from criminal responsibility. *Commonwealth v. McCloskey.*

III. Assault
A. Holding a bottle in one hand ten feet from the intended victim does not make it likely to end in the consummation of the crime of assault. *State v. Boutin.*

IV. Solicitation
A. The solicitor conceives the criminal idea and furthers its commission via another person by suggesting to, inducing, or manipulating that person. *State v. Mann.*
B. If a solicitor's message never reaches the person intended to be solicited, the act is criminal, but it must be prosecuted as an attempt to solicit. *State v. Cotton.*

V. Conspiracy
A. General Principles
1. A defendant may be convicted and punished for both the conspiracy and the substantive crime. *People v. Carter.*
2. Participation in the conspiracy is enough to sustain a conviction for the substantive offense in furtherance of the conspiracy. *Pinkerton v. United States.*
B. Criticisms of the Offense of Conspiracy
1. A statement made in furtherance of an

alleged implied but uncharged conspiracy to avoid criminal punishment is inadmissible under the hearsay rule. *Krulewitch v. United States.*
2. Conspiracy is a necessary doctrine in some respects, but also one that is overbroad and invites abuse. *The Unnecessary Crime of Conspiracy.*

C. Mens Rea
1. General Principles: A conviction of conspiracy to commit murder requires a finding of intent to kill, and cannot be based on a theory of implied malice. *People v. Swain.*
2. Intent: "Purpose" or "Knowledge"? The intent of a supplier who knows his supplies will be put to criminal use may be established by
    a. Direct evidence that he intends to participate, or
    b. Through an inference that he intends to participate based on
        (1) His special interest in the activity, or
        (2) The felonious nature of the crime itself. *People v. Lauria.*
3. Attendant Circumstances: A defendant need not be aware of the official status of his intended victim in order to be convicted for conspiracy to assault a federal officer. *United States v. Feola.*

D. Actus Reus
1. The agreement represents the actualization of the intent contemplated by the act-intent maxim. It is the "act" which expresses in concrete form the threat to society of an intent shared by two or more persons. *Conspiracy to Defraud the United States.*
2. Once conspiracy is established and upheld, a member of the conspiracy is also guilty of the criminal acts of his co-conspirators. *Commonwealth v. Azim.*
3. While proof of a tacit agreement to commit a crime may be enough to establish a conspiracy, a defendant cannot be convicted of conspiracy based solely on evidence tending to show his complicity as an accomplice

in the commission of the substantive crime. *Commonwealth v. Cook.*

E. Conspiracy: Bilateral or Unilateral?

1. Illinois legislation encompasses the bilateral theory of conspiracy, which requires the actual agreement of at least two participants. *People v. Foster.*

2. Acquittal of the sole alleged conspirator does not per se preclude the conviction of the remaining defendant, even if the defendants are jointly tried. *Commonwealth v. Byrd.*

F. Scope of an Agreement: Party and Object Dimensions

1. The scope problem is central to the concern of courts and commentators about the use of conspiracy, a concern based on the conflict between the need for effective means of prosecuting large criminal organizations, and the dangers of prejudice to individual defendants. *American Law Institute-Model Penal Code and Commentaries, Comment to Section 5.03.*

2. Hearsay testimony can only be admissible under the exception to the hearsay rule which provides that the out-of-court statements of one conspirator are admissible against all conspirators. *Kilgore v. State.*

3. The most common evidentiary issue in a wheel conspiracy is whether the separate transactions between the hub and individual spokes can be merged to form a single conspiracy. *People v. Macklowitz.*

4. A single agreement to commit acts in violation of several penal statutes must be punished as one conspiracy. *Braverman v. United States.*

G. Defenses

1. There is a recognized exception to Wharton's Rule which permits prosecution and punishment for both the substantive offense and the conspiracy. *Iannelli v. United States.*

2. A woman cannot be held criminally liable for conspiring to transport herself across state lines for illicit purposes, even when she consents to the substantive offense. *Gebardi v. United States.*

3. Withdrawal from a conspiracy avoids liability only for the target offense, or for any subsequent act committed by a co-conspirator in pursuance of the common plan. *People v. Sconce.*

H. RICO: The Sprawling Son-of-Conspiracy Statute

1. Definitions, prohibited activities and criminal penalties under the RICO statute. *Title 18, United States Code, Chapter 96-Racketeer Influenced and Corrupt Organizations (RICO)*

2. RICO prosecutions put before the jury charges that a particular defendant engaged in not just one but several, often very loosely related, crimes, and frequently also present an equally ill-assorted set of charges against codefendants. *RICO: The Crime of Being a Criminal, Parts I & II.*

3. In order to understand RICO's value in prosecuting diversified illicit enterprises, and the potential abuses of such prosecutions, we must first understand the limits imposed on criminal prosecutions by our conventional understanding of what a crime is, and the potential of RICO to explode those limitations. *RICO: The Crime of Being a Criminal, Parts II & IV.*

4. RICO allows a prosecutor to charge, in a single count, what might constitute multiple, smaller conspiracies. *United States v. Elliott.*

5. A conspiracy may exist even if a conspirator does not agree to commit or facilitate each and every part of the substantive offense. *Salinas v. United States.*

People v. Gentry

(State) v. (Firestarter)
157 Ill. App.3d 899, 109 Ill. Dec. 895, 510 N.E.2d 963 (1987)

M E M O R Y   G R A P H I C

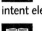

Instant Facts

Gentry (D) was convicted of attempted murder after spilling gasoline on his girlfriend during a fight which then ignited as she passed the stove.

Black Letter Rule

Only the specific intent to kill satisfies the intent element of the crime of attempted murder.

Case Vocabulary

ACTUS REUS: The physical criminal deed.
CULPABLE: Intentional wrong-doing.
SPECIFIC INTENT: Knowing and desiring certain consequences for a particular crime.

Procedural Basis: Appeal from defendant's conviction by a jury.

Facts: Gentry (D) and his girlfriend, Ruby Hill, were arguing in the apartment they shared together. They were both highly intoxicated and Gentry (D) spilled gasoline on Hill [*accidentally*, no doubt]. Hill passed by the stove and the gasoline ignited. Gentry (D) was able to smother the flames with a coat, but only after Hill had been severely burned. Hill testified to these events at Gentry's (D) trial. At the close of the presentation of evidence in this case, the court defined "attempt" as it relates to murder stating, a person "commits the offense of murder when he, *with intent to commit the offense of murder* does any act which constitutes a substantial step toward the commission of the offense of murder. The offense attempted need not have been completed." It also defined the crime of murder, including four culpable mental states. The court instructed the jury that a person commits the crime of murder "where he kills an individual if, in performing the acts which cause the death, he intends to kill *or* do great bodily harm to that individual; *or* he knows that such acts will cause death to that individual; *or* he knows that such acts create a strong probability of death or great bodily harm to that individual."

Issue: Is a finding of specific intent to kill a necessary element of the crime of attempted murder?

Decision and Rationale: (Linn, J.) Yes. Gentry (D) contends that the inclusion of all the alternative states of mind in the definitional murder instruction was erroneous because the crime of attempted murder requires a showing of specific intent to kill. Gentry (D) posits that inclusion of all four alternative states of mind permitted the jury to convict him of attempt upon a finding that he intended to harm Hill, or acted with knowledge that his conduct created a strong probability of death or great bodily harm to Hill, even if the jury believed that Gentry (D) did not act with specific intent to kill. We agree with Gentry's position that the jury was misinstructed in this case. Our supreme court has repeatedly held that a finding of specific intent to kill is a necessary element of the crime of attempted murder. Indeed, a trial court instructing a jury on the crime must make it clear that specific intent to kill is the pivotal element of that offense, and that intent to do bodily harm, or knowledge that the consequences of Gentry's (D) act may result in death or great bodily harm, is not enough. The State would read the attempt instruction as requiring a showing of any of the alternative mental states sufficient for a conviction of murder. In other words, the State makes no distinction between the mental state required to prove murder and the mental state required to prove attempted murder. We find the State's analysis and conclusion to be erroneous and lacking in legal substance since it fails to contain the judicial reasoning which recognizes the distinction between the intent elements of murder and attempted murder. Consequently, it is sufficient only for us to say that we recognize the distinction between the alternative states of mind delineated in the definitional murder instruction, as well as the fact that only the specific intent to kill satisfies the intent element of the crime of attempted murder. We reverse Gentry's (D) conviction and sentence, and remand this cause for a new trial in front of a properly instructed jury.

Analysis:

Criminal attempts really involve two different "intents" which merge as a practical matter. The actor must first intentionally commit the acts which constitute the actus reus of an attempt. Secondly, the actor must perform the acts with the specific intent to commit the substantive crime. It is a peculiarity in the common law that an attempt is usually punished less severely, and never more severely, than the intended offense, yet the mental state required for attempted murder is of a higher culpability than that required for the completed offense. This anomaly has been justified on the basis that the person intending to kill another is more dangerous because he may try again if unsuccessful the first time. Simply put, "the actor's unspent intent is a source of harm independent of his conduct." On the other hand, a person without that specific intent will either succeed in his quest the first time, thereby removing the threat posed, or else he may seek the result in a safer manner the second time. [We don't buy it either!]

THE STATE OF MARYLAND DOES NOT RECOGNIZE THE CRIME OF ATTEMPTED FELONY MURDER

Bruce v. State

(Store Robber) v. (State)
317 Md. 642, 566 A.2d 103 (1989)

M E M O R Y   G R A P H I C

Instant Facts
Bruce (D) was convicted of attempted felony murder, as well as other charges, for shooting a storekeeper he was attempting to rob at gunpoint.

Black Letter Rule
Attempted felony murder is not a crime in Maryland.

Case Vocabulary

CERTIORARI: Writ issued by a superior court to one of inferior jurisdiction so that the proceedings may be inspected to determine issues of importance.
FELONY MURDER: An unintentional death which occurs during the commission or attempted commission of a felony.

Procedural Basis: Certiorari granted on appeal from defendant's conviction by a jury in the trial court.

Facts: Bruce (D) and two other men entered Barry Tensor's shoe store. Bruce (D) was masked and armed with a handgun. He ordered Tensor to open the cash register. Upon finding it empty, Bruce (D) demanded to know where the money could be found. Tensor told Bruce (D) that that was all there was, and Bruce (D) aimed the gun at Tensor's head, telling him he was going to kill him. Tensor ducked down and moved forward. He testified that he thought he bumped into Bruce (D), and then Bruce (D) shot him [clearly self-defense]. Tensor was hospitalized for five weeks from a gunshot wound to his stomach. A jury found Bruce (D) guilty of attempted first degree felony murder, robbery with a deadly weapon, and two handgun charges. On appeal, Bruce (D) argued that attempted felony murder was not a crime in Maryland. The Court granted certiorari to consider the issue.

Issue: Is attempted felony murder a crime in Maryland?

Decision and Rationale: (Murphy, C.J.) No. To secure a conviction for first degree murder under the felony murder doctrine, the State is required to prove a specific intent to commit the underlying felony and that death occurred in the perpetration or attempt to perpetrate the felony; it is not necessary to prove a specific intent to kill or to demonstrate the existence of willfulness, deliberation, or premeditation. In determining whether attempted felony murder is a crime in Maryland, we note that criminal attempts are applicable to any existing crime, whether statutory or common law. Under Maryland law, a criminal attempt consists of a specific intent to commit the offense coupled with some overt act in furtherance of the intent which goes beyond mere preparation. Because a conviction for felony murder requires no specific intent to kill, it follows that because a criminal attempt is a specific intent crime, attempted felony murder is not a crime in Maryland.

Analysis:

The court in this case cites a previously decided case which held that there is an offense of attempted voluntary manslaughter, but no offense of attempted involuntary manslaughter. The reasoning behind this ruling is that the intent to kill is present in the former, but not in the latter, case. The outcome in this case follows from that because the court "recognizes" that an attempt crime requires specific intent (like the intent to kill in voluntary manslaughter), whereas felony murder involves an unintentional death (as does involuntary manslaughter).

United States v. Mandujano

(Government) v. (Not Stated)
499 F.2d 370 (1974)

M E M O R Y   G R A P H I C

Instant Facts

The court clarifies the definition of "attempt" as used in Section 846 of Title 21.

Black Letter Rule

For the crime of attempt, preparation alone is not enough, there must be some appreciable fragment of the crime committed.

Case Vocabulary

LOCUS POENITENTIAE: The opportunity for one to withdraw or renounce before the consummation of a crime.

MENS REA: The "guilty" mental state accompanying a criminal act.

Procedural Basis: None Stated.

Facts: None Stated.

Issue: Is preparation enough to constitute an "attempt" under Section 846 of Title 21?

Decision and Rationale: (Rives, C.J.) No. Apparently there is no legislative history indicating exactly what Congress meant when it used the word "attempt" in Section 846. It seems to be well settled that mere preparation is not sufficient to constitute an attempt to commit a crime, however it is also equally clear that the semantical distinction between preparation and attempt is one incapable of being formulated in a hard and fast rule. What might, in one factual situation, constitute preparation, may not under different facts. We have previously addressed the issue and concluded that the following test has been "frequently approved": Preparation alone is not enough, there must be some appreciable fragment of the crime committed, it must be in such progress that it will be consummated unless interrupted by circumstances independent of the will of the attempter, and the act must not be equivocal in nature.

Analysis:

While it may be well settled that mere preparation is not enough to constitute an attempt, there really is no clear-cut distinction between mere preparation and perpetration. The courts in many jurisdictions have tried to distinguish between the two, and the federal courts have confronted this issue on a number of occasions. Judge Learned Hand set forth a doctrine by which to test whether conduct still remains in the zone of mere preparation or if it has passed over to constitute an attempt. Hand stated that the test would be that the actor has done all that it is within his power to do, but has been prevented by outside intervention. In short, that he has passed beyond any locus poenitentiae. This doctrine, however, does not appear to be followed in our courts. Other courts have required that the objective acts of the defendant evidence commitment to the criminal venture and corroborate the mens rea. This way, the courts reason, it prevents the conviction of persons engaged in innocent acts on the basis of a mens rea proved through subjective, and thus less reliable, means. Every court seems to have a different delineation, however there does seem to be agreement on one point: the line between preparation and perpetration is a "murky twilight zone."

Commonwealth v. Peaslee

(State) v. (Arsonist)

177 Mass. 267, 59 N.E. 55 (1901)

M E M O R Y   G R A P H I C

Instant Facts

Peaslee (D) concocted a plan to burn a building and all its contents, but he changed his mind before the plan was accomplished.

Black Letter Rule

Collection and preparation of materials in a room for the purpose of setting fire to them, accompanied with a solicitation of another to set the fire, is near enough to the accomplishment of the substantive offense to be punishable.

Case Vocabulary

SOLICITATION: Requesting or encouraging another to engage in criminal acts.

Procedural Basis: Motion to quash the defendant's indictment and motion for a directed verdict for the defendant.

Facts: Peaslee (D) constructed and arranged combustibles in a building in such a way that they were ready to be lighted, and if lighted would have set fire to the building and its contents. The plan would have required a candle which was standing on a shelf six feet away to be placed on a piece of wood in a pan of turpentine and lighted [not one to keep it simple apparently]. Peaslee (D) offered to pay a younger man in his employment if he would go into the building, seemingly some miles from the place of the dialogue, and carry out the plan. This was refused. Later, Peaslee (D) and the young man drove towards the building, but when within a quarter of a mile, Peaslee (D) said that he had changed his mind and drove away. This is as near as he ever came to accomplishing what he had in contemplation.

Issue: Do Peaslee's acts come near enough to the accomplishment of the substantive offense to be punishable?

Decision and Rationale: (Holmes, C.J.) No. The most common types of an attempt are either an act which is intended to bring about the substantive crime, and which sets in motion natural forces that would bring it about in the expected course of events, but for the unforeseen interruption, as, in this case, if the candle had been set in its place and lighted, but had been put out by police, or an act which is intended to bring about the substantive crime, and would bring it about but for a mistake of judgment in a matter of estimate or experiment, as when a pistol is fired at a man, but misses, or when one tries to pick a pocket which turns out to be empty. [That was a mouthful!] On the pleadings in this case, which failed to allege the solicitation of the employee to set the fire, a mere collection and preparation of materials in a room for the purpose of setting fire to them, unaccompanied by any present intent to set the fire, would be too remote. If Peaslee (D) intended to rely upon his own hands to the end, he must be shown to have had a present intent to accomplish the crime without much delay, and to have had this intent at a time and place where he was able to carry it out. On the other hand, if the offense is to be made out by showing a preparation of the room and a solicitation of someone else to set the fire, which solicitation, if successful, would have been Peaslee's (D) last act, the solicitation must be alleged as one of the overt acts. If the indictment had been properly drawn, we have no question that Peaslee (D) might have been convicted. As it was drawn, however, Peaslee's (D) exceptions must be sustained.

Analysis:

That an overt act, although coupled with an intent to commit the crime, commonly is not punishable if further acts are contemplated as needful, is expressed in the familiar rule that preparation is not an attempt. Some preparations may amount to an attempt, however, and it is all just a question of degree. The degree of proximity of the preparation to the accomplishment of the act determines whether it will constitute an attempt, however the degree held sufficient may vary with circumstances. The key in this case, which lets Peaslee (D) off the hook, is that the prosecution did a poor job in drafting the indictment [ya just can't get good help these days!]. The prosecution omits the fact that Peaslee (D) solicited the young man to actually start the fire, and such omission is fatal to the State's (P) case. All of the acts Peaslee (D) did in preparation for the fire are futile without the final step of lighting the fire. Such first steps cannot be described as an attempt, because the acts alone are not sufficient to accomplish the end. If, however, the evidence of the solicitation had been included, it would have shown that Peaslee's (D) last act (the solicitation) was so close in proximity to the completed act that it would constitute attempt.

People v. Rizzo

(State) v. (Payroll Robber)
246 N.Y. 334, 158 N.E. 888 (1927)

OK, PAL.. TELL ME WHERE'S THE BANK, AND WHERE IS RAO?

M E M O R Y G R A P H I C

Instant Facts

Rizzo (D) and three others planned and looked for a man to rob a payroll from, but they were unable to find him before being arrested.

Black Letter Rule

For an act to constitute an attempt it must come very near to the accomplishment of the crime.

Case Vocabulary

RULE OF IMMEDIATE NEARNESS: An act constitutes an attempt when it comes very near to the accomplishment of the crime.

Procedural Basis: Appeal from the defendant's conviction and prison sentence.

Facts: Rizzo (D) and three others planned to rob Charles Rao of a payroll he was carrying to the bank valued at about $1,200. The four men, two of whom had firearms, set out in an automobile to find Rao or the man who was carrying the payroll on that day. Rizzo (D) claimed to be able to identify the man and was to point him out to the others who were to do the actual hold-up. After going to the bank and several buildings looking for Rao, they attracted the attention of two police officers, who began following and watching the four men. As Rizzo (D) jumped out of the car and went into a building, the four men were arrested [who needs probable cause?]. Neither Rao nor the man who was to actually carry the payroll that day were in the building where Rizzo (D) was arrested. The four men had not found nor seen the man they intended to rob; no person with a payroll was at any of the places where they had stopped and no one had been pointed out or identified by Rizzo (D) [now there's an airtight case!].

Issue: Do the acts performed by Rizzo (D) constitute the crime of an attempt to commit robbery in the first degree?

Decision and Rationale: (Crane, J.) No. The past case law states that in order for an act to constitute an attempt it must come very near to the accomplishment of the crime. How shall we apply this rule of immediate nearness to this case? To constitute the crime of robbery the money must have been taken from Rao by means of force or violence, or through fear. The crime of attempt to commit robbery was committed if Rizzo (D) and the others did an act tending to the commission of this robbery. Rao was not found, the men were still looking for him when they were arrested. No attempt to rob him could even be made until he came in sight. In short, Rizzo (D) and the other men had planned to commit a crime and were looking around the city for an opportunity to commit it, but the opportunity fortunately never came. For these reasons, the judgment of conviction of Rizzo (D) must be reversed and a new trial granted.

Analysis:

The court has repeatedly held that the act amounts to an attempt when it is so near to the result that the danger of success is very great. "There must be dangerous proximity to success." Thus it is no surprise that this case was decided the way it was on the facts presented. The quizzical part of this decision involves the facts surrounding the arrest scenario. Why did the police follow the four men to begin with, and what constituted the probable cause necessary for the arrests? How did the police find out about the mens' plan? Did they have prior knowledge? It seems there are a great deal of gaps left in the fact sequence which make it difficult to analyze and apply the ruling in this case to others.

People v. Miller

(State) v. (Rifleman)
2 Cal.2d 527, 42 P.2d 308 (1935)

M E M O R Y   G R A P H I C

Instant Facts

Miller (D) was convicted of attempted murder for threatening to kill Jeans and then later approaching him with a loaded rifle.

Black Letter Rule

Whenever the design of a person to commit crime is clearly shown, slight acts done in furtherance of this design will constitute and attempt.

Case Vocabulary

INFORMATION: Alternative to indictment as a means of starting a prosecution.
HOPS: A grain.
RES IPSA LOQUITUR: The thing speaks for itself.
UNEQUIVOCALITY DOCTRINE: An act does not constitute an attempt unless the actor's specific criminal purpose is evident from his conduct.

Procedural Basis: Appeal from jury's conviction of the defendant.

Facts: On the day in question, Miller (D), somewhat under the influence of liquor and in the presence of others at the town post office, threatened to kill Albert Jeans [drunk and postal!]. Jeans was employed on the hops ranch of the town constable, Ginochio. Miller (D), carrying a .22-caliber rifle, entered the hops field while Jeans, Ginochio and others were planting hops. Miller walked in a direct line towards Ginochio, who was 250 or 300 yards away. Jeans was about 30 yards beyond him. After Miller (D) had gone about 100 yards, he stopped and appeared to be loading his rifle. At no time did he raise the rifle as if to take aim. As soon as Jeans saw Miller (D), he fled on a line at about a right angle to Miller's (D) line of approach. When Miller (D) reached Ginochio, Ginochio took the rifle away from him, with Miller (D) offering no resistance. The rifle was found to be loaded with a high-speed cartridge.

Issue: Did Miller (D) commit acts in furtherance of his plan such that he is guilty of attempted murder?

Decision and Rationale: (Shenk, J.) No. We are mindful of the fact that case law requires that whenever the design of a person to commit crime is clearly shown, slight acts done in furtherance of this design will constitute an attempt. The reason for requiring evidence of a direct act, however slight, toward consummation of the intended crime, is that in the majority of cases, up to the time of the conduct of the defendant, consisting merely of acts of preparation, has never ceased to be equivocal; and this is necessarily so, irrespective of his declared intent. It is that quality of being equivocal that must be lacking before the act becomes one which may be said to be a commencement of the commission of the crime, or an overt act, or before any fragment of the crime itself has been committed, and this is so for the reason that, so long as the equivocal quality remains, no one can say with certainty what the intent of the defendant is. In the present case, up to the moment the gun was taken from Miller (D), no one could say with certainty whether Miller (D) had come into the field to carry out his threat to kill Jeans or merely to demand his arrest by the constable. Under the authorities, therefore, the acts of Miller (D) do not constitute an attempt to commit murder.

Analysis:

Strictly construing the unequivocality doctrine, statements made by the actor before, during, or after the incident are not considered reliable as to state of mind. This is because the actor may have been bluffing [do drunk men bluff?] or he may have considered the idea without actually acting on it, with the criminal act in question being motivated by a noncriminal purpose. The American Law Institute tries to justify this res ipsa loquitur rule by viewing it entirely as a matter of procedure. Whether the requirement of unequivocality is considered part of the substantive definition of attempt or as a separate rule of evidence, it can be realistically administered only by means of a procedural mechanism, that is, by excluding from the jury the actor's incriminating representations of purpose. It seems difficult to understand how the court could find Miller's (D) actions in this case to be equivocal, unless, once again, there are facts not mentioned in the case [leaving us in the dark again?].

JURY MAY FIND THAT AN ACTOR HAS TAKEN SUBSTANTIAL STEP TOWARD
COMMISSION OF A CRIME WHEN THE ACTOR POSSESSES REQUIRED MATERIALS
NEAR THE SCENE OF THE CRIME AND THE COURSE OF ACTION CORROBORATES THE
CRIMINAL PURPOSE

State v. Reeves

(State) v. (Teacher Killer)
916 S.W.2d 909 (1996)

M E M O R Y   G R A P H I C

Instant Facts
Reeves (D) and a friend devised and tried to carry out a plan to kill their homeroom teacher and steal her car.

Black Letter Rule
When an actor possesses materials to be used in the commission of a crime, at or near the scene of the crime, and where the possession of those materials can serve no lawful purpose of the actor under the circumstances, the jury is entitled, but not required, to find that the actor has taken a "substantial step" toward the commission of the crime if such action is strongly corroborative of the actor's overall purpose.

Case Vocabulary

INCHOATE CRIME: Offense not yet completed or finished.
STARE DECISIS: Principles announced in former judicial decisions which are upheld and followed unless there is a showing of good cause.

Procedural Basis: Appeal from the Circuit Court's affirmance of the juvenile court's delinquency conviction and sentencing of the defendant.

Facts: Tracie Reeves (D) and Molly Coffman, both twelve years old, talked on the telephone and decided to kill their homeroom teacher [what happened to talking about boys and crushes?]. The girls agreed that Coffman would bring rat poison to school the following day so that it could be placed in their teacher's drink. The girls also agreed that they would thereafter steal the teacher's car and drive to the Smoky Mountains [great getaway plan]. Reeves (D) then contacted Dean Foutch, a local high school student, informed him of the plan, and asked him to drive the car. Foutch refused this request. The next morning, Coffman placed a packet of rat poison in her purse and boarded the school bus. During the bus ride, Coffman told another student, Christy Hernandez, of the plan, and showed her the packet of rat poison. Upon their arrival at school, Hernandez told her homeroom teacher of the plan [tattle-tale]. The teacher then relayed the information to the principal, Claudia Argo. When Geiger entered her classroom that morning she saw Coffman and Reeves (D) leaning over her desk. When the girls noticed her, they giggled and ran back to their seats. At that time Geiger saw a purse lying next to her coffee cup on top of the desk. Shortly thereafter, Argo called Coffman to the principal's office. Rat poison was found in her purse and it was turned over to a Sheriff's Department investigator. Reeves (D) and Coffman were found to be delinquent by the Juvenile Court, and both appealed from that ruling to the Circuit Court. After a jury found that the girls attempted to commit second-degree murder, the trial court affirmed the juvenile court's order and sentenced the girls to the Department of Youth Development for an indefinite period. This appeal followed.

Issue: Does simply planning a crime and possessing materials required to commit such crime constitute a "substantial step" towards the commission of the crime?

Decision and Rationale: (Drowota, J.) Yes. Prior to the passage of reform legislation in 1989, the law of criminal attempt was judicially defined in *Dupuy v. State*. In *Dupuy* in order to submit an issue of criminal attempt to the jury, the State was required to present legally sufficient evidence of: (1) an intent to commit a specific crime; (2) an overt act toward the commission of that crime; and (3) a failure to consummate the crime. There was a sharp differentiation in *Dupuy* between "mere preparation" and "overt act," or the "act itself," which was characteristic of the pre-1989 attempt law. In 1989, however, the legislature enacted a general criminal attempt statute as part of its comprehensive overhaul of Tennessee's criminal law. The statute specifically requires, in part, that the conduct constitute a substantial step toward the commission of the offense. Furthermore, conduct will not constitute a *substantial step* unless the person's entire course of action is corroborative of the intent to commit the offense. Our task is to determine whether Reeves' (D) actions constitute a "substantial step" toward the commission of second-degree murder under the new statute. While we concede that a strong argument can be made that the conviction conflicts with *Dupuy* because Reeves (D) did not place the poison in the cup, but simply brought it to the crime scene, we are also well aware that the *Dupuy* approach to attempt law has been consistently and effectively criticized. Distinguishing between "mere preparation" and the "act itself" in a principled manner is a difficult, if not impossible, task. The other principal ground of criticism of the *Dupuy* approach bears directly on the primary objective of the law – that of preventing inchoate crimes from becoming full-blown ones. Failure to attach criminal responsibility to the actor until the actor is on the brink of consummating the crime endangers the

©2002 West Group. All Rights Reserved. Do not duplicate.

public and undermines the preventative goal of attempt law. After carefully weighing considerations of *stare decisis* against the persuasive criticisms of the *Dupuy* rule, we conclude that this artificial and potentially harmful rule must be abandoned. We hold that when an actor possesses materials to be used in the commission of a crime, at or near the scene of the crime, and where the possession of those materials can serve no lawful purpose of the actor under the circumstances, the jury is entitled, but not required, to find that the actor has taken a "substantial step" toward the commission of the crime if such action is strongly corroborative of the actor's overall purpose. For the foregoing reasons, the conviction is affirmed.

Concurrence and Dissent: (Birch, J.) The entire course of action of these two girls was not "strongly corroborative" of the intent to commit second-degree murder and the evidence was insufficient as a matter of law. These are twelve-year-old girls, not explosive-toting terrorists. Accordingly, while I concur in the majority's abandonment of the rule stated in *Dupuy*, I dissent from the conclusion of the majority in this case.

Analysis:

A jury could easily find that the girls took "substantial steps" toward the commission of the crime they had planned, that of killing their teacher. However, even if their conduct does seem to constitute a substantial step, it must be determined that those actions were "strongly corroborative" of their purpose to commit the crime. It seems possible in this case that an argument could be made that the girls' failure to actually put the poison in the coffee cup is indicative of a lack of genuine intent to kill their teacher. As the dissent points out, the girls are giggly and young; the plan to run off to the mountains seems particularly juvenile. Perhaps this was really more of a game to the girls than a seriously cold and calculated murder plot. On the other hand, in the world today, it seems a month can't go by without news of children killing others. The incidence of violence in the schools itself appears to be such that all threats and plans must be taken seriously and these children must be dealt with severely. Times have changed and the law must as well in order to keep up.

"THREATENING COMMUNICATIONS" [UNDER 18 U.S.C. §875(c)] MUST CONTAIN AN INTENT TO INFLICT HARM AS WELL AS FURTHERANCE OF A GOAL THROUGH INTIMIDATION

United States v. Alkhabaz

(Government) v. (Deviant Sex Freak)
104 F.3d 1492 (1997)

M E M O R Y   G R A P H I C

⚡ Instant Facts

Alkhabaz (D) was arrested for posting fictional stories involving the abduction, rape, torture, mutilation, and murder of women and young girls on the Internet.

⚖️ Black Letter Rule

To constitute "a communication containing a threat" under 18 U.S.C. Sec. 875(c), a communication must be such that a reasonable person (1) would take the statement as a serious expression of an intention to inflict bodily harm (the mens rea), and (2) would perceive such expression as being communicated to effect some change or achieve some goal through intimidation (the actus reus).

📖 Case Vocabulary

INTERSTATE COMMUNICATIONS: Either telephone, email or snail-mail, across state lines.

Procedural Basis: Appeal from the judgment of the district court quashing the defendant's indictment.

Facts: Over a period of about three months, Alkhabaz (D) (a.k.a. Jake Baker), and Gonda exchanged email messages over the Internet, the content of which expressed a sexual interest in violence against women and girls [a couple of real catches!]. Alkhabaz (D) used a computer in Michigan while Gonda (whose true identity and whereabouts remain unknown) used a computer in Ontario, Canada. Prior to this time, Alkhabaz (D) had posted a number of fictional stories to a popular interactive Usenet news group. His fictional stories generally involved the abduction, rape, torture, mutilation, and murder of women and young girls [not one to take home to meet your mother!]. One story he posted described the torture, rape, and murder of a young woman who shared the same name as one of Alkhabaz's (D) classmates at the University of Michigan. Alkhabaz was arrested and charged with violating 18 U.S.C. Sec. 875(c), which prohibits interstate communications containing threats to kidnap or injure another person.

Issue: Do fictional stories describing the torture, rape, and murder of women constitute "a communication containing a threat" under 18 U.S.C. Sec. 875(c)?

Decision and Rationale: (Martin, Jr., C.J.) No. To determine what type of action Congress intended to prohibit, it is necessary to consider the nature of a threat. At their core, threats are tools that are employed when one wishes to have some effect, or achieve some goal, through intimidation. This is true regardless of whether the goal is highly reprehensible or seemingly innocuous. Although it may offend our sensibilities, a communication objectively indicating a serious expression of an intention to inflict bodily harm cannot constitute a threat unless the communication also is conveyed for the purpose of furthering some goal through the use of intimidation. Accordingly, to achieve the intent of Congress, we hold that, to constitute "a communication containing a threat" under 18 U.S.C. Sec. 875(c), a communication must be such that a reasonable person (1) would take the statement as a serious expression of an intention to inflict bodily harm (the mens rea), and (2) would perceive such expression as being communicated to effect some change or achieve some goal through intimidation (the actus reus). The dissent argues that Congress did not intend to include as an element of the crime the furthering of some goal through the use of intimidation. Emphasizing the term "any" in the language of the statute, the dissent maintains that Congress did not limit the scope of communications that constitute criminal threats. While we agree that Congress chose inclusive language to identify the types of threats that it intended to prohibit, we cannot ignore the fact that Congress intended to forbid only those communications that in fact constitute a "threat." The conclusion that we reach here is one that the term "threat" necessarily implies. Applying our interpretation of the statute to the facts before us, we conclude that the communications between Alkhabaz (D) and Gonda do not constitute "Communications containing a threat" under Section 875(c). Even if a reasonable person would take the communications between the two as serious expressions of an intention to inflict bodily harm, no reasonable person would perceive such communications as being conveyed to effect some change or achieve some goal through intimidation. Quite the opposite, Alkhabaz (D) and Gonda apparently sent email messages to each other in an attempt to foster a friendship based on shared sexual fantasies. For the foregoing reasons, the judgment of the district court quashing the indictment is affirmed.

Dissent: (Krupansky, C.J.) The words in Section 875(c) are simple, clear, concise, and unambiguous. The plain, expressed statutory language commands only that the alleged communication must contain *any threat* to kidnap or physically injure *any person*, made for *any reason* or no reason. Section 875(c) by its terms does not confine the scope of criminalized communications to those directed to identified individuals and intended to effect some particular change or goal. Consequently, a communication which an objective, rational observer would tend to interpret, in its factual context, as a credible threat, is a "true threat" which may be punished by the government. Accordingly, I would reverse the district court's judgment which dismissed the superseding indictment as purportedly not alleging "true threats," and remand the cause to the lower court.

Analysis:

People cannot be punished for their thoughts, but how much further must a person go before the criminal law steps in? In this case, the woman whose name was used in the story knew nothing of the fantasy until the University and law enforcement notified her of the situation. It seems difficult to imagine then, that this fantasy could be threatening toward her [it sure makes you wonder who it is you're *really* dating though!]. But what is to ensure that the fantasy truly was nothing more than just a story? How can the criminal law deal with a person who seems to have a criminal disposition, but who may or may not ever act out his thoughts? It's a difficult line to walk, for as legislatures enlarge the scope of inchoate criminality, the risk of punishing innocent persons increases. This case shows one court's efforts to modify a statute to reach what it believes is a proper balance. The dissent only serves to underscore the immense controversy in this arena.

THE FACT THAT THE WOMAN WAS DEAD WHEN THE MEN HAD UNLAWFUL SEX WITH HER DOES NOT PRECLUDE CONVICTION FOR ATTEMPTED RAPE

United States v. Thomas

(Government) v. (Necrophiliac Rapist)
13 U.S.C.M.A. 278, 32 C.M.R. 278 (1962)

M E M O R Y   G R A P H I C

Instant Facts

Thomas (D) was convicted of attempted rape for having sex with a girl he thought was unconscious but in reality was dead.

Black Letter Rule

The fact that the female, upon whom the sexual acts were performed, was already dead at the time of their commission, is no bar to conviction for attempted rape.

Case Vocabulary

COURT-MARTIAL: Basic trial court of the military courts system.
FACTUAL IMPOSSIBILITY: Crime is impossible due to some physical impossibility unknown to the defendant.
LEGAL IMPOSSIBILITY: Act is not criminal therefore criminal liability cannot attach for an attempt to commit the act.

Procedural Basis: Certification to the Court of Military Appeals by the Acting Judge Advocate General of the Navy after the Board of Review set aside the defendant's conviction by general court martial.

Facts: Thomas (D) and two friends went on a "bar hopping" spree. After several stops, the trio entered a tavern where one of the men began dancing with a girl. Almost at once she collapsed in his arms. The three men volunteered to take her home [such nice young gentlemen]. They put the apparently unconscious female in their car and left. While driving, one of the men suggested they all have sexual intercourse with her as she was so drunk she would never know the difference [gee, how romantic]. Each of the three subsequently did or attempted to consummate this act and then started their return to town. The three became concerned as the woman had not regained consciousness. One of the men was dropped off at the USO, while the other two continued to take the woman home. They were unable to find her house, however, and they became more concerned about her condition. They stopped at a service station seeking help and the attendant called the police. When the police arrived at the service station they examined the girl and determined she was dead. An ambulance was called and she was taken to the hospital for further examination. An autopsy, later performed, revealed that she apparently died of a weakening of the heart muscles with edema and inflammation which occurs more in young people without its presence being suspected. It was the general undisputed opinion that her death probably occurred at the time she collapsed on the dance floor or very shortly thereafter. Thomas (D) and the others were unaware of the fact that she was dead. Thomas (D) and one of the other men (the third was granted immunity from prosecution and testified for the Government) were tried by court-martial. Each was charged with the offenses of conspiracy to commit rape, rape, and lewd and lascivious conduct, in violation of the Uniform Code of Military Justice. Each was acquitted of rape, but the court-martial found them guilty of attempted rape and the other two charges upon which they were brought to trial. The board of review set aside the convictions of attempted rape and conspiracy as to both men.

Issue: Can a person be convicted of attempted rape of a woman who was already dead at the time the sexual acts were consummated?

Decision and Rationale: (Kilday, J.) Yes. Before the board of review, Thomas' (D) counsel contended that the law officer erred in his instructions to the court. In support of that position, Thomas (D) argued that where circumstances beyond his control make it legally impossible to commit a crime, as distinguished from factual impossibility to do so, there can be no attempt to commit the substantive offense. Legal impossibility can be described as a situation where if the intended act is not criminal, there can be no criminal liability for an attempt to commit this act. Factual impossibility, on the other hand, is when the substantive crime is impossible of accomplishment because of some physical impossibility unknown to the accused. In a factual impossibility scenario, the elements of a criminal attempt are present. It is, however, most difficult to classify any particular state of facts as positively coming within one of these categories to the exclusion of the other. In substance, then, the question presented to the board of review was, whether the law officer was correct in his instructions to the court-martial that a finding the victim was alive was not essential to a conviction for attempt as a lesser included offense of rape. The American Law Institute has made clear in its draft of the Model Penal Code that the major purpose of the Article defining criminal attempts is to "extend the criminality of attempts by sweeping aside the defense of impossibility (including the distinction between so-called factual and legal impossibility)." After having given this entire question a great deal more than casual attention and study, we are forced to the conclusion that the law of attempts in military jurisprudence has tended toward the advanced and modern position, which position will be achieved for civilian jurisprudence if The American Law Institute is completely successful in its advocacy of this portion of the Model Penal Code. We hold, therefore, that in this instance the fact that the female, upon whom these detestable acts were performed, was already dead at the time of their commission, is no bar to conviction for attempted rape. The certified issue is answered in the negative, and the decision of the board of review is reversed.

Dissent: (Ferguson, J.) It should be noted at the outset that we are all in agreement that the offense of rape itself cannot be committed upon the body of a dead person. How then, could a person be convicted of an attempt to rape a dead person? I find nothing in the discussion of criminal attempts which indicates that it was believed that the defense of legal – as opposed to factual – impossibility was abolished upon enactment of the Uniform Code. Charges of attempted rape seem uniformly to have allowed legal impossibility as a defense when an impediment was found to prevent consummation of the crime. It seems to me that Thomas' (D) conviction of attempted rape must be vitiated on the basis of legal impossibility.

Analysis:

Note #1 after the case cites *United States v. Oviedo*, in which the Court states that legal impossibility occurs when the actions which the defendant performs or sets in motion, even if fully carried out as he desires, would not constitute a crime. Factual impossibility, on the other hand, occurs when the objective of the defendant is proscribed by the criminal law but a circumstance unknown to the actor prevents him from bringing about that objective. Based upon these definitions, it is possible to categorize *Thomas* as either a legal impossibility or a factual one. The defense will claim that a legal impossibility defense exists because the actions which Thomas (D) performed (having sex with a dead person), even if fully carried out would not constitute the crime of rape. The prosecution, on the other hand, will say the case is one of factual impossibility as a circumstance unknown to Thomas (D) (that the woman was dead) prevented him from bringing about his objective (the rape). The Court seems to take an easy way out in this case by reading an abolishment of the distinction between factual and legal impossibility into the Model Penal Code and applying that law to the court martial, much to the chagrin of the dissent.

Commonwealth v. McCloskey

(State) v. (Prisoner)
234 Pa.Super. 577, 341 A.2d 500 (1975)

M E M O R Y   G R A P H I C

Instant Facts
Prisoner planned a prison breach but abandoned the plan before leaving the prison and attempting the escape.

Black Letter Rule
A prisoner contemplating a prison breach, but still within a prison having not yet attempted the act, is in a position to abandon the criminal act voluntarily, thereby exonerating himself from criminal responsibility.

Case Vocabulary

BENCH TRIAL: Trial before a judge sitting without a jury.
SUB SILENTIO: Literally, under silence; a later opinion overrules a prior holding by necessary implication.

Procedural Basis: Appeal from the defendant's conviction in a bench trial.

Facts: McCloskey (D) was serving a one-to-three-year prison sentence for larceny. One early morning, at 12:15 a.m., James Larson, a Guard Supervisor at the Luzerne County Prison, heard an alarm go off that indicated that someone was attempting an escape in the recreation area of the prison. The alarm was designed so that it could be heard in the prison office, but not in the courtyard [can't let them know we're on to them]. Larson immediately contacted Guards Szmulo and Banik, who then checked the prison population but found no one missing. The three guards then checked the recreation area where the alarm had been tripped. They found one piece of barbed wire that had been cut, as well as a laundry bag filled with civilian clothing. A check revealed that the bag belonged to McCloskey (D). At approximately 5:15 a.m. that same morning, McCloskey (D) voluntarily approached Larson. He explained to Larson that he was going to make a break that night, but that he had changed his mind because he got scared and didn't want to shame his family any more [what a guy!]. The grand jury subsequently returned an indictment charging McCloskey (D) with prison breach. McCloskey (D) was found guilty in a bench trial of attempted prison breach.

Issue: Can a prisoner be convicted of attempted prison breach when he abandons the plan before ever leaving the prison?

Decision and Rationale: (Hoffman, J.) No. The evidence shows that McCloskey (D) scaled a fence within the prison walls that led to the recreation yard and then to the prison wall. The evidence supports McCloskey's (D) claim that he went only as far as the yard before giving up his plan to escape. Thus McCloskey (D) was still within the prison, still only contemplating a prison breach, and not yet attempting the act. He was thus in a position to abandon the criminal offense of attempted prison breach voluntarily, thereby exonerating himself from criminal responsibility. Judgment of sentence is vacated and McCloskey (D) ordered discharged on the conviction of attempted prison breach.

Concurrence: (Cercone, J.) I agree that the conviction should not be permitted to stand, however I disagree with the basis for the majority's conclusion. If voluntary abandonment is to be given effect in attempt cases, it should not be done covertly.

Analysis:

To better understand the majority and concurring opinions, it is necessary to note that McCloskey (D) was charged under the old Penal Code which did not speak to whether voluntary abandonment was a defense to a charge of attempt. It has long been recognized that plans voluntarily abandoned are less likely to be found to be attempts than are plans carried to the same point, but interrupted by the apprehension of the perpetrators. Unfortunately, in jurisdictions where voluntary abandonment or renunciation of a criminal purpose has not been recognized as an affirmative defense, the courts have sought to give effect to the defendant's abandonment, *sub silentio*, by characterizing his conduct as "preparatory." This is what the concurrence claims the majority did in this case, and this is what the concurrence disagrees with. The concurring opinion asserts that this preparation-perpetration dichotomy breeds superficially inconsistent results, and thus voluntary abandonment must be recognized as an affirmative defense itself. Additionally, there are policy reasons for recognizing abandonment in attempt cases. Voluntary abandonment negates the conclusion that the accused continues to be dangerous, and, the knowledge that voluntary abandonment exonerates one from criminal liability provides a motive to desist prior to completion of the crime.

State v. Boutin

(State) v. (Street Fighter)
133 Vt. 531, 346 A.2d 531 (1975)

M E M O R Y   G R A P H I C

Instant Facts

Boutin (D) and Moore got into a fight which was broken up by the police while the men were still ten feet from one another.

Black Letter Rule

Holding a bottle in one hand ten feet from the intended victim does not make it likely to end in the consummation of the crime of assault.

Case Vocabulary

ASSAULT: An attempt to cause bodily injury to another.

Procedural Basis: Appeal from defendant's trial and conviction after denial of the defendant's motion for a directed verdict.

Facts: Boutin (D) and Moore were involved in a scuffle in front of a pizza joint. Following the scuffle, Boutin (D) picked up a bottle from a nearby trash can, while Moore grabbed a rock from the street. Two town constables heard the disturbance and, upon investigating, found the two men ten feet apart, with Boutin walking towards Moore with the bottle raised above his head and Moore backing away across the street. The constables asked Boutin (D) to put down the bottle, at which time Boutin (D) turned on the officers [now *that's* a great idea]. At no time did Boutin (D) attempt to strike Moore or throw the bottle or lunge towards Moore, nor did he ever get closer than ten feet in proximity to Moore.

Issue: Is holding a bottle in one hand ten feet from the intended victim sufficient to find one guilty of assault?

Decision and Rationale: (Billings, J.) No. To constitute an attempt to commit a crime, the act must be of such a character as to advance the conduct of the actor beyond the sphere of mere intent. It must reach far enough towards the accomplishment of the desired result to amount to the commencement of the consummation. Here the holding of a bottle in one hand ten feet from the intended victim does not make it likely to end in the consummation of the crime intended. Although equivocal testimony did exist for the jury's evaluations, there first must be some testimony in a case evidencing criminal conduct as charged and sufficient to justify a finding of guilty beyond a reasonable doubt. Since the evidence failed to establish all of the elements essential to constitute the alleged offense, the trial court should have granted the motion for directed verdict. Reversed.

Analysis:

The assault statute referenced in this case indicates that a person is guilty of assault if he attempts to cause, or purposely, knowingly or recklessly causes bodily injury to another. The court is correct in deciding that Boutin's actions do not qualify under this statute. It would be a stretch to imagine that bodily injury could occur from the fact scenario presented in this case [unless he's got one heck of a long arm]. It is also interesting that Moore's action of picking up a rock was never addressed. It seems that a threat of being hit with a rock from ten feet would cause greater apprehension than that of a bottle. Or, at the least, it is a case of mutual aggression in which both parties had weapons. Perhaps Boutin (D) was trying to protect himself from a [vicious!] rock attack.

State v. Mann

(State) v. (Not Stated)
317 N.C. 164, 345 S.E. 2d 365 (1986)

M E M O R Y   G R A P H I C

Instant Facts
None Stated.

Black Letter Rule
The solicitor conceives the criminal idea and furthers its commission via another person by suggesting to, inducing, or manipulating that person.

Case Vocabulary

SOLICITATION: Asking, enticing, or encouraging another to commit a crime.

Procedural Basis: None Stated.

Facts: None Stated.

Issue: None Stated.

Decision and Rationale: (Martin, J.) Solicitation involves the asking, enticing, inducing, or counseling of another to commit a crime. The solicitor conceives the criminal idea and furthers its commission via another person by suggesting to, inducing, or manipulating that person. A solicitor may be more dangerous than a conspirator, as a conspirator may merely passively agree to a criminal scheme, while the solicitor plans, schemes, suggests, encourages, and incites the solicitation. Further, the solicitor is morally more culpable than a conspirator; he keeps himself from being at risk, hiding behind the actor.

Analysis:

There are many criticisms of the crime of solicitation. First, solicitations are said to be not in themselves dangerous, because no harm will occur unless the person solicited agrees. In that case, the conspiracy is proven, and there is no need for charging solicitation. Second, contrary to the assertions in this case, a solicitor is ordinarily *less* dangerous because of his reluctance to actually commit the crime himself [all talk, no action]. Finally, if solicitation is used over-zealously [do prosecutors *ever* do that?], it has been said that it will chill First Amendment free-speech rights.

TO BE CONVICTED OF SOLICITATION, THE MESSAGE MUST BE RECEIVED BY THE PERSON INTENDED TO BE SOLICITED

State v. Cotton

(State) v. (Sexually Abusive Stepfather)
109 N.M. 769, 790 P.2d 1050 (1990)

M E M O R Y   G R A P H I C

Instant Facts
Cotton (D) wrote letters to his wife, which she never received, trying to get her to convince his stepdaughter not to testify against him at trial.

Black Letter Rule
If a solicitor's message never reaches the person intended to be solicited, the act is criminal, but it must be prosecuted as an attempt to solicit.

Case Vocabulary
BONA FIDE: Good faith, genuine.

Facts: Cotton (D), his wife, five children and a stepdaughter moved to New Mexico. A few months later, Cotton's (D) wife and children moved back to Indiana. Shortly thereafter, the stepdaughter moved back to New Mexico to live with Cotton (D) [uh oh, now there's trouble!]. The next year, Cotton (D) was investigated by the Department of Human Services for allegations of misconduct involving him and his stepdaughter. He was subsequently arrested and charged with multiple counts of criminal sexual acts with a minor [surprise, surprise]. While in jail awaiting trial on those charges, Cotton (D) discussed with his cell-mate Dobbs his desire to persuade his stepdaughter not to testify against him. During his incarceration, Cotton wrote numerous letters to his wife discussing his strategy for defending against the charges. In one letter, Cotton (D) requested that his wife assist him in persuading his stepdaughter not to testify at his trial. He also urged his wife to contact his stepdaughter and influence her to return to Indiana or to give her money to leave the state so she would be unavailable to testify. After writing the letter, Cotton (D) gave the letter to Dobbs and asked him to obtain a stamp for it. Unknown to Cotton (D), Dobbs removed the letter from the envelope, replaced it with a blank sheet of paper, and returned the sealed stamped envelope to Cotton (D). Dobbs gave Cotton's (D) original letter to law enforcement authorities [what, no honor among thieves?]. Cotton (D) wrote another letter to his wife again telling her either to try to talk the stepdaughter out of testifying or to talk her into testifying favorably for Cotton (D). Cotton (D) also said his wife should warn his stepdaughter that if she did testify for the state "it won't be nice and she'll make the news." It is undisputed that neither letter was ever mailed nor received by Cotton's (D) wife.

Issue: Can a person be convicted of solicitation if the solicitor's message never reaches the person intended to be solicited?

Decision and Rationale: (Donnelly, J.) No. The offense of criminal solicitation is defined in part as: Except as to bona fide acts of persons authorized by law to investigate and detect the commission of offenses by others, a person is guilty of criminal solicitation if, with the intent that another person engage in conduct constituting a felony, he solicits, commands, requests, induces, employs or otherwise attempts to promote or facilitate another person to engage in conduct constituting a felony within or without the state. Cotton (D) contends that the record fails to contain the requisite evidence to support the charges of criminal solicitation against him because Cotton's (D) wife, the intended solicitee, never received the two letters. The state (P) reasons that proof of Cotton's (D) acts of writing the letters, and attempts to mail them, together with his specific intent to solicit the commission of a felony constitutes sufficient proof to sustain a charge of criminal solicitation. We disagree. As enacted by our legislature, the section defining criminal solicitation significantly omits one section of the Model Penal Code which pertains to the effect of an uncommunicated criminal solicitation. This omission, we conclude, indicates an implicit legislative intent that the offense of solicitation requires some form of actual communication from the defendant to either an intermediary or the person intended to be solicited, indicating the subject matter of the solicitation. We thus conclude that if the solicitor's message never reaches the person intended to be solicited, as where the intermediary fails to pass on the communication or the solicitee's letter is intercepted before it reaches the addressee, it does not constitute criminal solicitation. The act is criminal, however it may be that the solicitor must be prosecuted for an attempt to solicit on such facts. Cotton's (D) convictions for solicitation are reversed and the cause is remanded with instructions to set aside the convictions.

Analysis:

The Model Penal Code provides that conduct "designed to effect" communication of the culpable message is sufficient to constitute criminal solicitation and there is therefore no need for a crime of attempted solicitation. The New Mexico legislature deliberately omitted this language from its section regarding criminal solicitation, and the court interprets this to mean it specifically wanted some actual communication to take place before liability attaches. The prosecution in this case could have, however, seized upon the statutory language which reads "or otherwise *attempts* to promote or facilitate...." This phrase could have been used to cover the fact situation in this case and support the claim that uncommunicated solicitations are punishable as solicitations. [oops, dropped the ball!]

©2002 West Group. All Rights Reserved. Do not duplicate.

CONSPIRACY IS A CRIME SEPARATE AND DISTINCT FROM THE UNDERLYING
SUBSTANTIVE CRIME

People v. Carter

(State) v. (Not Stated)
415 Mich. 558, 330 N.W.2d 314 (1982)

M E M O R Y   G R A P H I C

Instant Facts
None Stated.

Black Letter Rule
A defendant may be convicted and punished
for both the conspiracy and the substantive crime.

Case Vocabulary
CONSPIRACY: A partnership in criminal purposes.

Procedural Basis: None Stated.

Facts: None Stated.

Issue: May a defendant be convicted and punished for both a conspiracy
and the substantive crime?

Decision and Rationale: (Moody, Jr., J.) Yes. Criminal
conspiracy is a mutual agreement or understanding, express or implied, between
two or more persons to commit a criminal act or accomplish a legal act by
unlawful means. The crime is complete upon formation of the agreement; it is
not necessary to establish any overt act in furtherance of the conspiracy as a
component of the crime. However, a twofold specific intent is required for
conviction: intent to combine with others, and intent to accomplish the illegal
objective. It is a settled principle of black-letter law that conspiracy is separate
and distinct from the substantive crime that is its object. A defendant may be
convicted and punished for both the conspiracy and the substantive crime.

Analysis:

As the court points out, the guilt or innocence of a conspirator does not depend upon the accomplishment of the goals of the conspiracy.
And, more importantly, a conviction of conspiracy does not merge with a conviction of the completed offense. This is why a defendant may
be convicted of both the conspiracy as well as the underlying substantive offense [two for the price of one]. Additionally, while conspiracy
is an inchoate offense, in most jurisdictions it also constitutes the basis for holding a person accountable for the completed crimes of others
(co-conspirators).]

Pinkerton v. United States

(IRS Scammer) v. (Government)

328 U.S. 640, 66 S.Ct. 1180, 90 L.Ed. 1489 (1946)

M E M O R Y   G R A P H I C

Instant Facts

Two brothers were convicted of both conspiracy and the substantive offense even though only one actually participated in committing the offense.

Black Letter Rule

Participation in the conspiracy is enough to sustain a conviction for the substantive offense in furtherance of the conspiracy.

Case Vocabulary

VICARIOUS LIABILITY: Imputing liability upon one person for the actions of another.

Procedural Basis: Appeal from jury's conviction of the defendant.

Facts: Walter and Daniel Pinkerton (D) are brothers who live a short distance from each other on Daniel's (D) farm. They were indicted for violations of the Internal Revenue Code. The indictment contained ten substantive counts and one conspiracy count. The jury found Walter guilty on nine of the substantive counts and on the conspiracy count. It found Daniel (D) guilty on six of the substantive counts and on the conspiracy count. A single conspiracy was charged and proved. Each of the substantive offenses found was committed pursuant to the conspiracy.

Issue: Is participation in a conspiracy enough to sustain a conviction for the substantive offense?

Decision and Rationale: (Douglas, J.) Yes. It is contended that there was insufficient evidence to implicate Daniel (D) in the conspiracy, but we think there was enough evidence for submission to the jury. There is, however, no evidence to show that Daniel (D) participated directly in the commission of the substantive offenses on which his conviction has been sustained, although there was evidence to show that these substantive offenses were committed by Walter in furtherance of the unlawful agreement or conspiracy existing between brothers. We take the view here that there was a continuous conspiracy which Daniel (D) never took any affirmative action to withdraw from. So long as the partnership in crime continues, the partners act for each other in carrying it forward. It is settled that an overt act of one partner may be the act of all without any new agreement specifically directed to that act. Thus we hold that Daniel's (D) participation in the conspiracy is enough to sustain his conviction for the substantive offense in furtherance of the conspiracy. Affirmed.

Dissent: (Rutledge, J.) The judgment concerning Daniel Pinkerton (D) should be reversed. It is my opinion that it is without precedent here and is a dangerous precedent to establish. The result is a vicarious criminal responsibility as broad as, or broader than, the vicarious civil liability of a partner for acts done by a co-partner in the course of the firm's business.

Analysis:

The court's decision in this case, taken at face value, appears sound [first clue that something's off]. However, the underlying facts make the judgment a bit harder to swallow. The proof showed that Walter alone committed the substantive crimes, and there was no proof that Daniel (D) even knew that he had done so. In fact, Daniel (D) was in prison for other crimes when some of Walter's crimes were committed [what?]. Walter and Daniel (D) became partners in crime by virtue of their agreement and, without more on his part, Daniel (D) became criminally liable for everything Walter did thereafter so long as there was no proof of a clear withdrawal or revocation from the agreement. The dissent correctly labels Daniel's (D) liability as vicarious, and it seems to be a better argument that vicarious liability should remain in the civil law, and not transferred to the criminal field.

STATEMENTS MADE BY CO-CONSPIRATORS TO HIDE THE FACTS OF THE CONSPIRACY MAY NOT BE ADMISSIBLE NOTWITHSTANDING THE CO-CONSPIRATOR EXCEPTION TO THE HEARSAY RULE

Krulewitch v. United States

(Pimp) v. (Government)
(1949) 336 U.S. 440, 69 S.Ct. 716, 93 L.Ed. 790

M E M O R Y   G R A P H I C

Instant Facts

The Government (P) introduced hearsay testimony about an effort by Krulewitch's (D) co-conspirators to help Krulewitch (D) avoid punishment.

Black Letter Rule

A statement made in furtherance of an alleged implied but uncharged conspiracy to avoid criminal punishment is inadmissible under the hearsay rule.

Case Vocabulary

HEARSAY: Testimony given by a person relating facts of which he does not have personal knowledge, but has learned or heard from another.

Facts: Krulewitch (D) and a woman defendant were indicted for (1) persuading another woman to go from New York to Miami for the purpose of prostitution; (2) transporting her to Miami for that purpose; and (3) conspiring to commit those offenses in violation of 18 U.S.C. § 371. Krulewitch (D) was convicted on all three counts, and the Court of Appeals affirmed. The Supreme Court granted certiorari to consider the admission of hearsay testimony. The testimony was from the woman who was induced and transported to Miami, and consisted of a narration of a conversation between her and the woman conspirator. Significantly, the conversation took place over one and one-half months after the crime and conspiracy occurred. It took place after arrest. The woman testified, "She asked me, she says, 'You didn't talk yet?' And I says, 'No.' And she says, 'Well don't . . . .. It would be better for us two girls to take the blame than Kay [Krulewitch (D)] because he couldn't stand it, he couldn't stand to take it.'" The Government (P) argues for admissibility of the hearsay declaration as one in furtherance of a continuing secondary objective of the conspiracy—the concealment of the conspiracy.

Issue: May hearsay evidence relating to an implied conspiracy to conceal a conspiracy be admitted at trial?

Decision and Rationale: (Black) No. We cannot accept the Government's (P) contention. Out-of-court statements by one conspirator against another are not admissible unless they are made in furtherance of the objectives of a going conspiracy. The Government (P) now asks us to expand this narrow exception to the hearsay rule to allow a statement made not in furtherance of the alleged criminal transportation conspiracy, but in furtherance of an implied conspiracy aimed at preventing detection and punishment. Under this rule, arguments could be made in conspiracy cases that most out-of-court statements admitted into evidence tended to shield co-conspirators. The rule would create a further breach of the general rule against the admission of hearsay evidence.

Concurrence: (Jackson) There is a growing habit of prosecuting for conspiracy in lieu of prosecuting the substantive offense itself. The modern crime of conspiracy is so vague that it almost defies definition. It is "predominantly mental in composition" because it consists of a meeting of minds and intent. The law has its place to prosecute dangerous group criminality, but it may also be trivialized where the conspiracy consists of a pimp and a prostitute going to Miami to ply their trade. At trial, a defendant charged with conspiracy is faced with a hodgepodge of facts and statements by others that he may not have authorized or even knew of, but which help convince the jury that the conspiracy existed. A conspiracy is often proved by evidence that is admissible only upon assumption that conspiracy existed. The naive assumption that prejudicial effects can be overcome by jury instructions is known by all practicing lawyers to be a fiction. A co-defendant may have difficulty in making his own case, especially where co-defendants can be prodded into accusing and contradicting each other. There is a strong temptation to relax rigid standards when they seem the only way to convict wrongdoers. But statutes authorize prosecution for substantive crimes for most wrongdoing, without the dangers to liberty and integrity of the judicial process inherent in conspiracy prosecutions. We should disapprove the doctrine of implied or constructive crime in its entirety.

Analysis:

Hearsay is generally not admitted in a criminal prosecution. An exception to the rule is the co-conspirator exception. An act or statement by one co-conspirator committed during and in furtherance of the conspiracy may be admitted against the other co-conspirators. Although *Krulewitch* indicates some limits on how much courts will allow, the requirement that the act or statement be in furtherance of the conspiracy is applied broadly. And, as Justice Jackson points out, jury instructions may not always temper the prejudicial effects brought on by admission of the evidence. Note that in this case the statements were not admitted to prove conspiracy to commit the original offense (crossing state lines for prostitution). Rather, they were admitted based upon a second conspiracy to hide the facts of the joint conspiracy. The prosecution argued that the latter was merely in furtherance of the original conspiracy.

People v. Swain

(State) v. (Drive-by Shooter)

12 Cal.4th 593, 49 Cal.Rptr.2d 390, 909 P.2d 994 (1996)

M E M O R Y   G R A P H I C

Instant Facts

Swain (D) was convicted of conspiracy to commit murder after his friend killed a young boy in a drive-by shooting.

Black Letter Rule

A conviction of conspiracy to commit murder requires a finding of intent to kill, and cannot be based on a theory of implied malice.

Case Vocabulary

CORPUS DELICTI: Body of the crime; proof a crime was committed.

IMPLIED MALICE: State of mind inferred from conduct and lacking in specific intent.

MALICE AFORETHOUGHT: Characteristic state of mind for murder; there is no justification or excuse, and no mitigating circumstances exist.

Procedural Basis: Appeal from defendant's conviction and sentence in a jury trial.

Facts: A brown van passing through a neighborhood at about 2:00 a.m. one morning slowed down near the spot where Saileele, a 15-year-old Samoan boy, and his friends were listening to music on the street [ever heard of curfews?]. A young black male was driving the van. Suddenly, several shots were fired from the front of the van. Chatman and another youth also fired guns from the rear of the van. One of the intended victims had yelled out "drive-by" as a warning of the impending shooting, so most of the people on the street ducked down [common occurrence in the neighborhood?]. Saileele, who was holding the radio from which the music was playing, was shot twice from behind. He died later in surgery. Afterward, Swain (D) was in jail boasting to jailmates about what good aim he had with a gun. He told them that he had shot the Samoan boy when they were in the van. At trial, Swain (D) testified that he had been in the van earlier in the evening, but that he had left prior to the incident because the smell of marijuana bothered him. At trial, Chatman admitted he had been in the van with his friends to retaliate for a car theft attributed to a neighborhood youth who was not the victim of the shooting. The original plan was allegedly to steal the car of the thief [that'll teach him!]. Chatman admitted he had fired shots, but claimed he fired wildly and only in self-defense [just a lucky shot]. He said he heard an initial shot and thought it was fired by someone outside the van shooting at him, so he returned fire. The jury returned a verdict finding Chatman guilty of second degree murder and conspiracy and, as instructed, made a finding that the target offense of the conspiracy was murder in the second degree. Several days later, the jury returned verdicts against Swain (D), finding him not guilty of murder or its lesser included offenses, but guilty of conspiracy.

Issue: Is intent to kill a required element of the crime of conspiracy to commit murder?

Decision and Rationale: (Baxter, A.J.) Yes. Swain (D) contends that the jury should have been instructed that proof of intent to kill is required to support a conviction of conspiracy to commit murder, whether the target offense of the conspiracy – murder – is determined to be in the first or second degree. More particularly, Swain (D) asserts it was error to instruct the jury on the principles of implied malice second degree murder in connection with the determination of whether he could be found guilty of conspiracy to commit murder, since implied malice does not require a finding of intent to kill. As we shall explain, we agree. Conspiracy is a specific intent crime. The specific intent required divides into two elements: (a) the intent to agree, or conspire, and (b) the intent to commit the offense which is the object of the conspiracy. To sustain a conviction for conspiracy to commit a particular offense, the prosecution must show not only that the conspirators intended to agree but also that they intended to commit the elements of that offense. We next turn to the elements of the target offense of the conspiracy here in issue. The crime of murder is defined as the unlawful killing of a human being with malice aforethought. The malice aforethought may be express or implied. This court has observed that proof of unlawful "intent to kill" is the functional equivalent of express malice. We have noted that conspiracy is a specific intent crime requiring an intent to agree or conspire, and a further intent to commit the target crime, here murder, the object of the conspiracy. Since murder committed with intent to kill is the functional equivalent of express malice murder, conceptually speaking, no conflict arises between the specific intent element of conspiracy and the specific intent requirement for such category of murders. Simply put, where the conspirators agree or conspire with specific intent to kill and commit an overt act in furtherance of such agreement, they are guilty of conspiracy to commit express malice murder.

The conceptual difficulty arises when the target offense of murder is founded on a theory of implied malice, which requires no intent to kill. Implied malice murder, in contrast to express malice, requires instead an intent to do some act, the natural consequences of which are dangerous to human life. Hence, under an implied malice theory of second degree murder, the requisite mental state for murder – malice aforethought – is by definition "implied," as a matter of law, from the specific intent to do some act dangerous to human life together with the circumstance that a killing has resulted from the doing of such act. Stated otherwise, all murders require, at the core of the corpus delicti of the offense, a "killing." But only in the case of *implied malice* murder is the requisite mental state – malice aforethought – implied from the specific intent to do some act *other than* an intentional killing *and* the resulting circumstance: a killing has in fact occurred as "the direct result of such an act." We conclude that a conviction of conspiracy to commit murder requires a finding of intent to kill, and cannot be based on a theory of implied malice.

Analysis:

This case is full of important principles, from the elements of the crime of conspiracy, to the reasoning behind making conspiracy a specific intent offense, to the requirement that two intents be proven: the intent to agree and the intent that the underlying offense be committed. This criminal intent element has long been a source of controversy. The Model Penal Code notes that the traditional definition of conspiracy said nothing about the actor's state of mind except insofar as the concept of agreement itself carries certain implications about his attitude toward the crime. Perhaps this is because the intent to agree is difficult to distinguish from the agreement itself. It is not sufficient to show that the conspirators intended to agree. It must be proved also that the conspirators intended to accomplish an unlawful objective, which is the object of the conspiracy. The elements of the unlawful objective must be met. It has been held repeatedly that a conspiracy to commit a particular substantive offense cannot exist without at least the degree of criminal intent necessary for the substantive offense itself. The Court does a good job in this case of breaking down the crime committed versus the crime intended in order to arrive at a reasonable and just solution. The bottom-line point to take from this case is that a person cannot be guilty of conspiring to commit an unintentional crime. This is because people cannot agree to commit an unintentional act, or intend an unintentional result.

A PERSON WHO SUPPLIES A PRODUCT OR SERVICE TO ANOTHER KNOWING THAT IT WILL BE USED AS PART OF A CRIME, MAY BE CONVICTED FOR CONSPIRACY UNLESS ONLY A MISDEMEANOR IS INVOLVED

People v. Lauria

(Government) v. (Telephone Answering Service Provider)
(1967) 251 Cal.App.2d 471, 59 Cal.Rptr. 628

M E M O R Y   G R A P H I C

Instant Facts
Lauria (D) ran a telephone answering service, which he knew was used by several prostitutes in their business ventures; Lauria (D) was indicted with the prostitutes for conspiracy to commit prostitution.

Black Letter Rule
The intent of a supplier who knows his supplies will be put to criminal use may be established by (1) direct evidence that he intends to participate, or (2) through an inference that he intends to participate based on (a) his special interest in the activity, or (b) the felonious nature of the crime itself.

Procedural Basis: Appeal by prosecution from order setting aside an indictment for conspiracy to commit prostitution.

Facts: In a prostitution investigation, police focused their attention on three prostitutes who used Lauria's (D) telephone service. An undercover policewoman, Stella Weeks, signed up for Lauria's (D) services. Weeks hinted that she was a prostitute, and wanted to conceal that fact from the police. Lauria (D) assured her that his service was discreet and safe. A few weeks later, Weeks called Lauria (D) and complained that because of his operation she had lost two "tricks." Lauria (D) claimed that her tricks probably lied about leaving messages for her. Lauria (D) did not respond to Weeks' hints that she needed more customers, other than to invite her over to become better acquainted. A couple of weeks later Weeks again complained that she had lost two tricks, and the office manager said she would investigate. Two weeks later, Lauria (D) and the three prostitutes were arrested. Lauria (D) testified before the Grand Jury that he only had 9 or 10 prostitutes using his service, and he kept records for known or suspected prostitutes for the convenience of police. However, Lauria (D) did not volunteer the information, but would give it when asked about a specific prostitute. He claimed that he tolerated the prostitutes so long as they paid their bills. Lauria (D) admitted having personal knowledge that some of his customers were prostitutes [use your imagination]. Lauria (D) and the three prostitutes were indicted for conspiracy to commit prostitution. The trial court set aside the indictment as having been brought without a showing of reasonable or probable cause. The Government (P) appeals claiming that a sufficient showing of an unlawful agreement to further prostitution was made. To establish agreement, the Government (P) need show no more than an implied mutual understanding, between co-conspirators, to accomplish an unlawful act.

Issue: Is a person criminally liable for conspiracy if he furnishes goods and services he knows will be used to assist in the operation of an illegal business?

Decision and Rationale: (Fleming) No. *United States v. Falcone* held that a seller's knowledge of the illegal use of the goods was insufficient to make the seller a participant in the conspiracy. In *Direct Sales Co. v. United States*, by contrast, the conviction on federal narcotics laws of a drug wholesaler was affirmed on a showing that the company had actively promoted the sale of morphine. In both cases, however, the element of knowledge of the illegal use of the goods or services and the element of intent to further that use must be present in order to make the supplier a participant in a criminal conspiracy. Proof of knowledge is ordinarily a question of fact. Lauria (D) admitted he knew that some of his customers were prostitutes. He probably knew that some of his customers were subscribing to his service in order to further their trade. The Government argues that this knowledge serves as a basis for concluding that Lauria (D) intended to participate in the criminal activities. We note some characteristic patterns in precedent cases: (1) intent may be inferred from knowledge, when the purveyor of the legal goods for illegal use has acquired a stake in the venture; (2) intent may be inferred from knowledge, when no legitimate use for the goods or services exists; and (3) intent may be inferred from knowledge, when the volume of business with the buyer is grossly disproportionate to any legitimate demand. In response to the first pattern, we note that Lauria (D) had no stake in the venture, and was not charging higher prices to the prostitutes. As to the second pattern, we note that nothing in the furnishing of telephone service implies that it will be used for prostitution, since all sorts of persons might use the service for completely legal activities. Finally, no evidence suggests any unusual volume of Lauria's (D) business was with prostitutes. In all three of these patterns, it can be said that in one way or another a supplier has a special interest in the operation of the criminal enterprise. There are cases in which it cannot be said that the supplier has a stake in the venture, yet still may be held liable based on knowledge alone. Some examples of this would be supplying cutting equipment to be used in a bank robbery, or supplying telephone service to persons involved in the extortion of ransom. Still, we do not believe that an inference of intent drawn from knowledge should apply to misdemeanors. Thus, with respect to misdemeanors, we conclude that positive knowledge of a supplier that his products will be used for illegal activities does not in itself establish intent to participate in the misdemeanor. However, with respect to felonies, we hold that in all felony cases, knowledge of criminal use alone may justify an inference of intent. From this analysis we deduce the following rule: the intent of a supplier who knows of the criminal use to which his supplies are put to participate in the criminal activity connected with the use of his supplies may be established by (1) direct evidence that he intends to participate, or (2) through an inference that he intends to participate based on (a) his special interest in the activity, or (b) the felonious nature of the crime itself. Lauria (D) took no direct action to further the activities of the prostitutes. There is no evidence of a special interest in the prostitutes' activities. The offense with which he has been charged is a misdemeanor. Thus the charges of conspiracy against Lauria (D) fail, and since the conspiracy theory was built around the activities of Lauria's (D) business, the charges against his co-conspirators must also fail. The order is affirmed.

Analysis:

It certainly can be argued that taking account of the seriousness of the criminal objective is appropriate in striking a balance between the conflicting interests of vendors (in regard to their freedom to engage in gainful and otherwise lawful activities without policing their vendees) and that of the community in preventing behavior that facilitates the commitment of crimes. A couple of arguments, offered on whether the specific mental state of conspiracy must be proved, demonstrate that a party has the intent, not just the knowledge, that the object of the conspiracy be achieved. Those who believe that proof of purpose should be required, argue that conspiracy laws should apply to those with criminal goals, rather than "seek to sweep within the dragnet of conspiracy all those who have been associated in any degree whatever with the main offenders." They argue that the law should not be extended to punish "legitimate businessmen" like Lauria (D). On the other hand, some argue that persons should be convicted solely on the basis of their knowledge that they are contributing to a criminal enterprise, even if they do not intend the same goals as the conspiracy. They argue that business people should not be immunized from criminal responsibility under the guise of free enterprise.

United States v. Feola

(Government) v. (Narcotics Rip-Off Conspirator)
(1975) 420 U.S. 671, 95 S.Ct. 1255, 43 L.Ed.2d 541

M E M O R Y   G R A P H I C

Instant Facts

Feola (D) and accomplices conspired to assault and assaulted federal agents posing as buyers in a drug transaction.

Black Letter Rule

A defendant need not be aware of the official status of his intended victim in order to be convicted for conspiracy to assault a federal officer.

Case Vocabulary

INCHOATE: Incomplete; in an early or even preparatory phase.

Procedural Basis: Appeal from reversal of conviction for conspiracy to assault a federal officer.

Facts: Feola (D) and his accomplices arranged to sell heroin to buyers who turned out to be undercover agents for the Bureau of Narcotics and Dangerous Drugs. Feola (D) and friends hoped to pass off sugar in place of heroin [this was before "Miami Vice," an 80's cop show in which the narcotics officers were always smart enough to taste the drugs before handing over the cash], and, if their ruse failed, they hoped to surprise their buyers and relieve them of their cash. The plan failed when an agent drew his revolver in time to counter an assault upon another agent. Feola (D) and his associates were charged with conspiring to assault, and with assaulting, federal officers, under 18 U.S.C.§ 371 and §111, respectively. At trial, the judge instructed the jury that, in order to find any of the defendants guilty on either the conspiracy or assault counts, they were not required to conclude that the defendants were aware that the buyers were federal officers. Feola (D) and associates were convicted. The Court of Appeals reversed the conspiracy convictions on a ground not advanced by Feola (D). The court approved the trial court's instructions as to the substantive offense, but concluded that the judge erred when instructing the jury that the victim's official identity must be proved in order to convict for conspiracy. The Court of Appeals felt bound by *United States v. Crimmins*, which holds that knowledge of a factual element that confers federal jurisdiction, while unnecessary for the conviction of the substantive offense, is required to sustain a conviction for conspiracy to commit the substantive offense.

Issue: Must a defendant be aware of the official status of his intended victim to be convicted for conspiracy to assault a federal officer?

Decision and Rationale: (Blackmun) No. The Government (P) urges that criminal liability under § 111 does not depend on whether the assailant meant to assault a federal officer: no knowledge requirement can be grafted on to § 371, the conspiracy statute. The Congressional purpose of the assault statute was to remove to federal courts the prosecution of criminals charged with assaulting federal officers, since local jurisdictions may not prosecute the crimes to the extent the federal government would. To effectuate the purpose of the statute should be construed to require that the accused intend to assault, and not that he be aware that his victim is a federal officer. In order to sustain a conviction of conspiracy, the Government (P) must prove at least the degree of criminal intent necessary for the substantive offense. In *Crimmins*, Judge Learned Hand offered a traffic light analogy: one may be guilty of running past a traffic light of whose existence he is unaware, but one cannot be held guilty of conspiring to run past such a light, for one cannot agree to run past a light unless one supposes that there is a light to run past. However, the traffic light analogy poses the question of whether it is fair to punish parties to an agreement to engage intentionally in apparently innocent conduct where the unintended result of the conduct is the violation of a criminal statute. This case does not require us to answer this question, and we decline to do so. But the *Crimmins* rule rests upon another foundation, that it is improper to find conspiratorial liability where the parties to the illicit agreement were not aware of the fact giving rise to federal jurisdiction, since the essence of conspiracy is agreement, and persons cannot be punished for acts that go beyond the scope of the agreement. This other reason states little more than a conclusion, since one may be guilty as a conspirator for acts that are not precisely known at the time of the agreement. The crucial question is whether the identity of the victim alters the legal character of the acts agreed to. Thus, the identity of the victim is irrelevant with respect to a conspiracy offense, as it is with the substantive offense, unless one of the values behind the imposition of conspiratorial liability is not served where the parties to the agreement are unaware that the intended target is a federal law enforcement official. There are two independent values served by the law of conspiracy. First, conspiracy laws protect society from the dangers of group criminal activity. The act of conspiracy to commit assault is no less dangerous because of the absence of a fact unnecessary to the formation of criminal intent. An "anti-federal" knowledge requirement, such as Feola (D) suggests, would only make it more difficult to convict on charges of conspiracy, a policy with no apparent purpose. The second value is that conspiracy is an inchoate crime, meaning that the likelihood of commission of the act is great and the criminal intent is sufficiently well formed to justify legal intervention. We do not see how imposition of an "anti-federal" knowledge requirement would relate to this purpose of conspiracy law. We hold that assault of a federal officer pursuant to an agreement to assault is not "beyond the reasonable intendment of the common understanding." The conspiratorial agreement is not enlarged, since knowledge of the official identity of the victim is irrelevant. We note that where the agreement calls for an attack on a specific individual, unknown to the conspirators as a federal officer, federal jurisdiction applies. If, however, the object of the attack is not identified with specificity so as to give rise to the conclusion that, had the attack been carried out, the victim would have been a federal officer, federal jurisdiction should not arise. In this situation, it would be impossible to assert that the mere fact of agreement to assault poses a significant threat to federal personnel. The judgment of the Court of Appeals with respect to the conspiracy conviction is reversed.

Analysis:

The Supreme Court's rejection of Hand's traffic light analogy in *Feola* has been justified by one commentator for several reasons. Among them, we note first that a traffic offense is not malum in se, but malum prohibitum, meaning that the crime is a regulatory violation, rather than a crime at common law. The court might be more willing to protect defendants in malum prohibitum cases. Second, the moral-wrong doctrine supports a distinction. A person who commits an assault knows that his activity is unlawful, while the driver in Hand's example is unaware of any wrongdoing on his part. Third, the attendant circumstance in *Feola* was a jurisdictional element, included in the definition of the crime solely to allow the federal government to prosecute the case in federal court. While the Court's decision in *Feola* seems heavy-handed, the Court limits its application somewhat. For example, if a group of individuals conspire to mug the next person who walks down the street, and the person happens to be a federal official, federal jurisdiction would not ordinarily apply. The group did not plan on attacking the federal official specifically—they just got the next person. A state court would thus probably decide the case.

Commonwealth v. Azim

(State) v. (Co-conspirator Driver)
313 Pa. Super. 310, 459 A.2d 1244 (1983)

M E M O R Y   G R A P H I C

Instant Facts

Azim (D) was the driver of a car which two friends jumped out of in order to beat and rob a man walking on the street.

Black Letter Rule

Once conspiracy is established and upheld, a member of the conspiracy is also guilty of the criminal acts of his co-conspirators.

Procedural Basis: Appeal from jury's conviction of the defendant.

Facts: Azim (D) drove a car in which two other men, James and Robinson, were passengers. Azim (D) pulled the car over to the side of the street, and Robinson called a passerby, Tennenbaum over to the car. When he refused, James and Robinson got out, beat and choked Tennenbaum, and took his wallet [nice guys]. Azim (D) sat at the wheel, with the engine running and lights on, and the car doors open, while the acts were committed in the vicinity of the car [But I didn't *know* what they were doing! *Really!*]. He then drove James and Robinson from the scene. Robinson and Azim (D) were tried and convicted as co-defendants. Azim (D) argues in this appeal that because his conspiracy conviction was not supported by sufficient evidence against him, the charges of assault and robbery must also fail.

Issue: Can a driver of the getaway car be considered a member of the conspiracy and thus guilty of the criminal acts of his co-conspirators?

Decision and Rationale: (Per Curiam) Yes. This court has maintained that the essence of criminal conspiracy is a common understanding, no matter how it came into being, that a particular criminal objective was to be accomplished. Among those circumstances relevant to proving conspiracy are association with alleged conspirators, knowledge of the commission of the crime, presence at the scene of the crime, and, at times, participation in the object of the conspiracy. We find no merit in Azim's (D) claim that he was merely a hired driver, with no knowledge of his passengers' criminal activity. We hold that a rational factfinder could find, beyond a reasonable doubt, that Azim (D) conspired with James and Robinson to commit assault and robbery. Once conspiracy is established and upheld, a member of the conspiracy is also guilty of the criminal acts of his co-conspirators.

Analysis:

Azim (D) argues that there was no evidence that he was a part of the conspiracy, as he did not participate in the actual criminal acts. However, by its very nature, the crime of conspiracy is frequently not susceptible of proof except by circumstantial evidence. And although a conspiracy cannot be based upon mere suspicion or conjecture, a conspiracy may be inferentially established by showing the relationship, conduct or circumstances of the parties, and the overt acts on the part of the co-conspirators have uniformly been held competent to prove that a wrongful alliance has in fact been formed.

EVIDENCE TENDING TO SHOW COMPLICITY AS AN ACCOMPLICE IN THE COMMISSION OF A SUBSTANTIVE CRIME IS NOT ENOUGH IN ITSELF TO CONVICT A DEFENDANT OF CONSPIRACY

Commonwealth v. Cook

(State) v. (Rape Accomplice)

10 Mass.App.Ct. 668, 411 N.E.2d 1326 (1980)

M E M O R Y   G R A P H I C

Instant Facts

Cook (D) and his brother met a girl and partied a bit, after which Cook's (D) brother forcibly raped her in the woods while Cook (D) watched.

Black Letter Rule

While proof of a tacit agreement to commit a crime may be enough to establish a conspiracy, a defendant cannot be convicted of conspiracy solely on evidence tending to show his complicity as an accomplice in the commission of the substantive crime.

Case Vocabulary

CONFEDERATION: Alliance.

Procedural Basis: Appeal from the trial court's denial of the defendant's motion for a required finding of not guilty, and subsequent conviction and sentence on the indictment.

Facts: Cook (D) and his brother, Maurice, were sitting in the common meeting area in a housing project, drinking and smoking marijuana. The victim, a seventeen-year-old girl, walked past them on her way to her boyfriend's home. The brothers tried to engage her in conversation, but she spurned their invitation to join them [smart]. Her boyfriend wasn't home, so on the way back past the brothers she decided to sit and talk to them while she waited for her boyfriend to return [uh oh]. The three sat for about forty-five minutes in the common area, several people were in the vicinity as well. The victim had a drink of beer but declined the marijuana. Cook (D) and his brother both identified themselves and told the girl where they worked; they even showed her their IDs, as she was having difficulty remembering their names. Maurice indicated that he was out of cigarettes and suggested the three walk to a convenience store located about a minute and a half away. The victim agreed. To reach the store, the trio proceeded along the street to a narrow path or trail located behind the project office [I can see where this is headed]. This path led down a hill through a wooded area to the rear of a well-lit service station adjacent to the convenience store. As they walked towards the path single file, the victim slipped and fell. She sat on the ground for a few seconds laughing when Maurice turned around and jumped on her. He told her she "was going to love it." After she screamed, Maurice covered her mouth with his hand, took off his belt and handed it to Cook (D), who was seated nearby. After some vile talk, Maurice forcibly raped her. During the assault the victim lost consciousness. She awoke a couple of hours later and went straight to her friends' home in the projects. The incident was reported to the police and the Cooks were arrested. Maurice was indicted for rape, and his brother (D), for accessory to rape and conspiracy to commit rape.

Issue: Can a defendant be convicted of conspiracy solely on evidence tending to show his complicity as an accomplice in the commission of the substantive crime?

Decision and Rationale: (Greaney, J.) No. Proof of a conspiracy may rest entirely or mainly on circumstantial evidence, but "some record evidence" is not enough, and an acquittal must be ordered if any essential element is left to surmise, conjecture or guesswork. We are of the opinion that the evidence, tested against the foregoing principles, was insufficient to establish a conspiracy. The circumstances under which the victim and Cook (D) met and socialized were not indicative of a preconceived plan between the brothers to commit a sexual assault. The brothers made special efforts to identify themselves to the girl, thus they could not be said to have attempted to lull her into a false sense of security. Moreover, since all the conversation took place in the victim's presence, no clandestine plan could have been formed. While openness will not automatically sanitize a conspiracy, highly visible conduct has to be considered inconsistent with the shadowy environment which usually shrouds the crime. The purpose for leaving the area was on its face innocuous and was suggested by Maurice, not Cook (D). The path was a short, reasonably direct route to a nearby, well-lit convenience store, visible from the hill. We do not think that the events up to the time the victim fell were sufficient to establish a criminal agreement or to warrant the jury in inferring the state of facts that the Commonwealth (P) claims to have existed. As to the attack itself, the fact that Maurice's attack began immediately after the victim found herself in a compromising situation suggests spontaneity of action on his part rather than the purposeful execution of a predetermined plan. From that point on, Cook's (D) actions fit the classic

HIGH COURT CASE SUMMARIES

©2002 West Group. All Rights Reserved. Do not duplicate.

paradigm of an accomplice adding encouragement to a crime in progress. The fact that Cook (D) may have aided and abetted the crime does not establish a conspiracy, particularly where the evidence shows that prior planning is not an inherent facet of the crime. In reaching our conclusion, we are mindful of the principle that proof of a tacit agreement to commit a crime may be enough to establish a conspiracy. But in this case it is just as reasonable to conclude that Cook (D) became implicated in the crime as an accomplice after it had commenced without any advance knowledge it was about to occur, as it is to infer that the minds of the parties had met in advance and agreed to commit the offense charged. The remaining question is whether Cook (D) can be convicted of conspiracy *solely* on evidence tending to show his complicity as an accomplice in the commission of the substantive crime. We think on the evidence in this case such a conclusion would be unjustified. Accomplice and conspiratorial liability are not synonymous, and one can be an accomplice aiding in the commission of a substantive offense without necessarily conspiring to commit it. Absent from the formulation of accomplice liability is the necessity of establishing an agreement or consensus in the same sense as those terms are used in describing the agreement or combination which hallmarks a conspiracy. Acts of aiding and abetting clearly make each actor a principal in the substantive offense but cannot, without more, also make each other a principal in the crime of conspiracy to commit such offense. We conclude that in this case the evidence of the confederation at the scene was insufficient to warrant Cook's (D) conviction of conspiracy.

Analysis:

The court states that proof of a tacit agreement to commit a crime may be enough to establish a conspiracy. However, the court is also careful to look carefully at the evidence to determine if the evidence is equivocal. For when the evidence tends to sustain either of two inconsistent propositions, neither can be said to have been established by legitimate proof. Additionally, as has already been discussed, the gist of conspiracy rests in the agreement between the conspirators to work in concert for the criminal or corrupt or unlawful purpose, and it is that agreement which constitutes the criminal act and which generally serves to manifest the requisite intent. When a defendant is convicted of conspiring with others to commit a crime, the conviction stems from, and is designed to punish, the unlawful agreement which preexists commission of the substantive offense. That is why proof of the conspiracy typically involves circumstantial evidence aimed at establishing a consensus prior to the commission of the target offense. Execution of the crime thus represents performance of the agreement, but beware: the offense does not substitute for the agreement. Bottom line: one can be an accomplice in a crime without being a conspirator.

People v. Foster

(State) v. (Robber)

99 Ill.2d 48, 75 Ill. Dec. 411, 457 N.E.2d 405 (1983)

M E M O R Y   G R A P H I C

 Instant Facts

Foster (D) devised a plan to rob an old man, however his co-conspirator really had reported him to the police and was just feigning agreement.

Black Letter Rule

The Illinois legislation encompasses the bilateral theory of conspiracy, which requires the actual agreement of at least two participants.

Case Vocabulary

BILATERAL THEORY OF CONSPIRACY: Requires actual agreement of at least two parties.

UNILATERAL THEORY OF CONSPIRACY: Only one conspirator needs to agree to the commission of the offense.

Procedural Basis: Appeal from the appellate court's reversal of the defendant's conviction.

Facts: Foster (D) initiated his plan to commit a robbery, approaching Ragsdale in a bar and asking him if he was "interested in making some money." Foster (D) told Ragsdale of an elderly man, Hedrick, who kept many valuables in his possession [not much of a challenge]. Although Ragsdale stated that he was interested in making money, he did not believe Foster (D) was serious until he returned to the bar the next day and discussed in detail his plan to rob Hedrick. In an effort to gather additional information, Ragsdale decided to feign agreement to Foster's (D) plan but did not contact the police. Two days later, Foster (D) went to Ragsdale's residence to find out if he was "ready to go." Since Ragsdale had not yet contacted the police, he told Foster (D) that he would not be ready until he found someone else to help them. Ragsdale informed the police of the planned robbery two days later [snitch!]. Foster (D) and Ragsdale met at Hedrick's residence the following day and were arrested. The appellate court determined that the Illinois conspiracy statute required actual agreement between at least two persons to support a conspiracy conviction. Reasoning that Ragsdale never intended to agree to Foster's (D) plan but merely feigned agreement, the court reversed Foster's (D) conviction. On appeal to this court, the State (P) argues that under the conspiracy statute it suffices if only one of the participants to the alleged conspiracy actually intends to commit the offense.

Issue: Did the Illinois legislature intend to adopt the unilateral theory of conspiracy?

Decision and Rationale: (Underwood, J.) No. The question is whether the Illinois legislature, in amending the conspiracy statute in 1961, intended to adopt the unilateral theory of conspiracy. Prior to the 1961 amendment, the statute clearly encompassed the traditional, bilateral theory. The former statute read in part "If any *two or more persons* conspire or *agree together* to do any illegal act they shall be deemed guilty of a conspiracy." The amended version provides that "*a person* commits conspiracy when, with the intent that an offense be committed, *he agrees* with another to the commission of that offense." The State (P) urges that the change in wording of the statute supports the argument that only one person need intend to agree to the commission of the offense. The unilateral/bilateral issue is not addressed in the comments to this statute, however, and we doubt that the drafters could have intended what represents a rather profound change in the law of conspiracy without mentioning it in the comments to the section. Illinois does have a solicitation statute which embraces virtually every situation in which one could be convicted of conspiracy under the unilateral theory. Moreover, the penalties for solicitation and conspiracy are substantially similar. There would appear to have been little need for the legislature to adopt the unilateral theory of conspiracy in light of the existence of the solicitation statute. We are also mindful of the rule of construction which requires us to resolve statutory ambiguities in favor of criminal defendants. For the above reasons, we conclude that the Illinois statute encompasses the bilateral theory of conspiracy.

Analysis:

The court found it significant that there was a statute for solicitation in Illinois, thus unilateral conspiracy was considered unnecessary. This is an important point, for some states only punish specific forms of solicitation and, as such, some defendants could slip through the cracks and go free unless conspiracy is deemed to be a unilateral offense. In those states without solicitation statutes, unilateral conspiracy fills in the gaps. This reasoning, however, can be a problem in that, generally speaking, solicitation statutes punish one who "commands, encourages, or requests *another to commit*" a crime. Thus, if Foster (D) intended Ragsdale to actually commit the robbery he would be guilty of solicitation, however if he merely wanted Ragsdale to help *him* commit the crime, the State (P) would need a unilateral conspiracy statute to reach Foster.

Kilgore v. State

(Freeway Shooter) v. (State)
251 Ga. 291, 305 S.E.2d 82 (1983)

M E M O R Y   G R A P H I C

Instant Facts

Kilgore (D) was convicted of shooting Norman twice in the head, killing him, while he was driving down the interstate.

Black Letter Rule

Hearsay testimony can only be admissible under the exception to the hearsay rule which provides that the out-of-court statements of one conspirator are admissible against all conspirators.

Case Vocabulary

CHAIN CONSPIRACY: A conspiracy in which there is successive communication and cooperation.
HEARSAY: Out-of-court statement not admissible as evidence.
HUB: Common source of the conspiracy.
SPOKE: Different persons involved in the conspiracy.
WHEEL CONSPIRACY: A conspiracy in which there is a single hub (conspiracy) and spokes (conspirators) who do not know each other.

Procedural Basis: Appeal from the defendant's conviction and life sentence.

Facts: Roger Norman was driving home on the Interstate in the early morning hours when he was shot twice in the head and killed. Kilgore (D) was arrested and tried for the crime. At trial, the state (P) introduced evidence of a conspiracy to kill Norman, including three previous attempts on Norman's life [third time's the charm!]. As to the first attempt, David Oldaker testified that earlier in the year, Greg Benton, his cousin, asked him to go with him to Norman's home. He testified that the purpose of the trip was to kill Norman for a crippled man named Tom who wanted Norman dead. This testimony was admitted over the hearsay objection of defense counsel. Tom Carden was Norman's brother-in-law, and a paraplegic, however he died before the case came to trial. Oldaker and Benton went to Norman's home, where they unsuccessfully tried to kill him. Kilgore (D) was in no way implicated in this attempt. Evidence did however directly connect Kilgore with the second attempt. Ed Williams, an employee of a truck stop located just off the interstate, testified that one month before the killing, he saw two cars traveling close to each other while crossing over a bridge. He heard sounds like a car backfiring, then Norman's car pulled into the truck stop while the other car turned north on the interstate. Norman, who had been on his way home from work, had been shot in the upper back [now might be a good time to go into hiding]. The police, based on what Norman told them, posted a lookout for a 1962 or 1963 Rambler with a dark bottom, white top, and Tennessee tags. Constance Chambers, Kilgore's (D) ex-girlfriend, testified that on that day, Kilgore (D) and his cousin, Lee Berry, borrowed her 1964 Rambler. It had a dark green body, white top, and Tennessee tags. She testified that Kilgore (D) returned to her apartment the next morning and told her they had killed a man. Later that day, Chambers testified that Kilgore (D) received a phone call from Tom Carden, during which she heard Kilgore (D) say "apparently we didn't get him." Chambers testimony further shows the continuation of a conspiracy to kill Norman. She testified to a phone call during which she heard Kilgore (D) tell Carden he needed more money to obtain a faster car and another man to help him. Shortly thereafter, Kilgore obtained the total of $16,500 from Carden. Chambers then drove Kilgore (D) to meet his friend, Bob Price, and the two drove off in Price's van after Kilgore (D) took his rifle from his car. Chambers testified that the day before the murder, Kilgore (D) and Price left her apartment in the evening driving separate vehicles [notifying the police would be out of the question?]. She next saw Kilgore (D) the next morning, and he was driving a blue Lincoln. Chambers testified that Kilgore told her that he and Price had killed a man on the interstate. Kilgore (D) was convicted and given a life sentence. He appeals from that judgment.

Issue: Was the hearsay testimony of Oldaker properly admitted in Kilgore's (D) trial as an exception to the hearsay rule which provides that the out-of-court statements of one conspirator are admissible against all conspirators?

Decision and Rationale: (Bell, J.) No. Kilgore (D) argues that the trial court erred in admitting over objection the hearsay testimony of Oldaker that Benton told him Tom was the man who wanted Norman killed. This testimony was the only evidence connecting Tom Carden to the attempt. For the reasons which follow, we find that this hearsay testimony was inadmissible. The testimony could only be admissible under the exception to the hearsay rule which provides that the out-of-court statements of one conspirator are admissible against all conspirators. Therefore, this testimony was only admissible if Oldaker, Benton, and Kilgore (D) were co-conspirators. To have a conspiracy, there must be an agreement between two or more persons to commit a crime. Here, there is no question that the evidence shows that Oldaker, Benton and Carden were co-conspirators in their attempt to kill Norman, and that Kilgore (D), Price and Carden were co-conspirators in the murder of Norman, but the question is whether Kilgore (D), who did not know of or communicate with Oldaker and Benton, and Oldaker and Benton, who likewise did not know of or communicate with Kilgore (D), can be considered to have agreed to and become co-conspirators in the murder of Norman. We find that they cannot. Limitations have been imposed upon the concept that persons who do not know each other can "agree" to commit a crime. An agreement, and thus one conspiracy, is more likely to be inferred in "chain" conspiracies usually involving drug distribution, in which there is successive communication or cooperation. It is more difficult to infer an agreement among the spokes of a "wheel" conspiracy because they are less likely to have a community of interest or reason to know of each other's existence since one spoke's success is usually not dependent on the other spokes' success, but instead on his dealings with the hub. In the instant case, we conclude that Kilgore (D) was not a co-conspirator of Benton and Oldaker. Here, there was no community of interests between Benton and Oldaker on the one hand and Kilgore (D) on the other. The success of Benton's and Oldaker's attempt to kill Norman was not dependent in any way on Kilgore (D). Likewise, the success of Kilgore's (D) attempt to kill Norman was not aided by Oldaker and Benton, especially considering that they did not assist in further efforts to kill Norman. In addition, Benton and Oldaker, as one spoke, and Kilgore (D), as another spoke, had no knowledge of and no reason to know of each other such that an agreement can be inferred between them. There was no reason for Kilgore to know of the previous attempt on Norman's life, as his success was not dependent on it. Likewise, Oldaker and Benton had no reason to know of another spoke. For the above reasons, we find that Kilgore and Oldaker and Benton were not co-conspirators. Consequently it was error to admit the hearsay testimony of Oldaker.

Analysis:

Kilgore also contended that the state (P) did not prove he actually committed the murder, and that consequently, it must have been proceeding on the theory that his guilt was based upon a conspiracy; yet, he argues, the state (P) did not prove a conspiracy because it did not prove an overt act occurred in Georgia. However, the conspiracy was merely an evidentiary tool used by the state (P) to help prove Kilgore (D) guilty of the murder of Norman. In fact, Kilgore could not have been tried for conspiracy since the object of the conspiracy was completed. As for the conspiracy itself, the type of agreement necessary to form a conspiracy is not the "meeting of the minds" necessary to form a contract and may be a mere tacit understanding between two or more people that they will pursue a particular criminal objective. It is possible for various persons to be parties to a single agreement (and thus one conspiracy) even though they do not know the identity of one another, and even though they are not all aware of the details of the plan of operation. It could be argued in this case that Oldaker and Benton should have known that if they failed Carden would find another spoke, and that, therefore, they can be deemed to have "agreed" with this spoke. However, this reasoning would be too speculative a ground on which to infer such an agreement.

Braverman v. United States

(Moonshiner) v. (Government)
317 U.S. 49, 63 S.Ct. 99, 87 L.Ed. 23 (1942)

M E M O R Y   G R A P H I C

Instant Facts

Braverman (D) and others were convicted of violating several statutes in the illicit manufacture, transportation, and distribution of distilled spirits.

Black Letter Rule

A single agreement to commit acts in violation of several penal statutes must be punished as one conspiracy.

Case Vocabulary

BILL OF EXCEPTIONS: Writing submitted to a trial court stating for the record objections to rulings made and instructions given by the trial judge.
ENVISAGES: Conceives.

Procedural Basis: Appeal from the Court of Appeals' affirmance of the trial court's conviction and sentence of the defendant after a jury trial.

Facts: The trial evidence showed that for a considerable period of time Braverman (D), and others, collaborated in the illicit manufacture, transportation, and distribution of distilled spirits involving the violations of statutes mentioned in the several counts of the indictment [pass the moonshine!]. At the close of the trial, Braverman (D) renewed a motion which was made at the beginning to require the Government (P) to elect one of the seven counts of the indictment upon which to proceed, contending that the proof could not and did not establish more than one agreement. In response, the Government (P) took the position that the seven counts of the indictment charged as distinct offenses the several illegal objects of one continuing conspiracy, that if the jury found such a conspiracy it might find Braverman (D) guilty of as many offenses as it had illegal objects, and that for each offense the two-year statutory penalty could be imposed [throw the book at them!]. The trial judge submitted the case to the jury on the Government's (P) theory. The jury returned with a general verdict finding Braverman (D) guilty as charged, and the court sentence was eight years imprisonment. On appeal, the Court of Appeals for the Sixth Circuit affirmed.

Issue: Can a single agreement to commit acts in violation of several penal statutes be punished as several conspiracies?

Decision and Rationale: (Stone, C.J.) No. Both courts below recognized that a single agreement to commit an offense does not become several conspiracies because it continues over a period of time, and that there may be a single continuing agreement to commit several offenses. But they thought that in the latter case each contemplated offense renders the agreement punishable as a separate conspiracy. Where each of the counts of an indictment alleges a conspiracy to violate a different penal statute it may be proper to conclude, in the absence of a bill of exceptions bringing up the evidence, that several conspiracies are charged rather than one, and that the conviction is for each. But it is a different matter to hold, as the court below appears to have done in this case, that even though a single agreement is entered into, the conspirators are guilty of as many offenses as the agreement has criminal objects. Whether the object of a single agreement is to commit one or many crimes, it is in either case that agreement which constitutes the conspiracy which the state punishes. The one agreement cannot be taken to be several agreements and hence several conspiracies because it envisages the violation of several statutes rather than one. Thus we hold that a single agreement to commit acts in violation of several penal statutes must be punished as one conspiracy.

Analysis:

Once again, it is pointed out that the gist of the crime of conspiracy as defined by the statute is the agreement or confederation of the conspirators to commit one or more unlawful acts [sound familiar yet?]. When a single agreement to commit one or more substantive crimes is evidenced by an overt act, as the statute requires, the precise nature and extent of the conspiracy must be determined by reference to the agreement which embraces and defines its objects. It is tempting to look at all the statutory violations and attach individual liability, as the lower courts did, however this Court correctly identified the bottom line, which is that the conspiracy is the crime which is being punished, and it is not relevant whether that agreement encompasses one or several substantive crimes. The single agreement constitutes a single conspiracy and it must be punished as such.

Iannelli v. United States

(Gambling Businessman) v. (Government)
420 U.S. 770, 95 S.Ct. 1284, 43 L.Ed.2d 616 (1975)

M E M O R Y   G R A P H I C

Instant Facts

Iannelli (D) was convicted and sentenced under both the substantive and conspiracy counts for gambling violations.

Black Letter Rule

There is a recognized exception to Wharton's Rule which permits prosecution and punishment for both the substantive offense and the conspiracy.

Case Vocabulary

DEMURRER: Request for dismissal of the action based only on the law.
INTER ALIA: Among other things.
PLURALITY: Significant number.
WHARTON'S RULE: Prevents conspiracy prosecuion for a crime that necessarily involves the participation of two or more persons.

Procedural Basis: Appeal from the Court of Appeal's affirmance of the trial court's conviction and sentence of the defendant.

Facts: Iannelli (D) was charged, along with seven others, seven unindicted co-conspirators, and six co-defendants, inter alia, with conspiring to violate and violating 18 U.S.C. Sec. 1955, a federal gambling statute making it a crime for five or more persons to conduct, finance, manage, supervise, direct, or own a gambling business prohibited by state law [too many cooks...]. Iannelli (D) and seven others were convicted of both offenses, and each was sentenced under both the substantive and conspiracy counts. The Court of Appeals for the Third Circuit affirmed, finding that a recognized exception to Wharton's Rule [rule that prohibits prosecution for conspiracy of crime that necessarily involves two or more persons] permitted prosecution and punishment for both offenses.

Issue: Is there a recognized exception to Wharton's Rule which permits prosecution and punishment for both the substantive offense of gambling and the conspiracy?

Decision and Rationale: (Powell, J.) Yes. The classic formulation of Wharton's Rule requires that the conspiracy indictment be dismissed before trial. Federal courts earlier adhered to this literal interpretation and thus sustained demurrers to conspiracy indictments. More recently, however, some federal courts have differed over whether Wharton's Rule requires initial dismissal of the conspiracy indictment. Federal courts likewise have disagreed as to the proper application of the recognized "third-party exception," which renders Wharton's Rule inapplicable when the conspiracy involves the cooperation of a greater number of persons than is required for commission of the substantive offense. The Courts of Appeals are at odds even over the fundamental question whether Wharton's Rule ever applies to a charge for conspiracy to violate Section 1955. This Court's prior decisions indicate that the broadly formulated Wharton's Rule has current vitality only as a judicial presumption, to be applied in the absence of legislative intent to the contrary. The conduct proscribed by Sec. 1955 is significantly different from the offenses to which the Rule traditionally has been applied. Wharton's Rule applies only to offenses that *require* concerted criminal activity, a plurality of criminal agents. In such cases, a closer relationship exists between the conspiracy and the substantive offense because *both* require collective criminal activity. The substantive offense therefore presents some of the same threats that the law of conspiracy normally is thought to guard against, and it cannot automatically be assumed that the Legislature intended the conspiracy and the substantive offense to remain as discrete crimes upon consummation of the latter. Thus, absent legislative intent to the contrary, the Rule supports a presumption that the two merge when the substantive offense is proved. But a legal principle commands less respect when extended beyond the logic that supports it. In this case, the significant differences in characteristics and consequences of the kinds of offenses that gave rise to Wharton's Rule and the activities proscribed by Sec. 1955 counsel against attributing significant weight to the presumption the Rule erects. More importantly, the Rule must defer to a discernible legislative judgment. Major gambling activities were a principal focus of congressional concern, as evidenced by passage of the Organized Crime Control Act of 1970. Large-scale gambling activities were seen to be both a substantial evil and a source of funds for other criminal conduct. We conclude, therefore, that the history and structure of the Organized Crime Control Act of 1970 manifest a clear and unmistakable legislative judgment that more than outweighs any presumption of merger between the conspiracy to violate Sec. 1955 and the consummation of that substantive offense. Affirmed.

Analysis:

Traditionally the law has considered conspiracy and the completed substantive offense to be separate crimes. Conspiracy is an inchoate offense, the essence of which is an agreement to commit an unlawful act. Unlike some crimes, the conspiracy to commit an offense and the subsequent commission of that crime normally do not merge into a single punishable act. Thus it is well recognized that in most cases separate sentences can be imposed for the conspiracy to do an act and for the subsequent accomplishment of that end. Indeed, the Court has even held that the conspiracy can be punished more harshly than the accomplishment of its purpose. Wharton's Rule first emerged at a time when the contours of the law of conspiracy were in the process of active formulation. The general question whether the conspiracy merged into the completed felony offense remained for some time a matter of uncertain resolution. That issue is now settled, however, and the Rule currently stands as an exception to the general principle that a conspiracy and the substantive offense that is its immediate end do not merge upon proof of the latter.

Gebardi v. United States

(Amorous Mann Act Violator) v. (Government)
(1932) 287 U.S. 112, 53 S.Ct. 35, 77 L.Ed. 206

M E M O R Y   G R A P H I C

Instant Facts

Gebardi (D) and a woman agreed to go across state lines for illicit purposes in violation of the Mann Act, and the two were charged with conspiracy to violate the Mann Act.

Black Letter Rule

A woman cannot be held criminally liable for conspiring to transport herself across state lines for illicit purposes, even where she consents to the substantive offense.

Case Vocabulary

ILLICIT: Illegal, unlawful; typically used in reference to sexual relations.

Procedural Basis: Certiorari granted to review conviction of a couple for conspiracy to transport a woman across state lines for illicit purposes.

Facts: Gebardi (D) and a woman agreed that Gebardi (D) would transport her across state lines for the purpose of having sexual intercourse. [No, other states weren't necessarily preferable for the purposes of sexual relations—Gebardi (D) was a mobster and when his girlfriend claimed they were out of town during the Valentine's Day Massacre of '29, in which Gebardi (D) allegedly supposedly was the gunman, the prosecutor pursued Mann Act charges against both of them.] Gebardi (D) purchased train tickets for at least one journey, though the couple went on several such trips together. Each time, in advance of the tickets' purchase, the woman voluntarily agreed to go on the trip in order to engage in illicit sexual relations. Gebardi (D) and the woman were both convicted of conspiracy to violate the Mann Act, which imposes a penalty on any person who knowingly transports any woman or girl for the purposes of prostitution or debauchery, or for any other immoral purpose. The trial court convicted on the authority of *United States v. Holte*, where the court argued that if a woman suggested the journey and carried out the journey by purchasing the tickets, in the hopes of blackmailing the man, the woman could be found guilty of conspiracy.

Issue: May a woman who consents to transportation across state lines for illicit purposes be convicted of conspiracy to violate the substantive offense of transporting herself across state lines?

Decision and Rationale: (Stone) No. First, the circumstances where a woman might violate the Mann Act are not present here. She did not purchase the tickets, nor does she appear to be the active and moving force in conceiving or carrying out the transportation. For a woman to be liable for violating the statute she must aid and assist in her transportation, meaning she must do more than consent—she must take an active role in the transportation. Second, just as by consenting the woman has not violated the Mann Act, she also is not guilty of conspiracy to violate the Mann Act. An incapacity to commit the substantive offense does not necessarily insulate one from being convicted of conspiracy to commit the offense. However, although Congress set out to deal with cases in which the woman frequently, if not normally, consents to the transportation, the consent to transportation was not made a crime under the Mann Act. The Mann Act does not condemn a woman's participation in transportation effected by her consent, so we take it as evidence that Congress meant to leave her acquiescence unpunished. On the evidence before us the woman has not violated the Mann Act, and is not guilty of conspiracy to do so. Since the man did not conspire with anyone else, his conviction on the conspiracy count must also be overturned. Judgments reversed.

Analysis:

Wharton's Rule states that where the very definition of a crime requires the agreement and voluntary participation of two persons, the two persons cannot be prosecuted as conspirators for the offense. For example, the crimes of bigamy, adultery, incest, and dueling are all crimes which require the willing participation of both parties. The rule is based on the premise that conspiracy laws seek to control the more dangerous nature of group criminality, yet these offenses require two people to commit them—there is no danger added by commission of the crime, and no extra need to control group criminality. There are some exceptions to the rule, however. A very important exception is the "third-party exception." The third-party exception provides that if more than the minimum number of persons needed to commit the offense agree to commit the offense, a conspiracy is formed, and Wharton's Rule does not apply. Wharton's rule was held not to apply in *Gebardi* because a woman may be taken away without her consent in violation of the Mann Act.

A CONSPIRACY IS COMPLETE AFTER AGREEMENT AND THE COMMISSION OF AN OVERT ACT, AND WITHDRAWAL IS NOT A VALID DEFENSE TO THE FORMATION OF THE CONSPIRACY

People v. Sconce

(State) v. (Murder Conspirator)
228 Cal.App.3d 693, 279 Cal.Rptr. 59 (1991)

M E M O R Y   G R A P H I C

Instant Facts

Sconce (D) hired someone to kill a man but before the murder was carried out he changed his mind and called it off.

Black Letter Rule

Withdrawal from a conspiracy avoids liability only for the target offense, or for any subsequent act committed by a co-conspirator in pursuance of the common plan, but liability for forming the conspiracy remains.

Case Vocabulary

LOCUS POENITENTIAE: An opportunity to withdraw from or terminate the agreement before the consummation of the crime.

Procedural Basis: Appeal from the trial court's setting aside of the information charging the defendant.

Facts: Sconce (D) offered Bob Garcia $10,000 to kill Elie Estephan, the estranged husband of Cindy Estephan [pretty cheap!]. Sconce (D) told Garcia that he, Cindy, and a man named Sallard were plotting the murder. Garcia agreed to find someone to kill Estephan or to do it himself. Garcia then contacted ex-convict Herbert Dutton and offered him $5,000 to carry out the killing [even more affordable, *and* an easy profit!]. Subsequently, Garcia and Dutton went to Estephan's house to inspect the area. They decided that Dutton would plant a bomb under Estephan's car. Approximately three weeks after Sconce's (D) initial conversation with Garcia, Sconce (D) "just called it off." He said to "just forget about it, disregard doing it." Garcia did not see Dutton after the night they drove to Estephan's house, and although Garcia did not know it at the time Sconce (D) told him not to kill Estephan, Dutton had been arrested on a parole violation. (The murder was not carried out.) The People (P) contend that the trial court erroneously set aside the information because Sconce's (D) withdrawal from the conspiracy, although it might insulate him from liability for future conspiratorial acts, does not constitute a defense to liability for the conspiracy itself.

Issue: Is withdrawal a valid defense to the completed crime of conspiracy?

Decision and Rationale: (Klein, P.J.) No. Under California law, withdrawal is a complete defense to conspiracy only if accomplished before the commission of an overt act, or where it is asserted in conjunction with the running of the statute of limitations. The requirement of an overt act exists to provide a locus poenitentiae to avoid punishment for the conspiracy. Obviously, the inverse of this rule is that once an overt act has been committed in furtherance of the conspiracy, the crime of conspiracy has been completed and no subsequent action by the conspirator can change that. Thus, even if it be assumed Sconce (D) effectively withdrew from the conspiracy, withdrawal merely precludes liability for subsequent acts committed by the members of the conspiracy. The withdrawal does not relate back to the criminal formation of the unlawful combination. In sum, conspiracy is complete upon the commission of an overt act. We are bound to follow the foregoing rule, and any change in the law is a matter for the legislature. The decision of the trial court is thus reversed.

Analysis:

It has been ruled that once one's participation in a conspiracy is shown, it will be presumed to continue unless he is able to prove, as a matter of defense, that he effectively withdrew from the conspiracy. Withdrawal from a conspiracy requires "an affirmative and bona fide rejection or repudiation of the conspiracy, communicated to the co-conspirators." The court speaks of communication to each and every co-conspirator, however this requirement appears to be onerous, and even impossible in the case of a large conspiracy where all members do not know each other. Thus, this requirement could remove any incentive the withdrawal defense may provide. The trial court relied upon this rationale in setting aside the information, as it encourages abandonment, thereby weakening the group. This Court, however, correctly recognizes that even if it is tempting to follow this rationale, the rule remains that withdrawal from a conspiracy avoids liability only for the target offense, or for any subsequent act committed by a co-conspirator in pursuance of the common plan. However, the change of mind is ineffectual as to the conspiracy crime itself, as one cannot undo that which he has already done.

United States v. Elliott

(Government) v. (RICO Conspirator)

571 F.2d 880 (1978)

M E M O R Y   G R A P H I C

Instant Facts

Elliott (D) and five others were charged with conspiring to violate the RICO statute.

Black Letter Rule

RICO allows a prosecutor to charge, in a single count, what might constitute multiple, smaller conspiracies.

Case Vocabulary

RICO: Racketeer Influenced and Corrupt Organizations Act; federal statute designed to eradicate organized crime.

TRIAL EN MASSE: Group trial.

Procedural Basis: Appeal from the lower court's conviction of the defendant.

Facts: The indictment charged Elliott (D) and five others with conspiring with each other, with 37 unindicted co-conspirators, and with "others to the grand jury known and unknown," to violate Section 1962, subsection (c), of RICO [that's one big party!]. The essence of the conspiracy charge was that Elliott (D) and the others agreed to participate, directly and indirectly, in the conduct of the affairs of an enterprise whose purposes were to commit thefts, fence stolen goods, illegally traffic in narcotics, obstruct justice, and engage in "other criminal activities." The evidence supported the Government's (P) claim that Elliott (D) and the others were involved in one or more of the criminal endeavors. However, at no time did more than three of the defendants participate in any specific criminal endeavor, although one person, J.C. Hawkins, was linked to all of the crimes. The thread tying all of these individuals together was the desire to make money.

Issue: Does RICO allow a prosecutor to charge in a single count what might constitute multiple, smaller conspiracies?

Decision and Rationale: (Simpson, C.J.) Yes. The Court has previously held that proof of multiple conspiracies under an indictment alleging a single conspiracy constituted a material variance requiring reversal where a defendant's substantial rights had been affected. At issue was the right not to be tried en masse for the conglomeration of distinct and separate offenses committed by others. This protects against the transference of guilt from members of one conspiracy to members of another. The impact of that decision was soon limited by the Court in a case where the chain conspiracy rationale was born. The Court reasoned that since the scheme which is the object of the conspiracy must depend on the successful operation of each link in the chain, an individual associating himself with this type of conspiracy knows that for its success it requires an organization wider than may be disclosed by his personal participation. This rationale applies only insofar as the alleged agreement has a common end or single unified purpose. The rationale falls apart, however, where the remote members of the alleged conspiracy are not truly interdependent or where the various activities sought to be tied together cannot reasonably be said to constitute a unified scheme. Applying pre-RICO conspiracy concepts to the facts of this case, we doubt that a single conspiracy could be demonstrated. The activities allegedly embraced by the illegal agreement in this case are simply too diverse to be tied together on the theory that participation in one activity necessarily implied awareness of others. In enacting RICO, Congress found that organized crime continues to grow in part because the sanctions and remedies available to the Government (P) are unnecessarily limited in scope and impact. Thus, one of the express purposes of the Act was to seek "eradication of organized crime by establishing new penal prohibitions, and by providing enhanced sanctions and new remedies to deal with the unlawful activities of those engaged in organized crime." Against this background, we are convinced that, through RICO, Congress intended to authorize the single prosecution of a multi-faceted, diversified conspiracy by replacing the inadequate "wheel" and "chain" rationales with a new statutory concept: the enterprise. The object of a RICO conspiracy is to violate a substantive RICO provision – here, to conduct or participate in the affairs of an enterprise through a pattern of racketeering activity – and not merely to commit each of the predicate crimes necessary to demonstrate a pattern of racketeering activity. Under the statute, it is irrelevant that each defendant participated in the enterprise's affairs through different, even unrelated crimes, so long as we may reasonably infer that each crime was intended to further the enterprise's affairs. To be convicted as a member of an enterprise conspiracy, an individual, by his

United States v. Elliott (Continued)

words or actions, must have objectively manifested an agreement to participate, directly or indirectly, in the affairs of an enterprise through the commission of two or more predicate crimes. In the instant case, it is clear that the essential nature of the plan was to associate for the purpose of making money from repeated criminal activity. Our society disdains mass prosecutions because we abhor the totalitarian doctrine of mass guilt. We nevertheless punish conspiracy as a distinct offense because we recognize that collective action toward an illegal end involves a greater risk to society than individual action toward the same end. That risk is greatly compounded when the conspirators contemplate not a single crime but a career of crime. The evidence could not be taken to support, to the exclusion of all other reasonable hypotheses, a conclusion by the jury that Elliott (D) agreed to participate, directly or indirectly, in the affairs of an enterprise through a pattern of racketeering activity. At best, the evidence shows he became peripherally involved in a stolen meat deal, which is not enough to prove that he knowingly and intentionally joined the broad conspiracy to violate RICO. Elliott (D) agreed to participate in the affairs of the enterprise, but not through a *pattern* of racketeering activity, hence, not in violation of the Act. The evidence relevant to Elliott (D) as we view the record, was not sufficient to permit the jury to conclude that he conspired with the five other defendants to violate the RICO statute. Accordingly, his conviction must be reversed.

Analysis:

This case holds that a series of agreements that under pre-RICO law would constitute multiple conspiracies could under RICO be tried as a single enterprise conspiracy. What ties these conspiracies together is not the mere fact that they involve the same enterprise, but is instead an agreement on an overall objective. What RICO does is to provide a new criminal objective by defining a new substantive crime. That crime consists of participation in an enterprise through a pattern of racketeering activity. Elliott (D) and the other defendants could not have been tried on a single conspiracy count under pre-RICO law because they had not agreed to commit any particular crime. They were properly tied together under RICO only because the evidence established an agreement to commit a substantive RICO offense. The agreement was an implicit one, but it was an agreement nonetheless.

Chapter 11

The law has long recognized criminal liability for people other than those who actually commit criminal acts. Individuals may assist, aid and abet, incite, or encourage others to commit criminal acts. Accomplices assume criminal liability in terms of their degree of participation in the criminal activity. They may receive a lesser punishment than the principal, depending upon the circumstances of the case.

The common law carefully classified parties to crimes. These categories were very important for procedural reasons, and they are retained in some statutes today. The categories are principal in the first degree, principal in the second degree, accessory before the fact, and accessory after the fact. Principals are those involved in the commission of a crime. Principals in the first degree are those who actually perpetrate crimes either through their own acts or by use of inanimate objects or innocent people. Principals in the second degree incite or abet the commission of crimes and are present either actually or constructively. Persons are constructively present when, without being actually present, they still are assisting the principals of the first degree at the moment the crimes are being committed. An example of this would be a "lookout" during a bank robbery who is posted away from the bank. An accessory before the fact incites or abets but is not actually or constructively present when the crime is committed. An example would be someone who provides counsel or tools for the commission of a crime. An accessory after the fact is one who, knowing that a felony has been committed, receives, relieves, comforts, or assists the felon for the purpose of hindering apprehension and conviction.

Generally, modern statutes do not distinguish between principals (either degree) and accessories before the fact. All three are treated as principals. Many of the statutes have abandoned the common-law terminology and specify that an accomplice is legally accountable for the conduct of another. Often a fine line is drawn between doing enough and not doing enough to constitute the act required for complicity; each case must be decided on its unique facts. Jurisdictions also differ regarding the mental state requirement of complicity. Generally, alleged accomplices are required at a minimum to have the mental state required for the offenses to which they are alleged to be accomplices. In addition, most jurisdictions require an intent to aid in the commission of a crime. Other courts have held that it is sufficient that accomplices know their acts will assist in the commission of crimes, although they do not necessarily desire that result. Still others permit finding that accomplices have the requisite criminal intent if they act recklessly knowing that that reckless behavior will facilitate the commission of a crime.

The scope of accomplice liability is another important issue. Traditionally, an accomplice has been held criminally liable for all crimes that might reasonably result in complicity, even though the principal's crimes go beyond those actually contemplated by the accomplice. It may be argued, however, that this position unreasonably extends criminal liability beyond the requirement of a criminal state of mind.

The defense of abandonment generally is recognized in accomplice liability. To sustain this defense, the defendant must show the complicity was abandoned in a timely manner. The actor must terminate the complicity before the commission of the offense and he must also attempt to prevent the crime from occurring.

Chapter 11

NOTE: THE PURPOSE OF THIS OUTLINE IS TO ORGANIZE THE CASES SO THAT ONE CAN QUICKLY UNDERSTAND THE RELEVANCE OF EACH CASE TO THE COURSE. NO ATTEMPT IS MADE IN THIS OVERVIEW TO ADDRESS EVERY CONCEPT THAT MUST BE STUDIED. BE SURE TO READ THE ENTIRE CASEBOOK AND/OR OTHER MATERIALS TO GAIN A FULL UNDERSTANDING OF ALL CONCEPTS.

I. Accomplice Liability
   A. General Principles
      1. Common Law Terminology and its significance
         a. An accessory cannot be tried, without his consent, before the principal, and an accessory cannot be convicted of a higher crime than his principal. *State v. Ward.*
      2. Theoretical Foundation: Derivative Liability
         a. Accessorial liability is derivative, that is, it is incurred due to the violation of law by the primary party to which the secondary party contributed.
   B. "Elements" of Accomplice Liability: In General
      1. The accused's response to the prosecutor's questions that "you could say" he was a lookout, standing completely alone, does not establish that the accused was an aider and abettor by participating in, and wishing to bring about the entering with intent to commit larceny. *State v. Hoselton.*
   C. Mens Rea
      1. Intent: "Purpose" or "Knowledge"?
         a. The intent of a supplier who knows his supplies will be put to criminal use may be established by direct evidence that he intends to participate in the crime, or through an inference that he intends to participate based upon either his special interest in the activity, or the felonious nature of the crime itself. *People v. Lauria.*
         b. By intentionally acting to further the criminal actions of another, the secondary party voluntarily identifies himself with the principal party. This intention to further the acts, thus creating criminal liability, is equivalent to manifesting consent to liability under the civil law. *Complicity, Cause and Blame: A Study in the Interpretation of Doctrine.*
      2. When Is "Intent" Not Required?
         a. Offenses Not Requiring Intent: A person may be held liable as an accessory to a criminally negligent act if he has the requisite culpable mental state for the commission of the substantive offense, and he intentionally aids another in the crime. *State v. Foster.*
         b. Natural-and-Probable-Consequences Doctrine:

A rule allowing for a murder conviction under a theory of accomplice liability based upon an *objective* standard, despite the absence of evidence that the defendant possessed the culpable *subjective* mental state that constitutes an element of the crime of murder, does not represent a departure from prior Maine law and, as such, is constitutional. *State v. Linscott.*
         c. Attendant Circumstances: There is a deliberate ambiguity as to whether the purpose requirement extends to circumstance elements of the contemplated offense or whether the policy of the substantive offense on this point should control.
   D. Actus Reus
      1. Difficult issues of fact and policy can arise when the secondary party's participation is relatively slight or when the Government seeks to hold the accomplice accountable for his omission, rather than his conduct.
      2. Accompaniment and observation are not sufficient acts to constitute "aid" so as to satisfy the elements necessary for accomplice liability or for any other crime. *State v. Vaillancourt.*
      3. Presence and payment to attend an illegal performance in order to attain benefit for oneself can constitute aiding and abetting the criminal act. *Wilcox v. Jeffrey.*
      4. A conviction may not be had upon the testimony of an accomplice unless his testimony is corroborated by such other evidence as tends to connect the defendant with the commission of the offense, and the corroboration is not sufficient if it merely shows the commission of the offense or the circumstances thereof. *State v. Helmenstein.*
      5. Accomplice law might be unjustified in ignoring causation, as it holds a person accountable for the actions of others. As a result, although the accomplice is punished because of his own conduct, he is punished to the extent of another's.
      6. A person cannot be convicted of aiding and abetting the commission of a crime when the underlying crime was never committed by anyone. *People v. Genoa.*
   E. Distinguishing Direct From Accomplice Liability
      1. One who effects a criminal act through an innocent or unwitting agent is a principal in the first degree. *Bailey v. Commonwealth.*
   F. Relationship of the Liability of the Accomplice to the Principal
      1. If the Principal Is Acquitted or Not Prosecuted

a. A principal's act, not criminal in nature when performed, cannot become criminal when imputed to an accomplice. *State v. Hayes.*

b. A defendant can be convicted of aiding and abetting even if the principal is not identified or convicted, however an aider or abettor may not be held liable absent proof that a criminal offense was committed by a principal. *United States v. Lopez.*

2. If the Principal Is Convicted

a. If there is only one offense committed, then the person who has requested that offense to be committed, or advised that the offense be committed, cannot be guilty of a graver offense than that in fact which was committed. *Regina v. Richards.*

G. Limits to Accomplice Liability

1. Where the Legislature has dealt with crimes which necessarily involve the joint actions of two or more persons, and where no punishment at all is provided for the conduct, or misconduct, of one of the participants, the party whose participation is not denounced by statute cannot be charged with criminal conduct on either a conspiracy or aiding and abetting theory. *In Re Meagan R.*

2. Withdrawal provisions of an accountability statute are ineffective to prevent liability for an attempted crime after the planning has already taken place. *People v. Brown.*

H. Special Problems: Aiding and Abetting Suicide and Euthanasia

1. Drawing Lines: When Does Suicide Assistance Constitute Murder?

a. Incitement to suicide, while morally reprehensible, is not criminal under the present state of the law. *People v. Campbell.*

b. Only where there is probable cause to believe that death was the direct and natural result of a defendant's act can the defendant be properly bound over on a charge of murder in an assisted suicide case. *People v. Kevorkian.*

2. Suicide Assistance and Euthanasia: Constitutional and Policy Issues

a. A statutory prohibition against causing or aiding a suicide does not offend the Fourteenth Amendment to the United States Constitution. *Washington v. Glucksberg.*

b. Disentangling the state's interest in the sanctity or intrinsic value of life from other policies served by the state's interest in the preservation of life is difficult. The phrase "sanctity of life" itself has many possible meanings. *The State's Interest in the Preservation of Life: From Quin-*

lan to Cruzan.

c. The quality of life argument focuses on a rational choice of euthanasia to exercise control over the end of life. *Euthanasia: Orchestrating "The Last Syllable of ... Time."*

d. There is a "slippery slope" concern that even if passive euthanasia is morally permissible, its toleration will lead to acceptance of voluntary euthanasia and, ultimately, to active *involuntary* euthanasia. *Some Non-Religious Views Against Proposed "Mercy-Killing" Legislation.*

e. Involuntary euthanasia is not an immediately practical problem that needs facing now. *"Mercy-Killing" Legislation – A Rejoinder.*

f. Perhaps a law should be enacted allowing physician-assisted suicide under certain circumstances. It is difficult to defend an absolute prohibition when it is not only expected that the prohibition will be violated in certain situations, but also that circumstances can be imagined where it would be understandable and even forgivable. *Yale Kamisar – Physician-Assisted Suicide: The Problems Presented by the Compelling, Heartwrenching Case.*

II. Vicarious Liability: An employer cannot be imprisoned under a theory of respondeat superior for the criminal acts of his employees committed on his premises without his presence, participation or knowledge. *Commonwealth v. Koczwara.*

III. Corporate Liability

A. A corporation may be prosecuted and convicted for the crimes of theft and forgery. *State v. Christy Pontiac-GMC, Inc.*

B. The critical weaknesses in both the traditional respondeat superior and MPC standards of liability is that they fail to sufficiently analyze corporate intent. *Pamela H. Bucy – Corporate Ethos: A Standard for Imposing Corporate Criminal Liability.*

C. A corporation can be "imprisoned," in that the Court restrains or immobilizes the corporation. The United States Marshal would seize the corporation's physical assets or part of the assets or restrict its actions or liberty in a particular manner. *United States v. Allegheny Bottling Company.*

D. Monetary penalties directed at the corporation will often prove inadequate to deter illegal behavior. *John C. Coffee, Jr. – "No Soul to Damn: No Body to Kick": An Unscandalized Inquiry Into the Problem of Corporate Punishment.*

ACCESSORY LIABILITY CANNOT BE DETERMINED PRIOR TO, AND CANNOT BE GREATER THAN, THE PRINCIPAL'S

State v. Ward

(State) v. (Not Stated)
284 Md. 189, 396 A.2d 1041 (1978)

M E M O R Y   G R A P H I C

Instant Facts
The court distinguishes and defines the common law treatment of felony principals and accessories.

Black Letter Rule
An accessory cannot be tried, without his consent, before the principal, and an accessory cannot be convicted of a higher crime than his principal.

Case Vocabulary

ABETTOR: Affirmative criminal conduct to assist in the commission of the felony.
ACCESSORY: The person who helps the perpetrator commit the felony. [Something added to spice up your wardrobe or placed on your dresser to make your room look nice.]
CRIMINAL PROTECTOR: Accomplice after the felony has been committed, who helps the felon in an attempt to prevent his apprehension or punishment.
INCITER: Accomplice not present during the commission of the felony, but who helped facilitate the crime.
PERPETRATOR: The person who actually commits the felony.

Procedural Basis: Not stated.

Facts: Not stated.

Issue: May an accessory to a felony be tried prior to the principal's trial and be convicted of a higher crime than his principal?

Decision and Rationale: (Orth, J.) No. The doctrine of accessoryship applicable to felonies developed through the common law of England. Maryland has not changed this doctrine by legislation or judicial decision, and it is presently in virtually the same form as it existed in the 18th century. The guilty parties are divided into principals, first degree (perpetrators) and second degree (abettors), and accessories, before the fact (inciters) and after the fact (criminal protectors). At the common law, the abettor may be tried and convicted prior to the trial of the perpetrator, or even after the perpetrator has been tried and acquitted. Furthermore, an abettor may be convicted of a higher crime or a lower crime than the perpetrator. The common law took a different path with regard to accessories, however. An accessory cannot be tried, without his consent, before the principal, and an accessory cannot be convicted of a higher crime than his principal.

Analysis:

There were also two other principal-accessory distinctions developed in the common law era. An accessory could only be prosecuted in the jurisdiction where the accessorial acts took place, rather than where the crime was committed. This rule did not apply, however, to principals in the second degree (abettors). Additionally, strict rules of pleading and proof prevented a defendant charged as an accessory from being convicted as a principal, and vice versa. Almost all states have abrogated, through legislation, the distinction between principals and accessories before the fact [k.i.s.s.]. Other states have permitted accessories before the fact to be tried and punished without regard to the status of the principal's prosecution, which reaches substantially the same result. Generally, the accessory after the fact is now treated as a separate and lesser offense, such as hindering prosecution or obstruction of justice, rather than being treated as a party to the crime committed by a perpetrator.

State v. Hoselton

(State) v. (Boat Burglar)
179 W.Va. 645, 371 S.E.2d 366 (1988)

M E M O R Y   G R A P H I C

Instant Facts

Hoselton (D) was charged and convicted as a principal in the first degree for acting as lookout while his friends broke into a boat's storage locker.

Black Letter Rule

The accused's response that "you could say" he was a lookout, standing completely alone, does not establish that the accused was an aider and abettor by participating in, and wishing to bring about the entering with intent to commit larceny.

Case Vocabulary

LARCENY: Theft.
PER CURIAM: Opinion of the court in which the author is not identified.

Procedural Basis: Appeal from the trial court's conviction and subsequent denial of the defendant's motions for acquittal and new trial.

Facts: When Hoselton (D) was eighteen years old, he and several friends went to a barge they frequently trespassed upon for fishing [boys will be boys]. His friends broke into the storage locker on the barge while Hoselton stood out at the end of the barge. His friends stole several items from the locker and loaded them into their car. Hoselton (D) took no part in assisting the others to load the goods into the car, and he was then driven immediately home. Hoselton (D) was charged and tried as a principal in the first degree for either breaking and entering or entering without breaking with intent to commit larceny. At the trial, Hoselton (D) testified that he didn't go into the storage locker. He was asked if he was keeping a lookout, and he said "You could say that. I just didn't want to go down in there." [Not the best coaching from his attorney!] Hoselton (D) was subsequently convicted of entering without breaking based upon his statement, which was the only evidence used to link him to the crime.

Issue: May a defendant's statements at trial be sufficient evidence to establish that he was a lookout, thus sustaining a conviction for breaking and entering as a principal in the first degree?

Decision and Rationale: (Per Curiam) No. A lookout is one who is "by prearrangement, keeping watch to avoid interception or detection or to provide warning during the perpetration of the crimes and thereby participating in the offenses charged." This Court has consistently held that lookouts are aiders and abettors, principals in the second degree who are punishable as principals in the first degree under State statute. An aider or abettor must "in some sort associate himself with the venture, that he participate in it as something that he wishes to bring about, that he seeks by his action to make it succeed." The prosecution must demonstrate that he or she shared the criminal intent of the principal in the first degree. Therefore, if the State establishes evidence that an accused acted as a lookout, it has necessarily established the requisite act and mental state to support a conviction of aiding and abetting. In both his voluntary statement and his testimony at trial, Hoselton (D) stated that he had no prior knowledge of his friends' intentions to steal anything from the barge. He did not help remove the goods from the barge and he never received any of the stolen property. The accused's response that "you could say" he was a lookout, standing completely alone, does not establish that the accused was an aider and abettor by participating in, and wishing to bring about the entering with intent to commit larceny. Viewed in the light most favorable to the prosecution, the State did not prove that Hoselton (D) was a lookout. We therefore reverse and set aside Hoselton's (D) conviction for entering without breaking.

Analysis:

Both the act and mental state must be present in order to support an accomplice liability theory. That is, one must give assistance or encouragement in the commission of the crime *along with* the intent that the aid promotes or facilitates the commission of the crime. The court focuses mostly on the idea that Hoselton's (D) statements show he did not have the requisite intent, but it is also important to the decision that he did not engage in any assistance of the crime. In fact, when he saw his friends removing the stolen items, he left the barge and waited in the car. Thus, neither prong of the standard was met in this case, and as such, Hoselton could not have been held liable for the crime.

People v. Lauria

(Government) v. (Telephone Answering Service Provider)

(1967) 251 Cal.App.2d 471, 59 Cal.Rptr. 628

M E M O R Y   G R A P H I C

Instant Facts

Lauria (D) ran a telephone answering service, which he knew was used by several prostitutes in their business ventures; Lauria (D) was indicted with the prostitutes for conspiracy to commit prostitution.

Black Letter Rule

The intent of a supplier who knows his supplies will be put to criminal use may be established by (1) direct evidence that he intends to participate, or (2) through an inference that he intends to participate based on (a) his special interest in the activity, or (b) the felonious nature of the crime itself.

Procedural Basis: Appeal by prosecution from order setting aside an indictment for conspiracy to commit prostitution.

Facts: In a prostitution investigation, police focused their attention on three prostitutes who used Lauria's (D) telephone service. An undercover policewoman, Stella Weeks, signed up for Lauria's (D) services. Weeks hinted that she was a prostitute, and wanted to conceal that fact from the police. Lauria (D) assured her that his service was discreet and safe. A few weeks later, Weeks called Lauria (D) and complained that because of his operation she had lost two "tricks." Lauria (D) claimed that her tricks probably lied about leaving messages for her. Lauria (D) did not respond to Weeks' hints that she needed more customers, other than to invite her over to become better acquainted. A couple of weeks later Weeks again complained that she had lost two tricks, and the office manager said she would investigate. Two weeks later, Lauria (D) and the three prostitutes were arrested. Lauria (D) testified before the Grand Jury that he only had 9 or 10 prostitutes using his service, and he kept records for known or suspected prostitutes for the convenience of police. However, Lauria (D) did not volunteer the information, but would give it when asked about a specific prostitute. He claimed that he tolerated the prostitutes so long as they paid their bills. Lauria (D) admitted having personal knowledge that some of his customers were prostitutes [use your imagination]. Lauria (D) and the three prostitutes were indicted for conspiracy to commit prostitution. The trial court set aside the indictment as having been brought without a showing of reasonable or probable cause. The Government (P) appeals claiming that a sufficient showing of an unlawful agreement to further prostitution was made. To establish agreement, the Government (P) need show no more than an implied mutual understanding, between co-conspirators, to accomplish an unlawful act.

Issue: Is a person criminally liable for conspiracy if he furnishes goods and services he knows will be used to assist in the operation of an illegal business?

Decision and Rationale: (Fleming) No. *United States v. Falcone* held that a seller's knowledge of the illegal use of the goods was insufficient to make the seller a participant in the conspiracy. In *Direct Sales Co. v. United States*, by contrast, the conviction on federal narcotics laws of a drug wholesaler was affirmed on a showing that the company had actively promoted the sale of morphine. In both cases, however, the element of knowledge of the illegal use of the goods or services and the element of intent to further that use must be present in order to make the supplier a participant in a criminal conspiracy. Proof of knowledge is ordinarily a question of fact. Lauria (D) admitted he knew that some of his customers were prostitutes. He probably knew that some of his customers were subscribing to his service in order to further their trade. The Government argues that this knowledge serves as a basis for concluding that Lauria (D) intended to participate in the criminal activities. We note some characteristic patterns in precedent cases: (1) intent may be inferred from knowledge, when the purveyor of the legal goods for illegal use has acquired a stake in the venture; (2) intent may be inferred from knowledge, when no legitimate use for the goods or services exists; and (3) intent may be inferred from knowledge, when the volume of business with the buyer is grossly disproportionate to any legitimate demand. In response to the first pattern, we note that Lauria (D) had no stake in the venture, and was not charging higher prices to the prostitutes. As to the second pattern, we note that nothing in the furnishing of telephone service implies that it will be used for prostitution, since all sorts of persons might use the service for completely legal activities. Finally, no evidence suggests any unusual volume of Lauria's (D) business was with prostitutes. In all three of these patterns, it can be said that in one way or another a supplier has a special interest in the operation of the criminal enterprise. There are cases in which it cannot be said that the supplier has a stake in the venture, yet still may be held liable based on knowledge alone. Some examples of this would be supplying cutting equipment to be used in a bank robbery, or supplying telephone service to persons involved in the extortion of ransom. Still, we do not believe that an inference of intent drawn from knowledge should apply to misdemeanors. Thus, with respect to misdemeanors, we conclude that positive knowledge of a supplier that his products will be used for illegal activities does not in itself establish intent to participate in the misdemeanor. However, with respect to felonies, we hold that in all felony cases, knowledge of criminal use alone may justify an inference of intent. From this analysis we deduce the following rule: the intent of a supplier who knows of the criminal use to which his supplies are put to participate in the criminal activity connected with the use of his supplies may be established by (1) direct evidence that he intends to participate, or (2) through an inference that he intends to participate based on (a) his special interest in the activity, or (b) the felonious nature of the crime itself. Lauria (D) took no direct action to further the activities of the prostitutes. There is no evidence of a special interest in the prostitutes' activities. The offense with which he has been charged is a misdemeanor. Thus the charges of conspiracy against Lauria (D) fail, and since the conspiracy theory was built around the activities of Lauria's (D) business, the charges against his co-conspirators must also fail. The order is affirmed.

Analysis:

It certainly can be argued that taking account of the seriousness of the criminal objective is appropriate in striking a balance between the conflicting interests of vendors (in regard to their freedom to engage in gainful and otherwise lawful activities without policing their vendees) and that of the community in preventing behavior that facilitates the commitment of crimes. A couple of arguments, offered on whether the specific mental state of conspiracy must be proved, demonstrate that a party has the intent, not just the knowledge, that the object of the conspiracy be achieved. Those who believe that proof of purpose should be required, argue that conspiracy laws should apply to those with criminal goals, rather than "seek to sweep within the dragnet of conspiracy all those who have been associated in any degree whatever with the main offenders." They argue that the law should not be extended to punish "legitimate businessmen" like Lauria (D). On the other hand, some argue that persons should be convicted solely on the basis of their knowledge that they are contributing to a criminal enterprise, even if they do not intend the same goals as the conspiracy. They argue that business people should not be immunized from criminal responsibility under the guise of free enterprise.

State v. Foster

(State) v. (Boyfriend of Raped Girl)
202 Conn. 520, 522 A.2d 277 (1987)

M E M O R Y   G R A P H I C

Instant Facts
Foster (D) was convicted of being an accessory to criminally negligent homicide after providing a knife to a friend who subsequently stabbed and killed a man.

Black Letter Rule
A person may be held liable as an accessory to a criminally negligent act if he has the requisite culpable mental state for the commission of the substantive offense, and he intentionally aids another in the crime.

Case Vocabulary

CULPABLE: Intentional wrong-doing.
DUAL INTENT: Intent to aid the principal *and* intent to commit the offense.

Procedural Basis: Appeal from the defendant's conviction and the trial court's denial of the defendant's post-trial motions for judgment of acquittal and in arrest of judgment.

Facts: Foster (D) lived with his girlfriend and their child in an apartment near a school. One evening, while walking near the school, Foster's (D) girlfriend was robbed and raped by a young black man who held a straight-edged razor to her throat. During the one half hour encounter, she observed her attacker's features and was able to describe him and his clothing to the police. She also described her attacker, with specific identifiable features, to Foster (D). Foster (D), angry about the attack, purposely went looking for his girlfriend's attacker [oh good, vigilante justice] A week later, Foster (D) and a friend, Cannon, went walking in the vicinity where the rape and robbery occurred. Near the school, Foster (D) saw a man he thought matched the description of the assailant. After telling Cannon who the man was, the pair confronted the suspected rapist (later identified as Middleton). Middleton denied any involvement in the robbery or rape and attempted to flee. A fight ensued, and Foster (D) beat Middleton with his fists and a blunt instrument, knocking him to the ground [beat first, ask questions later]. Foster (D) wanted to bring his girlfriend to the scene to make an identification, so he gave a knife to Cannon and told him to stay with Middleton to prevent his escape. While waiting for Foster (D) to return, Middleton reached into his pocket and charged at Cannon. As Middleton ran towards him, Cannon held out the knife Foster (D) had given him and fatally stabbed Middleton. Middleton had a straight-edged razor in his pocket which was later identified by Foster's (D) girlfriend as the one wielded by her assailant during the rape incident [well, at least they got the right guy]. Foster (D) was subsequently convicted in a jury trial of second-degree kidnapping, third-degree assault, and being an accessory to criminally negligent homicide. Foster (D) claims that the trial court erred in instructing the jury as to the crime of being an accessory to criminally negligent homicide, and in denying his post-trial motions for judgment of acquittal and in arrest of judgment.

Issue: Can a person be held liable as an accessory to a criminally negligent act?

Decision and Rationale: (Santaniello, A.J.) Yes. We have previously stated that a conviction under the statute at issue here requires proof of a dual intent that the accessory have the intent to *aid* the principal *and* that in so aiding he intend to *commit* the offense with which he is charged. Foster (D) relies on cases holding that a person cannot attempt or conspire to commit an offense that requires an unintended result, and argues that a person cannot be convicted as an accessory to criminally negligent homicide. We find Foster's (D) argument unpersuasive. Attempt and conspiratorial liability differ substantially from the liability imposed on an accessory. First, both attempt and conspiracy are offenses in and of themselves, while accessorial liability is not. Second, the intent required for attempt or conspiratorial liability is distinguishable from the requisite intent for accessorial liability. Unlike attempt and conspiratorial liability, accessorial liability does not require that a defendant act with the conscious objective to cause the result described by a statute. The statute in issue is not limited to cases where the substantive crime requires the specific intent to bring about a result. It merely requires that a defendant have the mental state required for the commission of a crime while intentionally aiding another. When a crime requires that a person act with criminal negligence, an accessory is liable if he acts with respect to a result or to a circumstance described by a statute defining an offense when he fails to perceive a substantial and unjustifiable risk that such result will occur or that such circumstance exists. Therefore, a person may be held liable as an accessory to a criminally negligent act if he has the requisite culpable mental state for the commission of the substantive offense, and he intentionally aids another in the crime. From the evidence presented, the jury could reasonably have found that Foster (D) intentionally aided Cannon by giving him the knife. Additionally, the jury could reasonably have inferred that Foster (D) had failed to perceive a substantial and unjustifiable risk that death would occur by handing Cannon the knife to prevent Middleton from escaping. Accordingly, the trial court did not err in denying Foster's (D) motion for judgment of acquittal. Affirmed.

Analysis:

The interpretation the court makes in this case is consistent with the underlying principles of accessorial liability. It is designed to punish a person who intentionally aids another in the commission of a crime and not one whose innocent acts in fact aid another who commits an offense. Accessorial liability is predicated upon the actor's state of mind at the time of his actions, and whether that state of mind is equivalent to the state of mind required for the commission of the offense. If a person, in intentionally aiding another, acts with the mental culpability required for the commission of the crime, he is liable for the commission of that crime.

State v. Linscott

(State) v. (Robber)
520 A.2d 1067 (1987)

M E M O R Y   G R A P H I C

Instant Facts

Linscott (D) was convicted of murder, under a theory of accomplice liability, when his friend shot and killed a man the two had intended to rob.

Black Letter Rule

A rule allowing for a murder conviction under a theory of accomplice liability based upon an *objective* standard, despite the absence of evidence that the defendant possessed the culpable *subjective* mental state that constitutes an element of the crime of murder, does not represent a departure from prior Maine law and, as such, is constitutional.

Case Vocabulary

FORESEEABLE CONSEQUENCE RULE: An accessory is liable for a criminal act which was the natural or probable consequence of the crime he intended, even though such consequence was not intended.

JURY-WAIVED TRIAL: Trial in front of a judge due to the defendant's exercising his right to waive a trial by jury.

Procedural Basis: Appeal from trial court's conviction of the defendant following a jury-waived trial.

Facts: Linscott (D), Willey, and Colby drove to Fuller's house to pick him up. Fuller came to the vehicle with a sawed-off shotgun in his possession. The four men next drove to Ackley's house, where Fuller obtained 12-gauge shotgun shells. Later that evening, Fuller suggested that the four men drive to the home of a reputed drug dealer, Norman Grenier, take Grenier by surprise, and rob him. Linscott (D) and the others agreed to the plan, reasoning that Grenier would be reluctant to call the police due to his being a reputed drug dealer. Fuller stated that Grenier had been seen with $50,000 in cash that day, and he guaranteed Linscott (D) $10,000 as his share of the proceeds of the robbery. The four men drove to Grenier's house and Linscott (D) and Fuller approached the house [the other two had a glimmer of sense]. Linscott (D) carried a hunting knife and switchblade, and Fuller was armed with the shotgun. Linscott (D) and Fuller walked around the back of the house; Grenier and his girlfriend were watching television in the front of the house. They wanted to break in the back door in order to place themselves between Grenier and the bedroom, where they believed Grenier kept a loaded shotgun. The back door was blocked by snow, however, so the men revised their plan and were to go in through the living room picture window [subtle]. Linscott (D) broke the living room window without otherwise entering the house. Fuller immediately fired a shot through the broken window, hitting Grenier in the chest. Fuller left through the broken window after having removed about $1,300 from Grenier's pants pocket [wow, jackpot!], later returning to the house to retrieve an empty shotgun casing. At a jury-waived trial, Linscott (D) testified that he knew Fuller to be a hunter and that it was not unusual for Fuller to carry a firearm. He stated that he had no knowledge of any reputation for violence that Fuller may have had, and that he had no intention of causing anyone's death in the course of the robbery. At the completion of the trial, the trial justice found Linscott (D) guilty of robbery and, on a theory of accomplice liability, found him guilty of murder. The court specifically found that Linscott (D) possessed the intent to commit the robbery, that Fuller intentionally or at least knowingly caused the death of Grenier, and that this murder was a reasonably foreseeable consequence of Linscott's (D) participation in the robbery. However, the court also found that Linscott did not intend to kill Grenier, and that he probably would not have participated in the robbery had he believed that Grenier would be killed in the course of the enterprise.

Issue: Does a rule allowing for a murder conviction under a theory of accomplice liability based upon an *objective* standard, despite the absence of evidence that the defendant possessed the culpable *subjective* mental state that constitutes an element of the crime of murder, represent a departure from prior Maine law and, as such, unconstitutionally violate a defendant's right to due process?

Decision and Rationale: (Scolnik, J.) No. The Due Process Clause protects the accused against conviction except upon proof beyond a reasonable doubt of every fact necessary to constitute the crime with which he is charged. Linscott (D) contends that the accomplice liability statute impermissibly allows the State to find him guilty of murder, which requires proof beyond a reasonable doubt that the murder was committed either intentionally or knowingly, without having to prove either of these two culpable mental states. Instead, Linscott (D) argues, the accomplice liability statute permits the State to employ only a mere negligence standard in convicting him of murder in violation of his right to due process. We find Linscott's (D) argument to be without merit. We have previously held that the "foreseeable consequence rule" of accomplice liability demands that accomplices be held liable for those crimes that were the reasonably foreseeable consequence of their criminal enterprise, *notwithstanding an absence on their part of the same culpability required for conviction as a principal to the crime.* We have consistently upheld this interpretation of the statute in issue here, and we discern no compelling reason to depart from this construction of the statute now. Furthermore, the foreseeable consequence rule merely carries over the objective standards of accomplice liability as used in the common law. Thus, a rule allowing for a murder conviction under a theory of accomplice liability based upon an *objective* standard, despite the absence of evidence that the defendant possessed the culpable *subjective* mental state that constitutes an element of the crime of murder, does not represent a departure from prior Maine law. We also do not find fundamentally unfair or disproportionate the grading scheme for sentencing purposes of murder premised on a theory of accomplice liability. The potential penalty of life imprisonment for murder under a theory of accomplice liability does not "shock the conscience." For the foregoing reasons, we find no constitutional defect in this statutory provision, nor any fundamental unfairness in its operation. Affirmed.

Analysis:

The "foreseeable consequence" or "natural and probable consequence" rule has been followed in many cases. The interpretation that this court alludes to is that liability for a "primary crime" (here, robbery) is established by proof that the actor intended to promote or facilitate that crime. Liability for any "secondary crime" (here, murder) that may have been committed by the principal is established upon a two-fold showing: first, that the actor intended to promote the *primary crime*, and second, that the commission of the secondary crime was a "foreseeable consequence" of the actor's participation in the primary crime. It seems a fair and logical result in the case at bar. [If you can't do the time, don't do the crime!]

State v. Vaillancourt

(State) v. (Alleged Burglar)
122 N.H. 1153, 453 A.2d 1327 (1982)

M E M O R Y   G R A P H I C

Instant Facts
The defendant challenged his indictment and conviction for burglary as he was merely present at the location of the crime and did not participate.

Black Letter Rule
Accompaniment and observation are not sufficient acts to constitute "aid" so as to satisfy the elements necessary for accomplice liability or for any other crime.

Procedural Basis: Appeal from a jury's conviction of the defendant after his pre-trial motion to dismiss was denied.

Facts: Vaillancourt (D) and a friend, Burhoe, were seen standing together on the O'Connors' front porch. The men were ringing the doorbell and conversing with one another [trick or treat?]. After remaining on the porch for approximately ten minutes, the neighbor who had seen them earlier became suspicious and began to watch them more closely [she obviously needs more excitement in her life]. She saw them walk around to the side of the house where Burhoe allegedly attempted to break into a basement window. Vaillancourt (D) allegedly stood by and watched Burhoe, talking to him intermittently while Burhoe tried to pry open the window. The neighbor called the police, who apprehended Vaillancourt (D) and Burhoe as they were fleeing the scene. Vaillancourt (D) was subsequently indicted and convicted for accomplice liability. He now contests the sufficiency of his indictment.

Issue: Are accompaniment and observation sufficient acts to constitute "aid" such as to satisfy the elements necessary for accomplice liability or for any other crime?

Decision and Rationale: (Per Curiam) No. Vaillancourt (D) bases his argument on the axiomatic principle that an indictment must allege some criminal activity. He specifically contends that his indictment was insufficient because, even if the facts alleged in it were true, they would not have satisfied the elements necessary for accomplice liability or for any other crime. We agree. The crime of accomplice liability requires the actor to have solicited, aided, agreed to aid, or attempted to aid the principal in planning or committing the offense. The crime thus necessitates some active participation by the accomplice. We have held that knowledge and mere presence at the scene of a crime could not support a conviction for accomplice liability because they did not constitute sufficient affirmative acts to satisfy the actus reus requirement of the accomplice liability statute. In the instant case, other than the requisite mens rea, the State alleged only that Vaillancourt (D) aided Burhoe by accompanying him to the location of the crime and watching. Consistent with our rulings with respect to "mere presence," we hold that accompaniment and observation are not sufficient acts to constitute "aid."

Dissent: (Bois, J.) Although I agree that "mere presence" would be an insufficient factual allegation, the indictment in this case alleged more than "mere presence." While not a customary form of assistance "accompaniment with the purpose of aiding" implies the furnishing of moral support and encouragement in the performance of a crime, thereby "aiding" a principal in the commission of an offense.

Analysis:

It seems that the line between "mere presence" which does not constitute aiding, and presence combined with some other factor which may constitute aiding, is a very fine one [makes it easier to justify seemingly inconsistent opinions!]. However the case law has been very consistent that even an undisclosed intention to render aid if needed will not suffice, nor is mental approval enough to impose accomplice liability. Additionally, mere presence plus flight has often been held insufficient to constitute aiding and abetting. The courts have been quite clear that presence is only equated to aiding and abetting when it designedly encourages the perpetrator, facilitates the unlawful deed, or when it stimulates others to render assistance to the criminal act.

Wilcox v. Jeffrey

(Magazine Proprietor) v. (Not Stated)
1 All England Law Reports 464 (1951)

M E M O R Y   G R A P H I C

Instant Facts
Reporter was convicted for aiding and abetting after he paid for and attended an illegal jazz concert to report on it for his jazz magazine.

Black Letter Rule
Presence and payment to attend an illegal performance in order to attain benefit for oneself can constitute aiding and abetting the criminal act.

Case Vocabulary
MAGISTRATE: England's version of a trial judge.

Procedural Basis: Appeal from the judgment of conviction.

Facts: Hawkins, an American saxophone player was invited by Curtis and Hughes to play at a jazz club in England. Curtis and Hughes applied for permission, as required by law, for Hawkins to "land," which was refused, but Hawkins nevertheless went to England with four other musicians [get out, Yank!]. Wilcox (D), who had no part in bringing the musicians to England, was at the airport when they arrived. He was there to report the arrival of these important musicians for the jazz magazine he wrote and sold for a living. Curtis and Hughes arranged for Hawkins to play a concert while he was in England (which was, apparently, illegal since Hawkins did not have permission to be in the country). Wilcox (D), along with many others, bought a ticket and attended the concert. He then wrote a most laudatory description of the concert in his magazine [uh oh, now you're in for it!].

Issue: Does one's presence at an illegal performance constitute aiding and abetting?

Decision and Rationale: (Lord Goddard, C.J.) Yes. Presence and payment to attend an illegal performance in order to attain benefit for oneself can constitute aiding and abetting the criminal act. There was not accidental presence in this case. Wilcox (D) paid to go to the concert and he went there because he wanted to report it. He must, therefore, be held to have been present, taking part, concurring, or encouraging, whichever word you like to use for expressing this conception. It was an illegal act on the part of Hawkins to play the concert. Wilcox (D) clearly knew that it was an unlawful act for Hawkins to play. Wilcox (D) had gone there to hear him; his presence and his payment to attend were encouragements for Hawkins to be there. He went there to make use of the performance to help sell his magazine. In those circumstances there was evidence on which the magistrate could find that Wilcox (D) aided and abetted, and for these reasons I am of the opinion that the appeal fails.

Analysis:

The court asserts that the result may have been entirely different if Wilcox (D) had gone to the concert and protested the illegality of the musicians playing there, and even perhaps attempted to stop the concert. The court goes on to say that if Wilcox (D) had "booed" at Hawkins it might have been evidence against the aiding and abetting charge. However, the court here appears to find the fact that Wilcox (D) used the unlawful performance to gain profit for his magazine to be the nail in his coffin. There were many other spectators who paid to attend the concert and who did not "boo" or create a disruption in protest, yet no one else was brought up on aiding and abetting charges. It seems that the case turns more on the fact that Wilcox profited from an illegal activity than the fact that he "encouraged" the performance, and aiding and abetting was simply the easiest way to prevent what the court viewed as spurious gain on the part of Wilcox (D).

State v. Helmenstein

(State) v. (Banana Burglar)
163 N.W.2d 85 (1968)

M E M O R Y   G R A P H I C

Instant Facts

Helmenstein (D) was convicted of burglary after he and his friends drove to a nearby town and broke into a store and stole beer and food.

Black Letter Rule

A conviction may not be had upon the testimony of an accomplice unless his testimony is corroborated by such other evidence as tends to connect the defendant with the commission of the offense, and the corroboration is not sufficient if it merely shows the commission of the offense or the circumstances thereof.

Case Vocabulary

CORROBORATION: Affirmation.
COUNTENANCED: Approved.
SINE QUA NON: The act without which the harm would not have occurred.

Procedural Basis: Appeal from the judgment of conviction and from an order denying the defendant's motion for new trial.

Facts: A group of young people were drinking beer in a town park. After a while, they all got into Helmenstein's (D) car and started driving around. Someone in the car suggested that they drive to a nearby town and break into a grocery store there. One girl in the party said she wanted some bananas [oh yummy, beer and bananas], and someone else expressed a desire for other items which could be obtained from the store. They drove to the town and parked the car some distance from the store. Three of the party, including Helmenstein (D), went to the store, broke in, and returned with beer, cigarettes, candy and bananas. They then drove back to their own town and, on the way, agreed on a story they would tell police if any of them was questioned [sure, that always works!]. They then divided the loot and separated. At trial, five of the people in the party testified against Helmenstein (D). The only witness other than those who were in the party on the night of the burglary was Harold Henke, the owner of the store that had been burglarized. His testimony in no way connected Helmenstein (D) with the offense, but merely established the fact that a crime had been committed. The trial court found Helmenstein (D) guilty and this appeal followed.

Issue: Is the testimony of an accomplice to a crime against another accomplice sufficient to sustain a conviction?

Decision and Rationale: (Strutz, J.) No. A conviction may not be had upon the testimony of an accomplice unless his testimony is corroborated by such other evidence as tends to connect the defendant with the commission of the offense, and the corroboration is not sufficient if it merely shows the commission of the offense or the circumstances thereof. To determine whether there was competent evidence against Helmenstein (D) sufficient to sustain the judgment of conviction, we must examine the record to determine the status of the witnesses the State called to testify against Helmenstein (D) who were members of the party on the night of the burglary. Carol Weiss was the one who wanted the bananas; we believe this makes her an accomplice. Janice Zahn admitted that she herself agreed to the burglary when it was suggested, thus she also is an accomplice. Kenneth Cahoon took part in the actual burglary with Helmenstein (D) so his status is clearly that of an accomplice. Glen Zahn was asleep in the car during the burglary, however he was awake when the three left for the store, and he helped make up the story to mislead the police. This makes him part of the offense as well. The record clearly shows that the burglary in this case was the result of a plan in which each of the parties had a part, and that each of these young people encouraged and countenanced the offense and that each of them was thus concerned with its commission. There is no evidence in this case, other than that of persons who are also accomplices, connecting Helmenstein (D) with the commission of the offense with which he is charged. Therefore the evidence against him is insufficient to sustain the judgment of conviction.

Analysis:

Most states have a rule similar to the corroboration rule in this case, or else require a jury instruction cautioning jurors to treat the testimony of accomplices with a cautious eye. It is important to note that the "assistance" of each of the accomplices does not need to contain a causal link to the offense. The courts have held that it is quite sufficient if the aid merely facilitated a result that would have transpired even without it. There have been criticisms of this approach, however, for in ignoring causation, persons are held accountable for the actions of others. As a result, although the accomplice is punished because of his own wrongful conduct, he is punished to the extent of another's. He can be punished for harm he was not the cause of. Sine qua non causation, on the other hand, ensures personal responsibility for crimes [is there still such a thing?]. It also is an assurance that those who are legally blameworthy are given their "just desserts." It serves as the link between the harm and the actor responsible for it, and ensures that both guilt and punishment are based proportionally on personal involvement.

People v. Genoa

(State) v. (Drug Financier)

188 Mich.App. 461, 470 N.W.2d 447 (1991)

M E M O R Y   G R A P H I C

Instant Facts

Genoa (D) was charged with aiding and abetting for giving money to an undercover agent to buy and then sell cocaine for a profit.

Black Letter Rule

A person cannot be convicted of aiding and abetting the commission of a crime when the underlying crime was never committed by anyone.

Case Vocabulary

ENTRAPMENT: Affirmative defense to a crime induced by governmental persuasion or trickery.

LEGAL IMPOSSIBILITY: Failure to commit a crime because of some underlying legal bar.

Procedural Basis: Appeal from the lower court's order dismissing charges against the defendant.

Facts: An undercover agent of the Michigan State Police met with Genoa (D) at a hotel and proposed that if Genoa (D) gave him $10,000 toward the purchase of a kilogram of cocaine, which the police agent claimed he would then sell, the agent would repay Genoa (D) the $10,000, plus $3,500 in profits and a client list [sounds like easy money!]. Genoa (D) accepted the proposal and later returned with the $10,000. After Genoa (D) left, the police agent turned the money over to the Michigan State Police, and Genoa (D) was subsequently arrested and charged with attempted possession with intent to deliver 650 grams or more of cocaine [I've been tricked!]. The district court judge dismissed the charge against Genoa (D) on the ground that because the police agent never intended to commit the contemplated crime and, indeed, never did commit it, Genoa (D), though he believed he was giving money for an illegal enterprise, financed nothing.

Issue: Can a person be convicted of aiding and abetting the commission of a crime when the underlying crime was never committed by anyone?

Decision and Rationale: (Shepherd, J.) No. The only theory by which Genoa (D) could be prosecuted was that he attempted to aid and abet the crime of possession with intent to deliver cocaine. Genoa (D) never attempted to constructively possess the cocaine himself, he simply helped to finance the proposed venture. While Michigan does not distinguish between principals and accessories for purposes of culpability, certain elements must be established to show someone aided and abetted the commission of a crime. One of those elements is that the underlying crime was committed by either the defendant or some other person. Thus, while the conviction of the principal is not necessary to a conviction of an accessory, the prosecution must prove that the underlying crime was actually committed. In the case at bar, it is clear that the underlying crime was never committed by anyone. The absence of this element made it legally impossible for Genoa (D) to have committed any offense. Affirmed.

Analysis:

Legal impossibility applies to situations where the actor does an act which would otherwise be criminal except that the facts render the crime impossible to commit. For example, it is impossible to murder someone who is already dead. It is impossible to commit the crime of receiving stolen property when the property was never stolen in the first place. It is impossible for Genoa (D) to have aided and abetted the crime of possession of cocaine when there was never any possession of cocaine. The court opines that the inability to charge or prosecute Genoa (D) results from a gap in legislation [pass the buck]. However, the court never even addresses the topic of entrapment which, from the facts of the case, could also have been a viable defense to prosecution in this case, issues of accomplice liability aside. The undercover agent set up the offense and induced Genoa (D) to participate in its commission. The prevailing "subjective" test of entrapment requires a comparison of the defendant's predisposition to commit the offense against the police conduct to determine whether the police can be said to have caused the crime. The alternative "objective" test looks solely to the police conduct used to induce the defendant to commit the crime. If Genoa could show that but for the police agent's encouragement he never would have violated the law, he could have successfully defended prosecution that way. Thus it seems that perhaps legal impossibility was not the only way out for Genoa (D) in this situation.

A SECONDARY PARTY MAY BE CONVICTED AS A PRINCIPAL IN THE FIRST DEGREE UNDER THE INNOCENT AGENCY DOCTRINE

Bailey v. Commonwealth

(Disgruntled Neighbor) v. (State)
229 Va. 258, 329 S.E.2d 37 (1985)

M E M O R Y   G R A P H I C

Instant Facts
Bailey (D) was convicted of manslaughter when his neighbor was shot by police responding to reports from Bailey (D) regarding his neighbor's behavior, which he instigated.

Black Letter Rule
One who effects a criminal act through an innocent or unwitting agent is a principal in the first degree.

Case Vocabulary

INNOCENT AGENCY DOCTRINE: A secondary party is a principal in the first degree if his acts cause a crime to be committed through an innocent agent.

Procedural Basis: Appeal from the defendant's conviction in a jury trial.

Facts: One night, Bailey (D) and Murdock, who were neighbors, were arguing over their citizens' band radios [10-4 good buddy!]. They were both drunk and began cursing and threatening each other. Bailey (D) told Murdock he was coming over to Murdock's house to injure or kill him. Bailey (D), who knew Murdock was visually impaired, told him to arm himself with his handgun and wait on his front porch for Bailey (D) to come. Murdock told Bailey (D) he would be waiting and implied he was going to kill him. Bailey (D) then made an anonymous phone call to the police, telling them that Murdock was out on his porch waving around a gun. A police car went to Murdock's house, but they did not see anything. Bailey (D) called Murdock again and chided him for not being out on his porch [sissy!]. They threatened each other some more, and Bailey (D) told Murdock to go out on the porch and wait because he was on his way. Bailey (D) then called the police again and said Murdock was waving his gun and threatening to shoot up the neighborhood. Three officers were dispatched to Murdock's house, and when they got there, no one was on the porch. A few minutes later, Murdock came out with something shiny in his hand. He sat on the porch with the shiny object beside him. One of the officers approached the porch and told Murdock to leave the gun on the porch and walk away from it. Murdock just sat there. The officer repeated the command, and Murdock cursed him. Murdock then got up with the gun and advanced in the officer's direction, firing. All three officers returned fire, and Murdock was struck. Lying on the porch, he said several times, "I didn't know you was the police." He died from the gunshot wounds. The trial court told the jury it should convict Bailey (D) if it found that his negligence or reckless conduct was so gross and culpable as to indicate a callous disregard for human life and that his actions were the proximate cause or a concurring cause of Murdock's death. The jury convicted Bailey (D) of involuntary manslaughter, and this appeal followed.

Issue: Can a person be convicted as a principal in the first degree if he was not the immediate perpetrator of a crime?

Decision and Rationale: (Carrico, J.) Yes. Bailey (D) argues that his conviction can be sustained only if he was a principal in the first degree, a principal in the second degree or an accessory before the fact to the killing of Murdock. The Attorney General agrees and maintains that he was a principal in the first degree. Bailey (D) counters that he could not be a principal in the first degree because only the immediate perpetrators of crime occupy that status, and the immediate perpetrators of Murdock's killing were the police officers who returned Murdock's fire. He was in his own home two miles away, Bailey (D) asserts, and did not control the actors in the confrontation at Murdock's home or otherwise participate in the events that occurred there. We have adopted the rule that one who effects a criminal act through an innocent or unwitting agent is a principal in the first degree. The question we must resolve is whether the police officers who responded to Bailey's (D) calls occupied that status, and, in resolving this question, we believe it is irrelevant whether Bailey (D) and the police shared a common scheme or goal. What is relevant is whether Bailey (D) undertook to cause Murdock harm and used the police to accomplish that purpose, a question which we believe must be answered affirmatively. Knowing Murdock was intoxicated, nearly blind and in an agitated state of mind, Bailey (D) orchestrated a scenario whose finale was bound to include harmful consequences to Murdock, either in the form of his arrest or his injury or death. Bailey (D) argues that Murdock's death was not the natural or probable result of Bailey's (D) conduct, but rather Murdock's own reckless and criminal conduct in opening fire upon the police. Alternatively he argues that the officers' return fire constituted an independent, intervening cause absolving Bailey (D) of guilt. We have held, however, that an intervening act which is reasonably foreseeable cannot be relied upon as breaking the chain of causal connection between an original act of negligence and subsequent injury. Here, under instructions not questioned on appeal, the jury determined that the fatal consequences of Bailey's (D) reckless conduct could reasonably have been foreseen and, accordingly, that Murdock's death was not the result of an independent, intervening cause, but rather arose out of Bailey's misconduct. Affirmed.

Analysis:

Bailey's (D) guilt in this case cannot be premised upon accomplice liability because of the fact that Bailey (D) could not be considered an accomplice of the police. The police were not guilty of any offense, therefore there is no guilt for Bailey (D) to derive from them. Bailey (D) used the police as his innocent agents, however there is a problem imputing the police officers' actions to Bailey (D). The police were justified in their actions, they returned fire in self-defense. Bailey (D) cannot take advantage of their self-defense claim, however, since he was the one who wrongfully created the emergency that required the police action. Bailey is guilty of an offense committed by his own conduct. It is his own culpability which determines the crime he has thus committed.

ACCOMPLICE CANNOT BE GUILTY OF A CRIME WHEN THE PRINCIPAL DOES NOT PERFORM A CRIMINAL ACT

State v. Hayes

(State) v. (Duped Burglar)
105 Mo. 76, 16 SW 514 (1891)

M E M O R Y   G R A P H I C

Instant Facts

Hayes (D) thought he and Hill were breaking into a store to steal, but Hill was setting him up with the police.

Black Letter Rule

A principal's act, not criminal in nature when performed, cannot become criminal when imputed to an accomplice.

Case Vocabulary

INCHOATE: Incomplete, attempted.

Procedural Basis: Not stated.

Facts: Hayes (D) proposed to Hill that Hill assist him in the burglary of a store. Unknown to Hayes (D), Hill was the stepson of the store owner [oops!]. Hill feigned agreement and informed his stepfather of Hayes' (D) intentions. On the night of the planned burglary, Hayes (D) opened a window and helped Hill inside. Hill picked up a side of bacon and handed it out to Hayes (D) [what a score!]. Hayes (D) assisted Hill out of the window, whereupon the men took 15 to 20 steps (with Hayes (D) holding the bacon) before the police arrived. Hayes (D) was convicted of burglary and larceny. Hill was not arrested.

Issue: Can an accomplice be convicted of the crime if the principal had no criminal intent and thus committed no crime?

Decision and Rationale: (Thomas, J.) No. Hill did not enter the warehouse with intent to steal, therefore we may assume that Hill committed no crime. The act of Hill was imputed to Hayes (D) by the trial court, and while it was not a criminal act when performed by Hill, it became criminal when imputed to Hayes (D) because of his felonious intent. This would probably be true if Hill had acted under the control and compulsion of Hayes (D), and as his passive and submissive agent in this transaction. But he was not a passive agent in this transaction. He was an active one, and he acted of his own volition. To make Hayes (D) responsible for the acts of Hill, they must have had a common motive and common design. The design and motives of the two men were not only distinct, but dissimilar, even antagonistic. The court should instruct the jury that if Hill broke into and entered the warehouse with a felonious intent, and Hayes (D) was present, aiding him with the same intent, then he is guilty; but if Hill entered the room with no design to steal, but simply to entrap Hayes (D) and capture him in the commission of a crime, and Hayes (D) did not enter the room himself, then he is not guilty of burglary and larceny as charged. Reversed.

Analysis:

Hill was the principal in the first degree in this situation, and Hayes (D) cannot be prosecuted as a principal through the innocent agency doctrine because Hayes (D) did not use Hill as his unwitting agent, it was the other way around! Hill had no criminal intent for either the burglary or the larceny, therefore Hayes (D) cannot be prosecuted because there was no guilt to be derived from Hill. The prosecutor tried to impute the act from Hill to Hayes (D) and thus change it to a criminal act, however this cannot work where the motives of the agent and the principal are antagonistic. In light of this result, it seems that if one wishes to ensnare a criminal "red handed" in a burglary, make the "bad guy" go into the building! Under these facts, Hayes (D) could be found guilty at common law of petty larceny (the bacon), or perhaps solicitation to commit burglary. If Hayes (D) had ever intended to enter the building himself, then perhaps his act of opening the window could be an attempted burglary at the common law, however under the facts here, Hayes (D) is not guilty of that inchoate crime. Under the Model Penal Code, however, Hayes (D) most likely would be found guilty of attempted burglary, as he attempted to aid and abet a burglary by Hill. Moral of the story? Find a better way to bring home the bacon!

U.S. v. Lopez

(Government) v. (Prison-Breaking Boyfriend)
662 F.Supp. 1083 (1987)

M E M O R Y   G R A P H I C

⚡ Instant Facts

Lopez's (D) boyfriend broke her out of prison by helicopter because her life was being threatened by prison authorities.

🔨 Black Letter Rule

A defendant can be convicted of aiding and abetting even if the principal is not identified or convicted, however an aider or abettor may not be held liable absent proof that a criminal offense was committed by a principal.

📖 Case Vocabulary

IN CAMERA: Proceedings held in a judge's chambers or where the public is not present.
MOTION IN LIMINE: Motion before trial to exclude reference to anticipated objectionable evidence.
"NECESSITY/DURESS" DEFENSE: Affirmative defense raised by the defendant which shows a just cause for an act so as to excuse liability.
PRIMA FACIE: On its face; doesn't require further evidence.

Procedural Basis: Excerpts from the trial court's ruling on the government's pretrial motion in limine.

Facts: McIntosh (D) landed a helicopter on the grounds of a federal prison in order to effect the escape of his girlfriend, Lopez (D), whose life allegedly was unlawfully threatened by prison authorities [if you're gonna do it, do it big!]. The two were apprehended and prosecuted for various offenses, including prison escape [at least they can sell the movie rights!]. Prior to their trial, McIntosh and Lopez (D) indicated their intent to raise a "necessity/duress" defense based upon the threats to Lopez's (D) life. This writing comes from excerpts from the trial court's ruling on the government's (P) motion in limine for an order barring the presentation of evidence on the defense of necessity or duress.

Issue: If a principal is found not guilty as the result of a successful affirmative defense can another party be found liable of aiding and abetting the principal?

Decision and Rationale: (Lynch, D.J.) No. In response to the government's (P) motion, each defendant has filed a written offer of proof in camera. By these offers of proof, McIntosh and Lopez (D) seek to establish the prima facie case required to be shown before they are entitled to an instruction on the defense of necessity/duress. The parties agree that if Lopez (D) makes a prima facie showing of each element of the necessity/duress defense, she will be entitled to an instruction on that defense. McIntosh (D) requests a jury instruction stating if Lopez (D) is found not guilty because she acted under necessity/duress, then McIntosh must also be found not guilty of aiding and abetting her alleged escape. The government (P) contents that McIntosh can be convicted of aiding and abetting Lopez's (D) escape even if Lopez (D) succeeds on her necessity/duress defense. The general rule is that a defendant can be convicted of aiding and abetting even if the principal is not identified or convicted, however an aider or abettor may not be held liable absent proof that a criminal offense was committed by a principal. This Court must therefore determine whether Lopez (D) committed a criminal offense if her necessity/duress defense succeeds. This determination requires first classifying Lopez's (D) defense as either a justification or an excuse. Justification defenses are those providing that, although the act was committed, it is not wrongful. When a defense is classified as an excuse, however, the result is that, although the act is wrongful, the actor will not be held accountable. The classification of a defense as a justification or an excuse has an important effect on the liability of one who aids and abets the act. A third party has the right to assist an actor in a justified act. In contrast, excuses are always personal to the actor and a third party can be convicted of aiding and abetting an actor in that case. The defense of duress or coercion traditionally arises when a person unlawfully commands another to do an unlawful act using the threat of death or serious bodily injury. The defense of necessity may be raised in a situation in which the pressure of natural physical forces compels an actor to choose between two evils. The actor may choose to violate the literal terms of the law in order to avoid a greater harm. The defense of necessity is categorized as a justification. In the context of prison escapes, the distinction between duress/coercion and necessity has been hopelessly blurred. In fact, courts seem to use the two terms interchangeably. This Court believes, however, that the defense asserted by Lopez (D), under the facts of this case, most nearly resembles necessity, which is a justification to an alleged crime. In the present case, Lopez's (D) claim is not that the alleged threats overwhelmed her will so that her inability to make the "correct" choice should be excused. Instead, Lopez (D) claims that she, in fact, did make the correct choice. Accordingly, if the jury finds Lopez (D) not guilty of escape by reason of her necessity defense, her criminal act will be justified. No criminal offense will have been committed by a principal, therefore McIntosh (D) would be entitled to his requested jury instruction.

Analysis:

Traditionally, the courts have been reluctant to permit the defenses of duress and necessity to be relied upon by escapees. This reluctance appears to have been primarily grounded upon considerations of public policy. Several recent decisions, however, have recognized the applicability of these defenses to prison escapes. Whether a defense is classified an excuse or a justification, liability is escaped by the principal actor. However, determining whether the defense is classified an excuse or justification holds significant importance to an accomplice of the principal. Basically, the important principle to take away from this case is that if the principal is acquitted on the basis of an excuse, the accomplice will not be protected from conviction. However, if the principal is acquitted because the action was justified, the accomplice cannot be convicted of aiding and abetting. This decision by the Court is a bit tough to swallow. It seems that if the principal actor is able to wriggle out of liability for any wrongdoing, then the person who helped her should not be left holding the bag. If it can be determined that although admittedly the act was wrongful, the perpetrator will not be punished for it, the logical conclusion would be that any who aided her in committing the wrongful, yet excusable, offense would also be immune from prosecution.

Regina v. Richards

(Government) v. (Unhappy Wife)
[1974] Q.B. 776 (1974)

M E M O R Y   G R A P H I C

 Instant Facts

Richards (D) hired two friends to beat up her husband. She was convicted of a more serious offense than the two men who actually beat him.

Black Letter Rule

If there is only one offense committed, then the person who has requested that the offense be committed, or advised that the offense be committed, cannot be guilty of a graver offense than that which was in fact committed.

Case Vocabulary

SPECIFIC INTENT: Desire to cause specific consequences.

Procedural Basis: Defendant's appeal from her conviction in the lower court.

Facts: Mrs. Richards (D) hired two of her friends to beat up her husband. Her marriage had been deteriorating, she had become very depressed and started drinking [it seemed like a good idea at the time....]. She told her friends to beat him up "bad enough to put him in the hospital for a month." [Because that will turn him into Mr. Wonderful!] One evening, Mr. Richards left his home to go to work. Shortly afterwards, in a lane not far away, he was attacked by two men (Mrs. Richards' (D) friends), who were wearing black balaclavas over their heads. He was struck on the back of his head. He tried to escape but was grabbed by the coat sleeves. Eventually he struggled free from his assailants. He sustained a laceration on the top of his head, which required two stitches, but the injury wasn't serious so he was not detained in the hospital. Mrs. Richards (D) was arrested the next day, and she admitted hiring the two men to attack her husband. She admitted that she had suggested the appropriate time for the attack to take place, and she had set up a signal system to alert the attackers of her husband's departure for work. The two men who actually attacked Mr. Richards were convicted of wounding without specific intent to do grievous bodily harm. Mrs. Richards (D), who committed no physical act upon her husband at all, was convicted of a more serious offense, wounding with intent to do grievous bodily harm.

Issue: Can a person who requested an offense to be committed be convicted of a graver offense than that which was actually committed?

Decision and Rationale: (James, J.) No. Looking at the facts of this case, the acts were perpetrated at some distance from where Mrs. Richards (D) was. She was not truly in a position as an abettor of those who did the acts. The evidence proved that one offense, and one offense only, was committed. That offense was wounding without the element of specific intent. We do not think it right that one could say that that which was done can be said to have been done with the intention of Mrs. Richards (D) who was not present at the time and whose intention did not go to the offense which was in fact committed. That is the short point in the case as we see it. If there is only one offense committed, then the person who has requested that offense to be committed, or advised that the offense be committed, cannot be guilty of a graver offense than that in fact which was committed.

Analysis:

This case has been highly criticized and, as a result, does not seem to be good law today. It has been suggested that the true principle in this case is that where the principal has caused an actus reus, the liability of each of the secondary parties should be assessed according to his own mens rea. The decision in this case is supportable, it is argued, on the ground that Mrs. Richards (D) did not *cause* the actions of the men. However culpable her intentions, she could not be blamed for an assault that did not take place. Thus the innocent-agency doctrine is inapplicable. Perhaps the best result would have been for Mrs. Richards (D) to have been prosecuted for solicitation to commit wounding with intent to do grievous bodily harm. The facts certainly support a finding of liability for that crime.

In Re Meagan R.

(State) v. (Teenage Girl)
42 Cal.App.4th 17, 49 Cal.Rptr.2d 325 (1996)

M E M O R Y   G R A P H I C

Instant Facts

Minor girl was convicted of burglary for breaking into a house with her boyfriend so they could have sex.

Black Letter Rule

Where the Legislature has dealt with crimes which necessarily involve the joint actions of two or more persons, and where no punishment at all is provided for the conduct, or misconduct, of one of the participants, the party whose participation is not denounced by statute cannot be charged with criminal conduct on either a conspiracy or aiding and abetting theory.

Case Vocabulary

STATUTORY RAPE: Having sexual intercourse with a female under an age set by statute, regardless of her consent.

Procedural Basis: Appeal from a judgment entered against the defendant in juvenile court.

Facts: Oscar Rodriguez broke into his ex-girlfriend's home, with the assistance of 14-year-old Meagan R. (D), in order for the two to have sexual intercourse in violation of a California statute proscribing statutory rape [gee, how romantic!]. The state attempted to prosecute Meagan R. (D) for burglary.

Issue: Can a minor girl be convicted of burglary predicated upon a finding that she entered a residence with the intent to aid and abet her own statutory rape?

Decision and Rationale: (Work, A.P.J.) No. Within the context of being an aider or abettor, there is a rule that where the Legislature has dealt with crimes which necessarily involve the joint actions of two or more persons, and where no punishment at all is provided for the conduct, or misconduct, of one of the participants, the party whose participation is not denounced by statute cannot be charged with criminal conduct on either a conspiracy or aiding and abetting theory. So, although generally a defendant may be liable to prosecution for conspiracy as an aider or abettor to commit a crime even though he or she is incapable of committing the crime itself, the rule does not apply where the statute defining the substantive offense discloses an affirmative legislative policy that the conduct of one of the parties shall go unpunished. Moreover, when the Legislature has imposed criminal penalties to protect a specific class of individuals, it can hardly have meant that a member of that very class should be punishable as either an aider and abettor or as a co-conspirator. The California statute has a provision designed to criminalize the exploitation of children rather than to penalize the children themselves. A ruling to the contrary that a child could be held responsible on a theory of aiding and abetting for violating such a statute would be contrary to express legislative intent. Consequently, Meagan (D), as the victim of the statutory rape, cannot be prosecuted on that charge, regardless of whether her culpability be predicated upon being a co-conspirator, an aider and abettor or an accomplice, given her protected status. Accordingly, the juvenile court cannot rely on the crime of statutory rape to serve as the predicate felony in a finding that Megan (D) committed burglary. When she entered the residence, she had no punishable intent, for she did not have the culpable state of mind required for burglary. The judgment is reversed.

Analysis:

The logic used in this case flows quite smoothly to the end result. The statutory rape statute was designed to punish only the male's criminal conduct, and the legislative intent was to protect the female [such favoritism!]. Therefore, a female may not be convicted of aiding and abetting her own statutory rape. Further, Meagan (D) could not be convicted of burglary as she had no intent to commit a felony which could be punished.

People v. Brown

(State) v. (Car Thief)

90 Ill.App.3d 742, 46 Ill.Dec. 591, 414 N.E.2d 75 (1980)

M E M O R Y   G R A P H I C

Instant Facts

Brown (D) and friends broke into a car dealership to steal a car, but changed their minds before actually entering the building and left.

Black Letter Rule

Withdrawal provisions of an accountability statute are ineffective to prevent liability for an attempted crime after the planning has already taken place.

Case Vocabulary

WITHDRAWAL: The separating of oneself from the criminal activity.

Procedural Basis: Appeal from a jury's conviction and sentence of four years imprisonment.

Facts: Brown (D) and a friend, Schultz, were driving around town in Schultz's truck. They picked up another man, Babcock, who was unknown to Brown (D). Babcock suggested that the three steal a car and go out and wreck it [now that's doing it up big!]. He said he knew a place where they could steal a car. Brown (D) testified that he and Schultz didn't really want to steal the car, but that they went along to Hillside Motors, the place where the theft was to occur. When they arrived there, Babcock told Brown and Schultz to go around the back and kick in the door while he stood lookout in front [the big risk-taker]. Brown (D) and Schultz did as planned, and Brown (D) kicked at the door twice [no leniency for being a wimp]. The door did not open, so Schultz kicked it once and it came open. At this time, Brown (D) got scared and decided he didn't want to participate anymore. He and Schultz went around to the front of the building and told Babcock they were leaving. Babcock didn't want to leave, but the other two told him they were going and the truck was too, so Babcock got in the truck. As they were leaving the parking lot next to Hillside Motors, the police arrived and stopped them. After a jury trial, in which Brown (D) was found guilty of attempted burglary, the trial court sentenced him to four years imprisonment. On appeal, Brown (D) argues his conviction should be overturned because the evidence established that he voluntarily abandoned his criminal activity and purpose.

Issue: Can a defendant relieve himself of liability by renouncing his intent and withdrawing from the commission of a crime after the crime has been planned and begun, but before the crime is completed?

Decision and Rationale: (Alloy, P.J.) No. Brown (D) first argues that his acts in kicking the door were a mere preparation and did not constitute a substantial step toward the commission of the burglary. We find, without difficulty, that the kicking in of the door was *not* merely preparation to the burglary but that it *was* a substantial step toward its completion. Once the door was open, the only step remaining was the entry into the building. Brown (D) next argues that even if the evidence was sufficient to show attempted burglary, the conviction should not have been entered because of the fact that Brown (D) was not acting as a principal and because he effectively withdrew from the criminal enterprise, while at the same time preventing its completion. The Illinois accountability statute removes accountability if before the commission of the offense, the person terminates his efforts to promote such commission and makes a proper effort to prevent the commission of the offense. The question of withdrawal must focus upon the offense or offenses which Brown (D) aided or abetted in the planning or commission of. In the factual context of this case, both burglary and attempted burglary are possible referents under the statute. As to the burglary offense, Brown's (D) withdrawal would have been effective, in that it occurred prior to the commission of any burglary. However, as to the offense of attempted burglary, his withdrawal was ineffective to prevent application of accountability to his actions, for the reason that such withdrawal did not occur before the commission of the attempted burglary. We conclude that the withdrawal provisions of the accountability statute were not applicable to the attempted burglary charge in that the evidence supported a finding that the offense had occurred prior to the time of Brown's (D) withdrawal. Affirmed.

Analysis:

The withdrawal provision is designed to provide an incentive to accomplices to back out of their criminal activity and block the commission of the crime by the remaining actors. The way the court in this case interprets the statute, however, there was no way for Brown (D) to have avoided criminal liability for the attempted burglary once he and Schultz kicked in the door [in for a penny in for a pound!]. This seems to be a flaw in the system, for unless there are two levels of punishment reserved for attempt vs. the completion, the court's reasoning appears to remove any incentive Brown (D) would have had to stop Babcock from completing the burglary. In fact, Illinois classifies burglary as a Class 2 felony, whereas attempted burglary is a Class 3 felony. Thus, there is a slight inducement to renounce in this case.

People v. Campbell

(State) v. (Gun Provider)
124 Mich.App. 333, 335 N.W.2d 27 (1983)

M E M O R Y   G R A P H I C

Instant Facts

Campbell (D) was charged with murder for giving a gun and bullets to a self-proclaimed suicidal friend who was also extremely drunk.

Black Letter Rule

Incitement to suicide, while morally reprehensible, is not criminal under the present state of the law.

Case Vocabulary

INFORMATION: Alternative to an indictment.
MOTION TO QUASH: Request for the court to vacate the indictment of the defendant.
PRELIMINARY EXAMINATION: Pre-trial hearing to determine whether probable cause exists to justify continuation of proceedings against a defendant.

Procedural Basis: Appeal from the circuit court's denial of the defendant's motion to quash the information and dismiss the defendant.

Facts: Campbell (D) was at Basnaw's house and they were drinking heavily. Two weeks before, Campbell (D) had walked in on Basnaw in bed with Campbell's (D) wife [well of course you'd make that person your drinking buddy!]. Late in the evening, Basnaw began talking about committing suicide, however he said that he didn't have a gun. Campbell (D) initially told Basnaw he couldn't borrow or buy one from him, but he later changed his mind and told Basnaw he would sell him a gun for whatever money he had in his possession [the wheels take a while to get going]. Basnaw then indicated that he did not want to buy a gun, but Campbell (D) continued to encourage him, and alternately ridiculed him. Basnaw finally relented, and Campbell (D) and Basnaw then drove to Campbell's (D) house to get the gun. Basnaw's girlfriend was present during the conversation, but when the two left to get the gun she didn't call anyone to report the plan. She said she believed Campbell (D) was just trying to get a ride home. Fifteen minutes later, the pair returned with a gun and bullets. Basnaw told his girlfriend to leave with Campbell (D) because he was going to kill himself. He then began to write a suicide note as the two left him alone [calling the bluff, eh?]. Campbell (D) told Basnaw's girlfriend not to worry, that the bullets were merely blanks and that the gun's firing pin didn't work. The next morning, Basnaw's roommate and a friend discovered him slumped at the kitchen table with the gun in his hand [oops]. The cause of death was listed as suicide – self-inflicted wound to the temple. Campbell (D) was charged with murder.

Issue: Can a defendant be convicted of murder for inciting another to suicide?

Decision and Rationale: (Hoehn, J.) No. The prosecutor argues that inciting to suicide, coupled with the overt act of furnishing a gun to an intoxicated person, in a state of depression, falls within a prohibition of "other wilful, deliberate and premeditated killing." We believe, however, that the term suicide by definition excludes a homicide. Simply put, Campbell (D) did not kill another person. Additionally, Campbell (D) had no present intention to kill. He provided the weapon and departed. He hoped Basnaw would kill himself, but hope alone is not the degree of intention requisite to a charge of murder. Incitement to suicide has not been held to be a crime in two-thirds of the States. In the states where incitement to suicide has been held to be a crime, there has been no unanimity as to the nature of severity of the crime. However no Legislature has classified such conduct as murder. While we find the conduct of Campbell (D) to be morally reprehensible, we do not find it to be criminal under the present state of the law. The trial court is reversed and the case is remanded with instructions to quash the information and warrant and discharge Campbell (D).

Analysis:

Causation appears to be the key consideration in the decision in this case. Campbell (D) certainly had reason to see Basnaw dead, due to the affair with Campbell's (D) wife. He encouraged and ridiculed Basnaw and then furnished him with a gun and ammunition, all while Basnaw was extremely intoxicated. The issue of causation is a close one, however, and the case for homicide must be examined more closely. Nonetheless, Basnaw began speaking about suicide on his own, and seemed committed to that outcome. This leads necessarily to a finding of suicide, not homicide. Campbell (D) did not force Basnaw to kill himself, therefore the court ruled correctly that the facts did not support a case for murder.

People v. Kevorkian

(State) v. (Dr. Death)

447 Mich. 436, 527 N.W.2d 714 (1994)

M E M O R Y   G R A P H I C

Instant Facts

Dr. Kevorkian (D) was charged with murder for assisting the suicides of two seriously ill women.

Black Letter Rule

Only where there is probable cause to believe that death was the direct and natural result of a defendant's act can the defendant be properly bound over on a charge of murder in an assisted suicide case.

Case Vocabulary

AFORETHOUGHT: Premeditated.
MALICE: Intent to cause harm.
PREPENSE: Deliberate.

Procedural Basis: Appeal from the Court of Appeals' reversal of the lower court's dismissal of charges against the defendant.

Facts: Dr. Kevorkian (D) created a "suicide machine," which was a device consisting of a board to which one's arm is strapped to prevent movement, a needle to be inserted into a blood vessel and attached to IV tubing, and containers of various chemicals that are to be released through the needle into the bloodstream [how pleasant]. Strings are tied to two of the fingers of the person who intends to die. The strings are attached to clips on the IV tubing that control the flow of the chemicals. The person raises that hand, releasing a drug called methohexital, a fast-acting barbiturate that is used to administer anesthesia rapidly. When the person falls asleep, the hand drops, pulling the other string, which releases another clip and allows potassium chloride to flow into the body in concentrations sufficient to cause death. Two women, Miller and Wantz, each contacted Dr. Kevorkian (D) for assistance in ending their lives. They were each suffering from extremely painful and disabling conditions. The women and several friends and relatives met Dr. Kevorkian (D) at a cabin to end their lives. Dr. Kevorkian tried, unsuccessfully , to hook up Miller to the "suicide machine." He eventually left and obtained a cylinder of carbon monoxide gas and a mask apparatus. He fashioned a lever to open the gas valve, and taught Miller how to operate it. Dr. Kevorkian (D) then turned his attention to Wantz. He was successful in hooking her up to the "suicide machine." He explained to her how to activate the device, which she did, and she died. Dr. Kevorkian then put the gas mask on Wantz and she opened the gas valve. The cause of her death was determined to be carbon-monoxide poisoning [surprise!]. Dr. Kevorkian was indicted on two counts of murder. He was bound over for trial following a preliminary examination. However, in circuit court, Dr. Kevorkian (D) moved to quash the information and dismiss the charges, and the court granted the motion. A divided Court of Appeals reversed, and this appeal followed.

Issue: Can a defendant be charged with murder for providing the means by which a person commits suicide?

Decision and Rationale: (Cavanagh, J.) No. Under the common-law definition, "murder is where a person of sound memory and discretion unlawfully kills any reasonable creature in being, in peace of the state, with malice prepense or aforethought, either express or implied." Implicit in this definition is a finding that the defendant performed an act that caused the death of another. To convict a defendant of criminal homicide, it must be proven that death occurred as a direct and natural result of the defendant's act. The modern statutory scheme in the majority of states treats assisted suicide as a separate crime, with penalties less onerous than those for murder. The courts generally have held that a person may be prosecuted for murder only if the person's acts went beyond the conduct that the assisted suicide statute was intended to cover. Accordingly, we overrule prior caselaw to the extent that it can be read to support the view that the common-law definition of murder encompasses the act of intentionally providing the means by which a person commits suicide. Only where there is probable cause to believe that death was the direct and natural result of a defendant's act can the defendant be properly bound over on a charge of murder. Where a defendant merely is involved in the events leading up to the death, such as providing the means, the proper charge is assisting in a suicide.

Analysis:

The ultimate issue in cases such as this one is whether the defendant's participation went beyond the scope of the jurisdiction's suicide-assistance law. A conviction of murder is proper if a defendant participates in the final overt act that causes death, such as firing a gun or pushing the plunger on a hypodermic needle. However, where a defendant simply participates in events leading up to the commission of the final overt act, a charge of murder is not appropriate.

Washington v. Glucksberg

(State) v. (Doctors)

521 U.S. 702, 117 S.Ct. 2258, 138 L.Ed.2d 772 (1997)

M E M O R Y   G R A P H I C

Instant Facts

A group of doctors challenged the constitutionality of the State's statutory prohibition against assisted suicide.

Black Letter Rule

A statutory prohibition against causing or aiding a suicide does not offend the Fourteenth Amendment to the United States Constitution.

Case Vocabulary

COURT PANEL: Part of the appellate court; division of three or more judges.

REHEARING EN BANC: Reconsideration of a panel's decision by the full court.

Procedural Basis: Appeal from the District Court's ruling that the State's assisted-suicide ban is unconstitutional. A panel of the Court of Appeals for the Ninth Circuit reversed. The Ninth Circuit reheard the case en banc, reversed the panel's decision, and affirmed the District Court.

Facts: A group of doctors (P) in Washington banded together to challenge the constitutionality of Washington's statute prohibiting the causing or aiding of a suicide [strength in numbers?]. These doctors (P) occasionally treat terminally ill, suffering patients, and declare that they would assist these patients in ending their lives if not for Washington's assisted-suicide ban. The doctors (P) asserted the existence of a liberty interest protected by the Fourteenth Amendment which extends to a personal choice by a mentally competent, terminally ill adult to commit physician-assisted suicide. The District Court agreed and concluded Washington's statute is unconstitutional because it places an undue burden on the exercise of that constitutionally protected liberty interest. A panel of the Court of Appeals for the Ninth Circuit reversed, emphasizing that "in the two hundred and five years of our existence no constitutional right to aid in killing oneself has ever been asserted and upheld by a court of final jurisdiction." [and by golly, change is bad!] The Ninth Circuit reheard the case en banc, reversed the panel's decision, and affirmed the District Court. After weighing and balancing the constitutionally recognized "right to die," against Washington's various interests, the court held that the State's assisted-suicide ban was unconstitutional as applied to terminally ill competent adults who wish to hasten their deaths with medication prescribed by their physicians.

Issue: Does a statutory prohibition against causing or aiding a suicide offend the Fourteenth Amendment to the United States Constitution?

Decision and Rationale: (Rehnquist, C.J.) No. In almost every State, it is a crime to assist a suicide. The States' assisted-suicide bans are not innovations, rather, they are longstanding expressions of the States' commitment to the protection and preservation of all human life. Further, the prohibitions against assisting suicide never contained exceptions for those who were near death. Rather, those terminally ill lives were under the protection of the law equally as the lives of those who were healthy. By the time the Fourteenth Amendment was ratified, it was a crime to assist a suicide in most states. Additionally, the Model Penal Code also prohibited "aiding" suicide, prompting many States to enact or revise their assisted-suicide bans. Our laws have consistently condemned, and continue to prohibit, assisting suicide. Despite changes in medical technology and notwithstanding an increased emphasis on the importance of end-of-life decisionmaking, we have not retreated from this prohibition. The Washington statute at issue in this case requires us to examine whether the "liberty" specially protected by the Due Process Clause includes a right to commit suicide which itself includes a right to assistance in doing so. In *Cruzan*, we concluded that there is a general right of a competent individual to refuse medical treatment. However, that case must be distinguished from this one because while the decision to commit suicide with the assistance of another may be just as personal and profound as the decision to refuse unwanted medical treatment, it has never enjoyed similar legal protection. The history of the law's treatment of assisted suicide in this country has been and continues to be one of the rejection of nearly all efforts to permit it. That being the case, our decisions lead us to conclude that the asserted "right" to assistance in committing suicide is not a fundamental liberty interest protected by the Due Process Clause. The Constitution also requires, however, that Washington's assisted-suicide ban be rationally related to legitimate government interests. As the court below recognized, Washington's ban on assisted suicide implicates a number of state interests, from an unqualified interest in the preservation of human life, to protecting the integrity and ethics of the medical profession. Additionally, there is a real risk of subtle coercion and undue influence in end-of-life situations, and there is also the fear that permitting assisted suicide will start us down the path to voluntary and perhaps even involuntary euthanasia. Washington, like most other States, reasonably ensures against these risks by banning, rather than regulating, assisted suicide. The decision of the en banc Court of Appeals is reversed, and the case is remanded for further proceedings consistent with this opinion.

Concurrence: (Souter, J.) The case for the slippery slope is fairly made out here, not because recognizing one due process right would leave a court with no principled basis to avoid recognizing another, but because there is a plausible case that the right claimed

would not be readily containable by reference to facts about the mind that are matters of difficult judgment, or by gatekeepers who are subject to temptation, noble or not.

Concurrence: (Stevens, J.) Just as our conclusion that capital punishment is not always unconstitutional did not preclude later decisions holding that it is sometimes impermissibly cruel, so is it equally clear that a decision upholding a general statutory prohibition of assisted suicide does not mean that every possible application of the statute would be valid.

Analysis:

There has been much criticism of the Court's decision regarding assisted suicide. Part of this criticism arises out of arguments that prohibiting assisted suicide violates the Equal Protection Clause because people on life-support machinery can accelerate their death by ending treatment, whereas other terminally ill people not on life-support machinery cannot hasten their deaths. Justice Rehnquist rejected this argument in *Vacco* by distinguishing the two situations. When a patient refuses life-sustaining medical treatment, he dies from an underlying fatal disease or pathology; but if a patient ingests lethal medication prescribed by a physician, he is killed by that medication. Justice Rehnquist also attempts to distinguish the intent in each case, however it seems that his reasoning is a bit stretched. Rehnquist tries to fashion an intent in the situation where a physician withholds or withdraws treatment, as one in which the physician is simply honoring a patient's wishes and ceasing to do useless and degrading things to patients who receive no benefit from them. The intent in assisted suicide, he contrasts, is simply to make the patient dead. In reality, however, the end intention and result is to quickly end the patient's suffering and hasten the patient's death, no matter how you try to dress it up.

EMPLOYER CANNOT BE IMPRISONED FOR THE CRIMINAL ACTS OF HIS EMPLOYEES COMMITTED ON HIS PREMISES WITHOUT HIS PRESENCE, PARTICIPATION OR KNOWLEDGE

Commonwealth v. Koczwara

(State) v. (Tavern Owner)
397 Pa. 575, 155 A.2d 825 (1959)

M E M O R Y   G R A P H I C

Instant Facts

Tavern owner and operator was fined and imprisoned for violations of the Liquor Code committed by his employees without his presence, participation or knowledge.

Black Letter Rule

An employer cannot be imprisoned (but can be fined) under a theory of respondeat superior for the criminal acts of his employees committed on his premises without his presence, participation or knowledge.

Case Vocabulary

DEMURRER: Request for dismissal because the opponent's argument is legally insufficient.
DIRECTED VERDICT: Verdict entered by the court, without consideration by the jury, because the facts presented during the trial make it clear that there is only one verdict which could reasonably be reached.
PLENARY POLICE POWER: Absolute power of the state to impose restrictions upon the public's private rights.
QUID PRO QUO: That which you get for that which you give.
RESPONDEAT SUPERIOR: Employer is responsible for the acts of his employees.

Procedural Basis: Appeal from the judgment sentencing the defendant to three months in jail, a fine of $500 and the costs of prosecution.

Facts: Koczwara (D) is the licensee and operator of an establishment known as J.K.'s Tavern. At that place he had a restaurant liquor license issued by the Pennsylvania Liquor Control Board. Koczwara (D) was indicted on four counts for violations of the Liquor Code. The first and second counts averred that Koczwara (D) permitted minors, unaccompanied by parents, guardians, or other supervisors, to frequent the tavern on two separate occasions [shocking!]. The third count charged Koczwara (D) with selling beer to minors, and the fourth charged him with permitting beer to be sold to minors. At the conclusion of the presentation of evidence, count three of the indictment was removed from the jury's consideration by the trial judge on the ground that there was no evidence that Koczwara (D) had personally participated in the sale or was present in the tavern when sales to the minors took place. Defense counsel demurred to the evidence as to the other three counts, but the demurrer was overruled. Koczwara (D) thereupon rested without presenting any evidence and moved for a directed verdict. The motion was denied, the case went to the jury, and the jury returned a verdict of guilty as to each of the remaining three counts.

Issue: Does a liquor code, which regulates and controls the use and sale of alcoholic beverages, intend to impose vicarious criminal liability on a licensee-principal for acts committed on his premises without his presence, participation or knowledge?

Decision and Rationale: (Cohen, J.) No. This case requires us to determine the criminal responsibility of a licensee of the Liquor Control Board for acts committed by his employees upon his premises, without his personal knowledge, participation, or presence, which acts violate a valid regulatory statute passed under the Commonwealth's police power. While an employer in almost all cases is not criminally responsible for the unlawful acts of his employees, unless he consents to, approves, or participates in such acts, courts all over the nation have struggled for years in applying this rule within the framework of "controlling the sale of intoxicating liquor." At common law, any attempt to invoke the doctrine of respondeat superior in a criminal case would have run afoul of our deeply ingrained notions of criminal jurisprudence that guilt must be personal and individual. In recent decades, however, many states have enacted detailed regulatory provisions in fields which are essentially non-criminal. Such statutes are generally enforceable by light penalties, and although violations are labeled crimes, the considerations applicable to them are totally different from those applicable to true crimes, which involve moral delinquency and which are punishable by imprisonment or another serious penalty. It is here that the social interest in the general well-being and security of the populace has been held to outweigh the individual interest of the particular defendant. The penalty is imposed despite the defendant's lack of a criminal intent or mens rea. Because of the peculiar nature of the business, one who applies for and receives permission to carry on the liquor trade assumes the highest degree of responsibility to his fellow citizens. This is the quid pro quo the Commonwealth demands in return for the privilege of entering the highly restricted and dangerous business of selling intoxicating liquor. Koczwara (D) argues that a statute imposing criminal responsibility should be construed strictly, with all doubts resolved in his favor. While he is entirely correct, we must remember that we are dealing with a statutory crime within the state's plenary police power. The question here raised is whether the legislature intended to impose vicarious criminal liability on the licensee-principal for acts committed on his premises without his presence, participation or knowledge. The language of the statute specifically omits the use of such words as "knowingly, wilfully, etc."

This omission is highly significant and it indicates a legislative intent to eliminate both knowledge and criminal intent as necessary ingredients of such offenses. We find that the intent of the legislature in enacting this Code was not only to eliminate the common law requirement of a mens rea, but also to place a very high degree of responsibility upon the holder of a liquor license to make certain that neither he nor anyone in his employ commit any of the prohibited acts upon the licensed premises. However, in this case, the trial court, of its own accord, imposed imprisonment as well as a fine for Koczwara's (D) violations of the Liquor Code. Such sentence of imprisonment in a case where liability is imposed vicariously cannot be sanctioned by this Court consistent with the State Constitution. Although to hold a principal criminally liable might possibly be an effective means of enforcing law and order, it would do violence to our more sophisticated modern-day concepts of justice. Liability for all true crimes, wherein an offense carries with it a jail sentence, must be based exclusively upon personal causation. It can be readily imagined that even a licensee who is meticulously careful in the choice of his employees cannot supervise every single act of the subordinates. A man's liberty cannot rest on so frail a reed as whether his employee will commit a mistake in judgment. We are holding that so much of the judgment as calls for imprisonment is invalid, and we are leaving intact the fine imposed in the lower court.

Dissent: (Musmanno, J.) The Majority's opinion is so novel, so unique, and so bizarre that one must put on his spectacles, remove them to wipe the lenses, and then put them on again in order to assure himself that whet he reads is a judicial decision. Without any justification anywhere, the Majority sustains the conviction of a person for acts admittedly not committed by him, not performed in his presence, not accomplished at his direction, and not even done within his knowledge. The Majority introduces into its discussion a proposition which is shocking to contemplate. Such a concept of "vicarious criminal liability" is as alien to American soil as the upas tree.

Analysis:

Strict liability allows for criminal liability without the element of mens rea found in the definition of most crimes. In contrast, vicarious liability eliminates the requirement of the actus reus and imputes the criminal act of one person to another. Vicarious liability is based solely on the relationship of the parties, as opposed to accomplice liability, where the justification for holding a secondary party liable for the actions of the primary party is that the accomplice has willingly participated in the criminal acts. This case is one of the earliest appellate decisions to consider the validity of vicarious liability, which helps to explain the vehement dissent [that's an understatement!].

State v. Christy Pontiac-GMC

(State) v. (Car Dealership)
354 N.W.2d 17 (1984)

M E M O R Y   G R A P H I C

Instant Facts

Car dealership was convicted of theft and forgery when its employees forged customer rebate forms and did not pass the rebates on to the customers.

Black Letter Rule

A corporation may be prosecuted and convicted for the crimes of theft and forgery.

Case Vocabulary

CORPORATE CRIMINAL LIABILITY: A corporation can commit a crime.

LEGAL FICTION: Assumption that certain facts exist, whether or not they actually do, so that a principle of law may be applied to achieve justice on the facts as they do exist.

THEFT BY SWINDLE: Stealing through trickery or deception.

Procedural Basis: Appeal from bench trial resulting in the defendant's four convictions.

Facts: Christy Pontiac (D) is a car dealership owned by James Christy, a sole stockholder, who serves as president and as director. In the spring of 1981, General Motors (GM) offered a cash rebate program for its dealers. A customer who purchased a new car delivered during the rebate period was entitled to a cash rebate, part paid by GM and part paid by the dealership. GM would pay the entire rebate amount initially and later charge back, against the dealer, the dealer's portion of the rebate. Apparently it was not uncommon for the dealer to give the customer the dealer's portion of the rebate in the form of a discount on the purchase price. Phil Hesli, a salesman and fleet manager for Christy Pontiac (D), sold two cars to different customers past the dates of the rebate periods. He told the customers they would not be able to get the rebate on the cars. Subsequently, it was discovered that Hesli had forged the customers' signatures on the rebate forms, backdated the forms to within the rebate period, and submitted the forms to GM [sure he's not a *used* car salesman?]. Both purchasers learned of the forged rebate applications when they received a copy of the application in the mail from Christy Pontiac (D). Both purchasers complained to James Christy, and in both instances the conversations ended in angry mutual recriminations. Christy did tell one of the customers that the rebate on his car was a "mistake" and offered half the rebate amount to "call it even." [or what others call "cover your a__"] After the Attorney General's office made an inquiry, Christy Pontiac (D) contacted GM and arranged for cancellation of one of the rebates that had been allowed to Christy Pontiac (D). Subsequent investigation disclosed that of 50 rebate transactions, only two sales involved irregularities [see, not *too* shady!]. In a separate trial, Phil Hesli was acquitted of three felony charges but found guilty on one count of theft and was given a misdemeanor disposition. An indictment against James Christy for theft by swindle was dismissed for lack of probable cause. Christy Pontiac (D), the corporation, was also indicted, and the appeal here is from the four convictions on those indictments (two counts of theft by swindle and two counts of aggravated forgery).

Issue: Can a corporation be prosecuted and convicted for the crimes of theft and forgery?

Decision and Rationale: (Simonett, J.) Yes. Christy Pontiac (D) argues that a corporation cannot be held criminally liable for a specific intent crime because the statutes refer only to natural persons and define a crime as "conduct which is prohibited by statute and for which the actor may be sentenced to imprisonment, with or without a fine." A corporation cannot be imprisoned, and cannot entertain a mental state so as to have the specific intent required for theft or forgery, Christy Pontiac (D) asserts. We are not persuaded by these arguments. The legislature has not expressly excluded corporations from criminal liability and, therefore, we take its intent to be that corporations are to be considered persons within the meaning of the Code, absent any clear indication to the contrary. We do not think the statutory definition of a crime was meant to exclude corporate criminal liability; rather, we construe that definition to mean conduct which is prohibited and, if committed, *may* result in imprisonment. We also have no trouble assigning specific intent to a corporation for theft or forgery. There was a time when the law declared that a legal fiction could not be a person for purposes of criminal liability, at least with respect to offenses involving specific intent, but that time is gone. Particularly apt candidates for corporate criminality are types of crime, like theft by swindle and forgery, which often occur in a business setting. We hold, therefore, that a corporation may be prosecuted and convicted for the crimes of theft and forgery. If a corporation is to be criminally liable, it is clear that the crime must not be a personal aberration of an employee acting on his own; the criminal activity must, in some sense, reflect corporate policy so that it is fair to say that the activity was the activity of the corporation.

What must be shown is that from all the facts and circumstances, those in positions of managerial authority or responsibility acted or failed to act in such a manner that the criminal activity reflects corporate policy, and it can be said, therefore, that the criminal act was authorized or tolerated or ratified by the corporation. We also hold that the evidence in this case is sufficient to sustain Christy Pontiac's (D) convictions. Hesli, the forger, had authority and responsibility in the business, and Christy Pontiac (D), not Hesli, received the rebate money; therefore Hesli was acting in furtherance of the corporation's business interests. The rebate money was obtained by Christy Pontiac (D) and kept by Christy Pontiac (D) until somebody blew the whistle. We conclude the evidence establishes that the theft by swindle and the forgeries constituted the acts of the corporation. Affirmed.

Analysis:

Most courts today recognize that corporations may be guilty of specific intent crimes. It is a logical conclusion, for if corporations can be liable in civil tort for both actual and punitive damages for libel, assault and battery, or fraud, it seems it should also be criminally liable for conduct requiring specific intent. As the court stated, for the corporation to be criminally liable, the crime must not be an employee acting on his own, it must, in some sense, reflect corporate policy so that it is fair to say that the activity was the activity of the corporation. The evidence showed that James Christy, as an individual, tried to negotiate a settlement when the customer complained, and that he did not contact GM headquarters about the problems until after the Attorney General's inquiry [what they don't know...]. The Court's logic seems to indicate that if James Christy had tried to correct the situation as soon as he learned of the wrongful conduct, the corporation may not have been liable, as that would have demonstrated that the corporation did not authorize, tolerate or ratify the employee Hesli's actions.

Perspective
Theft

Chapter 12

Theft law covers three basic offenses: larceny, embezzlement, and false pretenses. Larceny is a common law felony, but embezzlement and false pretenses arose from English misdemeanor statutes.

The legal history of theft law is an excellent example of how laws often become inadequate as people with dishonest intentions find new ways to avoid criminal punishment. In addition, theft laws also illustrate how laws can fail to keep pace with economic changes.

Early English common law did not punish theft, but prohibited the taking of another's property by force. As economic pressures changed in the Middle Ages, courts began to prohibit nonviolent, but nonconsensual, takings of property, resulting in the creation of common law larceny.

However, this expansion was slow and often convoluted. Under common law, larceny was a capital crime, and, like all capital crimes, punishable by death. Many courts, weary of capital punishment, were reluctant to broaden the law to include conduct that the economic conditions required. As a result, initially, larceny laws were narrowly defined. Strict definitions and technical rules accompanied concepts of possession. This also resulted in gaps in larceny law that were later filled either by expanded definitions of larceny or by legislative acts creating entirely new theft offenses.

The by-product of this history is that courts have had to struggle with various common law and statutory concepts and rules that often overlap or fail to cover certain dishonest conduct. Some of these concepts include possession, custody, trespass, intent, conversion, title, and fraud or misrepresentation. The following cases explore, define, or criticize these concepts and the rules that form the basis of theft law.

Chapter 12

NOTE: THE PURPOSE OF THIS OUTLINE IS TO ORGANIZE THE CASES SO THAT ONE CAN QUICKLY UNDERSTAND THE RELEVANCE OF EACH CASE TO THE COURSE. NO ATTEMPT IS MADE IN THIS OVERVIEW TO ADDRESS EVERY CONCEPT THAT MUST BE STUDIED. BE SURE TO READ THE ENTIRE CASEBOOK AND/OR OTHER MATERIALS TO GAIN A FULL UNDERSTANDING OF ALL CONCEPTS.

I. Larceny
  A. Larceny is the trespassory taking and carrying away of personal property of another with intent to steal. *Lee v. State.*
  B. The actus reus of larceny is a trespassory taking (caption) and carrying away (asportation) of the personal property of another.
    1. A person with limited or temporary control over another's property merely has custody of it. *Rex v. Chisser.*
      a. Employers who furnish their personal property to employees in furtherance of the employment relationship give their employees custody of the property. *United States v. Pruitt.*
      b. Common carriers delivering goods have possession of a package, but only hold custody of the contents of the package. *United States v. Mafnas.*
        (1) A delivery person who breaks open a package and takes its contents is guilty of larceny.
    2. An asportation occurs where the defendant carries away the property. Almost any movement of the property is sufficient .
    3. A trespass occurs where the defendant dispossesses another of property without consent.
      a. Trespass does not take place where the owner's property is taken at the request of or is facilitated by the owner. *Topolewski v. State.*
      b. Trespass takes place where possession is obtained by fraud. *Rex v. Pear.*
      c. Larceny of lost property does not take place unless the finder had a reasonable ground for finding the true owner and had an intent to steal the property at the time he or she takes possession of it. *Brooks v. State.*
      d. Trespass may include the misappropriation of property by the person receiving the property, even if it was obtained by the consent of the owner. *Lee v. State.*
    4. The defendant must take personal property possessed by another
      a. Traditionally, personal property did not include

labor or services provided by another. *Lund v. Commonwealth.*
      b. Personal property does not include real property (land).
  B. The mens rea of larceny is an intent to steal the property
    1. The defendant must intend to permanently deprive the owner of the property. *People v. Brown.*
      a. Under the continuing trespass doctrine, the intent to permanently deprive can arise at any time the wrongdoer remains in possession.
      b. A person is not guilty of larceny if she takes another's property believing that it belongs to her or that she has a right to legal possession (claim of right).
        (1) In most jurisdictions, a person cannot recover such property using force (e.g. robbery).
    2. An intent to steal is established where the taker's conduct creates a substantial risk of permanent loss. *People v. Davis.*

II. Embezzlement: Embezzlement is the fraudulent conversion of the property of another by one who is already in lawful possession. *Rex v. Bazeley.*

III. False Pretenses
  A. Theft by false pretenses occurs when the defendant makes a false representation of an existing fact with the intent to cheat or defraud the owner of his or her property. *People v. Ingram.*
  B. A misrepresentation can be explicit or implicit, and the misrepresentation must have caused the victim to transfer the property to the defendant. *People v. Whight.*

IV. Federal Mail, Wire, and Computer Fraud
  A. A scheme to defraud is shown where the defendant has a dishonest intent to deprive a person of their property by causing the owner some articulable harm or by intending to use the property for some gainful use. *United States v. Czubinksi.*
  B. A deprivation of honest services is found where the defendant fails or intends to fail to carry out his official tasks adequately for an employer or the public. *United States v. Czubinksi.*
  C. Computer fraud is found where the defendant makes an unauthorized access to a federal computer and gains anything of value in order to further an intent to defraud. *United States v. Czubinksi.*

Lee v. State

(Accused) v. (State)
(1984) 59 Md.App. 28, 474 A.2d 537

M E M O R Y   G R A P H I C

Instant Facts
None stated.

Black Letter Rule
Larceny is the trespassory taking and carrying away of personal property of another with intent to steal the same and may include the misappropriation of property by the person receiving the property, even if it was obtained by the consent of the owner.

Case Vocabulary

ASPORTATION: Where property has been moved.
BAILEE: A person who receives personal property of another but with no transfer of ownership.
CAPTION: Where a taking has occurred.
LARCENY: The trespassory taking and carrying away of personal property of another with an intent to steal.
MISAPPROPRIATION: Where someone dishonestly uses the property of another to his or her own benefit.
POSSESSION: Where someone has dominion (or authority) *and* control over a piece of property.
TRESPASSORY: An act or instance done wrongfully.

Procedural Basis: None stated.

Facts: None stated.

Issue: What is the *actus reus* of larceny?

Decision and Rationale: (Bell) Originally, common law courts designed theft-related offenses out of concern for crimes of violence and for protecting society against breaches of the peace. This then grew to include non-violent takings of property such as larceny, the trespassory taking and carrying away of personal property of another with intent to steal the same. A trespassory taking under traditional common law focused on the physical taking and possession of property, making larceny a crime against possession. Thus, if the owner willingly transferred property to another, the receiving party had "possessorial immunity" against punishment for receiving possession, misappropriation, or using the property in a manner inconsistent with the owner's expectations. However, courts gradually expanded the definition of larceny by manipulating the concept of possession to include misappropriation by the person receiving the property, even if the owner consented to the possession.

Analysis:

This opinion provides a brief outline of larceny's historical evolution. Originally, the common law only punished the taking of property that included the use of force. Larceny was created to include nonforcible, nonconsensual taking of property. This shifted the concept of theft away from being a crime against a person to being a crime against possession. Thus, it became a crime to nonviolently take the property of another without the owner's consent. However, this definition proved too narrow as those entrusted with property often misused it to the dismay of the owner. As a result, courts had to tinker with the concept of a possession to include such misuse.

Rex v. Chisser

(State) v. (Accused)

(1678) T. Raym,. 275, 83 Eng.Rep. 142

M E M O R Y   G R A P H I C

 ## Instant Facts

A person in a jewelry store asks the store-keeper to hand him some rings to inspect, but, instead of inspecting and paying for them, he runs off with the rings in hand.

Black Letter Rule

A person with limited or temporary control over another's property merely has custody of it.

Case Vocabulary

CONSTRUCTIVE POSSESSION: Where an owner of property may not have physical control over her property at that moment, but still retains dominion over it.

CREVATS: An old english word used for jewelry, especially rings.

Procedural Basis: A jury found the following facts to be true, and the court turned to the issue of whether the defendant's conduct was criminal.

Facts: Abraham Chisser (D) came to the jewelry store of Anne Charteris and asked her to show him two rings. Charteris placed the rings into Chisser's (D) hands, and Chisser (D) asked her their price. Charteris stated that the price was 7s, but Chisser (D) offered her 3s and then immediately ran out of the store with the rings in hand. He was caught [obviously Chisser (D) was no criminal mastermind] and brought to trial. A jury found the above facts to be true, and the court turned to the issue of whether the Chisser's (D) conduct was criminal.

Issue: Is mere custody of property enough to establish physical possession by a defendant for the purposes of larceny?

Decision and Rationale: (Court) No. Although the owner gave the property to Chisser (D), they were not out of her possession (and would not have been until they completed a contract for sale). In this case, no contract was concluded. Therefore, when Chisser (D) ran away with the goods, he committed a felony.

Analysis:

This opinion develops the distinction between custody of property and possession of property for the purposes of larceny. To understand the difference, we must look at the legal consequences entailing possession. The legal definition of possession is where someone has dominion *and* control over a piece of property. A person may possess property rightfully or wrongfully. This definition of possession is a function of the intent of the owner regarding the property and the circumstances. For example, if the owner of a photograph temporarily hands it to another to inspect, but does not intend to give away the photograph, then the receiver cannot be said to possess it. The receiver merely has temporary custody of the property. This means she has temporary physical control over it, but she does not have dominion or authority over it. She can hold it and look at it, but she can't tear it up, fold it, or draw mustaches on it. The owner retains dominion over the photograph while the receiver inspects it. On the other hand, if the receiver pockets the photograph and [makes a mad dash for the hills], the receiver has asserted dominion and control over the property. Thus, this person now has possession of the property, but holds it wrongfully. In this opinion, the accused is trying to argue that before he fled, he already had possession of the rings so his subsequent flight was not trespassory. After all, he didn't break into the display case and run off with the rings. The shopkeeper actually gave them to him. The court, therefore, had to fill a gap in larceny law and did so using the concepts of custody and constructive possession. For legal purposes, the accused did not have possession of the rings while he inspected them in the store. Despite her actions, the shopkeeper retained constructive possession of the rings even though she handed them over to the accused. This is because the Charteris gave him the rings, but did not intend to give him possession unless he paid for them. Therefore, she retained constructive possession of the rings, but gave the accused temporary custody of them for inspection. Consequently, at the moment he fled, he asserted control *and* dominion over the rings, and his actions became a trespassory taking. As a result, Chisser (D)'s custody of the rings converted into a wrongful possession as he fled. After fleeing, he had committed both a trespassory taking and a carrying away of property making him guilty of larceny.

United States v. Mafnas

(State) v. (Accused)
(1983) 701 F.2d 83

M E M O R Y   G R A P H I C

 Instant Facts

An armored car guard was arrested for taking money out of bank money bags while delivering them.

Black Letter Rule

Where an employer furnishes property to an employee in furtherance of the employment relationship, the employee has mere custody of the employer's goods.

Case Vocabulary

CONVERSION: The use or possession of another's property as if it were one's own.

Procedural Basis: Appeal from a district court for violation of a federal larceny statute.

Facts: Mafnas (D) was an employee of the Guam Armored Car Service whom the Bank of Hawaii and the Bank of America hired to deliver bags of money. On three occasions, Mafnas (D) opened the money bags and took money while making his deliveries. Mafnas' (D) [kleptomaniacal tendencies] were put to an end after he was caught. He was convicted in a district court under 18 U.S.C. § 2113(b) [which prohibits the taking "with intent to steal ... any money belonging to ... any bank"]. Mafnas (D) appealed to the United State's Court of Appeals for the Ninth Circuit.

Issue: Does an employee who receives property belonging to the employer during the scope of employment and converts the property to the employee's personal use commit larceny?

Decision and Rationale: (Court) Yes. If a person receives property for a temporary or limited purpose, that person is only acquiring custody, not possession in the legal sense. The owner retains constructive possession. Thus, a person hired to deliver the employer's property to another only has custody over the property in the course of the delivery. As a result, the decision of the employee to take the property for his own use is beyond the consent of the owner and constitutes larceny. See United States v. Pruitt [Larceny found where the defendant was a messenger who staged a fake robbery while he was delivering money for the bank]. However, Mafnas (D) distinguishes Pruitt by claiming he was an agent of the bank, not an employee, making him a bailee who had lawful possession over the money bags. See Lionberger v. United States [Holding that a bailee exists where the owner, while retaining title, gives property to the bailee for "some particular purpose upon an express or implied contract."]. Bailees are treated differently and are considered to have possession over their employer's goods. Nevertheless, a bailee may still commit larceny where the bailee "breaks bulk". Under this doctrine, the bailee-carrier is given lawful possession of a package, but not its contents. Thus, breaking open the package and taking a portion or all its contents is an act of larceny. As a result, under either theory, Mafnas (D) has committed larceny. In addition, the argument that the theft was from the service and not the banks has no merit. The money stolen was within the meaning of § 2113(b) since it was money "in the care, custody, control, management, or possession of any bank". Conviction is affirmed.

Analysis:

This opinion deals with the greedy employee who steals from the employer. To deal with this, courts have found that employees have mere custody of their employer's property, not full possession. A decision by the employee to keep the property for his or her own use and to take the property away is, therefore, larceny. However, some employers have employees that act as their agents. The classic example is delivery carriers. In such cases, the employer gives the property to a carrier, under contract, for delivery to another location. Courts initially saw this relationship as a lawful transfer of possession from the employer to the bailee-carrier. However, a problem developed. Some carriers, while in possession, wrongfully opened packages and stole some of all of its contents. Yet, since they were in lawful possession, they could not be guilty of larceny. Courts resolved this problem via the "breaking bulk" doctrine. Under this doctrine, bailees have lawful possession of the employer's package, but only have custody over its contents. Thus, breaking open a package and taking away any of its contents constitutes larceny. In the case at hand, Mafnas (D) tries to argue that he was a bailee in lawful possession of both the package and its contents. However, the "breaking bulk" doctrine prevents him from [beating the rap]. Nevertheless, the doctrine has its faults. For example, if Mafnas (D) had taken the bags of money unopened and brought them to his own bank for deposit, there would be no larceny. Mafnas (D) has lawful possession of the bags and did not break them open. His bank would not be guilty of larceny either. The bank will open the bags to make the deposit; but, at that point, the bank has lawful possession of the bags and its contents. This is because it received consensual possession of the bag from Mafnas (D), the bank is not a bailee, and the bank lacks the intent to steal. A better approach would be to treat the bailee as holding the package and its contents custodially or at least accept the notion that there may be persons with "possession" that nonetheless do not have total dominion over the property and can defraud others entitled to the property or its benefits. Thus, the employer would still have constructive possession over the package and its contents. This makes sense because the employer never intends the carrier to have title possession of the property. It only intends the carrier to ship the property to the requested destination.

Topolewski v. State

(Accused) v. (State)

(1906) 130 Wis. 244, 109 N.W. 1037

M E M O R Y   G R A P H I C

Instant Facts

A person was charged with stealing three barrels of meat from his employer, a meat packing company.

Black Letter Rule

A trespassory taking, for the purposes of larceny, does not take place where the taking is facilitated by the owner or at the owner's request.

Procedural Basis: The defendant was found guilty of larceny. The defendant appealed.

Facts: Topolewski (D) was an employee of the Plankinton Packing Company. Topolewski (D) wanted to collect a debt owed to him by a former employee of the meat packing company named Mat Dolan. Topolewski (D) approached Dolan for payment of the debt. However, Dolan was unable to make payment. Topolewski (D) conjured up a scheme for Dolan to satisfy his debt by helping Topolewski (D) steal some of the company's meat products. Topolewski (D) discussed the plan with Dolan, but Dolan [was a snitch and told the company about the scheme]. Dolan and the company agreed to set up Topolewski (D), so that he could be caught red handed. After Topolewski (D) and Dolan discussed a variety of possible schemes, the two arranged to meet and discuss the plan while an employee of the company listened in hiding. Dolan and Topolewski (D) agreed to a plan where Dolan would order some packages of meat to be placed on one of their loading platforms that was normally used to deliver meat to customers. Topolewski (D) would then arrive, pretending to be a customer, and pick up the meat. Dolan would make this arrangement at the company through Mr. Layer, the person in charge of its wholesale department. Mr.Layer was informed about the scheme and the plan to trap Topolewski (D). Mr.Layer ordered four barrels of meat to be packed and placed on the loading platform for Topolewski (D) to pick up. Mr.Layer notified the person in charge of the platform, Ernst Klotz, that a customer was to pick up the barrels. Topolewski (D) arrived, on schedule, to pick up the meat. Klotz allowed Topolewski (D) to load the barrels onto his wagon. Klotz consented to Topolewski's (D) actions, but did not actually help Topolewski (D) load the barrels onto the wagon. Topolewski (D) did not pick up the fourth barrel but told Klotz that he wanted it marked and sent to him with a bill. Topolewski (D) also told Klotz that he had ordered the barrels the night before through Dolan. Topolewski (D) then drove away with his [grand prize of] three barrels of meat, worth $55.20 while leaving the meat packing company [high and dry]. Topolewski (D) was caught and found guilty of having stolen three barrels of meat from the Plankinton packing company. Topolewski (D) appealed.

Issue: Is a person guilty of larceny where the owner of the property actually or constructively aids in the commission of the offense, as intended by the wrongdoer, by performing or rendering unnecessary some act in the transaction essential to the offense?

Decision and Rationale: (Marshall) No. The question in this case is whether the meat packing company consented to the taking of the barrels such that the element of trespass or nonconsent is not satisfied for the crime of larceny. The plan for stealing the property did originate with Topolewski (D). Nonetheless, the plan was impossible to achieve without the property being placed on the loading platform and Topolewski (D) being allowed to take it. However, neither Dolan nor the company explicitly consented to the misappropriation of the property. This case "is very a near the borderline, if not across it, between consent and nonconsent to the taking of the property." Larceny does not take place where property is delivered by a servant to a defendant under the direction of the master, regardless of the defendant's purposes. See *Reg v. Lawrence,* 4 Cox C.C. 438. This case is similar. The company placed the barrels on the loading platform with the knowledge that Topolewski (D) would arrive to pick it up. While Klotz did not assist Topolewski (D) in taking the barrels, he stood by and allowed Topolewski (D) to pick up the barrels, assisted him in arranging the wagon, and made provision for the fourth barrel. In addition, Klotz was instructed and had every reason to believe that Topolewski (D) had a right to take the property. His conduct amounted to a delivery of the three barrels to Topolewski (D). In *Rex v. Egginton,* 2 P. & P. 508, [a servant informed his master that he had been approached to

Topolewski v. State (Continued)

assist in the robbing of the master's house. The master instructed the servant to open the house to the thieves and allow them to steal certain items. The master intended to have the thieves arrested after they achieved their goal. However the court held that the crime of larceny was complete because the master did not direct the servant to deliver the property to the thieves or consent to its taking. The thieves "were neither induced to commit the crime nor was any act essential to the offense done by anyone but themselves."] The element of trespass is absent in this case. The company intended to set a trap for Topolewski (D), but the setting of the trap went too far by actually placing the company in the position of having consented to the taking. There can be no larceny without a trespass. Therefore, "where the owner of property by himself or his agent, actually or constructively, aids in the commission of the offense, as intended by the wrongdoer, by performing or rendering unnecessary some act in the transaction essential to the offense, the would be criminal is not guilty of all the elements of the offense." If Topolewski (D) had merely agreed with Dolan to improve the opportunity for the accused to steal the barrels of meat from the loading platform, then this case would have had a different result. Conviction reversed.

Analysis:

This opinion deals strictly with the element of trespass in larceny. This definition of trespass is different than the tort or crime of trespass to land. For the crime of larceny, there must be a taking and carrying away of property, but that taking and carrying away must be trespassory, or taken without the consent of the owner. Without this element, everyone who receives a gift would be a thief and every gift-giver a victim. A thief can only become a thief, if that person takes property without the owner's permission. The issue, again, focuses on the intent and actions of the owner. If an owner intends to give and actually does give property away, the owner cannot later claim that the recipient is a thief, even if the recipient had a criminal intent to steal. Criminal law recognizes that people should not be punished for criminal thoughts or intentions alone. Crimes only take place where the accused has the requisite *actus reus* along with the requisite *mens rea*. In this case, while the accused clearly had the proper *mens rea* for larceny, his *actus reus* was insufficient. The company allowed him to pick up the barrels, effectively allowing him to steal them. However, the company did not, in actuality, intend to give the barrels to the accused. In fact, it intended to temporarily give the accused the barrels, and then subsequently have him apprehended for his actions. Presumably, the company would then have its barrels returned. So, given that the company did not actually intend to give the accused the barrels permanently and he had the requisite *mens rea*, why let Topolewski (D) off? Criminal law is designed to prevent crime, not facilitate the commission of crime. Presume, for example, that without the company's assistance, it would be impossible for Topolewski (D) to take the barrels. In this case, Topolewski (D), while having criminal intentions, would never have been able to carry out his intent to steal. No crime would have taken place. If the court had found that Topolewski (D) had committed larceny in this case, this would give private persons the power to trap individuals into committing crime by encouraging and facilitating criminal behavior on the part of both the company and the accused. Instead of preventing crime, the law would encourage people to create crimes where they would not have otherwise existed. To thwart this undesirable result, the court applies a strict, literal meaning to the element of trespass. While the company did not actually intend or consent to a permanent deprivation of its property, its temporary consent, for the purpose of incriminating Topolewski (D), was not sufficient for larceny. However, the opinion is not very adept at demarcating the borderline between consent and nonconsent. The court distinguishes this case from the one in Egginton, apparently because the company specifically instrcuted its employees to give the accused the barrels. However, in both Egginton and this case, the owner intends the would-be thief to take the property. Is not the owner in Egginton, by instructing the servant to give the thieves access to the house and the property, also consenting to have the property taken? How is opening a door and leading the way different than allowing someone to load a wagon? Essentially, both the homeowner and the company are facilitating and encouraging criminal conduct. A better rule would be to find no consent where the owner, though aware of the wrongdoer's intentions, takes no action or omission to facilitate the theft.

Rex v. Pear

(State) v. (Accused)

(1779) 1 Leach 212, 168 Eng.Rep. 208

M E M O R Y   G R A P H I C

Instant Facts
A person rented a horse for the stated purpose of making a trip, but never returned it.

Black Letter Rule
Possession obtained by fraud is a trespassory taking for the purposes of larceny.

Case Vocabulary

SERIATIUM: When something occurs successively, one after another.

Procedural Basis: A jury found the following facts to be true, and the court turned to the issue of whether the defendant's conduct was criminal.

Facts: Samuel Finch was a stable keeper who rented a horse to Pear (D) on July 2, 1779. Pear (D) hired the horse telling the owner that he intended to ride to Surry, that he lived at 25 King-street, and that he would return with the horse at about 8 o'clock that same evening. Pear (D) did not go to Surry and did not return the horse. In fact, the very same day [after some horsing around], he sold the horse to someone else. Also, he was not living at the address that he gave to the owner. A jury found that the above facts were true and also found that Pear (D) had hired the horse with the fraudulent intention of selling it immediately. The case was then referred to the judges who had to decide whether Pear's (D) actions were a mere breach of trust or a felony.

Issue: Does possession obtained by fraud constitute larceny?

Decision and Rationale: (Court) Yes. The question of whether, at the time of the hiring, Pear (D) intended to steal and sell the horse, was decided by the jury. If no such intent existed, he must be acquitted. The jury concluded that Pear (D) hired the horse under the "mere pretense" to obtain possession and sell it. The judges found that the question regarding Pear 's (D) original intentions had been properly left to the jury. The judges then decided whether the pretense constituted a breach of trust or a felonious conversion. The judges concluded that the possession was obtained fraudulently and the true owner remained in possession at the time of the conversion. As a result, Pear (D) is guilty of a felony.

Analysis:

This is another opinion that deals with the element of trespass in larceny. This case is different because, while the owner did consent to Pear 's (D) possession of the horse, this consent was obtained fraudulently. This offense is now known as "larceny by trick". The opinion focuses on the timing of the intent of the accused. If the accused had no intention to steal and sell the horse at the time the owner gave it to him, than he could not be guilty of larceny. However, if the accused had the intent to steal and sell the horse at the time he obtained possession from the owner, then he could be held guilty. The opinion takes this approach because it needs to fit the facts of the case within the confines of traditional larceny law. Larceny is defined only as a crime of possession. Punishment is merited only if possession is wrongfully obtained. If Pear (D) was not lying when he asked to rent Finch's horse, then he used no fraud to obtain the horse and possession passed lawfully. At transfer, neither Pear (D) nor Finch had any knowledge about any "horseplay," unless, of course, Pear (D) later changed his mind and decided to steal it. However, does it make sense to allow a person who later develops the intention to steal the property to go free? Clearly, the law of larceny may be inadequate to cover this kind of behavior. In addition, this rule also creates the problem of determining when the crime actually occurs. Did the crime taken place the moment Pear (D) rode away after the owner gave him his horse, or did the offense occur when he failed to return the horse at 8 o'clock? Should we be able to arrest him immediately or allow the accused to change his or her mind and not perform an act inconsistent with the owner's intentions?

Brooks v. State

(Accused) v. (State)
(1878) Ohio St. 46

M E M O R Y   G R A P H I C

Instant Facts

A person found a wad of $200 in bills that someone else had lost a month earlier and spent the money for himself.

Black Letter Rule

Larceny of lost property does not take place unless the finder had a reasonable ground for finding the true owner and had an intent to steal the property at the time he or she takes possession of it.

Procedural Basis: Appeal of a jury verdict that found the defendant guilty of larceny.

Facts: Charles B. Newton, on October 24, 1878, rode into the city of Warren in a buggy to attend some business. He hitched his horse to a post and went to attend to his business matters. Later that afternoon, as he returned home, he discovered that he had lost a package of bank bills totaling $200. After an unsuccessful search for the money, Newton published an advertisement in two Warren newspapers regarding the missing money. On November 20, George Brooks (D), a resident of the city of Warren, found the roll of bank bills a few feet from the hitching post while he was working with several other laborers. None of the other laborers saw Brooks (D) find the money. However, to ward off any suspicion, Brooks (D) showed to the laborers a dollar bill which was wet and muddy. He then offered to sell the dollar bill to one of them for $0.25. A half-hour past his dinner break, he quit work and was paid off. Brooks (D) then spent part of the money that same day to buy a pair of boots and other items and gave $50.00 to Mrs. Lease to purchase furniture and other items for his wife. Brooks (D) and his wife, shortly afterward, then tried to sneak quietly out of town. The evidence does not show that Brooks (D) saw any of the newspaper notices regarding the lost money or that he knew of Newton's loss at the time he found the money. A jury found Brooks (D) guilty of larceny. Brooks (D) appealed.

Issue: Does a person commit larceny where he or she finds lost goods and takes them for his or her own use but has good grounds to believe that the owner can be found?

Decision and Rationale: (White) Yes. Larceny may be committed of lost property. Constructive possession still remains in the owner, unless the circumstances reveal that the owner abandoned the property. According to Baker v. The State, 29 Ohio St. 184, ["when a person finds goods that have actually been lost, and takes possession with intent to appropriate them to his own use, really believing, at the time, or having good ground to believe, than the owner can be found, it is larceny"]. This rule does not require the finder "to use diligence or to take pains" in finding the true owner. Lost property may be the subject of larceny if the finder has reasonable ground to believe, from the nature of the property, or the circumstances under which it is found, that if he deals with the item openly and honestly the owner will be discovered. In addition, the finder will be guilty of larceny if an intent to steal existed at the time he took the item into his possession. The case was properly submitted to the jury and the evidence reveals no ground to interfere with their decision. The judgment of the court below is affirmed.

Dissent: (Orey) I do not think the accused was properly convicted. The evidence fails to show that the accused had any information that someone had lost money or any information regarding the owner. The money had been left undiscovered for several weeks and its owner had stopped searching for it. The accused may have had been morally bound to take steps to find the owner, "but in violating the moral obligation, I do not think that the plaintiff incurred criminal liability." The obligation of dealing "honestly" with the money is far too indefinite with no guidance to the jury. "What one jury might think was honest dealing, another jury might think was the reverse."

Analysis:

This opinion is a classic legal analysis of the finders-keepers rule. It lays out two elements that must be established for a finder's conduct to be criminal. First, the finder must have had some reasonable grounds or clues regarding the owner of the property. Second, the finder must have an intent to steal the property at the time of discovery. A finder is not required to take responsibility to find the owner unless some clues exist or the nature of the property is such that disclosure of the discovery will reveal its owner. Absent these circumstances, the finder may keep the property, free of criminal liability. This is a balance between the interests of the owner and the economic interests of not hindering the use of property. If a person finds a 20-dollar bill blowing in the wind, requiring the finder to take steps, absent any clues, to find the owner, this would deter the use of the $20. On the other hand, if the bill is not blowing in the wind, but found inside a lost wallet with the owner clearly identified, it would not be fair to let the finder keep it. However, the intent to steal element is confusing. Practically speaking, does a person who finds and picks up a lost item, immediately, at that moment, form an intent to steal that item or does the intent develop later? An intent to steal can develop in only two ways. First, the finder may have a greedy propensity and, upon seeing the 20-dollar bill, immediately think, "That's my twenty bucks now," irrespective of any clues as to ownership. If there are good clues as to ownership, the finder would be guilty of larceny. Second, the finder may find the 20-dollar bill with a neutral intent and later discover good clues as to ownership but still decide to keep it. This person could not be criminally punished. The finder only developed an intent to steal *after* taking possession. Are you convinced that Brooks (D) had a wrongful intent at the moment he picked up the bills or did he develop it later? This question reveals loopholes in larceny law. What if Brooks (D) found the bills wrapped in brown paper, picked them up with a neutral intent, later unwrapped the paper to reveal the cash, and then decided to keep it? Because he lacked the intent to steal when he picked up the package, he would not be guilty of larceny. What if Brooks (D) found only an anonymous dollar bill blowing in the wind, picks it up not intending to steal it but knowing that there is no clue as to ownership, and learns five minutes later that a co-worker had just lost a dollar bill? Again, if he decided to keep the dollar bill, this would not be larceny because the intent to steal occurred after possession as a result of a new clue. However, is not his decision to keep the money just as deceptive and fraudulent as if he had picked up the bill with the intent to steal it in the first place?

Lund v. Commonwealth

(Accused) v. (State)

(1977) Va. 688, 232 S.E.2d 745

M E M O R Y   G R A P H I C

Instant Facts

A student used the computer services of his university without authorization or permission.

Black Letter Rule

Traditional common law does not prohibit the wrongful taking of labor or services.

Case Vocabulary

FALSE PRETENSE: A statement or conduct expressing a fact that is actually untrue.

Procedural Basis: The accused was found guilty of grand larceny and sentenced to two years and the accused appealed.

Facts: Charles Walter Lund (D) was a graduate student in statistics studying for his Ph.D. at Virginia Polytechnic Institute and State University. His dissertation required him to use a computer. The university had a computer center, but Lund's (D) faculty adviser neglected to arrange for Lund's (D) use of the computer facilities. [So, in the interests of science and earning that Ph.D.,] Lund (D) used the campus computer facilities without obtaining the proper authorization. The computers used by Lund (D) are leased by the university from IBM Corporation. The rental cost of the computers is shared by various departments within the university and is charged to the budget of each department. These departments are allocated computer credits based on a proportion of their budget. These departments receive a monthly statement showing the amount of computer time used to by each department and the remaining balance for each department. Each department receives their own account number and a key to a post office box where the computer center personnel store any printing jobs made under the account. Lund (D) came under surveillance on October 12, 1974 after complaints from departments of unauthorized charges to their computer accounts. Lund (D) was confronted by the university's investigator and initially denied use of the services, but later made an admission. He turned over seven keys for four post office boxes assigned to other persons. Lund (D) stated that he had received the keys from another student. In addition, a large number of computer cards and printouts were recovered from his apartment. The director of the computer center testified that the unauthorized use of the accounts totaled $ 5,065, and that Lund (D) used as much as $26,384.16 in unauthorized computer time, and furthermore, he stated that Lund's (D) computer cards and printouts had a value worth no more than scrap paper. Lund (D) testified that he used the computer without authorization, but he believed he did not do anything wrong because he was working on his dissertation. Four faculty members also testified in Lund's (D) behalf stating that the computer time used "probably would have been" or "would have been" given to Lund (D) if he had sought the proper authorization. Lund (D) was convicted under § 18.1-100 and § 18.1-118. § 18.1-100 [defines grand larceny as a taking from another of money or an item that is greater than $5 in value, or the taking not from the person of another goods and chattels greater than $100 in value]. § 18.1-118 [defines the crime of larceny by false pretense as a taking from another person money or other property through a false representation of an existing fact with knowledge of its falsity and with the intent to defraud]. Lund (D) argued that his conviction should be overturned because there was no evidence that articles were stolen or that they had a value of $100 or more and the computer time and services are not the subject of larceny under § 18.1-100 or 18.1-118.

Issue: Can the taking of labor or services be the subject of the crime of false pretense or larceny?

Decision and Rationale: (I'Anson) No. Under common law, larceny is a taking and carrying away of goods and chattels of another with intent to permanently deprive the owner of possession. Our statutes are no different. The phrase "goods and chattels" cannot be interpreted to include labor or services such as computer time. Criminal statutes must be strictly construed. Some jurisdictions have amended their criminal codes specifically to include the taking of labor or services by false pretense. However, no such amendments have been made to our statutes. Furthermore, the unauthorized use of the computer time cannot be the subject of larceny. Neither statute prohibits the use of the property of another. The statutes only refer to a taking and carrying away of a concrete piece of property. Labor, services, and the unauthorized use of property cannot be construed to be subjects of larceny under § 18.1-100 and 18.1-118. The commonwealth argues that even though the computer printouts have no market value, their value can be determined by the value of the computer time use to produce them. However, the cost of producing the printouts is not the proper method to ascertain the value here. If an article has no market value, the better rule is that the article's actual value should be proved. The evidence shows that the printouts had no monetary value to the university or the computer center and had no more value than scrap paper. As a result, the evidence was insufficient to convict under either § 18.1-100 or § 18.1-118. The judgment of the trial court is reversed and the indictment is quashed.

Analysis:

This opinion is an excellent example of how laws can sometimes fall behind the times. Traditional common law protected "goods and chattels". Intangible personal property was not protected under criminal law. Takings of intangible property were not the subject of criminal law because they were the subjects of contract and equity. If a person "stole" labor or services, the victim could recover under equitable theories of quasi-contract or unjust enrichment. A victim could be reimbursed for the value of the labor or services conveyed. However, as the economy evolved, labor and services became more or as valuable as tangible property, and pressure increased to include the "taking" of such intangibles within the scope of larceny. In this case, the accused stole intangibles valued over $30,000. Recognizing the problem, the opinion refused to expand its statutory definition of larceny, under § 18.1-100, or false pretense, under § 18.1-118, to include the use of computer services. Note, however, that the false pretense statute, § 18.1-118, does not use the language "taking and carrying away of the goods and chattels of another" found in § 18.1-100. Instead, the statute uses the language "obtain...money or other property which may be the subject or larceny" (Emphasis added). This statute does not refer to a taking or carrying away which may signify a legislative intent to include intangibles. Thus, either the opinion is using the "goods and chattels" definition for its "subject of larceny" from § 18.1-100 or it is transporting the traditional "take and carry away" meaning into the word "obtain". Finally, it is worth pointing out, that technically, Lund (D) did commit larceny by taking and carrying away the printouts. However, the court found that the value of the printouts was less than the $100 statutory minimum required under § 18.1-100.

People v. Brown

(State) v. Accused
(1894) 105 Cal. 66, 38 P. 518

M E M O R Y   G R A P H I C

Instant Facts

A boy took a bicycle from another boy intending to return it the same day.

Black Letter Rule

A felonious taking requires that the taking be with the intent to permanently deprive the owner of possession.

Procedural Basis: The defendant was convicted by a jury trial of the crime of burglary with intent to commit grand larceny and the defendant appealed.

Facts: Brown (D) was a seventeen-year-old boy who had been in an argument with another boy named Yount. Yount had thrown oranges at Brown (D), and Brown (D) wanted to get back at him. Brown (D) entered Yount's house and tried to take his bicycle, but took Frank's bicycle instead. Brown (D) claimed that he took the bicycle to get back at Yount, but intended to return the bike the next day. Brown (D) drove the bicycle into a grove, placed it on the ground, covered it with brush, and hid under it so that no one could find him until the evening when he planned to return the bike. However, Frank found him hiding under the bicycle and the brush. The trial court instructed the jury that larceny may take place even though the party taking the property only intended to temporarily deprive the owner of it. The trial judge compared the case to a man who takes a horse, not with the intent to take permanent possession of it, but only to ride to a particular destination, and then abandon it. The judge said this example was an example of conversion of property to one's own use, making the act a felony. The jury found Brown (D) guilty. Brown (D) appealed.

Issue: Does an intent to temporarily deprive the owner of his or her property constitute larceny?

Decision and Rationale: (Garoutte). No. The jury instruction was erroneous. The court instructed the jury that larceny may take place if the accused only intended to temporarily deprive the owner of the property. However, judicial authorities "form an unbroken line" holding that the felonious intent must be the intent to permanently deprive the owner of the property. The judge's example regarding the man taking the horse is too broad to accurately state what the law is. Under the judge's example, the man may or may not be guilty of larceny, and it would be a question of fact for the jury to decide. For there to have been felonious intent, the accused must have intended to permanently deprive the owner of his property and not just to convert the property to his own use. Judgment reversed.

Analysis:

This opinion illustrates requisite *mens rea* required for larceny. If a person takes another person's bicycle for a joyride and returns it, the joyrider cannot be guilty of larceny. However, in terms of the *actus reus*, a trespassory taking has still taken place. Nonetheless, the joyrider cannot be convicted of larceny because he lacked the required *mens rea*. It is apparent that the trial judge confused the concept of *animus furandi*, the intent to permanently deprive, with *lucria causa*, "for the sake of gain". If a joyrider takes a bicycle for a day to run his newspaper route, he may have gained from the taking, but his intent to return the bicycle does not create a felonious intent. On the other hand, if the joyrider takes the bicycle with the intent to wreck it beyond repair, he may not have received any pecuniary gain, but his intention to destroy it is *animus furandi*. Under traditional larceny law, a person who takes property temporarily, but later decides to permanently deprive the owner of it could not be found guilty of larceny because the proper *mens rea* did not exist at the time of taking. However, courts remedied this loophole by developing the legal fiction of "continuing trespass". Thus, if a person takes a bicycle intending to return it the next day, but decides the next day to keep the bicycle, then the initial trespass continues and the crime of larceny takes place at the moment the joyrider changes his mind.

People v. Davis

(State) v. (Accused)
(1998) 19 Cal.4th 301, 79 Cal.Rptr.2d 295, 965 P.2d 1165

M E M O R Y G R A P H I C

Instant Facts

A customer in a department store took a shirt off a rack, carried it to a sales counter, claimed it to be his own, and asked for a refund of cash or credit.

Black Letter Rule

An intent to steal is established where the taker's conduct creates a substantial risk of permanent loss.

Case Vocabulary

ANIMUS FURANDI: Where one intends to permanently deprive another of his or her property.

Procedural Basis: Appeal to the state supreme court of a conviction of petty theft.

Facts: Davis (D) entered a Mervyn's department store carrying a Mervyn's shopping bag. As he entered the store, he was placed under surveillance by a store security agent, named Carol German. German observed Davis (D) take a shirt off a rack and carry it to a sales counter in the women's department. Davis (D) told the cashier, Heather Smith, that he had previously bought the shirt for his father and that he wanted to return it now because it did not fit. Smith asked for a receipt, but Davis (D) said that he did not have one because "it was a gift." Smith informed Davis (D) that the store policy was not to issue cash refunds without a receipt for an amount more than $20.00, but she could issue a credit voucher. At this point, Smith was interrupted by a telephone call from the German who told Smith to issue Davis (D) a credit voucher. Smith issued the voucher which Davis (D) signed using a false name. German detained him as he walked away from the counter with the voucher. Davis (D) was convicted under penal code § 484 [which uses the common law definition of larceny]. Davis (D) appealed the conviction to the state supreme court.

Issue: Can an intent to steal exist if the primary purpose in taking the property is not to permanently deprive the owner of it?

Decision and Rationale: (Mosk) Yes. Davis (D) argues that the elements of trespass and intent to steal are lacking. First, Davis (D) argues that the element of trespass is not satisfied because the store, knowing how Davis (D) came into possession of the shirt, still consented to the issuance of the voucher. Davis (D) confuses the issue of consent. The issue is not consent regarding the voucher, but whether Mervyn's consented to Davis (D) taking the shirt. A department store impliedly consents to customers picking up, handling, and carrying to a sales counter an item for sale provided they have an intent to purchase the item. However, the store does not consent to a customer removing an item from a display with the intent to steal it. Second, Davis (D) argues that he lacked the intent to steal because he had no intent to permanently deprive Mervyn's of the shirt. He only intended to have the shirt long enough to receive a refund. Our research of case law reveals that the intent to steal may be found even though Davis' (D) purpose was not permanent deprivation. These cases are: (1) when the defendant intends to "sell" the property back to its owner, (2) when the defendant intends to claim a reward for "finding" the property, and three (3) when, as here, the defendant intends to return the property to its owner for a "refund". The "sale" cases offer three rationales for finding permanent deprivation. The first is that the deprivation would have been permanent unless the owner agreed to buy the property. The second rationale is that defendant's claim of the right to sell the property is also an assertion of the right of ownership and evidence of an intent to permanently deprive. Third, the act creates a substantial risk of permanent loss, because if the owner does not buy back his property the defendant will have "a powerful incentive to keep it in order to conceal the theft". See Perkins & Boyce, Criminal Law (3d ed 1982, at p. 329. The second line of cases involves a defendant who takes property for the purpose of later claiming a reward for "finding" the property. Courts, in these cases, have affirmed convictions of larceny on the theory that felonious intent existed because the defendant intended to deprive the owner of "a portion of the value of the property". The "portion of the value" in question involves the reward money paid. A second rationale is that the defendant makes the return of the property hinge on the offer of a satisfactory reward, and without the reward, the defendant would keep the property. Perkins, again, applies the rationale of a substantial risk of permanent loss to this scenario because a failure to give or offer a reward will also result in the permanent loss of the property. The third class of cases involves refunds much like the case at issue. Although these cases are similar factually, the opinions are less useful than the "sale" or "reward" cases. However, many of the rationales used in the "sale" and "reward" cases are also applicable to the "refund" cases. First, claiming a right to return an item, like claiming a right to sell an item, is an assertion of a right of ownership. Also, an intent to return an item to a store only if the store provides a refund is no less conditional than an intent to return an item based on the owner's reward. Therefore, a person "who takes an item from a store display with the intent to claim its ownership and restore it only on condition that the store pays a 'refund' must be deemed to intend to permanently deprive the store of the item within the meaning of the law of larceny." Second, the situation creates a substantial risk of permanent loss if the attempt to receive a refund of fails. Davis (D) has a strong incentive to keep the item in order to avoid drawing attention to the theft and avoid detection. As a result, we conclude that Mervyn's did not consent to Davis (D) taking possession of the shirt with the intent to steal it. Davis' (D) conduct was a trespassory taking. Furthermore, Davis' (D) intent to claim ownership of the shirt and to return it on condition of a payment of a refund is a felonious intent to permanently deprive Mervyn's within the meaning of larceny. Judgment of the court of appeal is affirmed.

Analysis:

As this opinion illustrates, there are situations where it is difficult to fit a defendat's conduct under the rubric of the intent to permanently deprive another of property. The "sale," "reward," and "refund" cases reveal new methods of theft. To deal with these new methods, courts created the doctrine of "a substantial risk of permanent loss". In these cases, an intent to permanently deprive, is said to exist if the defendant knew that his conduct would create a substantial risk of permanent loss. Therefore, if a person takes an automobile only for the purpose of driving it to a particular location, but abandons the automobile, than that person may create a substantial risk of permanent loss. Though the person may have an intent for the automobile to be eventually returned to its owner, by abandoning it the person creates the risk that the automobile may be stolen again. However, this risk does not necessarily lay on third parties; it may also lay on the person taking the property in the first place. In the "sale," "reward," and "refund" cases, the substantial risk of permanent loss rests on the taker. If the resale, reward, or refund is unsuccessful, the taker's temporary possession may turn into a permanent possession. In this case, it is highly likely that if Davis (D) was not able to obtain a refund, he would have walked out of the store with the shirt in his Mervyn's shopping bag. After all, he was claiming to own it. Finally, it is worth noting that the *mens rea* in this case is, in actuality, different than the *mens rea* of the intent to permanently deprive another of property. A person who shoplifts by pocketing an item and walking out of the store does have the intent to permanently deprive. However, a person who takes an item from the shelf and tries to receive a refund at the sales counter does not have the intent to permanently deprive at the time of taking. Instead, at the time of taking, the person intends either to wrongfully receive money for the item or, failing that, to walk out of the store with the item. Thus, Davis (D) is taking his chances and acting recklessly. However, for the purposes of larceny law both states of mind are treated as "intent to steal."

Rex v. Bazeley

(State) v. (Accused)

(1799) 2 Leach 835, 168 Eng.Rep. 517

M E M O R Y   G R A P H I C

Instant Facts

A bank teller decides to pocket a customer's deposit.

Black Letter Rule

An employee who receives property from a third person for delivery to the employer takes lawful possession upon delivery.

Case Vocabulary

DETINUE: An action against a person to recover wrongfully taken property.

EO INSTANTER: At that moment.

TROVER: An action against a person for damages due to the wrongful conversion of property.

Procedural Basis: The defendant is charged with larceny.

Facts: Bazeley (D) was the principal teller at a bank run by Esdaile & Hammet. In January 1799, he received bank notes and cash for deposit from William Gilbert through his employee, George Cock. Bazeley (D) credited Gilbert's account, but placed a bank note directly into his pocket. As is permitted in England, Esdaile & Hammet brought a criminal prosecution against Bazeley (D). Bazeley (D) was charged with larceny.

Issue: Does an employee who receives property from a third person for delivery to his employer take lawful possession upon delivery, thereby not constituting a trespassory taking?

Decision and Rationale: (Court) Yes. Defense counsel makes four different arguments. First, the argument is that the bank did not have constructive possession of the bank note at the time Bazeley (D) converted it to his own use. It is clear that at the time of taking the bank did not have actual possession of the note; therefore, we must decide whether the bank had constructive possession of the bank note. Sir William Blackstone defines possession as "both the right to, and also the occupation of, the property ". The bank may have had a right to possess the bank note; however, it was never under its custody or control. If, for example, Bazeley (D) had the bank note in his own custody and refused to turn it over to his employers, they could have recovered it by filing an action of trover or detinue. However, such actions assume that the person obtained possession of the property by lawful means, and that the right of possession of the property rests with the person bringing the action. In the case at hand, the note was delivered into Bazeley's (D) possession upon the bank's implied confidence that he would later deliver it into the bank's possession. If Bazeley (D) had deposited the bank note in the drawer kept for the receipt of deposits, it would have been a delivery of possession into the bank, but no such deposit was made. The facts support this. Second, the defense argues that, even assuming that the bank had possession of the note, Bazeley (D) did not have a felonious intention to steal it. The facts reveal no evidence that Bazeley (D) had any such intention at the time the note came into his hands. In addition, Bazeley (D) had given the bank a bond to insure the deposits he was handling. He also was the agent of a trading company and had the means to repay the bank the money that he took for his own use. In any case, Bazeley (D) must have had an intent to steal when the property came into his hands, but if he develops the intent afterwards, it is not larceny. Third, the defense argues that the situation at hand represents only a breach of trust between Bazeley (D) and the bank. Fourth, the defense argues that this is a breach of trust that has not been made punishable by the legislature. It is a settled point "that a breach of trust cannot by the rules of common law be converted into a felonious taking." There are only four statutes that convert such breaches of trust into a felony. Two of these statutes apply only to breaches of trust committed by employees of the post office. The third statute applies only to employees of the Bank of England. The fourth statute only applies to goods delivered by the employer to the employee. Therefore, none of these statutes are applicable to this case. The prosecution argues that the deposit made with Bazeley (D) was, in reality, a payment to the bank itself, not to Bazeley (D). The depositor entered the bank, and Bazeley (D), employed within the walls of the bank, was merely "one of the organs" of the bank who received the bank notes. Thus, payment to Bazeley (D) was, in effect, a payment to the bank. However, we disagree. Bazeley (D) should be pardoned.

Analysis:

This opinion highlights a gap in traditional common law and led to the development of the laws of embezzlement. Under traditional common law, an employee who takes property from a third person for delivery to the employer takes lawful possession of the property. This is different than an employee who is given property of the employer in furtherance of the working relationship. In this case, the employee merely takes custody of the property from the employer-owner. Thus, the employee may have temporary control of the property, but the employer had established dominion over the property before it was given to the employee and retains dominion over it while the employee uses it. This essentially prevents an employee from being able to [run off with the boss' dry cleaning]. However, if a third person gives property to the employee to hold and deliver to the employer, it is not possible to say that the employer has possession. Employer does not yet have control over the property. Instead, the third party has voluntarily given up possession and transferred it to the employee. Thus, the employee's holding cannot be described as custodial. During delivery, the employee is the only person with dominion and control over the property. The employer may have a right to the property, as the opinion states, but it simply never managed to obtain possession over it. Therefore, the legal definition of possession makes it impossible to call the holding custodial. However, as soon as the property enters into the hands of the employer, the employee loses possession. As a result, if Bazeley (D) had placed the bill into the bank drawer before pocketing it later, possession would have passed from the depositor to the bank. Bazeley's (D) subsequent taking would be a trespassory taking from the bank. In addition, the prosecution attempts to argue that since the depositor entered the bank and the defendant received the bank notes within the walls of the bank, Bazeley (D) was merely acting as its organ in collecting the deposit. Thus, the prosecution argues that the bank had *de facto* possession of the note when it was handed over to the defendant. The court refused this argument. While compelling, accepting this argument would have created new problems. What if Bazeley (D) had taken the deposit at Gilbert's home or just outside the bank's doors? Is the defendant still an organ of the bank? Can the identity of a bank be demarcated from the identity of its employees who may have their own individual intentions and criminal propensities? The court wisely absconded from enacting another bad rule and left it for the legislature to deal with. England responded by creating its first embezzlement statute which provided: "[I]f any servant or clerk, or any person employed … by virtue of such employment receive or take into his possession any money, goods, bond, bill, note, banker's draft, or other a valuable security, or effects, for or in the name or on the account of his master or master's, or employer or employers, and shall fraudulently embezzle, secrete, or make away with the same, or any part thereof … a [he] shall be deemed to have feloniously stolen the same." While embezzlement is a statutory crime and has a number of varying definitions, it is generally defined as the fraudulent conversion of the property of another by one who is already in lawful possession.

People v. Ingram

(State) v. (Accused)

(1998) 76 Cal.Rptr.2d 553

M E M O R Y   G R A P H I C

Instant Facts

A definition of the crime of false pretenses.

Black Letter Rule

Theft by false pretenses occurs when the defendant makes a false representation of an existing fact with the intent to cheat or defraud the owner of his or her property.

Case Vocabulary

TITLE: The legal right to use, control, or dispose of property.

Procedural Basis: None stated.

Facts: None stated.

Issue: What is the crime of false pretenses?

Decision and Rationale: (Haller) At issue here are two different forms of theft: larceny by trick and false pretenses. The crime of larceny by trick requires a trespassory taking where the defendant obtains possession, but not title to, another's property by fraud or trick. The fraud invalidates the consent, making the action a trespass. However, if the defendant obtains both possession and title through false representations with an intent to steal, there is no common law larceny. "The statutory crime of theft by false pretenses was created to fill the gap". The crime of false pretenses, while similar to larceny by trick, is a crime against *both* title and possession. "Theft by false pretenses occurs where the defendant makes a false representation with the intent to defraud the owner of his or her property, and the owner is in fact defrauded."

Analysis:

The crimes of larceny, embezzlement, and false pretenses may all take place as a result of fraud. However, the distinction between larceny by trick and false pretenses, as it relates to fraud, is a bit more difficult. As the opinion states, the primary difference between the two crimes is that false pretenses is a crime against title. A person may commit larceny by trick if she claims she wishes to rent a car but really intends to steal it. However, she drives off with possession of the car, but not with title to it. Title remains with the rental company. On the other hand, if she goes to a gas station with the intent to steal gas, fills up the tank, gives the station a bad check, and drives off, then she is guilty of the crime of false pretenses. The gas station gave her "ownership" to the gas free and clear, assuming that her check was good. As a result, since she fraudulently obtained title to the gas with a misrepresentation, she is guilty of false pretenses.

People v. Whight

(State) v. (Accused)

(1995) 36 Cal.App.4th 1143, 43 Cal.Rptr.2d 163

M E M O R Y   G R A P H I C

Instant Facts

Knowing that his bank account was no longer valid, a person continued to use his ATM card to obtain cash at several local grocery stores.

Black Letter Rule

A misrepresentation can be explicit or implicit, and the misrepresentation must have caused the victim to transfer the property to the defendant.

Procedural Basis: Appeal of a conviction of four counts of false pretenses.

Facts: Theodore Whight (D) opened a checking account at Tri-Counties Bank in January 1991. With this account, he was issued an ATM card which had no expiration date and was linked to his checking account. Whight (D) began the account with a deposit of $3,750.99. By June 1991 the account was overdrawn by $6.17. The bank mailed Whight (D) a letter notifying him that his account was overdue and that it would be closed if no deposits were made to make up for the overdraft. On July 10, 1991, with no deposits, the bank closed Whight's (D) account along with his ATM card. However, despite the cancellation, Whight (D) discovered that his ATM card continued to be valid at local Safeway stores. Safeway allows customers to make payments for items and receive cash back by using ATM cards. Safeway had a computer system that was used to verify ATM cards. Wells Fargo Bank operated this computer system. When a customer uses an ATM card at the Safeway check stand, a machine reads the magnetic strip on the back of the card. The information about the card is then sent by modem through telephone lines to Wells Fargo. Wells Fargo then sends the information to a banking network which links up with the customer's bank to verify the card. After the card is checked, a code is sent back to Safeway approving or disapproving the card. However, in some cases, Wells Fargo could not link up with the customer's bank or there would be a substantial delay in verifying the card. If this delay lasted more than 30 seconds, Wells Fargo would provide a "stand-in" code that would allow the transaction to take place without actually verifying the customer's information from the bank. Safeway would then automatically re-send the account information later in order to verify the account status. Safeway used "stand-in" codes for better customer service in order to speed transactions at the check stand. However, it also took the gamble that there would ultimately be a positive verification of the customer's account status. With Whight's (D) card, there was an error in the Wells Fargo computer system, which repeatedly returned a code to Safeway indicating that Whight's (D) bank could not be contacted. As a result, Safeway would repeatedly issue a "stand-in" code for Whight's (D) transactions. Whight (D) quickly realized that his ATM card was the modern-day equivalent of the "goose that laid the golden egg" and used the card on four different occasions to rack up a total of $19,000.00 [whoa!] in cash. After being caught [whew!], he admitted that he knew that his checking account had been closed. Whight (D) was convicted of four counts of false pretenses. Whight (D) appealed.

Issue: Can an implicit misrepresentation of fact cause the owner of property to transfer the property to the defendant for the purposes of the crime of false pretenses?

Decision and Rationale: (Sparks) Yes. Whight (D) argues that his convictions for theft under false pretenses should be reversed because Safeway did not rely on Whight's (D) implicit misrepresentation that his ATM card was valid, but did rely on the code issued by Wells Fargo Bank in approving Whight's (D) transactions. "This leaky contention cannot hold water". A conviction of theft by false pretenses must be supported by three elements: (1) the defendant made a misrepresentation or false pretense, (2) the defendant had an intent to use the representation to defraud the owner of his property, and (3) the owner is in fact defrauded because he gave up his property in reliance upon the misrepresentation. In this case, we are concerned with the issue of causation or reliance. The misrepresentation does not need to be expressed, oral, or written, but may involve conduct calculated and intended to deceive. Therefore, when Whight (D) offered his ATM card, he was making an implicit representation that it was valid. However, if the victim did not rely on the false pretense, a conviction cannot be made. Such reliance may be lacking in three typical situations: "(1) Where the complainant knew the representation was false, or did not believe it to be true. (2) Where, even if he believed it, he did not rely on it, but investigated it for himself or sought and relied on other advice. (3) Where, although some false representations are proved, the complainant parted with his money or property for other reasons or in reliance on other representations not shown to be false." In addition, the false pretense or misrepresentation does not need to be the sole reason causing the victim to part with his property, it must have materially influenced the owner. As long as the victim does not rest completely upon his own investigation, "sufficient reliance is shown if the victim relied in part upon the defendant's representations." Whight (D) claims that Safeway relied upon the computer authorization as opposed to his implicit representation that his ATM card was valid. This issue would normally be a question of fact for the jury to decide.

However, the evidence establishes that Safeway did not rely upon the computer authorization. The facts establish that Safeway had nothing to rely upon except Whight's (D) implicit representation that his ATM card was valid. Due to the glitch in the Wells Fargo computer system, Whight's (D) bank was not contacted and his account status was not verified. In fact, Wells Fargo kept returning a code to Safeway indicating that there was no response from Whight's (D) bank. As a result Safeway issued a "stand-in" code in order to facilitate the transaction. Consequently, the computer system never had the opportunity to verify Whight's (D) account. Therefore, it cannot be said that Safeway relied upon the computer system to verify the validity of his ATM card. "On this record, the element of reliance or causation was indisputably established." Conviction affirmed.

Analysis:

This opinion focuses on the elements of misrepresentation and reliance for the crime of false pretenses. According to the opinion, the misrepresentation can be implicit, based on words or conduct, as long as it was made with an intent to deceive. The reliance element requires that the victim actually rely on the misrepresentation. In other words, it must cause the victim to give up his or her property. If the victim knew the misrepresentation to be true or relied on evidence independent of the misrepresentation and still decided to give the property to the defendant, then the victim did not rely on the misrepresentation. Even if other independent evidence is used in the victim's decision, as long as the victim materially relied on the misrepresentation, the crime has been committed. In other words, the misrepresentation does not need to be the sole factor in the victim's decision to give up the property, but it should be the primary reason. In essence, the law only wants to punish the defendant's deceit to the extent that it causes another to do what they would not have otherwise. For example, take a customer who enters a store to buy a soda. She lies to the cashier by saying she is thirsty. The cashier hands her a soda, and the customer gives the cashier a dollar bill for the price of the soda and leaves. The customer obtained title and possession to the soda but also misrepresented a fact to the cashier. Nonetheless, the fact was probably not of the kind that the cashier relied on in making the transaction. The cashier was mainly concerned about receiving payment for the soda, which was properly made. Thus, her lie about thirst did not materially influence the cashier to sell her the soda. On the other hand, if the customer said she was dying of thirst and used that lie to get a free soda from the cashier, then this would be the crime of false pretenses. The cashier, relying on the belief the customer is in desperate need, gives up the soda without the $1. However, if a doctor happens to be in the store and the skeptical cashier calls on that doctor to confirm the customer's dehydrated state, then the issue of reliance may change. If the doctor mistakenly misdiagnoses the customer as severely dehydrated and the cashier believes the doctor and gives away the soda, then the defendant can't be prosecuted. The cashier did not rely on the customer's word, but relied on another source- the doctor. Similarly, the defendant in this case argues that the Safeway computer system was equivalent to the mistaken doctor in the above example. Safeway conducted its own investigation that approved the defendant's ATM card, and Safeway relied upon this information in issuing the defendant his cash. The court does not accept this and argues that Safeway attempted to conduct an investigation, but the investigation provided no information on whether the defendant's ATM card was valid or not. In essence, the court is arguing that the cashier sought the doctor's advice, but the doctor could offer no opinion. The Safeway computer system could not contact the customer's bank and a "stand-in" code was issued; as a result, Safeway had no other information to rely on except the defendant's representation that his card was valid. This interpretation poses a sticky factual problem. The facts of the case state that, if a transaction is denied, the Safeway screen at the check stand states "transaction declined". However, the facts of the case do not state what the screen at the check stand states when a "stand-in" code is issued and whether this is different than when a transaction is normally approved. If a "stand-in" code and an approved transaction both result in the message "transaction approved" on the Safeway screen at the check stand, then is it possible to state that Safeway had no information to rely upon besides the defendant's implicit representation? The Safeway cashier may read the "transaction approved" message and presume that the defendant's card was valid irrespective of the defendant's representation, explicit or implicit. The Safeway *computer* may have distinguished between a "stand-in" code and a genuine verification of the defendant's account, but did the cashier make such a distinction? If no such distinguishing message is displayed with a "stand-in" code, then the cashier may believe that the transaction was genuinely approved. This should make the defendant not guilty, unless the court believes that the Safeway agent to whom the defendant made the misrepresentation was the computer, not the cashier. Did Whight (D) fool the computer or the cashier?

A SCHEME TO DEFRAUD IS SHOWN WHERE THE DEFENDANT HAS A DISHONEST INTENT TO DEPRIVE A PERSON OF THEIR PROPERTY BY CAUSING THE OWNER SOME ARTICULABLE HARM OR BY INTENDING TO USE THE PROPERTY FOR SOME GAINFUL USE

United States v. Czubinksi

(State) v. (Accused)
(1997) 106 F.3d 1069

M E M O R Y   G R A P H I C

Instant Facts
An employee of the IRS looked through the personal taxpayer information of several people using unauthorized computer access.

Black Letter Rule
For the purposes of the federal wire and computer fraud statutes: 1) A scheme to defraud is shown where the defendant has a dishonest intent to deprive a person of their property by causing the owner some articulable harm or by intending to use the property for some gainful use; 2) A deprivation of honest services is found where the defendant fails or intends to fail to carry out his official tasks adequately for an employer or the public; 3) Computer fraud is found where the defendant makes an unauthorized access of a federal computer and gains anything of value in order to further an intent to defraud.

Case Vocabulary

A FORTIORI: By great force of logic.
ARTIFICE: A ruse, deception, or trick.
DEFRAUD: An act of deceit or dishonesty that causes the victim loss or injury.

Procedural Basis: Appeal of jury conviction on nine counts of wire fraud and four counts of computer fraud.

Facts: Richard Czubinski (D) was employed in the Boston office of the Internal Revenue Service ("IRS"). Czubinski (D) acted as a Contact Representative who answered questions from taxpayers regarding their returns. To retrieve information for inquiring taxpayers, Czubinski (D) routinely accessed information from one of the IRS computer systems known as the Integrated Data Retrieval System ("IDRS'), a database of taxpayer information. Czubinski (D) used a password (given to all IRS Contact Representatives), special search codes, and taxpayer social security numbers to retrieve the information of taxpayers on his computer screen in Boston. This information is permanently stored in a master file located in a computer in West Virginia. IRS rules prohibit an employee from accessing taxpayer information outside of the course of their official duties. In 1992, Czubinski (D) made unauthorized access of the IDRS files. He did so knowingly disregarding IRS rules. Internal IRS auditors discovered that Czubinski (D) made several unauthorized accesses of the IDRS. These unauthorized accesses involved information regarding: the tax returns of two David Duke presidential campaigners, the joint tax return of an assistant district attorney (who was prosecuting Czubinski's (D) wife on an unrelated charge) and his spouse, the tax return of a Boston city counselor or who had defeated Czubinski (D) in the previous election for a seat on the council, the tax return of one of his brother's instructors, the tax return of a police officer and his wife, and the tax return of a woman whom Czubinski (D) had dated a few times. Czubinski (D) also accessed the tax return information of other social acquaintances without authorization. [While Czubinski (D) was an electronic, peeping-tom IRS agent by day, at night he was the head of his own local invisible knights of the Ku Klux Klan chapter, no doubt making mom proud]. Neither the evidence nor the government argued that Czubinski (D) ever disclosed the information he accessed to any third party. The government's only evidence demonstrating an intent to use the confidential information for "nefarious ends" was the testimony of William A. Murray. Murray was briefly a member of Czubinski's (D) Klan chapter and worked with Czubinski (D) on the David Duke campaign. Murray testified that Czubinski (D) in early 1992 told a group that "he intended to use some of that information to build dossiers on people" who are involved in "the white supremacist movement". However, there was no evidence that Czubinski (D) created any dossiers or took any steps to create dossiers. In addition, he did not share any information in the following years with anyone. Czubinski (D) did not perform unauthorized accesses after 1992. He remained a Contact Representative for the IRS until June 1995 when a grand jury indicted him. The jury convicted him of nine counts of wire fraud and four counts of computer fraud under federal statutes. Czubinski (D) appealed to the First Circuit Court of Appeals.

Issue: Is merely accessing confidential information a sufficient deprivation of property for the purposes of wire fraud?

Decision and Rationale: (Torruella, J.) No. In order to establish a conviction for wire fraud, the government must prove beyond a reasonable doubt: (1) the accused participated knowingly and willingly in a plan to defraud with the specific intent to defraud, and (2) used interstate wire communications in furtherance of the plan. We find the first element dispositive of the case and conclude that the government failed to prove that Czubinski (D) participated in a plan to defraud within the meaning of the wire fraud statute. The government's case rested on two theories of wire fraud. The first is that Czubinski (D) defrauded the IRS of its property under section 1343, [which prohibits the transmission in interstate or foreign commerce "any writings, signs, signals, pictures, or sounds" for the purpose of carrying out a "scheme or artifice" (already created or intended to be created) to defraud or for obtaining money or property by false pretenses, representations, or promises], by acquiring confidential information for Czubinski's (D) intended personal use. The second is that Czubinski (D) defrauded individuals of their intangible right to honest government services under section 1346. Under the first theory, confidential information and its unauthorized distribution is "property" that an accused may deprive the owner of. Where the deprivation takes place through dishonest or deceitful means, a "scheme to defraud", is found within the meaning of the new wire fraud statute. As a result, it is necessary to show that Czubinski (D) intended to deprive another of this protected right. The government, however, fails to prove that a mere access of confidential information without any further use or intended use is sufficient to constitute a deprivation of IRS property, as it did in *Carpenter v. United States* [the court found a deprivation of property where the accused used confidential information regarding the contents of a newspaper article to his own benefit]. In contrast, Czubinski's (D) unauthorized browsing is not a deprivation within the meaning of the federal wire fraud statutes. In order to prove a deprivation of property, the owner must suffer some articulable harm from the unauthorized use or the accused must intend to have "some gainful use" of the information. While the government can prove that Czubinski (D) viewed the information deceitfully and without authorization, they cannot prove that Czubinski (D) gained from access to the information by using the information or that he intended to use the information. The only evidence regarding Czubinski's (D) intent to use any of the information rests on the testimony of Murray. Nevertheless, following Czubinski's (D) remark to Murray, Czubinski (D) did not create dossiers or even take steps to create such dossiers. Czubinski (D) did not record or print any of the taxpayer information nor did anyone else to testify as to Czubinski's (D) intent to use such confidential information. Therefore, since the evidence shows that Czubinski (D) never used, intended to use, or shared the information with anyone else, no rational jury could have found, beyond a reasonable doubt, that Czubinski (D) was browsing taxpayer files in furtherance of a scheme to use the information for his private gain. Regarding the second theory, Congress responded to a Supreme Court decision by enacting section 1364, [which expanded the term "scheme or artifice to defraud" to include "a scheme or artifice to deprive another of the intangible right of honest services"]. We hold that this section applies to the scope of the mail and wire fraud statutes. In *United States v. Sawyer*, we first noted that the definition

of honest services is uncertain, but should include instances of serious corruption of public officials such as embezzlement of public funds, bribery of public officials, or failure of public decision makers to disclose certain conflicts of interest. Second, we warned that deprivation of honest services should not include every instance of official misconduct that may result in the official's personal gain. Third, our holding in *Sawyer* found that the conduct of the official must intend to or actually deprive the public of its right to the official's honest services. Applying *Sawyer* to Czubinski's (D) case, "it is clear that his conviction cannot stand." First, his case falls outside of the class of fraud that is protected such as bribery, embezzlement, or disclosure of a conflict of interest. Second, finding Czubinski (D) culpable in this case would open the "threat" of "transforming governmental workplace violations into felonies." Czubinski's (D) conduct may have been troubling, but he received no indication that this workplace violation would be punishable by anything more than dismissal. Therefore, without a clear Congressional mandate, we cannot presume that Congress intended "to create what amounts to a draconian personnel regulation." Third, as discussed previously, there is no evidence that Czubinski (D) used the information or intended to use the information in a scheme to defraud. Czubinski (D), while committing wrongdoing in searching confidential information, did not deprive or intend to deprive the public of their right to his honest services. Czubinski (D) was also charged with four counts of computer fraud based on § 1030(a)(4) [which prohibits the fraudulent, unauthorized access of a federal interest computer that furthers an intended fraud and obtains anything of value]. While Czubinski (D) did make unauthorized access, the government failed to prove that he obtained anything of value. There is no evidence of an "end" to achieve other than Czubinski's (D) satisfaction of his curiosity. The legislative history of the statute further emphasizes that the statute was intended to include the theft of information for a specific use, rather than a mere unauthorized access. Finally, as a cautionary note, the broad language of the mail and wire fraud statutes makes them adaptable to new forms of criminal conduct, but also may result in the prosecution of behavior that may be "offensive to the morals or aesthetics of federal prosecutors". This should not be the basis of a federal felony. There is troubling evidence that this prosecution may have been motivated by Czubinski's (D) views, but the "wire fraud statute must not serve as a vehicle for prosecuting only those citizens whose views run against the tide, no matter how incorrect or uncivilized such views are". The convictions of nine counts of wire fraud and four counts of computer fraud are reversed.

Analysis:

This opinion provides a glimpse of the monster that theft laws have created. As the previous opinions have revealed, the laws of theft are a patchwork of imperfectly constructed rules that are often too rigid to cover new forms of dishonest conduct or present loopholes that wrongdoers may exploit. The wire fraud statute in this case was an attempt to deal with these problems. This federal statute essentially prohibits a person from defrauding or intending to defraud another using an electronic instrumentality of interstate commerce. The first part of this opinion focuses on the word "defraud" and its meaning within the wire fraud statute. The term "defraud" carries with it two concepts: deceit and loss. A person who defrauds another is actually doing two things. The defrauder is tricking the victim, and the victim, as a result of the deceit, is deprived of something or is injured. Therefore, while the wire fraud statute itself does not include the term "deprivation", the court rightfully understands that it is a necessary element of the term "defraud", which is used in the statute. In Czubinski's (D) case, it can be argued that he benefited from browsing the computer files. For example, he may have looked through the tax files of his enemies and either found information useful to him or no useful information. Even if he found useful information, the IRS (the victim in this case) did not suffer a loss or harm because Czubinski (D) did not put to use any of the information he came across. Traditional larceny law would state that Czubinski (D) did not "convert" the information to his own use. However, this poses an issue of when a crime actually takes place under the wire fraud statute. What if Czubinski (D), 20 years later, suddenly finds it in his interest to use information he remembered seeing 20 years ago on an IRS computer screen? Is this a continuing trespass that is immediately punishable or has the statute of limitations long expired? The wire and mail fraud statutes were drafted to be able to include new forms of dishonest conduct. But are they too broad? Note that the wire fraud statute covers not only schemes already put together, but also the intent to formulate a scheme. This would criminalize acts that are in their most infant stages. In the case at hand, Czubinski (D) did voice an intent to devise a scheme to defraud. However, the court failed to find sufficient the testimony of a single witness based on one incident. What if Czubinski (D) had written a letter to Murray instead, would that have been a more certain sign of his intent? If you e-mail a friend in another state telling her that you want to "get back at" your brother for spilling coffee on you, you are using an electronic instrumentality of interstate commerce to further an intent to devise a scheme to defraud someone. You can see how far reaching the statute can be. Nevertheless, the state can't punish everyone for such conduct, meaning it must pick and choose which acts merit prosecution. However, as the opinion warns, such a broad law does give prosecutors wide latitude to decide whom to prosecute for what, thereby making the personal whims of the prosecutor play a greater factor in how justice is administered.